Elizabeth Gundrey was well known as editor of Britain's first consumer magazine (*Shoppers' Guide*) long before she turned her keen eye for quality and value-for-money to the subject of travel. Of all her books, this one has been far the most popular, re-appearing every year in new enlarged editions, of which this is the thirteenth. She is also the author of *Running your own Bed and Breakfast* (Piatkus) for people who want to start doing this themselves; and of about 40 other books.

The British edition of *Cottages, B&Bs and Country Inns* is regularly the bestseller among Britain's accommodation guides. It is a book for all seasons.

Cottages, B&Bs and Country Inns of England and Wales

Published in Great Britain as *Staying Off the Beaten Track* (SOTBT)

ELIZABETH GUNDREY
with **WALTER GUNDREY**

*A personal selection of moderately priced
guest-houses, small hotels, farms and country houses*

13th EDITION

Edited by Jacqueline Krendel

Fodor's Travel Publications, Inc.
New York • Toronto • London • Sydney • Auckland

TO ANDREW, WITH LOVE

Acknowledgments

We acknowledge with much appreciation the assistance of the rest of the SOTBT team (Jennifer Christie, Andrew Cockburn, Jonathan May, Kate McCarney, Bob Vickers and Nancy Webber) as well as of all the proprietors of houses.

Elizabeth and Walter Gundrey

CONTENTS

NOTE: The houses in this book have been personally visited by Elizabeth (or, in the north, Walter) Gundrey. **At any of them (London excepted) you may stay for as little as £11–£20 (for bed-and-breakfast)** although at about a quarter of them the best rooms cost more. Prices may rise in high season. Owners, and prices, can change overnight; so check before you book. At many places, you can dine without staying: see entries under **'Dinner'**.

COMPLAINTS: If anything was not of reasonable standard (e.g. chilly bedroom or badly cooked food) you are entitled to claim a reduction on your bill, but *only if* you had previously told the proprietor and given him or her a chance to put matters right. We regularly inspect; and also will investigate complaints, showing your letter to the proprietor, **provided that you have first taken the matter up with him or her.** Owners are normally anxious to put right anything that is wrong. Please enclose International Reply Coupons if you want a reply.

Readers' comments quoted in the book are from letters sent to us: they are not supplied via the proprietors.

Telephoning Britain: Dial 011 44 then omit the '0' which precedes all telephone numbers in this book. Remember the big time differential: proprietors do not appreciate being awakened in the night!

GEOGRAPHICAL LISTINGS OF B&Bs AND COUNTRY INNS

A   **B**   **C**   **D**   **E**

1

2   SCOTLAND

N

3   Brampton

            Carlisle

             Penrith

          Cockermouth

4   CUMBRIA   Kirk Step

          Windermere

          Ulverston   Kendal

5

          Lancaster

          LANCASHI

          Clithe

          Preston

6   G MAN

        Isle   LIVERPOOL   MERSEY SIDE

        of

        Anglesey   Ma

7   N   Menai Bridge   Conwy   CHESHIRE

          Caernarfon   CLWYD   Ruthin   Chester   Nor

                       Nantwich

          Betws-y-Coed   Wrexham

              GWYNEDD   Bala   Oswestry

8   0   50 miles

              Dolgellau   Shrewsb

   0   75 km   Welshpool   Te

1

2

3

-Tweed

ck

eth

ND
R

ENGLAND

4

CLEVELAND
Darlington

Scarborough

YORKSHIRE

5

Thirsk

Pickering

Great
Driffield

rrogate   York

HUMBERSIDE
Beverley

6

EEDS

Hull

Scunthorpe

UTH
KSHIRE

Sheffield

Louth

7

Worksop

Chesterfield

ock   NOTTING-
HAMSHIRE

Lincoln

Newark   LINCOLNSHIRE

8

Derby   Nottingham

Grantham   Spalding

Fakenham

NORFOLK

Melton Mowbray   Oakham

King's Lynn

Norwich

LEICESTERSHIRE   Stamford

Swaffham

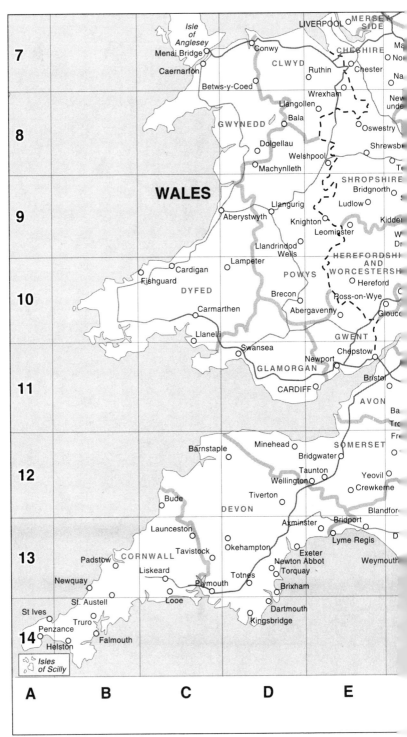

7

Isle
of
Anglesey
Menai Bridge○
Caernarfon○

○Conwy

LIVERPOOL○MERSEY
SIDE
Ma
CHESHIRE ○No
○Na

CLWYD

Ruthin
○

Chester

Betws-y-Coed○

Wrexham○

New
unde

8

GWYNEDD

Llangollen○
○Bala

Dolgellau
○
Welshpool○
○Machynlleth

○Oswestry

Shrewsb

T

WALES

SHROPSHIRE
Bridgnorth○

Llangurig○
Ludlow○

9

○Aberystwyth
Knighton○
Leominster○

Kidder

W
Dr

Llandrindod
Wells○
Lampeter○

HEREFORDSHI
AND
WORCESTERSH

○Cardigan
Fishguard○

DYFED

POWYS

○ Hereford

Brecon○
Ross-on-Wye○
C

10

Carmarthen○

Abergavenny○
Glouce

Llanelli○

GWENT

○Swansea
Chepstow○

Newport
○

11

GLAMORGAN

CARDIFF○

Bristol○

AVON

Ba
Tr
Fr

Barnstaple
○

Minehead ○

SOMERSET
○

Bridgwater○

12

Taunton
○
Wellington○

Yeovil ○
○ Crewkerne

Tiverton
○

Bude
○

DEVON

Blandfor

Axminster
○
Bridport○

13

Launceston
○

CORNWALL
Padstow○

Tavistock
○

Okehampton○

Lyme Regis○

Exeter○
Newton Abbot○
Torquay○

Weymouth

Newquay
○

Liskeard
○

Totnes○

St Ives○

St. Austell○

Looe○

Plymouth○

Brixham○

Dartmouth○

Truro○

Kingsbridge○

14○
Penzance
Helston○

Falmouth○

Isles
of Scilly

A   B   C   D   E

Sheffield
Worksop
Chesterfield
well
Y-
E
Newark
Lincoln
NOTTING-
HAMSHIRE
LINCOLNSHIRE
Louth
Derby
Nottingham
Grantham
Spalding
Fakenham
King's Lynn
Norwich
Melton
Mowbray
Oakham
Stamford
Swaffham
LEICESTERSHIRE
Market
Harborough
Peterborough
Thetford
Diss
NORFOLK
Coventry
NORTHAMPTON-
SHIRE
Kettering
Ely
CAMBRIDGE-
SHIRE
Bury St. Edmunds
SUFFOLK
Saxmundham
amington
pa
IRE
d-
voa
Northampton
Daventry
BEDFORD
SHIRE
Cambridge
Stowmarket
Ipswich
Brackley
Milton
Keynes
Bedford
Saffron
Walden
Sudbury
Woodbridge
Banbury
on-
Vold
BUCKING-
HAMSHIRE
HERTFORD-
SHIRE
Braintree
Bishop's
Stortford
Colchester
ESSEX
ord
Oxford
Aylesbury
Witney
Thame
Watford
Chelmsford
RDSHIRE
High Wycombe
Hampstead
Hornsey
Henley-
on-Thames
Reading
LONDON
Sittingbourne
BERKSHIRE
Newbury
Heathrow
Kingston-
upon-Thames
Faversham
Maidstone
Canterbury
SURREY
Sevenoaks
Tonbridge
Basingstoke
Dorking
Ashford
AMPSHIRE
Haslemere
E.Grinstead
Gatwick
Tunbridge
Wells
KENT
Dover
Winchester
Horsham
Tenterden
Petersfield
W.SUSSEX
Haywards Heath
Rye
Midhurst
Lewes
E.SUSSEX
Chichester
Hastings
wport
Portsmouth
Worthing
Brighton
Eastbourne
Bembridge
ENGLAND
Isle of
Wight
Shanklin
Ventnor

7

8

9

10

11

12

13

14

0   50 miles
0   75 km

H   J   K   L   M

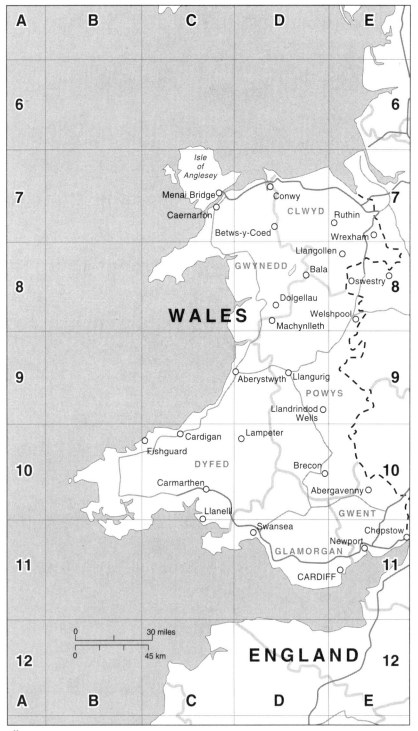

Isle of Anglesey

Menai Bridge
Caernarfon
Conwy
CLWYD
Ruthin
Betws-y-Coed
Wrexham
Llangollen
GWYNEDD
Bala
Oswestry
Dolgellau
Welshpool
WALES
Machynlleth
Aberystwyth
Llangurig
POWYS
Llandrindod Wells
Cardigan
Lampeter
Fishguard
DYFED
Brecon
Carmarthen
Abergavenny
Llanelli
GWENT
Swansea
Chepstow
GLAMORGAN
Newport
CARDIFF

0   30 miles
0   45 km

ENGLAND

B&Bs AND INNS LISTED BY TOWN

The B&Bs and inns in England appear in the main part of this book in alphabetical order, followed by those in Wales. However, for convenience in locating them, they are grouped in the following list according to towns. On the left is the nearest town (sometimes distant), with its map reference (see pages viii–xii), followed by the name of the B&B or inn and its nearest village.

ENGLAND

xix

WALES

B&Bs AND INNS LISTED BY COUNTY

The B&Bs and inns in England appear in the main part of this book in alphabetical order, followed by those in Wales. However, for convenience in locating them, they are grouped in the following list according to counties. On the left (in **bold** type) is the nearest town (sometimes distant), with its map reference (see pages viii–xii), followed by the name of the B&B or inn and its nearest village.

ENGLAND

Nearest town	Map ref. (see p. viii-xi)	Page
AVON		
Bath	**F.11**	
(Avonside, see Wiltshire)		12
(Bradford Old Windmill, see Wiltshire)		35
Bridge Cottage, Bathford		261
Granchen, Bitton		125
(Green Lane House, see Somerset)		131
Oldfields		357
The Orchard, Bathford		261
Paradise House		266
(Pickford House, see Somerset)		276
Somerset House		314
Wentworth House		357
Bristol	**F.11**	
Dornden, Old Sodbury		91
BEDFORDSHIRE		
Bedford	**J.10**	
Church Farm, Roxton		59
The Grange, Ravensden		129
Orchard Cottage, Wrestlingworth		118
BERKSHIRE		
Newbury	**G.11**	
Chamberhouse Mill, Thatcham		54
Marshgate Cottage Hotel, Hungerford		207
Nalderhill House, Wickham Heath		220
St Mary's House, Kintbury		302
(Woodlands Park Farm, see Hampshire)		54
Reading	**H.11**	
Boot Farm, Bradfield		32
Cherry Court, Burghfield Common		32
BUCKINGHAMSHIRE		
Aylesbury	**H.10**	
Foxhill, Kingsey		114
Poletrees Farm, Brill		279

Nearest town	Map ref. (see p. viii-xi)	Page
(Henley-on-Thames, Oxfordshire)	**H.11**	
Acha Pani, Bovingdon Green		192
Little Parmoor, Frieth		192
High Wycombe	**H.11**	
White House, Widmer End		83
Whites' Farmhouse, Radnage		365
Whitewebbs, Chalfont St Peter		367
Milton Keynes	**H.10**	
Chantry Farm, Hanslope		55
Grange Barn, Haversham		55
Richmond Lodge, Mursley		292
CAMBRIDGESHIRE		
Cambridge	**J.9**	
Glebe House, Longstowe		118
Old Rectory, Swaffham Bulbeck		306
Seven		306
Springfield, Linton		318
(Yardleys, see Essex)		318
Ely	**K.9**	
Old Egremont House		234
Spinney Abbey, Wicken		234
Peterborough	**J.9**	
(Castle Farm, see Northamptonshire)		51
CHESHIRE		
Chester	**E.7**	
Castle House		52
Hatton Hall, Hatton Heath		141
Newton Hall, Tattenhall		141
The Studio		52
Macclesfield	**F.7**	
Hardingland Farmhouse		140
Nantwich	**F.7**	
Burland Farm, Burland		46
Northwich	**F.7**	
Barratwich, Cuddington		46
(Wrexham, Clwyd, Wales)	**E.8**	
Tilston Lodge, Tilston		391

xxiii

WALES

Nearest town	Map ref. *(see p.xii)*	Page
CLWYD		
Llangollen	**E.8**	
Dee Farmhouse, Rhewl		416
Ruthin	**E.7**	
Eyarth Station, Llanfair-Dyffryn-Clwyd		397
(Welshpool, Powys)	**E.8**	
Bron Heulog,		
Llanrhaeadr-ym-Mochnant		387
Glyndwr, Pen-y-Bont-Fawr		387
Wrexham	**E.8**	
Buck Farmhouse, Hanmer		391
(Tilston Lodge, *see* Cheshire)		391
Wynn Hall, Penycae		416
DYFED		
Aberystwyth	**D.9**	
Brynarth Farmhouse, Lledrod		390
Cardigan	**C.10**	
Broniwan, Rhydlewis		389
Hendre Farm, Llangranog		404
Old Vicarage, Moylegrove		403
Park Hall, Cwmtydu		404
Carmarthen	**C.10**	
Cwmtwrch, Nantgaredig		394
Fferm-y-Felin, Llanpumsaint		394
Fishguard	**B.10**	
Coach House Cottage, Goodwick		393
Manor House Hotel		393
Mount Pleasant Farm, Penffordd		409
Tregynon, Pontfaen		409
Lampeter	**D.10**	
Erw Hen, Pumpsaint		401
Glanrannell Park Hotel, Crugybar		401
Llanelli	**C.10**	
Caernewydd Farm, Kidwelly		392
GWENT		
Abergavenny	**E.10**	
Thorntrees, Govilon		407
(Ty Croeso Hotel, *see* Powys)		410
Wenallt Farm, Gilwern		413
Chepstow	**E.11**	
(Upper Sedbury House,		
see Gloucestershire)		415
Wye Barn, Tintern		415
Newport	**E.11**	
West Usk Lighthouse,		
St Brides Wentlooge		414
GWYNEDD		
Bala	**D.8**	
Dewis Cyfarfod, Llandderfel		395
Melin Meloch		395
Betws-y-Coed	**D.7**	
Royal Oak Farmhouse & Cottage		411
Ty Gwyn		411
Caernarfon	**C.7**	
Bronant, Bontnewydd		388

Nearest town	Map ref. *(see p.xii)*	Page
Dolgellau	**D.8**	
Herongate, Arthog		402
Llwyndû Farmhouse Hotel,		
Llanaber		402
Menai Bridge	**C.7**	
Plas Trefarthen, Brynsiencyn,		
Isle of Anglesey		405
POWYS		
(Abergavenny, Gwent)	**E.10**	
Ty Croeso Hotel, Crickhowell		410
Brecon	**E.10**	
Aberyscir Old Rectory, Aberyscir		386
Trewalter House, Llangorse		412
Upper Trewalkin Farm,		
Pengenffordd		412
(Hereford, Herefordshire) E.10		
Tynllyne, Llanigon		142
Knighton	**E.9**	
(Monaughty Poeth, *see* Shropshire)		215
(Quarry House, *see* Shropshire)		287
(Woodside Old Farmhouse,		
see Shropshire)		287
Llandrindod Wells	**D.9**	
Argoed Fawr, Llanwrthwl		400
Ffaldau, Llandegley		399
Flickering Lamp, Elan Valley		400
Three Wells Farm Hotel, Howey		408
Llangurig	**D.9**	
Old Vicarage		406
Machynlleth	**D.8**	
Talbontdrain, Uwychygarreg		406
Welshpool	**E.8**	
(Bron Heulog, *see* Clwyd)		387
Burnt House, Trelydan		396
Dysserth Hall, by Powis Castle		396
(Glyndwr, *see* Clwyd)		387
WEST GLAMORGAN		
Swansea	**D.11**	
Fairfield Cottage, Knelston		398
Stoney Forge, Knelston		398

Entrance hall at Bron Heulog, Wales (see page 387)

INTRODUCTION

THIS BOOK has been appearing annually in Britain for thirteen years, where it has become a bestseller among accommodation guides. Its British title, *Staying Off the Beaten Track*, is so well known that regular users sometimes call themselves 'Gundrey's Trackies'!

I am delighted that it is now appearing in a third Fodor edition, so that even more overseas visitors using it will enjoy this country – which, although I am well travelled, still remains my own favourite holiday destination. With it and *Fodor's Great Britain* guide you have all you need for exploring highways and byways alike.

And, who knows, perhaps I will be meeting some of you when I myself stay at houses in this book during the year; for the revisiting of them (by myself or others I employ) is one of the behind-scenes activities which helps to ensure that standards remain as they were when I, or my brother, made the initial inspection, so that you may depend upon having an enjoyable time when you go exploring 'off the beaten track'.

For the benefit of overseas visitors, I have decided to use the introduction for a miscellany of useful information I've picked up in the course of many years' travelling for *Staying Off the Beaten Track*.

First, there is a telephone service in the UK well worth using before setting out on any journey. Dial 0836 and then one of the regional numbers listed below to get up-to-the-minute advice on both the weather and any traffic hold-ups in the area to which you are going:

All motorways: 401906

West Country: 401907	East Anglia: 401910
Wales: 401908	North-West: 401911
Midlands: 401909	North-East: 401912

In the south-east there are four numbers, covering roads between the M4 and M1 (401916); between the M1 and the Dartford Tunnel (401917); from the Dartford Tunnel to the M23 (401918); and from the M23 to the M4 (401919).

If you want to explore the country by rail or bus, follow the advice in *Fodor's Great Britain*:

A **BritRail Pass** gives you unlimited travel over the entire British Rail network. A variety of passes is offered. The adult first-class pass costs $299 for eight days, $489 for 15 days, $645 for 22 days, and $775 for one month. The adult second-class pass costs $219 for eight days, $339 for 15 days, $425 for 22 days, and $495 for one month. Senior citizens (over 60) can obtain a **Senior Citizen Pass**, which entitles the bearer to unlimited first-class or second-class travel. The first-class costs $279 for eight days, $455 for 15 days, $599 for 22 days, and $725 for one month. The second-class costs $199 for eight days, $305 for 15 days, $379 for 22 days, and $445 for one month. Young travellers (aged 16–25) can buy the **BritRail Youthpass**, which allows unlimited second-class travel. It costs $179 for eight days, $269 for 15 days, $339 for 22 days, and $395 for one month. There is also a **Flexipass** which can be used for travel during half of the days in a given period.

You *must* purchase the BritRail Pass before you leave home. They are available from most travel agents or from one of these BritRail Travel International offices:

1500 Broadway, New York, NY 10036, tel. 212/575-2667; 216 Young St., Toronto, Ontario, M4S 3A6, tel. 416/482-9196 or 800-387 7245.

If you want the flexibility of a car combined with the speed and comfort of the train, with **BritRail/Drive** (from around $293–$352 per person, based on two adults sharing a car, more for automatic transmission) you can have an eight-day BritRail Pass and four vouchers valid for Hertz car hire from over 80 BritRail stations and a further 40 'downtown' garage locations in other towns. This makes it possible to take the train to a major town, then use the car to get deep into the countryside to visit a stately home or other attraction. If you call your travel agency or Hertz's international desk at 800/654-3001, the car of your choice will be waiting for you at the station as you alight from your train. BritRail/Drive must be booked with your travel agent before leaving for Great Britain.

Once you're abroad, **Regional Rail Rover** tickets offer excellent value. They cost between £21.50 and £56 (depending on area covered) for a standard-class, three-day or seven-day pass, and can be bought at main stations and British Rail travel agents. Tickets are available for each of these areas: Scotland, Wales, Northwest England, the Northeast, Coast and Peaks (the Peak District and part of Snowdonia), Heart of England, East Anglia, East Midlands, and the Southwest. A separate series of tickets covers the Southeast and the London area. A seven-day **All-Line Rail Rover**, covering the whole country, costs £215. Ticket prises rise in January. Details of these and other BR facilities in Britain can be obtained from the **British Rail Travel Centre** (Euston Station, London NW1 1DF, tel. 071/387-7070).

Britain has a comprehensive bus (short haul) and coach (long distance) network, which offers an inexpensive way of seeing the country. Coaches are much cheaper than trains, usually about half the price or even less, but are generally slower, although some motorway services with the modern **Rapide** coaches reduce the margin considerably. Seats are comfortable, with meal and comfort stops usually arranged on longer trips. (Some coaches have toilet facilities on board.) A recorded guide to telephone numbers covering coach services throughout Britain can be obtained by calling 071/823-6567.

The British equivalent to Greyhound coaches is **National Express**. With its Scottish associate, **Caledonian Express**, it is by far the largest British operator. **Victoria Coach Station** (Buckingham Palace Rd., London SW1W 9TP) is the hub of the National Express network, serving around 1,500 destinations. Information is available from any of the company's 2,500 agents nationwide. In London, the main information point is the **Coach Travel Centre** (13 Lower Regent St., London SW1Y 4LR), near the British Travel Centre. Timetable information can also be obtained by calling 071/730-0202. There are National Express sales offices at London's Heathrow and Gatwick airport coach stations and in many towns.

National Express has two principal ticket offers for tourists. The **BritExpress Card** costs £12 and gives a 30% discount on all adult fares on National Express and Caledonian Express services over a 30-day period. There is also the **Tourist Trail Pass** costing £65 for 5 days, £90 for 8 days, £135 for 15 days, £160 for 22 days, and £190 for 30 days (discounts are available for children, students, and senior citizens). The pass allows unlimited travel on the company's services. The BritExpress Card and the Tourist Trail Pass can be bought in US dollars by mail from **British Travel Associates**, PO Box 299, Elkton, VA 22827, tel. 703/298-2232, or in person from 150 West Spotswood Avenue, Elkton, VA 22827. Both tickets can also be purchased in Canadian dollars from **Red Seal Tours**, 170 Evans Avenue, Suite 201, Toronto, Ontario, M8Z 5Y6, tel. 416/503-2233.

Overseas visitors can also buy a **Heritage Pass** (from travel agents at home or at selected Tourist Information Centres in the UK), giving free admission to about 600 stately homes and so forth. The pass is isssued by the British Tourist Authority.

A **Vacation Planner**, available free from **British Tourist Authority** offices in the US, provides a whole range of information on holidaying in Britain. The brochure includes a synopsis of the different regions, travel information, a diary of major events, places to eat and other useful contact addresses. It also lists a basic library of books, maps and videos which can be purchased in the US through mail order. Contact BTA offices at: 551 Fifth Avenue, New York, NY 10176, tel. 212/986-2200; 2580 Cumberland Parkway, Atlanta, GA 30339, tel. 404/432-9635; 625 North Michigan Avenue, Chicago, IL 60611, tel. 312/787-0490; World Trade Center, 350 South Figueroa Street, Los Angeles, CA 90071, tel. 213/628-3525.

In the UK, every regional tourist board annually publishes, free or for a small charge, well-produced and colourful directories of what to see in their area, with opening times, etc. For details of what's available, phone the region in which you are interested:

Cumbria: 05394 44444	East Midlands: 0522 531521
Northumbria (the North-East):	East Anglia: 0473 822922
091 3846905	West Country: 0392 76351
North-West: 0942 821222	Southern: 0703 620006
Yorkshire: 0904 707961	South-East: 0892 540766
Heart of England (the West	London: 071 730 3450
Midlands): 0905 763436	Wales: 0222 499909

Some more tips for overseas visitors: when writing to proprietors listed in this book, enclose three International Reply Coupons for an airmail reply; remember that 'bathroom' does not mean a toilet but a room with a bath, possibly with a shower; send a deposit in *sterling*, using a traveller's cheque (check), Eurocheque or International Money Order; make bookings before spring (I quote a typical reader's letter: 'When, at the beginning of August, I phoned all the places in Northumberland for a September booking, each was fully booked.'). Dates (on cheques, or when writing to book) can be confused if you put the month first, as in 1.12.94 for the 12th January 1994. In Britain, the day comes first: 12.1.94.

Things I have found useful to take with me when travelling: a compact kettle for bedroom tea-making; a clip-on book-light for reading in bed; an inflatable neck support for long car drives; car compass for the occasions when you lose your way in a maze of lanes.

Dining-room at Tregony House (see page 339)

'ENGLAND IN LITTLE . . .'

That is how a famous author described his own county '. . . lost in the midst of England'. Lost it certainly is as far as most tourists are concerned, who speed through on the M6 and never deviate to explore that county's wild moors or deep forests, its castles and mansions, mediaeval cathedral and countless ancient churches, antique and craft centres, inns and markets. One scenic valley has been called 'the English Rhineland'.

So, in this edition, I have singled out Staffordshire as my 'county of the year', for it is one of the most undervalued in Britain.

It has, for instance, so many outstanding gardens and parklands that there is even a special map to pinpoint them all. As well as innumerable footpaths – valley, hill, woodland or riverside – the 90-mile Staffordshire Way traverses the county, and on page xxvii you can find houses at which to stay close to its route. (There is not only a free map of this too but a substantial guidebook costing £3.50.)

In the north, the county extends into the Peak District National Park. Its moors, rugged crags and sparkling streams, with the Manifold Valley one of Britain's finest beauty-spots, contrast with the gentle Vale of Trent and leafy Cannock Chase, haunt of fallow deer, to the south. Only a small part of the county is occupied by Arnold Bennett's 'five towns' (actually six), the historic Potteries. They are best explored by the special china bus (Easter to November) which takes you from one famous name to another (Spode, Wedgwood, Doulton and all the rest) to tour factories and their museums, and buy bargains in crystal as well as china. The Stoke-on-Trent museum is exceptional and Stoke itself was nominated 'city of outstanding excellence' in 1990 (a ceramics festival is held there every November).

Other museums in the county – nearly thirty of them – include Chatterley Whitfield where ex-miners take you underground into a former coal mine; the Bass brewing museum where the great shire-horses are a special attraction; and a deer and forest museum in Cannock Chase. You can visit the houses of Samuel Johnson or Izaak Walton, a flint mill or a puppet theatre, Tamworth Castle, Roman sites or a vineyard (surprisingly far north), wildlife or rare breeds centres. Or abandon your car and take a rural canal trip, hire a bicycle or get on a steam train.

The free map/booklets mentioned above and many others are produced by the County Council's Tourism Group, and I have arranged for interested readers to be sent a complete information pack: just write a postcard mentioning this book (by its British title) to the Staffordshire Tourism Group, Shire Hall, Stafford; they will also provide a list of major events – from the big county agricultural show (in late May) to the traditional horn dance at Abbots Bromley (in September), balloon rallies (spring) to the music festival and fireworks in Lichfield (summer).

Other information leaflets can be obtained as follows: china factories, tel: 0782 284600; antique and mill shops, tel: 0538 381000 (there is also a book about the county's factory shops of all kinds, sold at Tourist Information Centres, £2.75); Arnold Bennett events, tel: 0782 834370.

Staffordshire's biggest attractions are Alton Towers – exciting rides in 500 acres of superlative gardens, Biddulph Grange Garden, and the stately homes of Weston Park and Shugborough, among many others. But some small and unusual sights are also worth seeking out – like the geology exhibition in a quarry near Waterhouses or the bird hides at Coombes Valley, James Brindley's watermill of 1752 in Leek – still working, or the 1914 pumping-station near Eccleshall.

Any reader who wants something different from the usual tourist areas should head for Staffordshire this year!

WHERE ELSE TO GO?

COASTAL TOURS   For a comprehensive free booklet, *Britain's Coasts*, telephone the British Tourist Authority (081-846 9000). 1994 is the 50th anniversary of D-Day, and its story, a map and details of related sites, forts, museums, etc. along the south coast are in a free booklet (tel: 0703 62006 for a copy, and for leaflets with discount vouchers, events programme).

GARDEN TOURS   Some counties are particularly well endowed, and the following county councils have free leaflets to guide you to outstanding gardens, obtainable by phoning the numbers given here: Bedfordshire (0234 363222), Cheshire (0244 603244), Cornwall (0872 74057), Cumbria (09662 4444), Dorset (0202 886116), East Anglia (0473 822922), Gloucestershire (0452 425676), Humberside (0482 211400), Isle of Wight (0983 524343), Kent (0622 696165), Lincolnshire (0522 526450), Northumbria (091 3846905), Nottinghamshire (0602 823823), Staffordshire (0782 712814), the South-East (0892 540766) and, in Wales, Gwynedd (0286 679548). The top ten National Trust gardens are in Cornwall (Lanhydrock), Gloucestershire (Hidcote), Kent (Chartwell and Sissinghurst), Surrey (Polesden Lacey), Sussex (Sheffield Park and Wakehurst), Wiltshire (Stourhead), Yorkshire (Fountains Abbey) and, in Wales, Gwynedd (Bodnant). The current 'Garden of the Year', a title awarded by the Historic Houses Association, is Forde Abbey (Dorset).

Every year, bookshops sell a new edition of the National Gardens Scheme guide to 3000 private gardens open (in aid of charity) on certain dates. Also recommended is the *Good Gardens Guide* by Rose and King (Vermilion). There is an excellent *Gardens Guide* by P. Taylor (Pavilion Books), covering the best nurseries too.

CYCLING TOURS   The British Tourist Authority has a booklet *Britain: Cycling* with 14 routes mapped; and information on bicycle hire, bicycles by public transport, etc. (tel: 081-846 9000).

CAR TOURS   A free book of motoring itineraries is issued by Budget Rent A Car in association with BTA (tel: 081-846 9000).

BIRDWATCHING   Good site guides are *Birdwatching in Britain* by Redman and Harrap and a regional series, all published by Helm.

COUNTRY WALKING Every town's Tourist Information Centre has leaflets, but for lesser-known possibilities obtain the Ministry of Defence's free booklet, which maps walks accessible on beautiful areas of the Ministry's lands: Dartmoor, Thorney Island (Sussex), Otterburn (Northumberland), Dorset, Salisbury Plain, Pembrokeshire. (Tel: 071-218 9000: public relations department.) A *Britain for Walkers* map-folder (61 long-distance paths and others) is available free from the BTA (tel: 081-846 9000).

OUTSTANDING SIGHTS Every year trophies are awarded for the best new tourism developments. To see all the latest ones, you could tour as follows: Dover (the White Cliffs Experience), Chatham (the Historic Dockyard), Greenwich (the Fan Museum), Grimsby (the Fishing Heritage Centre), Birmingham (the Symphony Hall, with orchestra conducted by Simon Rattle) and South Wales (Llancaiach Fawr at Nelson, a 17th-century 'time capsule', and the Maritime Quarter at Swansea).

HISTORIC BUILDINGS The counties with the greatest number of 'listed' buildings are Kent, Devon, Avon (Bath), and – surprise! – Essex. Conservation areas are another indicator of where the most picturesque villages and towns occur, namely in Kent, Devon, Hampshire, North and West Yorkshire, Norfolk, Wiltshire, Gloucestershire and Oxfordshire. The most famous individual structures outside London are, apart from cathedrals, (clockwise): the castles of Dover, Hever and Leeds in Kent; Brighton's Royal Pavilion in Sussex; Hampton Court in Surrey; Beaulieu in Hampshire, where there are also the ships *Victory* and *Mary Rose* at Portsmouth; Osborne House on the Isle of Wight; Stonehenge, Wiltshire; Roman baths and the Pump Room, Bath; Warwick Castle and the Shakespeare properties at Stratford-upon-Avon, Warwickshire; Blenheim Palace and Christchurch College, Oxfordshire; Windsor Castle, Berkshire; Woburn Abbey, Bedfordshire. Also, further north, Chatsworth in Derbyshire; Castle Howard and Fountains Abbey in North Yorkshire. For a free guide to 12 spa towns, tel: 081-748 0346.

INDUSTRIAL HERITAGE Sights to visit are shown on a series of free regional maps from the English Tourist Board (tel: 081-846 9000).

A NORTHERN TOUR There are finer scenery and lower prices in the north, yet fewer tourists. Here's an itinerary for a 10-day tour. Stage 1: Lake District (Bassenthwaite, Keswick, Thirlmere, Grasmere for Wordsworth's cottage, Ullswater) and Carlisle (cathedral and Tullie House). 2: Penrith, Alston, Haltwhistle (with Vindolanda on the Roman wall), Hexham, Blanchland, Beamish Open-Air Museum, Durham (cathedral). 3: Yorkshire Dales (Richmond, Leyburn, Askrigg, Aysgarth Falls, Buckden, Kettlewell, Grassington, Pateley Bridge, Ripley Castle, Fountains Abbey, Ripon, Harrogate, Knaresborough – in 1994, 8000 men are re-enacting the Battle of Marston Moor here, five centuries after the event, on 3–4 July). 4: York (minster, Viking Centre, Rail Museum, etc.) and Chester (cathedral, etc.).

MUSIC AND BOOKS Scores of towns have festivals annually, some outstandingly good. Programmes are obtainable through the British Arts Festivals Association (tel: 081-348 4117). As many arts festivals (40, big and small) are in the east, there is a free guide to these too (tel: 0473 822922). Other such events, in attractive venues, can be located through the Stately Homes Music Festival and Bailey's Summer Music – garden concerts with fireworks (for both, tel: 071-344 4444); English Heritage (tel: 071-973 3000); National Trust (tel: 071-222 9251); and the Festival of Music in Cathedrals (Box 1234, London SW2 2TG). Wine and music events in stately venues are run by the Wine Society (membership, tel: 0438 741177).

For other arts events, opera etc. throughout the country, see the quality newspapers; or ask the tourist boards for lists (England - tel: 081-846 9000; Wales – tel: 0222 499009) as well as for their leaflet, *Great British Art Galleries*, with programme of exhibitions. They can also tell you about major antique or craft fairs, arts centres and their events, and so on.

There are about a dozen regional tourist boards, too; as well as tourism departments in every county hall; and Tourist Information Centres in hundreds of towns – all excellent sources of information on these and every other topic of interest to travellers.

Enthusiasts for a particular author may be able to join a society dedicated to his/her works, each with not only a journal, etc. but also events in that author's locality – a good objective for a weekend away. Here are examples, with the county in which most events occur and the address of the society to which to send a subscription.

Hardy, Dorset (send £12 to the Hardy Society at Box 1348, Dorchester, DT1 1YH). **George Eliot,** Warwickshire (£7 to 71 Stepping Stones Road, Coventry, CV5 8JT). **Kipling,** Sussex (£6 to 24 Cedar Court, Haslemere, GU27 2BA). **Brontës,** West Yorkshire (£10 to Yorkshire Bank, Keighley, BD21 3SD). **Shaw,** Hertfordshire (£7 to 155A North View Road, London N8 7ND). **Mrs Gaskell,** Cheshire (£5 to Far Yew Tree House, Over Tabley, Knutsford, WA16 0HN). **Tennyson,** Lincolnshire (£6 to Central Library, Lincoln, LN2 1EZ). **Dickens,** Kent and London (£5 to 48 Doughty Street, London WC1N 2LF). **Housman,** Shropshire (£7.50 to 80 New Road, Bromsgrove, B60 2LA). **Edward Thomas,** Hampshire (£5 to 50 New Odiham Road, Alton, GU34 1QG). **Dorothy Sayers,** Essex (£7 to Rose Cottage, Malthouse Lane, Hurstpierpoint, BN6 9JY). **Charles Lamb,** London (£8 to 28 Grove Lane, London, SE5 8ST). **Arnold Bennett** (£4 to The Boatyard, Barlaston, ST12 9DJ).

This is only a selection. Other societies are dedicated to **Jane Austen, D. H. Lawrence, Trollope, E. F. Benson, Richard Jefferies, Parson Woodforde, Conan Doyle, Leo Walmsley, Lewis Carroll, Byron** . . . altogether there are about a hundred. Addresses can be had by phoning the Alliance of Literary Societies (tel: 021-236 3591).

Useful books are *Literary Walks of Britain* by D. Veale (Selecta) and *The Oxford Literary Guide to Britain* (OUP). To read as you go, take Blythe's *Places: An Anthology* (OUP) or Grigson's *Poems & Places* (Faber). In many areas, leaflets can be had at Tourist Information Centres describing places associated with local writers such as **Dickens** (Rochester, Kent), **George Eliot** (Nuneaton, Warwickshire), **Housman** (Bromsgrove, Worcestershire, and Ludlow, Shropshire), **Ellis Peters** – her 'Brother Cadfael' stories (Shropshire), **Bunyan** (Bedfordshire), **Shakespeare** (Warwickshire),and **Blackmore** (north Devon is Lorna Doone country). A variety of authors who lived in Hertfordshire and in other counties north or west of London are covered collectively in a couple of leaflets available from Tourist Information Centres. The British Tourist Authority (tel: 081-846 9000) has a free map-folder of *Literary Britain*.

GOLF AND FISHING Peerage publish guides to these with comprehensive gazetteers, £3.95 each from bookshops.

A ROOM WITH A VIEW

If you value a bedroom that has a particularly fine view, you will find plenty of choice in this book – and in great variety.

For a *sea view:* try the **Bosweddan** or **Marina Hotels, Acton Vean, Cliff House** or **Woodlands** (all in Cornwall), **The Wood** (Devon), **Red House** (Dorset), **Bank Cottage** (Scilly Isles), **Llwyndû** (Gwynedd), **Old Vicarage** (Dyfed), **Plas Trefarthen** (Gwynedd), **West Usk Lighthouse** (Gwent).

Lake or river views: **Old Granary** (Dorset), **Newbarn** (East Sussex), **Bickleigh Cottage** (Devon), **Pinksmoor Millhouse** (Somerset), **Kelleythorpe** (Humberside), **Pool House Hotel** (Worcestershire), **Glanrannell Park Hotel** (Dyfed), **Herongate** (Gwynedd), **Wye Barn** (Gwent).

Hills and valleys: **Barton Old Vicarage** (Cumbria), **Cottage Crest** (Hampshire), **Holmhead** (Northumberland), **Alfoxton Cottage** (Somerset), **Hardingland Farmhouse** (Cheshire), **Hermitage Manor** (Herefordshire), **Highlow Hall** (Derbyshire), **Jinlye** and **Woodside Old Farmhouse** (Shropshire), **Lamb Inn** and **Lower Green Farmhouse** (Gloucestershire), **Nalderhill House** (Berkshire), **Pillmead House** (Hampshire), **Park Hall** and **Broniwan** (Dyfed) **Flickering Lamp, Ty Croeso** and **Upper Trewalkin Farm** (Powys), **Wenallt Farm** and **Thorntrees** (Gwent).

Historic townscapes: **Old Vicarage,** Rye (East Sussex), **Cathedral Gate** (Kent; some rooms overlook Canterbury cathedral, floodlit at night), **Paradise House** (Avon; overlooks the whole of Bath), **Bradford Old Windmill** (Wiltshire), **Fortitude Cottage** (Hampshire; harbour view), **48 Water Street,** Lavenham (Suffolk).

These are only examples. And, obviously, only some rooms at each house have a fine view: check when booking.

KEEPING COSTS DOWN

Some 'sights' charge prohibitive prices now, so it is good to learn that Alton Towers (Staffordsire) – where one can spend days enjoying the gardens, rides, boats, 3-D cinema, cable-car and much else – offers a second day's entry for only £3 (normal price, £12). For half-price theatre tickets in London call at the Ticket Booth in Leicester Square on the day itself; or if you are a pensioner, call at the theatre or concert hall shortly before the performance; or get onto the mailing-list of Show Pairs (tel: 071-738 4488) which posts vouchers offering two seats for the price of one. Many museums are free, but even others have special offers – such as free admission after 4.30, or discounts for pensioners, etc.

Restaurants with the British Tourist Authority's 'fixed price' sticker provide a menu at about half the à la carte cost. Restaurants at cathedrals and churches serve excellent and often imaginative lunches for £5 or so (for a free guide to them, tel: 0727 864208). A recent addition to the many guides to budget restaurants is *The Gourmet's Guide to Fish and Chips* (Sutton, £6.95). The latest guide to inn food is the AA's *Britain's Best Pubs.*

Apex rail fares are cheap if booked a week ahead. To explore the many steam rail routes in Wales, buy a 4- or 8-day ticket for £20 or £27 (sold at all stations). The Royal Mail runs post-and-passenger buses to remote and beautiful places, particularly in Wales, the north and the south-east. Fares are modest, a book of timetables and maps is free (tel: 0246 556728).

YOUR HOSTS AND YOU

Most of the establishments recommended in this book are private houses, because I rarely find hotels which give such a genuine welcome and treat visitors as individuals – just as they might treat guests of the family. Many hosts get real pleasure, not just profit, from looking after you. Typical of the things they say are: 'So many visitors are gardening enthusiasts that it's always a pleasure to share their interest and several have produced good ideas for our garden.' (**Spursholt House**) 'We've had several family reunions here, and have laid on special dinners for ruby weddings. At birthdays, we provide free "bubbly" and an autographed drawing of our house as a memento: happy gatherings for our guests and ourselves too.' (**Shearings**) 'Some Americans stayed for five nights, which is unusual as most are one-night stays. But they were practised with your book and had learnt that it is better to get a good base and travel from it each day than face a daily round of packing.' (**Church Farm**, Bedfordshire) When visitors stay on for some days like this, they not only get a better knowledge of all the locality has to offer but often strike up a friendship with their hosts. One-nighters with whom contact is fleeting and impersonal are not too welcome at some houses; further, a one-night booking can prevent a longer one being accepted, at a substantial loss to the proprietor. This is why some now decline to make one-night bookings far in advance.

Although in many ways more responsive to guests' preferences than most hoteliers are, the owners of b & b or small guest-houses are in certain other ways more limited. Often they have few or no staff, that is why – in some places – meal times may be inflexible, and access to the house may not be permissible at all hours.

Dinner times are stated in the individual entries for the houses. Most serve dinner at or after 7pm; about two dozen, at 6.30pm. Even where non-residents are not accepted for meals (see entries), visitors' own friends are often welcome, by arrangement with the proprietor. As to breakfast, the most usual hour is around 8.30 – but with some, or even a great deal of, flexibility. Only a small number do not serve breakfast before 9am. Most proprietors can produce extra-early breakfasts for travellers in a hurry to be away (this may sometimes be just a coffee-and-toast tray); only a few, however, are prepared to serve breakfast after 9.30. If the time of breakfast is important to you, discuss this when booking.

It is also worth bearing in mind that few British people like bedrooms heated as warmly as in America, so if you travel north in winter, be prepared! Other differences to remember: only a few proprietors provide facecloths, ice cubes, bottled water and fresh-squeezed orange juice. Some are generous with their time when you want sightseeing advice but many are too busy running their house: every town has a Tourist Information Centre to help you. Ask for guidance when using electric appliances – never plug anything but a shaver into a shaver-socket, and nothing into a light socket.

Readers occasionally ask whether houses that are given shorter entries, following other much longer ones, are inferior. The answer is no. Space prevents my giving all entries a full page and where there are two alternatives in the same district, it seems reasonable to pair them. The second one may have fewer rooms, provide no dinners or have limited facilities; but this does not mean that its standards are necessarily lower. Some are, in fact, more 'posh' – if that is what you want.

On another page, you are invited to send in recommendations for possible new entries in later editions of this book. Occasionally I meet readers who say they fear publicity might 'spoil' their own particular finds. It has not, however, ↲ spoiled houses that have been in this book for years – and, in some cases, it has saved them from closing through lack of trade (or from letting standards slip through lack of income). For small proprietors, the fees charged to buy a page of advertising in most guides – and even to be inspected – can be prohibitive. They are heavily dependent upon the recommendations of satisfied visitors who write to me.

Finally, every year brings new threats to the continuance of that very English institution, bed-and-breakfast in private homes. Many now emanate from the bureaucracy in Brussels, issuing endless regulations. Some are primed by big hotel chains in an effort to stifle competition.

Certain regulations are sensible (such as fire precautions in houses where more than six visitors sleep). Others verge on the farcical – especially, food hygiene rules devised for factories and hospitals but enforced in domestic kitchens no different from your own kitchen at home. Commercial rates, levied locally, may be applied to all manner of things, from water supply to refuse collection. Fire-resistant mattresses and annually testing the safety of all electrical installations are two recent additions to the list of dos and don'ts, only some of which bring real benefits though all add to running costs. A number of b & b proprietors have gone out of business as a result.

Some readers may care to talk with their hosts about these issues.

Christopher Booker's *The Mad Officials: How the Bureaucrats are Strangling Britain* (Constable) is an exposure of all this.

YOU AND THE LAW

Once your booking has been confirmed – orally or in writing – a contract exists between you and the proprietor. He is legally bound to provide accommodation as booked; and you are legally bound to pay for this accommodation. If unable to take up the booking – even because of sickness – you still remain liable for a very substantial proportion of the charges (in addition to losing your deposit).

If you have to cancel, let the proprietor know as soon as possible; then he may be able to re-let the accommodation (in which case you would be liable to pay only a re-letting cost or forfeit your deposit). Phone if you are going to arrive late.

(**A note to American readers.** It may be an acceptable practice elsewhere to make bookings at several houses for the same date, choosing only later which one to patronize; but this way of doing things is not the British practice and you are legally liable to compensate any proprietors whom you let down in this way.)

READER PARTICIPATION

1 It would be very helpful if you will let me know your opinion of places from this book at which you have stayed. Please post this to: Elizabeth Gundrey, 19 Fitzjohns Avenue, London NW3 5JY (no phone calls please!). **If you wish for an acknowledgment please enclose International Reply Coupons and an addressed envelope.** Last year, it was **Toll Barn** (see page 291) and **Swainscombe** (see page 214) which prompted most letters of praise. Which house will it be this year?

Names of establishments

Your comments (with date of stay)

2 If you find other places in England, Wales or Scotland you think we should visit, for possible inclusion in a future edition, please will you send me your description (including price and address), with brochure. **No expensive places, please.** See overleaf.

Your name and address (capitals): _____

_____

Date: _____ Occupation (optional): _____

THANK YOU . . . to those who send details of their own finds, for possible future inclusion in the book. Do not be disappointed if your candidate does not appear in the very next edition. We never publish recommendations from unknown members of the public without verification, and it takes time to get round each part of England and Wales in turn.

Inevitably, there is a time-lag between visits and the appearance of what is written in book form. The details you send are always filed, under counties, until such time as we go to the county in question; and then they are a very great help, although there is never enough space for all of them to be used. Please, however, do not send details of houses already featured in many other guides, nor any that are more expensive than those in this book.

'NO VACANCIES' It is unreasonable to expect to find vacancies (particularly, the least expensive rooms) at short notice. A reader wrote to me on 6 February, saying: 'We stayed at five houses recommended in your book and would have stayed at more had we not been phoning ahead only one day or so at a time. An amazing number of your houses were fully booked even at this time of year.' And from one proprietor came this comment: 'So many people rang at very short notice that I just could not accommodate them, as most of my regular visitors book well in advance. I must have refused over 50 enquirers.' Another said: 'On just one day, I refused 17.' And, in early March, one wrote: 'I've just had an enquiry for Easter and it seems I was the tenth house unable to oblige.'

Dining-room at Holmhead (see page 159)

HOW TO HAVE A GOOD TIME

As the readership of this book grows so does the diversity of readers' tastes. My detailed descriptions are meant to help each one pick out the places that suit him or her best; but I still get readers who write to complain about bar or carpark noise at inns (so why pick an inn rather than a house without a bar?), and the presence of dogs (why go to a house with the code letter **D**, meaning dogs accepted, or to a farm where dogs are almost certainly kept?). Light sleepers should avoid rooms overlooking, for instance, a market square: not all houses in this book are rural.

Some people have very particular requirements; and it is up to them to discuss these when telephoning to book. Many hosts in this book are more flexible than big hotels, and all are eager to help if they can. I have in mind such things as: a bad back, needing a very *firm mattress* (I carry a folding bedboard from the Back Shop in London – tel: 071-935 9120); special *dietary* requirements, and *allergies* to feather pillows or animals; a strong preference for *separate tables* rather than a shared dining-table – or vice versa; *fewer courses* than on the fixed menu; *twin beds* rather than double beds – or vice versa; freedom to *smoke* – or freedom from it; a particular wish for *electric blanket, hot water-bottle*, etc. or a dislike of *duvets;* the need to arrive, depart or eat at *extra-early* or *extra-late* hours; an intention to pay by *credit card* (this should not be taken for granted, particularly at small guest-houses).

The code letters that appear after the name of each house will help you identify houses suitable for children, dogs, people with mobility problems, users of public transport, etc.: for full explanation, see page xlvi. Please also use the 'how to book' checklist on page xliv when telephoning.

It's best to stay at least 2–3 days: you cannot possibly appreciate an area if you only stay overnight (prices per night are often less, too, if you stay on). At some houses, 1-night bookings may be refused.

There is another important component in having an enjoyable experience: congenial company. I am struck by the number of readers who comment that, when they stay at one of our recommended houses, they find other visitors – also readers – very agreeable because they are compatible people. (Just occasionally there is an exception: the one who keeps aloof, or who loudly complains about trivia, for instance.)

When to go? Seaside resorts or other places suitable for children will be at their busiest (and dearest) in July–August and during half-term holidays (especially, in late May, which is also a bank holiday period). Houses which do *not* take children tend to have vacancies in July and August – even in the popular Cotswolds, for instance. Other peak periods are, of course, Easter, Christmas, New Year and the bank holiday in late August. There are local peaks, too (the Gold Cup races at Cheltenham or the regatta at Henley, for instance, are apt to fill hotels for miles around), and local troughs (Brighton, a conference centre, is least busy in high summer). In holiday areas, travel on any day other than a summer Saturday if you can. Make ferry, Motorail or coach/train reservations well in advance.

And one final tip on ensuring that you get all that you hope for: always use the most recent edition of *Cottages, B&Bs and Country Inns of England and Wales* that is available. Here's why this is so important. A reader wrote to me as follows: 'The house was dirty; room smelt damp; toilet-seat wobbly and stained; under-pillows had no cases; grubby carpets . . . (etc.)'. The house had changed hands years ago, and been dropped from my book as a consequence; but the reader was using an out-of-date edition. Prices change, so do telephone numbers and much else. Change of owner or inflated prices are the two most common reasons why I drop houses; a third is that I find somewhere better – or of better value – nearby.

TELEPHONING TO BOOK: A CHECKLIST

Book well ahead: many of these houses have few rooms. Further, at some houses, rooms (even if similarly priced) vary in size or amenities: early applicants get the cheapest and/or best ones. Mention that you are a reader of this book (called *Staying Off the Beaten Track* in Britain): sometimes there are discounts on offer exclusively for readers. Telephoning is preferable to writing to enquire about vacancies, and, in many cases, the best time is early evening (British time).

1. Ask for the owner by the *name* given in this edition. (If there has been a change, standards and prices may differ.)
2. Specify *your precise needs* (such as en suite bathroom, if available), see page xliii. (Do not turn up with children, dogs or disabilities if you have not checked that these are accepted or provided for.) Elderly people may wish to ensure that their room is not on the second floor.
3. Check *prices* – these, too, can change (particularly after spring). Ask whether there are any bargain breaks.
4. Ask what *deposit* to send (or quote a credit card number). Overseas visitors may be asked to pay up to 50 per cent.
5. State your intended *time of arrival*, what meals are wanted and at what times. (If you should then be late, telephone a warning – otherwise your room may be let to someone else. It is inconsiderate to arrive late for home-cooked meals prepared especially for you.) Most proprietors expect visitors to arrive about 5pm. In country lanes, finding your way after dark can be difficult.
6. Ask for precise instructions for *locating the house:* many are remote. Better still, ask for a brochure with map to be posted to you. Check where to park.
7. Few proprietors expect visitors to stay out of the house in the daytime; but if you want to stay in, check this when booking.

At houses where dinner is not served, a light supper can often be obtained (if ordered in advance), ranging from sandwiches to family 'pot luck'. (Packed lunches too.) Prices from about £2 to £8.

PRICES

This book came into being to provide a guide to good accommodation at prices suited to people of moderate means. That remains its policy.

In the current edition are houses at which it is possible to stay, at the time of publication, for as little as £11–£20 for b & b – that is, per person sharing a double room. (However, for the best rooms in the house, or later in the year, you may well be asked for more. **Check when booking.**)

The prices are as quoted to me when the book was in preparation during 1993. But sometimes unexpected costs force proprietors to increase their prices subsequently: becoming liable for VAT or business rates, for instance.

You can see from the text data when price rises occur. For instance, in the Isle of Wight few proprietors raise prices until summer (if then), while in the Lake District and Yorkshire Dales many put them up in spring.

Inclusive terms for dinner, bed-and-breakfast (particularly for a week) can be much lower than those quoted here for these items taken separately. Most houses in this book have bargain breaks or other discounts on offer, some exclusive to readers. A 'bargain break' is usually a 2- or 3-day booking including dinners, at a discount; sometimes at low season only.

READERS' COMMENTS
ON THE BRITISH EDITION

We have now stayed at well over 25 accommodations recommended in your various editions and have not had a bad one yet. We shall continue to use your book on our future visits to Britain.

A.J. Woodroffe
Mahwah, New Jersey

I must mention that my wife and I have stayed at a number of places recommended by you and we have never been disappointed. More than that, in almost all cases, our expectations have been exceeded. We look forward to more wonderful trips through England in the future which are made that much better by our staying off the beaten track.

Mr. and Mrs. J. Robert Hughes
Panama City, Florida

We wanted to take this opportunity during our current travels in the British Isles to express our thanks for your excellent book *Staying Off the Beaten Track*. It has been a great assistance in our bookings, and your evaluations and descriptions of the lodgings have been excellently portrayed.

Anne Manderson
Nokomis, Florida

Congratulations on *Staying Off the Beaten Track*! We have been devoted users of your book since 1983 and have never found your recommendations wrong. Your book has made each of our visits to England much more enjoyable.

Donald and Dorris Clopper
Sedona, Arizona

Found your book very helpful – much more complete than others published in the US.

Judith Wisnlewski
Devon, Pennsylvania

We were anxious to visit bed-and-breakfasts that were not in the heart of cities. Your suggestions were perfect.

Sharon Anderson
Fargo, North Dakota

We enjoy getting off the busy roads and are so pleased we found your book.

Eileen Spear
London, Ontario

EXPLANATION OF CODE LETTERS

*(These appear, where applicable, in alphabetical
order after the names of cottages, B&Bs and inns)*

C Suitable for families with children. Sometimes a minimum age is stipulated, in which case this is indicated by a numeral; thus **C(5)** means children over 5 years old are accepted. In most cases, houses that accept children offer reduced rates and special meals. They may provide cots, high chairs and even baby-sitting; or games and sports for older children. Please enquire when booking. And do not expect young children to be lodged free, as babies are. Many houses have playing-cards, board games, irons, hair-dryers, maps, gumboots, bicycles, and so forth – just ask. Families which pick establishments with plenty of games, swimming-pool, animals, etc., or that are near free museums, parks and walks, can save a lot on keeping youngsters entertained. (Readers wanting total quiet may wish to avoid houses coded **C**.)

D Dogs permitted. A charge is rarely made, but it is often a stipulation that you must ask before bringing one; the dog may have to sleep in your car, or be banned from public rooms.

M Suitable for those with mobility problems. Needs vary: whenever I have used the code letter **M**, this indicates that not only is there a ground-floor bedroom and bathroom, but these, and doorways, have sufficient width for a wheelchair, and steps are few. For precise details, ask when booking.

PT Accessible by public transport. It is not necessary to have a car in order to get off the beaten track because public transport is widely available; houses indicated by the code **PT** have a railway station or coach stop within a reasonable distance, from which you can walk or take a taxi (quite a number of hosts will even pick you up, free, in their own car). The symbol **PT** further indicates that there are also some buses for sightseeing, but these may be few. Ask when booking.

S Indicates those houses which charge single people no more, or only 10% more, than half the price of a double room (except, possibly, at peak periods).

X Visitors are accepted at Christmas, though Christmas meals are not necessarily provided. Some hotels and farms offer special Christmas holidays; but, unless otherwise indicated (by the code letter **X** at top of entry), those in this book will then be closed.

ALPHABETICAL DIRECTORY OF HOUSES AND HOTELS IN
ENGLAND

Prices are per person sharing a double room, at the beginning of the year. You may be quoted more later or for single occupancy.

Prices and other facts quoted at the head of each entry are as supplied by the proprietors.

Paradise House (see page 266)

ABBEY BRIDGE INN

C(5) **D M**

Lanercost, Cumbria, CA8 2HG   Tel: 06977 2224
North-east of Brampton. Nearest main road: A69 from Haltwhistle to
Brampton (and M6, junction 43).

7 **Bedrooms.** £19–£25. Bargain breaks.
Some have own bath/shower/toilet. Tea/
coffee facilities. Views of garden, country,
river. No smoking.
Dinner. A la carte, at 7–9pm. Vegetarian or
special diets if ordered. Wine can be
ordered. **Light suppers** available.
1 **Sitting-room.** With open fire, central
heating, TV. **Bar.**
Small garden

Where two rivers converge to the sound of rushing water, there is an old hump-
backed bridge of red sandstone built in the time of James II. The traffic ignores it,
hurrying across over a modern bridge further along. From it you can see part-
ruined Lanercost Priory, or leave it to walk along riverside paths. Right here, the
Sayers family (former lecturer Brian and his wife Sheila, together with their son –
a professional hotelier – and his wife) run the Abbey Bridge Inn. Its name has
been changed at least five times – once, when the reforming Countess of Carlisle
made it 'dry', it was called the Temperance Hotel.

It's a snug place to stay, particularly after a day's strenuous walking in the
Border hills. Most bedrooms (one on ground floor) are simply but pleasantly
furnished. Adjacent is the blacksmith's forge, dating back to the 17th century,
where meals (other than breakfast) are served to residents and non-residents. It is
a barn-like building with gnarled rafters and white-painted walls. The bar (with
real ales, and much used by locals) and sitting-area downstairs are made cosy by a
big iron stove. Up a specially made wrought-iron spiral staircase is a gallery where
one eats beneath wrought-iron chandeliers. You can have either very good bar
snacks; or a dinner including trout mousse, beef teriyaki (marinated in sherry and
ginger) and peach-brandy meringue, for instance, all freshly prepared. Sunday
lunch is also available.

Drinks or coffee can be enjoyed sitting under sun-umbrellas on the old bridge
itself, or in the garden.

As well as scenic walks or drives, and the beautiful priory, there is plenty to do
or see in the area: fishing in the River Irthing for brown trout or grayling; 14th-
century Naworth Castle, Hadrian's Wall with Roman forts, the Saxon church at
Over Denton, and historic villages like Gilsland and Bewcastle with Roman
remains. Bewcastle has a decorated stone cross which is one of Britain's greatest
Saxon treasures. In the river at Corby Castle on the way to Carlisle are salmon-
traps built by 12th-century monks and still in use today. The road from
Brampton to Alston is particularly attractive, running alongside the River South
Tyne, with views of the northernmost Pennines. The new 'dig' at Birdoswald
Roman fort is near the inn, an interesting site (with interpretation centre) where
one can see the dig in process.

Readers' comments: Glorious! Splendid. Made most welcome; excellent meals.
Excellent place, with superb food. Food very good. Nothing too much trouble.

ABBEY HOUSE

C(12) S

Monk Soham, Suffolk, IP13 7EN   Tel: 0728 685225
West of Saxmundham. Nearest main road: A1120 from Stowmarket to Yoxford.

3 Bedrooms. £17–£21 (less for 6 nights). Prices go up in May. All have own bath/toilet. Tea/coffee facilities. Views of garden, country. Washing machine on request.
Dinner. £12 for 4 courses and coffee, at 7.15pm (not Sundays). Vegetarian or special diets if ordered. Wine can be brought in. **Light suppers** if ordered.
1 Sitting-room. With open fire, central heating, TV.
Large garden
Closed from November to February.

'Fish, fish, do your duty!' the rector who lived here in the late 19th century used to admonish the inhabitants of his ponds (still there), which had originally provided Friday food for monks at the abbey (long vanished). This and other anecdotes of his life at Abbey House are in a book by his son which Sue Bagnall shows her visitors. It was he who planted the huge oaks, beeches and limes in the grounds. The architect was Teulon, a high-Victorian gothicist.

Sue and her husband have made the old rectory comfortable and have furnished it with antiques, keeping the atmosphere informal. Among fine old features they have restored is a magnificent cast-iron fireplace in the dining-room. Colours are soft (pale buff or shell pink, for instance). Sue cooks traditional English meals (using their own meat and vegetables) such as home-made soup or pâté, chicken in an orange and tarragon sauce, roast lamb, chocolate mousse and cheeses.

Guests are welcome to look at the livestock which includes Jersey cows (calves sometimes), sheep, chickens, ducks and peafowl. In the large garden, there is croquet and a swimming-pool.

The Norfolk Broads are within reach; historic Norwich; bird reserves along the coast; old-fashioned seaside towns like Southwold; Lowestoft with its sands and its busy fishing port. At nearby Snape Maltings, there are annual concerts, part of the Aldeburgh music festival.

Other sights include Somerleyton and Helmingham halls, Framlingham and Orford castles, Bressingham Steam Museum (with gardens), the Otter Trust, wildlife or farm parks, Saxtead windmill, rural crafts, vineyards and inns.

Readers' comments: Delightful. Excellent. Would be happy to make a return visit. The very best we have ever stayed in. House, food and hospitality outstanding.

The addresses of houses are geographically correct but postal addresses sometimes differ (for correspondence, the only essential element is the postcode).

Information about the nearest town and 'A' road helps you to locate the whereabouts of any village on a map; but before setting off it is necessary to get precise instructions from your host as many houses are very much 'off the beaten track'.

ACTON VEAN S
Trevean Lane, Rosudgeon, Cornwall, TR20 9PF Tel: 0736 762675
East of Penzance. Nearest main road: A394 from Helston towards Penzance.

2 **Bedrooms.** £20 (less for 2 nights). Tea/coffee facilities. TV. Views of garden, country, sea. Washing machine on request. **Light suppers** only if ordered. Wine can be brought in.
1 **Sitting-room.** With open fire, central heating, TV, record-player.
Small garden
Closed from December to February.

Down on the beach is a hollowed-out rock where, in the 18th century, Lady Susannah Acton used to take a seawater bath. Up on the secluded National Trust headland is the castellated mock-castle which her admiral husband built for her in 1725 (it is now converted into flats). And adjoining it one finds this very comfortable modern house with a sweeping panorama of Mount's Bay and the castle (NT) of St Michael's Mount. The coastal path wanders by, and down in the cove there is such a variety of seaweeds that naturalists flock to it.

David and Pamela Green have collected all kinds of things in and around their house – a granite altar, once in the castle's chapel, a ship's figurehead, a model of HMS *Victory*, embroidery pictures and tapestry cushions made by Pamela. The two ground-floor bedrooms (with shared bathroom) have pleasant views, mostly of the series of sloping gardens – one leading to another, some hidden behind hedges, one with lily-pool and fountain, the lowest with a wood settle from which to enjoy the sea view and spectacular sunsets. (Light snacks only.)

Rosudgeon is in the middle of a beautiful stretch of coast – sands, cliffs and coves. Nearby is the quaint seaside town of Marazion, from which one can walk across a causeway at low tide to visit the Mount. Beyond this lies Penzance and its antique shops, harbour (trips to the Scillies), ancient church and byways.

Readers' comments: A real treat! Comfortably spacious. They made you feel at home at once.

Few houses can be nearer to the sea than the **CHYMORVAH HOTEL**, situated on the outskirts of Marazion. Beyond its garden (where cream teas are served) is a beach of sand and rocks, with a close view of St Michael's Mount. Hazelmary Bull has furnished the bedrooms with lacy or colourful draperies and several have four-posters (one has a spa bath adjoining it). Sizes vary, the smallest being beamed attic rooms – by contrast with the rather grand main rooms in what was, a century ago, a mine-owner's granite mansion. A typical dinner menu:

vegetable soup, beef casserole, jam sponge with clotted cream (choices at every course). Coarse fishing, riding and trips to the Scilly Isles (sea angling free). £19.90–£22.65. [Tel: 0736 710497; postcode: TR17 0DQ]

ALBYNES

Nordley, Shropshire, WV16 4SX   Tel: 0746 762261
North-west of Bridgnorth. Nearest main road: A442 from Bridgnorth to
Telford.

Tea/coffee facilities. TV. Views of garden,
country. No smoking. Washing machine on
request.
Dinner (by arrangement). £8 for 3 courses
and coffee, at times to suit guests. Non-
residents not admitted. Vegetarian or
special diets if ordered. Wine can be
brought in. No smoking. **Light suppers** if
ordered.
1 Sitting-room. With open fire, central
heating, TV, record-player. No smoking
preferred.

2 Bedrooms. £16–£18 (less for 3 nights).
Both have own bath or shower/toilet.

Large garden
Closed in November and December.

Older readers may have grown up with the nature books of Frances Pitt: this is
the house where she lived and wrote them. As a child, she kept squirrels in the
attic here. (In nearby Dudmaston Hall there is a room exhibiting mementoes
from her life.)

The house was originally built in 1823 by John Smallman, a pupil of John
Nash (architect of London's Regent's Park terraces and of the Brighton Pavilion).
It was the home of the Burgher of Bridgnorth, who named it after his son
Albinius. The dining-room was designed to accommodate fine carved panelling
removed from a nearby Tudor house, and there is an elegant oak staircase that
spirals its way up to the bedrooms. Several of these overlook the lake (or far hills),
as does the sitting-room – furnished with antiques and gold brocade chairs.
Ducks waddle up from the water to peer at visitors; even pheasants and partridges
are bold and curious enough to stare in too. Twisting passages and steps, unusual
curved doors and round-arched alcoves add to the character of the house.

Cynthia Woolley collects old local pottery – both fine Coalport china (made at
Ironbridge) and jugs of Caughley earthenware, the clay for which came from
woods that are within view. She is an expert flower-arranger too, growing what
she needs in the informal garden around the big house. Her husband farms the
adjoining land – a mixture of arable fields and pastures for cattle or sheep. A
typical dinner may comprise: curried parsnip soup, grilled lamb chops with fresh
herbs and lemon-cream pudding with frosted green grapes.

On the other side of Bridgnorth
is **HARPSFORD MILL FARM,**
Oldbury. Clive Millington runs a
mixed farm here; but his great-uncle's
watermill on the Mor brook – next to
the farmhouse – no longer has a wheel
to turn. There is a pleasant sitting-
room with William Morris fabrics,
and a double bedroom overlooks the
bubbling stream. Through French
doors one can walk onto a terrace with
chairs or seek out waterside footpaths.
Upstairs, a surprise awaits visitors: a

huge double bath. (Suzanne serves
snack suppers only.) £16. [Tel:
074635 274; postcode: WV16 5NN]

5

ALDENHAM WEIR   C M PT X
Muckley Cross, Shropshire, WV16 4RR   Tel: 074631 352
North-west of Bridgnorth. On A458 from Bridgnorth to Shrewsbury.

5 Bedrooms. £18 (less for 6 nights). All have own shower/toilet. Tea/coffee facilities. TV. Views of garden, country. No smoking. Washing machine on request.
Light suppers if ordered. No smoking.
2 Sitting-rooms. With central heating, TV. No smoking.
Large garden

This lovely woodland location by the winding Mor brook, set well back from the road, enchanted the Coldicotts so much that a few years ago they built themselves and their children a very attractive, architect-designed house here. Once there had been a watermill – hence the weir and the old mill-race which are features of the beautiful site. Stephen, a plumbing engineer, did much of the work himself, to the highest standards; and Jennifer has furnished the house with equal care – using a lot of polished pine and rose-patterned fabrics in pink or blue. Older visitors may appreciate the two ground-floor bedrooms with French doors opening onto the garden, where there are rustic seats by the waterside from which to watch for kingfishers and woodpeckers. Alternatively, one can sit or even breakfast in the hexagonal conservatory, furnished with bamboo armchairs. As well as bedrooms, the upper floor of the house has a sitting-area for guests, containing television and tourist information. Children enjoy feeding the trout in the mill-race from one of the little bridges now spanning it.

The nearby market town of Bridgnorth is unusual – part is high up (here are half-timbered houses and the remains of a castle) and the rest so far below that a steep cliff-railway links the two. You can see traces of cave dwellings in the cliff, inhabited as late as this century.

The Severn Valley Railway, which steams 16 miles from Bridgnorth to Kidderminster, goes up and down through lovely riverside country – a relaxed way to enjoy the scenery. In a car you can deviate to visit not only the vintage cars (nearly a hundred) of Stanmore Hall and its beautiful park but also the flowery hilltop village of Claverley (black-and-white cottages and a church mural of 1200 showing knights in battle), Dudmaston Hall (Matisse and Henry Moore in an 18th-century setting), Upper Arley (another steep village leading down to the banks of the River Severn where there is a footbridge to the Old Harbour Inn) and historic Kinver (fine monuments in its ancient church, over which looms the stone ridge of Kinver Edge some 300 feet high – there are cave dwellings here and a dramatic view). The glades of Kingsford country park provide ideal spots for picnics. Further afield are the West Midland safari park, and Bewdley with a museum that comprises a cobbled byway with old craft workshops reconstructed (some modern craftsmen busy here too). Lovely Wyre Forest, with a nature reserve, is also in this direction.

ALFOXTON COTTAGE S

Holford, Somerset, TA5 1SG Tel: 0278 741418
West of Bridgwater. Nearest main road: A39 from Bridgwater to Minehead
(and M5, junction 23).

3 Bedrooms. £14–£16 (less for 4 nights).
Prices go up in June. Views of garden,
country. No smoking. Washing machine on
request.
Dinner. £15 for 4 courses and coffee, at
7pm. Non-residents not admitted. Wine can
be ordered or brought in. No smoking.
1 Sitting-room. With open fire, central
heating, piano, record-player. No smoking.
Small garden
Closed from December to February.

All round the cottage are the Quantock Hills and pretty hamlets, an area of outstanding natural beauty. Alfoxton House was tenanted by Wordsworth and his sister, and they used to walk along here to visit Coleridge (his cottage, now NT, is open).

The cottage is truly remote, up in the Quantock Hills with views across the Bristol Channel to Wales. You may believe you are never coming to it as you follow twists and turns up the small wooded lane to the top of the hill.

This little house is now the home of Richard and Angela Delderfield. Rooms are small and low but pleasantly furnished – for instance, bamboo or velvet bed-heads and a grandfather clock and flounced armchairs by the log fire in the white sitting-room, from which a door leads to the garden, woods, a trickling stream, donkeys and chickens.

Angela's cooking is one of the main attractions of staying here. She sometimes serves as a starter prawns in a creamy sauce containing whisky, or perhaps chilled lettuce soup. Chicken breasts will be stuffed with cashew and brazil nuts, raisins, herbs and lemon juice. Into her salads may go unusual ingredients such as spinach, sunflower seeds or hot crisp bacon with slivers of avocado. She makes flans of rhubarb and lemon, rum and almonds, or orange and almonds.

Readers' comments: A wonderful establishment. A lovely home in a beautiful area. Very hospitable, food and service excellent. Friendly and genuine people. Truly gifted cook. Delightful hostess. Very enjoyable stay.

At the foot of the hill is **QUANTOCK HOUSE**, a 17th-century cottage of stone and thatch; beams and huge inglenook inside, and outside a flowery garden, lawn and cobbled terrace beneath a fruitful vine. Pam Laidler (who qualified as a professional cook) produces such very English meals as lettuce soup, her own cheese-topped chicken dish, and fruit with clotted cream – all served on Portmeirion's botanical dishes. The samplers, embroidered cushions and patchwork spreads in the en suite bedrooms are all Pam's work. £17.

Readers' comments: 'Soaking up the atmosphere' is a holiday on its own! Mouth-watering food. Cannot praise too highly: I could have stayed for ever. Incomparable food. [Tel: 0278 741439; postcode: TA5 1RY]

APPLETREE COTTAGE

12 Shitterton, Bere Regis, Dorset, BH20 7HU   Tel: 0929 471686
East of Dorchester. Nearest main road: A35 from Dorchester to Poole.

rear view

2 Bedrooms. £16.50 (less for 4 nights). Price goes up at Easter. Views of garden, country. No smoking. Washing machine on request (at a small charge).
Light suppers by arrangement.
1 Sitting-room. With open fire, central heating, TV, piano. No smoking.
Garden

This is a real Hansel-and-Gretel style cottage – thick cob (clay) walls and thatched roof, with honeysuckle clambering round the front door. It was built in the 17th century and was a tiny inn when the little lane outside was a coaching road.

Inside, all ceilings are low, and walls slope. The breakfast-table is in the sitting-room, which has silky patchwork cushions on the velvet armchairs gathered around the inglenook with log stove. The very modern bathroom is also on the ground floor. Bedrooms have sprigged wallpapers, beams and board doors, and overlook the pretty garden with flagstone steps leading to the lawn. For evening meals, Beryl Wilson recommends the Royal Oak and the Greyhound.

Bere Regis is where the d'Urbervilles are buried and 'Tess' was filmed here. Hardy re-named it Kingsbere ('a little one-eyed, blinking sort o'place') and here the story begins with old Farmer Durbeyfield boasting, 'Under the church of that there parish lie my ancestors – hundreds of 'em – in coats of mail and jewels, in gr't lead coffins weighing tons and tons. There's not a man in the county of South Wessex that's got grander and nobler skillentons in his family than I.'

Bere is about half way between Poole and Dorchester, the environs of which are described elsewhere in this book. Lulworth Cove, T.E. Lawrence's cottage, Hardy country, good walks, pretty villages like Milton Abbas, seaside resorts and mellow old towns are all within easy reach as well as Bovington Tank Museum, Monkeyworld, Corfe Castle, Kingston Lacy house (and garden). Garden-lovers will enjoy Abbotsbury, Compton Acres, Athelhampton, and Wyevale garden centre. The area has many antique shops, and pick-your-own farms. An event which attracts visitors from all over the country is the Blandford Great Steam Fair.

The county town of Dorchester has a dinosaur museum with animated models, as well as traditional local history and military museums. Another new attraction is a reconstruction of Tutankhamun's tomb with facsimiles of all the treasures. You can visit the Old Crown Court (just as it was when the Tolpuddle Martyrs were condemned to transportation), Maumbury Rings (a 'coliseum' where Romans watched gladiators) and, by appointment, a local brewery at work. Near here is Palladian Came House, noted for its fine plasterwork and great Victorian conservatory. Southward lies Owermoigne with a working cider museum.

Readers' comments: An enjoyable holiday. Very pretty. Wonderful setting. Excellent cuisine. Very pleasant people. Spotless bathroom and excellent breakfast.

THE ARCHWAY
College Road, Windermere, Cumbria, LA23 1BY   Tel: 05394 45613
Nearest main road: A591 from Kendal to Ambleside.

C(10) **PT S X**

5 Bedrooms. £19–£20 (less for 3 nights). Prices go up in May. Bargain breaks. Most have own bath/shower/toilet. Tea/coffee facilities. TV. Views of garden, country. No smoking.
Dinner. £10.50 for 2 courses and coffee, at 6.45pm (not Sundays). 3 courses in winter. Non-residents not admitted. Vegetarian or special diets if ordered. Wine can be ordered. No smoking. **Light suppers** if ordered.
1 Sitting-room. With open fire, central heating. No smoking.
Small garden

The Windermere-Ambleside axis is the heart of the Lake District, for which many first-time visitors head. The Archway is in a side road close to the centre of Windermere (and conveniently near the railway station). It is in a Victorian terrace typical of those in Lake District towns, built of the green slate much used for houses hereabouts, and stands above road level behind a sloping garden.

A big semicircular arch divides the sitting-cum-dining room, which has stripped wood chairs and tables at one end and, at the other, cretonne-covered settees and chairs around a handsome fireplace. Walls are painted dusty pink; there are books everywhere; and on the walls here and throughout the house are prints, posters, Victorian engravings and other pictures, all chosen with a discriminating eye – not surprisingly, since Tony Greenhalgh has a degree in the history of art.

Anthony and Aurea, who share the cooking, are enthusiasts for food and wine. Breakfast could include home-made muesli, yogurt, granola, muffins and crumpets; and American pancakes or, more conventionally, kippers, Cumberland sausage or black pudding. A winter dinner might be cream of watercress soup or vegetable terrine; roast lamb with home-made rowanberry jelly; and such a pudding as franzipani tart or bread-and-butter pudding – sweets are a speciality.

Readers staying three nights receive a bottle of free elderflower wine and fudge at dinner.

Readers' comments: Pleasant atmosphere. Good food. They really know how to make guests happy. Attention to detail is perfect. Where else could you get such comfort, good food, good company? Truly excellent. A fabulous time. Hospitality and atmosphere excellent.

Troutbeck, near Windermere, is famous for Town End, a NT house, and the Mortal Man inn with its rhyming sign ('Thou mortal man that lives by bread/How comes thy nose to be so red?'). Near the inn is **STAMP HOWE**, Maureen Evans's spotless b & b house, where two of the rooms overlook the fells across the valley from the inn – which is where most guests dine very well. £15–£16.
Reader's comments: High calibre.

Bathroom immaculate, room bright, bed good. [Tel: 05394 33136; postcode: LA23 1PL]

9

ASHEN COPSE C S

Coleshill, Oxfordshire, SN6 7PU   Tel: 0367 240175

North-east of Swindon (Wiltshire). Nearest main road: A420 from Swindon towards Faringdon (and M4, junction 15).

2 Bedrooms. £16–£18 (less for 7 nights). Prices go up at Easter. One has own shower/toilet. Views of garden, country. No smoking.
Light suppers if ordered.
1 Sitting-room. With open fire, central heating, TV. No smoking.
Large garden

If you approach from the Faringdon direction there are panoramic views to the north of the road (and to the south the National Trust's celebrated stone barn at Great Coxwell – almost cathedral-like in its grandeur). A long, well-surfaced drive leads through pheasant woods to the 300-year-old house built of stone and brick; and around lie the 600 acres of the Hoddinotts' beef and arable farm (with a few pet lambs and a pony): all is owned by the National Trust. In this peaceful place, birdsong is usually the only sound.

It is an ideal house to bring children for a country holiday as there is a particularly good family room separate from the rest – very big and light, with its own shower room, and with windows on each side: one overlooks a lawn with magnolia, lilac and cherry trees (at their best in late spring) and the other the farmyard where calves and chickens are often to be seen. By the staircase to the other room are row upon row of colourful rosettes won at pony shows by the Hoddinotts' daughter every year since she was eight. From this bedroom you can look beyond the small swimming-pool (unheated) to the famous Uffington White Horse cut into the chalk of the hills and the prehistoric Ridgeway Path striding across the high horizon. Every room is immaculate; paintwork sparkling-white.

This is good walking country. From Ashen Copse there is a footpath all the way to Great Coxwell Barn, built by monks in the 13th century and one of the most impressive in Europe. Another goes all round Badbury Clump (site of an Iron Age fort), which is prettiest at bluebell time and from which there are fine views.

In the vicinity are attractive villages such as Highworth (17th-century houses and distant views), Buscot with a National Trust mansion of 1780 containing art treasures and watergardens running into a lake, Kelmscot (Tudor manor house where William Morris lived), Lechlade celebrated for its statue of Old Father Thames, old bridge and river locks, and picturesque Ashbury, worth a visit for the 14th-century brasses in its church and for 17th-century Ashdown House (the prehistoric site known as Wayland's Smithy is near here).

In this direction, too, are the gardens of Kingston Lisle, surrounding a fine manor house.

Readers' comments: Attractive house, pleasant welcome and attention.

Prices are per person in a double room at the beginning of the year.

ASHLANDS COTTAGE

Burwash, East Sussex, TN19 7HS   Tel: 0435 882207

North-west of Hastings. Nearest main road: A21 from Tunbridge Wells to Hastings.

C(12) **D PT S X**

2 Bedrooms. £16–£17 (less for 2 nights). Views of garden, country. Washing machine on request.
Light suppers if ordered.
1 Sitting-room. With central heating, TV.
Large garden

The garden of this pretty, lattice-paned cottage adjoins the estate of Batemans – a great 17th-century house that was Kipling's last home (it is now open to the public). Beyond its herbaceous beds and neat brick paths is a far view across the River Dudwell and buttercup meadows to Brightling Beacon. This is the scenery that inspired 'Pook's Song' ('See you the ferny ride that steals/Into the oakwoods far? . . . See you our little mill that clacks/So busy by the brook? . . . ') and you can glimpse Pook's Hill from the garden.

Trained as a singer and still keenly interested in the theatre, Nesta Harmer made her home here after many years spent in Bermuda. The pretty mahogany beds in one room were made there; and both rooms have wide views and a light, airy feel. Pine boards give the bathroom character, and the sitting-room has a restful colour scheme – predominantly pale sea-green.

Beyond the garden is a wood in which Nesta has cleared a glade and planted woodland flowers. She encourages visitors to picnic here, and some spend all day in this peaceful spot – others walk the local footpaths, or go birdwatching.

A full dinner is not available but the inns and restaurants of Burwash are two minutes' walk away.

Readers' comments: Beautifully furnished, magnificent views. Home-from-home service, restful and delightfully furnished.

Southward lies Herstmonceux and its romantic, moated castle close to which is **CLEAVERS LYNG** – an old, tile-hung yeoman's house (now a small hotel) with beams and inglenook in the dining-room where Sally Simpson serves such dinners (or Sunday lunches) as seafood cocktail, steak pie and orange mousse. Bedrooms are prettily furnished, some with balconies overlooking a garden with waterfall floodlit at night. Local craftsmen make

wrought iron and the famous Sussex 'trugs' (willow baskets). £19.75. [Tel: 0323 833131; postcode: BN27 1QJ]

AVONSIDE

C(10) **PT**

Winsley Hill, Limpley Stoke, Wiltshire, BA3 6EX   Tel: 0225 722547
South of Bath (Avon). Nearest main road: A36 from Bath to Warminster.

2 Bedrooms. £18–£20 (less for 4 nights or continental breakfast). Prices go up during summer. Tea/coffee facilities. Views of garden, country, river. Washing machine on request.
Dinner. £12 for 3 courses with aperitif and coffee, at 7.30pm. Non-residents not admitted. Wine can also be brought in.
Light suppers.
1 Sitting-room. With open fire, central heating, piano.
Large garden

A typical English country house, built of honey-coloured Bath stone, the Challens' secluded home stands on the banks of the River Avon: walks along it (or the nearby Kennet & Avon Canal) and coarse fishing are among the attractions of staying in this very scenic area.

Ursula has furnished the sitting-room with tangerine or pale lime armchairs, oriental rugs and antiques that show up well against walls painted peach, on which hang many paintings by Peter who, after serving as a major in the Gurkhas, turned to a completely different career as an artist. Through the bay window is a serene view of the well-kept lawn and landscaped grounds, with tennis and croquet.

Other rooms are equally pleasing, with attractive wallpapers and leafy views. The Challens treat visitors as if they were house-guests, offering them pre-dinner drinks (no extra charge). Typical of the kind of meal Ursula serves: avocado pâté; roast lamb with quince jelly and vegetables from the garden; a brûlée of brown sugar, cream and yogurt over raspberries. Alternatively, visitors can go out to the excellent Nightingales restaurant in the village or to the Hop Pole inn.

At Bradford-on-Avon steep roads converge to the mediaeval bridge with domed chapel-turned-lockup on it. It takes time to discover all Bradford's handsome houses, Saxon church, vast tithe barn and old inns. A few miles away is Bath, and northward, such other lovely spots as Corsham, Lacock (mediaeval abbey and museum of photographic history) and the Chippenham-Calne area. Garden-lovers head for Stourhead, antique-hunters for Bath. Malmesbury (on a hill almost surrounded by the River Avon) has its famous Norman abbey and handsome stone houses from the 17th and 18th centuries lining its streets and market square. Longleat, Dyrham Park and the historic American Museum are popular.

Readers' comments: Wonderful people, very friendly. Elegant; lovely meals. The Challens make one feel like their house guests. Excellent accommodation and food. A place of peace and comfort.

Book well ahead: many of these houses have few rooms. Do not expect dinner if you have not booked it or if you arrive late.

BANK COTTAGE

Bryher, Isles of Scilly, TR23 0PR   Tel: 0720 22612

C(7) **S**

rear view

5 **Bedrooms.** £19–£22. Prices go up in June. Some have own shower/toilet. Tea/coffee facilities. Views of garden, country, sea.
Dinner. £11.50 for 4 courses and coffee, at 7pm. Non-residents not admitted. Vegetarian or special diets if ordered. Wine can be ordered. No smoking. **Light suppers** if ordered.
1 **Sitting-room.** With central heating, TV. Bar.
Small garden
Closed from November to March.

Visitors here have a superb sandy beach (right outside) virtually all to themselves; beyond it is one of England's most beautiful seascapes, dotted with 22 islets.

Mac Mace works as a diver: sometimes diving for lobsters and crabs or for archaeological finds, including Spanish doubloons, on the many nearby wrecks; sometimes for sea urchins, the decorative shells of which are exported by the thousand. He and his wife Tracy take a few guests in their cottage (built at least 300 years ago, but with later additions). The attractive rooms have low ceilings and thick walls to keep winter's gales at bay. Bedrooms are cheerful and bright. One en suite bedroom has its own balcony with sea view.

Many visitors are content just to sit all day in the colourful garden (facing south-west) to enjoy the view of the bay, sheltered by the pink-flowered escallonia hedges; or they can use a small boat and go out fishing. The sunsets are outstanding. A gate opens onto the beach, but although the climate is warm here, the sea is not. The garden is at its most colourful in early summer (fuchsias, flowering cherries, tulips and arum lilies abound); the islets are best in late spring, when they are smothered in pink sea-thrift.

Vegetables and loganberries are home-grown, rolls home-baked, eggs from the Maces' hens. A typical meal cooked by Tracy may start with fish or fish pâté, followed by a roast or casserole. Tracy particularly enjoys making puddings like banana mousse or sherry trifle and her vegetarian meals are imaginative. Sometimes meals are served outdoors, using the granite barbecue.

Visitors arriving by boat from St Mary's are met and their baggage taken up for them by tractor or Landrover.

Readers' comments: Wished we could stay for ever! Felt completely at home; happy and relaxed atmosphere. Comfortable room, excellent food. Simply delighted, a marvellous time. Nothing is too much trouble. Excellent food and accommodation, good hosts. Now a regular and much-loved destination.

*View from
Bank Cottage*

13

BANK HOUSE
Cumberland Gardens, Castle Bytham, Lincolnshire, NG33 4SQ
Tel: 0780 410523
North of Stamford. Nearest main road: A1 from Stamford to Grantham.

2 Bedrooms. £20–£25 (less for 3 nights). Both have own bath/toilet. Tea/coffee facilities. TV. Views of garden, country. No smoking. Washing machine on request.
Dinner. From £12 for 3 courses (with choices), wine and coffee, at 7pm. Non-residents not admitted. Vegetarian or special diets if ordered. Wine can be brought in. No smoking. **Light suppers** if ordered.
2 Sitting-rooms. With open fire, central heating, TV, record-player. No smoking.
Large garden

Few b & b houses are run with the professionalism of Bank House: not surprising, as both Marian Foers and her husband trained and then had careers in catering.

Two large sitting-rooms, with windows on three sides, open into each other. From one, in which a mass of pot-plants surrounds bamboo seats, sliding glass doors open onto a paved terrace. In the other, Victoriana sets a different scene. Sometimes meals are served on the terrace – otherwise, in a dining-room furnished with antiques. All around is a lovingly tended garden which the Foers created from scratch, with views of Cabbage Hill and its woods.

All the soft-furnishings (and the floppy Pierrot dolls) in the bedrooms were made by Marian – the frilled or beribboned curtains and lacy spreads which complement thick carpets. 18th-century samplers hang on the walls. Bathrooms are pretty.

Meals, too, are of a high order, often comprising such dishes as a mousse of trout and smoked salmon, spiced chicken with almonds, summer pudding and local cheeses. Rolls are home-baked, and wine is included.

Castle Bytham is an exceptionally pretty village of mellow stone houses, Norman church and duck-pond (of the former castle, only the mound remains); and within easy reach are Burghley House with its celebrated horse trials each year, Belvoir Castle, Sandringham, Rutland Water (largest man-made lake in Europe), Boston, Spalding (thronged when the bulb-gardens are at their best), Lincoln, Peterborough and Southwell (its minster almost as outstanding as a cathedral). Stamford is a uniquely beautiful, mediaeval, limestone town.

Readers' comments: Superb meals. Tasteful luxury, friendliness and competence. A great feeling of space throughout.

Near Skillington is 18th-century **SPROXTON LODGE**, popular with walkers because the long Viking Way borders its fields. This is a homely, working farm – with silver ploughing-trophies won by Ted on display to prove it! He still has his very first tractor of 40 years ago, now almost a museum piece. Unpretentious comfort (and an enormous, carpeted bathroom) are what hospitable Eileen Whatton provides here, with such meals as home-

made chicken soup, sole stuffed with crab, and fruit pie. Vegetables are from the garden. £13–£14 (b & b). [Tel: 0476 860307; postcode: NG33 5HJ]

BANK VILLA
C(5) D

Masham, North Yorkshire, HG4 4DB Tel: 0765 689605
North-west of Ripon. Nearest main road: A6108 from Ripon to Leyburn.

7 Bedrooms. £17.50 (less for 7 nights).
Some have own shower. Views of garden,
country.
Dinner. £15 for 3 courses, at 7.30pm.
Non-residents not admitted. Vegetarian or
special diets if ordered. Wine can be
ordered.
2 Sitting-rooms. With central heating,
TV.
Large garden
Closed from November to February.

Good food is the principal attraction at Bank Villa, where Phillip Gill (former administrator of York's arts festival) is an inspired cook.

The villa is a late Georgian stone house set back from the busy road, with a steep terraced garden behind it (where there is a sunny summer-house in which to sit). Here are grown fruit and vegetables for the kitchen.

Dinner is served in a pleasant room – pretty 'Old Colonial' china and rush mats on the antique tables contrast with the William Morris 'chrysanthemum' wallpaper. Phillip cooks, and his partner Anton serves, such delicious menus as spinach-and-cheese soufflé as a starter, smoked pork cooked with Calvados, and iced Drambuie parfait.

Bedrooms, too, are attractive, many with floral wallpapers and pine furniture, and some with a glimpse of the River Ure at the foot of the hill. There are plenty of books around, and one of the sitting-rooms is for guests who like reading.

Masham, a little market town, has a church with interesting features; and, in mid-July, a traction-engine and steam fair. The town stands at the foot of Wensleydale, in an area of great historic as well as very varied scenic interest: within a few miles are two abbeys, three castles, one cathedral and a stately home. There are scenic roads, markets, the sight of racehorses exercising, waterfalls, a beautifully restored Georgian theatre (at Richmond) and fine gardens.

Bedale, which has had a market since the 13th century, is a town of pleasing buildings. Don't miss Fountains, finest of all the Yorkshire abbeys.

If you visit Ripon, you can hardly miss the big inscription over the market square: 'Except ye Lord keep ye cittie, ye Wakeman waketh in vain'. And if you are there at 9pm, you will see and hear the wakeman (i.e. watchman) blowing his buffalo horn and wearing a frock coat, a cocked hat, white gloves and a silver badge on his arm. The office dates back to Alfred the Great, who gave the city its first charter and a horn in AD 886. The wakeman was there to keep an all-night watch for Viking raiders, and he had to blow the horn to let the citizens know that he was on duty. The nocturnal patrol ceased centuries ago, but the horn-blowing continues. The wakeman's house, built in 1250, is now the city's tourist information centre. Below the cathedral is a Saxon crypt, all that remains of Ripon's first Christian church, which was destroyed by those same raiders, and in it is a fine monument to a wakeman of the past.

Readers' comments: A great start to our stages to Scotland: we'll be back. Food as good as in the priciest restaurants. Energetic, cheerful and efficient. Comfortable and welcoming. Excellent food and pleasant proprietors.

BARK HOUSE HOTEL   D
Oakfordbridge, Devon, EX16 9HZ   Tel: 03985 236
North of Tiverton. On A396 from Exeter to Minehead.

6 Bedrooms. £19–£28. Some have own bath/shower/toilet. TV. Views of garden, country, river. Washing machine on request. **Dinner.** £14.50 for 4 courses (with some choices) and coffee, at 8pm. Non-residents not admitted. Vegetarian or special diets if ordered. Wine can be ordered. **Light suppers** if ordered.
1 Sitting-room. With open fire, central heating.
Large garden
Closed from December to February.

In a wooded valley through which runs the River Exe is a stone building of unusual origin. It was once used as a tannery, the oak bark for which was brought from Exmoor Forest. (From powdered oak bark, rich in tannin, were made vats of liquor in which to soak hides – the tanning process. At Colyton this process is still in use.) Today, it has been handsomely converted; and Pauline and Douglas West provide visitors with complete comfort. Books, good pictures, thick Berber carpets, antiques, pot-plants and the flicker of a cheerful log fire set the scene.

In the dining-room brown and pink tablecloths contrast with white walls; around the tables are either pews or Windsor chairs. Every bedroom is different. No. 1 has a bow window with window-seat from which to enjoy the tranquil view; no. 4, art nouveau nymphs on the ceiling – however did *they* get there! No. 6 is a huge family room with its own ancient arched door to a rock garden with pool, and leaded casements. The garden is outstanding.

Dinner may begin with smoked salmon mousse or fish chowder or eggs en cocotte. With a daube of beef will be served potato galette and other vegetables. The fresh peach Melba has an orange-and-raspberry sauce. Because the Wests once lived in Provence, Pauline has many recipes from the region.

From Bark House there is a particularly scenic route over moors to Minehead in Somerset. Both Exmoor and the sea are near; and so are Exeter, Taunton and Barnstaple, all described elsewhere. The area has a great many stately homes to visit, such as Knightshayes (NT), and gardens (Killerton); as well as churches and castles. Dunster village and Dartington are other popular outings. South Molton, a market town, has a number of good 18th-century buildings and fine views; North Molton likewise (derelict copper mines here); Swimbridge, a particularly rich church; outside Rose Ash is pretty Cuckoo Mill Bridge.

Readers' comments: Beautiful setting; excellent cooking; friendly and cheerful hosts. Have stayed four times. Charming hotel and surroundings. Very comfortable. A delight in all respects. A wonderful find. Marvellous food. Welcoming. Lovely big room. We ended up good friends. Friendly and cheerful hosts. Food memorable. Wished we could have stayed longer.

For explanation of code letters (C, D, M, PT, S, X) see page xlvi.

BARN HOUSE
The Street, Rodmell, East Sussex, BN7 3HE   Tel: 0273 477865
South of Lewes. Nearest main road: A27 from Lewes to Brighton.

7 Bedrooms. £19–£25 (less for 3 nights). Price goes up at Easter. All have own bath/shower/toilet. Tea/coffee facilities. TV. Views of garden, country. No smoking. **Light suppers** if ordered.
1 Sitting-room
Large garden
Closed in February.

In the 'twenties a 17th-century flint barn was completely transformed into this modern house, at which the Queen Mother used to be a regular visitor – not the only royal connection, for Elizabeth I once owned a house in the picturesque village. Rodmell's most famous resident was, however, Virginia Woolf who lived at Monks House – now a National Trust property – until in 1941 she drowned herself in the river. (In her house you can see furniture painted by her sister Vanessa Bell and by Duncan Grant whose own home, Charleston, is also open to the public.) Dirk Bogarde, who grew up near here, has described Virginia marching about the watermeadows, wispy hair knotted under floppy hat, singing to herself and picking wildflowers. All around are views of water-meadows and of the high Downs beyond – good walking and birdwatching country.

In April 1920 Virginia wrote to Vanessa: 'Here we are with the bells ringing for church – daffodils out – apple trees in blossom – cows mooing – cocks crowing – thrushes chirping' (all just as it is today).

Bernadette Fraser has furnished Barn House well – some rooms have fabrics designed by Duncan Grant, and one has a four-poster. On many walls are flowery decorations which she has stencilled herself, and there are antiques, paintings and tapestries in the rooms. Bernadette will provide sandwich suppers; for a full dinner, it is necessary to go into Lewes or Brighton, where there are many restaurants, or to the local pub.

In the centre of Lewes itself is the **FELIX GALLERY**, down a quiet byway – Sun Street. The little gallery is devoted entirely to cats – craft-made or antique, western or oriental, metal, china or wood. On the floor above are simple but pleasant bedrooms, well-equipped. The Whiteheads do not serve dinners but have no objection to food being brought in; however, many visitors eat at the White Hart's carvery. The small house, which dates from

William IV's reign, is at the site of a Roman fort, long built over. £17–£18. [Tel: 0273 472668; postcode: BN7 2QB]

BARNFIELD FARM   C S
near Charing, Kent, TN27 0BN   Tel: 0233 712421
North-west of Ashford. Nearest main road: A20 from Maidstone to Ashford (and M20, junctions 8/9).

4–5 Bedrooms. £18–£20 (less for 7 nights). Tea/coffee facilities. Views of garden, country, river. No smoking. Washing machine on request.
Dinner. £12.50 for 3 courses and coffee, at 7pm. Non-residents not admitted. Vegetarian or special diets if ordered. Wine can be ordered or brought in. No smoking.
Light suppers if ordered.
2 Sitting-rooms. With central heating, TV, record-player. No smoking.
Large garden

This historic farmhouse was built about the time of the Battle of Agincourt (1415). It is so remarkable that sometimes coachloads of overseas visitors come to see it; and even individual visitors are given a tour round by Martin Pym, who grew up here, or by his wife Phillada.

One steps into a large hall, where the oak framework of the house is exposed to view (draped with hop bines) and a cask holding shepherds' crooks stands in one corner – for outside are sheep pastures, with arable fields beyond. The main sitting-room has an exceptionally large inglenook where logs blaze in front of a Cromwellian fireback; the original pot-hooks, soot-blackened, are still in place. Along one beam hangs a set of handbells, on which Christmas is rung in every year. The dining-room, too, has an open fire and ancient beams, with one especially fine door (linenfold panels contrasting with intricately carved foliage), made from a church chest. There is another sitting/dining-room for guests' use, comfortably furnished with deep cretonne armchairs, plenty of books and – like every room in the house – attractive objects.

The bedrooms are fresh and unpretentious, and in two one can see the construction of the house very clearly: massive treetrunks, rough-hewn to shape, curve up to support the roof. Some rooms overlook the River Stour.

Some of the furnishings were made by Martin's grandmother – for instance, a screen of Victorian scraps in one room, and an intricate embroidery commemorating two Pyms who died in the First World War. An old linen-press, chests, rocking-chairs – at every turn of the wandering corridors there is something interesting to see. Outside are lawns, herbaceous borders surrounding a pool guarded by four stone owls, a lake visited by Canada geese, and tennis court.

Phillada serves such meals as egg mayonnaise, casseroled lamb cutlets and chocolate mousse – loading a hot-tray on the sideboard for second helpings. Guests may be offered a glass of Martin's 'heady', home-brewed cider.

At Charing are remains of the archbishop's palace where Henry VIII stayed en route to the Field of the Cloth of Gold (1520), and from Charing Hill are views across the Weald. Pluckley is where *The Darling Buds of May* was filmed.

(In due course, this house may prove a handy stopover when going through the Channel Tunnel by train.)

Readers' comments: Enjoyed our stay very much; a warm welcome. Unobtrusive but charming hostess. Delightful house and garden. Excellent meal. Nicely secluded position. A house full of treasures and perfectly beautiful. Delightful.

BARROW HILL FARM

Ramsdean, Hampshire, GU32 1RW   Tel: 0730 823340

West of Petersfield. Nearest main road: A272 from Petersfield to Winchester.

rear view

3 **Bedrooms.** £18–£19 (less for 4 nights). One has own bath/shower/toilet. Tea/coffee free. Views of garden, country. No smoking. Washing machine on request. **Light suppers** if ordered. 1 **Sitting-room.** With open fire, central heating, TV. **Large garden** **Closed from November to February.**

A nearby hill with prehistoric burial-mound gives this beef- and dairy-farm its name. In the opposite direction it has a view of equally ancient Butser Hill, a windswept height well worth a visit.

The tile-hung house itself is beautifully furnished, with Victorian antiques shown at their best against well-chosen colour schemes and fabrics. The beamed sitting-rooms are divided by a see-through fireplace, and on the sills of the big windows all round is a profusion of pot-plants. Breakfast is served at a large oval table of mahogany in the dining-room. Bedrooms are excellent.

Everything is immaculate, outside as well as in, from carefully trained roses climbing up flint walls to the smooth lawns where one can sit to enjoy the setting sun amid the scent of catmint or lavender. Old chimney-pots have been used for planting petunias and lobelias. There are mementoes of Beatrix Potter – the very plates to be seen in the Tiggy-Winkle drawings: Mary Luff's aunt was the little girl illustrated in the story. For dinner Mary recommends the Seven Stars (Stroud) or Five Bells (Buriton).

Petersfield's 18th-century streets are pleasant; and at Greatham Mill is a lovely garden. All around are hills, woods and tranquil valleys of great beauty: a very agreeable area to explore by car or on foot. Jane Austen's home at Chawton and Gilbert White's at Selborne are only a few miles away. The Queen Elizabeth country park is an area of superb scenery. Beyond it is the Sir George Staunton Conservatory, a tropical rainforest under glass.

In green valleys amid the South Downs you will find churches that go back to Saxon times, flint-walled houses, and prehistoric burial-mounds. To the south are woodlands, remnants of the once-great Forest of Bere, and then comes Portsmouth Harbour. Despite heavy traffic on roads into the port, this is well worth a visit – to see Nelson's *Victory*, Henry VIII's *Mary Rose* and his Southsea Castle, and – the newest attraction – a big D-Day show.

Readers' comments: Excellent, very comfortable. A pleasant welcome. Huge, comfortable room. Excellent breakfast. A most generous and cheerful hostess. Delightful.

> **When writing to me, if you want a reply please enclose an International Reply Coupon.**

BARTON OLD VICARAGE

C D PT

Tirril, Cumbria, CA10 2LR   Tel: 07684 86307
South-west of Penrith. Nearest main road: A6 from Penrith to Shap
(and M6, junction 40).

3 Bedrooms. £17–£19 (less for 3 nights).
Prices go up in May. TV (in one). Views of
garden, country. No smoking. Washing
machine on request.
Dinner. £10 for 3 or 4 courses and coffee,
at 6–8pm. Non-residents not admitted.
Vegetarian or special diets if ordered. Wine
can be ordered or brought in. No smoking.
Light suppers.
2 Sitting-rooms. With open fire, central
heating, TV, piano, record-player.
Large garden

A mediaeval church and a Victorian vicarage make a familiar pair in the English
countryside, reminders that rural populations, church congregations and clerical
households all used to be much larger than they are today. Here, both isolated
church and vicarage lie almost buried in trees, some of the finest being in the
wooded part of the Walkers' big garden. The rooms too are big, with the heavy
pitch-pine joinery of the period. Sliding doors lead from the sitting-room, with its
view of Helvellyn, to the music room – which lives up to its name, as it contains a
Bechstein grand and music stands. Geyve Walker (a solicitor who is active in local
affairs) is the pianist, the children play stringed instruments, and friends or guests
sometimes join in as well. There is also a large collection of classical records and
the bookshelves are well filled too.

Scottish Sherie Walker is not only a linguist but a trained cook. Seated
round a circular dining-table, guests might eat watercress soup or fish mousse,
followed by pork en croûte; or (as foreign visitors in particular sometimes
request) a Cumbrian meal of farmhouse soup, smoked sausage, hotpot, and a
plate pie.

Bedrooms are large, with fine views towards the mountains of the Lake
District. Ullswater, the most beautiful of the larger lakes, is only a short drive
away, but there is plenty to enjoy in the vicinity without having to use the crowded roads which can spoil the Lake District at the height of the tourist season.
(Bicycles on loan.)

Places of interest include a working Victorian pottery, a birds-of-prey centre, a
trout farm and prehistoric remains (Mayburgh Henge and Arthur's Round
Table). At Brougham Hall, in process of restoration, are craft workshops and a
smokery. In a field outside the walls here was fought the last battle on English soil
– actually a skirmish with Jacobite stragglers. The little church, which has an
interesting and unusual interior, is one of the very few built during the
Commonwealth. Brougham Castle is an impressive ruin, and at Penrith, the local
market town, is another castle as well as a steam museum and a good pub where
Richard III stayed.

Readers' comments: We received a warm welcome, comfort, an excellent dinner
. . . The house stands in a lovely situation and is well furnished.

20

BATES GREEN

Arlington, Polegate, East Sussex, BN26 6SH Tel: 0323 482039
North-west of Eastbourne. Nearest main road: A22 from Eastbourne to East
Grinstead.

3 Bedrooms. £19–£20 (less for 4 nights
or, sometimes, mid-week). Prices may go up

in April. Bargain breaks. All have own
bath/shower/toilet. Tea/coffee facilities. TV
on request. Views of garden, country. No
smoking. Washing machine on request.
Dinner (in winter only). £11 for 3 courses
(with choice of puddings) and coffee, at
7.30pm. Non-residents not admitted.
Vegetarian or special diets if ordered. Wine
may be brought in. No smoking. **Light
suppers** if ordered (all year).
2 Sitting-rooms. With log fire, central
heating, TV, video. No smoking.
Large garden

Goliath poppies mingling with tiny blue borage: that is the kind of unexpected
juxtaposition of colour and scale which delights Carolyn McCutchan and makes
her lovely garden so memorable. It is open to the public annually under the
National Gardens Scheme, but visitors staying at the house can enjoy its colours
all the year round. There are stone paths and steps beside a lily-pond bordered by
rocks and shrubs, a herbaceous circle around a lawn with sundial, unusual plants
everywhere, a tennis court, and beyond all this a large pond frequented by ducks
and a big bluebell wood which is a carpet of colour every May. The McCutchans
have laid out woodland walks. This wood is very ancient and there is much of
interest to see. (Wellies on loan.) Sheep-farmer John McCutchan won a national
award for his conservation work here.

As to the house itself, tile-hung in traditional Sussex style, this began life in
the 18th century as a gamekeeper's cottage on the Michelham Priory estate, but
has since been much enlarged. There are two sitting-rooms, one beamed and
panelled with flowery cretonne armchairs around the log fire. The dining-room
has leaded casements opening onto the garden. From the brick-floored hall, stairs
rise to the pretty bedrooms (apricot or rosy bedspreads with matching curtains)
and bathrooms. The second sitting-room, upstairs, has fine views, particularly
when the sun is setting while you drink your coffee after dinner, which may consist of smoked salmon mousse, pork casserole with prunes stuffed with walnuts,
and chocolate roulade.

Alfriston – in the scenic valley which
the River Cuckmere has carved
through the Downs – is a showplace
village, but Winton Street is well
tucked away. Great, 300-year-old flint-
walled **WINTON BARN** is now run
as a b & b house by Fay Smith.
Upstairs is a homely suite – bedroom
plus sitting-room with sofa-bed (and
cooking facilities), bathroom in
between. Beyond the walled garden,
several Downs footpaths start. The
village has a celebrated restaurant,
Moonrakers, and several inns – as well

as enticing shops and a splendid
church. £16.
Readers' comments: Friendly and
helpful. Excellent value. Absolutely
delightful. [Tel: 0323 870407; postcode: BN26 5UJ]

BEECH VILLAS   C D PT S X

1–3 Borough Lane, Saffron Walden, Essex, CB11 4AF   Tel: 0799 523438

Nearest main road: A1053 from Saffron Walden to Braintree
(and M11, junction 9).

3 Bedrooms. £14–£14.50 (less for 7 nights). Some have own shower/toilet. TV. Views of garden. No smoking. Washing machine on request.
Dinner (if ordered). £8.50 for 3 courses or £6 for 2 courses and coffee, at 6.30–7.30pm. Non-residents not admitted. Vegetarian or special diets if ordered. Wine can be brought in. No smoking. **Light suppers** if ordered.
1 Sitting-room. With open fire, central heating, TV, piano, record-player. No smoking.
Small garden

This pair of pretty villas was built in 1820: their glass-roofed verandahs with iron columns are very typical of the period. Inside is a little sitting-room with pink velvet chairs (and occasionally a glimpse of trombone, horn or other instruments: the Butlers are a musical family). The bedrooms are pleasantly furnished with – for instance – stripped pine and ice-blue walls, blue bedspread of fringed brocade from Portugal, blue-and-white china and pretty 'Spice Island' curtains. A pine-and-white children's room has plentiful toys and books. There is also a cellar games room with darts and snooker.

Marilyn will produce such simple meals as home-made soup, lasagne and fruit salad (she has a wide range of vegetarian dishes); or you can eat well at the Eight Bells; or very well at the Saffron Hotel. Marilyn trained in aromatherapy, and you can book a session during your stay if you want a pleasurable and relaxing experience. Baby-sitting available.

Two miles into the countryside outside Saffron Walden are **GUNTER'S COTTAGES,** Thaxted Road, originally built in 1840 as homes for farmworkers' families, now combined and modernized. The special attraction of staying here is – surprise! – a heated, indoor swimming-pool built onto the back. This is directly accessible from the guests' self-contained suite of bedroom and bathroom. There is a spacious dining-room where Pat Goddard will serve sandwiches if you do not want to go into the town for a meal. An interesting feature of Gunter's is the pargeting: decorative exterior plasterwork, usually found only on the historic houses of Essex

and Suffolk but here a modern artist-craftsman has created some outstanding work – particularly the owl and the huntsman on, of all things, garage walls. No smoking. £15. [Tel: 0799 522091; messages: 0799 524784; postcode: CB10 2UT]

22

THE BEEHIVE
C(6) **D S**

Church Lane, Osmington, Dorset, DT3 6EL   Tel: 0305 834095

North-east of Weymouth. Nearest main road: A353 from Weymouth towards Wareham.

Easter. Bargain breaks. Some have own shower/toilet. Tea/coffee facilities. Views of garden, country. No smoking. Washing machine on request.
Dinner. £13 for 'Dorset dinner' or £9 for 3 courses and coffee, at 7.45pm (not in summer or on Sundays). Non-residents not admitted. Vegetarian or special diets if ordered. Wine can be brought in. No smoking. **Light suppers** by arrangement.
1 Sitting-room. With open fire, central heating. TV. No smoking.

3 Bedrooms. £15–£18.50 (less for 3 nights or continental breakfast). Prices go up at

Small garden

Closed in January.

Mary Kempe's father was Lord of the Manor at Osmington; and this little thatched stone cottage was the holiday home of her childhood. While the manorial lands passed into other hands, she was pursuing an academic career at the universities of Nairobi and London: the former accounts for the presence of African crafts in the old cottage, which is now her permanent home.

It is tucked away – in a pocket-handkerchief garden – down a lane leading to countryside of great beauty, with some lovely walks; to the south, fine coast scenery lies only a mile away (shingle beaches closest, sandy ones a little further).

The friendly sitting-room is a place of books and watercolours, lead-paned windows and comfortable sofas or chairs. Breakfast is served in the big, cork-floored kitchen warmed by a stove (you can buy jars of Mary's home-made jams). She produces, in the winter, imaginative dinners with many dishes based on traditional local recipes and produce – for instance, Martlemas (or Michaelmas) beef, which is marinaded in wine and vinegar then rubbed with spices before being baked, or Wessex chicken in a cider sauce. Before this might come Dorset pâté or a soup of carrots or lentils; and after it apple hedgehog, blueberry pie or buttered oranges. Or you can eat well at the nearby Smugglers' Inn. (Ask Mary for an excellent leaflet on where to buy Dorset local foods to take home.)

Birdwatchers go out from here to spend days at Radipole Lake, the Fleet or Studland nature reserve. Others tour the Thomas Hardy sites. Osmington, being roughly midway between Poole at one end of Dorset and Lyme Regis at the other, is a good centre from which to explore all parts of the county: see details elsewhere in this book. Further afield, one can visit such beauty-spots as Lulworth Cove and the Purbeck Hills; T. E. Lawrence's cottage at Clouds Hill; and picturesque villages like Wool which has *Tess of the d'Urbervilles* associations. Kingston Lacy House and gardens (National Trust) and Corfe Castle are also popular destinations. Nearby are good nurseries and garden centres, too.

To the attractions of a traditional seaside resort, Weymouth has in recent years added a Sea Life Centre; an outstanding butterfly farm; and a brewery converted into museum, restaurants and shops.

Readers' comments: Superb; delightful haven of peace; a marvellous hostess. One of the best meals we have ever sampled. A lovely welcome. Breakfast was excellent. A wonderful person.

37 Bridewell Street, Clare, Suffolk, CO10 8QD   Tel: 0787 277538
West of Sudbury. Nearest main road: A1092 from Long Melford to Clare.

2 Bedrooms. £16 (less for 7 nights). TV.
No smoking.
1 Sitting-room. With central heating. No
smoking.
Small garden

This small but historic house (once three cottages in a terrace) is filled
with antiques, paintings that include family portraits which go back to the 17th
century, all kinds of Victoriana and a great many books. At the back is a little
paved garden frequented by the Bells' three cats and their dogs. Around the
dining-table are ladderback chairs and a pine settle. Bedrooms are cottagey.

Clare is a place to explore on foot, to enjoy all the details of its ancient houses
– plasterwork decoration, exuberant inn signs, the old priory. It is close to
Cavendish, Sudbury and other attractive places in Suffolk such as Kentwell Hall
and gardens, Long Melford (good for antique-hunting, like Clare itself), Clare
country park, the Colne Valley steam railway, Gainsborough's house, Hedingham
Castle and Melford Hall. Bury St Edmunds and its abbey gardens are worth a
leisurely visit.

The area has several out-of-the ordinary museums – at Cotton, one devoted
to mechanical music, for instance; at Mildenhall, the Mildenhall Treasure
and RAF memorabilia under one roof; and the big National Horseracing
Museum at Newmarket (you can also go on conducted tours of the National
Stud here).

Readers' comments: Delightful hosts, charming house. Very good welcome. House
full of interesting things. So helpful.

In nearby Callis Street is the **SHIP
STORES**. Miles from the sea, this
one-time inn was originally called the
Sheep, not the Ship. Now it is a small
shop run by Colin and Deborah
Bowles, with a few en suite bedrooms
and an upstairs sitting-room for guests.
Secrets in this building, 400 years old,
have been uncovered: fireplaces long
boarded up, and the original brick
floor downstairs, for instance. It is a
place of low beams, creaking floors,
undulating roof and pink-plastered
front: full of character. In the dining-
room there is solid elm furniture locally
made. For dinner, Deborah serves
such meals as vegetable soup, lamb

chops, then fruit or a cream cake.
Bread and croissants are home-baked.
£17.50–£20 (b & b).
Readers' comments: A beautiful,
charming and superbly run establishment. [Tel: 0787 277834; postcode:
CO10 8PX]

BERE MARSH HOUSE

C(6) D S

Shillingstone, Dorset, DT11 0QY Tel: 0258 861133
North of Blandford Forum. Nearest main road: A350 from Blandford Forum
to Shaftesbury.

2 Bedrooms. £15.50–£16.50 (less for
2 nights and mid-week). Prices go up in
April. Tea/coffee facilities. Views of garden,
country, river. Washing machine on request.
Dinner. £13–£16 for 4 courses (with
choices) and coffee, from 7.30pm (not
Sundays and Mondays). Vegetarian or
special diets if ordered. Wine can be
ordered. **Light suppers** if ordered.
2 Sitting-rooms. With open fires, central
heating, piano, record-player (TV
available). Bar. Conservatory.
Large garden
Closed in January.

It is the food which brings most visitors here, for in the restaurant James and
Felicity Roe serve gourmet meals. In the past, Felicity used to cook directors'
lunches in London and then worked at the celebrated Peacock Vane hotel on the
Isle of Wight during its heyday.

There's a conservatory (with grapevine) where meals are usually served, and
armchairs surrounding a log stove in the hall of the 18th-century house. In the
garden are a tennis court, summer-house overlooking a rock garden in a dell and
a big vegetable garden. Beyond are far views over good walking country.

As to the meals, the Roes operate a sensible system. Although their repertoire
is very considerable, they let the first party to book dinner choose the menu for
that night, for all comers: that way, they can provide dishes from freshly bought
and cooked ingredients and (there being no waste) at a very reasonable price. So
it pays to make your reservation and study their list of dishes well in advance.
Most dishes are such classics as mushrooms à la grecque, boeuf Stroganoff and
crème brûlée.

There are plenty of good drives around here. For instance, one might go via
Sturminster Newton and Mere (which has a 16th-century inn that was a Royalist
stronghold during the Civil War) to visit the world-famous landscaped gardens
and lake of Stourhead and the 18th-century mansion itself (full of art treasures).
Alternatively, via Shaftesbury (described elsewhere) one could drive to Tollard
Royal on a road of hairpin bends that is an outstanding scenic route with superb
views when you get to the top. Along the way, lynchets can be seen – narrow
terraces constructed on the steep hillsides to make cultivation possible. This is
part of Cranborne Chase, for a thousand years a royal hunting forest: at Tollard
Royal the hunting-lodge of King John has been carefully preserved (the village
church is also worth a visit, particularly for its effigy of a knight in armour; and
also Larmer Grounds park when it is open – there are oriental temples and a
wooden theatre).

Other places of interest in the vicinity include the 15th-century manor house
at Purse Caundle and Sherborne for its golden abbey and two castles.

Prices are per person in a double room at the beginning of the year.

BICKFORD GRANGE   C D S
Bickford, Staffordshire, ST19 5QJ   Tel: 0785 841325
South of Stafford. Nearest main road: A449 from Stafford to Wolverhampton
(and M6, junction 12).

5 Bedrooms. £15–£17.50 (less for 4 nights). Some have own bath/shower/toilet. Tea/coffee facilities. Views of garden, country. No smoking.
Dinner. £8.50 for 3 courses and coffee, at times by arrangement. Non-residents not admitted. Vegetarian or special diets if ordered. Wine can be brought in. **Light suppers** if ordered.
1 Sitting-room. With open fire, central heating, TV, piano, record-player.
Large garden

Once a farm (hence the huge bell to call fieldworkers in to dinner), this Georgian house, which was built in 1800, still has a stone-flagged hall but its architectural features are grander, from a prettily plastered ceiling to the balustraded terrace overlooking its lawns: glass doors open onto this from the handsome blue sitting-room. The long dining-room, with mahogany and silver, has views of the fields. On the second floor is a suite of two double rooms that would be ideal for a family. Even the single bedroom here is spacious. Outside is a heated swimming-pool.

Gail Bryant enjoys cooking homely meals.

Lovely countryside surrounds the Grange, and there is much of interest to see – not only in this county but over the Shropshire border towards Telford and Ironbridge. Weston Park is one of many stately homes (full of art treasures and set in a Capability Brown deer park, at its best in azalea time – it was immortalized by P. G. Wodehouse as 'Blandings Castle'); others include Boscobel (Charles II's refuge) and Shugborough Hall. More places of interest include: Stuart Crystal, Wedgwood and other potteries, an aerospace museum, many gardens, ruined abbeys and castles, a working watermill and outside Stafford the continuing excavation of its Norman castle site (20 acres), with an interpretative trail for visitors.

Readers' comments: Really superb. Beautifully furnished.

Bedroom at Old Hall (see page 238)

BICKLEIGH COTTAGE HOTEL   S PT
Bickleigh, Devon, EX16 8RJ   Tel: 0884 855230
South of Tiverton. On A396 from Exeter to Tiverton (near M5, junction 27).

9 Bedrooms. £19.50–£23.50 (less for 7 nights). Most have own bath/shower/toilet. Tea/coffee facilities. Views of garden, country, river.
Dinner. £10.50 for 3 courses and coffee, at 7pm. Non-residents not admitted. Vegetarian dishes if ordered. Wine can be ordered. No smoking.
2 Sitting-rooms. With central heating, TV. **Bar.**
Large garden
Closed in winter.

Built about 1640 and later extended, this very picturesque thatched cottage has been run as a small hotel by the same family for over 60 years. It stands on a busy road by the River Exe, with a foaming weir a few yards downstream: everyone's ideal of a typically Devonian beauty-spot.

The rooms downstairs are full of antiques such as old chests and carved oak chairs, as well as a collection of blue glass and other interesting trifles including articles of Honiton lace made by Mrs Cochrane, which are for sale. The bedrooms are more simply furnished, though one has a four-poster bed. For total quiet, ask for a river-facing room (there are several). Outside is a pretty riverside garden with a fish-pond and glasshouses containing a collection of cacti and succulents.

Meals are of plain home cooking, a typical menu being smoked mackerel, roast lamb and pineapple meringue.

A good day's outing via Tiverton (which has a castle) would be along the Exe Valley (visiting opulent Knightshayes Court, lavishly designed by William Burges in 1869 amid beautiful gardens) to Dulverton – old woodlands giving way to open moors as you travel towards Exmoor. In Dulverton are mediaeval lanes and an ancient bridge, tempting shops, weavers' workshops and Exmoor's interpretation centre. There are good walks in Eggesford Forest on the way to the steep village of Lapford, in the church of which are outstanding Tudor woodcarvings. Crediton's stately church once had cathedral status (built of red sandstone, it has stained-glass windows depicting the life of its patron St Boniface). In the vicinity are other stately homes, such as Fursdon (Fursdons have lived in it from the 13th century to the present day) and Bickleigh Castle which, among other unusual exhibits, has espionage gadgets invented by the original of 'Q' in the James Bond novels. Bickleigh's watermill houses a craft centre. At South Molton (northward) you can see an exhibition of cider-making, and the Quince Honey Farm with bees busily at work. You can also take a trip on horse-drawn canal barges.

Readers' comments: Delightful. A favourite place. Beautiful position, good meals. Delightful cottage and scenery.

BIGGIN HALL   C D X

Biggin-by-Hartington, Derbyshire, SK17 0DH   Tel: 029 884 451

South of Buxton. Nearest main road: A515 from Ashbourne to Buxton.

12 Bedrooms. £19.50–£27.50 mid-week (more for a suite, and at weekends). Prices go up in April. Bargain breaks. All have own bath/shower/toilet. Tea/coffee facilities and TV in some. Views of garden, country. Washing machine on request.
Dinner. £14.50 for 4 courses (with some choices) and coffee, at 7pm. Non-residents not admitted. Vegetarian or special diets if ordered. Wine can be ordered. No smoking.
Light suppers if ordered.
2 Sitting-rooms. With open fire, central heating, TV, piano, record-player. Bar. No smoking in one.
Large garden

Charles II was on the throne when this handsome stone house with leaded windows was built, and it has changed little since his day (modern comforts apart). Logs blaze in the great stone fireplace, with cretonne-covered chairs grouped around on a quarry-tiled floor. Another sitting-room has one wall of bookshelves and glass doors opening onto the garden where children can play on the swing. Upstairs, one oak-panelled room has an oak-panelled half-tester bed (pink lilies on its blue draperies) and another a spectacular four-poster under the exposed beams – its bathroom is huge, carpeted and even equipped with a bidet. There are other rooms in an 18th-century stone annexe which are all equipped with fridges and microwaves. The Hall's owners, the Moffetts, used to be antique dealers.

In the dining-room (oriental rugs on flagstones, rush chairs, flowers on each table) breakfast is (unless you pay a little extra) continental-style, but this includes a choice of cereals, fruits and juices followed by home-made brioches, croissants and jams. In winter, cooked breakfast, packed lunch and mulled wine are free.

Evening meals may comprise a home-made soup, roast lamb with fresh vegetables, and queen of puddings, followed by cheese, fresh fruit and coffee.

In front of the house is a small stone-walled garden with poppies and peonies, and an old laburnum bowing low over its iron gates. A serene spot (slightly marred by telephone wires and a bright green plaque) in which to take one's tea or coffee.

Biggin is near the centre of the Peak District, 1000 feet up where the air is pure and fresh. Scenery is the main attraction here, but most visitors also go to see sights like the spa town of Buxton and varied attractions in or near it such as a museum with walk-through caves and barrows; the old lime-kilns in Miller's Dale; the Micrarium – insects under 40 microscopes; country park with view from 1500 feet up, interpretation centre and a cave with stalactites; and a steam railway centre.

Northward are the great peaks of Kinder Scout and Glossop where you will find another railway, a heritage centre and a scenic group of five reservoirs. On the way is Chapel-en-le-Frith with its sanctuary for owls and otters.

Westward lies Matlock, to the more famous attractions of which have been added craft workshops in Caudwell's mill; and two country parks.

Readers' comments: A wonderful weekend; warmly greeted, gorgeous furniture. The Moffetts are friendly, humorous and jovial. Warm and welcoming. A most enjoyable and memorable weekend. Setting delightful. Affable welcome.

BLACKWATER HOTEL   C D PT X
Church Road, West Mersea, Essex, CO5 8QH   Tel: 020638 3338
South of Colchester. Nearest main road: A12 from Colchester to Chelmsford.

7 Bedrooms. £19–£34 (less for 7 nights). Bargain breaks. Some have own bath/ shower/toilet. Tea/coffee facilities. TV. Washing machine on request.
Dinner. A la carte from £19 including coffee, from 7pm (not Sundays). Vegetarian or special diets if ordered. Wine can be ordered. **Light suppers** if ordered.
1 Sitting-room. With open fire, central heating. **Bar.**
Small garden
Closed in January.

The coastline here is a wilderness of creeks, islets and estuaries made colourful by the sails of small boats. A causeway now connects Mersea to the mainland, yet it still has the feel of an island with an identity all its own. There are Roman, Saxon and Norman remains – and, of course, the beds of Colchester oysters still flourish as they have done for centuries. Visitors go there, too, for all the usual seaside pleasures, for golf, sea-angling, riding or walking. At nearby Fingringhoe Wick is an outstanding bird reserve, with hides alongside its lakes.

Down a quiet side street is the creeper-covered Blackwater Hotel. Downstairs, beams and scarlet gingham tablecloths, copper pans and strings of onions, give the dining-room the informal air of a French bistro – these touches are Monique Chapleo's style. Here and in the small sitting-room with its tub chairs there are bowls of roses and pinks. All the bedrooms are very neat and fresh: wallpaper, curtains and bedspreads in matching sprigged patterns; bedheads of cane. Outside is a lawn with seats.

The food cooked by chef Roudesli is excellent, and the wine list is good. One might start with mushrooms champenoise or fish soup, to be followed by steak-and-kidney pie or calves' liver with mango and shallot sauce and a pudding such as floating island or French apple flan. There is a coffee-room that serves snacks.

Although so near London, there are plenty of rural rides in this part of Essex, and many sights to see within a few miles – such as the timbered village of Coggeshall (with Paycockes, a National Trust house, and antique shops), the historic city of Colchester founded by the Romans before London, St Osyth's Priory and East Bergholt (Constable country). Maldon is very near – an old port still frequented by the great sailing-barges. The oyster fishery and museum can be visited (tastings, boat trips – phone 0206 384141).

Colchester deserves several revisits because in addition to its more famous features there are in or near it such other sights as Oliver's Orchard (with cider-making as well as fruit-growing to see), Layer Marney Tower with its elaborate Italianate decorations, parrot and snake-handling shows at the zoo, a big steam railway museum, Bourne Mill (NT), two nature reserves (one in the historic Roman River conservation area), and no less than seven excellent museums in the city. West Mersea itself has a good local history museum.

Readers' comments: Charming hostess, excellent dinner and breakfast superb. Excellent cuisine. A real find – quite simply, perfect; charming patronne; superb meals; I don't think we have ever enjoyed a place so much. Outstanding. Food and service superb and everywhere spotless and gleaming.

29

BLACKWELL GRANGE

C(10) **M S**

Blackwell, Warwickshire, CV36 4PF   Tel: 0608 682357
South of Stratford-upon-Avon. Nearest main road: A3400 from Stratford towards Oxford (and M40, junctions 11/12).

3 Bedrooms. £20 (less for 5 nights). Price goes up in April. Bargain breaks. All have own bath/toilet. Tea/coffee facilities. Views of garden, country. No smoking. Washing machine on request.
Dinner. £14.50 for 4 courses (with choices) and coffee, at times to suit guests. Non-residents not admitted. Vegetarian or special diets if ordered. Wine can be brought in. No smoking. **Light suppers** if ordered.
1 Sitting-room. With open fire, central heating, TV.
Large garden

Stone-flagged floors and deep-set windows with chamfered mullions give this Cotswold house great character – but the Vernon-Millers had a tremendous task to give it modern comfort too. Liz has decorated the rooms with style – beribboned curtains in a shell-pink bedroom, for instance; fabric patterned with peonies and lilac; comfortable armchairs; very nice bathrooms. The many dried-flower arrangements come from Armscote Manor: one such fills a spotlit alcove. An inglenook fireplace is the setting for a collection of country bygones and Victorian kitchen tools. Dinner, by candlelight, could consist of such dishes as home-made pâté, game, damson ice cream (served with a platter of meringues) and cheeses.

Outside is a thatched barn, usually crammed full of hay for the thoroughbred horses, and their foals – to be seen in spring; and among the staddlestones (rick-stones) of the garden strut the miniature Wyandottes, white hens with feathery pantaloons down to their feet, which provide breakfast eggs.

Stratford-upon-Avon and Warwick are a few miles away; and the famous villages (Broadway, Chipping Campden, etc.) and gardens of the Cotswolds.

Readers' comments: Outstanding accommodation and warmth of hospitality.

Ilmington is all rose-covered cottages, complete with village green, ancient church and traditional inns. In Back Street is **FOLLY FARM COTTAGE**, once stables – now transformed and furnished with antiques. Bedrooms have four-posters or half-testers: roses and lace in one; bows and lavender in the next; pine and frilled drapes in a third. Each has a private bathroom and is provided with a table for meals. Sheila Lowe prepares such dishes as leek soup, plaice in a cream sauce and apple pie – available also to those in her adjacent self-catering cottages. £17 –£25 (b & b).

Readers' comments: Delightful and exquisite. Beautifully furnished. The very best in b & b. Highly recommended. Made very welcome. Most helpful. [Tel: 0608 682425; postcode: CV36 4LJ]

BOLEBROKE WATERMILL

C(7)

Edenbridge Road, Hartfield, East Sussex, TN7 4JP   Tel: 0892 770425
South-east of East Grinstead. Nearest main road: A624 from East Grinstead
to Tunbridge Wells.

5 **Bedrooms.** £19 (**to readers of this book only**)–£31.50 (less for 3 nights). Prices go up from Easter. All have own bath/shower/toilet. Tea/coffee facilities. TV. Views of millpond, country, garden. No smoking. Washing machine on request.
Dinner. £16 for 4 courses (with choices) and coffee, at 7.30pm (not Wednesdays and Sundays). Vegetarian or special diets if ordered. Wine can be brought in. No smoking. **Light suppers** if ordered.
2 **Sitting-rooms.** With central heating. No smoking.
Large grounds
Closed from November to February.

Remember that familiar scene? – Pooh, Piglet, Rabbit and Roo playing Pooh-sticks. The river that carried Pooh's sticks away feeds into the Medway as does the millstream that powered the wheel of this ancient mill, first recorded in Domesday Book.

Visitors here have the choice of staying in either the white weatherboarded watermill or the Elizabethan miller's barn. With just two bedrooms and a large sitting-room in each building, guests are assured of seclusion in rustic surroundings. If you stay in the mill, however, you will need to be nimble, for when David Cooper restored it he was careful to retain every original feature that he could – steep and narrow stairs to each bedroom, bathrooms tucked into what were once the big corn-bins, for instance. In the large sitting-room there are still millstones, the grain-hopper and overhead gear-wheels to be seen from the comfort of large armchairs or the bed that folds down from a wall. The bedrooms above are white and airy, with skylights; dried flowers hang from the rafters. For meals, guests descend through a hatch into the adjoining house.

For the less agile (and not too tall), the barn has a very pretty ground-floor bedroom and an upstairs 'hayloft' room with a four-poster.

In the evening, even a light supper may include a pheasant and cider broth, followed by local smoked trout and salad, a gooseberry and elderflower tart and Sussex cheeses.

Readers' comments: Food beautifully cooked and served. Friendliest welcome, service excellent. Beautiful room.

Set back from the High Street of picturesque Hartfield village is 17th-century **STAIRS FARM** where not only its own organic produce but that of other farms too is sold by Geraldine Pring: meat as well as vegetables, cheeses, etc. – used for meals too. At breakfast, visitors enjoy through leaded panes a view of the landscaped garden. No sitting-room, but there are sofas or armchairs in the pleasant, spacious bedrooms. £18–£20. [Tel: 0892 770793; postcode: TN7 4AB]

31

BOOT FARM

C(10) **PT X**

Southend Road, Bradfield, Berkshire, RG7 6ES   Tel: 0734 744298
West of Reading. Nearest main road: M4 (junction 12).

4 Bedrooms. £16–£18.50 (less for 3 nights or continental breakfast if ordered). Bargain breaks. Some have own shower/toilet. Tea/coffee facilities. TV. Views of garden, country. No smoking. Washing machine on request.
Light suppers if ordered. No smoking.
1 Sitting-room. With open fire, central heating, record-player. No smoking.
Large garden

This is a working farm with the addition of a very busy livery yard for riders. High teas here are substantial and very good value – for instance, ham salad, omelette or Welsh rarebit followed by home-made cakes and jams. (Patricia Dawes recommends several local inns for those who want a full dinner.)

There is a large and very comfortable sitting-room, its pastel fabrics complementing peach walls, a log fire blazing on cold days, casements open to the garden in summer. Bedrooms are attractive and the bathroom is exceptional; toilet as well as bath has a flowery pattern. In the dining-room, hand-stitched roses on tapestry chairs are part of an all-pink colour scheme.

Visitors come for the open-air theatre of Bradfield College, for the trout lakes, to ride, or for the many golf courses in the county. East Berkshire has been described under other entries; to the west lies picturesque Hungerford, famous for it scores of antique shops (many open even on Sundays). Nearby are the windswept heights of the Berkshire Downs where racehorses train, and you can walk along the prehistoric Ridgeway Path. The sites of Iron Age forts or burial mounds dot the area. The Kennet Valley is in complete contrast – fertile meadows with birch and oak woods beyond, a great area for birdwatchers. The villages here have flint-and-brick cottages roofed with thatch. In and around both Lambourn and Newbury are historic buildings, stately homes and pretty villages. London, Windsor, Oxford, Pangbourne and Henley are all within easy reach.

CHERRY COURT (in Hollybush Lane, Burghfield Common – towards Reading) is very typical of its county and its period (turn-of-the-century): spacious, solid and dignified. Rooms are well carpeted and furnished, mostly in pinks and greens. A log fire crackles on chilly days, and for sunny ones there is a heated swimming-pool in the grounds. Fruit and eggs are home-produced. A sunken garden is full of roses – when not eaten by deer. Jacqueline Levey serves such meals as pâté, salmon hollandaise and fresh fruit salad (with wine), after which one can relax in a small sun-room – grapevine overhead. Heathrow is a

half-hour taxi ride, and you can park your car at Cherry Court while you are abroad. £19–£22.50.
Readers' comments: Remarkably hospitable and friendly. [Tel: 0734 832404; postcode: RG7 3JS]

BOSWEDDAN HOUSE HOTEL   C D S X
Cape Cornwall, St Just, Cornwall, TR19 7NJ   Tel: 0736 788733
West of Penzance. Nearest main road: A3071 from Penzance to St Just.

8 Bedrooms. £17 (less for 7 nights). Most have own shower/toilet. Views of garden, country, sea.
Dinner. £8.75 for 4 courses and coffee, at 7pm. Non-residents not admitted. Vegetarian or special diets if ordered. Wine can be ordered. **Light suppers** if ordered.
1 Sitting-room. With open fire, central heating, TV, piano. **Bar.**
Large garden
Closed in January.

Once the mansion of an 18th-century mine-owner, this house is kept immaculate by Mary Stokes and Sheila Bond, from the bedrooms (some overlooking the sea) to the sitting-room and dining-room, both with big windows to make the most of the sunny views. There is double-glazing as well as a log fire for winter comfort. Dinners are traditionally English – for instance, carrot soup, roast beef, trifle and cheeses.

This far part of Cornwall is so different from the rest of England that it feels like another country (it has much in common with Brittany): wild, ancient, beautiful and mysterious. Land's End is only a few miles away, also the cliffside Minack Theatre, coastal beauty-spots between fishing villages like Mousehole and such sandy coves as Lamorna on the south side of the peninsula.

Northward one passes Botallack and an area peppered with disued tin mines ('Poldark' country). Gurnard's Head, Morvah and Sennen Cove are all interesting places – particularly the last, with its silvery sands and view back to Cape Cornwall.

Along the lanes are high banks gay with pink campion and herb Robert, celandines, violets or wild garlic flowers – even the occasional palm tree to contrast with tiny streams among ferns and homely cottage-gardens. That is Cornwall's prettier face, but it can be wild and dramatic too, with barren granite rocks looming over bleak moors, or Atlantic gales whipping the sea into a boiling cauldron and contorting gorse permanently into witch-like shapes: between this coast and America there is nothing but 3000 miles of pounding ocean.

For prehistoric remains go inland. For walks with magnificent views, follow stretches of the coastal footpath that goes all round Cornwall (or take buses all the way round).

Readers' comments: Very high standard. Nothing too much trouble. Perfect hotel and surroundings. Excellent accommodation. Like being with friends at home.

BOUCHERS FARMHOUSE

C(5) S

Bentham, Gloucestershire, GL51 5TZ   Tel: 0452 862373
South-west of Cheltenham. Nearest main road: A46 from Cheltenham to
Stroud (and M5, junction 11).

2 Bedrooms. £13. Views of garden, country. No smoking.
1 Sitting-room. With open fire, central heating. TV. No smoking.
Large garden

Previously a farm, Bouchers is still surrounded by hayfields just beyond the garden, where rock doves fly across the lawns to a graceful weeping willow. A sundial on one wall declares the date of the house, 1661, and of the old cider-house which is now Bruce's workshop.

Inside all is immaculate and very comfortable, and you will get a warm welcome from Anne Daniels as you step through the front door straight into the big U-shaped living-room. Here plenty of velvet armchairs are grouped round the hearth where an open fire crackles in winter, and a grandfather clock ticks the time away. Round the other side of the U is the dining-room, for breakfast only (visitors eat other meals at local inns or at one of the innumerable restaurants in Cheltenham).

Bentham, on the edge of the Cotswolds, is close to the route south to Bath. Gloucester with its cathedral, historic Cirencester (don't miss the Roman museum) and the Forest of Dean are all within easy reach, as are Prinknash Abbey and the Wye Valley. Also in the area are Slimbridge Wildfowl Trust, Westonbirt Arboretum, Badminton House (a Palladian mansion, where the Queen is often seen at the spring horse trials), 12th-century Berkeley Castle in its lovely grounds. Cheltenham and Tewkesbury are both near.

The Cotswolds is a rich hunting-ground for antique collectors and there is an illustrated guide to about 50 of its antique shops (with map, on which to base a tour) obtainable from the Cotswold Antique Dealers Association – tel: 0386 700280. This describes the speciality of each shop, its opening hours and (briefly) the sightseeing possibilities nearby.

Cheltenham has many such shops – and others of every conceivable kind. Its Regency houses date from its heyday as a fashionable spa: the Duke of Wellington regularly came here whenever rheumatism or the affairs of state got him down. The town needs repeated visits to see everything: the birthplace of composer Gustav Holst, the Pump Room (where you still can 'take the waters'), the elegant Promenade and Montpellier area, 14th-century church, distinguished art gallery, very lovely gardens and Pittville Park (costume museum). Racegoers throng here at Gold Cup time; others come for various arts festivals.

Readers' comments: Service excellent – the sort for which you would expect to pay double the price. Will go there again. Very satisfied. Excellent value. Wonderful hosts, fantastic setting. Did everything possible for us.

BRADFORD OLD WINDMILL
C(6) **S PT X**

Masons Lane, Bradford-on-Avon, Wiltshire, BA15 1QN   Tel: 0225 866842

East of Bath (Avon). Nearest main road: A363 from Bath to Trowbridge (and M4, junction 17).

4 Bedrooms. £19 (**one room for readers of this book only**)–£32.50. Less for 2 nights or mid-week. Prices go up in April. Bargain breaks. Some have own bath/shower/toilet. Tea/coffee facilities. TV. Views of garden, country. No smoking. Washing machine on request.

Dinner. £18 for 3 vegetarian courses and coffee, at 8pm (on Monday, Thursday and Saturday only). Non-residents not admitted. Special diets if ordered. Wine can be brought in. No smoking. **Light suppers** if ordered.

1 Sitting-room. With open fire, central heating. No smoking.

Small garden

The Napoleonic wars brought prosperity to this area (where cloth for uniforms was woven) but with peace came depression. As a result, the baker who in 1807 had built a windmill here went broke. In 1817 the mill ceased to function, and its sails and machinery were removed. Today its stump is simply a very unusual stone house, perched on a hillside within picturesque Bradford-on-Avon. From it there is a view full of interest, overlooking a higgledy-piggledy array of old roofs.

It is now in the imaginative care of Peter and Priscilla Roberts, a much-travelled couple (engineer and teacher) who have brought back finds from the Far East, New Zealand, Tahiti and Australia which now decorate the rooms – as do pictures and mementoes of their other enthusiasms, from canal boats to whales.

Every room has its own character and shape: some are circular. In the sitting-room, William Morris sofas and furniture of stripped pine face a log fire and there are maps on the walls. One bedroom (with the best roofscape view of all, through a pair of deep-set pointed windows) has a circular bed with a spread patterned with wildflowers and butterflies. In another, there are windmill pictures, arrangements of dried flowers and tea things laid out on top of an old barrel. Draped Tahitian fabrics contrast with pieces of driftwood, and there is even a water-bed covered with a patchwork bedspread.

Their cooking, too, is eclectic (even breakfasts are imaginative with such options as hash browns, muffins or croissants, and home-made yogurts). Meals range from wholesome 'soup trays' (with cheese and apple juice too) to an occasional Thai meal which may include eggs in a spicy coconut sauce; fresh green or purple broccoli stir-fried in sesame oil and spiced with ginger; bananas baked in citrus juices and honey, garnished with toasted almonds. Less exotic dinners are normally available too, but all evening meals must be booked in advance.

There is a tiny, Victorian-style garden around the foot of the mill stump and from it one gets a good view of Bradford's notable buildings – a panorama that includes a colossal 14th-century tithe barn, river bridge with one-cell prison actually on it, and an 18th-century cloth mill.

The Roberts may take you on a tour of the newly restored sail gallery.

Readers' comments: Everything you could want. Very friendly, I thoroughly enjoyed my visit.

35

BRAMWOOD

C PT S

19 Hallgarth, Pickering, North Yorkshire, YO18 7AW   Tel: 0751 474066
Off A170 from Thirsk to Scarborough.

rear view

6 Bedrooms. £14–£16 (less for 7 nights). Bargain breaks. Some have own shower. Tea/coffee facilities. No smoking.
Dinner. £9 for 3 courses and coffee, at 6.30pm. Non-residents not admitted. Vegetarian or special diets if ordered. Wine can be brought in. No smoking.
1 Sitting-room. With open fire, central heating, TV. No smoking.
Small garden

The best approach to this 18th-century guest-house is from the back, through an old archway built for coaches – racks for the horses' tack and an old forge still survive, but beyond what was once the stable yard there is now a pretty and secluded garden, with clematis scrambling up old walls and an apple tree; in one part vegetables are grown for the table.

All the bedrooms are immaculate, some of them spacious, and many have cane rocking-chairs. The white-and-green and cream-and-blue colour schemes downstairs are tranquil and refreshing. Ann Lane, who used to enjoy cooking 'for recreation', has put her enthusiasm to good use here, providing visitors with such meals as egg and mushroom bake, pork medallions served with sage-and-apple sauce, and Yorkshire curd tart. She finds old-fashioned puddings are very popular with guests, particularly at the end of a strenuous day's walking, cycling, bird-watching or even gliding. Her home-made chutneys and marmalades are on sale.

In the vicinity are lovely Staindale and many moorland villages tucked away which are well worth seeking. Lastingham, for instance, which has fountain and crypt dating back to the 11th century. Two hundred years ago, its inn, the Blacksmiths' Arms, was run by its curate: when the bishop objected, he said he had thirteen children to support! Thornton Dale is very picturesque: trout swim in the clear stream that curves through the village and under the little footbridges that lead to each 17th- or 18th-century house and its flowery cottage-garden. Hutton-le-Hole, which has the region's folk museum, was once a refuge for persecuted Quakers. Through the middle of its cluster of pale stone houses is a ravine carved by a stream that descends, with cascades, from the high moors.

This area has some of the most spectacular abbey ruins: Rievaulx, Byland, etc. In 1536 over 800 monasteries flourished in Britain; by 1540 Henry VIII had the whole lot destroyed or closed. In the north's loveliest of solitary places were sited great abbeys built in the Cistercians' heyday (the 12th century). Some were wealthy and owned vast lands, but monastic life was already in decline when Henry helped himself to their properties.

When looking round these ruins it is hard to imagine them bustling with monks, pilgrims and beggars seeking bed and board, scholars in their libraries and schools, and the comings-and-goings of any big property-owning institution – all combined with ceaseless prayer, seven church services a day, and observance of St Benedict's strict Rule (no meat, no baths, no letters, no idleness).

Readers' comments: Excellent food, friendly. Lovely rooms. Most accommodating. Charming hospitality. Very good food. Comfortable bedroom. Absolutely loved it.

BRATTLE HOUSE
C(12)

Cranbrook Road, Tenterden, Kent, TN30 6UL   Tel: 01580 63565

Nearest main road: A28 from Ashford to Hastings.

side view

3 Bedrooms. £18.75–£27 (less for 4 nights or continental breakfast). Bargain breaks. All have own shower/toilet. Tea/coffee facilities. Views of garden, country. No smoking. Washing machine on request.
Dinner. £15.50 for 4 courses and coffee, at 7.30pm. Non-residents not admitted. Vegetarian or special diets if ordered. Wine can be brought in. No smoking. **Light suppers** if ordered.
1 Sitting-room. With central heating. No smoking.
Large garden

Reputedly this was once the home of Horatia, illegitimate but much-loved daughter of Nelson and Lady Hamilton, who was only five when Nelson died.

The tile-hung house (parts of which date back to the 17th century) has great dignity – white marble fireplace from the 18th century; wide, panelled doors with handsome brass fittings; bay windows with leaded casements. The Rawlinsons have furnished the rooms in suitable style with, for instance, a pale thick carpet contrasting with a dusky pink wallcovering in the dining-room, and many pot-plants everywhere.

Bedrooms are equally handsome. There are two very large rooms at the front with window-seats, brick hearths and draped bedheads. From these, one can enjoy a view of the church where Horatia's husband was vicar, and of the steam train which occasionally puffs by: a scene at its most lovely when the sun goes down. Another is all roses and cream, with a little black iron grate, sloping floors, and an old brick chimney thrusting up through its bathroom.

Although the Rawlinsons are themselves vegetarian, Maureen cooks such three-course meals as sweet-sour cucumber, lamb with apricots and almonds, and chocolate roulade. They usually dine with their guests. Breakfast may be served in the conservatory.

Readers' comments: Excellent service. Tasty and imaginative food. Elegant, gracious house in beautiful countryside. Delightful couple. Enjoyed every minute. So nicely furnished. Dinner up to Michelin star standard.

At the quieter end of Tenterden's main street is **WEST CROSS HOUSE HOTEL**, a part-Tudor building with an 18th-century façade. Bedrooms are simply furnished, but spacious and well carpeted. There are antiques and a huge fireplace in the big sitting-room. (Marguerite May provides light suppers only.) £15–£17.
Readers' comments: Lovely house. Good value. [Tel: 05806 2224; postcode: TN30 6JL]

BROAD OAKS

C(5) **PT**

Haverthwaite, Cumbria, LA12 8AL   Tel: 05395 31756
North-east of Ulverston. Nearest main road: A590 from Barrow towards
Kendal (and M6, junction 36).

2 Bedrooms. £17–£18 (less for 3 nights).
Prices go up from Easter. Bargain breaks.
Both have own bath/shower/toilet. Tea/
coffee facilities. TV. Views of garden,
country.
Dinner. £10 for 3 courses (with choices)
and coffee, at 7pm. Non-residents not
admitted. Vegetarian or special diets if
ordered. Wine can be brought in.
1 Sitting-room. With open fire, central
heating.
Large garden
Closed in November and December.

The unusual arrangement of Broad Oaks, with the bedrooms on the ground floor
and the living-rooms above, is easily explained: when it was built, it was for a doctor, and the guests' accommodation is in what was the surgery. The house is a
neat piece of modern architecture, with lots of massive pine joinery.

Sitting- and dining-rooms run into each other around a big brick fireplace,
centrally placed in Scandinavian style. Some paintings are by the Emmetts'
talented son, who teaches English in Tokyo and is the source of the Japanese
objects. In the bedrooms (where there may be a little traffic noise), pillows hanging from brass rails make unusual bedheads. (Baby-sitting available.)

The first course at dinner is a choice between soup, pâté or something fishy.
Then might come steak, a casserole or a pork dish. The puddings – crème
caramel, queen of puddings, profiteroles – offer a choice between something light
and something filling.

The house is in wooded country near the south end of Windermere, which
tends to be less crowded in summer than the area at the top of the lake. Close
by is one terminus of the well-known Lakeside & Haverthwaite Railway, so it is
possible to take a steam train to the other station and thence a cruise on a lake
steamer.

Readers' comments: Charming, friendly hosts, hospitality is excellent, food is very
good, nicely presented, attractive rooms with all facilities, a haven of delight.
Extremely helpful and pleasant; good food. A truly wonderful reception.

A few miles eastward is Levens village.
In Cinderbarrow Lane is a converted
barn called **BIRSLACK GRANGE**
where Jean Carrington-Birch offers
comfortable accommodation overlooking the Lyth Valley, famous for
damsons. Evening meals (such as
home-made vegetable soup, beef in
wine, and apple sponge and cream)
can be provided. The house is close
to two mansions: Levens Hall and
Sizergh Castle, both of which have fine

gardens. Kendal's attractions range from
bargain shoes to fine art. £13– £15.
Readers' comments: Good fortune to
stay. Delicious breakfast. [Tel: 05395
60989; postcode: LA8 8PA]

BROOKFIELD FARM HOTEL   C D M PT X
Winterpit Lane, Plummers Plain, West Sussex, RH13 6LU
Tel: 0403 891568

South-east of Horsham. Nearest main road: A281 from Horsham to Brighton (and M23, junction 11).

rear view

25 Bedrooms. £19–£32. All have own bath or shower and toilet. Tea/coffee facilities. TV. Views of garden, country, lake. Washing machine on request. **Dinner.** £12 for 3 courses and coffee, at 6.30–9pm. Vegetarian or special diets if ordered. Wine can be ordered. **Bar snacks. 1 Sitting-room.** With open fire, central heating, TV, video, record-player. **Bar. Large garden**

Over the years, John Christian has added to and improved his farmhouse extensively, creating a busy, small hotel (his sons farm the surrounding land). Apart from the well-equipped bedrooms, some small and two on the ground floor, and the comfortable sitting-room with its open fire and array of brass and copper, there are now several dining areas, a bar opening out to the garden, a billiards room, a sauna and small gym, fishing and a big play area at one side for children – who can also enjoy paddle-boats on the lake and riding the donkeys. There is a six-hole golf course and golf-driving range, and a minibus for escorted tours.

Manager Carol and her chefs set high standards of home-style cooking – on various occasions I have enjoyed a filling soup with home-cured ham in it, a really good steak pie, and a beautifully presented and copious prawn cocktail.

Travellers using Gatwick appreciate the convenience (and economy) of parking their car at Brookfield while away; and, no matter how early or late their flight, the Brookfield minibus takes them to or from the airport. Honeymooners like the four-poster suite with Jacuzzi for at least their first night of wedded bliss!

Readers' comments: Cheerful surroundings, friendly hospitality.

An elegant Victorian house, **WEST-LANDS** on Brighton Road at Monk's Gate, has been very well furnished by Kathleen Ticktum, with much emphasis on light colours and complete comfort. There is a very lovely flower garden with terrace and lily-pool (floodlit at night). A good choice for anyone who values peace, spaciousness and high standards. Only light snacks provided: there are nearby inns for meals. No smoking. Parking (and taxi-service) for visitors flying from Gatwick. £18.50–£20.

Readers' comments: Immaculate. Friendly. Most outstanding accommodation. Warm hospitality. [Tel: 0403 891383; postcode: RH13 6JD]

BROOKLAND   C S

Peacock Lane, Middle Tysoe, Warwickshire, CV35 0SG Tel: 0295 680202
South-east of Stratford-upon-Avon. Nearest main road: A422 from
Stratford-upon-Avon to Banbury.

3 Bedrooms. £15.50 (less for 3 nights).
Tea/coffee facilities. Views of garden,
country. No smoking. Washing machine on
request.
Dinner (if ordered in advance). £11.50 for
3 courses and coffee, at 6.30pm. Non-
residents not admitted. Vegetarian or
special diets if ordered. Wine can be
brought in. No smoking. **Light suppers** if
ordered.
1 Sitting-room. With open fire, central
heating, TV, record-player.
Small garden

The first battle of the Civil War was fought nearby at Edgehill (in 1642, not long
before this cottage was built), a dramatically sharp ridge on the border of
Oxfordshire and a fine car-drive today. Charles I narrowly missed a defeat that
could have prevented his army from moving on to London and all the long
struggles which followed until he was beheaded in 1649. It is difficult to imagine
such violent deeds while enjoying this tranquil spot today.

When I visited Brookland, my first impression was of flowers everywhere,
butterflies thronging the tall yellow spires of verbascum, stone troughs brimming
with colourful blooms. There is a little sun-lounge where one can sit under a vine
to enjoy the morning sunshine, while inside grandfather clocks tick peacefully.
The old stone cottage still retains many of its original features, such as the tinder-
box cupboard built into an inglenook fireplace; and Topsy Trought has furnished
the dining-room with carved, cane chairs in William-and-Mary style.

Topsy makes wedding- and birthday-cakes for local families, but it is Tim who
does the elaborate and colourful decorations of sugar fruit and vegetables. Topsy
says her most popular meal is a peach-and-pineapple starter, gamekeeper's
casserole and loganberry mousse. A homely and hospitable atmosphere.

As to sightseeing, most visitors head first – of course – for Stratford-upon-
Avon, but Warwick and its castle, Leamington Spa and Coventry are all near.
Tysoe is named after the same Saxon god whose name was given to Tuesday.

Readers' comments: Outstanding. Most beautiful and interesting. Lovely hosts.
Fresh, attractive. Charming hosts. First class.

Bloxham village (Oxfordshire) is a web
of steep and twisting lanes, greens, a
stream, thatch, flowers, old pumps and
richly golden stone walls. **THE
KNOLL**, perched above Little Bridge
Road, is an 18th-century guest-house
in a pretty walled garden (one big
bedroom is in an annexe here). I
particularly liked room 4, with its
mulberry Laura Ashley decor; and a
single room. Wendy Woodward serves

only light snacks, but two inns are
near. £15–£18. [Tel: 0295 720843;
postcode: OX15 4PU]

BROOKSIDE

CDS

Lustleigh, Bovey Tracey, Devon, TQ13 9TJ Tel: 06477 310
North-west of Newton Abbot. Nearest main road: A382 from Bovey Tracey to
Moretonhampstead.

rear view

3 Bedrooms. £17 (less for 7 nights).
Tea/coffee facilities. Views of garden,
country, river. No smoking. Washing
machine on request.
Light suppers if ordered. Wine can be
brought in.
1 Sitting-room. With central heating,
wood stove, TV. No smoking.
Garden

A show village of the Dartmoor National Park, Lustleigh is sometimes crowded
with sightseers – but even then Brookside, well tucked away, is peaceful. It looks
across its garden to the village cricket field: the visitors' TV room upstairs has a
balcony from which one can watch matches being played.

The landscaped garden is raised up on what was once a railway embankment.
Round it winds the River Wrey, and one can sit above its waters on the little
bridge across which trains once puffed their way. As a backdrop to all this are the
high moors where the famous Dartmoor ponies roam free.

One enters Judy Halsey's old house through a combined sitting/breakfast-
room, which has a great granite hearth (with wood stove) at one end. A twisting
stair rises to bedrooms furnished in simple cottage style. The house was originally
a thatched cottage belonging to a 15th-century farm, now the Cleave Inn, which
serves good dinners.

This is an excellent area for birdwatching: among 67 species spotted by one
visitor were whinchats, ring ouzels, wood warblers and rock pipits. Mountain
bicycles, guided walks and maps are available.

Lustleigh has an ancient history: there are prehistoric remains, King Alfred
bequeathed it to his youngest son and its church is in part 13th-century.

Also in the Dartmoor National Park is
an exceptionally pretty, 450-year-old
cottage of white walls and thatch:
CORBYNS BRIMLEY, Higher
Brimley, near Bovey Tracey. It has
been attractively furnished by Hazel
White in a style that is in keeping with
its age. Snack suppers, or visitors may
eat at the Toby Jug, Bickington; the
Rock Inn, Haytor Vale; or at the
Rumbling Tum. £19–£20.
Readers' comments: Superb views,
splendid accommodation, caring

proprietors; shall return again and
again. [Tel: 0626 833332; postcode:
TQ13 9JT]

BROWNHILL HOUSE

C PT S X

Ruyton XI Towns, Shropshire, SY4 1LR   Tel: 0939 260626
South-east of Oswestry. Nearest main road: A5 from Shrewsbury to Oswestry.

3 Bedrooms. £14–£16 (**less to readers of this book** and for 3 nights). Prices go up at Easter. One has own bath/shower/toilet. Tea/coffee facilities. Views of garden, country, river. Clothes-washing on request.
Dinner. £7.50, at 6.30pm. Vegetarian or special diets if ordered. Wine can be brought in. **Light suppers** if ordered.
1 **Sitting-room.** With open fire, central heating.
Large garden

It is the garden which brings most visitors here. Although when they moved in Roger and Yoland Brown had not the slightest interest in gardening, they have since created an outstanding garden on the steep site – or rather, a series of gardens. By the use of steps, paths, walls and banks they have provided a variety of experiences for the visitor – here a paved walk, there wild woodland, 500 different shrubs, 20 kinds of fruit or nut, a vegetable garden with glasshouses. They visit great gardens here and abroad, coming home with new ideas: a Roman garden with pond and gazebo; a Thai miniature garden; a laburnum walk inspired by one at Bodnant; parterres, walks, follies, rock gardens, statuary and a bog garden, all contributing different scenes which unfold as one wanders around. At the foot is the River Perry (free fishing available). Plants are on sale.

As to the house itself, the bedrooms are comfortable – redecorated and improved annually. The beamed sitting-room has a huge stone fireplace. Meals are served in the large farmhouse-style kitchen, and may comprise such things as soup made from the garden's vegetables or salade niçoise, stuffed pork with a crisp crumb coating, and a compote of garden fruit. Breakfasts are exceptional. Fruit juice will be freshly squeezed (from the Browns' own berries or peaches, for example), bread is baked in the village and jams are home-made by Yoland. Among breakfast choices are pancakes, omelettes and home-made fishcakes.

About 1150, eleven hamlets here amalgamated: hence the strange name of the village, the history of which has been written by Yoland.

Readers' comments: Most generous hosts, excellent hospitality. Very warm welcome and a really delicious meal. Wished we could have stayed longer.

In peaceful Yeaton Lane, Baschurch, **FRANKBROOK** was an old cottage and cow-house, now much modernized and surrounded by a flowery, sheltered garden with a view of the Berwyn Mountains. The Pickups are a musical family – hence the spinet, clavichord, etc. which are to be seen (and heard, on madrigal evenings). In the beamed sitting/dining-room, Eileen – a friendly and helpful hostess – serves (using garden produce) such meals as egg mayonnaise, chicken in wine and

rear view

mushroom sauce, raspberries and Shropshire cheeses. Home-made marmalade, jams and pot-pourri for sale. £13–£13.50. [Tel: 0939 260778; postcode: SY4 2HZ]

BUCKYETTE
Littlehempston, Devon, TQ9 6ND   Tel: 080 376 2638

North of Totnes. Nearest main road: A381 from Newton Abbot to Totnes.

C S

6 Bedrooms. £16.75 (less for 7 nights). Price goes up in June. All have own bath/shower/toilet. Tea/coffee facilities. Views of garden, country.
Dinner. £8.50 for 3 courses (with choices) and coffee, at 6.30pm. Non-residents not admitted. Vegetarian or special diets if ordered. Wine can be ordered. **Light suppers** if ordered.
1 Sitting-room. With open fire, TV, piano.
Garden
Closed from November to February.

The curious name of this house appears in the Domesday Book and is believed to be a Saxon word meaning 'head of spring': the spring is still there, and in use. The present building, made from stone quarried on the farm, dates from 1860. It is on a commanding site with far views, and is furnished with Edwardian pieces suited to the scale of the lofty rooms. In the sitting-room is a log fire for chilly days, and for sunny ones tall French doors open onto a wisteria-hung verandah. The peppermint-pink dining-room has particularly handsome tables, which Roger Miller himself made from timber on the estate, and pictures of theatrical costumes. Bedrooms are not elegant but comfortable.

Elizabeth Miller serves such meals as lentil soup, chicken in a crisp cheese-and-garlic coating and queen of puddings; with home-baked bread. The garden provides asparagus, strawberries and other produce. Everything about the house is solid, comfortable, unpretentious, and very English. Children are particularly welcome and baby-sitting is available.

Littlehempston is well placed for a family holiday because the safe sands of Torbay are so near – as are Paignton's zoo, miniature gardens, a scenic steam railway and river trips. There are plenty of inns, theatres and concerts including those at Dartington's celebrated arts and crafts centres. Totnes, a centre for complementary medecine, has its castle and streets of ancient buildings, with interesting little shops. In the church is an especially fine rood-screen. At Buckfast Abbey the monks sell their wine and honey to visitors. Ashburton is a pretty hill town, with all of Dartmoor beyond – its most famous beauty-spot is Dartmeet where two rivers converge and there is an old 'clapper' bridge of stones by which to cross the water, a typical Devon feature. Widecombe, of 'Uncle Tom Cobleigh' fame, still has its celebrated fair high up on the moor every September. Princetown (large, bleak and weather-beaten) is where the big Dartmoor Prison is, originally built by and for Napoleonic prisoners-of-war.

The west country has many prehistoric sites. These are well explained at the Prehistoric Hill Settlement museum near Dartmouth. There are several vineyards in the area which welcome visitors.

Readers' comments: Amazingly good welcome. Beautifully served food. Very charming lady – I will go again.

BULMER FARM   C(12) **D M S X**

Holmbury St Mary, Surrey, RH5 6LG   Tel: 0306 730210

South-west of Dorking. Nearest main road: A25 from Dorking to Guildford
(and M25, junction 9).

8 Bedrooms. £17–£19. Some have own
shower/toilet and TV. All have tea/coffee
facilities. Views of garden, country, lake.
Washing machine on request.
1 Sitting-room. With open fire, TV,
record-player.
Large garden

In the folds of Surrey's high North Downs (most of which are so scenic that they
are in National Trust protection) a number of very picturesque villages lie hidden,
and Holmbury is one. Near the centre stands Bulmer Farm, built about 1680.
One steps straight into a large dining-room with gleaming furniture, and through
this to an attractive sitting-room – a room of pink walls and old beams, chairs
covered in cretonne patterned with pink poppies, logs crackling in front of the
cherubs and harps of an old iron fireback in the inglenook. It opens onto the large
garden.

Upstairs are pleasant, spacious bedrooms with cottage-style furnishings. Five
additional and very comfortable rooms (with en suite showers) have been created
in outbuildings.

Outdoors, a Dutch barn is crammed with hay and David Hill will show you
the lake he created a few years ago, now a haven for herons, kingfishers, Canada
geese, snipe and other wildfowl: it won a conservation award.

B & b only, but the area is full of inns offering good meals, such as the Royal
Oak (300 yards away), the Parrot at Forest Green and the Stephan Langton at
Friday Street.

Some tourists find this a good area in which to stay while visiting London –
train day-tickets cost very little, and the journey takes three-quarters of an hour
(from Dorking).

The surrounding area of woodland and hills is one of the finest beauty-spots
near the capital, truly rural, and dotted with footpaths to follow, historic churches
and villages with craft shops, trout farms, antiques and the like. Dorking and
Guildford (the latter with castle ruins, river trips and a good theatre) are each well
worth a day's visit. The Royal Horticultural Society's gardens at Wisley are near,
too; so are Leith Hill (walks), Clandon and Polesden Lacey (stately homes), and
Hatchlands (NT house with an interesting collection of old musical instruments).
Several fine gardens open to view. Beautiful Shere has monthly antique fairs.

You can go via pleasant lanes to reach Farnham, a largely 18th-century town
at the foot of a mound with castle: the local museum has William Cobbett
memorabilia, while another (at nearby Tilford) has an open-air display of old
agricultural machinery. Birdworld is an exceptionally good park with exotic birds,
and attached to it is Underwaterworld with unusual fish.

Readers' comments: One's every wish is catered for. So warm and friendly. Made
so welcome, made to feel like one of the family. Picturesque, restful. Ultra quiet.
Friendly, helpful owners. Good food. A great time.

BULMER TYE HOUSE   C S

Bulmer Tye, Essex, CO10 7ED   Tel: 0787 269315

South-west of Sudbury (Suffolk). Nearest main road: A131 from Halstead to Sudbury.

4 Bedrooms. £15. Some have own bath/toilet. Views of garden. No smoking. Washing machine on request.
Dinner (only if pre-booked). £7.50 for 2 or 3 courses and coffee (time by arrangement). Non-residents not admitted. Vegetarian or special diets if ordered. Wine can be brought in. No smoking. **Light suppers** if ordered.
3 Sitting-rooms. With open fires, central heating, TV, piano, record-player. No smoking.
Large garden

One of Gainsborough's most famous paintings is of the Andrews family whom he knew when he lived in Suffolk. It was one of their sons, a parson, who in the 18th century 'modernized' this house, most of which dates back to the reign of Elizabeth I, by putting in huge sash windows and so forth.

Today its old timbers resonate to the sound of music (played by family or guests), for Peter Owen is a maker of very fine clavichords – and much of the interesting furniture seen in the rooms. A hexagonal table with a complex pattern of end-grain triangles is his; so is a throne-like chair of elm, its joints secured with wood pegs only; and also a dolls' house – which is in fact a scale replica of Bulmer Tye House itself.

His wife is an authority on antiques, about which she writes articles and books (under her pen-name of Noël Riley); so not surprisingly there are some unusual period pieces in the house. Instead of using furnishing fabrics with a traditional look, the Owens have contrasted the antiques with strong modern patterns – a Bauhaus design for curtains in one room, an Aztec-style pattern in another, in colours such as tangerine and blue. A Chinese sunshade, inverted, makes an unusual ceiling lightshade. There is a large Bechstein in one of the sitting-rooms and log fires in all three. In one bedroom, with a handsome bed, 19th-century Persian curtains and a Laura Ashley pattern co-exist happily.

The quarry-tiled kitchen is decorated in brilliant primary colours and on one wall screen-printed Spanish tiles give a trompe l'oeil effect. Here guests eat with the family round a huge pine table and are apt to get drawn into family life, including anything from duets to political debates. Garden produce often goes into the making of soups and of fruit puddings; wine, lemonade and elderflower cordial are all home-made and Peter bakes the bread. Some of the dishes guests enjoy most are beef-and-lentil flan, Roman cobbler (pork and mushrooms with a topping of semolina and cheese), fish pie and, for vegetarians in particular, a cheesy bread-and-butter pudding served with stir-fried vegetables. For breakfast, you will be offered home-made muesli, bread and marmalade, as well as free-range eggs (no fry-ups).

The large garden is notable for its fine trees (some are 200 years old) which include copper beeches, walnuts, cedars and yews, as well as a number of unusual plants. There is a grass tennis court.

Readers' comments: Characterful house, beautiful garden, very informal and friendly.

BURLAND FARM   C(10) **D S**
Wrexham Road, Burland, Cheshire, CW5 8ND   Tel: 0270 74210
North-west of Nantwich. On A534 from Nantwich to Wrexham (near M6, junction 16).

3 Bedrooms. £19 **to readers of this book only** (less for continental breakfast by arrangement). Price goes up at Easter. All have own bath/shower/toilet. Tea/coffee facilities. TV. Views of garden, country.
Light suppers by arrangement.
2 Sitting-rooms. With open fire, central heating, piano.
Small garden

This early Victorian house, surrounded by lawn and trees, is in the pretty *cottage ornée* style that was once fashionable: windows are lozenge-paned, the gable is decorated with woodwork, hinges are of wrought iron.

The Allwoods' furnishings complement this well. Their huge dining-table and cupboard were made from oaks felled on the farm, and other antiques have been added, such as spindleback chairs. Colour schemes are pleasant – a pink and grey bedroom, for instance, with a white tapestry bedspread from Portugal.

Sandra usually bakes her own bread, and will make American-style muffins for breakfast if requested. She will also supply guests with scenic routes for drives, and give advice on local gardens and unusual churches.

Readers' comments: Warmly recommended, superb meal. Everything was done for us with a delightful, open friendliness. We cannot speak too highly of the experience and can heartily recommend it to others. Spacious, comfortable rooms.

Just beyond the Delamere Forest, in Cuddington village is **BARRATWICH**, Cuddington Lane, a Victorian cottage with a large garden from which to enjoy the fine views. These include a valley trout lake that, like many other Cheshire meres (old marl diggings), attracts unusual birds – and birdwatchers. Visitors enter a white and celadon hall with galleried staircase leading to fresh, cottagey bedrooms – one with white boarded wall, another with stencilled decoration. There is a pink sitting-room opening into a prettily tiled conservatory, many antiques and a wall with five generations of family photos (some ancestors further back in time were burnt at the stake during persecutions of Catholics). On tables laid with pink linen and silver, Mary Riley – an expert

cook – serves such meals as carrot and orange soup (one of John Tovey's recipes), chicken Véronique and lemon pudding. Among more famous sights close by, seek out picturesque Great Budworth – familiar to Hinge and Bracket fans, for much filming was done here; the unusual salt museum at Northwich; and the mansions of Arley Hall and Marbury Park. £15. [Tel: 0606 882412; postcode: CW8 2SZ]

BURLEIGH FARM   C S X

Bladon Road, Cassington, Oxfordshire, OX8 1EA   Tel: 0865 881352
North-west of Oxford. Nearest main road: A40 from Oxford to Witney.

2 Bedrooms. £17.50–£18 (less for 3 nights). Both have own bath/shower/toilet. Tea/coffee facilities. TV. Views of garden, country. No smoking.
Light suppers if ordered.
1 Sitting-room. With open fire, central heating, TV, piano, record-player. No smoking.
Large garden

In the 18th century, the farming scene was drastically changed by the Enclosure Acts. Not only were villagers no longer allowed to cultivate wide open spaces under the traditional 'strip' system, but there was constant encroachment on their common grazing-pastures by the local lord's multiplying flocks of sheep – 'growth industry' of the time. Hedges were planted to enclose fields, and farmhouses were built in remote spots among them, into which villagers moved as tenants of the lord. They then paid rent to farm his fields, each field being as large as one team of oxen could plough in a day.

Burleigh was one such 'enclosure farm' on the great Blenheim estate. It is still owned by the Duke of Marlborough, and farmed by the Cooks, who keep a herd of pedigree Friesian cows.

The stone house combines historic character (stone floors, log fires) with modern comfort. From some bedrooms there are distant glimpses of Oxford's spires and from others Blenheim Palace, a romantic prospect when the setting sun glints on the far windows. Visitors are welcome to look round the farm and to follow footpaths through its fields to Bladon church, where Churchill is buried. Another footpath, to Wychwood Forest, was Charles I's escape route when he and his men fled unnoticed while the Roundheads kept watch round Oxford. Little Cassington itself is even more historic – Bronze and Iron Age relics have recently been found, and the church (with murals) is Norman. Its name means 'watercress town': there is still cress in the stream which flows into the Thames.

Readers' comments: Very efficient and well furnished. Warm welcome.

At 17th-century **OLD FARMHOUSE** on Station Hill, Long Hanborough, Vanessa Maundrell serves light suppers (vegetables come from the garden) in a stone-flagged dining-room with a dresser full of blue Spode china. One of the sitting-rooms has her collection of some 40 pot-lids over the inglenook. Beams, rugged stone walls and deep-set windows with far views are comple-mented by flowery fabrics, Victorian bedspreads and family treasures.

Outside is a pretty cottage-garden with old iron pump among the foxgloves. £17–£19. [Tel: 0993 882097; post-code: OX8 8JZ]

BUTTONS GREEN FARM

C D PT S

Cockfield, Suffolk, IP30 0JF Tel: 0284 828229
South of Bury St Edmunds. Nearest main road: A1141 from Lavenham
towards Bury St Edmunds.

3 **Bedrooms.** £15–£16. Tea/coffee facilities.
Views of garden, country. Washing machine
on request.
Dinner. £10 for 3 courses and coffee, from
6.30pm. Vegetarian or special diets if
ordered. Wine can be brought in. **Light
suppers** if ordered.
1 **Sitting-room.** With open fire, central
heating. TV.
Large garden
Closed from November to mid-March.

Behind a big duck-pond and masses of roses stands an apricot-coloured house
built around 1400, the centre of an 80-acre farm of grain and beet fields. It has
mullioned windows and a Tudor fireplace upstairs.

In Margaret Slater's sitting-room, with large sash windows on two sides, a pale
carpet and silky wallpaper make a light background to the antiques and velvet
armchairs grouped round a big log stove. The dining-room, too, has a log-burn-
ing stove in the brick inglenook, and leather-seated chairs are drawn up at a big
oak table. Here Margaret serves meals with home-grown or home-made produce,
her own chutneys and marmalade. Among her most popular starters are egg
mayonnaise and home-made pâté. A chicken or other roast may follow and then,
for instance, chocolate soufflé or raspberries and cream.

Twisting stairs lead to big beamed bedrooms with sloping floors, which Mrs
Slater has furnished with flowery fabrics, pot-plants and good furniture.

The farm is only a few minutes from Lavenham, one of the county's show
villages – very beautiful (but, in summer, often very crowded), with a guildhall
owned by the National Trust and a spectacular church.

Readers' comments: Lovely house. Charming hosts. Good home cooking. Just
perfect. Delightful, friendly, comfortable. Very good value. Good meals. Very
nice people.

Just the other side of Lavenham is
Brent Eleigh and **STREET FARM**,
its apricot walls half-timbered, its
garden well-groomed. Inside are
beamed ceilings and fine furnishings –
big velvet armchairs, and Hepplewhite-
style chairs in the dining-room, for
instance. Bedrooms are spacious and
immaculate, with good private bathrooms. There are pleasant country
views. £18.
Readers' comments: Very friendly.
Comfortable. Beautifully maintained,
very quiet. Best b & b we've had.

Everything to make one feel welcome.
Beautiful surroundings. [Tel: 0787
247 271; postcode: CO10 9NU]

48

CARN WARVEL
Church Road, St Mary's, Isles of Scilly, TR21 0NA   Tel: 0720 22111

5 Bedrooms. £19. Price goes up in April. All have own bath/shower/toilet. Tea/coffee facilities. TV. Views of garden, country. Washing machine on request.
Dinner. £10 for 4 courses (with choices) and coffee, at 6.30pm. Non-residents not admitted. Vegetarian or special diets if ordered. Wine can be ordered. No smoking.
Light suppers if ordered.
1 Sitting-room. With open fire, central heating, record-player. Bar.
Large garden
Closed from December to February.

If a suntrap were needed on Scilly, this 200-year-old granite house is one, tucked away down a lane and surrounded by trees. Once two cottages, it has been in its time the home of a miller and of a farrier; and a farmhouse. Downstairs, the beamed ceilings are low, and so are the doorways.

Neil and Jenny Hedges ran a guest-house in little Hugh Town before taking on the renovation of what was almost a ruin. They have carried it out very well, tucking built-in fitments into stone-lintelled fireplaces in the character-ful bedrooms, leaving outcrops of granite here and there, and lining walls with pine.

The cosy sitting-room opens onto a terrace surrounded by lush garden. Here, once a week during summer, guests eat from a big help-yourself salad buffet laid out indoors, with fruit cup to accompany it. Other evening meals consist of, for instance, local prawn cocktail, roast beef, and apple pie with Cornish cream. In season, grapes come from the vine in the big conservatory. (Those in the self-catering accommodation can dine in, if they wish.)

The main attractions of the Isles of Scilly are their unspoilt beauty, mild climate, low rainfall, and pure air. Storms are brief, sunny days long. Visitors to St Mary's (the largest island) get about on foot, by bus or taxi, and with hired bicycles (it is the only island with anything that could be called traffic).

Readers' comments: Made extremely welcome. Lovely house. Excellent food.

Of the off islands, St Martin's (the second largest) is particularly well provided with sandy beaches. John and Barbara Clarke holidayed on Scilly for decades before they bought **GLENMOOR COTTAGE**, where they run a small guest-house and a gift shop. (Wind-surfing boards on loan.) The view is panoramic, though the rooms are rather small; there is a shower but no bath. Barbara is an enthusiastic cook. A typical dinner: fresh local crab, roast lamb and five vegetables, raspberry mousse. £16 (b & b).

Readers' comments: Good food, good accommodation. [Tel: 0720 22816; postcode: TR25 0QL]

49

CARNWETHERS   C(7) **S**
Green Lane, Pelistry Bay, St Mary's, Isles of Scilly, TR21 0NX
Tel: 0720 22415

rear view

9 Bedrooms. £17–£25 (less for 7 nights with dinner). Prices go up in May. Bargain breaks. All have own bath/shower/toilet. Tea/coffee facilities. TV. Views of garden, country, sea.
Dinner. A la carte or £14 for 4 courses (with choices) and coffee, at 6.30pm. Non-residents not admitted. Wine can be ordered. No smoking.
2 Sitting-rooms. With open fire, central heating, TV. **Bar.** No smoking.
Large garden
Closed from November to March.

St Mary's, the principal island in the Scillies, is only three miles long. Even its centre of action, Hugh Town, can hardly be called busy by mainland standards (though it does receive tides of day-visitors during high summer), and so it is easy to find any number of unfrequented coves or beaches close by. Pelistry Bay is one of these – sheltered from wind, calm and unspoilt. Around it are pines and ferns, coastal footpaths and nature trails.

Carnwethers is more than an ordinary guest-house (and a very good one, at that). Its owner is Roy Graham, well known in the island and beyond as an under-water explorer and photographer, and a marine archaeologist – with 30 years in the Navy before he came here. Even non-experts appreciate his library of books on maritime subjects (wrecks, shipping, fish, wildlife, boats) and his immense knowledge of Scillonian history and ecology. His illustrated lectures in St Mary's twice a week should not be missed. He has assembled a number of videos about the islands which he shows to visitors, and can advise on boating or diving.

As to the house itself, this was once a farmhouse, but has been modernized. It is still surrounded by fields. Every room is as neat as a new pin. There is a bar and lengthy list of good-value wines, a heated 30-foot swimming-pool within sight of the sea itself but sheltered by granite walls and flowering shrubs, solarium, sauna, games room (for table tennis, darts, pool, etc.) and croquet lawn.

Meal times fit in with the times of the buses that take visitors into Hugh Town for slide shows which are usually packed out, concerts and the pubs.

Local produce is much used by the chef for meals: fish (obviously), new potatoes, free-range eggs, home-grown vegetables and home-made marmalade, for example. A typical meal might comprise soup or fruit juice, roast turkey and roly-poly pudding or fudge cake. Breakfasts include options like kedgeree and kippers. The dining-room has hanging-plants, a stove for cold days and views of the fields with cows, flowers or potatoes in them according to season. Here and in the sitting-room, there are pictures of ships and seascapes. Bedrooms are agreeably decorated; colours are pretty, cupboards have louvred doors.

Day trips to each of the other islands are well worth taking. Among these, Tresco is world-famous for its romantic gardens planted with subtropical flowers from every continent; it contains an outdoor museum of ships' figureheads.

Diving, boating and fishing can also be arranged.

Readers' comments: Happy, friendly atmosphere. Could not ask for more. Nothing is too much trouble. Complete satisfaction.

CASTLE FARM   **C M X**

Fotheringhay, Northamptonshire, PE8 5HZ   Tel: 08326 200

South-west of Peterborough (Cambridgeshire). Nearest main road: A605 from
Peterborough to Oundle.

have own bath/shower/toilet. Tea/coffee facilities. TV. Views of garden, country, river. No smoking. Washing machine on request.
Dinner. £9 for 2 courses and coffee, at 7pm (not Sundays). Non-residents not admitted. Vegetarian or special diets if ordered. Wine can be brought in. **Light suppers** if ordered.
1 Sitting-room. With open fire, central heating, TV.

6 Bedrooms. £16.50–£23 (less for 5 nights). Prices may go up in June. All

Large garden

In the castle that was once here, Richard III was born – later to gain an infamous and probably unjustified reputation as murderer of 'the princes in the Tower'. Here, too, in that grim keep surrounded by two moats (a maximum-security prison) Mary Queen of Scots was, after many similar imprisonments, confined at the end of her life – to be tried for conspiracy against Elizabeth I. Forget the romantic picture of the lovely young queen. Ageing, lined and bent after long years of captivity, she limped pathetically with rheumatism to her execution on a scaffold she had earlier heard being hammered together in the courtyard, leaving 'this world out of which I am very glad to go' at daybreak on a bright, wintry morning: 8 February 1587. When the executioner lifted her head away from the body (clad in the scarlet of martyrdom), its wig fell off to reveal the balding head beneath. She had wished to be buried in Catholic France; but after interment by night in Peterborough cathedral her headless corpse was later re-interred by her son, James I, in Westminster Abbey.

Her heart had been secretly buried, however, in the mound on which the castle, now long gone, was built: part of the land belonging to Castle Farm today. The thistles that grow here are called Queen Mary's tears.

At the Victorian farm, one steps straight into Stephanie Gould's huge quarry-tiled kitchen where a pine staircase rises to spacious bedrooms that are spick-and-span, all with good views (one of them looks onto the farmyard in one direction and to the ancient church in the other). There are very good bath- or shower-rooms, and much stripped pine. The big, comfortable sitting-room, too, has a view to enjoy – of the swift River Nene beyond the lawn, and a picturesque bridge. The Goulds have converted outbuildings to make more bedrooms. (Baby-sitting available.)

Stephanie produces traditional meals of two courses (such as lamb navarin with three or four vegetables including, for instance, home-grown asparagus, followed by sticky pear-gingerbread) or one can eat well at the nearby Falcon Inn.

Fotheringhay church is particularly fine, and contains interesting tombs. To the south is Oundle, famous for its public school (a delightful little town within a loop of the river, on which you can go boating). The whole area is dotted with undisturbed woods and fields watered by the winding rivers.

Readers' comments: Very relaxed. Good breakfast. Lovely view. Beautifully furnished. Excellent room. Friendly young hostess. Could not have been more hospitable. Rooms excellent and very up-market.

CASTLE HOUSE   **C D PT X**
23 Castle Street, Chester, Cheshire, CH1 2DS   Tel: 0244 350354
Nearest main road: A483 from Wrexham to Chester.

5 Bedrooms. £19–£20 (less for 5 nights). From April **£20 to readers of this book only.** (Sunday half-price if part of 3-night booking.) Some have own bath/shower/ toilet. Tea/coffee facilities. TV. Washing machine on request.
1 Sitting-room. With open fire, central heating. Bar.
Small garden

Right in the middle of the city but in a quiet by-road, this interesting house has a breakfast-room which dates from 1540 behind an 18th-century frontage and stair-case. The arms of Elizabeth I (with English lion and Welsh dragon) are over the fireplace. It is both the Marls' own home and a guest-house with modern bed-rooms that are exceptionally well furnished and equipped. Bed-and-breakfast only, for Chester has so many good restaurants; but visitors are welcome to use the kitchen. Newspapers and local phone calls are free – as are help-yourself drinks from a small bar. Coyle Marl, a local businessman, is an enthusiast for Chester and loves to tell visitors about its lesser-known charms, which can be toured in a horse-drawn hansom cab if you wish.

The city is, of course, of outstanding interest – second only to Bath and York in what there is to see. It is surrounded by ancient walls of red sandstone, just outside which is a large Roman amphitheatre. The most unusual feature, however, is the Rows: here, steps from street level lead up to balustraded galleries overhanging the pavements, serving a second level of small shops above the ones below. Chester's cathedral of red stone dates back to the 14th century and its zoo is outstanding.

Readers' comments: Welcoming. Breakfasts absolutely first-class. Excellent room and hospitality. Delightful hosts.

Down a cobbled cul-de-sac in the city centre, one finds **THE STUDIO** restaurant (at 2 Abbey Green), with rooms above. The secluded 18th-century house now belongs to Peter and Barbara Reynolds whose elegant home is **Dewis Cyfarfod** in Wales. They restored fine features such as panelled doors and shuttered windows (a handsome old cooking-range, too) and furnished the house with 'Bloomsbury' overtones. Arts events are held. Outside is a walled garden, small but romantic, with barbecue. Typical dishes: lamb steaks in

mushroom or redcurrant sauce, lime-marinaded beef with chillies and coriander, salmon with emerald sauce. £18–£25 (b & b). [Tel: 0244 311616 or 313522; postcode: CH1 2JH]

CATHEDRAL GATE HOTEL   C D PT X
36 Burgate, Canterbury, Kent, CT1 2HA   Tel: 0227 464381
(M2, junction 7, is near.)

24 Bedrooms. £20 (**to readers of this book only**)–£34.25. Prices go up in April. Bargain breaks. Some have own bath/shower/toilet. Tea/coffee facilities. TV. Views of cathedral (some). Washing machine on request.
Dinner. A la carte for about £9.50 for 3 courses, at 7–9pm. Non-residents not admitted. Vegetarian or special diets if ordered. Wine can be ordered. No smoking.
2 Sitting-rooms. With central heating. Bar.

The cathedral has a great, sculpted, mediaeval gateway. Tucked beside it is a row of shops and restaurants, above part of which is this upstairs guest-house (which has direct access to the cathedral precincts), not luxurious but characterful.

Even in Saxon times there was some kind of hospice here; and when the martyrdom of Thomas Becket in 1170 began to bring pilgrims to Canterbury in their thousands, it was in these beamy rooms that many of them stayed.

The bedrooms are reached via a maze of narrow corridors and creaking stairways which twist this way and that. All are quiet (for Burgate is now semi-pedestrianized); and some at the top have superlative views across the cathedral precincts to the great tower and south transept – floodlit at night (during summer).

When the small hotel was taken over by Caroline Jubber and her husband, they greatly improved most bedrooms – some of them reached via a rooftop walkway – while retaining ancient beams, leaded casements and bow windows. There are now two sitting-rooms, which include a bar, and one splendid 'mediaeval' bathroom where modern tiles contrast with dark beams. Breakfast (continental, unless you pay extra) is brought to you in the small dining-room or in your bedroom. A modest evening meal is available, as well as full afternoon teas. (Many good restaurants close by.) Bedrooms are well equipped and comfortable. One has a four-poster. Some look across undulating old roofs and red chimney-pots where pigeons perch. The hotel's locked carpark is several minutes' walk away.

It is, of course, the cathedral which brings most visitors to Canterbury: one of Britain's finest and most colourful, with many historical associations. It is the site of Becket's martyrdom (commemorated in some of the finest stained glass in the world) and houses the splendid tomb of the Black Prince, and much more.

The ancient walled city still has many surviving mediaeval and Tudor buildings, the beautiful River Stour, old churches and inns, Roman remains, a very good theatre, and lovely shops in its small lanes. The Heritage Museum is well worth a visit to see some of the city's most important treasures.

This is a useful place to stay before or after a ferry-crossing to the continent – or as a base from which to explore the historic south Kent coast, the Cinque Ports, Dover Castle and Dover's famous Roman 'Painted House', the Minster Abbey at Ramsgate, or the Kent countryside, the garden of England.

Readers' comments: Incredible situation. Very nice people. Location superb. Delicious breakfasts. We can't wait to return.

CHAMBERHOUSE MILL
Thatcham, Berkshire, RG13 4NU   Tel: 0635 865930
East of Newbury. Nearest main road: A4 from Newbury to Reading
(and M4, junction 13).

rear view

1 Bedroom. £17.50. With bathroom. Tea/coffee facilities. TV. View of garden, country, river. Washing machine on request. **Dinner.** £12.50 for 3 courses and coffee, at about 8pm. Vegetarian or special diets if ordered. Wine can be brought in. **Light suppers** if ordered.
1 Sitting-room. With central heating, TV.
Large garden
Closed in January and February.

The huge watermill, where from at least 1086 to 1969 grain used to be ground into flour, has been skilfully converted into a number of very comfortable modern houses. Betty de Wit, her husband and six cats live at no.2, right over one of the two great wooden wheels – the sound of rushing water is always present.

One crosses footbridges and a big sluice to reach their hidden garden, enclosed by box hedges. Here there is a summer-house on the riverbank from which to watch the grebes and ducks: one of Britain's biggest swan colonies frequents these waters, too. All around are great old trees – cedar, copper beech and others.

The second-floor guest-room is neat as a ship's cabin but more spacious, a room-divider of louvred fitments separating the bed end from the other, where there is a William Morris sofa, television and a small refrigerator. Walls are of varnished pine. Here and elsewhere are Betty's landscape photographs: a Fellow of the Royal Photographic Society, she exhibits and lectures to camera clubs.

Both she and Gerry enjoy cooking the meals which they serve in their own dining-kitchen – beamed, with rush chairs, pine fitments and pot-plants. Dinners, have a Provençal influence, as the de Wits regularly visit France.

Readers' comments: Felt very much at home. Cosy and comfortable. A real delight. Room was great, snug. Mrs de Wit extremely pleasant.

Carol Freeman's 18th-century home, **WOODLANDS PARK FARM** at Ashford Hill – near Newbury, though the house is actually in Hampshire – is a typical farmhouse, very well kept. There are two spacious downstairs bedrooms (creamy silk duvets complement satinwood furniture, old china adorns the walls), and two upstairs, one with Paisley fabrics and big sash windows – remote-control TV is an extra indulgence. The generous dinners are very good value: typically, chicken and bacon pie followed by (if you are in luck) a succulent courgette-

and-chocolate cake with cream. Beyond the garden (tree-house and sandpit for children) cattle graze. £19 –£20. [Tel: 0635 268258 or 0734 814821; postcode: RG15 8AY]

54

CHANTRY FARM

C(5) **D S**

Higham Cross Road, Pindon End, Hanslope, Buckinghamshire, MK19 7HL
Tel: 0908 510269 (Messages: 0908 510413)
North of Milton Keynes. Nearest main road: A508 from Milton Keynes to
Northampton (and M1, junctions 14/15).

3 Bedrooms. £17–£20. Some have own shower. Tea/coffee facilities. TV. Views of garden, country. Washing machine on request.
Light suppers if ordered.
1 Sitting-room. With open fire, central heating, TV.
Large garden

The stone quarried to build this house in 1650 left a deep hole, now a pond to one side of it. From this stone was also made the big inglenook fireplace with bread oven, the main feature of the sitting-room. In what was once a cattle-yard there is a heated swimming-pool, with table tennis in the adjoining stable. Out in the fields you will see sheep, cattle and possibly deer (farmed for venison). Further off is a trout lake which Wake Adams created a few years ago – and which, like the rest of the farm, helps to provide the ingredients for the meals which Chuff produces for her visitors. Even her snacks are excellent: I particularly enjoyed a Stilton quiche. (Clay-pigeon shooting by arrangement; croquet.)

Rooms are pleasantly furnished – oriental rugs on tiled floors, rush ladder-back chairs in the salmon-pink dining-room (with oak butter-churn), hefty iron keys dug up in the grounds – where the remains of an ancient prison have been found.

GRANGE BARN, Haversham, was elegantly converted to become the home of Mike Kilby (author and former MEP). From the attractive hall (raspberry walls and embroidered curtains) a door opens onto the walled garden, and an iron stair spirals up to the bedrooms. One, with rose wallpaper and walnut bedhead, goes from front to back of the house – very light and spacious. On a refectory table with rush ladderback chairs, Mary will serve light suppers by arrange-

ment. £15– £19 (b & b). Minimum 2 nights. [Tel: 0908 313613; postcode: MK19 7DX]

Some proprietors stipulate a minimum stay of two nights at weekends or peak seasons; or they will accept one-nighters only at short notice (that is, only if no lengthier booking has yet been made).

CHASE LODGE   C D M PT X

Park Road, Hampton Wick, Surrey, KT1 4AS   Tel: 081-943 1862

North of Kingston-upon-Thames. Nearest main road: A308 from Staines to
Surbiton (the M25, M3 and M4 are also near).

10 Bedrooms. £17.50–£40 (less for 3
nights and at weekends). Some have own
bath/shower/toilet. Tea/coffee facilities. TV.
Refrigerator. No smoking (in one).
Dinner. £12 for 3 courses (with choices)
and coffee, from 8–10pm. Vegetarian or
special diets if ordered. Wine can be ordered.
No smoking. **Light suppers** if ordered.
Sunday 'carvery', summer barbecues.
2 Sitting-rooms. With open fire, central
heating. TV, video. **Bar.**
Small garden

Not only can you garage your car here and be taken to and from Heathrow
Airport, but it is also a very handy place at which to stay in order to explore the
'royal' stretch of the Thames Valley (monarchs chose nearby Richmond,
Hampton Court, Kew and Windsor for their palaces). Park Road is in a quiet
conservation area, a street of pretty little Victorian villas with cottage-gardens, yet
only a minute or two from a railway station, buses and the excellent shops of
Kingston.

Chase Lodge has been redecorated with interesting pieces of Victorian furniture and decorative trifles in its sitting-room and elsewhere. There are African
violets and other pot-plants in some rooms. One has a tented scarlet-and-green
ceiling and a mural of a crusader castle in its bathroom. Another, a four-poster
with lace. Most have very good en suite showers or bathrooms.

For dinner, Nigel Stafford-Haworth, formerly chef at a 5-star hotel, prepares
either à la carte or table d'hôte menus. (Supper trays and Sunday lunch available,
too.) As all bedrooms have phones, breakfast can be ordered in bed. Free parking
permits on request.

At the back is a tiny, sun-trapping patio with a few seats among the flowers.

I was greatly impressed by Denise's attention to detail and the immense
trouble she takes. Not many far more costly hotels provide room-service free, and
complimentary carafes of sherry. Baby-sitting can also be arranged.

There is an enormous amount to see and do in the neighbourhood: walks
among the deer and chestnut trees of Bushey Park or along the towpaths,
Hampton Court – with *son-et-lumière* shows at night – and its gardens (with
maze), horse-racing at Kempdown and Sandhurst, tennis at Wimbledon, rugby at
Twickenham, and any number of regattas and festivals in summer. Richmond
deserves at least a day to itself, to explore the byways and curio shops off the
green, the stunning river view from the top of the hill, and the 3000 acres of
Richmond Park. There are also Georgian or earlier mansions in fine grounds
(Ham House, Orleans House, Marble Hill, Syon Park, Chiswick House,
Hogarth's house and Osterley Park).

The river trips from nearby Kingston Bridge are particularly worth taking, and
you can go all the way to Oxford through exceptional scenery.

Readers' comments: Superb hosts. Very comfortable. Without fault. Best b & b ever!
Friendly and attentive. Great attention given. Delightfully furnished and all the
facilities expected. Food of highest quality, in unusual and attractive dining-room.

CHIMNEYS   C(5) PT S

Main Street, Chideock, Dorset, DT6 6JH   Tel: 0297 89368 (Messages: 0705 594704)

West of Bridport. On A35 from Axminster to Bridport.

5 Bedrooms. £16–£25 (less for 3 nights). Most have own shower/toilet. Tea/coffee facilities. Views of garden, country. No smoking. Washing machine on request.
Dinner. £12.50–£14.50 for 4 courses and coffee, at 7.15pm every other night. Vegetarian diets if ordered. Wine can be ordered. No smoking.
1 Sitting-room. With open fire, central heating, TV, video. Bar. No smoking.
Large garden
Closed in November and January.

This pretty thatched cottage in its old-fashioned garden is on the road between 18th-century Bridport and historic Lyme Regis. Built in the 17th century, the guest-house has been furnished in keeping with its age. The sitting-room and bar are beamed and have log fires in winter. One bedroom has a four-poster, and several are beamed (the ones at the back are quiet, front ones are double-glazed).

For dinner you might get a home-made soup, duckling in orange sauce, ice cream made with Cointreau, cheese, Rombouts coffee (and free house liqueur), on a table with lace cloth, cut glass and Wedgwood or Royal Worcester china. For breakfast, try the coddled eggs or one of many other imaginative options. Cream teas sometimes available.

Ann and Brian Hardy lend visitors Ordnance Survey maps and give advice. For example, they can tell you where to find fossils easily plucked from the Blue Lias clay, or where the best walks are on clifftops or through valleys – and if you want a lift back at the end of a walk, they are willing to come and fetch you in their car. They also show a film of Dorset.

Car washing and vacuuming facilities are free for you to use.

Chideock itself is a very pretty village of thatched cottages, in a fold of the west Dorset hills designated an area of outstanding natural beauty. At nearby Morcomblake, you can visit Moores Biscuit Bakery (famous for Dorset Knobs) and its shop selling west country products. The sea is close and much of the coastline hereabouts belongs to the National Trust. Within a short distance are Lyme Regis, Charmouth, Abbotsbury (swannery and subtropical gardens), Chesil Beach, Portland and Weymouth – all on the coast. Among the hills and vales, the farmlands and streams, are Sherborne (castle and abbey), Parnham House and Cricket St Thomas, Cerne Abbas (abbey, and the giant cut in the chalk hills nearly two thousand years ago) and Beaminster (Georgian houses). There are fine gardens at Forde Abbey and Clapton Court.

Readers' comments: Beautifully appointed house, historic without detracting from 20th-century comforts, comfortable, friendly, good food. Very helpful and pleasant, well prepared food but not too exotic. Charming house and owners. A delight; meal was exceptionally good value, owners have warmth and humour. Comfortable room, excellent meals, many little extra touches. Delicious breakfasts.

CHITHURST FARM   C S
Chithurst Lane, Horne, Smallfield, Horley, Surrey, RH6 9JU
Tel: 0342 842487
East of Gatwick (West Sussex). Nearest main road: A22 from Godstone to
East Grinstead (also M23, junction 9; and M25, junction 6).

3 Bedrooms. £14–£14.50 (less for 6
nights). Prices go up in May. Tea/coffee
facilities. Views of garden, country. No
smoking.
Light suppers if ordered.
1 Sitting-room. With wood burner, TV.
No smoking.
Large garden
Closed in December and January.

Despite being so near Gatwick (and even London is only 35 minutes from the
nearest rail station), this farm seems truly remote, reached by a long and winding
lane. Built in the 16th century, it has tile-hung walls of mellow red brick against
which the japonica flowers in spring.

Inside are low beams and a twisting staircase leading to simple but spacious
bedrooms. These have double-glazing so that the sound of aircraft (numerous
only during the day in summer) is not disturbing, with air-conditioners providing
fresh air. In the visitors' sitting/dining-room, armchairs and a rocking-chair are
grouped around a huge inglenook fireplace, its original spit-rack still in place.

Visitors are welcome to watch cows being milked, and to buy home-made
jams and crafts. This is a good area for walking in the North Downs. There are
several stately homes, gardens (such as Wakehurst), and bird or wildlife parks
nearby. Even Brighton in one direction, and the Kentish Weald in the other, are
soon reached. Old towns like Horsham, East Grinstead and Dorking are worth
exploring. Churchill's house (Chartwell), the Bluebell steam railway, Hever
Castle, Tunbridge Wells and Ashdown Forest are all very popular, as are the
many pick-your-own fruit farms. Chessington World of Adventures, a 65-acre site
comprising a zoo and entertainments, is half an hour away.

Some people stay at the farm before flying from Gatwick, and if necessary Mrs
Tucker will leave early breakfasts ready. A nearby garage will house your car, with
free transport (24 hours a day) to and from the airport – where parking would
cost you far more.

In the vicinity are Standen House, a National Trust property, full of
William Morris furnishings, and Gatwick zoo where you can walk inside the
big aviary and the butterfly garden. The monkey island is another popular
feature there.

Mrs Tucker does not provide full evening meals, but has a list of recommended local restaurants, etc. which do, such as the Hedgehog Inn. Chithurst Farm is
remarkably good value for this area.

A car is essential as there is no public transport and taxis from the nearest railway station (4 miles away) are expensive.

Readers' comments: Charming. Pleasant attention.

CHURCH FARM   C D PT S X

High Street, Roxton, Bedfordshire, MK44 3EB   Tel: 0234 870234
North-east of Bedford. Nearest main road: A428 from Bedford towards
St Neots.

2 Bedrooms. £15–£18 (less for 7 nights or continental breakfast). Tea/coffee facilities. TV. Views of garden. No smoking. Washing machine on request.
1 Sitting-room. With open fire, central heating, TV. No smoking.
Large garden

It is a surprise to find such a peaceful village (a thatched church as well as thatched cottages) only a mile from the busy Great North Road, the A1, and in it this house – part 17th- and part 18th-century. One bedroom has a royal coat-of-arms carved in the wall, dating from Stuart times.

A beautiful breakfast-room has a Chippendale-style table and a sideboard with its original brass rails. The bedrooms are in a guest wing (one has a particularly handsome wardrobe); all rooms are furnished with an informal mixture of family antiques. There is a pleasant sitting-room in shades of cream and brown with a log fire. (For dinner, Janet Must recommends restaurants in either St Neots or Bedford, but visitors are welcome to bring their own snack suppers in.)

Visitors who stay here are often surprised to discover Bedfordshire's little-publicized charms, particularly its pretty villages, many of which are sited on wandering streams. Popular outings include not only Bedford (with the John Bunyan museum, the art collection in the Cecil Higgins gallery, a church with carved angels in the roof and pretty riverside lawns) and Cambridge, but the English Heritage properties of Wrest Park and Bushmead Priory, Shuttleworth's historic aircraft collection, the Swiss Garden, stately homes (such as Luton Hoo, Woburn Abbey and Hatfield House), Grafham Water and Olney (for its antique shops and boutiques). Sandy has the RSPB's headquarters and bird reserve, Huntingdon its Cromwell associations. Many towns or villages of Bedfordshire have antique shops; there are also a number of pick-your-own fruit farms, first-class garden centres, and good but not strenuous walks. Near Luton is an exhibition of horse-drawn vehicles through the ages.

Almost the whole of Bunyan's life was played out in Bedfordshire, and it is possible to follow a Bunyan trail, starting at Elstow (where he was born in 1628 and grew up to follow his father's trade – a tinker, a mender of cooking- pots and suchlike). It was at Lower Samshill that he was first arrested for preaching; and at Bedford that he spent much of his life in prison. Mementoes (including his portable anvil) are in the Bunyan Museum, near the meeting-house which has scenes from *The Pilgrim's Progress* in bas-relief on its doors.

Book well ahead: many of these houses have few rooms. Do not expect dinner if you have not booked it or if you arrive late.

CHURCH HOUSE   C(12) X
Grittleton, Wiltshire, SN14 6AP   Tel: 0249 782562
North-west of Chippenham. Nearest main road: M4 (junctions 17/18).

4 Bedrooms. £18.50–£24.50. Bargain breaks. All have own bath/shower/toilet. Tea/coffee facilities. TV. Views of garden, country. Washing machine on request.
Dinner. £14 for 4 courses (with wine) and coffee, at 8pm. Vegetarian or special diets sometimes. **Light suppers** if ordered.
2 Sitting-rooms. With open fire, central heating, piano.
Large garden

This little-known but very beautiful village lies just off the M4 midway between London and Wales: a cluster of elegant houses, a great Tudor-style mansion and church, all built from golden Cotswold limestone.

Church House began life in 1740 as a huge rectory, which it took six servants to run. Around it are lawns with immense copper beeches (floodlit at night), an orchard, fields of sheep and a covered swimming-pool, well heated in summer (84°) as well as a walled vegetable and fruit garden which provides organic produce for the kitchen, where Anna Moore produces imaginative meals if these are ordered in advance. A typical menu might comprise sorrel soup, chicken in a creamy apricot-and-curry mayonnaise, a tart of fresh peaches, English cheeses, fruit and wine (included in the price).

She and her family treat all visitors as house-guests. If you want to meet Grittleton people, she will invite some to dinner, and she often escorts overseas visitors on sightseeing tours. Some she takes to the Royal Shakespeare Theatre (Stratford is 1½ hours away), with a champagne picnic supper on the banks of the Avon afterwards. The Moores are a musical family, and occasionally arrange music evenings – there is one huge room with a grand piano used for this purpose. Watching polo can be arranged. There is a croquet lawn and a sun-bed.

The house has handsome and finely proportioned rooms. In the yellow sitting-room (which has an immense bay window overlooking the garden) are antique furniture, interesting paintings and a large log stove. The dining-room is equally handsome: raspberry walls, an Adam fireplace of inlaid marble and, on the long mahogany table, silver candelabra and Victorian Spode Copeland china. The most impressive architectural feature is the graceful staircase that curves its way up to the second floor, where the guest-rooms are furnished with antiques; some have their bathroom facilities behind screens.

There is an immense amount to see and do in the neighbourhood. Close by is Badminton (celebrated for the annual horse trials, attended by the royal family); Bath is only 12 miles away; and the many historic (and prehistoric) sites of Wiltshire, such as Avebury, are all around. Both the west country and the Cotswolds are accessible from Grittleton. Malmesbury Abbey, Castle Combe and Westonbirt Arboretum are favourite sights.

Readers' comments: Anna Moore is an excellent cook. Bedrooms spacious and most comfortable. Peaceful. Lovely beds, charming house. Happy memories.

CHURCH HOUSE   C PT
Lyonshall, Herefordshire, HR5 3HR   Tel: 05448 350
West of Leominster. Nearest main road: A44 from Leominster to Kington.

3 Bedrooms. £15–£18 (less for 3 nights). Bargain breaks. Some have own bath/toilet. Tea/coffee facilities. Views of garden, country. No smoking. Washing machine on request.
Dinner. £8.50 for 3 courses and coffee, at 7.30pm. Non-residents not admitted. Vegetarian or special diets if ordered. Wine can be brought in. **Light suppers** if ordered.
1 Sitting-room. With open fire, central heating, TV. No smoking.
Large garden

Venture into the sitting-room here and you may be tempted to order a unique creation: a pin-tucked blouse, lace- or ribbon-trimmed in Edwardian style, each specially designed for its recipient by Eileen Dilley (formerly a London fashion designer). Now she uses the room for a display of these and other crafts – all in Edwardian style: other garments (including children's), lavender bags, dolls, cushions.

The 18th-century house, too, is filled with her work and with Edwardiana she and her husband have collected. Most of the furnishings are from that period, with bedrooms named after celebrities of the time such as Baden-Powell, Nellie Melba and Conan Doyle (who lived near here while writing *The Hound of the Baskervilles*, using a well-known local name in its title). Every room has frilled curtain-ties or cushions she has made; fans, fashion prints or valentines she has collected. In one of the large bedrooms is a four-poster. In her Victorian-style dining-room, Eileen serves such dinners as a pear and Stilton starter, beef in burgundy and chocolate fudge cake. There is much emphasis on local produce and recipes.

Outside are donkeys in a paddock, many trees including a specimen copper beech in the garden, spring lambs and fine views beyond the haha.

Whichever way you drive there is plenty to see. Hereford (with cathedral and its unique treasure, the Mappa Mundi, which was saved by a whisker from sale abroad in 1989), Leominster (market town, with many antique shops), hilly mid-Wales, the Elan Valley, Llandrindod Wells (old-fashioned spa), Welsh seaside resorts, the black-and-white villages typical of Herefordshire, several stately homes (Croft Castle, Berrington Hall and Burton Court, for instance). Clee Hill is a well-known beauty-spot in the direction of historic Ludlow and the outstanding castle of Stokesay. Symonds Yat is a celebrated viewpoint above the Wye Valley. Walkers head for Offa's Dyke, bookworms for Hay-on-Wye, garden-lovers for Hergest Croft.

Readers' comments: Excellent quality. Highly recommended, excellent food; I have been four times in one year. Superior to lots of hotels. Superb meals. Delighted with the reception we received.

For explanation of code letters (C, D, M, PT, S, X) see page xlvi.

61

THE CITADEL   C
Weston-under-Redcastle, Shropshire, SY4 5JY   Tel: 063084 204
North of Shrewsbury. Nearest main road: A49 from Shrewsbury to
Whitchurch.

3 Bedrooms. £20–£30 (less for 3 nights). All have own bath/shower/toilet. TV. Views of garden, country. Washing machine on request.
Dinner. £16.50 for 4 courses (with choices) and coffee, at 7.30pm (not Sundays). Non-residents not admitted. Vegetarian or special diets if ordered. Wine can be brought in. **Light suppers** if ordered.
1 Sitting-room. With open fire, central heating, TV, piano.
Large garden
Closed from November to March, except for 2-day or longer bookings of 4–6 people.

The castellated turrets of this unusual red sandstone mansion have never known a shot fired in battle. Erected in 1820 when the fashion for mock-Gothic architecture was at its peak, it was built as the dower house of Hawkstone Hall.

The interior is equally striking: some rooms – including one guest bedroom – are round, windows are deep-set, and ceilings are particularly decorative.

One enters through a round hall with an inlaid octagonal table; the ceiling has decorative ribs and bosses. In the huge celadon-green dining-room the coffered ceiling is embellished with plasterwork vines. There is a sitting-room (chocolate and cream) which houses a grand piano; as well as a billiard room with terracotta ceiling. An unusual stone staircase leads up to the turret bedrooms.

Sylvia Griffiths serves such dinners as cheese and asparagus flan to start with, jugged pheasant and chocolate roulade.

Readers' comments: Most interesting house. Delightful stay. Superb setting. Excellent. The most luxurious of our stops.

Well tucked away in Foxleigh Drive in the little market town of Wem is handsome **FOXLEIGH HOUSE**, the most memorable feature of which is the fine sitting-room. Its cocoa walls, coffee ceiling and Chinese carpet are an excellent setting for antiques that include inlaid tables and a series of Hogarth prints. Bay windows open onto the croquet lawn and its towering Wellingtonia. In the dining-room, Barbara Barnes serves such meals as melon, lamb, trifle and cheeses. The bedrooms have 'thirties suites of

figured maple, and the hall a gallery of ancestral portraits. £17–£18. [Tel: 0939 233528; postcode: SY4 5BP]

CLAY LANE HEAD FARMHOUSE   C PT
Cabus, Garstang, Lancashire, PR3 1WL   Tel: 0995 603132
North of Preston. On A6 from Preston to Lancaster (and near M6, junctions 32/33).

3 Bedrooms. £14–£18 (less for 7 nights). Two have their own bath/shower/toilet. Tea/coffee facilities. Views of garden, country.
Light suppers (not Wednesdays).
1 Sitting-room. With open fire, TV, piano, record-player.
Small garden
Closed in January and February.

Though hardly off the beaten track – it stands on the A6 – Clay Lane Head Farmhouse could easily be missed as one sped by, on the way to or from Scotland or the Lake District. It would be a good place to break a long journey, though it deserves more than a brief overnight visit, for both the house and the surroundings have much to offer visitors who like an easygoing atmosphere.

The stone house, which is more characterful than it appears to be from the outside, is basically 16th-century, and some of the internal walls are of plastered reeds. It is a rambling, beamy old place, full of family antiques and Victoriana, with a book-lined sitting-room to sprawl in (it has a log fire); and it has not been modernized. The rooms face away from the main road. Although this is no longer a working dairy-farm, there are cattle, goats and sheep.

Joan Higginson, a pharmacist, dispenses good food, home-made from fresh ingredients.

Start by visiting the Garstang Discovery Centre before you investigate the hinterland – notably the Trough of Bowland, which is like a miniature Lake District without the lakes. The steep, heather-covered hills here are excellent for walking and picnicking, and there are picturesque stone villages and mansions to visit. One such is Browsholme Hall, a little-altered Jacobean house still in the possession of the family which provided the hereditary Bowbearer of Bowland. Historic towns such as Lancaster and Clitheroe are not far, and the Lake District and the resorts of the Lancashire coast are within an easy day trip. Other popular outings include Lancaster Castle, Cockersand Abbey, Sunderland Point, Beacon Fell country park and Brock Bottom nature trail.

Because the M6 motorway is near, it is easy to get to Lancashire's great cities which, although no great pleasure in themselves, do house a number of places of considerable interest – such as the restored Albert Dock and an outpost of London's Tate Gallery at Liverpool, and the outstanding Museum of Science and Granada Studios in Manchester. Blackpool, with its famous tower and miles of sands, is near: the latest attraction there is a huge, tropical, indoor swimming-pool. In this direction, too, are Fleetwood (port and fishmarket) and the pleasant resort of Lytham St Anne's.

Readers' comments: Very enjoyable. Attentive service. Concerned for our every comfort, spotless rooms. Interesting place. Very satisfactory. Friendly and bright. Very comfortable, excellent food.

CLAYBATCH FARMHOUSE   S
Blatchbridge, Somerset, BA11 5EF   Tel: 0373 461193
South of Frome. Nearest main road: A361 from Frome to Shepton Mallet.

rear view

2 Bedrooms. £17–£19 (less for 4 nights or continental breakfast). Prices go up from

April. Both have own bath/shower/toilet. Tea/coffee facilities. Views of garden, country. No smoking. Washing machine on request.
Dinner (by arrangement). £12.50 for 4 courses, and coffee, at 7.30pm. Non-residents not admitted. Special diets if ordered. No smoking. **Light suppers** sometimes.
1 Sitting-room. With open fire, central heating, TV, piano. No smoking.
Large garden
Closed from mid-December to mid-January.

Jacqueline George, a professional cook, has another outstanding talent: a flair for combining beautiful colours. Her early 18th-century home is a perfect setting for both her skills.

The big sitting-room is memorable. Duck-egg blue walls and the mellow patina of walnut furniture contrast with the brilliance of apricot chairs grouped round a stone fireplace – their colour echoed in Warners' pheasant and peony fabric on the sofas. (When I was there Jackie had put a great bowl of matching roses on a table.) Big casement doors open onto a sloping lawn, flowerbeds and watergarden. The dining-room has Chippendale-style chairs (Prince of Wales' feathers decorate their backs) with tapestry seats made by her aunt; and on the coral walls hang oil paintings. Here Jackie serves such dinners (on your night of arrival only) as smoked trout pâté; pork fillet with juniper berries and garden vegetables; profiteroles; and cheeses (pre-dinner drinks are included). On other nights, guests can eat well in Frome, or at local pubs.

Bedrooms, too, are charming with little rosebuds on one bedspread, Chinese pavilions on another, for example.

Claybatch used to be part of the Longleat estate. The great Elizabethan mansion of Longleat is one of England's stateliest homes, full of art treasures and famous for its free-ranging lions in part of the grounds landscaped by Capability Brown. Stourhead, too, is near: a Palladian mansion with fine gardens.

Somerset is a county of great beauty, its landscape punctuated by impressive church towers from the resplendent Perpendicular period of mediaeval architecture, big stone barns and little stone villages, with Bath itself just over the county boundary to the north; Wells and Salisbury are close. Geology is what accounts for its great variety, with buildings made of stone that ranges from lilac to gold (for every quarry is different), and a landscape of hills and levels contrasting with one another. Monks drained marshes (still crisscrossed with their ancient ditches) between hills of great beauty but quite dissimilar from one another – the Mendips, the Quantocks and Exmoor. Where streams carved their way through rock there are gorges and caves.

Readers' comments: Made most welcome, delicious meals, beautiful home.

CLIFF HOUSE   C PT S X

Devonport Hill, Kingsand, Cornwall, PL10 1NJ Tel: 0752 823110

South-west of Plymouth (Devon). Nearest main road: A374 from Plymouth towards Looe.

3 Bedrooms. £15–£19 (less for 3 nights). Prices may go up at Easter. One has own bath/toilet. Tea/coffee facilities. Views of garden, country, sea. No smoking. Washing machine on request.

Dinner. £16 for 4 courses, coffee and wine, at 7pm. Vegetarian or special diets if ordered. Wine can be brought in. No smoking. **Light suppers** if ordered.

2 Sitting-rooms. With open fire, central heating, TV, CD player, video. Balcony. No smoking. Piano.

Small garden

Just across the Devon/Cornwall border lies a neck of land that is almost an island and which most tourists pass by. But if one leaves the main road to follow a woodland route along the winding banks of the River Lynher (frequented by swans), one comes to a little world of billowing green hills and high-banked lanes that plunge up and down until, right at the tip, one reaches the Mount Edgcumbe estate and the point at which ferries (car or pedestrian) arrive from Plymouth as they have done since time immemorial. This is the Rame peninsula, an area of outstanding natural beauty; and here, in a fishing village of coloured or red sandstone cottages, a maze of tortuous byways, small shops and bistros, is 17th-century Cliff House – perched high above the sea and within a few yards of the south Cornwall coastal path.

From its hexagonal bay windows or the verandah, one can watch naval ships passing in and out of Plymouth Sound or, in the opposite direction, children playing on the sands of Cawsand Bay. To make the most of these views, the sitting-room (with sofas and log stove, the television end curtained off) is on the first floor. On the walls of the house are paintings by local artists that are for sale, and theatrical posters. Some bedrooms, too, enjoy the fine views – the largest having armchairs in the bay window. There is one with a cupboard full of books for children. (Baby-sitting is also available.)

Ann Heasman is not only a fount of information about the locality but an enthusiastic wholefood cook – of such meals as lentil pâté with spiced fruit salad, carbonnade of beef or local venison, and chocolate roulade or rhubarb fool – and she bakes her own bread.

The house is on the edge of the Mount Edgcumbe country park, at its heart a much restored Tudor mansion and fine gardens, both landscaped and formal. As well as developing the gardens, successive generations created such adornments as an orangery, shell fountain, conservatories, a fern dell, pavilions and memorials. There are also fortifications, Tudor and Napoleonic, to guard the sea approaches.

The whole peninsula is so full of interest that it would take a long holiday to explore it all. Every walk has unusual views: from the obelisk near Cremyll, one looks across to the most historic part of Devonport dockyard; at Empacombe, a path goes by an 1812 redoubt (with lake view); there are all sorts of 'finds' to be made – a mediaeval well-house, a track where hundreds of glow-worms glow . . .

Readers' comments: Delightful owner, made us so at home. All standards excellent, breakfast marvellous. Didn't want to leave.

CLOW BECK HOUSE
Monk End, Croft-on-Tees, North Yorkshire, DL2 2SW   Tel: 0325 721075
South of Darlington (County Durham). Nearest main road: A167 from
Northallerton to Darlington.

5 Bedrooms. £18.50–£23.50. All have own
bath/shower//toilet. Tea/coffee facilities. TV.
Views of garden, country. Washing machine
on request.
1 Sitting-room. With open fire, central
heating, TV, record-player.
Large garden

Heather Armstrong being a teacher of beauty therapy, it is not surprising that
the rooms in Clow Beck House have been decorated and furnished with some
flamboyance! The big sitting-room is in shades of the royal blue of the Chinese
carpet, with white details such as Adam-style panels on walls and alcoves by
the fireplace. A chandelier hangs over the armchairs and settee, which have
carved wooden frames and blue velvet upholstery, and the swagged curtains are
also in blue.

There is another chandelier in the marble-floored hall with its big gilt mirror.
Up the oak staircase, one bedroom, in pink, has a tented fabric ceiling and a satin
bedhead. The en suite double bedroom, in blue, has a canopied bed and rattan
furniture, and the twin room is in shades of yellow.

Even the large and luxurious bathroom has been equipped in style – dark
blue carpet, fawn dado, and shell-shaped washbasin. In the dining-room, the
oak furniture is from one of the craftsmen for whom North Yorkshire is well
known.

Though hardly typical, this is indeed a farmhouse, and from it David
Armstrong runs a mixed holding which – though the house is less than 10 years
old – has been in his family for generations. Unlike most farmers, he is a keen
gardener and puts a lot of time into the big open garden he is developing in front
of the house.

'Lewis Carroll ' (Charles Dodgson) spent his early life in Croft, where his
father was the rector. The village is not far from Darlington, famous in railway
history, a greener and pleasanter place than those who do not know it might
suppose, and with an arts centre.

Bedroom at Bishop Garth (see page 195)

COACH HOUSE   C D M PT S X

Belton-by-Grantham, Lincolnshire, NG32 2LS   Tel: 0476 73636
North of Grantham. Nearest main road: A607 from Grantham to Lincoln.

4 Bedrooms. £15–£17.50 (less for 3 nights). Prices go up from Easter. All have own bath/shower/toilet. Tea/coffee facilities. TV. Views of garden, country. No smoking. Washing machine on request.
Dinner (if ordered). £10 for 3 courses and coffee, at about 7pm. Wine can be ordered or brought in. No smoking. **Light suppers.**
1 Sitting-room. With central heating, TV, video. No smoking.
Large garden

Along the High Dyke nearby, the Romans built a road which was still in use, centuries later, as a stagecoach route. For an overnight stop on the long haul from Cambridge to York the coaches paused here at an inn, next door to which the buildings of Ancaster stone that are now the Nortons' home were stables surrounding a coach yard. All very different today, with tubs of petunias where the coaches used to clatter in and out. And very peaceful, even though the busy A1 is only five minutes away.

Bernard Norton spends every spare hour improving his house, and himself created such attractive features as a second, sun-trapping courtyard with a fountain in the centre of a circle of blue-brick paving: an attractive view to enjoy while dining. There are ground-floor bedrooms (one with courtyard view, one with none) and others upstairs – be prepared for rafters and steps – which have roof-lights. Sue has made ruffled pelmets and, on one bed, a prettily draped corona, using silky pink or rose-patterned fabrics.

For dinner she may offer you minestrone, lemon chicken and strawberries, for instance.

All around the conservation village is National Trust land to provide good walks, a plethora of golf courses including one with 45(!) holes and, just up the road, the exceptionally fine mansion of Belton House: in its collection of coaches are some that used to do the Cambridge-York run. There is a particularly good garden centre nearby.

Belton is in an attractively wooded part of the county, well placed to visit the splendid Vale of Belvoir in one direction and historic Lincoln in the other. Grantham itself has treasures hidden away: a National Trust house, ornate church – full of angels – which owes much of its magnificence to the same masons who built Salisbury cathedral, an excellent local museum with Isaac Newton memorabilia (he was born here, so was Margaret Thatcher: her father's grocery is now a restaurant), and the 13th-century Angel Hotel which three mediaeval kings are known to have visited.

Readers' comments: Delightfully situated, very attractively furnished. Meals cooked to perfection.

When writing to me, if you want a reply please enclose an International Reply Coupon.

COACH HOUSE   C D M S

Crookham, Northumberland, TD12 4TD   Tel: 0890 820293 (Messages: 089082 373)

South-west of Berwick-upon-Tweed. On A697 from Wooler to Coldstream.

9 Bedrooms. £19–£29. Some have own bath/shower/toilet. Tea/coffee facilities. Views of garden, country. Washing machine on request.
Dinner. £14.50 for 4 courses (with choices) and coffee, at 7.30pm. Non-residents not admitted. Vegetarian or special diets if ordered. Wine can be ordered. No smoking.
2 Sitting-rooms. With open fire, central heating, TV, record-player.
Large garden
Closed from December to February.

This is almost on the border of Scotland, and very close to the site of Flodden Field, where in 1513 Henry VIII's armies slaughtered the King of Scotland and 10,000 of his followers: the very last mediaeval battle with knights wearing armour, and swords or arrows the principal weapons. Each August there is a tremendously emotive spectacle commemorating it.

The Coach House is a group of several old farm buildings forming a square around a courtyard which traps the sun. What was the coach house itself is now a highly individual sitting-room, with lofty beamed ceiling and great arched windows where there used to be doors for the carriages. One looks onto an orchard. Colours are light and cheerful, and there is a log fire in an enormous brick fireplace.

An old dower house has panelled doors of stripped pine, pointed 'gothick' windows, rare chestnut beams, an old Victorian kitchen-range, two immensely high attic bedrooms and a dining-room (one of two).

In the main part, some of the ground-floor bedrooms look onto paddocks where goats graze. All are light and airy, with interesting paintings and a file of leaflets on the many local places worth visiting. They have fridges which guests find useful for a variety of purposes (baby's feeds, dog's meat, insulin or soft drinks) and toasters; there are reduced prices for people who make their own breakfast.

The owner, Lynne Anderson, used to travel a great deal when she was a singer and so has a lot of practical ideas about what travellers need – disabled travellers in particular. She had doorways made wide, and steps eliminated.

Porridge is properly made from pinhead oatmeal, and breakfast includes bacon from an Edinburgh smokery, beef sausages from a local butcher, and free-range eggs. Dinner has a choice of six starters; a roast or casserole; puddings like lemon meringue pie or one of 15 home-made ice creams; cheese and coffee. Organic produce is used increasingly. (There is also a small gift shop where you can buy food products prepared in the Coach House kitchens, as well as local specialities.)

Readers' comments: Very friendly and welcoming, exceptionally well organized; most impressed. Warm and friendly owner; professional efficiency. A great success! Wonderful. So much room, the very best breakfast, and Lynne is exceptionally good at making guests at ease with one another.

COACH HOUSE   C(16) S
Whorlton, County Durham, DL12 8XQ Tel: 0833 627237
East of Barnard Castle. Nearest main road: A67 from Darlington to
Barnard Castle.

2 Bedrooms. £17.50. Tea/coffee facilities.
TV. Views of garden, country. No smoking.
Washing machine on request.
Dinner. £12 for 4 courses and coffee,
at 7.30pm. Non-residents not admitted.
Vegetarian or special diets if ordered.
Wine can be brought in. **Light suppers** if
ordered.
2 Sitting-rooms. With open fire, central
heating, TV, record-player.
Small garden
Closed in February.

Off a big village green and near a pretty Victorian church, the drive to the Coach
House runs past the mansion which it once served. The painted-brick house, with
its recently added conservatory, has on one side a neat garden with heathers and
conifers; on the other there is a steep drop to a rushing stream, which one of the
bedrooms overlooks.

Helen Calder's big collection of cookery books bears witness to her
enthusiasm for cooking; a typical meal might comprise river trout, then stuffed
lamb cutlets and a fruity pudding (bread is home-baked). Sometimes dinner is
served in the new conservatory; otherwise guests dine at the big Hepplewhite-style
table where they take breakfast. In season, game and fish are likely to appear on
the menu, for her husband is a keen shot and angler.

Upstairs, as well as the bedrooms, is a small sitting-room for guests, with
television and books. There are many antiques and prints about the house.

Cosy as it is, the village is close to what David Bellamy has called, with a little
exaggeration, England's last wilderness. It is not far before the Teesdale road
starts to climb up the side of the Pennines through deserted hills until even the
scattered farmhouses are left behind, and only sheep and birds inhabit the slopes.

Readers' comments: Incredible kindness, superb food; superbly appointed home.
Excellent in every way. . . the welcome and attention.

Piercebridge is a carefully conserved
village quite close to the busy A1 near
Darlington. **HOLME HOUSE** is just
outside it, over the North Yorkshire
border by a matter of yards. Down a
metalled farm road, it is a spacious
Georgian house furnished with
antiques and with many sporting prints
and watercolours around. Guests
breakfast at a long stripped-pine farmhouse table (most dine at the George
in the village). Anne Graham's family
are animal-lovers (hamsters to horses),
and there is a variety of livestock at the

adjoining farm, which is managed by
her husband. The two bedrooms have
splendid views of open countryside,
and there are interesting Roman
remains nearby. £14–£15. [Tel: 0325
374280; postcode: DL2 3SY]

COASTGUARDS

St Agnes, Isles of Scilly, TR22 0PL   Tel: 0720 22373

CDS

3 **Bedrooms.** £13.50–£15.50 (less for continental breakfast). Prices go up in April. One has own bathroom. All have tea/coffee facilities. Views of sea. Laundry done (within reason) for week-long visitors. No smoking.
Dinner. £8.50 for 4 courses and coffee, at 7pm. Non-residents not admitted. Vegetarian or special diets if ordered. Wine can be brought in. No smoking. **Light suppers.**
1 **Sitting-room.** With open fire. No smoking.
Garden
Closed in December.

There are very few coastguards living in the many coastguard cottages still left around the shores of England: electronic surveillance has taken over from the man with the spyglass. Needless to say, such cottages were always well sited for sea views, on coasts where high seas and jagged rocks make spectacular scenery but are hazards for ships, and where coves and inlets were an attraction to smugglers.

One such group of cottages stands on a high point of St Agnes, a little island so unspoilt that there are no cars and no hotel – only a small shop with a good selection of drinks and books. It is a paradise for those who want nothing more than sunshine early or late in the year, wildflowers, walks, birdwatching and peace.

Wendy and Danny Hick provide accommodation for guests in two adjacent cottages. They have furnished the rooms simply but attractively, with interesting objects around. The sitting-room has a William Morris suite and views out to the sea, polished board floors, many books on the shelves and an open fire for chilly evenings. The pieces of iron-studded furniture are from Curaçao, where Danny's father was a mining engineer. The collection of old bottles (from inkwells to flasks that contained sheep-cures) are mostly local finds. Danny makes ship models sold in London's West End galleries and abroad.

The food is all of a very good, homely style: bread is home-baked, soups home-made, clotted cream is from a friendly neighbourhood cow, fish (of course) straight out of the sea, and new potatoes from the fields around.

Visitors reach St Agnes via St Mary's, from which boats take them in 15 minutes to the little quay at St Agnes. (Wendy will supply all the times etc. for getting to Scilly by rail and boat or helicopter.) Luggage is conveyed for them up the steep track that leads to the few cottages; past the Turk's Head inn (for a really succulent Cornish pasty, pause here!) and past Rose Cottage and Covean which serve Cornish cream teas and light lunches. Whatever track you follow, there is a superlative view at every turn. This is a great place for birdwatchers, particularly in autumn when rare migrants arrive. But even at other times it is a pleasure to watch the red-legged oystercatchers, for instance, scuttling like busy mice among the rock-pools on the shore.

Readers' comments: Excellent in every respect. Good food, lovely scenery, such nice people. Warmly welcomed, well looked after, delicious food, excellent value; beautiful and peaceful place. Superb food and hospitality.

COCKETT'S HOTEL   D X
Market Place, Hawes, North Yorkshire, DL8 3RD   Tel: 0969 667312
Nearest main road: A684 from Sedbergh to Leyburn.

8 Bedrooms. £20–£30 (less for 7 nights). Prices go up from Easter. Bargain breaks. Some have own bath/shower/toilet. Tea/coffee facilities. TV. Views of garden, country. No smoking.
Dinner. A la carte or £14 for 3 courses (with choices) and coffee, at 7pm. Vegetarian or special diets if ordered. Wine can be ordered. No smoking.
1 Sitting-room. With central heating. **Bar.** Small garden
Closed from mid-November to end of December.

'God being with us Who can be against' is carved deep into the stone lintel of a door, together with the date 1668. It was the main entrance to a hostel once used by Quakers travelling to distant meeting-houses.

Things are different now. One steps from the paved forecourt into a snug little bar with comfortable chairs and an ornate French cast-iron stove. There is another quiet sitting-room elsewhere, and a small writing-room.

In the dining-room, on lace-covered tables are served imaginative dinners (and lunches sometimes), cooked by a chef who has been with the hotel for several years. There are four choices at each course on the table d'hôte. They might include fennel and cucumber soup, or baked trout fillet with hazelnuts and dill; roast half-duck with jasmin and raisin sauce, or venison medallions; home-made coffee-and-walnut ice cream, or black cherry frangipane. The cheeseboard might have as many as eight different Yorkshire cheeses.

Every room has interesting furniture, too; one four-poster, with barley-sugar posts, is covered in a scarlet dragon fabric; another, of pine, has pale green chintz. One's eye is caught by interesting details everywhere: satinwood bedside cupboards, art nouveau fingerplates on the doors. For quiet, ask for a back room.

When genial Fred and Mary Bedford took over the hotel, they extended it into an adjoining cottage. Here are the two least expensive bedrooms, which would make an ideal suite for a family wanting to be self-contained. One bedroom, with its own door to the outside, is for dog-owners.

Hawes, its buildings clustered around a stream, is near the head of Wensleydale from which the spectacular Buttertubs Pass leads to Swaledale: the 'butter tubs' are curious holes in the rock. The dale's crags and waterfalls, castles and history museums, attract visitors from all over the world.

Readers' comments: Food excellent. Interesting food. Cuisine excellent. Excellent dinner. The epitome of the perfect inn-keepers! Every detail is given attention. Chef is outstanding. A very special place, we hope to return many times. A definite cut above the ordinary.

Prices are per person in a double room at the beginning of the year.

COOMBE FARMHOUSE
Widegates, Cornwall, PL13 1QN Tel: 05034 223
North-east of Looe. On B3253 from Looe to Widegates.

C(5) **D M S**

10 Bedrooms. £16.50–£18.50 (less for 2 nights if dinner is taken). Prices go up in June. All have own shower/toilet. Tea/coffee facilities. TV. Views of garden, country, sea. No smoking. Washing machine on request.
Dinner. £10.50 for 4 courses and coffee, usually about 7pm. Non-residents not admitted. Vegetarian or special diets if ordered. Wine can be ordered. No smoking.
Light suppers if ordered.
1 Sitting-room. With open fire, central heating, TV, video films. Bar. No smoking.
Large garden
Closed from November to February.

At this spacious and comfortable guest-house, built on a marvellous site with a distant sea view, Alex and Sally Low provide many extras such as a swimming-pool, croquet and a stone-walled games room for snooker and table tennis. Antiques, paintings and interesting objects fill the house.

From a glassed-in verandah are views of terraced lawns where peacocks roam, and of a pond (one of several) frequented by ducks and coots. Elsewhere, geese and ponies graze, there are rhododendron woods and camellias grow wild. My bedroom opened onto this garden; others upstairs have armchairs or sofa from which to enjoy the view. Visitors can picnic in the garden.

A typical dinner may comprise something like home-made soup, roast duck and a fruit sponge with Cornish clotted cream. Visitors help themselves to drinks, writing down in a book what they have had.

Readers' comments: Excellent! Friendliness and warmth. A wonderful experience. Place superb, hospitality gracious. A haven of peace. Excellent food.

The **OLD RECTORY**, high up in Duloe Road, St Keyne, is an early 19th-century building with very handsome architectural features, and fine furniture in keeping with this.

In the sitting-room (with glass doors to the garden) are capacious velvet sofas and, through an arch, a turquoise and cherry bar. Two bedrooms have lacy, modern four-posters; one bedroom is on the ground floor.

Ron and Kate Wolfe offer such dishes as Stilton and celery soup, lamb's kidneys in red wine, and orange brandy crêpes. B & b: £20 (one room, **to readers of this book only**) –£30.
Readers' comments: Excellent cooking with quality ingredients; warm and

welcoming. Charming atmosphere of true repose and Victorian elegance. Food exceptional. Very good; nice people. Very well furnished; food beautifully cooked. Quite exceptional. [Tel: 0579 342617; postcode: PL14 4RL]

CORFIELD HOUSE   C M S

Sporle, Norfolk, PE32 2EA   Tel: 0760 723636
North-east of Swaffham. Nearest main road: A47 from King's Lynn to
Norwich.

5 Bedrooms. £18.50–£19.50 (less for 6
nights half-board). All have own
bath/shower/toilet. Tea/coffee facilities. TV.
Views of garden, country. No smoking.
Dinner. £11.50 for 4 courses and coffee, at
7.30pm. Vegetarian or special diets if
ordered. Wine can be ordered. No smoking.
Light suppers if ordered.
1 Sitting-room. With open fire, central
heating. No smoking.
Small garden
Closed from January to March.

Turning their backs on the London rat-race, and arming themselves with Delia
Smith's cookery books plus a lot of determination, Linda and Martin Hickey
moved here with their little daughter to build a new life running their own guest-
house. Much hard work went into adapting the early Victorian farmhouse and
creating a particularly pretty garden, its path to the front door bordered with roses
and lavender and its apple-trees a froth of pink in spring.

Inside, Linda has used delicately patterned wallpapers, much pine and rattan
furniture, soft blues and pinks. There is a ground-floor room with bathroom that
would particularly suit any disabled person.

A typical dinner might comprise crab and avocado salad, beef bourguignonne,
raspberry clafouti (a type of pancake) and some unusual cheeses from Swaffham's
Saturday market – all served on rose-patterned Doulton china.

Martin runs the Swaffham Tourist Information Centre and both he and Linda
are mines of information about the area. Nearby Swaffham has a huge market
square, many 18th-century buildings and a good local history museum.

Readers' comments: Strongly recommended. Excellent value. Superb breakfast.
First-class. Outstanding dinners. Most efficient but with the personal touch.

Southward lies Thompson where
priests used to live in **COLLEGE
FARMHOUSE** until Henry VIII dis-
banded them. Later owners added oak
panelling, a coat-of-arms and other
features. There are Gothic windows;
walls (some three feet thick) have odd
curves. Lavender Garnier has collected
interesting furniture, family portraits
(it was an ancestor who, when taking
part in the Oxford and Cambridge
boat race, selected dark blue as
Oxford's now famous colour), and
attractive fabrics for bedrooms that
have armchairs and TV (no sitting-
room). A lovely garden slopes down to
eel-ponds, with flint walls a perfect

background to roses. Inn food one
mile away. £16–£17.
Readers' comments: Warm hospitality.
Magical peace in a beautiful house.
Very comfortable, warm and friendly.
Breakfasts were a joy. [Tel: 0953
483318; postcode: IP24 1QG]

THE COTTAGE   C
Westbrook, Bromham, Wiltshire, SN15 2EE   Tel: 0380 850255
South of Chippenham. On A3102 from Calne to Melksham.

3 Bedrooms. £19–£20 (less for 7 nights).
All have own shower/toilet. Tea/coffee
facilities. TV. Views of garden, country.
Breakfast/sitting-room. With central
heating.
Large garden

Converted stables, weatherboarded and pantiled, provide the accommodation
here, in a quiet hamlet once the home of Thomas Moore, the Irish poet. The
adjoining mediaeval cottage was originally a coaching inn.

Inside, the roof beams are still visible. The bedrooms (on ground floor) have
been furnished in keeping with the style of the building and Gloria Steed has
added such decorative touches as patchwork cushions and pincushions which she
made herself. Through the bedroom windows one can sometimes see deer and
rabbits, with a distant landscape created by Capability Brown in the 18th century.

At breakfast (in a room with rough white walls, small William Morris armchairs and beautifully arranged flowers) there will be local produce, home-made
muesli and compotes of fruit. For other meals, Gloria can show you menus from
inns and restaurants within a few miles (I ate very well at the Lysley Arms).
Occasionally she invites guests to a barbecue or to enjoy 9-hole putting.

This is very lovely walking country, and with lots of sightseeing possibilities
too (Lacock, Avebury and Bath are all within a few miles; and Bowood House is
close – an Adam building in superb grounds, with lake and cascade).
Chippenham and Devizes are historic market towns, with fine churches and other
buildings of golden stone. Castle Combe is a much-photographed village in a
dramatic setting.

Readers' comments: Full of charm and character. We couldn't have asked for more.

Very different is homely **SEEND-
BRIDGE FARMHOUSE** at nearby
Seend: a place for anyone who values
good food above all else. Judy Podger
is a dedicated cook, self-taught but to a
highly professional standard which has
won accolades. She runs the whole
ground floor as a restaurant (and has
another one in Devizes, called
Wharfside) and therefore provides the
large bedrooms with their own sofas
and armchairs. When you book
accommodation, you are given a
lengthy menu from which to select
your dinner. (Example: mushrooms in
smoked ham, duck breast in bramble
sauce, baked Alaska. Bring your own
wine.) This system, by avoiding waste,
keeps the price well down – and
enables Judy to buy ingredients fresh
every morning. Bedrooms have recently been refurbished: I liked the big,
rosy family room in which a wall
divides the double bed from two singles. £14–£15. [Tel: 0380 828534;
postcode: SN12 6RY]

COVE HOUSE (No. 2) **C D**

Ashton Keynes, Wiltshire, SN6 6NS Tel: 0285 861221

North-west of Swindon. Nearest main road: A419 from Swindon to Cirencester (and M4, junctions 15/16).

3 Bedrooms. £19–£25 (less for 2 nights). Discounts for repeat bookings. Two have own bath or shower and toilet. Tea/coffee facilities. TV (in one). Views of garden.
Dinner. £16.50 for 3 courses and coffee, at 7.30pm (not Sundays). Non-residents not admitted. Vegetarian or special diets if ordered. Wine can be brought in. **Light suppers** if ordered.
2 Sitting-rooms. With open fire, central heating, TV.
Large garden

The narrow trickle running through this little village is in fact the infant Thames; you can walk right to its source from here. All around is a chain of large pools (originally gravel-diggings) now known as the Cotswold Water Park, which more or less encloses Ashton Keynes as if it were an island: birdwatchers come here to view the waterfowl.

Here Peter and Elizabeth Hartland live in one half of a 17th-century manor house (with later alterations) surrounded by a particularly lovely and secluded garden which has a succession of lawns and a paved carriage yard with barbecue beside its lily-pool. One of its previous owners was Puritan John Richmond, who had a part in founding Taunton, Massachusetts.

Indoors is a large, friendly sitting-room; a dining-room that has antiques and huge heirloom paintings; and Elizabeth's lovely flower arrangements everywhere. In the small library is an alcove lined with a large-scale, illuminated map of the area. Here Peter keeps a collection of packs for visitors, each full of carefully compiled information about various day outings and his own 'good food guide' to local eating-places. Yet another sitting-room, upstairs, is for TV and viewing a video of local sights.

Bedrooms have individuality – one green-and-white sprigged; another very flowery; a third (turquoise, with brass bedheads) has an unusual domed ceiling. Flowers are usually present.

Elizabeth uses garden produce for meals, at which the Hartlands dine with their guests. You might start with gazpacho or home-made pâté, perhaps; to be followed by a roast or salmon mayonnaise and then perhaps fruit sorbet or rhubarb-and-orange pudding.

Ashton Keynes is on the edge of the Cotswolds. Among other sightseeing possibilities the following are within an easy drive: Cheltenham, Oxford, Burford, Avebury, Bath, Stratford-upon-Avon, Marlborough, Blenheim, Cirencester, Malmesbury, Bibury village – also the gardens of Hidcote, Barnsley House and Kiftsgate. Ashton Keynes has an outstanding farm shop (meat etc.), with fruit and trout farms nearby. Antique shops are numerous.

Readers' comments: Stayed several times. Excellent in all respects. Beautiful house, relaxed and friendly hosts. They could not have been kinder or more welcoming. The best breakfast I've ever had. Superb.

COWLEIGH PARK FARMHOUSE
C(5) **D PT**

Cowleigh Road, Great Malvern, Worcestershire, WR13 5HJ

Tel: 0684 566750

Nearest main road: A449 from Worcester to Ross-on-Wye (and the junction of the M5 with M50).

3 **Bedrooms.** £19.50 (less for 3 nights). Bargain breaks. All have own bath/shower/toilet. TV. Tea/coffee facilities. Views of garden, country. No smoking. Washing machine on request.

Dinner. £13 for 3 courses and coffee, at 7pm (Monday–Friday only). Non-residents not admitted. Vegetarian or special diets if ordered. Wine can be ordered or brought in. No smoking. **Light suppers** if ordered.

2 **Sitting-rooms.** With open fire, central heating, piano, record-player.

Large garden

The half-timbered house is 350 years old, and some of its beams even older (taken from a 13th-century moated manor house which once stood in the field behind it). Approaching it from the high Malvern Hills, one passes along lanes of larches and crags, shadows alternating with sunshine, the distant landscape vanishing into a soft haze. On driving up to the door, there is a tranquil scene – snowy alyssum spreading over old stone walls, an ancient cider-press on the brick terrace. (The Worcestershire Way starts here.)

Beyond the slate-flagged hall, Sue Stringer has furnished the low-beamed rooms attractively – comfortable antique chairs are placed around a large inglenook in the main dining/sitting-room, in one corner of which stands a grand piano. Meals are taken at a yew refectory table with 18th-century rush-seated chairs, near the window so that guests can enjoy the view of the garden. Bedrooms have deep-pile carpets, stripped pine, board-and-latch doors, and soft colours. One has a particularly pretty view, of lily-pool and rock-garden.

Sue's dinners are imaginative – starting with, for instance, Stilton-and-apple soup or salade niçoise; possibly with goulash to follow and blackcurrant gâteau.

The house has its own piped Malvern water.

Readers' comments: Warm, hospitable and friendly. Wished we could have stayed longer. Very relaxing and comfortable home. Pretty rooms. Charming home. Made very welcome. Food excellent and plentiful.

Sitting-room at Upton House (see page 347)

CRAB AND LOBSTER INN   C PT S
Foreland, Isle of Wight, PO35 5TR Tel: 098387 2244
East of Bembridge. Nearest main road: A3055 from Ryde to Shanklin.

5 Bedrooms. £15–£16 (minimum booking, 2 nights). Less for 7 nights. Tea/coffee facilities. Some have sea views.
Dinner. A la carte, from 7pm. Vegetarian or special diets if ordered. Wine can be ordered. **Light suppers.**
1 Sitting-room. With central heating, TV.
Bars.
Closed in January and February.

This old inn perched on a clifftop provides simple accommodation and spectacular views over the Channel. David Hill will tell you the inn was not named after the plentiful local shellfish but a New Zealand shrub (Puniceus) which has flowers that look like crab or lobster claws and which grows by its walls. Before he took over the inn he used to have the job of advising hotels on their wine, so naturally his are good value. Good straightforward food – big lobsters straight from the sea.

The inn started in 1810 as tea-rooms, but one day the clifftop garden fell into the sea. The dining-room, with big windows, is very attractively decorated (as is the adjoining bar); its walls are white-painted boards, and there are pot-plants everywhere. In the main bar are casks of sherry, peach and apricot wine, mead and scrumpy alongside more conventional drinks. There is a second bar with darts etc.

Outside are the watchtower of the coastguards who keep a careful eye on the reef below, footpaths along the clifftop or down to the sands, and, out in the sea, the enormous old Nab Tower that was built in Southampton and towed to its site in the days when French invasion was feared, later to be used for suspending anti-submarine nets across the approaches to the Solent. David and the coastguards who frequent the bar are full of anecdotes about such local oddities, and about some of his past visitors ('we get prince and pauper here'), who have included the French Ambassador on one occasion, and Edward Heath with the crew of *Morning Cloud* on others. The inn is very busy in high summer.

Bembridge itself is an interesting little place with a lifeboat house open to the public, sailing harbour and a particularly good maritime museum. Coast and rolling countryside are equally lovely here. Although it is at the east end of the island where most of the resorts are, it is not difficult to get to the wilder west end. There is a lot to visit here; many stately homes, fossils around Sandown (visit the geology museum to identify your finds), a first-rate wildlife park, botanical gardens with an intriguing museum of smuggling, Queen Victoria's house outside the sailing centre of Cowes, beautiful Blackgang Chine with one lovely garden after another, a centre with dozens of craftsmen at work, Carisbrooke Castle.

Readers' comments: Food excellent; service most attentive.

CRACROP FARM
Kirkcambeck, Cumbria, CA8 2BW Tel: 06978 245
North of Brampton. Nearest main road: A6071 from Brampton to Longtown.

Tea/coffee facilities. TV. Views of garden, country. No smoking.
Dinner. £12 for 3 courses and coffee, at 6.30pm. Vegetarian or special diets if ordered. Wine can be brought in. No smoking. **Light suppers** if ordered.
1 Sitting-room. With central heating, TV, record-player. No smoking.
Large garden

3 Bedrooms. £18 (less for continental breakfast). All have own shower/toilet.

Agriculture and forestry still predominate in the Border hills, truly unspoiled countryside. The rolling western marches are less bleak than those to the north-east, being well watered by streams and small rivers, and having plenty of woodland, rich in wildlife.

Typically for the area, Cracrop is principally a stock farm, where the friendly Stobarts are pleased if visitors take an interest in the work. Semi-finalists in a local conservation competition, they have produced an excellent farm trail leaflet which gives an insight into the holding and its interesting past, and also leaflets for walks of a few miles from the house. Sturdier walkers have plenty of routes to follow, too.

If walking is not exertion enough, in the Victorian house are an exercise bike and a rowing-machine (and a snooker table), and to recuperate in, a sauna (for an extra charge) and a spa bath.

Bedrooms are sizeable, two giving views of the northern Pennines and the Lake District hills, the other of the farmyard. Walls are pleasantly plain-coloured, and the downstairs rooms are comfortably furnished in conventional style.

Typical of one of Marjorie Stobart's dinners is a choice of salmon mousse, leek soup, or fruit juice; a roast, chops or trout; and fruit crumble, lemon meringue pie or a gâteau.

Though so out of the way, Cracrop is a good centre for outings long or short: to see the notable Saxon cross at Bewcastle a few miles away; Hadrian's Wall, Lanercost Priory and Naworth Castle; or Kielder Water and the Border Forest Park (see other pages) which are a little further. There are the Lake District, Carlisle for its castle and museum (newly rearranged by the firm which designed Jorvik at York), and the castles and mansions of Northumberland.

Readers' comments: Superior accommodation, meals outstanding.

At **BANK END FARMHOUSE,** Roadhead, there is a suite of twin bedroom, well-equipped sitting-room upstairs (with good views) and bathroom. A typical meal by Dorothy Downer might be trout mousse, chicken in leek-and-onion sauce, vegetables from the garden or the locality, and Normandy apple tart (available also to those in the self-catering cottage). This 18th-century farmhouse, on a quiet and tree-lined lane, has a pleasant

rear view

garden with bird- and bat-boxes. It drops down to the little River Lyne, where one can fish for brown trout. No smoking. £18–£20. [Tel: 06977 48644; postcode: CA6 6NU]

CRANDON HOUSE
Avon Dassett, Warwickshire, CV33 0AA   Tel: 0295 770652
South-east of Leamington Spa. Nearest main road: A423 from Banbury to
Coventry (and M40, junctions 11/12).

3 Bedrooms. £17–£19 (less for 6 nights).
All have own bath/shower/toilet. Tea/coffee
facilities. TV. Views of garden, country. No
smoking. Washing machine on request.
Dinner (by arrangement). From £11.50 for
3 courses (with some choices) and coffee, at
7pm. Vegetarian or special diets if ordered.
Wine can be brought in. No smoking. **Light
suppers** if ordered.
2 Sitting-rooms. With wood stove, central
heating, TV.
Large garden

A 'hostess of the year' award was once won by Deborah Lea – the most unassuming of people – who with her brother runs this guest-house on a smallholding where a few rare British white cattle, sheep and poultry roam free. One can sit in the glass sun-room to watch the geese and ducks enjoying life, with a view of hills beyond. There is a separate television room with log stove, and a terrace outside; in another direction, the small disused quarry (now overgrown) from which Crandon stone was hewn is a picturesque feature. Everything about the house, built in the 1950s, is solidly comfortable. The pink or blue bedrooms (with en suite bathrooms) have nice pieces of furniture (a walnut suite, for instance, and a shellback brocade chair) and large windows.

Deborah uses much home produce in the 'old-fashioned food' which her guests love. A typical menu: garlic mushrooms, roast lamb and chocolate mousse – quality and presentation are outstanding. Breakfast options include kippers and smoked haddock.

Readers' comments: We felt extremely welcome, no detail was overlooked.

The beautiful village of Warmington, near Banbury and the M40, is so tucked away that few tourists find it. Around a sloping green with duck-pond are ranged rows of cottages built from local stone, and **POND COTTAGE** is one of these. Vi Viljoen has furnished its rooms with great elegance – gleaming antique furniture and silver contrast with the rugged stones of the sitting-room walls. One pretty bedroom is all blue – from the silk bedspread to the flowery Victorian wallpaper. Vi serves such meals as home-made soup, chicken with almond sauce, a tart of her own fruit or home-made ice cream. £16.50 (b & b).

Readers' comments: Delicious food, extremely good value. Like staying with a friend, every need anticipated. [Tel: 029589 682; *changing to:* 0295690 682 in spring 1994; post-code: OX17 1BU]

CRASKEN
C(14) D S

Falmouth Road, Helston, Cornwall, TR13 0PF   Tel: 0326 572670

Nearest main road: A394 from Helston to Falmouth.

6 Bedrooms. £15.50–£25 (less for 5 nights or continental breakfast; **5% less to readers of this book staying 4 or more days**). Some have own bath/shower/toilet. Views of garden, country. No smoking. Washing machine on request.
Dinner. £12.50 for 3 courses and coffee, at 7–9pm. Non-residents not admitted. Vegetarian or special diets if ordered. Wine can be brought in. **Light suppers** if ordered.
1 Sitting-room. With open fire, central heating, TV.
Large garden

Down a very long drive is a rare survival – a 17th-century farmhouse built court-yard-style, rather French, with its granary and old carpentry-shop adjoining it (some of these outbuildings have been converted for visitors to use on either a b & b or a self-catering basis). The ancient midden (for dung), a 'listed' structure, is now a pretty, low-walled garden. And in the grounds a prehistoric site has been discovered – the name 'Crasken' is Celtic for 'settlement'. The granite walls of the house are two feet thick, a handsome background to tubs of flowers outside and arrangements of dried flowers within. The rooms are full of 'unconsidered trifles', from rag dolls to an array of willow-pattern plates, nosegays of wildflowers to log-cabin patchwork, Victorian crochet and jugs, rag rugs, pots of begonias.

Jenny Ingram is a very good cook, of such meals (if ordered in advance) as crab and broccoli au gratin, chicken in lemon sauce and meringues with gooseberry cream – the eating of which can be accompanied by a continuing soap-opera just outside the window, the never-ending domestic strife of a family of white ducks and one black intruder. Elsewhere you will find goats and donkeys as well as, in spring, a wonderful variety of wildflowers. In addition to some unusual plants, such as crinodendron and Himalayan honeysuckle, the garden has a grapevine.

Readers' comments: Best I have visited. Peaceful, picturesque and very welcoming. Uniquely decorated, secluded and peaceful. Most friendly, kind and thoughtful.

Near the centre of the lovely Lizard peninsula is **ROSEVEAR BRIDGE COTTAGE**, west of Mawgan, on a little tributary of the River Helford. A white house with neat brown shutters, it began life as a cowman's cottage centuries ago. Everything, including the sloping garden, is trim, the windows are low and deep-set, and an open-tread staircase rises through the sitting-room to immaculate bedrooms, varying in size. Hazel Howard uses garden produce for such homely meals

as chicken pie and trifle. £13–£13.50 (b & b).
Reader's comment: Absolutely loved it. [Tel: 0326 221672; postcode: TR12 6AZ]

THE CRAVEN C M S X
Fernham Road, Uffington, Oxfordshire, SN7 7RD   Tel: 0367 820449
South-west of Oxford. Nearest main road: A420 from Oxford to Swindon (and M4, junction 14).

7 Bedrooms. £17.50–£27 (less for 7 nights). Some have own bath/shower/toilet.

Tea/coffee facilities. Views of garden, country, river. No smoking. Washing machine on request.
Dinner. £12.50 for 3 courses (with choices) and coffee, at 7pm. Non-residents not admitted. Vegetarian or special diets if ordered. Wine can be ordered or brought in. No smoking. **Light suppers** if ordered.
2 Sitting-rooms. With open fire, central heating, TV, video, record-player. No smoking preferred. Piano.
Large garden

Three hundred years ago, this cream-walled and thatched house was a hostelry – some rooms are in what were once brewhouse and stables – which is described in *Tom Brown's Schooldays* as 'a low-lying wayside inn' (its author, Thomas Hughes, lived in the village). It was named after the local landowner, Lord Craven, who fell in love with the widowed Queen of Bohemia and brought her here.

One of the best bedrooms is on the ground floor – its four-poster hung with cabbage-rose chintz, its pillows in embroidered Victorian pillowslips; in the pretty bathroom is an antique weighing-machine. Upstairs, where passages and steps turn this way and that, are other beamed rooms, equally attractive – for example, a white iron half-tester bed is draped with white voile and covered with a white lace spread, in a room with blue sprigged wallpaper. The single rooms are as attractive as the double ones, and the bathrooms too – one, stone-walled, is all yellow.

The beamed sitting-room, with a log fire in its inglenook, has among other antiques a particularly splendid grandfather clock made in Lincolnshire.

Carol Wadsworth serves dinners at a big pine table in her huge L-shaped kitchen with scarlet walls and a dresser of blue-and-white china – or occasionally in the brick-paved courtyard among tubs of plants. A typical dinner: watercress soup, chicken in cheese sauce and chocolate rum gâteau.

Centuries ago, all was swamp hereabouts, dotted with islands – on each a village. That's how the tiny hamlet of Lyford began (its name means 'flax island') with **LYFORD MANOR** (1480) at its heart, on the green. The Manor belongs to St John's College, Oxford, and has been tenanted for 300 years by the same family, the Pikes. Some spacious, lattice-paned and beamed rooms are in the house, more modern ones (ground-floor) in former stables. Mary Pike does snack suppers only, served in a hexagonal conservatory. Outside the handsome house are a lawn and walled

herbaceous beds, stone dovecote, old iron pump and the cows which visitors enjoy seeing milked. £18.
Readers' comments: Wonderfully quiet and pretty. Extremely friendly and helpful. [Tel: 0235 868204; postcode: OX12 0EG]

CRIB FARM   C(7)

Long Causeway, Luddenden Foot, West Yorkshire, HX2 6JJ
Tel: 0422 883285 (Messages: 0422 886230)
West of Halifax. Nearest main road: A58 from Rochdale to Halifax
(and M62, junction 24).

4 Bedrooms. £12.50–£15 (less for 3
nights). Some have own bath/shower/toilet.
Views of garden, country. No smoking.
Dinner (not in winter). £7.50 for 3 courses
(with some choices) and coffee, at 6.30pm.
Vegetarian or special diets if ordered. Wine
can be ordered or brought in.
1 Sitting-room. With open fire, central
heating, TV, piano. Bar.
Large garden
Closed in November and December.

A necessary break to change horses on the long cross-Pennine journey from
Lancashire to Yorkshire brought this 17th-century moorland house into being, for
originally it was a coaching inn. Centuries later it became – and still is – a dairy-
farm, though its role as a haven for travellers continues too, even though they now
arrive by car, by train (to Halifax) or even by air (to Leeds). The Hitchen family
have been here since 1815 and a framed auction notice on the wall proves it.

The old house has a warm and hospitable atmosphere, with rooms decorated in
light and cheerful colours. Comfortable and unpretentious, it was first recommended to me by friends who also praised Pauline's cooking. A typical menu:
melon or home-made asparagus soup, home-reared turkey with garden vegetables,
a choice of puddings from strawberries and cream to apple pie, or cheeses.

Luddenden Foot, which lies below the farm, once had a railway station, where
Branwell Brontë worked as a clerk, and the village will be familiar also to viewers
of Thora Hird's 'In Loving Memory'. From the farm there are sweeping views to
the wild uplands of Midgley Moor, but down below Branwell found his station
dank and depressing – 'hacked out of a great black rock-face', as Lynne Reid
Banks describes it in *Dark Quartet*. He, the rich son of a local mill-owner, and Irish
labourers together drank themselves silly at local inns; and it was at Luddenden
that he first took drugs too, stealing money from the station till to pay for them.

Readers' comments: A welcoming farming family. Very comfortable and easy. A
very happy week.

Terraced houses used to be built one
on top of another to fit the steep slopes
of Hebden Bridge. A pair of these form
PROSPECT END (8 Prospect
Terrace, Savile Road), where the
guest-rooms are approached through
the garden, while the kitchen/break-
fast-room above them is at street level
and the sitting-room windows look
onto treetops. The two bedrooms,
predominantly pale pink, are neat
and well equipped. Ann Anthon can
provide dinners, but most guests go
to the many restaurants in the town,

which has become something of a
cultural centre for the south Pennines
and has some interesting shops. £15.
[Tel: 0422 843586; postcode: HX7
6NA]

CROFTBANK
32 Grovewood Close, Chorleywood, Hertfordshire, WD3 5PX
Tel: 0923 284989

West of Watford. Nearest main road: A404 from London to Amersham (also M25, junctions 17/18; and M1, junction 5).

rear view

2 Bedrooms. £17. Prices go up from Easter. Tea/coffee facilities. TV. Views of woodland. No smoking. Washing machine on request.
Light suppers if ordered.
1 Sitting-room. With central heating, TV, piano. No smoking.
Small garden
Closed from October to December.

'Dame Nature's fingers have lingered long in setting out this beautiful array of trout stream, wooded slope, meadow and hilltop sites,' wrote John Betjeman; and as you approach Chorleywood through undulating woods and wide greens, past old flint walls and leafy bridleways, it is hard to believe that west London is only half an hour away (and Heathrow little more). Londoners really do not need to feel they have to drive for hours when they want to take a short break off the beaten track.

Croftbank, a modern house, is the home of an accomplished oboist, Deirdre Dods, whose work as a music-examiner had taken her all over England – using this book to find accommodation – before she decided to start offering b & b herself, on the same friendly and welcoming lines as she had experienced in the homes of other proprietors.

After a light supper in her book-lined dining-room, guests can either retire to one of her pine-furnished bedrooms, each with easy-chairs and television, or take coffee in the big sitting-room which opens onto a lawn surrounded by tall larches. Comfort and peace are the keynotes of a stay here.

Hertfordshire may not seem an obvious choice for a holiday, but within a few miles of Croftbank there is a multitude of things to see and do (a number ideal for children). It is on the edge of the lovely Chiltern Hills, with innumerable good walks and pretty villages to discover – such as Sarratt, Chipperfield and the Chalfonts, each having an inn, ancient church, cricket green or duck-pond, as its focal point.

A few miles westward is **WHITE HOUSE** (North Road, Widmer End, Buckinghamshire) which actually comprises three 17th-century farmworkers' cottages, but visitors sleep in an adjoining self-contained suite. From the bedroom, with its view of grazing sheep, one descends via a staircase of exposed beams and brickwork to the breakfast-room in the old part of the cottage. No dinners (the Vaughans will provide light snacks if ordered in advance) but there are good inns nearby and plenty of restaurants in the old quarter of Amersham. £16.

Readers' comments: Very comfortable, warm and friendly. Every comfort thought of. Really nice, big bedroom. Friendly and good value. [Tel: 0494 712221; postcode: HP15 6ND]

83

CROSSWAYS FARM

C D PT S X

Raikes Lane, Abinger, Surrey, RH5 6PZ Tel: 0306 730173
South-west of Dorking. Nearest main road: A25 from Guildford to Dorking (and M25, junction 9).

3 Bedrooms. £14–£18 (less for 5 nights). Prices go up at Easter. Some have own bath/toilet. Tea/coffee facilities. Views of garden, country. No smoking. Washing machine on request.
Dinner. £10 for 2–3 courses and coffee, at 7pm. Non-residents not admitted. Vegetarian or special diets if ordered. Wine can be brought in. No smoking. **Light suppers** if ordered.
1 Sitting-room. With open fire, central heating, TV, piano, record-player.
Small garden

Meredith's *Diana of the Crossways* (one of those books most people have heard of and few have read) took its title from this historic building of unusual architectural interest, which featured in a film about the 17th-century diarist John Evelyn.

One steps through the arched door in a high wall to find a small, enclosed garden with a flagged path leading to the wide front door of the house. In its façade decorative brickwork combines with local sandstone, and Dutch-style arches curve over the small-paned windows. There is an immense chimney-stack towering above – 30 feet in circumference. But the most striking feature of all is the great oak staircase inside, its two flights leading up to large, beamed bedrooms, simply but comfortably furnished (there is a suite consisting of a double and a twin room with bathroom); the balusters and newels are handsomely carved.

The house has had many owners since it was built about 1620. For the last 30 years, the Hughes family have farmed here, producing beef and corn. By arrangement, Sheila Hughes serves homely farmhouse meals (like Irish stew, fish pie, roast chicken etc.), usually with garden vegetables; or you can eat well at, for instance, nearby Wootton Hatch. Breakfast options include, if ordered in advance, such extras as fishcakes or kidneys. There is a croquet lawn.

Readers' comments: Warm welcome. Comfortable.

A mile or so westward is one of Surrey's beauty-spots, picturesque Shere with old cottages around a stream. Here is **CHERRY TREES**, in Gomshall Lane, a traditional 'twenties brick and tile-hung house in a garden of winding flowerbeds and colourful shrubs (with seats in leafy nooks from which to enjoy hill views). One of the bedrooms is on the ground floor, in former stables overlooking the pretty garden. There is also a swimming-pool. Breakfast is served in a cream-walled room with oak dresser and leaded casements; for dinner,

Olwen Warren recommends the White Horse inn a few yards away. No sitting-room for guests. No smoking. £15–£18.50. [Tel: 048641 2288; postcode: GU5 9HE]

CROWDY MILL   C M

Bow Road, Harbertonford, Devon, TQ9 7HU   Tel: 0803 732340

South of Totnes. Nearest main road: A381 from Totnes to Kingsbridge.

7 Bedrooms. £17.50–£25. Bargain breaks. All have own bath/shower/toilet. Tea/coffee facilities. Views of garden, country, river. No smoking. Washing machine on request.
Dinner. £10.50–£13.50 for 3 courses (with choices) and coffee, at 7.15pm. Non-residents not admitted. Vegetarian or special diets if ordered. Wine can be ordered. No smoking. **Light suppers** if ordered.
2 Sitting-rooms. With stoves, central heating, TV, record-player. No smoking.
Large garden

You will not go home empty-handed for this is still a working watermill (600 years old) and its organic stoneground flour is on sale here (as well as in such prestigious shops as Fortnum & Mason). You can also buy Don and Ann Benton-Barnes' flavoursome home-baked bread, jams and unusual mueslis as well as honey from Crowdy's bees, and eggs from the free-ranging hens. You can see the mill in action, enjoy the very best of Devon cream teas in a former barn, and maybe have a bread-making lesson too. Or just enjoy the scenery of this sunny, sheltered valley frequented by kingfishers, buzzards and dippers.

Some bedrooms are in the mill cottage itself, where meals are usually served (and there is a sitting-room); two bedrooms are upstairs in the barn and another is in a separate cottage. My favourite is a ground-floor suite with stone-flagged floor and the water of the mill-leat rushing by right outside: a door opens onto a little paved garden with duck-pond beyond. But every room is attractive, with views of the River Harbourne, a trout stream, on its way to join the Dart and then the sea. All have modern pine or antique furniture, simple country-cottage fabrics and interesting pictures on the walls.

As well as particularly good breakfasts (beginning with orange juice freshly squeezed), Ann – an outstanding cook – offers visitors a wide choice of dishes at dinner. One orders in advance from a long list: for instance, there are 18 main-course options ranging from fish pie to rack of lamb, chicken in yogurt and garlic to fresh asparagus quiche. All individually cooked that day, nothing frozen, and served with a complimentary glass of wine.

Within a few miles are the historic market town of Totnes and its castle, Blackpool sands, Slapton nature reserve, picturesque Dartmouth (go to it by boat from Totnes), the resorts along Tor Bay and Dartmoor.

Bedroom at Sampsons Farm (see page 303)

CWM CRAIG FARM C S X
Bolston Road, Little Dewchurch, Herefordshire, HR2 6PS
Tel: 0432 840250
North-west of Ross-on-Wye. Nearest main road: A49 from Ross to Hereford
(and M50, junction 4).

3 **Bedrooms.** £14–£15 (less for 3 nights).
Tea/coffee facilities. Views of garden,
country.
Light suppers if ordered.
1 **Sitting-room.** With open fire, central
heating, TV, piano.
Large garden

The 18th-century farm near the River Wye would be a good choice for a family.
Children can watch very tame, hand-reared calves being fed, and use the games
room which has a snooker table and dartboard. A good family room (with
figured walnut suite and shapely bevelled mirrors) has books and games; also a
particularly good bath- and shower-room. There is a second dining-room (with
kitchen) reserved for those who want to bring in their own food; and a utility
room for clothes-washing. (Baby-sitting available.)

All rooms are high and light, kept in immaculate condition by Gladys
Lee, with far views through their large sash windows. Fine architectural details
including marble fireplaces, arches and panelled doors are complemented by pink
velvet wing chairs or others in William Morris covers.

In the attractive garden, an old stone cider-press is now planted with colourful
busy Lizzies.

Readers' comments: Beautiful and quiet house, tastefully furnished, comfortable
beds: quite wonderful. Lovely friendly people. Amazing attention to detail – three
kinds of marmalade, and even the shower is computerized! Quite entranced: I
defy anyone to better it.

Picturesque Hoarwithy, on the River
Wye, has not only an exceptional
Italianate church (you can recognize
the pulpit of Fiesole's cathedral, the
lamps of St Mark's at Venice and
carvings from Ravenna – all faithfully
copied in marble, porphyry and other
exotic materials) but a good guest-
house in an 18th-century building
called the **OLD MILL**. The mill-race
flows through the garden, clematis and
roses grow up the front of the cream-
painted house. Beyond a tiled and
stone-walled hall is a beamed sitting-
room with log fire and a dining-room
of scarlet-clothed tables (a typical

meal: melon-and-prawn cocktail,
chicken casserole, chocolate roulade).
Carol Probart has furnished the bedrooms in cottage style. £14–£15.
Readers' comments: Hospitable and
helpful. [Tel: 0432 840602; postcode:
HR2 6QH]

St Andrews Lane, Cranford, Northamptonshire, NN14 4AQ
Tel: 053678 273
East of Kettering. Nearest main road: A14 from Kettering towards Cambridge.

coffee facilities. TV. Views of garden, country. No smoking. Washing machine on request.
Dinner. £10 for 3 courses (with choices) and coffee, at 7pm. Non-residents not admitted. Vegetarian or special diets if ordered. Wine can be brought in. No smoking. **Light suppers** if ordered.
1 Sitting-room. With open fire, central heating, TV, record-player. No smoking.
Garden

3 Bedrooms. £18–£22 (less for 5 nights). Some have own bath/shower/toilet. Tea/

This is not in fact a dairy-farm but arable and sheep. Its name derives from the old dairy around which the manor house was built, in 1610. It is a fine building with mullioned lattice windows in limestone walls and a thatched roof. Its noble chimney-stacks, finials on the gables, dormer windows and dignified porch give it great character. In the grounds stands a circular stone dovecote (mediaeval) with unique rotating ladder inside, used for collecting the birds from the 400 pigeon-holes that line it.

Audrey and John Clarke have hung old family portraits in the sitting-room, and furnished the house with things like an oak dresser, chests and ladderback chairs that are in keeping with it. Some bedrooms, one with four-poster, overlook church and mansion nearby.

Meals consist of straightforward home cooking – soups, roasts, fruit pies – using fruit and vegetables from the garden. Mrs Clarke also does a cordon bleu menu, which costs a little more and has to be ordered ahead.

Visitors enjoy croquet, and walks (by a willow-fringed stream, across-country, or simply to the Woolpack Inn). This is good cycling country, too. Sightseeing possibilities include Burghley House, Rockingham Castle, the mediaeval stone town of Stamford, Althorp (home of the Princess of Wales's brother), Lamport and Kirby Halls, Peterborough cathedral, Cambridge, Uppingham and Oundle. And at Kettering, Wicksteed Park is an ideal place to take children. Oundle is as attractive as many old Cotswold towns, for the local stone is the same, but much less frequented by tourists. The buildings of its famous public school are like an Oxford college. One can take boat trips on the River Nene, and visit watermills and a country park just on the outskirts, or the gardens at Coton Manor. For the equestrian-minded, there are the Burghley horse trials in September.

The farm is close to the borders of both Cambridgeshire and Bedfordshire which means that it is also easy to visit such places of interest as Elton Hall, Hinchingbrooke House (a much altered Norman nunnery) and 18th-century Island Hall; or Bromham watermill on the banks of the Ouse, Stevington wind-mill, Stagsden bird gardens and all the Bunyan sights in and around Bedford (which has the exceptional Cecil Higgins art gallery too). Grafham Water is a big, naturalized reservoir. Huntingdon has a Cromwell museum.

Readers' comments: Very special, will return. Delicious food; peaceful; attentive hosts. Very kind, food plentiful, peaceful. Delightful house and setting.

DAMSELLS LODGE   C D M PT
The Park, Painswick, Gloucestershire, GL6 6SR   Tel: 0452 813777
North of Stroud. Nearest main road: A46 from Stroud to Cheltenham
(and M5, junction 13).

3 **Bedrooms.** £18–£19.50 (less for 3 nights). One has own shower/toilet. Tea/coffee facilities. TV. Views of garden, country. Washing machine on request. **Light suppers**
1 **Sitting-room.** With log stove, central heating, TV, piano.
Small garden

This very comfortable house was originally the lodge to the nearby mansion. It is in a peaceful rural lane and has truly spectacular views from every window across a small garden of lawns, stone terrace and flowering shrubs. Only breakfast and snack suppers are provided – guests eat dinner at the nearby Royal William or in one of Painswick's restaurants: the Royal Oak or Country Elephant, for instance.

Judy Cooke is a welcoming hostess who soon makes friends with her visitors. She has made the Lodge immaculate and very comfortable. The huge sitting-room has windows on three sides, and a big log stove. Everywhere there are thick carpets and good furniture (even the bathroom is pretty luxurious). In my view, the best bedroom is one separate from the house: it is in a one-floor garden cottage, with huge sliding windows through which to step straight onto the lawn or to view the distant hills while still in bed, and ideal for anyone who finds stairs difficult. (Baby-sitting available.)

Painswick church is famous for its 99 enormous yews, centuries old, clipped into arches or other neat shapes, and for its fine peal of twelve bells. In an ancient ceremony every September, children dance and sing round the church. The village has many antique shops. To the north lies the cathedral city of Gloucester (it houses the outstanding National Waterways Museum, among many other sights), and to the south the wooded Cotswold Hills, with particularly spectacular views from Minchinhampton and Rodborough commons (National Trust land). Go west for the Severn estuary with its throngs of seabirds and geese.

The steep ups and downs of this hilly area mean there are many scenic car rides – for instance, in the direction of Prinknash Abbey (part mediaeval, part modern – with a viewing gallery above the monks' pottery and a collection of exotic birds) from which there are views to the River Severn – or go to the observation point high above the beech woods of Cooper's Hill, topped by a maypole. Further on is Crickley Hill (with three trails to choose from – geological, archaeological or ecological – and more superb views). You could return via Birdlip and Sheepscombe; or take the Ermine Way (a Roman road, straight as a spear) to Cirencester (described elsewhere), perhaps returning via Sapperton, sited on a steep ridge which overlooks the 'Golden Valley' of the River Frome – truly golden in the autumn, when the beech woods turn colour. (The church at Sapperton has splendid carvings and several houses were designed by Gimson and his associates who lived here.)

Readers' comments: Excellent accommodation; the place and the owners delightful. Immaculate; lovely setting, gorgeous view; helpful. Friendly. Always lovely.

DEEPLEIGH

C S X

Langley Marsh, Somerset, TA4 2UU   Tel: 0984 23379

North-west of Taunton. Nearest main road: B3227 from Taunton to Wiveliscombe (and M5, junction 26).

5 **Bedrooms.** £20 (less for 2 nights). Weekend price goes up in April. Bargain breaks. All have own bath/shower/toilet. Tea/coffee facilities. TV. Views of garden, country. No smoking. Washing machine on request.

Dinner. £15 for 4 courses (with choices) and coffee, at 7.30pm. Vegetarian or special diets if ordered. Wine can be ordered. **Light suppers** if ordered.

1 **Sitting-room.** With open fire, central heating, record-player. **Bar.**

Large garden

Through high banks of red earth smothered with honeysuckle and foxgloves, I made my way into a little frequented yet very lovely part of Somerset to find this mediaeval house perched on a hillside. Its cream walls make a perfect backdrop to tubs of petunias; and from the chairs on its paved terrace are fine views.

Christine Lymer has furnished the hotel most attractively. In one room, a pretty blue-and-white bordered wallpaper matches frilled curtains with blue ribbons; in the beamed sitting-room (which has a wall of oak planks at one end and an inglenook at the other) there are a number of rosy sofas, shell-pink walls and Chinese carpets to match. Each bedroom is different – pale blue roses in one, silky peach fabrics in another, rosebuds and white wicker in a third (with bathroom and child's room adjoining). Baby-sitting available.

Many paths converge here, from what were once quarries (now picturesquely overgrown). Previously, Deepleigh was a cider-house frequented by the thirsty quarrymen. The room where the cider-press once stood is now filled with diningtables, and here Christine serves such meals as smoked haddock and watercress mousse; lamb braised in a sauce of white wine, mustard and cream; rich chocolate and vanilla pudding; and cheeses – all served on fine white china and linen.

Readers' comments: Hospitality, food and surroundings very acceptable.

It is the River Tone which gives 18th-century **WATERCOMBE HOUSE** (at Huish Champflower) its name, for it flows through the valley garden – in and out of a trout pool. A glass sun-room (used for breakfast) overlooks the shrubs, paths and nooks of the garden. Moira Garner-Richards is a cordon bleu trained cook, and serves such dinners as pears with Roquefort, beef cooked in Somerset cider (accompanied by such vegetables as celery julienne, creamed spinach and potatoes dauphinoise) and baked cheesecake. £17.50–£19.50 (b & b).
Readers' comments: A place to unwind

in. Simply furnished but with individual touches. Delicious breakfast (with fresh-picked raspberries!). Everything done for our comfort. Friendly and most helpful. [Tel: 0984 23725; messages: 0935 83351; postcode: TA4 2EE]

89

DEERFELL
Blackdown Park, Fernden Lane, West Sussex, GU27 3LA
Tel: 0428 653409
South of Haslemere. Nearest main road: A286 from Haslemere to Midhurst.

bath/shower/toilet. Tea/coffee facilities. TV. Views of garden. No smoking. Washing machine on request.
Dinner. £8.50 for 2 courses (with choices) and coffee, from 6.30pm (not Sundays). Non-residents not admitted. Vegetarian or special diets if ordered. Wine can be brought in. No smoking. **Light suppers** if ordered.
1 Sitting-room. With open fire, central heating, record-player. No smoking. Piano.
Large garden
Closed from 20 December to 7 January.

2 Bedrooms. £17.50 (less for 3 nights or continental breakfast). Both have own

The Black Down, a Stone Age stronghold 8000 years ago, rises to nearly 1000 feet. The ferny lane that winds up it, beech trees arching overhead, gives way to sandy heathland where, in Tudor times, iron nodules were grubbed up to be forged into guns, pots and the decorative firebacks that are to be seen in old houses for miles around. To provide power for their forges, the ironworkers dammed streams – hence the chain of 'furnace ponds' which one passes on the way up.

One of the wealthiest ironmasters built himself in 1607 a mansion that is still here (and Deerfell was originally its coach house, erected three centuries later). Cromwell occupied it during the Civil War, and Tennyson was a frequent visitor; you can see the home he built and where he died, at the National Trust carpark on the other side of the Down.

As to Deerfell, its conversion from coach house to home was well done, retaining such features as stone-mullioned windows and latched board doors, but with such modern additions as a glass sun-room and a fireplace of green marble. Elizabeth Carmichael has furnished it with antiques, old rugs and colour schemes which are predominantly soft brown and cream. Bedrooms are comfortable and spacious. Meals (which are usually served in the handsome dining-room with grandfather clock, piano and an ancestral portrait of William IV's physician) are well-cooked, ample and unpretentious – for instance, moussaka and treacle tart or chocolate cheesecake. Breakfast sometimes includes wild mushrooms.

London is only 45 minutes away by train from Haslemere.

Bedroom at Welam House (see page 95)

DORNDEN
C D

Church Lane, Old Sodbury, Avon, BS17 6NB   Tel: 0454 313325
North-east of Bristol. Nearest main road: A432 from Bristol to Old Sodbury
(and M4, junction 18).

9 Bedrooms. £19.50–£23 (less for 2 nights at weekends or 4 mid-week). Prices go up at Easter. Bargain breaks. Some have own bath/shower/toilet. TV. Views of garden, country. Washing machine on request.
Dinner. £8.50 for 3 courses (with choices of sweet) and coffee, at 6.45pm. Non-residents not admitted. Vegetarian or special diets if ordered. Wine can be brought in.
1 Sitting-room. With central heating, piano.
Large garden
Closed in October.

An immaculate garden surrounds the big guest-house – flowerbeds and box-hedges in trim and neat array, with a large vegetable and fruit garden to supply the kitchen. From its lawns and grass tennis court, set high up, there are splendid views.

This is the place for a quiet stay, well placed for exploring the scenic counties of Avon, Somerset, Wiltshire and Gloucestershire around it. All the rooms are sedate and comfortable in a style appropriate to what it was, in mid-Victorian days, a vicarage and with features of the period still retained – from the beautifully polished tiles of the hall to the terrace onto which the sitting-room opens.

Daphne Paz serves traditional favourites at dinner – such as roasts, steak-and-kidney pie or trout with almonds, followed by a choice of, say, sticky toffee pudding, pies or crumbles, and fresh soft fruit from the garden in summer, and then cheeses: very moderately priced.

Old Sodbury is conveniently placed near a motorway yet is a quiet retreat at the south end of the Cotswolds. In its immediate vicinity are 17th-century Dyrham Park (which the National Trust regards as one of its most spectacular properties – its tapestries and its gardens are outstanding), and Westonbirt Arboretum.

Quickly reached from, for instance, London, it is also well placed as a centre from which to go sightseeing. Bath and Bristol are near, and Wales only a short hop across the Severn estuary; while, using the M5, one can quickly arrive in Somerset, Devon and the rest of the west country. But there is no need to go far.

Close by is Castle Combe – a most picturesque village, nestling in a valley around which wooded hills climb high (it's a place of mellow stone houses, a turreted church with lovely fan-vaulting, canopied market cross, and a twisting brook that flows under its ancient bridge). Other lovely villages include Biddestone and Badminton in particular. Two things contributed to the beauty of north-west Wiltshire: the fact that wealth (from wool weaving) was amassed during a period of fine architectural style, and the availability of lovely gold or creamy stone with which to build. Rivers watered fertile pastures and carved out valleys where woodlands flourish.

Readers' comments: Strongly recommended. Cooking of high standard. Excellent value. Very friendly.

DOWN COURT
Steanbridge Lane, Slad, Gloucestershire, GL6 7QE   Tel: 0452 812427
North of Stroud. Nearest main road: A46 from Stroud to Cheltenham (and M5, junction 15).

D PT

2 Bedrooms. £16.50 (less for 7 nights). Price goes up in April. Tea/coffee facilities. Views of garden, country. No smoking. Washing machine on request.
Dinner. £12.50 for 3 courses and coffee, from 7.30pm. Non-residents not admitted. Vegetarian or special diets if ordered. Wine can be ordered or brought in. **Light suppers** if ordered.
2 Sitting-rooms. With open fire, central heating, TV, video, piano, record-player.
Large garden

Slad is the hamlet where Laurie Lee grew up (he still lives near the inn), and on your way to Down Court you may pass many of the scenes in his *Cider with Rosie*.

When the BBC filmed *Cider with Rosie* (1971), they used Down Court for the interior shots and its paddock for the final haymaking scene with the memorable cider; and on the video which the Mills show interested guests you may recognize details like the big cheval mirror in your bedroom. Village children acted the parts of the Lee children. Anne Mills assisted with props and other help during the year-long filming, and has many behind-scenes stories to tell. There are autographed copies of *Cider with Rosie* which visitors can buy.

As to Down Court, it began life in 1620 as five little cottages in a courtyard for farm workers' families, with a communal well outside. Walls are two feet thick, windows stone-mullioned, ceilings low and beamed, fires set in huge stone inglenooks. Now there are fine antiques (unusual French chairs, for instance, and a single-handed clock that dates back to the 17th century), and a high standard of comfort. Anne has made many of the furnishings herself, particularly patchwork cushions and window-seats in the attractive bedrooms from which there are tranquil hill views. In the larger of the two sitting-rooms is an Erard grand piano (1820). Baby-sitting can be arranged.

After qualifying at Bath Catering College, Anne was at the Dorchester Hotel for a while, later doing private catering of a high order. For five years she worked for Prince and Princess Michael of Kent who – like other royals – live near here. Today visitors to her home enjoy the same high standard of cooking.

I selected courgette soup, chicken in a creamy lemon sauce and a deliciously light summer pudding. Most vegetables and fruit come from the garden.

Readers' comments: Excellent hospitality, faultless service. We altered our itinerary in order to return again! Excellent food, environment peaceful. Idyllic; glorious views. A perfect stay; wonderfully comfortable rooms. Highly recommended. Every comfort; delicious meals.

DRAYTON LODGE

C D M S X

Daventry, Northamptonshire, NN11 4NL   Tel: 0327 702449 or 76365
Nearest main road: A425 from Daventry to Leamington (also M1, junctions 16/17).

5 Bedrooms. £17.50–£20 (less for 7 nights). All have own bath/shower/toilet. Tea/coffee facilities. TV. Views of garden or farmyard. No smoking.
Dinner. £12 for 4 courses (with some choices) and coffee, at 7pm. Non-residents not admitted. Vegetarian or special diets if ordered. Wine can be brought in. No smoking. **Light suppers** if ordered.
1 Sitting-room. With open fire, central heating, TV. No smoking.
Large garden

A sculpture of a sow, blissful with piglets, is in the white sitting-room, the walls of which are filled with paintings of well-fed farm animals. Ann Spicer had given me a beaming welcome; and the whole house, built in 1800, seemed to have a happy and bountiful atmosphere.

In the striped dining-room, a pretty lacquer whatnot holds china and a display-case is filled with 'thirties or older jewellery – jumble-sale bargains collected over the years. Here Ann serves such dinners as fish pâté, roast lamb with garden vegetables and chocolate mousse.

A steep stair leads to some of the bedrooms (others are in a converted barn), attractively decorated with, for instance, poppy wallpaper or a green trellis one, brass or mahogany beds with pretty duvets.

One could easily spend a week here to sample the little-known pleasures of the area. Rolling countryside surrounds the market town of Daventry with rivers and reservoirs adding to its beauty. The landscape is dotted with stately homes such as Canons Ashby (Dryden), Sulgrave Manor (Washington family), Althorp (where the Princess of Wales' brother lives), Holdenby (Charles I was imprisoned there) and Lamport Hall. The Naseby battlefield has its own museum. This is good walking country (it includes two long-distance paths) with old inns to spur you on, found in tranquil and historic villages – such as Ashby St Ledgers – built of stone that is geologically the same as the Cotswolds'. You can hire your own canal boat, or take an evening trip on a passenger-boat; drive to Stratford-upon-Avon in about an hour; or wander in the varied gardens at Coton Manor. Church-fanciers should go to those at Great Brington and Brixworth, among others.

Just south of Daventry is the pleasant ironstone village of Badby and the thatched **WINDMILL INN**, now a small hotel, as well as a 14th-century church, a green and a nearby bluebell wood. Although John Freeman and the Suttons have kept the bar and one of the dining-rooms traditional, even to the stone-flagged floor and cricketing prints, their well-equipped bedrooms are spacious and modern, with blue flowery fabrics, mahogany suites and power-showers. From a wide

choice, one can dine on such meals as tuna-and-bean salad, chicken cooked in apple juice and cream, and treacle tart. £17.50–£23.50 (b & b). [Tel: 0327 702363; postcode: NN11 6AN]

93

DRYLANDS FARM   C

Molash, Kent, CT4 8HP   Tel: 0233 740205

South-west of Canterbury. Nearest main road: A252 from Canterbury to
Charing (also M20, junction 9; and M2, junction 6).

2 Bedrooms. £19–£22.50 (the latter is less for 3 nights). Both have own bath/shower/toilet. Tea/coffee facilities. TV. Views of garden, country. Washing machine on request.
1 Sitting-room. With open fire, central heating, TV, record-player.
Large garden

The minute you enter the pink-carpeted hall with its huge copper vat of
dried hydrangeas, you realize that this is a house of exceptional standards.
Built in the 18th century but much 'Victorianized' later, it is at the heart of a
large farm.

There is a large pink sitting-room with doors to terrace and lawn, where a
tall Wellingtonia casts its long shadow. On chilly nights, a log fire crackles in
the marbled fireplace. I particularly liked a bedroom of pale green and pink
with hydrangea curtains and a very lovely bathroom adjoining it. Outstanding
views.

Sally Holmes (a professional tennis coach) provides bed-and-breakfast only.
(Baby-sitting also available.)

Although most people staying here make for Canterbury (only a quarter-hour
away), even nearer is old Chilham and its castle. The half-timbered houses
surround a square on the hilltop. All but the Norman keep of the castle was
built in 1616: now there are mediaeval banquets in the keep, and falconry
displays outside in a park that was landscaped by Capability Brown.

Readers' comments: Made my family very welcome. High standards.

There is no formality at 15th-century
RIPPLE FARM, Crundale, where the
Baurs grow organic produce. They are
an artistic family: Chagall posters are
pinned on the walls, hop bines or
bunches of dried flowers hang from
ceilings, floors are of polished boards,
and there is much use of stripped pine.
In one of the bedrooms there is a
platform (plus ladder) for children's
beds above their parents'. The bathroom is on the ground floor, along
with the sitting/dining-room for guests.
This is a simple room with shuttered
windows, pyjama-stripe wallpaper and
log stove. Outside are an 18th-century

rear view

barn, now a games room, and the
remains of three oast houses – hop
kilns. (Maggie does light suppers
only.) £15.50–£16.50. [Tel: 0227
730748; messages: 0227 730762;
postcode: CT4 7EB]

EASTCOTT MANOR   C D S
Eastcott, Wiltshire, SN10 4PL   Tel: 0380 813313
South of Devizes. Nearest main road: A360 from Devizes to Salisbury.

4 Bedrooms. £18–£20 (less for 3 nights; and **15% reduction to readers of this book in winter**). Some have own bath/shower/toilet. Tea/coffee facilities. TV. Views of garden, country. No smoking preferred. Washing machine on request.
Dinner (if ordered in advance). £12 for 4 courses and coffee, at 7.30pm. Non-residents not admitted. **Light suppers** if ordered.
1 Sitting-room. With open fire.
Large garden

As early as 1150 there was a house on this spot. The present building has parts dating back to the 16th century, but every century since has added its contribution. Furnishings vary. Some are fine antiques – the refectory table in the dining-room (its walls hung with ancestral portraits) is 400 years old, for instance; and one alcove houses Crown Derby and other porcelain. Up the oak staircase with barley-sugar balusters are bedrooms of which the most attractive has peach-and-white panelled walls with big sash windows at each end and rural views.

In outbuildings or paddocks are always some of the Firths' horses: they have trained such horses as Lucinda Green's. Janet's other great interest is cookery, for which she has a number of diplomas. A typical meal, served on a generous help-yourself basis: fish soufflé, lamb provençale, caramelized fruit and cheeses (eggs, vegetables and fruit are home-produced). Jam and cordials for sale.

Readers' comments: Lovely house. Friendly and helpful. Delicious food. Very much enjoyed. Kind and welcoming. Delicious supper.

Westward lies West Ashton, the former vicarage of which is **WELAM HOUSE**, in Bratton Road. It was built from Bath stone in 1840 in the 'goth-ick' style so fashionable then – hence the pointed windows, arched fireplaces and stained glass in the hall (with the crest of Lord Long, a great local landowner at the time). There is exceptionally decorative plasterwork, particularly in the sitting-room added in 1865, which has pomegranates on the ceiling and massive Jacobean-style pendants. Outside is a lawn with lily-pool, bowling green and putting; alter-natively, there is the shady canopy of a

weeping cherry under which to recline in a deckchair on a sunny day. Bedrooms are comfortably furnished. (Elizabeth Cronan serves only light suppers.) £16.
Readers' comments: Very comfortable. Excellent value. [Tel: 0225 755908; postcode: BA14 6AZ]

EASTON FARMHOUSE

C S

Bishops Cannings, Wiltshire, SN10 2LR   Tel: 0380 860228
North-east of Devizes. Nearest main road: A361 from Devizes towards
Avebury.

2 Bedrooms. £16–£17 (less for 4 nights).
Tea/coffee facilities. Views of garden,
country. No smoking. Washing machine on
request.
Light suppers if ordered.
1 Sitting-room. With open fire, central
heating, TV.
Large garden

The first sight is of a really outstanding rock garden with flowery shrubs, created
with the help of sarsen stones which ploughs often turn up in this county (a
sarsen is a boulder peculiar to the Wiltshire Downs – big ones are found in the
stone circles of Avebury and Stonehenge; the latest theory is that they are relics
of a tropical desert past). There are also staddle- (or rick-) stones – those big
'mushrooms' on which granaries were often perched, to confound even the
nimblest rats. Stone troughs brim with flowers, a century-old weeping ash weeps
over the lawn, and at the back there is a goldfish pond and a summer-house from
which to enjoy the lovely garden there – created by Ann Horton's indefatigable
efforts. There is also a tennis court.

The Victorian house is immaculate, the traditional furnishings in the big
rooms comfortable and well complemented by Ann's flower arrangements. There
are large windows from which to enjoy the peaceful views, a very pretty pink
bathroom, and here and there inlaid Edwardian furniture in keeping with the
architectural style of the house. Ann will provide (if it is ordered) a simple
supper – soup, a meat salad and fruit, for instance – or you can dine at the
Crown Inn in the village or go to Devizes (for the Bear Hotel, a wine bar
and other options). Milk and yogurt are home-produced, and food is served on
Spode china.

This is an excellent area for walks: the Kennet & Avon Canal (with towpath
flanked by wildflowers) is easily accessible; and through the farmlands in the
Downs to the north passes the Wansdyke – a 25-foot-high earthwork built by the
last of the Romans as a defence against the Saxons (it runs from here to the
Bristol Channel).

The 60-mile Kennet & Avon Canal was built in 1794, during 'canal mania', to
link the River Kennet at Newbury with the Avon at Bath: a very wide canal,
designed with locks for far bigger boats than other canals. It took gangs of navvies
from far parts – a riotous lot, the locals found – some sixteen years to complete
the great task, the hardest part being the long flight of locks to be seen at Devizes.
Until trains took trade away in the 1830s the canal was thronged with loads of
Somerset coal, Bath stone, hay and corn. By 1960, it was a miserable sight of
mud, weeds and rotting lock-gates. Then restoration began, to be completed only
in 1990, once more making the waterway clear and navigable.

Readers' comments: The highest praise. Spacious, comfortable, beautifully
appointed, lovely antiques. Charming and welcoming. Very pleasant, warm
and comfortable. Breakfast beyond praise. Most welcoming. Attractively
decorated.

EASTON HOUSE

CDS

Chidham Lane, Chidham, West Sussex, PO18 8TF   Tel: 0243 572514
West of Chichester. Nearest main road: A259 from Chichester towards Portsmouth.

2 Bedrooms. £16–£18 (less for continental breakfast). Prices go up in April. One has own bath/toilet. Tea/coffee facilities. Views of garden, country, sea. No smoking. Washing machine on request.
1 Sitting-room. With log stove, central heating, TV, video, piano, record-player.
Small garden

Every corner of this Tudor house has been filled by Mary Hartley with unusual antiques and trifles. A modern white-and-red poppy wallpaper contrasts with old beams, oriental rugs with stone-flagged floor, scarlet folkweave curtains with antique furniture. All around is a fine collection of mirrors (Spanish, art deco, rococo – every conceivable kind) and pictures of cats; Mary is musical, and guests are welcome to play on the Bechstein or join in chamber music sessions. It's a free-and-easy atmosphere, a house full of character and cats. Bathrooms are pretty.

Although only breakfast is served (one can dine well in Chichester, particularly at Thompson's, at the Old House at Home in Chidham, or in nearby Emsworth), visitors are welcome to linger in the comfortable lime-green sitting-room with its log stove (where tea is served on arrival); or in the garden, under the shade of magnolia and walnut trees.

Peaceful Chidham looks across an inlet to ancient Bosham, one of the most picturesque sailing villages on the winding shores of Chichester's lovely natural harbour (with boat trips): very popular and crowded in summer. Chichester itself is near. It has a mediaeval cathedral, Georgian houses and a theatre.

Wherever you drive or walk there is fine scenery; and plenty of interesting sights within a few miles – such as the Weald and Downland Open-Air Museum (acres of ancient buildings reconstructed and an open-air theatre), the huge Roman palace of Fishbourne, a brass-rubbing centre in Chichester, crafts complex in Bosham and fine gardens at West Dean. Around Chidham harbour are lovely walks.

Readers' comments: Peaceful house with great character, very reasonably priced. A marvellous place. Mrs Hartley anticipates her guests' every need. Excellent.

Opposite the church is the **OLD RECTORY**, built in 1830 and now well furnished by Peter and Anna Blencowe in traditional country-house style (all rooms have en suite bathrooms). The large garden has a swimming-pool (unheated) and the elegant sitting-room a grand piano. Bed-and-breakfast only. £19–£22.
Readers' comments: Wonderful garden and furniture. [Tel: 0243 572088; postcode: PO18 8TA]

97

EASTWATER COTTAGE   C D

Wells Road, Priddy, Somerset, BA5 3AZ   Tel: 0749 676252
North of Wells. Nearest main road: A39 from Wells to Bath.

4 Bedrooms. £14 (less for 7 nights). All have tea/coffee facilities. TV. Views of garden, country. Washing machine on request.
Dinner. £9 for 3 courses (with choices) and coffee, at 6.30pm. Non-residents not admitted. Vegetarian or special diets if ordered. Wine can be brought in. **Light suppers** if ordered.
Small garden

This whitewashed cottage is named after one of the greatest of many impressive caverns in the Mendip Hills, a scenic area famous for the Cheddar Gorge and the strange formations within Wookey Hole, and where slate used to be quarried – you can see some of it on the floors of the cottage – as well as the stone from which were built the 28-inch thick walls nearly 300 years ago. When you stay here, you may find other guests are cavers or pot-holers who have come to explore the Mendips' underground mysteries.

This was originally a long-house (family at one end, their livestock at the other), deliberately built without any windows on the north-east side to ensure that it was warm in winter (cool, too, in even the hottest summer). Jennie Clements has added double-glazing and a log stove to ensure that, high up as her cottage is, guests will be snug during the winter months.

There are two dining-areas, one adjoining the open-plan kitchen: pine and scarlet chairs surround the table and on the dresser are blue willow-pattern plates. A glass of Jennie's home-made wine will be offered to you with your dinner, which might perhaps comprise home-made mushroom soup, game pie or lamb in a sauce made from Somerset's famous apples, and bread-and-butter pudding.

Bedrooms have white or stone walls, pine furniture, comfortable armchairs, Welsh tapestry bedspreads and low windows. (Baby-sitting available.)

Beyond the Mendips is Wells – with Europe's oldest mediaeval street, 13th-century cathedral with 300 statues on the front, and bishop's palace. Glastonbury is famous for the high Tor (where the Holy Grail was reputedly buried), Chewton for its Cheddar cheese dairy, Longleat House for its lions. Bath and Bristol are both close. The coast is also nearby and the resort of Weston-super-Mare with its vast, sandy beach and, among other diversions, an Edwardian gaslight workshop, old chemist's shop and other nostalgia; a helicopter museum; and a heritage centre. At Brean Down is a large tropical bird garden and, in the same area, a country park with farm animals including rare breeds. There are several wildlife reserves or trails to explore; vineyards; and magnificent scenery on the walks through Ebbor Gorge.

And when you get back to Priddy, you may sometimes find Morris dancers gambolling on the village green or, in late August, an immense sheep fair.

Readers' comments: So comfortable. Marvellous food. Friendly. Very enjoyable. Comfortable and pleasant. Very helpful.

EDGCOTT HOUSE

CDSX

Porlock Road, Exford, Somerset, TA24 7QG   Tel: 064383 495
South-west of Minehead. Nearest main road: A396 from Tiverton to Dunster.

4 Bedrooms. £17–£20 (less for 3 nights **to readers of this book only,** or 7 nights). Prices go up in April. One has own bath/shower/toilet. Views of garden, country. Washing machine on request.
Dinner. £10 for 4 courses (with choices) and coffee, at 7.30pm. Non-residents not admitted. Vegetarian or special diets if ordered. Wine can be brought in.
1 Sitting-room. With open fire, central heating, TV, piano.
Large garden

Trompe l'oeil murals, in 'Strawberry Hill gothick' style, cover the walls of the long dining/sitting-room. They were painted in the 1940s by George Oakes, who became a director of the distinguished interior decorating firm of Colefax & Fowler. The tall bay windows of this room open onto a tiled terrace from which there is a fine hill view beyond the old, rambling garden where yellow Welsh poppies grow in profusion, and wisteria clambers over the pink walls of the house. In the long entrance hall (red quarry-tiled floor contrasting with whitewashed stone walls) are Persian rugs and unusual clocks. Bedrooms are homely; throughout there is a mix of antique and merely old furniture, with more trompe l'oeil alcoves or doors.

Gillian Lamble's style of cooking is traditionally English and she serves such meals as mackerel pâté, roast lamb, lemon meringue pie and cheeses.

Readers' comments: Mrs Lamble is kindness itself. A house of character. She went out of her way to be helpful. Food excellent. Will definitely return. A lovely house. A favourite. One of the best.

Outside nearby Luckwell Bridge, in a lovely position, is an 18th-century farm with apricot walls: **CUTTHORNE,** where Ann Durbin produces candlelit dinners with much home produce (meat and game). Bedrooms in the house vary (some have bathrooms), and one has a carved and tapestry-hung four-poster. In the sitting- and dining-rooms are antique rugs, log fires and brass-rubbings.

There is a courtyard where chickens roam, a pond with exotic species of ducks and geese, and swings in a children's play area. Trout fishing, shooting and Landrover safaris available. £17.50–£25. (Two cottages have their own kitchens and dining facilities for either b & b or self-catering: guests can dine in the main house.)

Readers' comments: Excellent food, kind hosts, quiet setting. Attractive rooms, comprehensively equipped. The Durbins were most helpful. Good food, well presented. [Tel: 064383 255; postcode: TA24 7EW]

EDGEHILL HOTEL   C D PT
2 High Street, Hadleigh, Suffolk, IP7 5AP   Tel: 0473 822458
West of Ipswich. Nearest main road: A1071 from Ipswich towards Sudbury.

12 Bedrooms. £18.25–£33.75 (less for 2 nights). Bargain breaks. Most have own bath/shower/toilet. Tea/coffee facilities. TV. Views of garden, country. No smoking in one room. Washing machine on request.
Dinner. £13.50 for 3 courses (with choices) and coffee, at 7pm (not Sundays). Vegetarian or special diets if ordered. Wine can be ordered. No smoking. **Light suppers** if ordered.
1 Sitting-room. With central heating.
Large garden

Hadleigh, once a rich wool town, went through bad times but is now prospering again. As a result, its very lengthy High Street is full of shops enjoying a new life as wine bars, antique shops and so forth. It is a street of colourful façades, pargeting (decorative plasterwork), overhanging bay windows, carved wood details, ornamental porches and fanlights over the doors. Behind lie river meadows.

One of the High Street's many fine historic buildings to have been rejuvenated is a Tudor house with Georgian façade which is now this private hotel. Rodney Rolfe, formerly the manager of a motor dealer's, took over Edgehill Hotel in 1976 and began to convert it. The well-proportioned rooms have been furnished with style, and attractive wallpapers chosen for each one. In all the spacious bedrooms there are thick-pile carpets and good furniture. The sitting-room has glass doors opening onto the walled garden where an annexe has some bedrooms.

Angela Rolfe, previously a teacher, and her mother do all the cooking and use home-grown raspberries, strawberries, vegetables and other produce from the kitchen garden. She serves soup, roasts, organic vegetables and desserts such as raspberry pavlova, ginger meringues, rhubarb and ginger fool (not on Sunday; and ordering ahead is always necessary). She is not only a good cook, but also makes and sells crafts. (Baby-sitting can be arranged.)

This is a good base from which to explore the very pretty countryside and villages nearby, and such well-known beauty-spots as mediaeval Lavenham, Dedham, Woodbridge on the Deben estuary, Kersey and Long Melford.

In addition, Suffolk has a tremendous variety of interest for garden-lovers. For instance, there are in the vicinity of Hadleigh and Ipswich a council-house garden shown on 'Gardener's World' (at Charsfield), colourful woodland gardens at Little Blakenham with a number of rarities, the seed-trial fields of Thompson and Morgan and formal riverside gardens around Letheringsett's watermill.

Wind- and water-mills are a particular feature of the Suffolk countryside. Some notable ones are Bardwell windmill where you can buy stoneground flour (occasionally, the mill is operated by steam); Buttrums 6-storey windmill at Woodbridge – where there is also the famous watermill operated by the movement of the tides; the marsh drainage mill at Herringfleet on the edge of the Broads; and a superb 18th-century windmill at Saxtead.

Readers' comments: Absolutely excellent. High standard.

EXPLANATION OF CODE LETTERS

(These appear, where applicable, in alphabetical order after the names of houses)

C   Suitable for families with children. Sometimes a minimum age is stipulated, in which case this is indicated by a numeral; thus **C(5)** means children over 5 years old are accepted. In most cases, houses that accept children offer reduced rates and special meals. They may provide cots, high chairs and even baby-sitting; or games and sports for older children. Please enquire when booking. And do not expect young children to be lodged free, as babies are. Many houses have playing-cards, board games, irons, hair-dryers, maps, gumboots, bicycles, and so forth – just ask. Families which pick establishments with plenty of games, swimming-pool, animals, etc., or that are near free museums, parks and walks, can save a lot on keeping youngsters entertained. (Readers wanting total quiet may wish to avoid houses coded **C**.)

D   Dogs permitted. A charge is rarely made, but it is often a stipulation that you must ask before bringing one; the dog may have to sleep in your car, or be banned from public rooms.

M   Suitable for those with mobility problems. Needs vary: whenever I have used the code letter **M**, this indicates that not only is there a ground-floor bedroom and bathroom, but these, and doorways, have sufficient width for a wheelchair, and steps are few. For precise details, ask when booking.

PT   Accessible by public transport. It is not necessary to have a car in order to get off the beaten track because public transport is widely available; houses indicated by the code **PT** have a railway station or coach stop within a reasonable distance, from which you can walk or take a taxi (quite a number of hosts will even pick you up, free, in their own car). The symbol **PT** further indicates that there are also some buses for sightseeing, but these may be few. Ask when booking.

S   Indicates those houses which charge single people no more, or only 10% more, than half the price of a double room (except, possibly, at peak periods).

X   Visitors are accepted at Christmas, though Christmas meals are not necessarily provided. Some hotels and farms offer special Christmas holidays; but, unless otherwise indicated (by the code letter **X** at top of entry), those in this book will then be closed.

ELM HOUSE   C D PT S
14 Upper Holt Street, Earls Colne, Essex, CO6 2PG   Tel: 0787 222197
West of Colchester. On A604 from Colchester to Cambridge.

3 Bedrooms. £18–£25 (less for 3 nights). Prices may go up in April. Bargain breaks for return visits. Some have own bath/toilet. Tea/coffee facilities. TV. Views of garden. Washing machine on request.
Dinner. £10–£12 for 4 courses (with choice of puddings) and coffee, at about 7.30pm. Vegetarian or special diets if ordered. Wine can be brought in. **Light suppers** if ordered.
2 Sitting-rooms. With open fire, central heating, TV.
Garden

This gracious 18th-century house has been furnished with suitable elegance. The moss-green and pale gold sitting-room is furnished with antiques (its high French doors open onto a very attractive garden where meals are occasionally served). In the dining-room, which is sage-green, the mahogany table is laid with white-and-gold Spode and silver candelabra at dinner time. There is also a reading/writing-room for guests who want complete quiet.

Although on a main road, the house provides quiet bedrooms at the back, overlooking the walled garden (windows are double-glazed). I liked the coffee-and-white room with William Morris curtains; another is huge, with windows on three sides. There are pretty, antique, iron beds (painted white or black, with bright brass knobs) coupled with the modern comfort of warm duvets. Details like brass curtain-poles and decorative fanlights catch one's eye.

Lady Larcom so much enjoyed entertaining that she started to take guests in Elm House. Dinners here are therefore rather special. They may begin with bouillabaisse or smoked haddock soup, for example, followed perhaps by beef bourguignonne or stuffed peppers (baked in tomato and mushroom sauce, topped with sour cream, and served with wild rice and salad), then may come iced coffee soufflé or gooseberry mousse and cheeses.

Earls Colne is in one of the best parts of Essex – the north-east. This is a region of peaceful watermeadows with willows, outstanding churches and great historic interest. Colchester is an exceptional Roman/Norman city, described else-where. All down the coast are winding creeks and wildernesses that attract migrant waterfowl. Where once the Vikings sailed in to plunder, boat enthusiasts now go yachting. There is very varied scenery to explore inland: heaths, woods and villages that once prospered from weaving wool and are still beautiful today.

The area has, too, plenty of sightseeing possibilities. For instance: Gosfield Hall (Tudor), the historic walled and watergardens of Saling Hall, the world's oldest timber-framed barn at Coggeshall (Norman), 16th-century Paycockes, the working silk-mill at Braintree, boat trips on Gosfield Lake, walks in ancient Chalkney Wood, and a variety of local museums or galleries – from Braintree's heritage centre to the art exhibitions in Finchingfield's Guildhall, and bygones in Great Bardfield's charity cottage.

Readers' comments: Lady Larcom was most hospitable, her home is very comfort-able, and every meal was a delight. Exceptional value. The food was excellent. Memorable stay, outstanding meals.

102

ENFORD HOUSE

C D PT S

Enford, Wiltshire, SN9 6DJ Tel: 0980 70414

South-east of Devizes. Nearest main road: A345 from Marlborough to Salisbury.

3 Bedrooms. £15 (less for 3 nights). Price goes up in April. Tea/coffee facilities. Views of garden. Washing machine on request.
Dinner (when available). £13 for 4 courses (with choices) and coffee, at 7–8pm (must be ordered by lunchtime). Wine can be brought in. **Light suppers** if ordered.
1 Sitting-room. With open fire, central heating, TV.
Garden

The latest in telecommunications and 4000-year-old mysteries oddly combine in the telephone number of this house – Stonehenge 70414: this world-famous monument is only a few miles away. In fact, Enford (being in Salisbury Plain) is surrounded by prehistoric remains of many kinds.

The 18th-century house (once a rectory) and its garden are enclosed by thatch-topped walls – a feature one often finds in those parts of Wiltshire where, stone being non-existent, a mix of earth and dung with horsehair or else chalk blocks were used to build walls (which then needed protection from rain). The house has pointed 'gothick' windows on one side, doors to the garden on another. Antiques furnish the panelled sitting-room, which has a crackling fire on chilly nights. Bedrooms are simple, fresh and conventionally furnished.

Sarah Campbell serves, on pretty Watteau china, soups that she makes from garden vegetables, roasts, puddings such as gooseberry fool or lemon soufflé, then cheeses. The Campbells tell their guests a great deal about the area – not just its historic sights for they are knowledgeable about its wildlife (Salisbury Plain has a tremendous variety of wildflowers as well as larks and lapwings), where to go for the finest views from the surrounding downs and the best walks.

Readers' comments: Everything quite delightful. A charming hostess and excellent food. Very comfortable. Pleasant and relaxed time.

Southwards, in the scenic Woodford Valley, at Lower Woodford, are **MANOR FARM COTTAGES** where a party of visitors could have their own cottage – thatched and mediaeval or flint-walled and Victorian; gathering together with others in one of these for breakfasts and the light suppers Elva Randall provides on request (unless you prefer to cook your own in the fully equipped kitchen available in each cottage; or to eat at the Wheatsheaf Inn close by, which has an excellent chef). The cottages are simply but pleasantly furnished, well carpeted, and with restful colour schemes of pink or

blue. All have gardens, sitting-rooms, washing machines. (Baby-sitting can be arranged.) £17–£19.
Reader's comment: Excellent in all respects. [Tel: 0722 73393; postcode: SP4 6NQ]

ESHTON GRANGE   C(8) **S X**
Eshton Road, Gargrave, North Yorkshire, BD23 3QE   Tel: 0756 749 383
North-west of Skipton. Nearest main road: A65 from Skipton to Settle.

4 Bedrooms. £18–£20 (less for return visits). All have own bath/shower/toilet. Tea/coffee facilities. TV. Views of garden, country, river. Washing machine on request.
Dinner (by arrangement). £10–£12 for 3–4 courses (with choices) and coffee, at 6.30–8pm. Vegetarian or special diets if ordered. Wine can be brought in. **Light suppers** if ordered.
1 Sitting-room. With open fire, central heating, TV.
Large garden

Inquisitive brown eyes watched my arrival: two of the Eshton Grange stud of tiny Shetland ponies were in a paddock overlooking the courtyard.

Judy and Terry Shelmerdine have created a comfortable, informal atmosphere in their home even though it is furnished with fine antiques and good paintings, many by Judy. It has stone inglenooks, chintz or tapestry chairs and deep-set windows. In the garden is a croquet lawn.

The beamed bedrooms are on two floors – at the top is a big attic room ideal for a family, for children shin up a ladder to their beds in the apex of the roof, tucked away above the king-post which supports it. It's a higgledy-piggledy room, with pretty trellis wallpaper, a circular window, and in one corner a cooker useful for preparing the children's supper.

Dinners are traditionally English – home-made soup, roast chicken with all the accompaniments, sherry trifle, and cheese, for example. You help yourself to as much as you want. (Must be ordered in advance.) Those who occupy the Grange's self-catering accommodation may dine in too.

Eshton is surrounded by beautiful views. It is near Malham (in Airedale), famous for its massive crags, tarn (lake) belonging to the National Trust, and cove – a huge circular cliff. Go to Gordale Scar for the sight of twin waterfalls in a 300-foot gorge. There is a moorland road through wooded Littondale to Arncliffe and Litton, villages with quaint houses, ancient churches, and swirling rivers.

Readers' comments: Owners, room, food and views fantastic! A good place, very reasonably priced. Bang on! – have stayed twice. A charming couple, dinner was excellent, and very good value for money. Most comfortable. Beautiful setting. Judy's cooking is very good, bounteous and wholesome. Beautiful house. Delighted by the welcome.

Shetland ponies at Eshton Grange

ESTATE HOUSE   C(5) S
Ford, Northumberland, TD15 2QG   Tel: 0890 820297
South-west of Berwick-upon-Tweed. Nearest main road: A697 from Wooler
to Coldstream (Scotland).

2 Bedrooms. £14. Tea/coffee facilities. Views of country, village. No smoking.
Dinner. £8 for 3 courses and coffee, at 7pm. Non-residents not admitted. Vegetarian or special diets if ordered. Wine can be brought in. No smoking.
1 Sitting-room. With open fire, central heating, TV. No smoking.
Small garden
Closed in December and January.

Ford is a model village built by the owners of Ford Castle and its estate (the name probably comes from that of a Norman owner and has nothing to do with a river crossing). Most of it was the creation in the 1850s of Lady Waterford (a temperance campaigner, so there is no pub), who was also a gifted amateur painter. Her biblical murals adorn what was the village school and is now a gallery devoted to her works.

The Estate House was built at the turn of the century, and to an Edwardian standard: rooms are large and high-ceilinged, with tall windows, some overlooking the garden with its big lawn. This runs down to the grounds of the 13th-century castle (now used by the county council and not open to the public).

Judith and John Bradley were both biology teachers. He now manages the nearby working cornmill, where you can learn to operate a watermill, and also hire bicycles; she runs a craft shop adjoining the house, when she is not gardening, tending her flourishing house-plants, or preparing such meals as Eyemouth sole with loganberries, roast Cheviot lamb and fresh fruit salad, most of the produce being from the garden or the locality.

This is an area rich in history, most of it savage (George Macdonald Fraser's *The Steel Bonnets* is recommended reading); nearby Berwick-upon-Tweed, with its 16th-century fortifications, is a reminder of shifting allegiances (the county of Berwickshire is in Scotland). Now the rolling countryside is extremely tranquil and well provided with craftsmen (furniture-makers, blacksmith, potters) and garden nurseries.

On the road to Etal (another model village) is **HAY FARMHOUSE**, also a spacious turn-of-the-century house, the home of retired farmers John and Margaret Chisholm. The big rooms give splendid views of Ford Castle and the distant Cheviots. No basins in the bedrooms but a huge contemporary tub in the bathroom! There is pub grub at Etal and elsewhere and more elaborate restaurants (including a Lebanese one) in Berwick, a quarter of an hour's drive away. (No smoking.)

£15. [Tel: 0890 820315; postcode: TD12 4TR]

105

FAIRFIELD HOUSE

C D M PT

44 High Street, Corsham, Wiltshire, SN13 0HT   Tel: 0249 712992
South-west of Chippenham. On A4 from Bath to Chippenham
(and M4, junction 17).

3 Bedrooms. £15–£17 (less for 7 nights).
All have tea/coffee facilities. TV. Washing
machine on request.
Small garden

Within a peacock's cry of Corsham Court (a palatial Elizabethan mansion with a
famous collection of paintings and other treasures) is a quiet and picturesque
street, a backwater despite its name – which, in the 17th century, was lined with
the cottages and workrooms of Flemish weavers. Fairfield House is one of few to
have survived from then, for an explosion of gunpowder stored nearby (during the
building of Brunel's Box Hill railway tunnel, one of his greatest feats) devastated
some of the street.

During the building of the two-mile tunnel (1836–41), every spare bed in
Corsham was occupied by railway navvies working on the 'monstrous and
extraordinary, most dangerous and impracticable tunnel'. Men and horses were
the only power available to get through the rock (solid Bath stone for much of the
way), working by candlelight; every week, a ton of candles and a ton of gunpowder were used; and, in all, 30 million bricks to line the tunnel which the sceptics
said Brunel could never complete. Today's high-speed travellers whisk through it
with little thought of how it was built.

At Fairfield House, one steps straight into a low, white breakfast-room with
jade paintwork and curtains, beyond which lie two bedrooms and bathroom,
with more upstairs. Christine Reid has furnished all of these with exceptional
grace – using either silky cream duvets or pretty patchwork (made by her
mother) on the beds, wallpapers patterned with small roses or with Chinese-
style pheasants. White-shuttered windows are set in deep embrasures; fresh or
dried flower arrangements are everywhere. This is altogether an exceptionally
attractive small house. Breakfast only; for dinner, visitors go to the Copperfield,
Jaipur, Methuen Arms or other restaurants in the little High Street. (Baby-sitting
can be arranged.)

Wiltshire is, I feel, an undervalued county, for in addition to its rolling
countryside there is so much to see – outstandingly, its 4500 prehistoric sites
(of which Stonehenge may be the most famous but is less impressive than
Avebury). Great houses include Wilton, Stourhead, Mompesson House (within
the precincts of Salisbury cathedral); even nearer, Bowood, Lacock Abbey and
Longleat. In fact, the county has more listed buildings than any other, and
many of its villages are little beauties. Corsham has the unusual Bath Stone
Quarry Museum.

Readers' comments: Delightful; great food; very welcoming. Excellent.

FAIRSEAT HOUSE
Station Road, Newick, East Sussex, BN8 4PJ   Tel: 0825 722263
East of Haywards Heath (West Sussex). On A272 from Haywards Heath to Uckfield.

3 Bedrooms. £19. All have own bath/shower/toilet. Tea/coffee facilities. Views of garden, country. No smoking. Washing machine on request.
Dinner. £17.50 for 4 courses, wine and coffee, at any convenient time. Vegetarian or special diets if ordered. Wine can be ordered or brought in. **Light suppers** if ordered.
1 Sitting-room. With open fire, central heating, TV. Library with piano, cassette recorder. Also a quiet sitting/writing area.
Large garden

Readers who previously enjoyed Roy and Carol Pontifex's hospitality at Old Cudwells will be glad to know they are still doing b & b at their new home, which is only three miles away. It is a big, yellow stucco Edwardian house – large and light – with a striking two-storey, arched window. It stands in its own spacious grounds, which have a covered and heated swimming-pool available for most of the year. The library's big French windows open onto the garden, which faces south, and occasionally dinner is served on the terrace.

As before, visitors will enjoy Carol's decorative touches, the buttoned velvet chesterfields, Persian rugs, fiddleback chairs and a number of particularly interesting 18th-century portraits: one ancestor was Robert Chambers (of dictionary fame) and a painting of his daughter, Lady Priestley, hangs on a wall. Carol wove some floor-rugs herself, on an old outsize loom from Scandinavia. Everywhere handsome Edwardian fittings – from fireplaces to lamps – have been retained or installed.

Up the wide staircase are attractive bedrooms and good bathrooms – one has a Victorian rolltopped bath, another has a hip-bath with overhead shower.

Carol and Roy have always enjoyed meeting people, and entertaining: so those visitors who order a full dinner are treated to such meals as salmon mousse, fillet of beef, a savoury which might be mushrooms on toast, and lemon pie (wine included). Alternatively, they can have fewer courses or even a light supper such as quiche and salad, and this too would be served by candlelight. Breakfast eggs are as fresh as ever, for when the Pontifexes moved their Buff Orpingtons came too. Also in the grounds is a flock of Gotland sheep.

London is ¾-hour away by train (cheap day-tickets available); Gatwick Airport the same, by car. In the area there is plenty to enjoy (in addition, the south coast is soon reached): Ashdown Forest, the beauty-spot of Ditchling Beacon, the 'Jack and Jill' pair of windmills, pretty villages like Lindfield, the Bluebell Line steam train, and such sights as Standen House, Chartwell (Churchill's Tudor house), Batemans (Kipling's) and the castles of Bodiam, Hever and Lewes. Brighton, with the Prince Regent's oriental Pavilion is near; Eastbourne and Tunbridge Wells too. Then there are all the great gardens for which Sussex is famous: Wakehurst, Sheffield Park, Borde Hill, Nymans, Leonardslee and Heaselands. Newick itself is celebrated for the bonfire and firework display held on its green every Guy Fawkes night – the 'guys' now usually include unpopular politicians or even local busybodies!

THE FALCONRY
Sprinks Lane, Kingsley, Staffordshire, ST10 2BX   Tel: 0538 754784
North-east of Cheadle. Nearest main road: A52 from Stoke-on-Trent to
Ashbourne.

2 Bedrooms. £17–£18 (less for 4 nights).
Prices go up from June. One has own
shower/toilet. Tea/coffee facilities. Views
of garden, country, river. Balcony. No
smoking. Washing machine on request.
Light suppers if ordered.
1 Sitting-room. With open fire, central
heating, TV.

Here you can encounter otters as well as eagles, owls and many other birds rarely
seen in close-up. For on a steep site overlooking the lovely Churnet valley is a
wildlife sanctuary where the Hodges family have established a refuge for ailing or
orphaned wildlife: their animal ambulance is regularly called out. You can join a
course on birds of prey (1 or 2 days) or have a guided tour.

The accommodation is in Val Hodges' modern, single-storey house, its huge
sliding glass doors opening onto a verandah high above a steep wooded gorge that
has been likened to Rhineland. Not only the Churnet below but the 18th-century
canal that accompanies much of it can be explored on foot, or in a tug-drawn
boat.

Light meals are available in the comfortable sitting/dining-room, its walls full
of wildlife pictures. Water comes from a spring so pure that once there was a
bottling-plant here.

Kingsley is near the Peak District National Park in one direction and
Stoke-on-Trent in the other – the traffic of the latter is well worth braving to
seek out the exceptional china museum, the famous-name factory shops (a bus
circulates among them to save you driving), the Gladstone working Victorian
pottery and the underground experience of the Chatterley Whitfield coal
mine museum.

The name of **OLD FURNACE
FARM** at Oakamoor derives from the
time when the 'iron valley' that lies
below it echoed to the sound of
smelters at work. Now no sound louder
than cackling geese is heard, the smelt-
ing mill is a coffee-shop and foxgloves
throng undisturbed lanes. One steps
into a sitting-room with huge, oak-
armed sofas around the log fire. From
it, a wooden staircase rises to big
bedrooms, where you can sit on a
sofa to enjoy the spectacular view.
Everywhere are pot-plants, Victorian
prints, copper or old silver.
Occasionally such dinners as Stilton
soup, chicken in cream sauce, apple

pie and cheeses are available, but more
often Maggie Wheeler does light
snacks only. And outdoors there is the
'hobby farm' to explore (guinea-fowl,
sheep, a peacock) as well as a trout
lake. £18–£20. [Tel: 0538 702442;
postcode: ST10 3AP]

FITZ MANOR

Fitz, Bomere Heath, Shropshire, SY4 3AS   Tel: 0743 850295
North-west of Shrewsbury. Nearest main road: A5 from Shrewsbury to
Llangollen.

3 Bedrooms. £16–£20 (less for 7 nights).
Tea/coffee facilities. Views of garden,
country. Washing machine on request.
Dinner. £12.50 for 4 courses and coffee, at
times to suit guests. Non-residents not
admitted. Vegetarian or special diets if
ordered. Wine can be brought in. **Light
suppers** if ordered.
2 Sitting-rooms. With open fire, central
heating, TV, record-player.
Large garden

This outstanding manor house was built about 1450 in traditional Shropshire
style – black timbers and white walls. It is at the heart of a large arable farm.

The interior is one of the most impressive in this book. A vast, deep blue dining-room with parquet floor and Persian carpet overlooks rosebeds, pergolas and
yew hedges. It is furnished with antiques, paintings by John Piper and a collection
of Crown Derby. In the oak-panelled sitting-room there are damask and pink velvet armchairs around the log fire (or guests can use the glass sun-room). Between
these two rooms are the arched hall and a winding oak staircase; one door here is
carved with strapwork and vines, on the tiled floor are Persian rugs and oak chests.

Bedrooms differ in size. For instance, adjoining one huge room with armchairs
from which to enjoy views of the Severn Valley and Welsh hills is a white cottage-
style bedroom – a useful combination for a family (and there is a playroom).

Dawn Baly's candlelit dinners often start with home-made pâté or soup;
casseroled pheasant or wild duck sometimes appear as the main course, with
home-grown vegetables; puddings may be fruit pies, meringues or chocolate
mousse; and then there are cheeses – unless visitors want only a light supper.

The garden is still much as it was when laid out in Tudor times, although now
there is a heated swimming-pool and croquet lawn. Guests are encouraged to use
the land – for barbecues, picnics, swimming or fishing in the river.

Readers' comments: Lovely place – quite magical. Dinner was extremely well
cooked, abundant and well presented. No attention to detail spared.

Leaton's **OLD VICARAGE** was built
in 1859 for an archdeacon, by a master
of High Victorian style: hence the
many pointed or trefoil-arched windows, the arcading in the sitting-room,
handsome floor-tiles and doors of
ecclesiastical design. One very big
room has a bay window and another
an oriel from which to enjoy views of
the garden, where there is an immense
Wellingtonia – or Washingtonia, as
Americans would say. One Victorian
bathroom is particularly attractive.

(Joan Mansell-Jones serves snack suppers only.) £14–£16. [Tel: 0939
290989; postcode: SY4 3AP]

FOLDGATE FARM   C S
Corney, Cumbria, LA19 5TN   Tel: 0299 718660
North-west of Ulverston. Nearest main road: A595 from Whitehaven towards Millom.

3 Bedrooms. £12.50–£13.50 (less for 3 nights or continental breakfast). Views of country, sea, river. No smoking. Washing machine on request.
Dinner. £8 for 3 courses and coffee, at 6pm (or later by arrangement). Non-residents not admitted. Vegetarian or special diets if ordered. Wine can be brought in. No smoking. **Light suppers** if ordered.
1 Sitting-room. With open fire, central heating, TV. No smoking.
Small garden
Closed in December.

A real Cumbrian farm near Millom, and well outside the main tourist areas, it covers 100 acres on which are kept Swaledale and Herdwick sheep as well as some cattle. The approach to the farm is through a cobbled yard, with a great stone byre and stables at one side, Muscovy ducks perching on a dry-stone wall, and sundry old iron pots and kettles filled with stonecrop, London pride or primroses. A stream slips quietly by. Pat, the sheepdog, comes bounding out to greet visitors.

The rooms have old furniture. Guests sometimes eat with the family, by a dresser where mugs hang, the clothes airer suspended overhead and a grandfather clock ticking in one corner. There are bacon-hooks in the ceiling, old horn-handled shepherds' crooks stacked in the hall, and a bright coal fire in the evenings. Mary Hogg does most of the talking as she serves guests a proper farmhouse meal, and her husband is glad to tell visitors about his sheep and all the local goings-on – guests are welcome to watch the life of the farm, and to join in at haymaking time in July or August.

You'll get real country fare here: Cumberland sausage, 'tatie pot', plum pudding with rum sauce, farm duckling, Herdwick lamb or mutton, rum butter on bread, currant cake with tea on arrival and at bedtime, and jams made from local bilberries, pears, or marrow and ginger. There are free-range eggs for breakfast. This is a thoroughly unpretentious, homely and friendly place to stay.

As to the countryside around, there are the moors of Corney Fell close by and roads winding up and down, with sea views. An unusual attraction is a smokery (for meats) where visitors are welcome.

Up the coast from Corney is Ravenglass, a port from Roman times but long since silted up. It is the terminus of a narrow-gauge railway, built to transport iron ore but now a very popular tourist ride. Take it to Boot for a drink at the pub and a look round the craft gallery and the cornmill (not working), then return to the mill at Muncaster (which is working during the summer). At Muncaster Castle, they breed and release owls, which you can see. Transport enthusiasts will want to visit the railway museum at Ravenglass and the motor museum at Holker Hall. At Sellafield, the visitor centre of the nuclear industry has become a popular tourist attraction.

Readers' comments: Excellent food, good company. Good food. Lovely welcome. A great success. Never a dull moment! Food, atmosphere and welcome couldn't be faulted. Delighted with our welcome, the food and all the local attractions.

FOREST FARMHOUSE
Mount Road, Marsden, West Yorkshire, HD7 6NN   Tel: 0484 842687
South-west of Huddersfield. Nearest main road: A62 from Oldham to
Huddersfield.

3 Bedrooms. £13.50–£15 (less for 7 nights). Tea/coffee facilities. Views of country. Washing machine on request.
Dinner. £6 for 3 courses (with choices) and coffee, at 7pm. Vegetarian or special diets if ordered. Wine can be brought in.
Light suppers if ordered.
1 Sitting-room. With open fire, central heating, TV, organ, record-player.

The Industrial Revolution concentrated the textile industries into the mechanized mills which are still to be seen all over Yorkshire and Lancashire. Until then, spinning and weaving were done in people's homes, whole families working together and often combining weaving with farming. Forest Farmhouse was just such a dual-purpose home.

Standing at 1000 feet, the house is now surrounded by a golf course (which visitors can often use) and moorland, much of it owned by the National Trust, at the top of the Peak District National Park. There was never a forest: the word is used in its sense of a hunting-ground and, at least according to the deeds of the house, the royal family still has the right to use it. This is a typical farmhouse of its kind, built of dark gritstone at least 200 years ago, with mullioned windows and stone-slated roof. Inside, the beamed wooden ceilings are low and the guests' sitting-room has a big stone fireplace. Seamus, the enormous and friendly Irish wolfhound, sometimes ambles about. Bedrooms, some with exposed masonry, have pine fittings.

Genial Ted and May Fussey run the place with walkers in mind (the open moors and the nearness of the Pennine Way attract them here). May provides, for example, home-made soup or grilled grapefruit, pork steak in breadcrumbs with fresh vegetables, and chocolate pudding with white sauce. All bread is home-made: 'If I can't make it, I won't buy it!', she says.

Climbing, angling and hang-gliding are some of the pastimes available nearby. The area is also of interest for its industrial and social history. The Luddites used to plan their campaigns in an inn that stood up the road from Forest Farmhouse. Many of the mills they attempted to sabotage are still working, producing yarn or worsted, and there are plans to open a nearby one to visitors. The country's longest canal tunnel starts near Marsden and is being restored. There are museums, exhibitions, canal-boat trips, and walks both waymarked and guided, to help to bring the past to life. Marsden, which has its own theatre company, is where much of the television series 'The Last of the Summer Wine' was filmed. Holmfirth, where the series is based, is only a few miles away.

Facts (prices, etc.) at the top of entries are supplied by the proprietors themselves. While every effort is made to ensure that these are correct at the time of going to press, they may alter thereafter: please check when you book.

FORTH HOUSE   C D M PT X
44 High Street, Warwick, CV34 4AX   Tel: 0926 401512
(M40, junction 15, is near.)

2 Bedrooms. £19–£24 (less for 3 nights or continental breakfast). Prices go up in April. Both have own bath/shower/toilet. Tea/coffee facilities. TV. Refrigerator. Views of garden. No smoking. Washing machine on request.
Dinner. £8 for 3 courses and coffee, at times to suit guests. Non-residents not admitted. Special diets if ordered. Wine can be brought in. No smoking. **Light suppers** if ordered.
2 Sitting-rooms. With open fire, central heating, TV, record-player. No smoking.
Small garden

Past the antique and craft shops of the busy High Street is a terrace of trim Georgian houses; overhead looms Warwick Castle. Not exactly 'off the beaten track'. But behind no. 44 lies a secret place: a long garden stretching far back. Stone steps and paths flank the lawn, rosebeds and pool; an ancient wisteria clambers high. Here is found an entire garden-suite for visitors: virtually a flat, and all on the ground floor. It is not only spacious but very pretty – roses and ribbons on the bathroom curtains, the bath's sides made of pine; and in bedroom and sitting-room 'Country House' or Laura Ashley fabrics.

There's another bedroom at the back of the house, on the first floor. This has a pine table and rush chairs for meals (if you want to take these in privacy), and a sofa. Elsewhere are carved marble fireplaces, huge bouquets of dried flowers, prettily ruffled curtains in big bay windows.

An extra bonus for many guests is often the sight of Labrador pups at play – Elizabeth Draisey breeds them as guide dogs for the blind.

As to her dinners, a typical menu might comprise a melon and grape cocktail, pork in tarragon and cider sauce, and a gâteau. (Visitors in the self-catering accommodation can dine in the main house; baby-sitting available too.)

West of Warwick is Claverdon, and Doreen Bromilow's home, **WOODSIDE** in Langley Road, with its own wildlife reserve. Hillside woods, untouched since mediaeval times, have rare old trees and traces of the farming techniques used before the Black Death killed off the local people. Daffodils and bluebells abound in spring. Furnished with antiques, Woodside has a good bedroom on the ground floor; others, including a pretty family room with fine views, are upstairs; and through the picture-windows of the dining-room, inquisitive cows watch you eat such

meals as melon, chicken casserole (in help-yourself quantity) and apple pie. And after dinner? Croquet in summer, a log fire in winter. Bridge for beginners and creative embroidery weekends are also organized. £15–£17. [Tel: 0926 842446; postcode: CV35 8PJ]

FORTITUDE COTTAGE

51 Broad Street, Old Portsmouth, Hampshire, PO1 2JD Tel: 0705 823748

Nearest main road: A3 from London to Portsmouth.

3 Bedrooms. £18–£20. Prices go up at Easter. Some have own bath/shower/toilet. Tea/coffee facilities. TV. Views of sea. No smoking.

Light suppers if ordered.

Carol Harbeck's little cottage – one room piled on top of another – backs onto her mother's (also a guest-house), with a flowery little courtyard and fountain between the two: its appearance has won it awards. It is named for the Fortitude Inn, once next door; itself named for HMS *Fortitude*, a ship-of-war which ended as a prison hulk – overlooked by the big bay window of Carol's first-floor sitting-room. This is Portsmouth's most historic area. From here, Richard Lionheart embarked for the Crusades, Henry V for Agincourt, and the first settlers for Australia. It's a place of ramparts and bastions, quaint buildings and byways, much coming-and-going of ships and little boats. The waterbus leaves from the quay just outside.

All the rooms in the cottage are prettily furnished – even the bathroom. One can dine well at Becketts or the Talisman. Handy as a stopover for people using Portsmouth's port, Fortitude Cottage deserves a longer stay, for Portsmouth (and its adjoining Victorian resort, Southsea) have so much to offer: HMS *Victory*, the *Mary Rose*, HMS *Warrior*, the Royal Navy's museum and that of the Marines, cathedral and historic garrison church, Henry VIII's Southsea Castle, the D-Day museum, Hayling Island and the wild places of Chichester Harbour, clifftop Victorian forts, Roman/Norman Portchester Castle, submarine museum at Gosport, a big new leisure centre, other museums (including Dickens' birth-place), the Searchlight Tattoo every September, trips to the Isle of Wight, and fine downland countryside to explore inland.

Readers' comments: Excellent accommodation, spotless. Absolutely excellent, high standard. Delightfully unusual. What a find! Particularly enjoyable.

Near the city is Denmead and in Hambledon Road you will find **FOREST GATE**, the graceful 18th-century house of Torfrida Cox and her husband, with a large garden. It is on the 70-mile Wayfarers' Walk. This is an informal home furnished with antiques. Meals (which have to be ordered in advance) include such dishes as Armenian lamb pilaff or moussaka, mousses or lemon meringue pie. Each bedroom has a bath or

shower. £16–£18. [Tel: 0705 255901; postcode: PO7 6EX]

113

Kingsey, Buckinghamshire, HP17 8LZ   Tel: 0844 291650
South-west of Aylesbury. On A4129 from Princes Risborough to Thame
(and near M40, junctions 7/8).

3 Bedrooms. £18–£19. Some have own shower. Tea/coffee facilities. TV. Views of garden, country. No smoking.
Light suppers if ordered.
2 Sitting-rooms. With central heating, TV. No smoking.
Large garden
Closed in December and January.

The instant impression is delightful: sparkling white house beyond green lawns where Muscovy ducks waddle with their young towards a pool crossed by an arching stone bridge. The gnarled remains of an immense 500-year-old elm tree stand beside the drive. At the back of the house is a garden with heated swimming-pool, against a distant view of the Chiltern Hills.

The interior is just as attractive. The house having been the home of architect Nick Hooper and his family for many years, it is not surprising that its modernization was done with imagination and with care to respect its 17th-century origins. In the hall, floored with polished red quarry-tiles, a wrought-iron staircase leads up to bedrooms with beamed ceilings, attractive wallpapers and rugs, and restful colour schemes. Board doors have the original iron latches. The breakfast-room (which also serves as a sitting-room) has brown gingham tablecloths and rush-seated chairs. Here Mary-Joyce – a warm, gentle hostess – usually serves only breakfast, recommending for other meals restaurants in the ancient market town of Thame, only a few minutes away.

Thame is a lively place in autumn when the mile-long market place at its heart is filled with stalls for the annual fair, and is a mecca for gourmets; beyond lie all the attractions of Oxfordshire described elsewhere in this book. In west Buckinghamshire, too, there is plenty – from the wooded hills of the Chilterns down into the fertile Vale of Aylesbury. Early in the year there are bluebells and cherry blossom; in autumn the beech woods blaze with colour.

The centre of Aylesbury is picturesque, threaded with pathways and courtyards to explore on foot (one of the many inns, the King's Head, belongs to the National Trust). Of many villages worth visiting, go to Long Crendon not only for the near-by lovely bridge and rose-covered cottages but for two 15th-century houses (one belonged to Catherine of Aragon and is now owned by the National Trust). At Waddesdon is the Rothschild mansion, looking like a French château (also National Trust property); at Upper Winchendon, high up, a dramatic view of the Thames; Cuxham, in good walking country, has a stream through the middle. Hughenden Manor was Disraeli's house. Waterperry's gardens are outstanding.

All these are very near. Visitors staying for some time can also from here explore Oxford, West Wycombe, old Amersham, Henley and other Thames-side towns (even Windsor), and any number of castles, stately homes, museums, antique shops, etc. London is only an hour away.

Readers' comments: Wonderfully kind hosts, lovely home, top of out list! Beautiful house, meticulously kept; charming, friendly and helpful. The Hoopers and their home are charming. A good welcome and nice house.

FRIAR HALL FARM

C S

Caldbeck, Cumbria, CA7 8DS Tel: 06974 78633
South-west of Carlisle. Nearest main road: A595 from Carlisle to
Cockermouth.

3 Bedrooms. £15–£16 (less for 4 nights).
Tea-making facilities. Views of garden,
country, river. No smoking. Washing
machine on request.
Light suppers if ordered.
1 Sitting-room. With open fire, central
heating, TV.
Small garden
Closed from December to February.

As the name suggests, this farmhouse has a long history. The Prior of Carlisle
built a hospital here, which was dissolved in the reign of King John. The 12th-
century part of the house was once the monks' refectory (hence the name 'hall'),
with the hospital proper next door.

Today it is the centre of a 140-acre sheep- and dairy-farm. Caldbeck Fells rise
up above the village where John Peel was born and is buried (the little churchyard
is right opposite Friar Hall, across a tiny humpback stone bridge spanning a tum-
bling stream with a weir). The Blencathra foot-hounds still roam these fells in
winter, just as they once did with John Peel – but now hang-gliders go up there
too.

Guests use a snug sitting/dining-room with big leather armchairs, crimson
velvet curtains and, on wintry evenings, logs blazing in a fireplace made of green-
ish Buttermere slate, casting a flicker on the gleaming brass fire-irons. The ceiling
is beamed, the walls are thick.

All the bedrooms look across the tiny garden and the stream to the far hills
beyond, and to a sky of scudding clouds when the wind blows. Fresh paint and
light colours make them attractive; carpets are good; colour schemes simple.

For dinner most visitors go to the village inn, the Oddfellow's Arms, or
to Park End restaurant, as Dorothy Coulthard serves only breakfast and light
suppers.

Caldbeck is one of the Lake District's prettiest villages, with a pond (used by
Muscovy ducks), an old inn, and a Wesleyan chapel carved with the reminder
'Remember NOW thy creator'. The approach from the north is particularly
lovely, driving across a heath with gorse towards a view of a green valley.

In the graveyard of the pleasant church of St Kentigern (a.k.a. St Mungo) lie
not only John Peel but the real-life original of the heroine of Melvyn Bragg's novel
The Maid of Buttermere. To the south of the village, Carrock Fell is known for the
variety of minerals which can be found.

Readers' comments: Beautiful view; comfortable bedroom. Good home cooking;
made very welcome; pretty view of the beck. Thoroughly enjoyed our visit,
well looked after. Food excellent, house delightful, shall return. Most enjoyable,
excellent food, will return. Superb. Splendid.

115

FRITH FARM HOUSE
Otterden, Kent, ME13 0DD   Tel: 0795 890701

C(10) **X**

South-west of Faversham. Nearest main road: A20 from Maidstone to
Charing (and M2, junction 6).

3 **Bedrooms.** £19.50–£24.50. All have
own shower/toilet. Tea/coffee facilities. TV.
Views of garden, country. No smoking.
Washing machine on request.
Dinner. £15 for 4 courses (with choices),
wine and coffee, at 7.30pm (not Sundays).
Non-residents not admitted. Vegetarian or
special diets if ordered. Wine can be
brought in. **Light suppers** if ordered.
1 **Sitting-room.** With open fire, central
heating, record-player. Piano.
Large garden

Once, there were cherry orchards as far as the eye could see: now Frith has only
six acres. (From their fruit – 'If I can grab it before the birds do!' – Susan
Chesterfield makes sorbets for her gourmet dinners.)

They say money doesn't grow on trees. Not true, for those cherry trees
financed the building in 1820 of this very fine house where a fountain plays outside the pillared front door. Maroon damask wallpapers and sofas are in keeping
with its style. The bedrooms are beautifully decorated and very well equipped
(one has a four-poster).

In a very lovely dining-room, fiddleback chairs and a collection of antique
plates contrast with a bold geometrical 'Kazak' print (Liberty's) used for the
curtains, and with the white dishes of German bone china on which Susan serves
such meals as avocado with taramosalata, sorbet, lamb steaks with capers,
meringues glacés and cheeses (wine included).

A recent addition is a polygonal conservatory where Susan provides not only
breakfast but dinner parties for local people.

The house is so high up on the North Downs (an area of outstanding natural
beauty) that its views across orchards and woods extend – in the case of one of
the pretty bedrooms – as far as the Isle of Sheppey, which is a distant twinkle of
bright lights after darkness falls. The Downs can be explored at the pace of
bygone days in the Chesterfields' landau: details on request.

Canterbury is, of course, the magnet which draws most visitors here but there
is a great deal more to east Kent than this. For a scenic drive, go across the North
Downs to the valley of the River Stour, the Tudor village of Chilham (with castle,
grounds and Battle of Britain museum) and then to Hastingleigh.

There is a particularly pretty little
cottage at Eastling, in the Faversham
direction: **PLANTATION HOUSE**,
where Dany Fraser takes visitors for
bed-and-breakfast and will provide
light suppers if ordered in advance.
Half-timbered and with low beams,
a Tudor brick hearth and French
provincial furniture, it has an unusually
large and wandering garden concealed
behind it. (Tuition in French avail-

able.) £12–£14. [Tel: 0795 890315;
postcode: ME13 0AZ]

GEORGIAN TOWN HOUSE   C
11 Crossgate, Durham, DH1 4PS   Tel: 091 386 8070
Nearest main road: A690 from Crook to Durham.

rear view

6 Bedrooms. £20–£22.50. Prices go up in May. All have own bath/shower/toilet. Tea/coffee facilities. TV. Views of garden, cathedral.
1 Sitting-room. With open fire, central heating.
Closed from mid-December to mid-January.

Minutes by foot from the centre of the city, Crossgate is a fairly quiet street of mainly Georgian-fronted houses. This is one (or rather two) such.

Architect's wife Jane Weil has decorated her six bedrooms with great flair, from the simple beamed attic to the more elaborate rooms below, with swags of fabric over windows and bedheads. Downstairs, the sitting-cum-breakfast room has dark green walls, leaf green carpet, and soft-furnishings in red, green and cream – a bold and agreeable colour scheme. A polygonal sun-room with white cast-iron furniture (sometimes used for breakfast) leads to a tiny garden. Ingenious decorative arrangements include stencilled classical columns with ivy swags.

Two pubs are close (for which reason the back bedrooms might be preferable, at least on Fridays and Saturdays). Downhill is the 12th-century church of St Margaret of Antioch and the river. Durham is surprisingly badly off for good restaurants, but Mrs Weil can direct visitors to the best there are.

The city is best known for its Norman cathedral (one of the gems of European architecture) and castle, which surmount what is almost an island in a loop of the River Wear. The riverside walk is very attractive, or one can hire a boat. There are some good museums too, such as the Gulbenkian collection of oriental art, which is attached to the university; a visit here also gives an opportunity of seeing some interesting modern architecture.

The city centre has many pleasant old streets. Go to the covered market for bric-a-brac and very fresh fish from the east coast.

Readers' comments: Most friendly atmosphere. Converted most tastefully.

A little further up Crossgate is **COLE-BRICK** (no. 21), which possesses the considerable advantages for this area of having private parking space and of being set back from the road behind a front garden. The bedrooms and the bathroom are on the ground floor. There are splendid views from the Mellanbys' large, first-floor sitting-room (with balcony) of the cathedral and castle. Breakfast is served on Minton china, with linen napkins. No

smoking. £20. [Tel: 091 384 9585; postcode: DH1 4PS]

117

GLEBE HOUSE C

Park Lane, Longstowe, Cambridgeshire, CB3 7UJ Tel: 0954 719509

West of Cambridge. Nearest main road: A1198 from Huntingdon to Royston (and M11, junction 12).

2 **Bedrooms.** £18 (less for 7 nights). Price goes up in April. Both have own bath/shower/toilet. Tea/coffee facilities. TV. Views of garden, country. No smoking. Washing machine on request.
Dinner. £15 for 3 courses and coffee (or £8.50 for 2), at 5–8pm. Vegetarian or special diets if ordered. Wine can be brought in. No smoking. **Light suppers** if ordered.
Small garden

Scalloped white bargeboards round the roof are like a demure lace collar on the pink walls of this secluded 16th-century house. A former owner added architectural finds, such as the bas-relief of a ram which decorates one gable. In summer, poppies, clematis and peonies contribute colourful touches; and moorhens nest below the briar roses surrounding the garden pond. Over the old lych-gate honeysuckle climbs. The house was (as 'glebe' indicates) church property.

Charlotte Murray has decorated all the rooms attractively, using soft pinks and greens in the bedrooms and deep mulberry for the dining-room where, on Wedgwood's 'Devon Rose' china, she serves either simple meals or dinners cooked to professional standard – for Charlotte, after training at the Cordon Bleu Cookery School in London, used to cook for City directors' dining-rooms. She chooses dishes to suit her guests' tastes, one popular menu being carrot-and-coriander soup, pork tenderloin stuffed with mushrooms, and almond applecake. When children stay, she can do a separate and early meal with simpler food.

Another of her skills is making dried flower arrangements, and she offers produce and crafts for sale.

Most visitors come here as a base from which to visit Cambridge (only ¼-hour away). Also within easy reach are Newmarket and Ely, with its cathedral.

Readers' comments: Absolutely lovely. Beautiful house, warm and comfortable. Terrific supper. Friendly, helpful. Lovely food, helpful hostess. Very comfortable, warm and tasteful. Lovely supper. Nice hostess.

Another talented lady lives at Wrestlingworth, in the direction of Sandy (Bedfordshire). At thatched **ORCHARD COTTAGE,** once the village bakery, Joan Strong makes bobbin-lace – an old craft for which the area was once famous – while some of the furniture in the house was made by her husband, Owen. The pleasant rooms have views of fields, or of the garden enclosed by high cupressus hedges. From the large sitting/dining-room (with log fire) glass doors open onto a terrace. For dinner, sample the many inns in this area. £14.50–£16.

Readers' comments: Very good value, spotless and comfortable. [Tel: 0767 631355; postcode: SG19 2EW]

118

GLENWOOD

Croxton, Staffordshire, ST21 6PF   Tel: 063082 238
North-west of Stafford. Nearest main road: A5013 from Eccleshall to Stafford
(and M6, junction 14).

3 **Bedrooms.** £13–£17. One has own
shower/toilet. Tea/coffee facilities. TV in
one. Views of garden, country. No smoking.
Washing machine on request.
Light suppers if ordered.
1 **Sitting-room.** With central heating. TV.
No smoking.
Small garden

The quiet road outside was once a main coaching route to Chester, and this
house (built in 1650) was then a coaching inn. The beamed sitting-room overlooks a large garden and all the bedrooms, neat and with pine beds, are on the
ground floor. Ann Thorpe serves light snacks only, so many visitors go to dine in
the market town of Eccleshall which has romantic castle ruins, the moat now
turned into gardens.

Izaak Walton's cottage is near here (with angling memorabilia). Also in this
direction are Doxey Marshes, a wetland wildlife reserve; and in Stafford the
largest half-timbered house in any English town. On your way to Trentham
Gardens or to the Wedgwood Visitor Centre (outside Stoke-on-Trent), stop to
look inside Swynnerton's church for a Norman sculpture of Christ, eight-feet tall.
Ingestre's church has a magnificent Wren interior. This is an area with plenty of
castles and stately homes to visit, canal trips, and such historic industrial sights as
watermills, a steam pumping-station and working pottery kilns. Quite a number
of fine gardens and farm or wildlife centres too.

The inventor of Hovis bread lived at a
watermill (now a hotel) in the market
town of Stone, the name of which
refers to a cairn of stones that marked
the grave of two Saxon princes mur-
dered by their father here. Close to a
lock on the long Trent & Mersey
Canal stands the **BOAT HOUSE** in
Newcastle Road, also built in the 18th
century, as a bargees' inn. It is not 'off
the beaten track' but one of the
immaculate bedrooms overlooking Jill
Adams' landscaped garden would suit
light sleepers. The sliding glass doors
of the beige-and-white sitting-room,

rear view

with its buttoned velvet chairs, open
onto the lawn. There is a towpath walk
outside, and boat trips are available.
£17.50. [Tel: 0785 815389 or 813137;
postcode: ST15 8LD]

**Book well ahead: many of these houses have few rooms. Do not
expect dinner if you have not booked it or if you arrive late.**

GOBLANDS FARM
Court Lane, Hadlow, Kent, TN11 0LT Tel: 0732 850853
North-east of Tonbridge. Nearest main road: A26 from Tonbridge to
Maidstone.

3 Bedrooms. £15–£17. Tea/coffee
facilities. TV. Views of garden, country.
No smoking. Washing machine on request.
1 Sitting-room. With central heating, TV.

The strawberries, apples and beans in your supermarket might have been grown
on the Pierces' 700 acres. But, like many farmers, they have had to diversify, and
so guests staying here are intrigued to discover varied crafts being carried on in
one outbuilding, and a gamekeeper's pens of young partridges and pheasants
behind this. Another outbuilding houses a games room for visitors, there is a
sheltered swimming-pool (heated to 80°), and you can view Richard's collection
of vintage traction-engines.

Accommodation is in a huge converted barn, 200 years old. There is under-
floor heating beneath the York stone slabs which cover the ground floor, and light
floods in through a vast glass wall rising from ground to roof. Where once corn
was winnowed there now stands the long refectory table of the dining-room – the
corn-grinding shaft is still overhead and, here and in the little sitting-room, the
brick or board walls are exposed to view, with high rafters overhead. The cottage-
style bedrooms are on the ground floor. All are light and airy, with board floors,
and a pleasant single room has its own armchair and desk.

Marilyn will drive visitors to and from Hadlow's various restaurants if
they wish (or they can use the barbecue on the paved patio overlooking
the fields). The farm is on the estate of so-called Hadlow Castle (an ornate
early-Victorian mansion of which only a spectacular 'gothick' tower remains,
looming nearly 200 feet high). Its builder, William May, has an elaborate
mausoleum by the ancient church. Hadlow itself, a village of Saxon origin, is
where Caxton was born.

Some people come here when walking the long-distance Weald Way
which runs through the farm, on its 80-mile way from the Thames estuary to
Beachy Head at Eastbourne. Another house in this book is on its route
(**Number 10**, Modest Corner), so a not too taxing walk could take you from
one bed to another, and back the next day – with some of the finest stretches
of the footpath along your route, and wildlife to spot. It is well provided with
direction signs.

> The addresses of houses are geographically correct but postal
> addresses sometimes differ (for correspondence, the only essential
> element is the postcode).
>
> Information about the nearest town and 'A' road helps you to
> locate the whereabouts of any village on a map; but before setting
> off it is necessary to get precise instructions from your host as
> many houses are very much 'off the beaten track'.

GOODMANS HOUSE

C D X

Furley, Devon, EX13 7TU   Tel: 040488 690

North-west of Axminster. Nearest main road: A30 from Honiton to Chard
(and M5, junction 25).

6 Bedrooms. £17.50–£24 (less for 2 nights
or continental breakfast). Prices go up in
May. Bargain breaks. All have own bath/
toilet. Tea/coffee facilities. TV. Views of
garden, country.
Dinner. £14 for 3 courses (with choices),
aperitif and coffee, at 7pm. Vegetarian or
special diets if ordered. Wine can be
ordered or brought in. No smoking. **Light
suppers** sometimes.
2 Sitting-rooms. With open fire, central
heating. No smoking in one.
Large garden
Closed in January.

This is the model of what a small country-house hotel should be: in every respect,
Robert and Pat Spencer have got things exactly right.

They sold their previous, larger hotel to pursue the ideal of 'smaller is better'
and give every guest personal attention.

The house (mostly 18th-century, some parts much older) had been steadily
crumbling away for the last 80 years. Much of the renovation was done by the
Spencers, after which it was completely transformed with well-chosen furnishings
to create an ambience that is elegant without being formal. Complimentary
aperitifs are served in a sitting-room with the pale colours of stone and lichen
complementing the greenery of pot-plants and the glow from logs in a Minster
fireplace, before a candlelit dinner in a long, arched dining-room with inglenooks
at each end. Or, one may sit in the conservatory to enjoy the fine views – it is
furnished with wicker chairs and festoon blinds. The bedrooms are some of the
most attractive in this book, with handsome bathrooms.

Alternatively, some families prefer to have accommodation in garden cottages
– sometimes let on a wholly self-catering basis but also used for those who want
to take meals in and enjoy the amenities of the main house. Even though these
have their own kitchens and living-rooms, they cost less per head than bedrooms
in the house. Dinner can, if you prefer, be brought on a trolley to your cottage.

Pat qualified with a first-class pass at her catering college, and every meal she
produces is a memorable experience, using their own produce (which includes
sheep and poultry) and also local, organically reared meat – as Bob used to be a
butcher, he buys expertly. Occasionally there are barbecues beside one of the
three lily- and fish-pools in the grounds. A typical menu: seafood and mango
platter, pork with apricot and orange stuffing (imaginatively prepared vegetables),
hazelnut meringues with raspberries. On Mondays and Tuesdays there is a
discount on the already very reasonable charge for meals.

Early in spring, the azaleas and magnolias burst into flower: there are even a
palm and a jacaranda to testify to the mildness of the climate here. In autumn,
the fiery and varied colours of foliage are a delight. There are orchards and ponds.

Readers' comments: Very special warmth and hospitality. Very high standard of
catering – the best value in Britain! Superb setting, luxurious rooms, full of character. A welcome that makes you feel one of the family. Delicious food – large
portions too. We've yet to find a place as good as Goodmans. Beautifully done.

121

GORSELANDS FARMHOUSE   C D X
Boddington Lane, East End, Oxfordshire, OX8 6PU   Tel: 0993 881895
North-east of Witney. Nearest main road: A4095 from Woodstock to Witney.

5 Bedrooms. £13.75–£17.50 (less for 5 nights). Prices go up in June. Bargain breaks. Some have own bath/shower/toilet. Tea/coffee facilities. TV. Views of garden, country. No smoking. Washing machine on request.
Dinner. £9.95 for 4 courses (with choices) and coffee, from 7–9pm. Non-residents not admitted. Vegetarian or special diets if ordered. Wine can be ordered. No smoking.
Light suppers if ordered.
2 Sitting-rooms. With open fire, central heating, TV, piano. No smoking.
Large garden
Closed in March and April.

Within a short stroll of North Leigh's Roman villa (it had 60 rooms, and is famous for the intricate mosaic floor and well-preserved central heating system) is this comfortable home of Cotswold stone, the oldest part originally a barn. Today it is run as a guest-house by Barbara Newcombe-Jones. Beyond the stone-flagged hall are sitting-rooms (one with satellite TV, one with log fire), a games room with full-size billiard table, and a conservatory where Barbara's staff serve such meals as melon with Parma ham, coq au vin, cheeses and chocolate mousse.

Bedrooms, simply furnished but comfortable, are spacious and in the bathroom of one is an oval bathtub. Well-behaved children are welcome; and Barbara can arrange for a baby-sitter. There is a tennis court.

Gorselands is close to both Oxford and historic Woodstock; spectacular Blenheim Palace (in baroque style, set in grounds landscaped by Capability Brown and now with a huge new maze, as well as boats on its lake); the Cotswold Wildlife Park where exotic animals roam in the gardens and park of an old manor house; Churchill's grave at Bladon (Blenheim, his birthplace, has a Churchill exhibition); and Cogges Farm Museum where life on a Victorian farm is recreated.

Oxford itself – its colleges, churches and museums – needs no description, but there is always something new to be seen for those who stay several days. In 'The Oxford Story' you ride (literally) back through 800 years of history; Curioxity is a 'hands-on' science gallery. Latest addition (at Magdalen College) is a version of Leonardo's 'Last Supper', even better – some say – than the one in Milan.

The blacksmith from the Blenheim estate once lived in 18th-century **MAYFIELD COTTAGE** (at West End in the pretty village of Combe), the home of Rosemary and Stan Fox. They discovered a little inglenook hidden in a wall, a feature of which is the salt ledge – to keep that precious commodity dry in times when homes were incurably damp. Breakfasts and light suppers are served at one end of this room, chinoiserie sofas furnish the other, and in the middle an open-tread

staircase rises to the bedrooms. Doorways are low and ceilings beamed. £15–£17. [Tel: 0993 898298; postcode: OX8 8NP]

GRAFTON VILLA FARM
Grafton, Herefordshire, HR2 8ED Tel: 0432 268689
South of Hereford. On A49 from Hereford to Ross-on-Wye.

C D PT X

3 Bedrooms. £16–£18.50 (less for 4 nights). One has own bath/shower/toilet. All have tea/coffee facilities. TV. Views of garden, country. No smoking. Washing machine on request.
Dinner. £12 for 4 courses (with choices) and coffee, at 7pm (not Wednesdays). Non-residents not admitted. Vegetarian or special diets if ordered. Wine can be brought in. No smoking. **Light suppers** if ordered.
1 Sitting-room. With open fire, central heating, TV.
Large garden

The 18th-century farmhouse, set well back from the road, is furnished with antiques and well-chosen fabrics. Each bedroom is named after the woodland of which it has a view (Aconbury, Dinedor, Haywood), for the panoramic scenery in every direction is one of the attractions of staying here. The pretty family room also overlooks the farmyard with its free-ranging chickens and ducks – sometimes, foals too. Bath- and shower-rooms are good; the little sitting-room snug, its velvet chairs grouped around the fire. The sunny dining-room looks onto patio and garden from which come vegetables for the table.

At dinner, portions are generous. Jennie Layton's meals often feature cider soup, chicken breasts in tarragon sauce and a hazelnut meringue gâteau with which she serves hot apricot sauce. Her vegetables are imaginatively prepared: carrots may be cooked in orange juice, beetroots appear in Stilton sauce, courgettes with tomatoes and basil. As well as conventional breakfast choices, she may offer you fruit compote, poached haddock and croissants. (Sunday lunch can be provided. Baby-sitting available.)

The house is close to the cathedral city of Hereford and within a few miles there are other historic towns such as Ledbury, Ross-on-Wye and Hay-on-Wye ('book city') as well as picturesque villages like Weobley, Eardisland and Pembridge. Such beauty-spots as Symonds Yat, the Black Mountains, the Malvern Hills and the River Wye are all close, too.

Close to the Welsh border, and at one end of the Golden Valley (with spectacular views of the Black Mountains on the way) is **ROWLESTONE COURT**, Rowlestone. It began life in the 14th century or earlier as a 'long-house', and was enlarged in the 17th century. A flagstoned lavender path to the front door passes a garden that has eight-foot-high Scottish thistles, stone troughs of flowers and a goldfish pond. What was once a cheese room in the farmhouse is now part of the raftered, stone-walled sitting-room, furnished with coral and turquoise sofas and antiques. The equally big, 14th-century dining-room has log stove, grand piano

and a fine dresser. Each of the chairs, made in Yorkshire in the 17th century, has a different carved portrait-head on it. Up a wide oak stair are bedrooms that have views of Offa's Dyke, the Black Mountains and the Sugarloaf. (Margaret Williams does snack suppers only.) £14. [Tel: 0981 240322; postcode: HR2 0DW]

THE GRANARY   M S
Main Street, Clanfield, Oxfordshire, OX18 2SH   Tel: 036781 266
South-west of Witney. Nearest main road: A4095 from Witney to Faringdon.

3 Bedrooms. £15–£17 (less for 7 nights or continental breakfast). Prices go up from June. Bargain breaks. Some have own bath/toilet. Tea/coffee facilities. Views of garden, country, river. No smoking. Washing machine on request.
1 Sitting-room. With central heating, TV. No smoking.
Small garden

A willow-fringed stream runs alongside the village road as it pursues its course to the Thames. On the other side are an 18th-century cottage, Victorian shop and old granary that have been turned into a guest-house. There is a beamed dining-room, and guests have their own sitting-room. The best and quietest bedroom is on the ground floor (with its own bathroom); the others are above. Throughout, Rosina Payne's house is spotless, airy and decorated in light and pretty colours. (B & b only; good bar meals are available at the Clanfield Tavern.)

This part of the Cotswolds is full of interest. One drives through a landscape threaded with streams, among fields where cows or sheep doze in the sun. In late spring, Queen Anne's lace billows along every verge, and apple-blossom dances in sugar-pink against bright blue skies. The lanes lead one to such famous sights as Bourton-on-the-Water, Stow-on-the-Wold, Bibury watermill, Burford (and its wildlife park), Witney's farm museum or old Minster Lovell Hall. Further afield are Cirencester, Cheltenham, Oxford and Woodstock (with Blenheim Palace). But there is no need to go far for interesting things to do. Just along the road is Radcot and the oldest bridge over the Thames, from which (in summer) narrow-boat trips set out for 18th-century Lechlade.

Readers' comments: Warm and friendly. Accommodation excellent, breakfast delicious. We couldn't praise enough.

At **MORAR FARM**, Weald Street, in nearby Bampton, Janet and Terry Rouse take exceptional care of their guests – whether it is by involving them in their many activities (Morris-dancing, bell-ringing, spinning wool) or by their close attention to detail (two fresh towels provided daily, unlimited fruit juices at breakfast, fill-ing vacuum flasks free of charge, etc.). Their home is a modern stone house, comfortable and trim, which stands in an attractive garden. During winter, Janet may serve a meal comprising home-made soup, beef with Yorkshire pudding and six vegetables, Bakewell

pudding and fruit to follow. No smok-ing. £15–£19 (b & b).
Reader's comments: Excellent! Janet is a delight. Sunday bell-ringing was a highlight of our trip. [Tel: 0993 850162; postcode: OX18 2HL]]

124

Church Road, Bitton, Avon, BS15 6LJ   Tel: 0272 322423
North-west of Bath. Nearest main road: A431 from Bristol to Bath
(and M4, junction 18).

3 Bedrooms. £14–£16 (less for 3 nights or continental breakfast). Views of garden, country. No smoking. Washing machine on request.
Dinner. £9 for 4 courses and coffee, at times to suit guests (not Thursdays). Non-residents not admitted. Wine can be brought in. No smoking.
1 Sitting-room. With open fire, central heating, TV, piano. No smoking.
Small garden
Closed in January and February.

Where once the Romans had a camp, the Normans built a manor house – now called the Grange – with a vast, separate kitchen (and a big, stone pigeon-house to supply the table). Granchen is that kitchen: it was altered by John Wood, the celebrated 18th-century architect of Bath, who gave it the distinctive round windows and triple arches which make its façade unique. (He lived at the Grange while working on nearby Bath.) The ruined pigeon-house can be seen in the lovely walled garden, in the shadow of the church's great, crocketted tower (adorned with the heads of Edward III and his queen, in whose time it was built), among the gargoyles of which kestrels sometimes nest.

The stone-flagged sitting-room is dominated by an enormous arched, stone inglenook – it looks big enough to spit-roast an ox. Liberty curtains in glowing colours contrast with pale blue walls, Valerie Atkins' patchwork cushions match the russet tones of the oriental rugs, and to one side of the hearth are her elegant appliqué pictures of farm gates and hedgerows (she trained at art school and some of her creations are on sale at Granchen). On Thursday evenings, a local madrigal group gathers round her Bechstein to practise with her.

Valerie's other accomplishments include cooking. Using garden produce, she prepares such meals as chicken-and-lentil soup, baked gammon with cauliflower cheese, and redcurrant fool. Meals are served in a coral dining-room (with unusual, carved stickback chairs from Canada) which looks through a pilastered archway into her kitchen.

Everywhere there are interesting touches – wildflower wallpaper in a bathroom, a dresser with blue-and-white china and, in the garden, clematis scrambling through the boughs of a rare apple-tree which bears red-fleshed fruit.

Readers' comments: Perfect. Lovely house, made very welcome. Charming atmosphere. Beautiful house. A lovely time.

Some proprietors stipulate a minimum stay of two nights at weekends or peak seasons; or they will accept one-nighters only at short notice (that is, only if no lengthier booking has yet been made).

THE GRANGE   **C PT S**
Alverstone, Isle of Wight, PO36 0EZ   Tel: 0983 403729
North of Shanklin. Nearest main road: A3055 from Ryde to Ventnor.

7 **Bedrooms.** £18.50–£20.50 (less for 4 nights). Prices go up in June. All have own bath/shower/toilet. Tea/coffee facilities. Views of country.
Dinner. From £13.50 for 4 courses (with choices) and coffee, at 6.30–7.30pm. Non-residents not admitted. Vegetarian or special diets if ordered. Wine can be brought in. No smoking. **Light suppers** if ordered.
1 **Sitting-room.** With open fire, central heating, TV, piano. No smoking.
Garden
Closed in December and January.

This immaculate guest-house, with light and modern rooms, was once the hunting-lodge of Lord Alverstone – MP for the island and Lord Chief Justice at the turn of the century. He built the whole village (around an old mill recorded in Domesday Book), the first in England to have water piped to each house because he banned strong drink in his village, which is why there is still no inn.

Geraldine Watling not only provides very good meals (she is a qualified cook) but is most helpful with books and maps for walkers: the island is threaded with scenic footpaths. In winter, she organizes activity weekends such as fossil-hunting with the local dinosaur expert. (Baby-sitting can also be arranged.)

Meals usually comprise a soup such as carrot and barley, a roast or a dish such as boeuf bourguignonne, and then a traditional pudding (like steamed apple and syrup pudding) with the option of a light alternative such as lemon chiffon.

Readers' comments: Effortless efficiency. Relaxed and happy atmosphere. Imaginative cooking. Warm and welcoming. Excellent accommodation, wonderful food.

In Shanklin itself is **CAVENDISH HOUSE**, Eastmount Road, with particularly pretty rooms, Laura Ashley fabrics and well-chosen colours complementing antiques. Lesley Peters has emphasized the architectural features of the Victorian house by, for instance, painting the plasterwork vine of one ceiling blue, and filling an old tiled fireplace with pot-plants. Each bedroom has a table and chairs for breakfast as there is no dining-room. For other meals, guests go into Shanklin. A nearby cliff-lift takes you down to the sands, or you can

walk through the famous scenic chine (a steep ravine). Buses go to all parts of the island. Outstanding sights are Osborne House and Carisbrooke Castle. £15–£16.50. [Tel: 0983 862460; postcode: PO37 6DN]

126

THE GRANGE
New Road, Burton Lazars, Leicestershire, LE14 2UU   Tel: 0664 60775
South-east of Melton Mowbray. Nearest main road: A606 from Melton
Mowbray to Oakham.

3 **Bedrooms.** £18.50 **to readers of this book only.** All have own bath/shower/toilet. Tea/coffee facilities. TV. Views of garden, country. Balcony (one). No smoking. Washing machine on request.
Dinner. £12.50 for 4 courses and coffee, from 7pm. Non-residents not admitted. Vegetarian or special diets if ordered. Wine can be brought in. **Light suppers** if ordered.
2 **Sitting-rooms.** With open fire, central heating, TV. No smoking in one.
Large garden

Until recently this was the home of the McAlpine family – a creeper-covered country mansion in 18th-century style with such features as leaded window-panes, arches, prettily plastered ceiling and barley-sugar banisters on the oak staircase.

Pam Holden has decorated the rooms with imagination, and hung the walls with good paintings. In one aquamarine sitting-room are shell-pink armchairs; in another, snug and with an open fire, is Chinese-style wallpaper. There is one rosy ground-floor bedroom with a large bathroom; a yellow bedroom upstairs has its own balcony. The four-poster room has a particularly good bathroom (and every guest is provided with an outsize bath-sheet).

Landscaped grounds include a sunken garden, orchard with pony, and paved terrace with chairs from which to enjoy the view across terraced lawns to the Vale of Stapleford, tea- or coffee-cup in hand.

Pam, a trained cook, enjoys preparing such dinners as melon with straw-berries, chicken tarragon, pecan pie and cheeses.

As to the strange name of the village, in the Middle Ages it was a leper (lazar) colony, established here because of the reputedly healing properties of the local spring water.

Melton Mowbray, of pork-pie and fox-hunting fame, has had a market from Saxon times and this is still carried on in the big Market Square. Its church is the finest in the county. In the great mansion of Stapleford Park are treasures that include a collection of 400 Staffordshire statuettes; other stately homes are Burghley (on a hilltop with fine views), the mediaeval Bede House at Lyddington; and, of course, great Belvoir Castle which dominates the Vale of Belvoir below it. Rutland Water is near. There are magnificent tombs in Bottesford's church and an exceptional carved arch in Tickencote's. Wing has a rare mediaeval maze; Waltham-on-the-Wolds, a smock windmill; Uppingham, the 16th-century courts and quadrangles of its famous school; Oakham, a market square still with stocks and butter-cross. All around are undulating hills (wolds), with small woods among sheep pastures threaded by a maze of lanes and cottages of pinkish stone which have slate or thatched roofs.

For explanation of code letters (C, D, M, PT, S, X) see page xlvi.

127

THE GRANGE   C(12)

Torrington Lane, East Barkwith, Lincolnshire, LN3 5RY   Tel: 0673 858249

North-east of Lincoln. Nearest main road: A157 from Wragby to Louth.

Views of garden, country. No smoking. Washing machine on request.
Dinner. £12 for 3–4 courses (with choices), sherry and coffee, at 7pm. Vegetarian or special diets if ordered. Wine can be brought in. No smoking. **Light suppers** if ordered.
1 Sitting-room. With open fire, central heating, piano. No smoking – another room is kept for smokers.
Large garden

3 Bedrooms. £18. All have own bath/shower/toilet. Tea/coffee facilities. TV.

Anne Stamp frequents salerooms for the 'unconsidered trifles' which give so much character to her home – such things as the looking-glass painted with flowers, the Victoriana in the sitting-room, the old baskets which, along with dried flowers, hang from kitchen beams, china in the alcoves, and chairs with heraldic lions.

The house deserves all the thought she puts into it. Built in 1820, it has a pink-walled hall with stained glass door, black-and-white floor tiles and a graceful staircase. Sash windows are deep-set in shuttered embrasures. Anne has furnished the sitting-room with pink and blue flowery sofas and prettily draped curtains. A second (family) sitting-room, with television, leads to a conservatory full of flowery pot-plants and a lawn with swing-settee, croquet and tennis.

Along a Turkey-carpeted corridor are equally attractive bedrooms – for instance, one has William Morris tiger-lilies on blinds, wallpaper and bedspread (and a sparkling, all-white shower room); another, delicate lace and roses; a third, cream satin (its gold-tapped bath is oval).

Anne (who writes short stories for women's magazines when not looking after her guests) serves such well-chosen menus as cucumber soup, pheasant, and half-melons filled with raspberries (there are choices of starters and puddings). And when a long-stay visitor suggested she might want a night off, she declined – saying she preferred to stay in and enjoy her guests.

The Grange has won a major conservation award; and there are nature trails with 'Walkman' commentary.

Lincolnshire is the county to choose if you want to unwind in the peace of a remote and solitary countryside, where the skies are open wide and the pace is slow-changing. One can motor at leisure untroubled by other traffic.

Caistor is high enough up in the Wolds to have views of distant Lincoln cathedral. It developed from a Roman camp to a peaceful market town. In its part-Saxon church is a fine Crusader tomb. Kingerby, too, has outstanding church monuments and woodlands full of wildflowers in spring. Tealby is a particularly beautiful Wolds village by the River Rase where Tennyson often walked to Hainton where there is a park that was landscaped by Capability Brown.

Readers' comments: Most enjoyable, strongly recommended. The standard of food, presentation, etc. could not have been bettered. Very comfortable house, beautifully furnished. Welcomed as friends; excellent food. Wonderful ambience, perfect hosts. Perfect: impossible to find fault. A real joy. Comfort, hospitality and food first-class. Truly delightful.

THE GRANGE
C(5) **S X**

Sunderland Hill, Ravensden, Bedfordshire, MK44 2SH Tel: 0234 771771

North of Bedford. Nearest main road: A428 from Bedford towards St Neots
(and M1, junction 14).

rear view

3 Bedrooms. £17–£18 (less for 4 nights or continental breakfast). Some have own bath/shower/toilet. Tea/coffee facilities. TV. Views of garden, country. No smoking. Washing machine on request.
Dinner. £12.50 for 3 courses (with choices), sherry and coffee, from 6pm. Vegetarian or special diets if ordered. Wine can be brought in. No smoking. **Light suppers** if ordered.
2 Sitting-rooms. With log stoves, central heating, TV, video, cassette-player.
Large garden

This large manor house has been divided into three dwellings, of which No. 1 is the handsome home of Patricia Roberts, with views downhill of terraced lawns and great cedars, flowering shrubs and a copper beech. Patricia has furnished the rooms in keeping with the architectural style. Good paintings (some by her daughter) hang on silky coral walls; silver, big velvet armchairs and Chippendale furniture are in one room; in another the tulips and pinks of curtain and sofa fabric have inspired the colour scheme for the whole room. Even the bathrooms are carpeted and have flowery wallpaper. The snug little dining-room is in fact a book-lined alcove behind a blue satin curtain (sometimes another is brought into use when there are two families being accommodated). Baby-sitting facilities.

Dinner is very attractively presented. Salmon and pheasant often appear on the menu but guests can have whatever they like if it is ordered in advance. Beans, asparagus, strawberries and spinach are among the produce grown in the garden. (Sunday lunch also available.)

Patricia has much information to share about sightseeing in Bedfordshire, and about the best places in which to hunt for antiques. A squadron of the US Air Force was based at the Grange during the Second World War.

It is still possible to identify, in and around Bedford, places which inspired passages in Bunyan's *The Pilgrim's Progress*. Bedford has, in addition to its Bunyan Museum and a notable church, a good traffic-free shopping centre, twice-weekly market and fast trains to London. There are long garden walks beside the lovely River Ouse (boat trips, too). All around the town are pretty villages. At Cardington one can see ballooning and the giant sheds which once housed airships. Elstow (Bunyan's birthplace) has an old moot hall with museum, and half-timbered houses; Felmersham is a boating centre; Harrold has an ancient bridge and country park, Odell castle grounds, Podington old cottages and Hinwick Hall. A nature reserve in gravel-pits is at Sharnbrook, bird gardens at Stagsden, a windmill at Stevington, and an extraordinary Tudor dovecote (for 1500 birds) at Willington. A little further afield, Woburn Abbey (and safari park), Whipsnade Zoo, Dunstable Downs (to watch gliders), Wrest Park gardens, Luton Hoo (art treasures), Bedford's country park and Grafham Water are sights worth half a day.

Readers' comments: Nothing too much trouble. Food delicious. Charming hostess. Wished we could have stayed longer. Dinners imaginatively prepared. Elegantly furnished, and every comfort. Kind welcome, we felt at home. Excellent.

129

GRASSFIELDS

CDS

Wath Road, Pateley Bridge, North Yorkshire, HG3 5HL   Tel: 0423 711412
North of Harrogate. Nearest main road: A59 from Harrogate to Skipton.

9 Bedrooms. £19 (**to readers of this book only**) – £22. Less for 3 nights. Prices go up in April. Bargain breaks. All have own bath/shower/toilet. Tea/coffee facilities. TV. Views of garden, country. Washing machine on request.
Dinner. £12 for 3 courses and coffee, at 7pm. Non-residents not admitted. Vegetarian or special diets if ordered. Wine can be ordered. **Light suppers** if ordered.
2 Sitting-rooms. With open fire, central heating, TV. Bar.
Large garden
Closed in December and January.

This country house is set back from the road, in its own gardens: it is a handsome Georgian building surrounded by lawns and trees. All the rooms are spacious and comfortably furnished. Barbara Garforth studies her visitors' interests and provides helpful information on local areas of interest, including many local walks. There is a tranquil and informal atmosphere.

Meals are prepared from local vegetables and produce wherever possible, including free-range eggs and Nidderdale lamb. A typical menu: pear and cream cheese salad, local beef, apple and mincemeat tart – all in generous quantities. There is a wide selection of wines.

Pateley Bridge is an interesting small town (in an area of outstanding natural beauty) with a number of good shops, set on a junction of several roads, which makes it a fine centre from which to go sightseeing. Grassfields is in the heart of Nidderdale, where there are crags, glens, lakes and How Stean gorge.

Lovely Nidderdale, being outside the National Park area, is less frequented than some other dales. It has some very old reservoirs created by damming the River Nidd, now well naturalized and full of ducks, geese, herons and other birds (200 species have been recorded, including some rare migrants). The effect is reminiscent of the Lake District. How Stean is a romantic gorge with a stream cascading into a rocky cleft 70 feet deep (good home-made cakes at the modest café nearby). From the churchyard at Middlemoor, high up at the head of the dale, there are spectacular views down the length of it.

From here one can easily motor to a number of Yorkshire's spectacular abbeys – Bolton, Jervaulx, and Byland. Also Harewood Hall, Newby Hall and garden, and half a dozen castles; as well as the strange natural formations of Brimham Rocks.

Readers' comments: Stayed twice: excellent. Most comfortable and quiet. Most helpful. Very fine food. Well furnished. Good food and plenty of it. Thoroughly enjoyed our stay, and every mouthful. Wonderful.

> **When writing to me, if you want a reply please enclose an International Reply Coupon.**

GREEN LANE HOUSE

C D PT X

Green Lane, Hinton Charterhouse, Somerset, BA3 6BL   Tel: 0225 723631
South of Bath (Avon). Nearest main road: A36 from Bath to Warminster.

4 Bedrooms. £18.50–£24.50 (less for 3 nights). Some have own shower/toilet. Tea/coffee facilities. Views of garden. Washing machine on request.
Light suppers if ordered.
1 Sitting-room. With open fire, central heating, TV.
Small garden

The hilly village of stone houses with colourful gardens gets its name from the Carthusian ('charter house') monks who in the 13th century had a priory here, its remains still to be seen though not open to the public. The house (originally three cottages) dates from 1725 and descendants of the family who inhabited it then still live in the village.

Today it belongs to Christopher Davies and his wife Juliet who previously spent nearly 30 years in hotel management overseas.

Past owners had restored such features as an old fireplace in one room and a massive stone inglenook in another, board doors and round-arched, wood-shuttered windows: these contrast with more modern furnishings and colour schemes – huge, white cutwork ginger-jars as bedroom lamps, lyre-back dining-chairs, bamboo-patterned tiles in a very pretty bathroom, comfortable Parker Knoll chairs in the bedrooms. The Davieses have added mementoes from their years overseas, including alabaster from Oman, papyrus paintings from Egypt, curiously shaped palm fruits from the Seychelles and an ostrich egg from Tanzania. There is a walled cottage-garden.

Sitting-room at Deepleigh (see page 89)

131

GREENHAM HALL

CDX

Greenham, Somerset, TA21 0JJ   Tel: 0823 672603

West of Wellington. Nearest main road: A38 from Wellington towards Exeter (and M5, junctions 26/27).

6 Bedrooms. £17.50–£20 (less for 4 nights). Some have own shower/toilet. Views of garden, country. Washing machine on request.
Light suppers if ordered.
2 Sitting-rooms. With open fire, central heating, TV, piano.
Large garden

This great castellated pile with buttresses topped by barley-sugar finials stands on a commanding hilltop site. It was built at the height of the Gothic Revival period, but fell on hard times – in some of its splendid, high-ceilinged rooms, hay and even tractors were stored. Then the Ayre family came here and restored the mansion including the west wing (to left of picture) where extra bedrooms are available.

Rooms have impressive floor-to-ceiling windows, arched and stone-mullioned; solidly made, panelled doors; and ogee arches. From the huge galleried hall (with log stove, concert piano and the biggest dresser I have ever seen – carved and inlaid), a staircase with 'gothick' banisters and stained-glass windows rises to the bedrooms. The very large family room is especially impressive, with carved bed-heads and a bay window-seat from which to enjoy the sight of terrace, lawn and stately trees. (Weekend courses – from painting and creative writing to the Alexander technique.)

Readers' comments: Very comfortable and pleasant.

PINKSMOOR MILLHOUSE is a complete contrast (at nearby Pinksmoor, closer to Wellington), parts of it dating back to the 13th century. The river and mill leat provide an attractive setting (with herons, kingfishers, snipe and dragonflies to be seen – occasionally, badgers too). The Ashes won a wildlife conservation award. Comfortable furniture and an inglenook fireplace give the rooms character. There is a particularly good room (en suite) from which you can watch pedigree cows being milked; and a twin-bedded room with beams and a sofa from which to birdwatch through the picture-windows. Old mill gear can still be seen in an outhouse, and a col-

lection of vintage tractors. For dinner, Nancy Ash serves such dishes as grapefruit with rum and brown sugar, roast beef with home-grown vegetables, a choice of puddings such as rhubarb crumble and cheeses. £17 (b & b). [Tel: 0823 672361; postcode: TA21 0HD]

GREY GABLES   C D
Norwich Road, near Cawston, Norfolk, NR10 4EY   Tel: 0603 871259
North-west of Norwich. Nearest main road: B1149 from Norwich to Holt.

6 Bedrooms. £19–£28 (less for 2 nights). Prices go up in March. Bargain breaks. All have own bath/shower/toilet. Tea/coffee facilities. TV. Views of garden, country.
Dinner. £15.50 for 3 courses (with choices) and coffee, at 7pm. Vegetarian or special diets if ordered. Wine can be ordered. No smoking. **Light suppers.**
2 Sitting-rooms. With open fire, central heating. **Bar.**
Large garden

Every year James and Rosalind Snaith travel in Europe looking for interesting new wines and recipes to add to their repertoire, for this former rectory is no ordinary guest-house. There is a choice of a three-course dinner or five-course feast that may include, after an hors d'oeuvre, creamed salmon or Italian bean soup, chicken Wellington with apricots in puff pastry, or fillet steak with Marsala sauce, choux filled with lemon curd and cream, and then cheeses.

They have rung the changes on blue-and-beige colour schemes in nearly every room from the Victorian-style sitting-room and up the elegant mahogany staircase to the bedrooms. Dinner is eaten at mahogany tables with velvet-upholstered chairs; silver, rosy Royal Albert china and candles make it an elegant occasion. I was looking at a needlework sampler made by Rosalind's great-aunt in the 'twenties when her mother told me embroidery had been a family tradition through at least four generations of craftswomen ('We never buy anything if we can embroider it ourselves!'): Rosalind herself continues it.

My favourite bedroom is no. 1: pretty fireplace, big bay windows.

There is a grass tennis court.

Readers' comments: Excellent; marvellous food. Very friendly, good food. Very comfortable and friendly.

At 17th-century **ROOKERY FARM**, in Church Street, Reepham (a handsome conservation village), there is indeed a lively rookery – horses too; a pool; and drifts of wild daffodils in spring. Stripped pine doors and shuttered windows give character to rooms that have green and white or pink colour schemes. Bedrooms are reached via a curving staircase. Gill Goff's breakfasts include home-baked bread. Baby-sitting and use of kitchen available. £16–£17.
Readers' comments: Helpful, friendly.

Large and attractive rooms; we extended our stay from two to six nights. Very pleasant and comfortable. Very high standards. [Tel: 0603 871847; postcode: NR10 4JW]

GREYS

C(10) **S**

Margaret Roding, Essex, CM6 1QR   Tel: 0245 231509

North-west of Chelmsford. Nearest main road: A1060 from Bishop's Stortford to Chelmsford.

3 Bedrooms. £16–£18 (less for 3 nights or continental breakfast). Prices may go up in April. Tea/coffee available. Views of garden, country. No smoking.
Light suppers if ordered.
1 Sitting-room. With central heating, TV. No smoking.
Large garden

Once a pair of farmworkers' cottages, Greys became the Matthews' home when they moved out of their large farmhouse to let their son take over management of the farm. They painted the exterior apricot – in typical East Anglian style – and furnished the rooms simply (a mixture of Habitat and antiques) and with light, clear colours. The beamed breakfast-room has pine furniture and honeysuckle-patterned curtains; from the sitting-room, a glass door opens onto the large garden.

'It's lovely when guests book in for one night and then stay for several,' says Joyce. This often happens because so many people think Essex consists of Dagenham's motorworks, Southend's trippers and little else – then, when they come here, find a revelation.

The eight Roding villages include some of England's prettiest, in an area of winding streams and lanes, flowery inns, colourwashed houses with pargeted walls (decorative plasterwork) under thatched roofs. Many visitors arrive at Harwich or at Stansted Airport, then base themselves here to visit London (¾-hour by train from Epping), Cambridge, Roman Colchester and the rest of East Anglia. But there is much to enjoy close by, including picturesque Thaxted (which has music festivals and a church of cathedral-like splendour), old Dunmow which still has the four-yearly award of the Dunmow Flitch to happily married couples – the next ceremony, complete with bewigged judge, will be in 1996, Greenstead (unique Saxon church made of wood), and the attractive towns of Saffron Walden and Bishop's Stortford.

These are only a beginning. Go to Waltham Abbey for the enormous church where King Harold was buried after defeat by William the Conqueror. To Maldon to see great, russet-sailed sailing-barges along the picturesque waterfront. To Mersea for the oysterage. To Clacton for the pleasures of an old-fashioned seaside resort. At Mountfichet Castle you might find a wildflower festival in full swing or a herbal weekend; in one of many fine manor gardens, a typical country fête; on village greens, Morris dancers; windmills in full sail; great shire horses on show at Toppesfield; displays of sheep-shearing; exhibitions by the many local craftsmen and artists; guided walks. The area also has the Imperial War Museum's collection of historic aircraft, etc. (at Duxford), two wildlife parks and numerous National Trust properties within easy reach. Saffron Walden has a museum internationally renowned for its 'worlds of man' gallery, particularly the Aborigine exhibits.

Every night you could dine at a different, excellent local inn: the Black Bull at Fyfield, the Cock & Bell at High Easter, and many others.

Reader's comment: Warmth and good food.

134

GROVE HOUSE   C(5) S
Hamsterley Forest, County Durham, DL13 3NL   Tel: 0388 488203
West of Bishop Auckland. Nearest main road: A68 from Darlington to
Consett.

3 **Bedrooms.** £19.50 (less for 7 nights).
Tea/coffee facilities. Views of garden,
country. No smoking. Washing machine on
request.
Dinner. £11 for 4 courses and coffee,
at 7.30pm. Vegetarian or special diets if
ordered. Wine can be brought in. No
smoking. **Light suppers** if ordered.
2 **Sitting-rooms.** With open fire, central
heating, TV, record-player. Bar. No
smoking.
Large garden
Closed in December.

Hamsterley Forest is a 5000-acre Forestry Commission holding in the hills of
County Durham. Much of it consists of commercial conifers, but down one side
lie 1000 acres of old mixed woodland, which the Forestry Commission manages
for recreational purposes, with drives, waymarked walks, two rivers, a visitor
centre and so on. A few houses are buried in this beautiful forest, among them
Grove House, once an aristocrat's shooting-box; another is the home of
David Bellamy.

Grove House is now the home of businessman Russell Close, his wife Helene
and their three children. It is a peaceful place, surrounded by its own big gardens
and reached only by a forest road (private but metalled). The windows of the
prettily furnished guest-rooms look across the lawn into the forest, where you may
see woodpeckers at work. Birdsong is the loudest sound you will hear.

The downstairs rooms have a touch of aristocratic grandeur, with the
addition of some unusual fittings brought from Germany by Helene's grand-
parents, from whom she inherited them (notice the art deco doorhandles).
Settees and armchairs in the enormous sitting-room are covered in William
Morris fabrics.

Helene prepares all the food from fresh ingredients. Meals usually consist of
a first course such as a fish gratin; home-made soup; followed by a main
course which is often game from the forest; and then a cold sweet such as
meringues with ice cream and hot chocolate sauce. She discusses guests'
preferences beforehand.

Visitors using the self-catering cottage can take meals in the house.

Bicycle hire and pony trekking are available, but should you tire of walking,
driving, cycling or simply sitting in the forest, there is a huge expanse of deserted
heather moorland a few miles away. The other attractions of this little-known
county include High Force waterfall, Raby Castle, the magnificent Bowes
Museum (château-style), Beamish open-air museum and of course Durham
cathedral.

Readers' comments: Delicious, imaginative food. Fairytale house in beautiful setting. Good value. Greeted as old friends. A wonderful 'find'; it was perfect.
Idyllic. Exceptionally varied menus, beautifully cooked. Excellent. Marvellous
situation, food and welcome. Absolutely charming. A trip to paradise!

GUITING GUEST-HOUSE   C D PT S
Post Office Lane, Guiting Power, Gloucestershire, GL54 5TZ
Tel: 0451 850470
West of Stow-on-the-Wold. Nearest main road: A436 from Andoversford towards Stow-on-the-Wold.

3 Bedrooms. £18.50–£22 (less for 4 nights). Prices go up at Easter. All have own shower/toilet. Tea/coffee facilities. TV. Views of garden, country. Washing machine on request.
Dinner. A la carte or £15 for 3 courses (with choices) and coffee, at 7pm. Non-residents not admitted. Vegetarian or special diets if ordered. Wine can be brought in. No smoking. **Light suppers** if ordered.
2 Sitting-rooms. With open fire, central heating, TV, record-player.
Small garden

This is a quintessential Cotswold village with stone cross on a green, mossy roofs, roses and wisteria clambering up mellow, sun-soaked walls – much of it just the same as four centuries ago. The name refers to the River Windrush which flows by ('gyting' is Saxon for a rushing brook) and to a 13th-century magnate, le Poer, who owned the village at the time when wool-weaving was beginning to prosper.

The village once had five inns – of which this house, then known as the Bell, was one – thronged with beer-drinkers during the Whitsuntide Fair. It still has its celebratory occasions but of a quite different kind: an annual music festival every July. And there are still hill sheep with particularly fine, white fleece – though preserved as a rare breed now, at the nearby farm park (see below). All around are lanes or footpaths with a great variety of wildflowers.

Changes to the 450-year-old guest-house have been done with sensitivity. New pine doors have wood latches; the dining-room floor is made of solid elm planks from Wychwood Forest; logs blaze in a stone fireplace with ogee arch; and in the snug sitting-room are flagstones with oriental rugs (elsewhere in the house are rag rugs which Yvonne Sylvester made herself). Yvonne has filled a bay window with begonias and shelves with china that she collects; her meals are served on wildflower-patterned china. Bedrooms are pleasantly decorated, with such touches as beribboned cushions or an old cane-backed rocking-chair, and four-posters. I particularly liked no. 2: through its stone-mullioned window is a view of another cottage made colourful by hanging flower-baskets.

As to dinner, Yvonne will cook whatever you want but a favourite menu is trout from a nearby fish farm, chicken in a lime and ginger sauce, strawberry baskets with cream, and cheeses.

The Cotswold Farm Park just north of the village is home to the Rare Breeds Survival Trust which exists to preserve historic breeds of farm animals that might otherwise die out, and here you can spend a day among, for instance, little Soay sheep first domesticated by Stone Age man and striped piglets of a prehistoric strain. Children can stroke baby animals in Pets Corner, adults can follow farm trails or watch various husbandry demonstrations.

Readers' comments: Extremely welcoming, nothing was too much trouble. Went out of their way to look after us. Charming house; spotless and tastefully decorated. Outstanding in every way. Marvellous hosts.

GUY WELLS

Eastgate (road), Whaplode, Lincolnshire, PE12 6TZ   Tel: 0406 422239

East of Spalding. Nearest main road: A151 from Spalding to King's Lynn.

3 Bedrooms. £16–£18.50 (less for 4 nights). Prices go up in April. One has own shower/toilet. Tea/coffee facilities. TV (by request). Views of garden, country. No smoking.

Dinner. £11.50 for 3 courses (with choices) and coffee, at 7 pm. Vegetarian or special diets if ordered. Wine can be brought in. No smoking. **Light suppers** if ordered.

1 Sitting-room. With log stove, central heating, TV, video. No smoking.

Large garden

Springs in the land around this Queen Anne house are what gave it its name. It is in a lovely and secluded position, surrounded by a traditional garden, trees, and beyond that the Fens. The Thompsons have daffodil and tulip fields as well as glasshouses where they cultivate spring flowers and lilies. Tour them with Richard, and buy flowers or bulbs to take home.

The interior of the house is full of imaginative touches – like the addition of an alcove with domed top and scallop-edged shelves to one side of the brick hearth where a log stove stands. Raspberry velvet tub chairs contrast with homely stripped-pine doors. And there is no sound louder than a slow-ticking clock.

Hall and staircase are pretty (with sprigged wallpaper, an old cedar chest, prints and bouquets of flowerheads dried by Anne), leading to the bedrooms – one of which is huge, with antique bedhead and en suite shower room. The best one of all has a spread with tucks and pink ribbons, and windows on two sides. One has a half-tester bed. Needlepoint weekends are run occasionally.

Visitors who choose Guy Wells do so in order to explore the superb churches of the county, to enjoy its birdlife or the spring flowers, for the easy cycling (it's a level area) or just for the peace.

And for Anne's wholefood cooking (using their own vegetables, honey and eggs). She makes all her own pâtés, soups, quiches or ratatouille for starters; a traditional roast or casserole may follow; and puddings like raspberry pavlova, cheesecake or (a speciality I found delectable) a crème brûlée in which yogurt combines with cream as a topping to brandied grapes.

From Whaplode, one can easily explore most of Lincolnshire and much of Cambridgeshire, too – Peterborough, in particular, is worth a day for its cathedral, river trips, local museums and shopping centre, all described elsewhere. Also easily accessible are King's Lynn, and royal Sandringham House which is now open to the public during the summer. Go to Boston for its great church and the Guildhall (museum, and the cells where the Pilgrim Fathers were imprisoned). Great houses in the vicinity include magnificent Belton and Burghley, Harlaxton Manor (its huge conservatory stocked by Kew Gardens), mediaeval Grantham House, and Woolsthorpe Manor (birthplace of Isaac Newton).

Readers' comments: Lovely people. Enjoyed the cooking so much. Delightful lady, friendly, excellent cook, very pleasant house. Lovely place, superb food, nice lady. Very warm welcome, happy atmosphere, glorious food. Interesting part of the country, have visited twice. Welcoming couple, pleasant place.

THE HALL
C(5) D PT S

Great Hucklow, Derbyshire, SK17 8RG   Tel: 0298 871175

North-east of Buxton. Nearest main road: A623 from Chapel-en-le-Frith towards Chesterfield.

3 Bedrooms. £18 (less for 4 nights). Price goes up in May. Views of garden, country.
Dinner. £13 for 3 courses and coffee, at 7pm. Vegetarian or special diets if ordered. Wine can be brought in.
1 Sitting-room. With wood stove. No smoking.
Large garden
Closed from December to February.

This, like many Derbyshire villages, is famous for summer 'well-dressings': huge mosaics of flower-petals depicting religious themes, each ushered in by a blessing of the well. To enjoy this floral event, stay at The Hall, where you can also see the Whatleys' south-facing garden when it is at its most colourful (Angela grows the vegetables, her mother-in-law – who lives in the Hall's converted barn – the flowers). Tourist Information Centres issue a leaflet with dates of all the well-dressings.

The sandstone Hall was built – on mediaeval foundations – soon after Charles I became King. Like **Highlow Hall** (see elsewhere), it was one of several in similar style which a Derbyshire farmer (Bagshaw, in this case) provided for each of his sons. Rows of small, mullioned windows give it particular charm, and in the former kitchen (now a sitting-room) the original fireplace, which would have housed a great spit, has been exposed. Walls three feet thick, which keep the house warm in winter and cool in summer, have here been painted cream, a good foil to the handsome furniture and unusual mirrors (some for sale) which John makes in his spare time. He has restored an unusual, very narrow, cellar-to-attic window (diamond-paned) which lights the staircase.

His craftsmanship is evident in the bedrooms too. For instance, in one of the very big family rooms there is a huge cockerel he carved, as well as stools and bedside tables made by him. The bath- and shower-rooms (cork, pitch-pine and unusual tiles) have more of his decorative mirrors.

Angela is a discriminating cook, using fresh garden produce, local game, and imaginative recipes. A typical dinner might comprise her own pâté (with watercress and toast); chicken pie accompanied by ratatouille, boulangère potatoes and plenty of other vegetables; then unusual water-ices (such as gooseberry and elderflower) accompanied by home-made biscuits. 'Proper' puddings are a speciality.

All around are the hills and lovely valleys of the Peak District and such sights as Chatsworth (and its garden centre), Haddon Hall and Monsal Dale. Lea Gardens are noted for rhododendrons. Buxton, over 1000 feet up in the hills, is a spa that was laid out in the 18th century to rival Bath. You can drink the waters (palatable – unlike many!) which well up, hot, from underground springs.

Readers' comments: More than satisfied. Dinner one of the most superb meals I have ever had, quite perfect. Most friendly welcome. Most enjoyable. Very comfortable. Excellent food. In a beautiful setting. Charming people. We couldn't have been better fed and looked after if we had been staying at the Ritz.

138

HALL FARMHOUSE
Gonalston, Nottinghamshire, NG14 7JA   Tel: 0602 663112
North-east of Nottingham. Nearest main road: A612 from Nottingham to
Southwell.

3 Bedrooms. £17.50 (less for 3 nights).
Some have own bath/shower/toilet. Tea/
coffee facilities. Views of garden. No
smoking. Washing machine on request.
Dinner (by arrangement). £12.50 for 3
courses (with choices), drinks and coffee,
7.30–8.45pm. Non-residents normally not
admitted. Vegetarian or special diets if
ordered. Wine can be ordered or brought in.
Light suppers if ordered.
2 Sitting-rooms. With open fires, central
heating, TV, piano, cassette-player.
Large garden

To the attractions of the house itself, which was built early in the 18th century,
are added the varied pleasures of a pretty garden which include rosebeds, an
aviary of budgerigars, a large heated swimming-pool, tennis court, fish-pond and
vegetable garden from which come asparagus and other produce for the dinner-
table. Stables have been converted to provide a games room (with table tennis).
Nearby are fields with Suffolk sheep that win prizes.

Rosemary Smith's visitors eat either in the beamed and quarry-tiled dining-
room (its French doors open onto the garden) or in the big kitchen. She uses a
lot of Prue Leith and Delia Smith recipes. (A typical dinner: tomato vinaigrette,
chicken Florida with rice and salad, applecake with clotted cream, and cheeses –
wine included.)

The sitting-rooms, also beamed and with oak floors, have antiques and, in
one, mallard-patterned sofas around the brick fireplace. A feature of the attractive
bedrooms are spreads Rosemary bought at the auction of a Sherwood Forest
mansion, Thoresby Hall.

Visitors come for a variety of reasons – to enjoy the National Watersports
Centre, to browse through the many antique shops, follow riverside walks, or visit
innumerable stately homes, such historic towns as Southwell and Newark, and
the Robin Hood exhibition in Sherwood Forest. Nottingham itself is full of
interest: the castle (now a fine museum – I enjoyed the jewellery department
especially) is perched on a 130-foot crag of stone riddled with tunnels and caves,
the lace museum is outstanding, there are some very ancient inns, and an 18th-
century quarter is well worth exploring on foot. There are trips on the River
Trent, a splendid natural history museum (in Elizabethan Wollaton Hall,
surrounded by a deer park), a good theatre, and, in Brewhouse Yard, a recreation
of bygone life in a group of old cottages. Other museums are devoted to canal
history, the Salvation Army (Booth's birthplace), costume and, at Eastwood,
D. H. Lawrence (his birthplace). At the pretty village of Papplewick is an
outstandingly ornate Victorian pumping-station.

Prices are per person in a double room at the beginning of the year.

HARDINGLAND FARMHOUSE
Macclesfield Forest, Cheshire, SK11 0ND Tel: 0625 425759
East of Macclesfield. Nearest main road: A537 from Macclesfield towards
Buxton.

3 Bedrooms. £17.50–£19. Some have own
bath. Tea/coffee facilities. Views of garden,
country. Washing machine on request.
Dinner. £12.50 for 3 courses (with choices)
and coffee, at 7pm (not Sundays). Non-
residents not admitted. Vegetarian or special
diets if ordered. Wine can be brought in.
Light suppers if ordered.
1 Sitting-room. With open fire, central
heating, TV.
Large garden
Closed from December to February.

It is exceptional to find at one house outstanding surroundings, food and furnishings: Hardingland is just such a place.

The secluded house is perched high up on the fringe of the Peak District, on a
hillside with stupendous panoramic views below. Anne Read's reputation is so
high that she has cooked for such demanding clients as the Manchester Stock
Exchange. *And* her 18th-century house has been furnished with style.

Before her marriage, Anne was a professional caterer, winning an award at
Buxton's Salon Culinaire in 1989. She uses a great many of John Tovey's Miller
Howe recipes when she prepares for her visitors such meals as: tarragon apples
with Boursin cheese; lamb cutlets in ginger and orange sauce; an array of imaginative vegetables like French beans with almonds, caramelized carrots, herbed
potatoes and orange and sunflower-seed salad; chocolate pots. The Reads' own
smallholding provides beef and lamb; venison comes from forest deer.

The large sitting-room has comfortable sofas covered in a William Morris
satin. Between the deep-set windows watercolours hang on the walls. The
beamed dining-room is furnished in Regency-style, and one of the bedrooms has
an attractive apricot and pale turquoise colour scheme. Bathrooms are excellent.

Outside, wide stone steps beside a lily-pool lead to a paved garden and lawn
sheltered by a stone-walled herbaceous bed. The garden is high above a deep
valley across which are hills and the pine plantations of Macclesfield Forest.

Readers' comments: Food excellent. Went to so much trouble. Whole atmosphere
very good, will go again. Beautifully furnished.

North of Leek (Staffordshire), in the
rural hamlet of Heaton, near Rudyard,
is 17th-century **FAIRBOROUGHS
FARM**. From the mullioned windows
of every spacious room are lovely views.
In the big, beamed dining-room
Elizabeth Lowe serves such typical farmhouse meals as home-made mushroom
soup, roast beef and fruit pies (beside a
crackling fire when evenings are cool).
One of the two bedrooms has an antique
Scottish pine bed. £12.50–£14.

Readers' comments: A charming couple.
Highly recommended. [Tel: 0260
226341; postcode: ST13 8PR]

140

HATTON HALL
C(10) **D X**

Hatton Hall Lane, Hatton Heath, Cheshire, CH3 9AP   Tel: 0829 70601

South-east of Chester. Nearest main road: A41 from Chester to Whitchurch.

4 Bedrooms. £16–£18 (less for 3 nights). One has own bath/shower/toilet. Tea/coffee facilities. TV. Views of garden, country, moat. Washing machine on request. **Light suppers** if ordered.
Large garden

A moat dug by Normans surrounds this large 18th-century house, at the heart of a big dairy-farm. Once there was even a drawbridge.

The bedrooms are beautifully decorated and particularly well equipped (bathrooms quite luxurious). Australian-born Shirley Woolley likes, for instance, traditional rosy cretonnes, country Chippendale chairs, an abundance of dried flowers, antique bedspreads of white crochet. One room has a chair from the Prince of Wales' investiture at Caernarfon Castle at which Shirley's father-in-law (Lord Woolley, former president of the NFU) was a guest.

Visitors dine in Chester or at local inns, as Shirley serves only breakfast (though for women travelling singly, she will do dinners), which includes unusual home-made jams (such as sloe-and-ginger or strawberry-and-loganberry) as well as honey 'which I steal from my bees at great risk to my person!'

Beyond the garden and the rose-bordered moat are stables with horses trained to compete at horse shows, as well as geese and free-ranging chickens ('I would use my own eggs if only I could find them!').

Readers' comments: Delightful. Genuinely friendly. A pleasure to stay. Beautiful house, wonderful hostess.

At nearby Tattenhall is a big dairy-farm and a 300-year-old house, **NEWTON HALL**, surrounded by gardens and fine views of both Beeston and Peckforton castles. Anne Arden's rooms have an air of solid comfort (the blue bedroom is particularly beautiful, with handsome Victorian mahogany furniture and an en suite bathroom). In the breakfast-room are wheelback chairs, oak table and dresser, the original quarry tiles, a brick fireplace, huge beams and oak doors with great iron hinges. Like those in the sitting-room, its casements open onto sweeping lawns.

(Snack suppers if ordered.) £16.50–£17.50.

Readers' comments: Exceptionally charming. Hostess of great care. Most warmly received. Outstanding. Very pleasant. Exceeded our expectations. [Tel: 0829 70153; messages: 0829 70215; postcode: CH3 9AY]

THE HAVEN   C D M PT S
Hardwicke, Herefordshire, HR3 5TA   Tel: 0497 831254
West of Hereford. Nearest main road: A438 from Hereford to Brecon.

6 Bedrooms. £19.50–£24.50 (less for 5 nights). Prices go up in April. Some have own bath/shower/toilet. Tea/coffee facilities. TV. Views of garden, country. No smoking. Washing machine on request.
Dinner. £11.50 for 4 courses (with choices) and coffee, at 7.30pm. Non-residents not admitted. Vegetarian or special diets if ordered. Wine can be ordered. No smoking.
Light suppers if ordered.
2 Sitting-rooms. With open fire, central heating, piano. No smoking in one. Bar.
Large garden
Closed in December and January.

Kilvert, a frequent visitor to this house when it was a vicarage and its garden much used for charity fêtes, wrote in his now famous diary that paintings done by the vicar's wife were auctioned – but her flowers and birds still adorn the door to one of the sitting-rooms. Here, through shuttered windows, are views of the hills.

There is a ground-floor bedroom (with bathroom) equipped to suit disabled people – even a wheelchair for use under the shower – and with a view of the unheated swimming-pool in the garden. Janet Robinson has stencilled the walls with a waterlily pattern to match the Liberty fabrics used in the furnishings.

In every room her flair for decoration is evident – a pretty chinoiserie wall-paper here, a sweet-pea paper there, cane bedhead in one room and a huge four-poster in another. One bathroom (raspberry and gold, with sunken bath, bidet and two basins) is not so much a bathroom as an event.

Meals are unusually imaginative: a nut-and-herb roulade might be followed by beef casseroled with ginger and then a creamy fool.

The Robinsons occasionally run special activity weekends on such subjects as Kilvert's diary, book-collecting (Hay-on-Wye is near) or 'hidden treasures'.

Readers' comments: Exceptional, have booked to go again. Kind and genuine hospitality. Very comfortable; food lovely. Very thoughtful, cooking outstanding. First-class room, food excellent. Friendly and stimulating company.

Just over the Welsh border, at Llanigon, is a dairy-farm with a big H-shaped house built in the year of the Spanish Armada: **TYNLLYNE** – 'house by the lake'. Low beams, three-foot-thick stone (or oak plank) walls and the turned balusters of the wide oak stair all date from that period. One bedroom has a high brass bed with broderie anglaise and a big carpeted bathroom. Outside is a terrace (with barbecue), an immaculate lawn, and a stream-and-woodland nature trail. For dinner, Lynda Price might serve melon with port, venison or a carbonnade of

beef, treacle pudding or chocolate mousse – always with many choices. £18 (b & b).
Readers' comments: The best food I have tasted, beautiful bathroom. [Tel: 0497 847342; postcode: HR3 5QF]

HAZEL TREE FARMHOUSE

C M S

Hassell Street, Hastingleigh, Kent, TN25 5JE   Tel: 0233 750324

North-east of Ashford. Nearest main road: A20 from Folkestone to Ashford.

5 Bedrooms. £16–£18 (less for 3 nights or continental breakfast). One has own wash-basin/toilet. Tea/coffee facilities. TV. Views of garden, country. Washing machine on request.

Dinner. £10 for 3 courses (with choices) and coffee, at 7.30pm. Non-residents not admitted. Vegetarian or special diets if ordered. Wine can be brought in. **Light suppers** if ordered.

1 Sitting-room. With open fire, central heating, TV, piano.

Large garden

Closed from December to March.

Small though this is, it is a true hall house: that is to say, an early mediaeval structure in which the ground floor consisted of one high communal room originally rising to the roof, with only a screen wall separating it from the dairy.

Christine Gorell Barnes and her artistic family have contributed greatly to the character of the old house, filling it with their paintings, tapestries and the results of a lifetime of collecting. There are old chests in a corridor, patchwork curtains and spreads on old brass beds, bunches of dried flowers and hop bines over a brick inglenook, books everywhere, and on the landing many generations of dolls, dolls' house and toys which young visitors are allowed to play with. One unusual treasure is an old dulcitone – a keyboard instrument in which the hammers strike a graduated row of steel tuning-forks, with bell-like sounds. Bedrooms are furnished in simple cottage style. Outside is a willow-fringed pool and a field with Christine's 14 sheep. (Painting weekends with tuition available.)

Meals are, like the old house itself, out of the ordinary. When I called, Christine was preparing borscht (beetroot soup), chicken baked with courgettes and accompanied by dauphinoise potatoes, and a spicy pumpkin pie.

WALNUT TREE FARMHOUSE at Lynsore Bottom, Upper Hardres, south of Canterbury, has one of the prettiest exteriors in Kent. Inside, too, it is full of charm. Gerald Wilton makes furniture, very decorative carved signboards, colourful decoy ducks and much else – including the long oak table which looks as if it, like the house itself, dates from the 14th century.

Guests' bedrooms (some in the house and others in a converted barn) are reached by broad step-ladders. Every wall and floor slopes a little. Crisp white fabrics, flower-sprigged, and pine fitments combine to give rooms an airy, cottagey feel. An attic one with low windows has the ancient king-post that supports the whole structure. No smoking. Swimming-pool. (B & b only; for evening meals, Sheila Wilton recommends the nearby Duck inn.) £18.50.

Readers' comments: Have returned many times, most exceptional. A lot of thought and care; made most welcome. Beautifully furnished. Made to feel like guests of the family. [Tel: 022787 375; messages: 022783 0931; postcode: CT4 6EG]

THE HAZELWOOD   **C M PT S** (in winter) **X**
24–25 Portland Street, York, YO3 7EH   Tel: 0904 626548
Nearest main road: A19 from Thirsk to York.

16 Bedrooms. £17–£23.50 (less for 7 nights). Prices go up from April. Most have own bath/shower/toilet. All have tea/coffee facilities. TV. Views of garden. No smoking. Washing on request.
1 Sitting-room. With central heating. Drinks can be ordered. No smoking.
Small garden

Being in a cul-de-sac leading only to the grounds of a public school, The Hazelwood is quiet despite its central position. So the noise of the busy York streets is not a problem for visitors to this pair of tall grey-brick houses in an 1860s terrace. And just across the main road is the largely pedestrianized heart of this historic city.

Joy and Peter Cox, who are most thoughtful hosts, both used to work in educational drama, and both are art-lovers: their collection, much of which is displayed on the walls of the public areas, is eclectic and interesting, and there are stories to be told about many of the paintings. Redouté rose prints decorate the bedrooms, most of which have silvery relief wallpaper and pink velvet furnishings (some have four-poster beds). The breakfast-room (no smoking) and the sitting-room contain lots of house-plants and interesting bits and pieces. At the back of the house is a small courtyard with tables and chairs – and one hazel tree. The Coxes keep menus from recommended restaurants. For early arrivals, there is some private parking – an advantage in central York.

Readers' comments: Excellently run, with good facilities, plus great courtesy and friendliness, and very quiet. Worth every penny.

Just outside the city walls, a little further from the minster but close to historic Clifford's Tower and the interesting Castle Museum, is **THE DAIRY** (3 Scarcroft Road), which was just that until only about 15 years ago: to prove it, a milk churn now planted with flowers stands in the creeper-hung yard at the back. Rooms are cottagey in style, with original Victorian joinery, plasterwork and fireplaces, furnished with sprigged fabrics and stripped pine. One of the best, off the yard, is the room where Yorkshire curd was made; another has the use of a big

Victorian bath. Breakfasts can be of wholefood. For dinner, there is an award-winning restaurant next door, or a big choice within walking distance. £15–£19. [Tel: 0904 639367; postcode: YO2 1ND]

144

HEATH HOUSE
Scords Lane, Toys Hill, Kent, TN16 1QE   Tel: 0732 750631
South-west of Sevenoaks. Nearest main road: A25 from Sevenoaks to Reigate
(and M25, junction 6).

2 Bedrooms. £15–£17.50 (less for 4 nights). TV. Views of garden, country. No smoking. Washing machine on request.
Light suppers if ordered.
Large garden

Octavia Hill, co-founder of the National Trust, lived near here (at Crockham Hill) – gardening, mapping the innumerable footpaths needing preservation, and ultimately presenting to the Trust the top of Toys Hill, which commands a superb view over the Weald of Kent. She followed this gift with Ide Hill 'for the people of England for ever . . . a breezy hill, wide view, woodland glades, tiny spring, all yours and mine and every citizen's for all time to come'. And so it all remains today, together with hundreds' more lovely acres in the area that are now in the Trust's possession. At her death in 1912, the government offered a Westminster Abbey funeral, but she is buried at her beloved Crockham.

It is over the scenery which she preserved that Heath House looks out, and from close by is one of the footpaths to Ide Hill which she mapped – a very pretty walk.

Two hundred years ago, it was just a cottage for workers at Scords Farm but it has been extended by Mike Murkin's own hard work to make the lovely home it is today. The original walls were built of 'Sevenoaks greenstone' quarried in the garden and, there being no more of this, Mike bought part of a demolished house made from it so that the new wing should be indistinguishable from the old, with clematis and honeysuckle climbing up both. Bedrooms have fresh, pale colour schemes. The sunny breakfast-room opens onto a paved terrace, a lawn with seats, and a view across a pond towards Ashdown Forest. If you want something more than one of Patricia's snack suppers, you can take the footpath to Four Elms and a good restaurant.

At Bough Beech, on the road to Tonbridge, is 15th-century **JESSOPS,** home of artist Frank Stark whose landscapes line the walls. Every room has unusual antiques and other interesting finds from afar. There are beams and lattice windows, pot-plants and bouquets of dried flowers, a buttoned leather sofa and grand piano in one room, William Morris sofa in another. Outside are a flowery garden and the Starks' pets: geese, ducks and dogs. Judith's excellent breakfasts include varied home-made breads, croissants

and her own marmalade. (Snack suppers by arrangement.) £15–£17.50. [Tel: 0892 870428; postcode: TN8 7AU]

HEAVERS   **C D**

Chapel Street, Ryarsh, West Malling, Kent, ME19 5JU   Tel: 0732 842074

West of Maidstone. Nearest main road: A228 from Tonbridge to Rochester
(and M20, junction 4).

2 Bedrooms. £15–£17 (less for 2 nights or continental breakfast). Prices go up in June. Bargain breaks. Tea/coffee facilities. Views of garden, country. No smoking. Washing machine on request.

Dinner (must be ordered in advance). £12 for 4 courses (with choices) and coffee, at 7.30pm. Non-residents not admitted. Vegetarian or special diets if ordered. Wine can be brought in. No smoking. **Light suppers** if ordered.

1 Sitting-room. With open fire, central heating, TV, video, piano, record-player. No smoking.

Large garden

Perched on a hilltop, this red brick farmhouse with dormer windows in the roof and clematis around the porch is at the heart of a smallholding which provides much of the produce that Jean Edwards (once a health visitor) enjoys cooking for her guests. Until a few decades ago, the old house was occupied by generations of the same farming family which built it in the 17th century. All around are country lanes, fields, woodlands and two long-distance footpaths.

The little sitting-room has very comfortable armchairs grouped around the brick hearth (stacked with logs), which still has the old bread oven alongside. It's a cosy room, with the soothing sound of clocks ticking, Gem (the Edwards' Jack Russell terrier) snoozing on the hearth, a collection of china pigs and good books.

Jean enjoys cooking a wide repertoire of dishes (whenever she travels in France, she always returns with new recipes). She bakes her own bread; honey, eggs and lamb are home-produced.

Beamed bedrooms with white-boarded, latched doors are prettily furnished with Laura Ashley fabrics and attractive colour schemes (pink or blue and white, or blue and yellow). The Edwards have collected stuffed birds and maps for the walls, and pot-plants for every window-sill. Through the windows are views of the Downs or of the garden which, even in winter, is colourful with witch hazel, holly berries and winter-flowering cherry trees. There's an old pump in it, a swing-seat on the brick patio, and a children's swing. Rooms are small. (Baby-sitting and bread-making tuition are available.)

Although only an hour from South London (Heathrow and Gatwick airports are even closer), this is a good centre from which to explore rural Kent, the mediaeval bridges of the upper Medway, and any number of castles – Allington, Leeds, Hever, Rochester – and historic buildings – Boughton Monchelsea house, the friary at Aylesford, Sissinghurst with its famous gardens, the Archbishop's Palace at Maidstone, Chartwell (Churchill's home) and Ightham Mote. There's county cricket, boating and sailing, and a famous collection of carriages at Maidstone. But the scenery is the main thing: hills, orchards, streams, hop gardens with their conical oast houses (you can visit Whitbread's hop farm), and picturesque villages.

Readers' comments: Very good indeed. As charming as could be; convivial hosts; mouth-watering and plentiful food. Charming house, food delicious.

HERMITAGE MANOR

Canon Pyon, Herefordshire, HR4 8NR   Tel: 0432 760317

North-west of Hereford. Nearest main road: A4110 from Hereford to Knighton.

3 Bedrooms. £18.50–£23 (less for continental breakfast). All have own bath/shower/toilet. Tea/coffee facilities. TV. Views of garden, country. No smoking. Washing machine on request.
Light suppers if ordered.
3 Sitting-rooms. With open fire, central heating, TV, piano. No smoking.
Large garden
Closed from December to February.

An *escalier d'honneur* sweeps grandly up to the front door which opens into a room of baronial splendour, its ceiling decorated with Tudor roses and strapwork, motifs which are repeated on the oak-panelled walls. Through stone-mullioned bay windows are some of the finest views from any house in this book. There is also a very lovely music room (damask walls and velvet chairs are in soft blue; the limewood fireplace has carved garlands). Throughout, carpets and other furnishings are of equal quality to the architecture.

The bedrooms, and their bathrooms, are of the highest standard and very large. No. 6 has a view of a hillside spring flowing through stepped pools of pinkish limestone (from a quarry in the area) which Shirley Hickling created when she was converting this exceptional house. She serves bed-and-breakfast and snack suppers only – but there are good inns nearby, and Hereford is only ten minutes away. (Croquet in the garden.)

Walking and watching the deer or birds are main attractions in this scenic area – the Wye Valley (with Symonds Yat viewpoint), Malvern Hills, Welsh border, Offa's Dyke path, Brecon Beacons and Black Mountains are all accessible. In addition there are historic houses to visit, rural museums, castles and abbeys.

Readers' comments: Magnificent view, magnificent bedrooms. So outstanding that we stayed several times this year and last.

Judy Seaborne's very good home cooking is the main attraction of **STONE HOUSE FARM**, Tillington. The setting is very peaceful, with fine views, and children in particular enjoy spring visits when there are lambs, calves and foals to be seen. A typical meal: homemade soup, a roast (the farm's own meat), fruit pie – served from Royal Worcester dishes, in a dining-room with log stove. (Sunday lunch and baby-sitting available, too.) Made of solid stone, the house is well away from any road, and has fine greenery beyond its small orchard. There is an old pump in the front garden. £16.

Readers' comments: Well fed and received with great friendliness. Food of high quality and ample. Most welcoming; excellent cook. [Tel: 0432 760631; postcode: HR4 8LP]

HIGH GREEN HOUSE

CDMSX

Nowton, Suffolk, IP29 2LZ   Tel: 0284 386293
South of Bury St Edmunds. Nearest main road: A134 from Bury St Edmunds
to Sudbury.

5 Bedrooms. £18–£22 (less for 7 nights or for continental breakfast). Prices go up in April. Bargain breaks. All have own shower/toilet. Tea/coffee facilities. TV. Views of garden, country. No smoking. Washing machine on request.
Dinner. £12.50 for 4 courses (with choices) and coffee, at times to suit guests. Non-residents not admitted. Vegetarian or special diets if ordered. Wine can be ordered. No smoking. **Light suppers** if ordered.
1 Sitting-room. With open fire, central heating, TV. Bar.
Large garden

Part Tudor and part Victorian, this delightful house is truly secluded – surrounded by brimming herbaceous borders, a paddock of geese and an old well, with wheatfields beyond. There are a lily-pool (it is all that remains of a moat), troughs of begonias and fuchsias, and, where only the great frame of a mediaeval barn survives, Rosemary Thew has created a sun-trap in which to sit, training scented roses and wisteria over the timbers and placing seats to face the view.

The interior of the house is full of nooks and crannies, cabinets of old china and glass, antique furniture and low beams. There are oriel and mullioned windows, a brick fireplace, and wrought-iron hinges on bedroom doors. Some bedrooms are small and simple; but one has a four-poster, windows on three sides, a carved chest and a cheval mirror with painted flowers. Rosemary (who worked with physically handicapped people until her retirement) has also provided a downstairs bedroom ideal for a disabled person. Baby-sitting available too.

Dinner can comprise a chicken vol-au-vent as a starter, then a good roast joint, profiteroles and cheese. She is a genial, informal lady with whom one immediately feels at home; and, because she was formerly clerk to the local council, she is a mine of information about the area (and its people).

Bury and its environs are described elsewhere. Also within easy reach are the great houses of Ickworth and Melford; pretty villages like Clare and Cavendish; the gardens at Bressingham – and antique shops everywhere.

Readers' comments: Warm welcome and excellent food. Most tranquil house. Miss Thew is delightful. Charming building; a bargain; Miss Thew is a character. Peaceful and friendly, nothing too much trouble. Warm welcome and personal attention. Took a lot of trouble; fed us royally. Lovely garden. Good food. Very good; charming lady. Splendid. Fascinating house; wonderful food. A hilarious time with kindred spirits. Excellent food.

HIGH GREENRIGG HOUSE   C D M S

Caldbeck, Cumbria, CA7 8HD   Tel: 06974 78430
South-west of Carlisle. Nearest main road: A595 from Carlisle to
Cockermouth.

7 Bedrooms. £17–£20 (less for 7 nights).
All have own bath/shower/toilet. Tea/coffee
facilities. Views of garden, country. No
smoking. Washing machine on request.
Dinner. £8 for 3 courses and coffee, at
7pm. Vegetarian or special diets if ordered.
Wine can be ordered. No smoking.
3 Sitting-rooms. With open fire, central
heating, TV, record-player. **Bar.**
Large garden
Closed in January and February.

Hidden in the moors three and a half miles above the village, this 17th-century
house has great character, with low doorways and stone lintels. Inside, modern
furnishings have been well chosen to suit the beamed interior with no attempt at a
'ye-olde' effect. Pine and cane predominate in the dining-room; in the sitting-
room, once a cow byre (now carpeted and very warm), there is a self-service
alcove where visitors can make unlimited tea and coffee. The bedrooms (which
include some on the ground floor) have pine fittings and bedheads, and they give
fine views of the surrounding fells. Good food is a speciality of Robin and Fran
Jacobs (who used to be an engineer and a social worker respectively). They share
the cooking and make their own bread, marmalade, ice cream, soups, etc. Their
buffet meals are designed to be light and healthy.

There is plenty of room for quiet relaxation in the evening; or one can go to a
games room with a mezzanine bar, where plate glass has replaced the barn doors.
This being an outstanding area for walkers, well away from the crowded part
of the Lake District, the Jacobs, with the help of a National Park ranger, have
prepared a well-produced booklet of recommended routes.

Readers' comments: Most enjoyable. Food superb. Will stay again. Excellent place
with superb food. Stayed several times. Fran and Robin delightful.

In the tiny, remote hamlet of High
Ireby, **FELL EDGE**, which was built
in the 18th century as a chapel, is the
home of the highly musical Allison
family. This is a place for people who
appreciate quietness and views – of the
northern fells in one direction and,
across the garden which Arthur Allison
is landscaping, as far as Dumfries in
the other. The garden contributes to
such dinner menus as celery soup,
roast beef, and raspberry flan. Apart
from the northern Lake District, the
area is worth exploring for the rather
fen-like Solway Plain (an area of outstanding natural beauty) and the
deserted coast. No smoking. £14.

Readers' comments: Stayed there twice
and been very satisfied. Wonderful
hospitality. Very interesting people.
Each meal well cooked and well presented. [Tel: 06973 71397; postcode:
CA5 1HF]

Hinton, Blythburgh, Suffolk, IP17 3RJ Tel: 050270 528
North-east of Saxmundham. Nearest main road: A12 from Ipswich to
Lowestoft.

3 Bedrooms. £18–£20 (less for 7 nights). One has own bath/shower/toilet. No smoking. Washing machine on request. **Dinner.** £15 for 3 courses, wine and coffee, at 8pm. Vegetarian or special diets if ordered. Wine can be brought in. No smoking. **Light suppers** if ordered. **1 Sitting-room.** With open fire, central heating, TV. **Small garden**

For four centuries, right up to 1976, the same family, Blois, farmed here: there are memorials to them in Blythburgh church. The latest of the Blois still live nearby, at Cockfield Hall.

Now the half-timbered house is Mary Montague's home. She has furnished it with unusual antiques such as a Spanish dresser, a collector's cabinet from the 18th century, country dining-chairs and sofas upholstered in an art nouveau Liberty fabric. On the dining-room floor are heavy tiles of Spanish clay; and up winding stairs are big bedrooms (one of which has exposed joists separating two single beds) with, for instance, pink patchwork spreads and cushions, and particularly good bathrooms.

Mary loves cooking, and for dinner might prepare such meals as mushrooms in garlic or Cromer crabs to start with; roast beef or sole stuffed with mushrooms and prawns; then Belvoir pudding (a steamed lemon pudding with meringue and apple surrounding it) or crème caramel; wine is included.

Hinton is in P. D. James' country, an area where wildlife still flourishes – barn owls nest in the lane, you may hear nightingales, and there are masses of such wildflowers as cowslips, scabious and primroses. Mary's own pond is frequented by herons, kingfishers and ducks.

The hamlet lies a little way inland from Suffolk's 'heritage coast', now carefully conserved as an area of outstanding natural beauty: stretching from the fishing port and sandy resort of Lowestoft in the north, via the old-fashioned seaside towns of Southwold (a flowery place, with a series of village greens) and Aldeburgh, to the big Victorian resort of Felixstowe in the south. The sea constantly erodes this coast (go to nearby Dunwich to see this most dramatically – the whole of the mediaeval port has been lost to the tides).

Among the crops are villages of great variety, some houses with walls of flint, others of brick – with pantiled roofs and shapely gables as in Holland, just across the sea from here – and still others of colourwashed plaster, often with thatched roofs. Barns are typically black with red roofs; surviving windmills, sparkling white. At Blythburgh is a great church with huge clerestory through which you can see the sky, rearing up above a sandy heath of dunes.

Readers' comments: One of the best. Charming and helpful. Delightful. Delicious dinner. Very warm and friendly.

HIGH WINSLEY COTTAGE   X
Burnt Yates, North Yorkshire, HG3 3EP   Tel: 0423 770 662
North-west of Harrogate. Nearest main road: A61 from Harrogate to Ripon.

5 Bedrooms. £18 (less for 7 nights). Price goes up at Easter. All have own bath/shower/toilet. Tea/coffee facilities. Views of garden, country. No smoking.
Dinner. £11.50 for 3 courses and coffee, at 7pm. Non-residents not admitted. Vegetarian or special diets if ordered. Wine can be ordered.
2 Sitting-rooms. With open fire, central heating, TV. No smoking in one.
Large garden
Closed in January and February.

Weird shapes loom above the moors – a 50-acre outcrop of stone which wind and rain have carved into surreal forms: Brimham Rocks.

Off the road leading to these is a one-time farm cottage now much extended, which has been modernized with care by Clive and Gill King. From the parquet-floored dining-room one steps down to a sitting-room where rosy sofas face a log fire and sliding glass doors open onto a terrace with views to the far hills. Lawn, flowers, orchard and a population of bantams and guinea-fowl add to the charm.

Colour schemes have been well chosen, here and upstairs. A blue-and-white bedroom has a matching bathroom; Laura Ashley briar-roses predominate in another, furnished with antiques; and I particularly liked a large room with windows on two sides and comfortable armchairs from which to enjoy the views.

Gill was once one of 'Miss Gray's young ladies' at the Bay Tree, Burford: those readers who knew the cooking standards there will rightly guess that High Winsley Cottage, too, can be depended upon for good and imaginative food. Gill also lived, and cooked, in Paris for a while.

She puts as much care into making the simplest dishes as into a dinner such as lemons with a stuffing of smoked fish, pork in a spiced orange sauce, and apple jalousie. Her own or local produce is used; bread is home-baked.

Burnt Yates is not only in the middle of a very scenic area (Nidderdale is among the loveliest yet least frequented of the Yorkshire Dales, and popular Wharfedale is not far away) but is also close to several traditional spa towns – Harrogate (described elsewhere), Ripon (with cathedral) and, one of my favourites, Ilkley, a delightful little town in the valley of the River Wharfe. It is particularly pretty in spring when the cherry-blossom is out on the trees that line its shopping streets, and the riverside gardens are coming into flower. The town has excellent restaurants, tea-rooms and bakers; a grocer specializing in cheeses and ham on the bone for picnics; plenty of bookshops, antique and craft shops; and historical interest, from ancient Saxon monuments to Tudor and 18th-century buildings. The invaluable local guide (free from the Tourist Information Centre in the library) gives maps for walks, short and long; tells you where to watch fell-racing, hang-gliding or international tennis. It lists other places for outings: caverns, ruins, picturesque villages and much else. North Yorkshire is a county that offers great variety to the visitor.

Readers' comments: Excellent in every respect. Hospitality and food superlative. Excellent, considerate hosts. Room delightful. Like being entertained by friends.

151

HIGHFIELD PT S X
Ivington Road, Leominster, Herefordshire, HR6 8QD   Tel: 0568 613216
Nearest main road: A44 from Worcester to Leominster.

3 Bedrooms. £18.50–£20 (less for 2 nights). Prices go up in April. All have own bath/shower/toilet. Tea/coffee facilities. Views of garden, country. No smoking. Washing machine on request.
Dinner. A la carte or £10 for 3 courses (with choices) and coffee, at 7–7.30pm or when requested. Vegetarian or special diets if ordered. Wine can be ordered. **Light suppers** if ordered.
2 Sitting-rooms. With open fire, central heating, TV, record-player. No smoking in one.
Large garden

Twin sisters Catherine and Marguerite Fothergill so loved cooking and entertaining that they gave up London careers to come here and make a full-time occupation of these pursuits. They learnt cooking from Robert Carrier and Prue Leith.

The big comfortable house, built in Edwardian times, stands among fields just outside the old market town of Leominster. The sisters have furnished it handsomely – Chippendale-style chairs in the dining-room, for instance, scalloped pink tablemats and napkins (with flowers and candles to match), Eternal Beau china, William Morris armchairs. Outside are sunny rosebeds and, on a paved terrace, white cast-iron chairs from which to enjoy the scene, drink in hand.

Not only are dinners very special but breakfasts too can be memorable – with such options as home-made brioches, fishcakes, kedgeree, home-cooked ham.

As to other meals, residents can choose from the house menu or (after their first night) a gourmet one (or have a snack). Gourmet choices include Marsala chicken-liver puffs or mixed seafood cocktail in curried mayonnaise to start the meal; then cider-baked gammon with orange sauce or Burgundy beef pie; profiteroles, home-made ice creams or pear pie with brandy cream to finish.

Readers' comments: Nothing was too much trouble. Cooking, service and friendliness made my stay seem like a house party. Excellent food and attention. Ideal.

MAUND COURT, near Bodenham, is a 15th-century red sandstone house at the heart of a large mixed farm. Some of the bedrooms overlook the swimming-pool, heated to 76°. One (en suite) is on the ground floor. Although there are good eating-places in the area, Pauline Edwards will, by arrangement, provide such dinners as prawns in sherry sauce, pheasant and profiteroles. There is a beamed dining-room and a sitting-room with an oak-beamed fireplace. Plenty of local maps on loan. Guests can enjoy the large garden, patio and croquet lawn. £16.

Readers' comments: Very pleasant and welcoming, a hearty breakfast, we will go again. Friendly and welcoming atmosphere, excellent breakfast. Absolutely excellent. Incomparable. [Tel: 056884 282; postcode: HR1 3JA]

HIGHLOW HALL

C D S

near Hathersage, Derbyshire, S30 1AX   Tel: 0433 650393
West of Sheffield (South Yorkshire). Nearest main road: A619/A623 from
Chesterfield to Chapel-en-le-Frith.

6 Bedrooms. £20–£25 (less for 7 nights). Prices may go up in April. Some with own bath/toilet. Tea/coffee facilities. Views of garden, country. Washing machine on request.
Dinner. £11.95 for 3 courses and coffee, at 7.30pm. Wine can be ordered.
1 Sitting-room. With open fire, TV.
Large garden

At the heart of this huge farm (raising sheep and cattle) is a castellated, stone manor house of considerable historic interest – complete with not one but four ghost stories. It is one of several similar ones in the Peak District built by a 16th-century farmer for each of his sons: his name, Eyre, is now famous because Charlotte Brontë, who stayed at Hathersage vicarage, took it for her heroine Jane Eyre. (And in the locality was a house which had burned down with, reputedly, a mad woman in it – inspiration for Thornfield Hall.) In the square porch is a massive front door with old iron studs and hinges; the windows have stone mullions and small panes; and above the walls of gritstone is a roof of dark stone slates. It is as if the house grew out of the land itself, for this is the northern (or 'dark') part of the Peak District, in contrast to 'white' limestone further south.

The sitting-room was added in Georgian times, so it has large sash windows with views of the far moors, where the Wains' sheep graze, rising to slopes brilliant with heather in September and rusty bracken in October. Deep, velvety chairs are grouped round a blazing fire on cold days. Adjoining is the dining-room, with comfortably upholstered chairs around each table. Here Julie Wain, who is a trained cook, serves such meals as smoked mackerel with horseradish sauce, steak and mushroom pie, and fresh fruit pavlova with cream.

Bedrooms are roomy and comfortable, some with ancient stonework and all with fine views – not another building is in sight. The house is 800 feet above sea level (its name derives from 'high hlaw', meaning 'high hill'). One may wake in autumn to frost-sugared grass and grazing sheep.

Philip or Julie will show you the most ancient part of the house: the huge stone-flagged hall with great oak staircase. This was once the kitchen, and it still has an old stone sink, stone cheese-press, and ancient chest.

Many visitors come here simply for the scenery and the peace; but there are plenty of places worth visiting (and, of course, glorious walks – the Pennine Way starts in the Peak District). There are the Blue John caverns, the summer 'well-dressing' ceremonies in the many historic villages, interesting old towns such as Buxton and Bakewell, and the city of Sheffield – a great deal more than just an industrial centre (its art gallery, cathedral and theatre are all good).

Readers' comments: Quite delightful; beautifully furnished; friendly and obliging; very impressed – made most welcome. Very hospitable; comfortable, quiet and in beautiful countryside. A wonderful experience; a beautiful setting. Friendly welcome. Good food. Excellent scenery. Most welcoming and comfortable.

153

HILL FARMHOUSE

Bury Road, Hitcham, Suffolk, IP7 7PT   Tel: 0449 740 651
North-west of Ipswich. Nearest main road: A1141 from Hadleigh towards Bury St Edmunds.

3 Bedrooms. £14.50–£16.50 (less for 5 nights). All have own bath/toilet. Tea/coffee facilities. TV. Views of garden, country.
Dinner. £10 for 3 courses (with choices) and coffee, at times to suit guests. Non-residents not admitted. Vegetarian or special diets if ordered. Wine can be brought in. No smoking.
3 Sitting-rooms. With open fire, central heating.
Large garden
Closed from November to February.

Part Tudor, part early Victorian, this handsome house provides a choice between the spacious, traditional bedroom at the front of the house (with cornfield views); or the snug low-beamed ones at the back, with little oak-mullioned windows and rugs on brick floors. Downstairs is a kitchenette; the brick oven and hearth of Tudor times are now a decorative feature which Pippa McLardy fills with arrangements of dried flowers.

One enters the main house through a hall of powder-blue and white, with cherry-carpeted staircase. Pale pink sitting- and dining-rooms have mahogany antiques, a carved pine fireplace and views of countryside or garden (there are duck-ponds, a freestanding swimming-pool and slides etc. for children). Pippa is an imaginative cook: for dinner one might choose between fennel Mornay or stuffed vineleaves; pork normande or Scotch salmon; raspberry-and-cream choux or lemon sorbet. Eggs and vegetables are often home-produced.

Hitcham is centrally placed within a triangle of historic towns (Bury St Edmunds, Sudbury – Gainsborough's birthplace – and Ipswich) and surrounded by very lovely countryside, ideal for walking as well as touring. The great mediaeval 'wool' churches of the area are justly famous.

This unspoilt region is a patchwork of farmland and fens, low hills and a varying shoreline (much favoured by birdwatchers), secretive valleys and wild heaths.

On the other side of Hitcham is **MILL HOUSE** where peacocks roam the grounds and black swans grace the ornamental lake. Judith White has furnished the bedrooms with rose-sprigged fabrics and velvet bedheads, the stone-walled dining-room with maple furniture. There is no sitting-room, but guests often linger in the sunny conservatory overlooking the large landscaped garden and tennis court. (Light suppers only, but there is

good food at the White Horse down the road.) £12.50–£13. [Tel: 0449 740 315; postcode: SK17 8SN]

HOATH HOUSE   C S
Penshurst Road, Chiddingstone Hoath, Kent, TN8 7DB   Tel: 0342 850362
North-west of Tunbridge Wells. Nearest main road: A264 from Tunbridge
Wells to East Grinstead.

2 Bedrooms. £13.50–£19.50 (less for 2 nights). Tea/coffee facilities. TV. Views of garden, country. No smoking. Washing machine on request.
Light suppers if ordered.
1 Sitting-room. With open fire, central heating, piano. No smoking.
Large garden

Chiddingstone Castle, near the very pretty mediaeval village of the same name, was for four centuries the seat of the Streatfeild family. The senior branch of the remaining Streatfeilds now live in Hoath House – a building of exceptional mediaeval interest which, starting as a simple hall house, has had wings and other additions built on through the centuries. The result is rambling and characterful.

One enters through a high hall, originally the mediaeval hall house. On a Breton sideboard in the oak-panelled dining-room are carved lively scenes of cider-making and other country pursuits. The massive, chamfered beams of the sitting-room, its lattice-paned windows and the plastered walls where the handprints of the Tudor builders can still be seen, are impressive – contrasting with the homely presence of family photographs and board-games.

To reach the bedrooms one passes through passages with 18th-century ancestral portraits, despatch-boxes, writing-cases still containing letters from Queen Alexandra, huge chests and a great Grenadier Guards drum: all family heirlooms. The rooms vary – one vast bedroom has a sofa in the bay window (from which there are views over the old red roofs of outbuildings to distant Ashdown Forest). There is an enormous bathroom in 'thirties style. For your own snack suppers, one room has refrigerator amd table.

Readers' comments: Our favourite. Exceptionally friendly and helpful. Fascinating house.

On a wooded hillside close to Tunbridge Wells is a hidden hamlet, well-called Modest Corner. Here is **NUMBER TEN**, home of Dutch-born picture-framer Anneke Leemhuis. The ground-floor bedrooms are simple, furnished with pine and Laura Ashley fabrics; the bathroom is good. Meals (such as lamb with ratatouille followed by trifle) are eaten in Anneke's kitchen. Her dog has proved an excellent guide for visitors exploring the many footpaths. Only five minutes from a station with fast trains to London. £16–£18.

Readers' comments: Homely atmosphere, wonderful walks. Unequalled hospitality and helpfulness. I have stayed four times and am continually impressed. [Tel: 0892 522450; postcode: TN4 0LS]

HOE HILL   C(5) **S X**
Swinhope, Binbrook, Lincolnshire, LN3 6HX   Tel: 0472 398206
North-west of Louth. Nearest main road: A16 from Louth to Grimsby (and
M180, junction 5).

3 Bedrooms. £14–£15 (less for 2 nights).
Prices go up from May. Tea/coffee facilities.
Views of garden, country. No smoking.
Washing machine on request.
Dinner (by arrangement). £10 for 3 courses
(with choices) and coffee, at 7–7.30pm.
Vegetarian or special diets if ordered. Wine
can be brought in. No smoking. **Light
suppers** if ordered.
1 Sitting-room. With open fire, central
heating, TV.
Large garden

'You're lucky to be going there!' said the garage proprietor from whom I asked
the way. So good is Erica Curd's cooking that she often gives demonstrations to
groups of six in her impressive kitchen which has a U-shaped counter.

One enters the white house, built in 1780, through a porch filled with
geraniums. Off a poppy-papered hall is the large and attractive sitting-room, its
light pink and clear blue scheme picking up the colours from a Raoul Dufy
print of Nice. Antiques and a marble fireplace contrast with modern furniture
of bamboo. Glass doors open onto a terrace and croquet lawn shaded by a big
chestnut tree.

As to the meals which have won Erica so much local renown, you might
be offered a choice of cheese-stuffed mushrooms or watercress soup with home-
baked rolls before, for instance, roast duck (or fish straight from Grimsby, or
local game perhaps). The choice of puddings might be a home-made sorbet
accompanying melon and crème de menthe or a traditional favourite such as
bread-and-butter pudding. With the coffee come chocolates. Breakfasts, too, are
impressive, with such options as Lincolnshire sausages, kippers, kidneys in bacon,
kedgeree and occasionally Arbroath smokies.

For those who like to seek out lovely but little frequented parts of England,
the Wolds - where Swinhope lies - will come as a pleasant surprise.

The vast county of Lincolnshire could easily be three, each with its own
character. The northern part, Lindsey, has forty miles of chalk hills, once wooded
but now farmed (totally different from the huge expanse of flat fens to the south,
drained long ago to provide the richest agricultural soil in Britain).

The northern Wolds rise high and have extensive views, but the southern part
is 'Tennyson country' (he used to play skittles in the White Hart at Tetford). To
either side of the Wolds are attractive old market towns: 18th-century Louth
(which not only has a fine market hall but a 16th-century church with the tallest
spire in England), and Market Rasen, originally a Roman settlement. Somersby
has Tennyson's birthplace and the garden that inspired him to write 'Come into
the garden, Maud'. The area is one of woods and streams.

There is a particularly fine drive to the coast, 'the bluestone route', and a new
National Fishing Heritage Centre at Grimsby.

Readers' comments: Absolutely first-rate, the best I have found. Meals excellent,
greeting warm and sincere. We have made this a regular venue for family
get-togethers.

HOLEBROOK FARM   C M

Lydlinch, Sturminster Newton, Dorset, DT10 2JB   Tel: 0258 817348
South-west of Shaftesbury. Nearest main road: A357 from Sturminster
Newton to Stalbridge.

6 Bedrooms. £19–£21 (less for 4 nights).
Prices go up at Easter. Some have own
shower/toilet. Tea/coffee facilities. TV.
Balcony (one). Views of garden, country.
Washing machine on request.
Dinner. About £10.50 for 3 courses and
coffee, at 7pm (not Mondays). Non-
residents not admitted. Wine can be ordered.
1 Sitting-room. With open fire, central
heating, TV.
Small garden

A long track brings one into the yard behind this large farm; on one side are
stables handsomely converted into bedrooms and on the other, a new wing where
there are more bedrooms. You are likely to enter via the big old kitchen, with its
original flagged floor and stone ovens carefully preserved – it is here that Sally
Wingate-Saul serves dinner. (The main course may be anything from lasagne to –
once a week – pheasant; puddings include such calorific treats as chocolate
roulade or treacle tart with sultanas and lemon; and there are always prize-
winning local cheeses too.) Those booking self-catering accommodation may dine
in the house if they wish.

From a gracious sitting-room (shell-pink walls, pale blue damask chairs, log
fire) deep-set, pine-shuttered windows overlook the lawn at the front of the house
beyond which are apple trees and a kitchen garden. Clematis and roses clamber
up the walls. The house is full of interesting objects which the Wingate-Sauls
acquired on travels to the Seychelles, the Pitcairns and Australia; and in a huge
attic bathroom is a varied collection of hats (to which visitors have contributed).

The stable rooms include some that are enormous, each with sitting-room and
bathroom. Stripped pine has been used a lot, and old horse-stalls retained as
room-dividers. Small concealed kitchens are useful for visitors who want to prepare any meals themselves, and there are plenty of armchairs. There are also a
games room with pool table, a swimming-pool and clay-pigeon shooting; and
baby-sitting is available. There is a low-season programme of 'activity' weekends,
such as cookery demonstrations.

Readers' comments: Made so welcome and had a lot of fun. Very good, organized
hosts. Relaxed and helpful. Excellent accommodation, helpfully equipped. Meal
delicious and outdoor pool a boon. Very good value. Had a wonderful stay. Like
part of the family.

STRAWBERRY COTTAGE at
Packers Hill, Holwell, is even older, a
cottage of thatch, stone and brick, with
modern furnishings of high standard.
There is a comfortable TV room which
is well supplied with tourist literature;
one bedroom is en suite. The cottage is
situated in quiet countryside near
Sherborne. (As well as excellent breakfasts, Vivienne Powell provides light

suppers if ordered.) £15.50–£16.50.
[Tel: 0963 23629; postcode: DT9 5LN]

HOLLY TREE

East Witton, North Yorkshire, DL8 4LS   Tel: 0969 22383

South-east of Leyburn. Nearest main road: A6108 from Masham to Leyburn.

C(10) **S**

4 Bedrooms. £18–£20 (less for 7 nights). All have own bath/shower/toilet. Views of garden, country. No smoking. Washing machine on request.

Dinner. £12 for 5 courses (with choices) and coffee, at 7.30pm. Non-residents not admitted. Vegetarian or special diets if ordered. Wine can be ordered. No smoking. **Light suppers** if ordered.

2 Sitting-rooms. With open fire, central heating, TV. No smoking.

Small garden

Closed from December to February.

This is one of Wensleydale's more peaceful villages, a pretty group of cottages around a green, where sometimes strings of racehorses trot by on their way to exercising on the moors. All around is some of England's most magnificent scenery – the Yorkshire Dales – and towns which are honeypots for antique collectors. In the 12th century, part of the house provided stabling for the horses of monks travelling between the great Cistercian abbeys which are a feature of this area. A curiously shaped breakfast-room, with built-in settle and window-seat, was the 'snug' when the house used to be an inn.

Beyond the sitting-room, which has a crackling fire and huge grandfather clock, are two small garden-rooms with glass doors opening onto terrace and lawn with seats from which to enjoy the far view. The formal dining-room has scarlet walls and curtains contrasting with white shutters, green alcoves filled with flowers, and antique furniture. Everywhere there are steps and odd angles.

Bedrooms are particularly pretty. One, for instance, has a brass bed with white and apricot draperies; in its bathroom (blue wallpaper, pale blue curtains) are two basins and a bidet. Another has a rose-swagged frieze, pink-and-white beds, and a green chaise longue skilfully upholstered by Andrea Robson herself. There is also a garden bedroom with its own shower, basin, toilet and foyer.

Andrea Robson's greatest skill is cookery (she won the Gas Boards' 'Cook of the Year' award in 1981). Typically, one of her dinners (preceded by free sherry) might comprise salmon mousse and then her own recipe for chicken breast en croûte (it has a mushroom stuffing and a coat of pâté and ham, inside a flaky-pastry crust). The pudding might then be pears – stuffed with walnuts and cherries, coated with chocolate and brandy, and served with cream.

Altogether, this is a house that has everything – memorable food, attractive rooms, and lovely surroundings. (Horse riding can be arranged.)

Wensleydale is described more fully elsewhere. The nearest small town is Middleham: 18th-century houses cluster around the market place, there's a ruined castle, and racehorses can be seen exercising on the surrounding moors. Well worth a visit are Wensley's riverside church, Ushaw bridge, Jervaulx Abbey and an inn (at Carlton, in Coverdale) with a Saxon burial-mound in its yard. Richmond (with castle), Ripon (cathedral) and Newby Hall are all near.

Readers' comments: More than comfortable. Food truly excellent. Rooms delightful. A lovely home. Very warm welcome. Wonderful food and accommodation. Very comfortable, superb cuisine, delightful house. Cannot be faulted. Everything was just perfect. Freshly decorated and very comfortable. Fun to be with!

HOLMHEAD   C PT

Greenhead, Northumberland, CA6 7HY   Tel: 06977 47402

East of Brampton (Cumbria). Nearest main road: A69 from Carlisle to Hexham.

4 Bedrooms. £18.90 **to readers of this book only** (less for 3 nights). Price goes up in April. Bargain breaks. All have own shower/toilet. Tea/coffee facilities. Views of garden, country, river. No smoking. Washing machine on request.

Dinner. £12–£15 for 3 courses and coffee, at 7.30pm. Non-residents not admitted. Vegetarian or special diets if ordered. Wine can be ordered. No smoking.

2 Sitting-rooms. With central heating, TV, video, record-player. Bar. No smoking.

Large garden

Beside a salmon river, just where the walkers' Pennine Way crosses the Roman wall, this remote house has the ruins of Thirlwall Castle looming overhead (Edward I once stayed there). Just outside are the remains of a Roman turret, somewhere under the lawn or sunken garden, awaiting excavation; and some Roman stones were re-used when the house was built. All this, with the distant moors, is within view through the windows of the guests' large and comfortable sitting-room upstairs – copiously equipped with games, toys and facilities to make unlimited hot drinks. Pauline Staff used to be a tour guide, and so is immensely helpful with advice on sightseeing. She occasionally gives visitors talks with slides, or may even show them around. In winter, guided walks and discounts on tickets to museums are available.

There is now a bridge over the river which used almost to isolate the house; farm gates may need to be opened as one crosses the fields.

Although some of the bedrooms are small, there are all kinds of unexpected 'extras' in this out-of-the-way house: a foot-massager for weary walkers; pure spring water; table tennis; snooker; snacks at any hour; and the company of Rex, a Hungarian visla hound. Pauline likes to cook local dishes and has even experimented with Roman recipes cooked in the area around AD 300 (one favourite is honey-roast ham in pastry). She makes all the preserves, chutneys, cakes, bread and scones. A typical dinner might comprise: melon with kiwi fruit; trout in hollandaise sauce; almond meringue with wild raspberries in whipped cream (eaten at a big candle-lit table). Out of season, a ground-floor self-catering flat is available for b & b.

Breakfast choices include haggis, black pudding, kedgeree, muffins, crumpets and occasionally a Scandinavian buffet.

This is a splendid area for walks (with or without a National Park guide). The Northumberland National Park starts here; there are associations with Walter Scott and Catherine Cookson. You can look at working shire horses, Roman forts or prehistoric remains (including rock carvings), four castles, Hexham Abbey, Lanercost Priory, Beamish's celebrated open-air museum, stately homes. Some of the most popular sights include the Roman Army Museum, Naworth Castle and Talkin Tarn. But it is, of course, Hadrian's Wall that is the biggest attraction of all.

Readers' comments: Food very good, Mrs Staff a marvellous help. Enjoyable. Well cared for and well fed. Fell for it completely. Orderly and civilized. Very helpful and knowledgeable hostess.

HOME FARM   **C D PT**
Church Lane, Old Dalby, Leicestershire, LE14 3LB   Tel: 0664 822622
(Messages: 0664 822633)
North-west of Melton Mowbray. Nearest main road: A46 from Leicester to
Newark-on-Trent.

5 **Bedrooms.** £17.50 (less for 5 nights).
Price goes up from Easter. Singles have own
bath/shower/toilet. Tea/coffee facilities. TV.
Views of garden, country. No smoking.
Washing machine on request.
Light suppers if ordered.
1 **Sitting-room.** With open fire, central
heating, TV, piano. No smoking.
Small garden

Set in an idyllic garden and facing the church, this 18th-century house (extended
in 1835) has great charm and an atmosphere of peace. Clematis and quinces grow
up its walls. Beyond espaliered apples and herbaceous beds are lawns and a
kitchen garden. (It is no longer a farm.) Two single en suite bedrooms are in a
barn.

Indoors, every room has old furniture, pot-plants and white walls. Country-
style dining-chairs surround the long table where breakfast is served, a fire
crackling on chilly mornings. Val Anderson's collection of 'twenties and
'thirties photographs of local hunting personalities hangs here (including one
of the then Prince of Wales, who first met Mrs Simpson at nearby
Burrough Court).

Normally, Val serves only breakfast as the award-winning Crown Inn nearby is
popular for other meals: 'the best food in the Vale of Belvoir', Val says. However,
she is prepared to offer guests snack-type meals (soup, quiche, salad, cheese or
pâté) if booked in advance. Home-grown fruit is served at breakfast.

Guests at Home Farm find plenty to do in the area, visiting Belton and
Burghley Houses, Belvoir Castle, Newstead Abbey (Byron's house), Wollaton
Hall, Whatton Gardens and the Donington Motor Museum. Calke Abbey, with a
famous state bed, has fine grounds laid out in 1772. The National Watersports
Centre, Vale of Belvoir, Trent Bridge and Rutland Water are other attractions.

Loughborough is worth a visit to see round the bell-foundry and its museum;
also the steam railway, and, in the vicinity, one of the county's several farm trails
or farm parks (Broomriggs Farm). Beyond Loughborough lie Desford's tropical
bird gardens, Ashby-de-la-Zouch castle, and Staunton Harold's extensive crafts
centre (there is an unusual Cromwellian church here, too). The county has an
industrial heritage trail of which the Moira blast furnace near Ashby is an outstanding feature. Ancient Charnwood Forest, too, is in this direction.

Leicester itself is an unlovely city with little left from the past except its
mediaeval guildhall and much altered cathedral but it has about a dozen
museums, some with a technological emphasis – there is even one devoted to the
history of gas! – and botanical gardens run by the university. In this direction are
Belgrave Hall (Queen Anne), the ruins of Bradgate Hall – associated with Lady
Jane Grey, Kirby Muxloe castle and, in the city, a Victorian brewery.

Readers' comments: Excellent. Good welcome and breakfast. Warm welcome,
friendly atmosphere. Better than being at home!

HONEY COTTAGE
The Green, Upton, Nottinghamshire, NG23 5SU   Tel: 0636 813318
West of Newark.   On the A612 from Southwell towards Newark.

2 Bedrooms. £18 (less for 7 nights). Both have own bath/shower/toilet. Tea/coffee facilities. TV. Views of garden. No smoking. Washing machine on request.
Small garden

Upton Hall is now occupied by the National Horological Institute (whose collection of clocks can be visited at weekends), but when it was a private home the estate's gamekeeper lived in this cottage opposite. Since much extended, the cottage now stretches back from the road (which means that light sleepers can have a room at the back, facing the quiet garden).

Kate Ellis serves light suppers only, but one can dine well at the French Horn or Cross Keys along the road.

Nearby Newark is a town well worth exploring. The dramatic ruins of a 12th-century castle destroyed during the Civil War are reflected in the waters of the broad River Trent (boat trips available). There's a vast cobbled market place with grandiose town hall, colonnade and mediaeval inns – one with carved angels. More angels (painted and gilded) in the lofty church, too, which has stained glass and monuments. There are byways to explore, a museum of quaint mementoes from the town's turbulent past, the house where Prince Rupert stayed after defeat at Marston Moor, and much else.

In the vicinity, black-and-white villages can be discovered and such church treasures as the 14th-century Easter sepulchre at Hawton – and, of course, the wonderful stone carvings in Southwell Minster. Laxton is celebrated for having retained to this day the strip-farming system which prevailed in the Middle Ages: fields are divided into strips, and each farmer is allotted a number of these. Newstead Abbey (1170) was Byron's home (he is buried at Hucknall) and still contains possessions of his; there are lakes in its extensive grounds. By contrast, D. H. Lawrence's childhood home at Eastwood is a miner's cottage – also open to the public. Many scenes in his *Sons and Lovers* can be identified in the neighbourhood. To the east lies historic Lincoln (dramatically sited cathedral, castle, Norman and Roman remains).

Bedroom at Beechenhill Farm (see page 320)

161

HOOK GREEN POTTERY
Clay Hill Road, Hook Green, Lamberhurst, Kent, TN3 8LR

C D PT

Tel: 0892 890504

East of Tunbridge Wells. Nearest main road: A21 from Tonbridge to Hastings (and M25, junction 5).

2 or 3 Bedrooms. £10–£18 (less for 4 nights). Prices go up in April. Tea/coffee available. Views of garden, country. Non-smokers preferred. Washing machine on request.
Dinner (if ordered). £8 for 3 courses and coffee, from 7pm. Non-residents not admitted. Vegetarian or special diets if ordered. Wine can be brought in. **Light suppers** if ordered.
1 Sitting-room. With log stove, central heating. No smoking.
Large garden

After 20 years as a London art director, Don Morgan trained as a potter at Dartington in Devon for two years and then returned to this house – tile-hung in typical Kent style – as both home and studio. You can buy his wares here.

Outside are geese and a croquet lawn; jasmine, fuchsias and climbing geraniums. One enters through Don's brick-floored showroom, via the kitchen, to a dining-room which has a large table at the window and a log stove on the great hearth of nooks and crannies. In the cosy sitting-room, its walls decorated with a bold William Morris wallpaper, there are plenty of books. Upstairs is an old four-poster, broderie anglaise draping the top, in a room with French flowery blue wallpaper and an old Victorian fireplace complete with trivet. There's a view of the local inn, a picturesque half-timbered building. Sometimes the Morgans let one of their sons' bedrooms to teenage guests. (Baby-sitting available.)

As to dinner (served on – what else! – Don's pottery), Ruth produces such meals as a help-yourself chicken casserole or moussaka with garlic bread; black-currant crumble or home-grown raspberries and cream, then cheeses.

On the outskirts of Lamberhurst, in Furnace Lane, is **FURNACE FARM**, surrounded by acres of strawberry fields. Bedrooms are light and spacious, with pretty floral fabrics and excellent en suite bathrooms; one beamed bedroom (with shower) has wheelchair access. In addition to the comfortable sitting-room, which has a brick fireplace and an iron fireback dated 1641, there are two dining-rooms (one with piano and attractive displays of dried flowers). Here, Mary Barnes serves such dinners as melon with Parma ham, then beef in wine (with garden vegetables), and straw-

berries often appear in mousses or other puddings. £17–£19 (b & b).
Readers' comments: Very welcoming. Food excellent and plentiful. Outstanding accommodation, warm hospitality. [Tel: 0892 890788; postcode: TN3 8LE]

HOPE BOWDLER HALL   C(14) PT S
Hope Bowdler, Church Stretton, Shropshire, SY6 7DD   Tel: 0694 722041
North of Ludlow. Nearest main road: A49 from Shrewsbury to Ludlow.

2 Bedrooms. £16–£17.50. Tea/coffee facilities. Views of garden, country. No smoking. Washing machine on request. **Light suppers** if ordered. No smoking.
1 Sitting-room. With open fire, central heating, TV. No smoking.
Large garden
Closed from December to February.

The ancient, stone manor house was 'Georgianized' in the 18th century – hence the handsome sash windows and graceful staircase, though older features such as stone-flagged floors still remain.

Rosaleen Inglis has decorated the sitting-room in apricot, furnished the dining-room with a fine mahogany table and damask wallpaper, and for one of the bathrooms found tiles with Shropshire views.

The big engraving of officers at the Siege of Lucknow (1857–8) and the impressive ceremonial sword were possessions of John's great-grandfather who commanded the garrison during the siege of Lucknow, one of the major events in the Indian Mutiny. (The then Mrs Inglis had to live for months, with the other wives, in rat-infested cellars: some kept prussic acid at hand in case the mutineers succeeded in taking Lucknow.) Among his other ancestors was the first Bishop of Nova Scotia.

Outside is a large garden with pool frequented by a mallard, a hard tennis court and bluebell wood.

Hope Bowdler is ideally placed for walkers, lying between those famous Shropshire hills, the Long Mynd and Wenlock Edge. Shrewsbury and Ludlow are both near – also Stokesay Castle, the Acton Scott farm museum, Ironbridge (with the Coalport china museum), and the outstanding gardens of Hodnet Hall, Burford House (Tenbury) and great Powis Castle.

The legendary Celtic leader Caractacus fought his final battle against the Romans in these hills: his fortress was on a hilltop near here, one of the many pre-historic or Roman sites in the area. Now more peaceful activities prevail: rambling in the beautiful Carding Mill Valley, for instance; golfing on one of the country's highest courses; gliding; sampling Church Stretton's many restaurants and antique shops; or birdwatching.

Readers' comments: Accommodation charming, proprietress most hospitable. Enjoyed an excellent week.

HORSLEYGATE HALL   C(5)
Horsleygate Lane, Holmesfield, Derbyshire, S18 5WD   Tel: 0742 890333
North-west of Chesterfield. Nearest main road: A61 from Chesterfield to
Sheffield.

3 Bedrooms. £17–£19.50 (less for 4 nights). Some have own bath/shower/toilet. Tea/coffee facilities. Views of garden, country. No smoking. Washing machine on request.
Light suppers sometimes if ordered.
1 Sitting-room. With open fire, central heating, TV. No smoking.
Large garden
Closed in December and January.

Garden enthusiasts, in particular, will enjoy staying here to see the transformation wrought by Margaret Ford on a sloping site which was an overgrown wilderness when she took over. The house too (part early Victorian, part Georgian) had hardly been touched for generations: in some ways an advantage, for its original features were intact and have now been carefully restored – even to the stone-slabbed floors.

The Fords painted the panelling in the sitting-room apricot and grey, with fabrics to match. What was once the children's schoolroom (where they found a large bottle of ink still lingering, and one of the desks) is now a breakfast-room – where, incidentally, you may be lucky enough to have garden raspberries offered. Here and elsewhere are Margaret's various 'flea market' finds which add to the character of the house.

There are spacious bedrooms, some with armchairs from which to enjoy the superb Peak District scenery (you would not guess that the centre of Sheffield is only 20 minutes away). Stripped pine doors, beribboned curtains and baths set in alcoves are features of the house.

Margaret serves only snack suppers because she is too busy to cook: busy, that is, with her consuming passion – the garden. She started as a complete novice, but within a few years created a fascinating terraced garden of stone walls, hidden patios, woodland paths, rock garden descending to a lily-pool, herbaceous beds and brimming stone troughs: one pleasure after another reveals itself as you wander round.

By way of an extra bonus, there lives in part of the house a qualified masseuse who can revive you with aromatherapy or reflexology after a day's strenuous sightseeing.

If you want more than just the hill scenery, there are stately homes to visit (Chatsworth, Hardwick and Haddon Hall), the market town of Bakewell, and Sheffield for its many and varied attractions: excellent art gallery, cathedral, industrial heritage museum with steel craftsmen (the 'little mesters') at work, an industrial hamlet (bellows and waterwheel still active), and one of the prisons of Mary Queen of Scots.

Readers' comments: Very impressed. Picturesque and quiet location, with good views. Friendly and helpful. Enjoyed our stay tremendously.

164

HOWARDS GORHUISH   C(10) S
Northlew, Devon, EX20 3BT   Tel: 0837 53301
North-west of Okehampton. Nearest main road: A30 from Okehampton to
Launceston.

4 Bedrooms. £15–£18. Some have own bath/shower/toilet. Tea/coffee facilities. TV. Views of garden, country. No smoking. Washing machine on request.
Dinner. £8 for 3 courses and coffee, at 7pm (not Sundays, Tuesdays or Thursdays). Non-residents not admitted. Vegetarian or special diets if ordered. Wine can be brought in. No smoking.
1 Sitting-room. With open fire, central heating, TV, video. No smoking.
Large garden
Closed in December.

Not long ago, this 'long-house' was still being used as its 16th-century builders intended: cattle at one end, living quarters in the centre, and storage at the other.

Rugged stone walls, inglenook, low doorways and many steps are a reminder of its past. The contrasting decor, of oriental furnishings (which the Richards brought back from Hong Kong) and English antiques, marries surprisingly well with this background. All around the remote, pink-walled house are acres of garden, organic vegetable beds and orchard and beyond these spectacular views of Dartmoor's tors. And in an outbuilding is an excellent games room for children – adults too – with table tennis, sofas, and books.

On four evenings a week, Heather serves dinner – with such imaginative dishes as prawn-and-lobster bisque, lemon chicken, a brandy sponge into which also go chocolate and cream, and cheeses.

She is an accomplished quilter: every room has examples of her work and such sparkling colour schemes as peppermint and white or coral and white. A particularly good bathroom has pretty tiles complementing the pine fitments.

Readers' comments: Superb. A very charming couple, delightfully attentive. Wonderful location, fine accommodation.

Overlooking the market place at nearby Hatherleigh is 15th-century **TALLY HO INN**, now owned by Gianni and Annamaria Scoz. Their cosy bar (with wooden beams and huge open fireplaces) serves ale from their own brew-house, open to view at the back. Bedrooms have stripped pine furniture and bathrooms are excellent. In addition to an à la carte restaurant, there is a good selection of bar snacks, and a thatched barbecue in the small garden where summer evening meals can be enjoyed. £20 (b & b).

Readers' comments: Most comfortable, kind and welcoming. Food fantastic. [Tel: 0837 810306; postcode: EX20 3JN]

HULLERBANK

C(10) PT

Talkin, Cumbria, CA8 1LB Tel: 06977 46668
South of Brampton. Nearest main road: A69 from Carlisle to Brampton (and M6, junction 43).

3 Bedrooms. £17.50 (less for 7 nights). All have own bath/shower/toilet. Tea/coffee facilities. Views of garden, country. No smoking.
Dinner. £10 for 3 courses (with choices) and coffee, at 7pm. Vegetarian or special diets if ordered. Wine can be ordered or brought in. No smoking. **Light suppers** if ordered.
1 Sitting-room. With open fire, central heating, TV. No smoking.
Small garden

Little Talkin village is in an interesting part of the country, surrounded by fells that are popular with walkers and near a country park and tarn with various watersports. Hadrian's Wall is also quite near: the most interesting parts at this end of it are the Banks Burn stretch and the fort at Birdoswald. The Scottish border country and the Lake District are easily reached too, and the beautiful Eden Valley lies to the south. Brampton is an old market town; Alston and the city of Carlisle are not far. Talkin used to be a stopping-place for monks making their way to Lanercost Priory: part of this is in ruins, but the lovely nave is still used as a church and what was the guests' solar is a village hall.

For railway enthusiasts, nearby are vestiges of the track of a railway which pre-dates the steam age, where Stephenson's *Rocket* ended its working life, and the station where printed tickets were invented by a stationmaster who tired of filling in each ticket by hand.

Hullerbank is in a secluded spot only half a mile from the village, and offers farmhouse accommodation at its most comfortable. Though this is only a 14-acre smallholding, Brian and Sheila Stobbart are farming people. The sheep they raise provide the chops and joints which guests greatly appreciate. Lamb (or other straightforward farmhouse dishes, all entirely home-made) might be preceded by soup, or grapefruit or prawn-and-mushroom parcels, and followed by apple pie, for example, or blackcurrant meringues, to which the orchard and garden have contributed. When trout is on the menu, it is from a local fish farm.

Readers' comments: Comfortable facilities, friendly hosts, a lovely part of the country. We are definitely planning a return visit. Very friendly. I can definitely recommend Hullerbank. Very comfortable and spotlessly clean. Delightful house, every comfort. Dinners and breakfasts exceptionally good.

The addresses of houses are geographically correct but postal addresses sometimes differ (for correspondence, the only essential element is the postcode).

Information about the nearest town and 'A' road helps you to locate the whereabouts of any village on a map; but before setting off it is necessary to get precise instructions from your host as many houses are very much 'off the beaten track'.

HUNTHOUSE FARM C(8) S
Frith Common, Worcestershire, WR15 8JY Tel: 0299 832277
West of Kidderminster. Nearest main road: A456 from Tenbury Wells to
Kidderminster.

3 Bedrooms. £15–£16. All have own bath/shower/toilet. Tea/coffee facilities. Views of garden, country. No smoking.
Light suppers if ordered.
1 Sitting-room. With open fire, central heating, TV, record-player.
Large garden
Closed in December.

In this part of England, very fine black-and-white timbered houses are a characteristic sight – evidence of agricultural wealth in centuries past. This one is typical: inside, antiques complement the oak beams and big fireplaces (in front of which you will be offered tea and home-made cake when you arrive); and outside is rural peace with fine views on all sides – the Clee Hills in one direction, the Teme Valley in the other. There are horses and sheep on the farm lands. Bedrooms are trim and freshly decorated, the dining-room spacious – Jane Keel serves snack suppers here if these are ordered.

There are innumerable good walks in this hilly northern part of Worcestershire, particularly in Wyre Forest, and plenty of 'sights' to visit – such as Witley Court (with its exceptional baroque church), the Elgar Museum (his house is at Lower Brockhampton) and the gardens of Burford House. In addition to exploring the historic towns of the area (Ludlow, Bewdley and Worcester), shop for bargains in glass at the Stuart and Brierley factories, for china at Royal Worcester, and carpets in Kidderminster.

In whichever direction you go, your drive will usually be traffic-free and scenic whatever the season.

In the historic village of Abberley, **CHURCH FARM** sits, as you might guess, right by the church. It is a big yet unpretentious Victorian building from which the same family has farmed ever since it was built, on a site inhabited for perhaps two thousand years or more. A guest with a metal-detector dug up Roman coins as well as 17th- and 18th-century buckles and horse-brasses in the grounds – these finds are now on display indoors. In the homely living-room, bacon hooks still hang down from the ceiling and a log fire crackles on cool evenings. Around are orchards, duck-ponds with bulrushes, fields of cattle and the Abberley Hills (beautiful walking

country). In the bedrooms (each with bathroom), Sally Neath has used flowery fabrics that have a homely Victorian air. (Snack suppers only.) £16. [Tel: 0299 896316; postcode: WR6 6BP]

HURDON FARM   C M S
Hurdon, Cornwall, PL15 9LS   Tel: 0566 772955
South of Launceston. Nearest main road: A30 from Launceston to Bodmin.

6 Bedrooms. £14–£18 (less for 4 nights). Some have own bath/toilet. Tea/coffee facilities. TV. Views of garden, country.
Dinner. £9 for 4 courses and coffee, at 6.30pm (not Sundays). Non-residents not admitted. Vegetarian or special diets if ordered. Wine can be brought in. No smoking. **Light suppers** if ordered.
1 Sitting-room. With open fire, central heating, TV.
Large garden
Closed from November to mid-April.

The 18th-century stone house is in a picturesque area, not far from Dartmoor and Bodmin Moor (both the north and south coasts are within reach, too). It has large sash windows with the original panelled shutters and built-in dressers in the dining-room. The sitting-room has large and comfortable chairs and a great log stove. The most interesting room is, however, the big kitchen-scullery where an old slate sink and pump stand alongside the modern washing machine, and in the granite fireplace is an array of old jacks, trivets, and a built-in Dutch oven.

Upstairs, all is spick-and-span with fresh paintwork and light, bright colour schemes in the bedrooms. There is also a family suite (made pretty by an old-fashioned rosebud wallpaper) on the ground floor, where the dairy used to be.

Meals, often prepared by Margaret Smith's daughter Nicola, are above average 'farmhouse fare', with imaginative starters, in particular. Her soups are accompanied by home-made rolls; lamb or coq au vin by such vegetables as courgettes au gratin, cabbage cooked with onion and bacon, potatoes dauphinoise (with milk and cheese) or creamed turnips; her puddings include raspberry pavlovas, chocolate rouleaux and home-made ice creams – always followed by cheeses. She uses the farm's own organic produce and clotted cream.

Visitors can join in farming activities. Some even rise at 6am to give J.R. his bottle; *this* J.R., too, is a black sheep but the bottle contains milk not whisky!

From Launceston you can visit the majestic and romantic north Cornish coast, described elsewhere in this book, or head inland to wild Bodmin Moor to discover hidden, unspoilt villages. The coast has stark cliffs, waterfalls and wide sands; the moor, high tors that can be reached only on foot or horseback. Don't miss the elaborately carved church (St Mary's) in Launceston itself, an old-world market town. The area is full of Arthurian legends; and Daphne du Maurier's Jamaica Inn is on the moor. An otter park, a steam railway, Lydford Gorge and Launceston Castle add to the interest of the region.

Cotehele and Lanhydrock are two very impressive National Trust houses in the vicinity, and most visitors also enjoy Morwellham Quay, Dobwalls theme park near Liskeard, and the National Shire Horse Centre at Yealmpton.

Readers' comments: Charming lady. Recommended for value, friendliness and atmosphere. Fantastic, very good value. Lovely room. Superb atmosphere. Idyllic – we were spoilt! Excellent meals, very comfortable, very reasonable. Enjoyable and relaxing. We return year after year. Well above average farm cooking. Food of the highest standard. Everything immaculate. Superb food.

HUXTABLE FARM   C M
West Buckland, Devon, EX32 0SR   Tel: 0598 760254
East of Barnstaple. Nearest main road: A361 from South Molton to Barnstaple.

6 Bedrooms. £19–£22 (less for 3 nights outside high season). All have own bath/shower/toilet. Tea/coffee facilities. TV (in some). Views of garden, country. Washing machine on request.
Dinner. £11 for 4 courses (with choices) and coffee, at 7.30pm. Non-residents not admitted. Vegetarian or special diets if ordered. Wine can be brought in. No smoking.
2 Sitting-rooms. With open fire, central heating, TV.
Small garden and farmland.

Oak beams and screen panelling, bricks for open fireplaces and bread-ovens, flagstones for the floors – all are still to be seen in this house, built in 1520 and capable of lasting another four centuries.

The main room of Huxtable Farm was originally a hall house before being converted into a long-house (that is to say, rooms at one end, cattle byre at the other, all in one long row), and around it were added outbuildings that include a barn and roundhouse (now providing extra accommodation). Today it is the very comfortable home of Antony and Jackie Payne who farm the land and manage the accommodation. It is also the home of Antony's parents, Freddie and Barbara, a doctor and a teacher, both much-travelled – which accounts for the presence of such touches as carved window-frets from the Yemen.

On the farm are sheep (in April, lambs), rabbits, a Shetland pony, and a kitchen garden with vegetables, fruit and herbs. Children are encouraged to feed the animals, pick wild strawberries from the banks of a private lane, and get up early to spot deer which stray in from the adjoining woods. There is a stream to paddle in – and a particularly well-equipped games room and sauna. From here, visitors can join the 'Tarka Country Trail' which passes by the farm.

The Paynes really do welcome even the smallest children, not just tolerate them; and provide not only cot and high chair but even a baby alarm and night-light in the big family room; and kitchen high-teas and breakfasts specially for children. There are also ride-on toys, sandpit, Wendy-house and swings.

Bedrooms in the farmhouse are cottagey in style (those in the barn have modern louvred pine cupboards and a light, airy look: pink and white, with bamboo furniture; bathrooms are as beautiful as the bedrooms).

Jackie uses produce from Exmoor and Dartmoor, as well as from the Paynes' own extensive garden. A typical 4-course candlelit dinner starts with, perhaps, a choice of artichoke soup or mackerel pâté made with the farm's own cottage cheese; then there might be roast lamb and vegetables (both from the farm) with an interesting sauce; followed by the choice of a creamy dessert, possibly using whortleberries picked on the moors, or a hot fruit pudding – you help yourself from a sidetable – and cheeses. With coffee there is home-made fudge. Bread is home-baked, and with your meal is offered a complimentary glass of Freddie's home-made wine (elderberry, rhubarb or raspberry).

Readers' comments: Excellent. Very good evening meals. Wished we could stay longer. Lovely setting. Delightful hostess. Very relaxed atmosphere.

ING HILL LODGE

CDX

Mallerstang Dale, Cumbria, CA17 4JT Tel: 07683 71153
South of Kirkby Stephen. Nearest main road: A685 from Tebay to Brough.

4 Bedrooms. £20 **for readers of this book** (less for 7 nights). Bargain breaks. All have own shower/toilet. Tea/coffee facilities. TV. Views of garden, country, river. No smoking. Washing machine on request.
Dinners. £12.50 for 3 courses and coffee, at 7pm. Non-residents not admitted. Vegetarian dishes if ordered. Wine can be ordered. No smoking. **Light suppers.**
1 Sitting-room. With open fire, central heating, record-player. Bar.
Large garden

Mallerstang must be the Cumbrian valley least known to tourists. Yet it is rich in associations, real or legendary: King Arthur, Dick Turpin, the Romans and the Vikings, Thomas Becket, Michael Faraday. Along one side of the valley runs the famous Settle to Carlisle railway, and on the fells above the last wild boar in England was reputed to have been killed.

Ing Hill – probably built as a hunting-lodge, in 1820 – stands above the valley floor, and the views are splendid, especially from the bedrooms. The latter have neatly co-ordinated fabrics and ingenious bedheads-cum-backrests designed by Tony Sawyer. A retired surveyor, he has done all the design and conversion work in the house himself, and he occasionally offers courses in advanced DIY.

Sheelagh Sawyer provides menus to suit the appetites of the walkers who stay here: typically, mushroom soup, steak pie, and blackberry crumble with cream. The 'butler's pantry' upstairs is well equipped for hot drinks and biscuits.

As a change from exploring the upper reaches of the River Eden, which rises at the valley head, visit Kirkby Stephen for its antique shops and interesting mediaeval church approached through a curious classical colonnade. Short or longer drives lead to one of England's highest waterfalls, or into the Yorkshire Dales.

Readers' comments: Warm welcome, excellent hospitality, beautiful surroundings. Standard of a top hotel. Food plain but delicious. Thrilled by standard of accommodation. Marvellous hospitality. Delightful furnishings and location.

Sitting-room at Low Hall (see page 196)

IOLANTHE
86 Wildwood Road, Hampstead, London, NW11 6UJ Tel: 081-455 1417
(M1, junction 1, is near.)

C PT X

4 Bedrooms. £17.70. Tea/coffee facilities. TV. Views of garden, heath. No smoking. Laundry service.
Light suppers if ordered.
Small garden

For country quiet while in London, this is the place to be. The Hampstead Garden Suburb was founded by the philanthropist Henrietta Barnett in 1907 when, appalled at the housing conditions of London's poor, she determined that as the Underground spread northward a new all-classes community should be built there – green and leafy, with cottages and manor houses in 16th- and 17th-century styles.

At its centre is St Jude's, a great Lutyens church, low-eaved without and frescoed within. Alas, for Dame Henrietta's idealism: today only the well-to-do can buy even the smallest cottage.

Situated right by Hampstead Heath, Iolanthe is a Lutyens-designed house and one of the oldest in the Suburb. Here, Rosy Gill provides breakfast and snack suppers either in visitors' rooms or downstairs – overlooking or even on the terrace of the garden. (No sitting-room, but there is also a first-floor terrace which guests are welcome to use.)

Bedrooms are light and airy, with cottage-style furnishings and fresh white walls. (Baby-sitting can be arranged.)

Central London is 20 minutes away by Underground.

On the summit of Muswell Hill is a 500-acre park with stupendous views. Here, in 1873, was built the great 'people's palace': Alexandra Palace – still worth a visit even when there are no special exhibitions, antique fairs or concerts. In the neighbouring streets is **MIDDLE HOUSE**, 21 Palace Road, Hornsey, the attractive home of Patrick and Susie Power. For guests, there is an elegant, lemon-yellow sitting-room with some fine antiques, a fresh, simply furnished bedroom and a very pretty bathroom. Meals are served in a dining-kitchen on Spode china at a round table; French windows open onto a narrow but secluded garden. A

typical dinner: chicken in cream and tarragon followed by syllabub; wine included. No smoking. £17 (b & b).
Reader's comment: Greatly enjoyed our stay. [Tel: 081-341 6154; postcode: N8 8QL]

171

IRELANDS FARM D
Irelands Lane, near Henley-in-Arden, Warwickshire, B95 5SA
Tel: 0564 792476
South-east of Birmingham (West Midlands). Nearest main road: A3400 from
Birmingham to Stratford-upon-Avon.

3 Bedrooms. £17.50–£20 (less for 3
nights). All have own bath/shower/toilet.
Tea/coffee facilities. TV. Views of garden,
country. No smoking. Washing machine on
request.
Light suppers if ordered.
1 Sitting-room. With central heating, TV,
piano, record-player. No smoking.
Large garden

In the middle of Shakespeare's Forest of Arden was built ancient Lapworth Hall,
later re-named after the family who extended it. A copy of the first Ireland's will
(1559) hangs in the house; in it he wrote 'I bequeath my soul to almighty God, to
the parishioners a cow, to my wife all the corne, six pieces of pewter, two potts
and two pannes . . . the salt meat in the rouffe . . . ' and so on. Stone-flagged
floors have survived the centuries, but much of the present house was built in
1820.

All around are the Shaws' fields (arable or pasture) and downhill lies the
Tapster Brook: the whole area is one of undulating hills with small hidden valleys
and a history that goes back to Saxon, Roman and even prehistoric times. Boats
on the Birmingham–Stratford canal add touches of bright colour to the scene.

In the house, stairs twist up and down to bedrooms that are light, roomy and
comfortable. One has a sofa and a pretty little Victorian fireplace. There are
pleasant, farmhouse-style furnishings (much oak in the dining-room). Although
picturesque Henley has a dozen eating-places as well as many antique and craft
shops, notable church, etc., Pamela will prepare snacks for anybody who does not
want to dine out – exhausted, perhaps, by a day at the National Exhibition Centre
(only ¼-hour away); or in Birmingham, Warwick or Stratford-upon-Avon; or
spent walking the nearby Heart of England Way which links the Pennines to the
Cotswolds.

Bedroom at Irelands Farm

JINLYE   C M X
Castle Hill, All Stretton, Shropshire, SY6 6JP   Tel: 0694 723243
South of Shrewsbury. Nearest main road: A49 from Shrewsbury to Ludlow.

3 Bedrooms. £16–£24 (less for 3 nights). Tea/coffee facilities. Views of garden, country. No smoking. Washing machine on request.
Dinner. £12.50 for 4 courses and coffee, at 7pm. Non-residents not admitted. Vegetarian or special diets if ordered. Wine can be brought in. No smoking. **Light suppers** if ordered.
2 Sitting-rooms. With open fire, central heating, TV, piano. No smoking in one.
Large garden

This area calls itself 'the Shropshire Highlands': it is the country of A. E. Housman and Mary Webb. One of its most towering heights is the primeval ridge called Long Mynd and on these windy and magnificent moors you can see for miles. It is here, 1400 feet high and surrounded by 6000 acres of National Trust land, that Jan Tory has her guest-house, built in traditional style with stones from an old demolished building. Around it is a spectacular landscaped garden.

The big, front sitting-room with woodblock floor and velvet chairs has a deceptively old look: its beams came from an ancient barn, its windows are lattice-paned, the walls are of exposed stone. Jan has added a lot of brassware and copper. This room opens onto a sheltered terrace. Pretty bedrooms have superb views.

Teas are served in a conservatory – the delicious cakes are home-baked and the tea made with spring water. A second sitting-room at the back has blue chinoiserie sofas around the fireplace, and in the dining-room are sideboards of carved oak. Here visitors enjoy specialities like lamb larded with ham and simmered in wine, or chicken (a half-bird each) with port and mushroom sauce. You help yourself from an array of puddings: chocolate and nut gâteau, charlottes, and so forth. Cheeses follow, and then liqueurs with your coffee. (Sunday lunch also available.)

As to the strange name, this is much older than the house itself: *lye* (or *ley*) is an Old English word for a clearing in a wood.

In the foothills of the Long Mynd, **RECTORY FARM** stands near the village green of Woolstaston. It is a fine half-timbered house surrounded by big clipped yews that may be 400 years old. Inside is panelling elaborately carved with pomegranates and roses. Three sitting-rooms open into one another, and all bedrooms are spacious, immaculate and with fine views – particularly one from which you can see the Wrekin beyond the lawns, rosebeds and lead nymphs of the garden. There is a long oak table in the dining-room used for breakfast

(Jeanette Davies serves no other meals, so visitors go to the restaurants of Church Stretton). £18.
Readers' comments: A delightful home.
[Tel: 0694 751306; postcode: SY6 6NN]

KARSLAKE HOUSE HOTEL

C D S

Halse Lane, Winsford, Somerset, TA24 7JE   Tel: 064 385 242

South of Minehead. Nearest main road: A396 from Minehead to Exeter.

7 Bedrooms. £19–£24.50 (less for 4 nights). Prices go up from April. Bargain breaks. 5% **off to readers carrying this book.** Some have own bath/shower/toilet. Tea/coffee facilities. TV. Views of garden, country. No smoking. Washing machine on request.
Dinner. £14.50 for 4 courses (with choices) and coffee, at 7.30pm. Vegetarian or special diets if ordered. Wine can be ordered. No smoking.
1 Sitting-room. With open fire. **Bar.**
Small garden
Closed from December to February.

This one-time malthouse (parts of it date from the 15th century) is now run very professionally by Fred Alderton and Jane Young. June is an ideal time to visit, when high Exmoor, unlike some places has few visitors.

Beyond the large, light dining-room is a small bar; and, for residents, a sitting-room. Narrow, scarlet-carpeted passages twist and turn. Upstairs are pleasant bedrooms – two have views of the garden lawn and herbaceous borders. The bathrooms are attractive. There is one ground-floor bedroom.

There are always choices on the 4-course menu: I chose a delectable carrot and coriander soup, tender Exmoor lamb (garden vegetables included snapper peas), farmhouse Stilton, then raspberry and almond tart – all cooked to perfection.

Winsford, an ancient village (and birthplace of Ernest Bevin), has eight bridges over the several streams which converge here, thatched cottages, a craft centre in an 18th-century chapel, and the Royal Oak inn (12th-century) which provided material for Blackmore's book *Lorna Doone*. It is a good centre from which to explore Exmoor: quite near are the Caractacus Stone, a 5th-century memorial to a nephew of Caradoc, one of the most valiant defenders of Britain against the Romans; prehistoric burial mounds; and Tarr Steps, a prehistoric bridge.

Towards the Devon border is 'Lorna Doone country' (Oare church, in lovely woods, was the scene of her wedding); and also Dunster Castle with its working watermill.

Readers' comments: High standards, we were delighted. Charming and hospitable, food excellent, rooms spotless and comfortable. Excellent food, lovely rooms. A truly delightful place. Everything first class. Excellent hosts. Food of the highest gastronomic standard. Efficient, courteous, friendly, helpful. Food and accommodation excellent. Good food, comfortable, most helpful and welcoming.

15th-century **OLD MANOR** at Lower Marsh, Dunster, stands on marshes that lead to the sea. There is a chapel over the front porch: its barrel-vaulted roof has carved bosses.

Gillian Hill's bedrooms differ, the most striking being the huge rooms with the wood pegging of the cruck-beamed roof open to view. Breakfasts here are exceptional, with home-grown fruits. (Light snacks only.) £18.50–£23.

Reader's comment: A most enjoyable two weeks. [Tel: 0643 821216; postcode: TA24 6PJ]

KELLEYTHORPE CDS
Driffield, Humberside, YO25 9DW Tel: 0377 42297
South-west of Great Driffield. On A163 from Market Weighton to Great Driffield.

3 Bedrooms. £15–£18 (less for 7 nights). Prices go up in April. Some have own shower/toilet. Tea/coffee facilities. Views of garden, country, lake. Washing machine on request.
Dinner. £10 for 4 courses (with choices) and coffee, at 7pm. Non-residents not admitted. Vegetarian or special diets if ordered. Wine can be brought in. **Light suppers** if ordered.
1 Sitting-room. With open fire, central heating, TV.
Large garden

This big 18th-century farmhouse, partly rebuilt after wartime bombing, has been in the Hopper family since the early 1800s. It takes its name from 'kell', the Anglo-Saxon word for spring, many of which rise in the small lake just at the back of the house. The bay window of the large sitting/dining-room overlooks the lake (as does one bedroom), and there is a terrace with chairs from which guests can watch the ducks and – with luck – kingfishers. This is the source of the River Hull, which gives the downstream city its name. There are lakeside and woodland walks on the 200-acre farm.

In spite of the size of the house, with its wide staircase hung with oil paintings, this is not a formal place, and family antiques – old furniture, pewter and silver – are scattered around almost casually. (Baby-sitting available.)

Dinner here might consist of smoked trout or asparagus; pork fillet en croûte (much of which would have been produced on this or the family's other farm); and a fruit pudding. It must be ordered in advance.

Walking is popular in this part of the world, which is on the edge of the Wolds. Other attractions are the coastal scenery, historic York and Beverley (see other pages of this book), and such mansions as Burton Agnes (Elizabethan) and Sledmere (Georgian). Factories for pottery (at Hornsea) and rock – the peppermint kind – (at Carnaby) actively encourage visitors.

North-east of Driffield are the resort of Bridlington and the spectacular cliffs at Flamborough Head. On the way there, in the unpretentious farming village of Harpham, is the **ST QUINTIN ARMS**. This 250-year-old inn is run by the Curtis family, who provide food which is much more interesting than the usual run of pub meals – fried clams, for example, and daily specials which might include beef and mushroom stir-fry. The pleasantly furnished bedrooms include one with a brass-framed half-tester bed.

£15.50–£18.50. [Tel: 0262 490329; postcode: YO25 0QY]

KIMBERLEY HOME FARM

C S

Wymondham, Norfolk, NR18 0RW   Tel: 0953 603137
South-west of Norwich. Nearest main road: A11 from Norwich to Thetford.

4 Bedrooms. £18. Some have own bath/shower/toilet. Tea/coffee facilities. TV. Views of garden, country. Washing machine on request.
Dinner. £11.50 for 3 courses and coffee, at guests' convenience. Wine can be brought in. **Light suppers** if ordered.
1 Sitting-room. With open fire, central heating, TV, record-player.
Large garden
Closed from December to March.

This is a beautifully furnished farmhouse with stables at the front and a large garden at the back, onto which the glass doors of the large sitting-room open. There is a pond with ducks, and a hard tennis court. Apart from the hundreds of acres of crops, the main activity at Kimberley is training and racing horses.

The bedrooms are particularly pretty, the bathroom excellent, and the dining-room has a long Regency table. Jenny Bloom is not only a superb cook but a generous one, leaving pheasants or joints of meat on a hot-tray from which guests may help themselves, and she is apt to whisk away a half-demolished chicken merely in order to replace it with a fresh one. Starters are imaginative (avocado mousse, for instance), and puddings delicious.

You can have the exclusive use of rooms if you wish, or get more involved with the family and the activities of the farm. There is a very good attic family-suite.

Norwich is one of the most beautiful of mediaeval cities, complete with castle and cathedral, full of craft and antique shops in cobbled byways. The county has a great many stately homes and even statelier churches, wonderful landscapes and seascapes, and, of course, the Broads. The Sainsbury Art Centre outside Norwich is exceptional. The Norfolk coast, King's Lynn and Cambridge are all about one hour away.

This is an excellent spot from which to explore in all directions. Bressingham Hall has fine gardens and steam engines. Beyond Diss (market on Fridays) are the very colourful villages of Burston and Shelfanger. East Dereham has an unusual town sign (two legendary does), an interesting church, an archaeological museum in cottages with decorative plasterwork. Go to the Norfolk Wildlife Park to see bears and otters, to Harleston for spring blossom or summer roses and the River Waveney. Further afield, in Suffolk, there are historic Bungay and Earl Soham, riverside Debenham, Framlingham Castle, Heveningham Hall and a museum of rural life at Stowmarket. Yoxford village is famous for its cottage-gardens. Farming is done on a prairie-size scale, but villages with their little greens, and occasional windmills, are a pretty sight.

The Broads are near (a steam train runs between Wroxham and Aylsham). At Tasburgh are the gardens of Elizabethan Rainthorpe Hall, with trees of botanical interest; at Badley Moor, a butterfly centre; in the direction of Diss, a monkey sanctuary; and near Fakenham one of the world's largest waterfowl collections.

Readers' comments: Total peace, comfortable rooms, delicious food. Comfortable, and very good food. Excellent.

KING'S LODGE   C D S

Long Marston, Warwickshire, CV37 8RL   Tel: 0789 720705
South-west of Stratford-upon-Avon. Nearest main road: B439 from Stratford
towards Evesham (and M40, junction 15).

4 Bedrooms. £17–£24 (less for 3 nights).
Some have own bath/toilet. Tea/coffee
facilities. Views of garden.
Light suppers. Wine can be ordered. No
smoking.
2 Sitting-rooms. With open fire, central
heating, TV. Bar.
Large garden
Closed in December and January.

With his father beheaded and Cromwell ruling England, young Charles II (only
twenty-one) made a desperate attempt in 1651 to regain the throne. Badly defeated
at Worcester, however, he became a fugitive on the run – for weeks eluding
escape by means of disguises and hiding-places, as he made his way to the coast
and France.

To get through Stratford-upon-Avon, swarming with Cromwellian troops, he
dressed himself as the manservant of Miss Jane Lane (sister of one of his
colonels), and together they rode to Long Marston and the house of her kinsman,
John Tomes. This was on 10 September; and I stayed there on almost the same
date, breakfasting in the hall with great inglenook where he had a narrow escape:
on being asked by the cook to wind up the jack that operated the roasting-spit, his
ignorance of this homely task nearly gave the game away. Although other parts of
the Tudor house have changed, this room is much as it was when he stayed here –
and outside, too, the scene has altered very little. Probably, the willow-fringed
duck-pond and the mulberry and pear trees are very like what he saw.

When the house came up for sale many years ago, George and Angela Jenkins
(who lived locally) could not resist buying it, even though it was very neglected
and rather too large for their family. To pay for its restoration and upkeep, they
decided to take paying guests.

One bedroom has a four-poster made from elms felled in the grounds and
a fine stone fireplace on which the Tomes children inscribed their initials over
three centuries ago. The house is full of old pictures and trifles which the
Jenkins have collected, many relating to Charles II or the Tomes family who
sheltered him.

Angela sometimes serves light suppers in the garden; croquet available.

The house is ideally placed for visiting the beauty-spots, gardens and historic
sights of three counties – Warwickshire, Gloucestershire (the Cotswolds), and
Oxfordshire. Head for Evesham if you want pick-your-own fruit and to Stratford
for its Shakespeare sights. Close to King's Lodge is an antiques' warehouse.

Readers' comments: Delighted with situation, food and hospitality. Enjoyable and
interesting. Very good value. Have returned because of friendly, unassuming
service. Lovely house, good accommodation and food. Very nice people.

177

LAMB INN   C D PT
Great Rissington, Gloucestershire, GL54 2LP   Tel: 0451 820388
East of Cheltenham. Nearest main road: A40 from Oxford to Cheltenham.

13 Bedrooms. £19–£35 (Sunday nights free to over-60s). Prices go up in April. Bargain breaks. All have own bath/shower/toilet; tea/coffee facilities. Views of garden, country. No smoking. Washing machine on request.
Dinner. A la carte (about £12–£15), at 7pm. Vegetarian or special diets if ordered. Wine can be ordered. No smoking. **Light suppers** if ordered.
1 Sitting-room. With open fire, central heating, TV. **Bar.**
Large garden

This is exactly what one asks of a typical old Cotswold inn! It is a place of little windows, zigzag corridors and stairs, quaint oak doors, thick stone walls; outside are magnificent views of the countryside, looking across to some of the highest Cotswolds. Kate and Richard Cleverly have furnished the bedrooms with care – restful colours, everything neat, a pretty tulip wallpaper in one room, and in the dining-room pine chairs at polished tables with candle-lamps lit at night. The menu is à la carte, with such dishes as Stilton-topped fillet steaks, veal-and-sweet-corn pies, salmon-and-prawn mousse, lamb with apricots. Outside is a landscaped garden from which to enjoy the summer view with a glass of 'real ale' in hand; a covered swimming-pool (heated to 80°) and a summer-house. In cold weather, there is a log fire in the bar, and in the attractive residents' sitting-room. The restaurant extension was created from an old barn and is furnished with Laura Ashley fabrics. There is also a four-poster suite on the ground floor.

Richard is an imaginative as well as skilled craftsman: the carving of a lamb over the sitting-room fire is his, and so are the conversions of old doors, pews and school desks to new uses. He has even made a four-poster with carved decorations. In former stables are two double bedrooms, with en suite showers. Both have exposed stone walls, beams and chintz curtains.

Readers' comments: Excellent. Clean, friendly and comfortable. The food varied, well-cooked and plentiful. Superb accommodation, very friendly.

Close to Burford (Oxfordshire), on Westhall Hill, Fulbrook, is the **DOWER HOUSE**, another handsome house of golden stone, which Diana Westall has furnished with flair. You might sleep in a four-poster, or a brass bed with porcelain panels in a room with panoramic views on two sides and a bathroom which, like other rooms, has William Morris wallpaper. (Light suppers only: plenty of restaurants in Burford.) £16.
Readers' comments: Highlight of our

trip. Perfect hostess. [Tel: 099382 2596; postcode: OX18 4BJ]

LANE END HOUSE C(10) D M PT X
Green Lane, Tansley, Derbyshire, DE4 5FJ   Tel: 0629 583981
East of Matlock. Nearest main road: A615 from Matlock to Alfreton
(and M1, junction 28).

3 Bedrooms. £19–£21.50 (less for 2 nights). Prices go up in April. Bargain breaks. All have own bath or shower and toilet. Tea/coffee facilities. TV. Views of garden, country. No smoking. Washing machine on request.
Dinner. £13.50 for 4 courses and coffee, at 7.30pm. Non-residents not admitted. Vegetarian or special diets if ordered. Wine can be ordered. No smoking. **Light suppers** if ordered.
Small garden

Even the 18th-century pigsty is a 'listed' building here! But to the old house, opposite the Gate Inn, a new wing has been added, in which there is a big picture-window opening onto a stone terrace with lawn and flowers beyond. Antiques and ample sofas encourage one to linger indoors, but croquet awaits in the landscaped garden from which there is a spectacular view of gaunt Riber Castle looming over the horizon. Outside the dining-room's French windows is a watergarden.

One bedroom is on the ground floor, attractively furnished with silky mulberry quilts, while from the dining-room an open-tread staircase rises to others which have fine views of the wonderful scenery all around. One particularly pleasant room has a draped bedhead and figured walnut suite, with a rather splendid Victorian bathtub and cistern in its bathroom. The pink-and-green room enjoys windows on three sides – and houses part of Marion Smith's vast collection of pottery hedgehogs. Every detail has been thought out with much care, from Vanitory units neatly concealed behind louvred cupboard doors to the provision of towelling bathrobes, maps, videos of the Peak District and even tape-recorders with a selection of tapes.

Marion Smith and her husband, who used to run a large Leicestershire hotel, apply professional standards to everything they do – particularly the meals (including a very varied breakfast). From a wide choice, one might possibly start with a chicken vol-au-vent or mushrooms à la grecque; to be followed by a sorbet and then trout with a honey, orange and raisin sauce or chicken with four garden vegetables and potatoes lyonnaise; and finally perhaps individual sticky-toffee puddings or a roulade. Vegetarian options are numerous and imaginative. Yogurt and muesli are home-made, stoneground flour is used for pastry, there is much emphasis on low-fat foods, low-sugar jams, and syrup-free compotes, for instance. There is a long wine-list.

Readers' comments: Very warm welcome, food excellent, most comfortable. First-class, imaginative menus. Wines of excellent provenance. Most welcoming. Charming house and interesting garden. A gourmet's delight. Attentive and friendly proprietors. Delightful surroundings. Most peaceful, and so many personal touches. Meticulous care and attention. Home cooking at its very best. Exceptional in every way. Food beautifully cooked and served.

LANGORF HOTEL   C PT X

20 Frognal, Hampstead, London, NW3 6AG Tel: 071-794 4483
(Toll-free from USA on: 1-800-925-4731)
Nearest main road: A41 (Finchley Road) from London to Aylesbury
(M1, junction 1, is near).

32 Bedrooms. £24 (or £21 at weekends) **to readers of this book only** (prices may rise in April). All have own bath/shower/toilet. Tea/coffee facilities. TV. Washing/cleaning service. **Light suppers** etc. (24 hours). **Bar.**

For readers visiting London, I have negotiated a very special price (just over half the usual cost) at a small but luxurious hotel.

Its quiet residential road, at the top of which Hampstead had its beginnings in Saxon times, has housed such famous residents as Stephen Spender (at no. 10), Kate Greenaway (no. 39), Charles de Gaulle (no. 99) and Ramsay MacDonald (no. 103); and walking up it – to Hampstead village, the church where Constable is buried and the famous Heath – you will pass many fine 18th-century houses.

Within yards is busy Finchley Road with its shops, buses into Central London, Underground station (Jubilee and Metropolitan lines) and British Rail (to the City in one direction, Richmond and Kew Gardens in the other). The hotel is particularly well placed for visiting the art treasures of Kenwood House, Regent's Park (with the Zoo), Keats' house, the shops of Baker Street and Oxford Street (Selfridges, etc.), the Wallace Collection, Madame Tussauds, the Planetarium, West End theatres and cinemas, Lord's cricket ground and much else.

The bedrooms are elegant, and have every convenience that you might expect of a top hotel. Modern limewood furniture is complemented by excellent soft-furnishings such as coral fabrics on armchairs and padded bedheads, and silver-grey quilts on the beds. All bathroom and other fitments are of the highest quality: high-pressure showers, for example, and solid brass fittings on the white, panelled doors. There are remote-control satellite television sets in each room, direct-dial telephones, hair-dryers, etc. Some bedrooms are on the ground floor, others are served by a lift. Twenty-four-hour room-service for snacks and drinks.

Downstairs, an attractive blue-and-white reception/sitting-area, with sofas of navy buttoned leather and prettily draped curtains, leads into the airy breakfast-room, which overlooks a leafy garden. Here one helps oneself from a buffet of some two dozen items that include melon and other fruits, ham, cheeses, croissants and much else (cooked breakfasts are extra). Throughout the rest of the day, light meals are available – such as quiches and salads – and a bar. Individual dietary requirements can be catered for, if the hotel is forewarned. Special dinner menus have been arranged at two very good restaurants nearby.

The young manager, Nigel Walker, who came here after working in the big hotels of Trust House Forte and Grand Metropolitan, aims to provide a very personal service – as far as possible, getting to know each guest himself and catering for their individual needs: so different from most city hotels.

Readers' comments: Compliments of the highest order to Nigel Walker and his entire staff. Very pleased.

LANNARDS
Okehurst Lane, Billingshurst, West Sussex, RH14 9HR   Tel: 040 3782692
South-west of Horsham. Nearest main road: A29 from London to Chichester.

3 Bedrooms. £16. Tea/coffee facilities. TV. Views of garden, country. No smoking. Washing machine on request.
Light suppers if ordered.
1 Sitting/dining-room. With central heating. No smoking.
Small garden

This is one for collectors of contemporary art – paintings, ceramics and silver – or of antiques. Adjoining the house of cedar shingles where guests are accommodated is an octagonal gallery of pine and glass where a discriminating display of fine arts is exhibited for sale. It is the brainchild of Betty Sims on whose husband's farm is this unusual gallery-cum-guest-house. As to antiques, within yards is an outpost of Sothebys (a Tudor mansion where auctions are held).

All bedrooms are on the ground floor – neat, compact rooms with pale colours and built-in cupboards. There is a comfortable sitting-room, lawn with tables and rural views all round.

Nearby Billingshurst is one of many pretty Sussex villages, sited on the road the Romans called Stane Street (it ran from London to Chichester). It is well placed to visit – to the south – Brighton (Pavilion, etc.) and other coastal resorts beyond the South Downs. Arundel (castle, wildfowl reserve) and also innumerable stately homes such as Petworth, Parham and Hever Castle are near. The countryside is lovely; and Gatwick Airport about half an hour away.

In pretty Billingshurst itself (in East Street), right by the mediaeval church, is a beamy 17th-century house, **CHURCHGATE**, which Sheila Butcher has furnished in traditional country-house style. Views from its windows (double-glazed in case light sleepers are disturbed by bell-ringing or passing cars) are of a flowery little garden and the church. Dinner (to be ordered in advance) might typically be pâté, coq au vin, home-made desserts and cheeses (choices are offered). In the sitting-room is a piano which guests are welcome to play, television,

video and a good selection of books. £15–£17.50.

Readers' comments: Excellent, personal service. A most delightful place. Superb atmosphere and excellent food. [Tel: 0403 782 733; postcode: RH14 9PY]

For explanation of code letters (C, D, M, PT, S, X) see page xlvi.

LANSCOMBE HOUSE

Cockington Lane, Cockington, Devon, TQ2 6XA   Tel: 0803 606938
West of Torquay. Nearest main road: A379 from Torquay to Paignton.

7 Bedrooms. £18–£20 (less for 5 nights). Prices go up from June. All have own bath/shower/toilet. Tea/coffee facilities. TV. Views of garden (some). No smoking in some.
Light suppers if ordered.
1 Sitting-room. With open fire, central heating, record-player. No smoking. **Bar.**
Large garden
Closed in November.

An ideal spot for anyone who wants that 'off the beaten track' feel while being close to all the amenities of a major seaside resort. Picturesque and secluded, Cockington village has just survived being swallowed up by the spread of Torquay's palms and promenades.

The life of the thatched village, complete with its blacksmith's forge and ancient church, used to be dominated by a great house set in a park, Cockington Court (now a Rural Skills Centre, where you can watch traditional crafts being taught). Pink-walled Lanscombe was its dower house: when each lord of the manor died, his widow would move out of the Court to live here. It was built in the early 18th century and has the features of that very fine architectural period – for instance, the floor-to-ceiling sash windows in the dining-room. Here Pat Perryman serves not only breakfasts and snack suppers but Devon cream teas during the summer season. This and other rooms overlook the secluded garden with pools fed by a stream that flows to the sea some 300 yards away.

Bedrooms are spacious, decorated in soft pastel colours and with flowery fabrics. Several of the beds have prettily draped coronas or pelmets, and one is a four-poster. Some rooms have armchairs.

Botanists are impressed by the huge magnolia (probably as old as the house) which usually flowers from July to the end of December – this coastline is well called 'the English Riviera'.

Those who want more than a light supper can stroll to the Thatched Drum nearby, the only inn to have been designed by Lutyens.

Just north of Torquay is Maidencombe, a conservation village, and , perched on Steep Hill (where no traffic goes), **THE BEEHIVE** – with stunning views across Lyme Bay which is at the foot of the hill. This modern house was designed by its owner Norman Sibthorp to handsome standards and is furnished immaculately. Comfort within is complemented by a beautifully tended, steep garden reached via a terrace of red sandstone outside the sliding glass doors of the dining-room. A few yards downhill is the Thatched Tavern for meals; just beyond this, a sandy cove – one of

many – and the coastal footpath to Teignmouth. No smoking. £15–£16.
Readers' comments: Beautifully decorated. Never met hosts who were kinder and more anxious to please. Thoroughly enjoyed our stay. Superb quality, exceptional hospitality. [Tel: 0803 314647; postcode: TQ1 4TS]

LANSDOWNE HOUSE
C(5) M PT S
Clarendon Street, Leamington Spa, Warwickshire, CV32 4PF
Tel: 0926 450505 or 421313

Nearest main road: A425 from Warwick to Southam (and M40, junctions 13/14).

15 Bedrooms. £19.45–£24.95 (less for 2 nights). **If included in a 3-night half-board stay, Sunday's accommodation is free to readers of this book; and in high summer 15% off.** Prices go up in September. Bargain breaks. Some have own bath/shower/toilet. Tea/coffee facilities. TV. Laundry and dry-cleaning: 8-hour service.
Dinner. £16 for 3 courses (with choices) and coffee, at 6.30–8.30pm. Vegetarian or special diets if ordered. Wine can be ordered. No smoking. **Light suppers** if ordered.
2 Sitting-rooms. With open fire, central heating, TV. **Bar.**

A pretty creeper-covered house built in the 18th-century, this small hotel cannot be described as truly 'off the beaten track' for it stands at a crossroads not far from the centre of Leamington. But bedroom windows are double-glazed to reduce any sound from traffic – and the hotel is of such excellence that I wanted to include it.

When David and Gillian Allen took it over they decided to furnish it to a very high standard and in keeping with its architecture. There is a particularly pretty sitting-room with sea-green and strawberry Victorian sofas, for example; in the small dining-room, meals are served on fluted Rosenthal china and wine in elegant glasses; the bar has cherry buttoned seats; and every bedroom is attractively decorated in soft colours with well-chosen fabrics, stripped-pine furniture and thick, moss-green carpet. (No. 2 is the quietest, with roof-light not windows.)

The same care goes into the food. David, who trained as a chef in Switzerland, is a perfectionist. He sends to Scotland for his steaks, to the Cotswolds for his trout, has coffee specially blended to his taste, and damson and other sorbets made for him on a fruit farm nearby. Connoisseurs will appreciate some little-known wines among his very good selection, and the range of malt whiskies.

There are always several choices of good English dishes at dinner. Starters include particularly imaginative soups (such as celery-and-walnut or cream of parsnip), while main courses are likely to be such things as roast pork with freshly chopped rosemary or liver and bacon with fresh sage. Puddings might include walnut-and-chocolate fudge pudding or fruit cobbler.

Royal Leamington Spa is a health resort with a saline spring. It has fine Georgian terraces and lovely riverside gardens. A good base from which to visit not only Warwick and Kenilworth castles, described elsewhere, but also Coventry (modern cathedral, some historic buildings), Southam (old market town), Stoneleigh (mediaeval village and the great National Agricultural Centre) and fine countryside towards Stratford-upon-Avon.

For residents there are discounts at Warwick Castle (where Tussaud's 'royal house party' is a superb show) and many other sights. Free guided local walks.

Readers' comments: Excellent. Charming features, food excellent. The personal touch made such a difference.

LASKILL FARM   C D M PT S X
Hawnby, North Yorkshire, YO6 5NB   Tel: 0439 798268
North-west of Pickering. Nearest main road: A170 from Thirsk to Helmsley.

7 Bedrooms. £15.50–£18.50 (less for 3 nights). Prices go up from Easter. Some have own bath/shower/toilet. Tea/coffee facilities. TV. Views of garden, country, river. Washing machine on request.
Dinner. £10.50 for 4 courses and coffee, at 7pm (not Sundays). Non-residents not admitted. Vegetarian or special diets if ordered. Wine can be ordered.
1 Sitting-room. With open fire, central heating, TV.
Large garden

This stone farmhouse lies in a hilly, wooded area of great scenic splendour ('Herriot country'), and close to famous Rievaulx Abbey. Its courtyard is made pretty with stone troughs, flowers and rocks; and around lie 600 acres with cattle and sheep. There are white iron chairs in the garden, and a duck-pond.

In the sitting/dining-room is oak furniture hand-carved by local craftsmen, each of whom 'signs' his work with his own particular symbol – an acorn, a beaver or a stag's head. Here Sue Smith serves home-made soup or pâté before a main course which is likely to comprise meat and vegetables from the farm, followed by (for instance) lemon meringue pie or a fruit fool, and then an interesting selection of cheeses. Often there is a chance to see James Herriot himself, as he sometimes opens fêtes or gives talks. Television's 'Heart Beat' was filmed nearby.

Two bedrooms are in a beamy outbuilding and open onto the lawn. Two others, more recently converted, are in another farm building, stone-built and red-tiled, and face across the yard. These rooms have their own bathrooms.

The North York Moors are one of England's finest national parks: whether you walk or drive, the views are spectacular, particularly when the heather blooms.

Readers' comments: Comfortable, welcoming, and good food. Excellent meals, complete relaxation. Charming and considerate hostess. Delightful; everything perfect. Mrs Smith was so welcoming and easy to get on with. Food excellent. Beautiful location. Comfort, good food and congenial company. Delightful room. Extremely comfortable. Food generous. A welcoming hostess.

Sitting-room at Bishop Garth (see page 195)

LEWORTHY FARMHOUSE   C M S X

Leworthy, Holsworthy, Devon, EX22 6SJ   Tel: 0409 253488

East of Bude (Cornwall). Nearest main road: A3072 from Holsworthy to Bude.

12 Bedrooms. £15–£18 (less for 7 nights). Bargain breaks. Some have own shower/toilet. Tea/coffee facilities. Views of garden, country. Coin-operated laundry.
Dinner. £9.50 for 4 courses (with choices) and coffee, at 7pm. Vegetarian or special diets if ordered. Wine can be ordered. No smoking. **Light suppers** if ordered.
2 Sitting-rooms. With open fire, central heating, TV, video, piano, record-player.
Bar.
Garden

Guests greatly appreciate genial Eric Cornish, and he goes to considerable lengths to give them a good time – young children in particular. Dozens of their drawings and letters to him are pinned up around the bar.

He has added to the rooms in the farmhouse to provide more accommodation in a bungalow close by, and sometimes has as many as forty people staying – laying on for this huge house-party all kinds of evening entertainments (games, dancing, conjuror, film) for which there is no extra charge. This is obviously appreciated by families tired of the spend-spend-spend involved in keeping youngsters entertained in most resorts. Eric also takes visitors on tractor-drawn hay-rides (dogs following) to see the crops, sheep, beef-cattle, lake, river and woods, while explaining to them what work is going on. It's a place where parents can leave their older children to go their own way – they find plenty to do, like organizing table tennis or badminton competitions. There are deer, herons and even otters to be spotted; abundant wildflowers; and lots of good picnic spots within the farm estate. Clay-pigeon shooting, fishing, pitch-and-putt, riding, tennis and pub skittle-matches are also available. And there is a wheelchair.

Something new is always afoot, so Eric and Marion keep in touch with past guests by means of a circular letter with news of what has been happening to the various pets and the family. Many guests become lifelong friends, and most get involved in one way or another (the gumboot rack was made by a group of dads).

Marion produces typical farmhouse meals such as soup, roast beef, fruit pie and cream, cheese, coffee. Visitors in the self-catering accommodation may dine in the main house if they wish.

There is so much going on that many people hardly stir. However, within a short drive are the beaches of Bude and superb clifftop views, Hartland's dramatic reefs and lighthouse and quaint Clovelly. Holsworthy is only three miles away.

Readers' comments: Very much enjoyed the Cornishes' company; they make you feel welcome. A delightful couple who spared nothing to see that everyone had a good time. We had a high time! So genial and helpful; constant laughter. The very best type of English cooking. The atmosphere was more that of a party of friends than paying guests. Shall be back at the first opportunity! Wonderful holiday, a big house-party. Holiday of a lifetime. Enjoyed our stay tremendously.

THE LIMES   **C PT X**

23 Stankelt Road, Silverdale, Lancashire, LA5 0TF   Tel: 0524 701454
North of Lancaster. Nearest main road: A6 from Carnforth to Kendal
(and M6, junction 35).

3 Bedrooms. £18.50 (less for 3 nights). All have own bath/shower/toilet. Tea/coffee facilities. TV. Views of country. No smoking. Washing machine on request. **Dinner.** £11.50 for 5 courses, dessert wine and coffee, at 7–8pm. Vegetarian or special diets if ordered. Wine can be brought in. No smoking. **Light suppers** if ordered.
1 Sitting-room with conservatory.
Large garden

Near Carnforth (where railway enthusiasts will want to visit Steam Town) is an area of outstanding natural beauty, quite different from the Lake District National Park, whose boundary it meets. Almost at sea level, this is wooded countryside rich in wildlife, most of it protected in nature reserves. In nearby Warton, ancestral home of the Washingtons since the 13th century, the stars and stripes on their coat of arms in the church inspired the American flag.

The Limes is a Victorian house run by Noel and Andrée Livesey. From the tented conservatory with its basketwork chairs to the one attic bedroom, with its sunken bathroom, they have decorated the rooms with flair. The dining-room reflects their travels and their interest in art and antiques.

A typical dinner (of which guests in the self-catering accommodation may also partake) might be hot brandied grapefruit; chestnut and broad-bean soup; steak and smoked oyster pie with vegetables; baked apple stuffed with vine fruits (served with dessert wine); and cheese. (Country club facilities nearby, including swimming and fishing, free.)

Readers' comments: Candlelit meal impeccably served. No restaurant could have been better. Most friendly, helpful and attentive. Imaginative dinners, delicious and meticulously prepared. Very comfortable. Superlative dinners. Warm welcome. Couldn't do enough for us. Comfortable, spotless, what a delight!

A little inland is the small village of Yealand Conyers and **THE BOWER**, built as a farmhouse in 1745 and later gentrified. The cast-iron porch is handsome. There is a modern harpsichord in the entrance hall and hi-fi in both the sitting-room and the dining-room (as well as a piano in the former), for Michael Rothwell teaches music (also bridge). Sally-Ann serves for dinner such dishes as pâté or mousse, a casserole or a roast, and fruit pie. The colours in the rooms are mostly muted greys and pinks, with elaborate floral curtains at the tall windows. These give views across a big garden, to the summit of

Ingleborough. No smoking. £19.95–£32.65 **for readers of this book.**
Readers' comments: Charming young couple, charming garden, comfortable dining-room, superb bedroom with every convenience. Most enjoyable in every respect. [Tel: 0524 734585; postcode: LA5 9SF]

LINDEN HOUSE

14 Church Street, Ross-on-Wye, Herefordshire, HR9 5HN Tel: 0989 65373
Nearest main road: A40 from Gloucester to Monmouth (and M50, junction 4.)

8 Bedrooms. £17–£21. Some have own shower/toilet. All have tea/coffee facilities. TV. No smoking.
Dinner. £11 for 3 courses (with choices) and coffee, at 6.30pm (by arrangement). Non-residents not admitted. Vegetarian or special diets if ordered. Wine can be ordered. No smoking. **Light suppers** sometimes.
Small garden

Although close to the central market square of this historic town, the guest-house is in a quiet street with little sound except the chiming of the church clock opposite. It was built in 1680 but its façade was altered in the 18th century. At every sash window there is a window-box ablaze with geraniums during summer.

Indoors, Clare O'Reilly has stencilled fuchsias up the staircase and on bedroom walls. Some of the rooms are small (and there is no sitting-room) but all are pretty, and there is one with an attractive view of the old churchyard. A number of rooms have brass beds.

Much is home-made, from the marmalades and jams at breakfast to the cream teas served on some afternoons. At dinner, options may include celery and cashewnut soup, pork in a cream and mustard sauce (or a good vegetarian dish) and chocolate-orange cheesecake. Most produce is locally grown.

The old market town of Ross is ideally placed for touring some of the best parts of England and Wales, midway in a scenic corridor between Hereford and Chepstow. One could easily spend a fortnight here without exhausting all the possibilities.

For every visitor, a trip to Symonds Yat is a 'must': around the foot of this rock, 500 feet high, the great River Wye makes a loop that almost turns it into an island and in every direction are superb views of river, wooded slopes and fields. Also in this direction is Goodrich Castle, the red towers and walls of which seem almost part of the rock on which it stands, a moat deep-hewn around – and it, too, is perched high above a meander of the River Wye. (It was built in 1160 to mount guard over a crossing of what was then a strategically important waterway. It proved impregnable until, during the Civil Wars of the 17th century, the 200-lb cannon balls of 'Roaring Meg' battered it into submission: 'Meg' still exists, on Hereford's Castle Green.)

Visitors come to Ross not only for the surrounding scenery (the Black Mountains, Malvern Hills and Forest of Dean) but to go antique-hunting in the town itself and to see the 'lost streets' museum (old shops preserved and re-erected). There are also many fine gardens in the county – such as those of Westbury Court (the pavilion reflected in clear water and the formal beds in Dutch style have been restored exactly as they were in the 17th century); and 18th-century Berrington Hall with grounds designed by Capability Brown on a commanding site – the house itself, classical without, is elaborately decorated within.

LINK HOUSE

C(8) M S

Bassenthwaite Lake, Cumbria, CA13 9YD Tel: 07687 76291
East of Cockermouth. Nearest main road: A66 from Keswick to Cockermouth.

8 Bedrooms. £19–£23 (less for 7 nights). Prices go up at Easter. Bargain breaks. All have own shower/toilet. Tea/coffee facilities. TV. Views of garden, country.
Dinner. £12.50 for 5 courses (with choices) and coffee, at 7pm. Vegetarian or special diets if ordered. Wine can be ordered.
2 Sitting-rooms. With open fire, central heating. **Bar.**
Small garden
Closed in December and January.

Teacher May Smith so much enjoyed cookery as a hobby that eventually she gave up her career to start a new one, running a guest-house. That is why Link House, outwardly similar to many others in the Lake District, is in fact very different in the kind of meals that are served.

The small Victorian house stands in a garden near the north end of the lake. Everything inside is spick-and-span. One bay-windowed sitting-room has a log fire and comfortable chairs; the other, a conservatory bar, is attractively furnished, with cane seats and tiled floor. Beyond this is the dining-room where tables are laid with fine linen napkins, Wedgwood china, decorative silver and Cumbria crystal goblets; it is a light room with windows on two sides. The bedrooms are equally pleasant: pine woodwork and pale shades in one, modern furniture and cheerful colours in another, and so on. All around are fells and forests.

Dinner is a five-course meal with coffee. Peach and tarragon cream cheese might be followed by tomato and pimento soup, venison, rum and pineapple trifle, and then cheeses (with choices at most courses). Bread is home-made.

Bassenthwaite Lake is the most northerly of the lakes and the only one with the word 'lake' in its name, the rest being 'meres' or 'waters'. On one side is the great peak of Skiddaw and on the other Thornthwaite Forest, with a visitor centre provided by the Forestry Commission. By it is Mirehouse, one of the least intimidating of mansions: children have been known to be led to find a sweet in a secret drawer in a bureau, and the sound of the grand piano is heard on occasion. It is still in the possession of the family whose ancestors entertained Tennyson and Carlyle there. As well as maintaining a domestic atmosphere in the house itself, they have provided an adventure playground in the grounds.

Westward is Cockermouth, Wordsworth's birthplace. Less crowded than other Lake District towns, it has plenty of antique shops. On the way there, Wythop Mill, with a display of old woodworking and wheelwrighting tools, is a good stop for tea or coffee, as is Thornthwaite Gallery off the same road, where there is an outstanding choice of crafts and pictures. Near Keswick, pleasant but often crowded during the tourist season, are a stone circle and the famous Manesty Gardens. Beautiful Derwent Water is to the south.

Readers' comments: Could not have been more helpful; food ample and delicious. Food, service and friendly atmosphere truly excellent. Lovely setting. Lovely meals.

LISLE COMBE

C PT S

Undercliff Drive, St Lawrence, Isle of Wight, PO38 1UW
Tel: 0983 852 582
West of Ventnor. Nearest main road: A3055 from Ventnor to Niton.

3 Bedrooms. £15–£16.50. Prices go up in July. Tea/coffee facilities. Views of garden, country, sea. No smoking.
Light suppers if ordered.
1 Sitting-room. With open fire, TV.
Large garden

'East of the garden, a wild glen glimmers with foxgloves,
And there, through the heat of the day,
In a fern-shadowed elf-ring of sand, with pine logs round it,
Three bird-voiced children play,
With a palm to shelter their golden heads from the sun,
When the noon-sun grows too strong . . . '

One of Alfred Noyes' 'bird-voiced children' about whom he wrote this poem in 1936 now owns that garden, glen and the family home. Hugh Noyes grew up to become *The Times* parliamentary correspondent until 1982, but is now occupied in dairy-farming and breeding rare species of waterfowl. He has also been High Sheriff of the Isle. Surrounding the house is his rare breeds and waterfowl park (in 30 acres of outstanding natural beauty) to which guests have free access.

Visitors staying at Lisle Combe see not only the scenes which inspired so many poems but many of the poet's possessions, such as a series of watercolours by Frederick Weld (who became New Zealand's first Prime Minister); and all his papers are preserved in his still intact library.

The house itself is exceptional. It was built in the early 19th century – but in Elizabethan style, by the same Lord Yarborough whose monument dominates one of the island's hills (he was a considerable landowner on the island – Pelham Woods, opposite the house, carries his family's name).

It has barley-sugar chimneys and lozenge-paned bay windows, many overlooking the English Channel; and a paved verandah with grapevine where breakfast is sometimes served. Hugh's mother brought to the house some very exceptional furniture and paintings that were salvaged when, in the 'thirties, her former home – Lulworth Castle (in Dorset) – was burnt down. One of the most attractive rooms is a small, pale-blue sitting-room with sea views. Through the garden and among palm trees, pools and streams a path leads down to the sandy beach.

(No dinners: Judy recommends such nearby inns as the Crown at Shorwell.)

Lisle Combe is close to Ventnor's botanical gardens, full of subtropical flowers, and with an excellent museum of smuggling through the centuries. This south-facing part of the coast is the warmest, and Ventnor itself looks rather Mediterranean because the houses are built on terraces zigzagging steeply down to the sea.

Readers' comments: Beautiful house and setting. Warm, welcoming feeling. Helpful and courteous; interesting and delightful; friendly welcome. Memorably happy.

189

LITTLE LODGE FARMHOUSE   C(6)
Broughton Green, Hanbury, Worcestershire, WR9 7EE   Tel: 0527 821305
East of Droitwich. Nearest main road: A38 from Birmingham to Worcester
(and M5, junction 5).

3 Bedrooms. £19–£21 (less for 3 nights).
Prices go up in June. All have own
bath/shower/toilet.   Tea/coffee   facilities.
Views of garden, country. No smoking.
Washing machine on request.
Dinner. £14 for 3 courses and coffee, at
7pm (Tuesdays and Thursdays only). Non-
residents not admitted. Wine can be
brought in.
1 Sitting-room. With open fire, central
heating, TV.
Large garden
Closed in December.

Once there was a great deer forest all around a mere woodland clearing where this secluded house, originally a hunting-lodge, was built about 1650. Now, nearly all the oaks gone, its surroundings are a patchwork of farmlands and fields for the thoroughbred horses which the Chuggs breed (Robert used to be a jockey), with a distant view of the Clent Hills. In the grounds is a tiny building that was once a schoolroom for local children.

The beamed sitting-room with inglenook fireplace is on two levels and, like all rooms here, has very lovely fabrics to complement the antique furniture. There are hedgerow fruits in the dining-room fabrics, Warner peonies in the coral and green sitting-room, Colefax roses in one bedroom and Jane Churchill garlands in another.

In a very pretty attic room, Jackie herself stencilled the ribbons that decorate the walls. Everywhere she has placed decorative arrangements of dried flowers.

Another of her talents is cookery (she trained at the celebrated Tante Marie School), and at each meal she offers – if it is arranged in advance – a choice of such dishes as egg-and-prawn mousse, duck with Morello cherry sauce and gâteau Diane (which is chocolate-filled meringue). Even breakfasts are rather special, with such options as fromage frais to accompany fruits, granary bread, black pudding from Stornoway, etc.

Worcestershire is one of England's loveliest counties (particularly to the south). The highest point is in the Clent Hills, rising to 1000 feet, among which you can drive or walk to explore their woodlands and pools; and there are hills to the west, too. The Severn is a lovely river to follow down from Stourport to where, beyond the cathedral city of Worcester, it joins the pretty River Teme in an area well-known for its orchards, hops, dairy-cattle and lush meadows. At Droitwich, water saltier than the Dead Sea is pumped up from subterranean sources 200 feet down – so buoyant that visitors bathing in it float unsinkably.

Readers' comments: A marvellous place. I could not find fault anywhere.

**Book well ahead: many of these houses have few rooms. Do not
expect dinner if you have not booked it or if you arrive late.**

LITTLE OREHAM FARM   M
Horn Lane, Henfield, West Sussex, BN5 9SB   Tel: 0273 492931
North-west of Brighton (East Sussex). Nearest main road: A281 from
Horsham towards Shoreham.

3 Bedrooms. £17.50–£18 (less for 7 nights). Bargain breaks. All have own bath/shower/toilet. Tea/coffee facilities. TV. Views of garden, country. No smoking. **Dinner.** £12 for 3 courses and coffee, at about 6.30pm. Non-residents not admitted. Vegetarian or special diets if ordered. Wine can be brought in. No smoking. **Light suppers** if ordered.
1 Sitting-room. With open fire, central heating, TV, video. No smoking.
Large garden
Closed in January.

Inside this brick and timbered house, 300 years old, rooms have beams and oak-mullioned or lattice-paned windows. There is a great inglenook fireplace with iron fireback as old as the house itself (a collection of big copper vessels is housed on its slate hearth), and red tiles cover the dining-room floor.

Most of the well-furnished bedrooms for visitors (pine furniture and sprigged fabrics) are in the converted outbuildings, but meals are taken in the house itself: typically Josie Forbes provides (if these are ordered in advance) such dinners as antipasto, roast pork with an apple and nut stuffing, and pumpkin pie with ice cream.

Readers' comments: Beautiful surroundings; most charming lady and a marvellous cook; made me so welcome I am planning to return. Very friendly and warm. Peaceful.

At Wineham, also near Henfield, is **GREAT WAPSES**, a farmhouse which, having been extended in 1720 from a 16th-century building, has all the elegance of that period – pine-panelled walls and doors, for example, and shuttered windows. One ground-floor bedroom is lined with white and apricot panelling to which Eleanor Wilkin has matched the brocade bed-spreads, contrasting with a moss-green carpet and velvet chesterfield from which to enjoy the view of the trees and duck-pond. (There is also a tennis court.) Another bedroom has a lacy four-poster; while (for those nimble enough to manage the twists and turns up to the sloping attic floor) there is a suite which includes a sitting-room with homely furniture.

Eleanor provides simple but gener-ous meals if ordered: often a roast (as much as you want) and then perhaps chocolate mousse. £17–£18 (b & b). [Tel: 0273 492544; postcode: BN5 9BJ]

LITTLE PARMOOR

C(5) **S X**

Parmoor Lane, Frieth, Buckinghamshire, RG9 6NL   Tel: 0494 881447

North-east of Henley-on-Thames (Oxfordshire). Nearest main road: A40 from Oxford to High Wycombe (also M40, junctions 4/5; and M4, junctions 8/9).

3 Bedrooms. £18–£22.50 (less for 4 nights). Tea/coffee facilities. TV. Views of garden, country. No smoking. Washing machine on request.
Dinner. £13.50 for 3 courses and coffee, at 7.30pm (if booked in advance). Non-residents not admitted. Vegetarian or special diets if ordered. Wine can be brought in. No smoking. **Light suppers** if ordered.
1 Sitting-room. With open fire, central heating. No smoking.
Large garden

Within a mere half-hour of Heathrow (and little further to London) is a peaceful spot among the lovely Chiltern Hills, and in it this attractive house built in 1724. (It used to be the house of the estate manager who looked after the lands of Sir Stafford Cripps' father, Lord Parmoor, when he occupied the nearby great house.)

Inside are pale green and white panelling, log fires and watercolours painted by Wynyard Wallace's grandfather. An elegant pine staircase leads to one pretty white-panelled bedroom and another, single, that is very good – unlike so many single bedrooms. Children particularly like the attic rooms above, with circular windows and sloping ceilings. Julia provides breakfast (sometimes taken under the vine outside) and dinners which may include such dishes as home-made vegetable or fish soup, Chiltern game pie with locally grown vegetables, and lemon meringue pie. Also, within five miles are ten inns, all of which serve good food.

Although so many busy roads skirt this area, it is very secluded and few motorists explore its narrow lanes where boughs reach overhead, pheasants dart from hedges or vanish into the glades, beech woods turn to fiery colours in autumn, and one finds unknown villages tucked away, built in flint and brick.

Southward is one of the finest and most winding stretches of the River Thames – from Sonning through Henley (of regatta fame) and Maidenhead to Windsor, best explored by boat – arguably at its best in uncrowded autumn when the hills descend to the river in a blaze of colour.

Readers' comments: Made us feel part of the family. Lovely. Most impressed by the warmth of welcome, the comfort and the outstanding quality of the meals. Excellent. Charming people. Thoughtful, caring hospitality. Kindness itself.

Tucked away in Bovingdon Green is **ACHA PANI** (Urdu for 'good waters'), a modern house with a polygonal sun-room for breakfast. Bedrooms, neat and well-equipped, have garden views. Mary Cowling serves such meals as home-made soup, chops and chocolate mousse, with wine. She gives walkers lifts at the start and finish of their walks: this scenic area is full of footpaths. £14–£15.

[Tel: 0628 483435; postcode: SL7 2JL]

LODGE FARM

C(6) **D S**

Fersfield, Bressingham, Norfolk, IP22 2BQ   Tel: 037988 629
West of Diss. Nearest main road: A1066 from Thetford to Diss.

3 **Bedrooms.** £15–£17. Tea/coffee facilities.
Views of garden, country. Washing machine
on request.
Light suppers if ordered.
2 **Sitting-rooms.** With open fire, central
heating, record-player.
Large garden

Henry VIII had a 'palace' for hunting near here and at the boundaries of his great
estate were lodges, of which this was one. Its windows and pink walls give little
hint that the house goes back so far, for each subsequent century saw additions
and alterations. But inside are chamfered beams, low ceilings, odd steps and
angles.

David and Pat Bateson have furniture that is very much in keeping – for
instance, a wedding-chest dated 1682; a great refectory table; and an iron fireback
of 1582 which furnishes the great inglenook where logs blaze on chilly nights.
Bedrooms are cottagey in style, one lime-and-white, one (with brass bed) pink-
and-white. Another is connected by a very low passage to its own sitting-room
and a winding stair up to two attic rooms: an ideal suite for a family (with bathroom and even a kitchen below). Indeed, this is a marvellous place for a family
holiday (with plenty of sightseeing outings likely to appeal to older children).
Outside is a garden and the Batesons' smallholding (they keep sheep, ducks and
horses). There is also accommodation in a converted coach house which can be
booked on a b & b or self-catering basis.

Breakfast and light suppers only; for a full dinner, most visitors walk or drive
(one mile) to the Garden House Inn or the Fox at Garboldisham (4 miles).

Bressingham is famous for its live steam museum, and acres of very lovely
gardens. Among the hundreds of exhibits is the *Royal Scot*. Historic Diss hums
with life on market day (Friday) but the lanes and meres remain peaceful.

Readers' comments: Made so welcome. Delightful weekend. Reasonable bill.

A few miles north of Diss, at Gissing,
is **OLD RECTORY**, a solidly handsome 19th-century building which is
the home of Ian and Jill Gillam. Its
rooms are well furnished with good
colour schemes and fabrics, and decorated with Ian's unusual collection of
architectural drawings. Outside is a
very large garden with terrace and
conservatory. There is also a heated
indoor swimming-pool. Jill serves such
meals as iced lettuce soup, cod-and-
prawn pie, chocolate mousse and

cheeses. (No smoking in dining-room
or bedrooms.) £19–£27. [Tel: 037977
575; postcode: IP22 3XB]

LOW BARNS   **C D M PT X**
Thornbrough, Corbridge, Northumberland, NE45 5LX   Tel: 0434 632408
East of Hexham. Nearest main road: A69 from Hexham to Newcastle.

3 Bedrooms. £18–£20 (less for 7 nights). Prices go up from April. All have own bath/shower/toilet. Tea/coffee facilities. TV. Views of garden, country. Washing machine on request.
Dinner. £13.50 for 4 courses (with choices) and coffee, at 7pm (not Sundays). Non-residents not admitted. Vegetarian or special diets if ordered. Wine can be brought in. No smoking. **Light suppers** if ordered.
1 Sitting-room. With central heating.
Large garden

With a history that goes back to the Romans, picturesque Corbridge is a large residential village where there are good pubs and superior shops. A little way outside it is Low Barns, once a farmhouse and still surrounded by rolling arable farmland. Typically for the area, it is long in plan and built of stone – exposed in some of the bedrooms, which have sloping beamed ceilings and good views. (The downstairs one is accessible by wheelchair). Colour schemes are fresh and bright, with plain carpets.

One of Sue Jones's dinner menus might consist of asparagus, steak braised in stout, trifle, and cheese. Guests eat at a long pine table in the big kitchen with a grandfather clock. A glazed door leads into a pleasant garden (with cornfields beyond), from part of which Tom Jones produces most of the fruit and vegetables for the table. On the other side of the house, a gravelled yard is a sun-trap where fuchsias flourish. (Visitors in the self-catering accommodation may dine in the main house if they wish.)

The big attraction here is Hadrian's Wall, some of the best sites being close. Not far away are the birthplaces of George Stephenson and of Thomas Bewick. At the latter, you can see prints being made and buy works taken from his original boxwood blocks.

On the other side of Corbridge, and well placed not only for the Roman wall but also Newcastle Airport (at Ponteland), is **DALTON HOUSE**, Anna Trevelyan's family home. Hidden in trees by the hamlet of Dalton (near Newcastle-upon-Tyne), this large Georgian house is replete with antiques, including the bedsteads in the twin rooms (respectively brass and mahogany) and the chairs round the open fireplace in the big sitting-room. A grandfather clock looks down on the dining-table, where Mrs Trevelyan serves (for instance) home- made soup, a meat course cooked with plenty of wine and herbs, and chocolate rum charlotte or home-made ice cream. Almost all the fruit and vegetables are grown by her. £16 (b & b). [Tel: 0661 886225; postcode: NE18 0AA]

LOW GREEN HOUSE

C D

Thoralby, Bishopdale, North Yorkshire, DL8 3SZ   Tel: 0969 663623
East of Hawes. Nearest main road: A684 from Leyburn to Hawes.

4 Bedrooms. £18. Price goes up at Easter. All have own shower/toilet. Tea/coffee facilities. TV. Views of garden, country. No smoking.
Dinner. £10 for 4 courses and coffee, at 6.45pm (not Thursdays). Non-residents not admitted. Vegetarian or special diets if ordered. Wine can be brought in. No smoking.
1 Sitting-room. With open fire, central heating. No smoking.
Small garden

This stone house in a tiny hamlet is the home of Tony and Marilyn Philpott, who are founts of information on where to walk and what to see.

Within rugged walls are particularly comfortable and pretty rooms. (Two bedrooms are in a 17th-century cottage annexe.) I had a pink-and-white bedroom with deep brown carpet; the bathroom was excellent; and in the sitting/dining-room (which runs from front to back of the house, with a picture-window looking towards Wensleydale), soft colours, deep armchairs around a log fire and plentiful books provide a relaxed atmosphere. For dinner Marilyn served – with decorative flourishes – local smoked trout, pork cooked with cream and mushrooms, blue Wensleydale cheese, and raspberry torte. With the coffee came a dish of chocolates. (All carefully prepared, and remarkably good value.)

The Yorkshire Dales have many peaks over 2000 feet high: wild and windy, with lonely farms on their foothills, and waterfalls rushing down the valleys.

Readers' comments: Comfort, hospitality and value cannot be bettered. Lovely hosts. Food was a delight, breakfasts huge and dinners delicious. A Gundrey gem! A happy welcome. Friendly attention. Very comfortable, delicious meals. Very comfortable and friendly. Good value. Exceptional hosts. A divine cook. A most special place.

Newbiggin-in-Bishopdale is a hamlet of ancient stone houses on a no-through-road a few miles away. First 'modernized' in 1767, **BISHOP GARTH** is the home of two well-travelled professional ladies, Meriel Overton and Barbara Marsden. They are developing a wild garden on part of the six acres that go with the house, where they also grow fruit and vegetables. In the house, the stairs are a little tricky but the bedrooms are neat and quiet. Downstairs, the rooms are low and beamy and well provided with books and comfortable armchairs. A typical dinner: fish and cheese pancakes; ham with Cumberland sauce;

raspberry meringues; cheese. £15–£18 (b & b).
Readers' comments: Excellent hostesses. Tastefully furnished and very comfortable. Food beautifully cooked and imaginative. The house and garden create an atmosphere of beauty and tranquillity. [Tel: 0969 663429; postcode DL8 3TD]

195

LOW HALL C(10) **D**
Brandlingill, Cumbria, CA13 0RE Tel: 0900 826654
South of Cockermouth. Nearest main road: A66 from Keswick to Cockermouth.

6 Bedrooms. £20–£21.50 (less for 3 nights). Prices go up at Easter. All have own bath/shower/toilet. Tea/coffee facilities. Views of garden, country, river. No smoking.
Dinner. £14.50 for 5 courses (with choices) and coffee, at 7–7.30pm. Non-residents not admitted. Vegetarian dishes. Wine can be ordered. No smoking.
2 Sitting-rooms. With open fire, central heating, TV, piano. Bar. No smoking.
Large garden
Closed from November to February.

Low Hall is mostly of 17th-century origin but was enlarged to accommodate a big Victorian family. When the previous owners renovated it, they uncovered a huge fireplace in what was the dairy and is now the dining-room, where candlelit dinners are accompanied by classical music. Current owners are Hugh and Enid Davies, respectively an anaesthetist and an ex-teacher.

There is one big sitting-room with log fire and grand piano, and a second smaller one for television addicts.

The bedrooms, most of which are spacious, give views of the Lorton fells in the north-western corner of the Lake District or of the grounds of the house. This is an area of great beauty, wooded rather than rugged, where the Cumbrian mountains start their descent to sea level. It is never overrun by tourists, yet the well-known parts of the Lake District are only a short drive away. Guided walks available.

The menus always include a vegetarian or fish alternative to the meat course. A typical menu: avocado and prawn mousse; soup; pork celeste or baked trout, or courgette and carrot crumble; and a choice of puddings, followed by cheese. Breakfasts are much more interesting than the usual egg-and-bacon routine. Preserves, rolls and ice cream are home-made.

Readers' comments: So impressed with the quality and imaginative cooking . . . delightful base for walking. Fantastic food, super couple. Incredibly well looked after. A real winner. A happy house-party. Perfect in every detail. Meals a delight. Food as good as in any top-class restaurant. Everything one could wish for.

A few miles away, on the edge of High Lorton, Ann Roberts provides dinner, bed-and-breakfast at **OWL BROOK**, Whinlatter Pass, all the year round. This architect-designed and attractive bungalow of green lakeland slate with pine ceilings was built a few years ago, and all the airy bedrooms have fine views. Dinner might comprise soup, risotto, and fresh fruit salad, using wholefood ingredients. £16–£17.50 (b & b).

Readers' comments: Beautiful views and utter tranquillity. Breakfasts were superb. Very friendly family atmosphere. [Tel: 090085 333; postcode: CA13 9TX]

LOW JOCK SCAR   D M

Selside, Cumbria, LA8 9LE   Tel: 05398 3259
North of Kendal. On A6 from Kendal to Penrith.

5 Bedrooms. £18–£21 (less for 6 nights). Some have own bath/shower/toilet. Tea/ coffee facilities. Views of garden, country, river. No smoking.
Dinner. £12.50 for 4 courses (some choices) and coffee, at 7.30pm. Non-residents not admitted. Vegetarian or special diets if ordered. Wine can be ordered. No smoking.
1 Sitting-room. With open fire, central heating, TV, piano. No smoking.
Large garden
Closed from December to February.

Low Jock Scar is only a couple of decades old, but it stands on the site of a much older cottage. One doorstep is an immovable lump of pink Shap granite, but most of the house is built of the green slate much used in what was once Westmorland, and the style of building is traditional.

Not so traditional is the large conservatory at the back, with big pot-plants against the wall. This is where guests breakfast and dine on oak tables and chairs, looking out across the lawn to a picturesque stone bridge among trees.

The conservatory is off a large sitting-room with deep armchairs, a slate fire-place which might date back to the original cottage, a piano, plenty of books and games, and some interesting pictures.

Also on the ground floor is one bedroom. As in the one immediately above it, windows on two sides give views of the beck which runs between wooded banks and of the footbridge across it, which leads into the grounds of the house, mostly natural woodland. There is plenty of scope for walking here or further afield. Another bedroom at the front of the house overlooks a rock garden with heathers and conifers planted around massive boulders.

Alison Midwinter offers a choice of first courses for dinner (such as broccoli and cheese soup, garlic mushrooms or a terrine of four cheeses); then roast lamb with garlic and herb stuffing, or beef in beer; a choice of puddings (lemon meringue pie, raspberry crumble, or lemon sorbet) and cheese.

Readers' comments: Absolutely charming. Very attractive house, warm and comfortable. Excellent dinner and breakfast. Very thoughtful hosts.

On the edge of Kendal, **HOLM-FIELD** (41 Kendal Green) is a large Edwardian house off an open space. The big sitting/dining-room, decorated in pastel colours and with an inglenook at one end, overlooks a fine garden with a croquet lawn, swimming-pool, and summer-house, as well as fruit trees and flowerbeds. Eileen Kettle's rooms give pleasant views across the garden and valley towards the Lake District hills. No smoking. £15–£17.
Readers' comments: Elegant house,

panoramic views, nice rooms, friendly welcome, outstanding decor. [Tel: 0539 720790; postcode: LA9 5PP]

LOXLEY FARMHOUSE   C D M

Stratford Road, Loxley, Warwickshire, CV35 9JN   Tel: 0789 840265
South-east of Stratford-upon-Avon. Nearest main road: A422 from Stratford
to Banbury (and M40, junction 15).

2–3 Bedrooms. £19.50 (less for 7 nights).
Price goes up at Easter. All have own
bath/shower/toilet. Tea/coffee facilities. TV.
Views of garden, country.
Light suppers if ordered. Vegetarian or
special diets. Wine can be brought in.
2 Sitting-rooms. With open fire (one),
central heating, TV.
Large garden

Loxley is a hilltop village with diminutive church. From a seat on its sloping
green, where crab-apple trees are bright in autumn, there are far views across
woodland and fields of red earth. Just downhill from here Loxley Farm is tucked
away: a picture-postcard house of half-timbering and thatch, parts dating back to
the 13th century. Perhaps Robin Hood ('Robin of Loxley') knew the house;
there's a worn stone in the churchyard on which, tradition has it, he and his
companions used to sharpen their arrow-tips. And certainly Charles I stayed here
after the nearby Battle of Edgehill.

Inside, everything is in keeping with the style of the ancient house: low
ceilings with pewter pots hanging from the beams, flagged floors, small-paned
windows, log fires, oak doors. You can see the cruck construction of the house –
at its heart, the unhewn trunks of two trees support the roof timbers. There
is not a single straight wall or floor. Anne Horton has furnished the rooms in
appropriate style. In the dining-room, leather chairs surround a large oak table;
here, breakfast – with home-made muesli and buns – and suppers such as
smoked salmon soup, lamb hotpot and, a National Trust recipe, lemon pudding
are served.

Two of the bedrooms are in a separate, half-timbered, thatched barn conversion, together with a sitting-room and kitchen. Both have en suite bathrooms. In
the main house is a family suite (sometimes available for guests) which has its
own sitting-room furnished with deep armchairs, Staffordshire figures, copper
and brasses, lavender and dried flowers.

The broad River Avon gives character to the peaceful countryside: cattle grazing in green meadows where once Shakespeare's Forest of Arden spread for miles
around. It is easy to visit Stratford-upon-Avon from here, the Cotswolds and
Oxford. It is also worth travelling to Dudley to see the excellent new Black
Country Museum. Warwick Castle, Blenheim Palace, Charlecote, Hidcote (and
many other great gardens) make this area a tourist honeypot.

Readers' comments: Idyllic surroundings. Much care and attention. Generous,
flavoursome fare. Most welcoming and comfortable. Not a jarring note. The most
delightful of all. Have enjoyed Mrs Horton's hospitality over the past ten years.
Pleasant place and very pleasant people.

MACHINE COTTAGE

Hill Furze, Bishampton, Worcestershire, WR10 2NE   Tel: 0386 860963
North-west of Evesham. Nearest main road: A44 from Evesham to Worcester.

3 Bedrooms. £15–£17.50 (less for 3 nights). Bargain breaks. One has own shower/toilet. Tea/coffee facilities. TV. Views of garden, country. Washing machine on request.
Dinner. £10 for 3 courses and coffee, at 7pm (not Saturdays). Non-residents not admitted. Vegetarian or special diets if ordered. Wine can be brought in. **Light suppers** if ordered.
1 Sitting-room. With open fire, central heating, TV, video.
Large garden

There are still a few damson trees left from what was once a vast acreage here: they used to be grown to provide purple dye for the textile industry, until synthetic dyes took over. They and the apple orchards (this crop goes to Hereford, where Bulmer's cider is produced) make a lovely sight around April – and Machine Cottage is right on the Vale of Evesham's official 'blossom trail'.

At any season Machine Cottage is worth seeking out, for there is year-round colour in the garden – lovingly tended by the Broomes, who are also a mine of information on all matters horticultural in the fruitful vale and beyond. They will direct you to such great gardens as Hidcote, Spetchley, Bredon Springs, Kemerton Priory and Sezincote, and to the national clematis and pelargonium collections. The cottage is at its loveliest in early summer when roses, honeysuckle and clematis clamber up and baskets brim with flowers. The garden's vegetables are served with roasts, its fruits go into gâteaux and cheesecakes.

In the living-room are pretty, curved sofas around the fire and a pine table made by Roger at the other end, with windows on three sides. This, like the pine-furnished bedrooms, is immaculate. There is a sunken bath in the plant-filled bathroom. (Baby-sitting available.)

As to the unusual name, the cottage was built in 1872 to house workers at nearby Machine Farm: one of the earliest to mechanize work in the fields.

Readers' comments: Beautiful house and garden, and good breakfast.

A few miles southward lies Little Comberton, and in Wick Road is **WINDRUSH** where two thatched 17th-century cottages have been combined as one, with a particularly pretty garden created around them. Rooms are low-beamed, and the inexpensive little bedrooms furnished in appropriately cottagey style. Altogether, a really 'old world' effect. Light suppers only, but there is good food to be had at the Mill (Elmley Castle) or the Fox and Hounds (Bredon). £12.

Readers' comments: Beautifully preserved; garden a joy. A gem of a find. Mrs Lewis is charming and friendly. Warm welcome and hospitality. [Tel: 0386 710284; postcode: WR10 3EG]

MANOR FARM
Adstone, Northamptonshire, NN12 6DT   Tel: 0327 860284
South of Daventry. Nearest main road: A4525 from Banbury to Northampton.

3 Bedrooms. £15–£18 (less for 5 nights). Some with own bath/shower/toilet. Tea/coffee facilities. TV. Views of garden, country. Washing machine on request.
Dinner. From £9 for 3 courses and coffee, from 7pm. Non-residents not admitted. Vegetarian or special diets if ordered. Wine can be brought in. **Light suppers** if ordered.
1 Sitting-room. With open fire, central heating, TV, record-player. No smoking.
Garden

It was an ancestor of George Washington who, in 1656, built Manor Farm. Within its stone walls are attractively decorated rooms that have hill views beyond the walled garden and the fields where calves graze. In the red-tiled and leather-seated dining-room, Liz Paton serves such two-course meals as lamb with onion sauce and lemon soufflé.

All the family can learn clay-pigeon shooting here. Alongside are a tiny Norman church; and woodland walks where bluebells and wild orchids grow.

The Stars and Stripes flies over nearby Sulgrave Manor, its design inspired by the stars and bars in the family coat-of-arms over the porch of the manor house. For this was the home (built in the reign of Elizabeth I) of Lawrence Washington – ancestor of George Washington, some of whose possessions are on show at the house.

Northamptonshire is an underrated county. Because its geology is identical with the Cotswolds, its old buildings are of the same lovely, honey-coloured stone and its landscape just as scenic. In addition, it has the Grand Union Canal with its colourful boats, river scenes, bluebell woods, old coaching inns (some described by Dickens), thatched cottages, ancient churches and much more. Yet, when the famous Cotswolds are over-busy with tourists, this little-known area remains undisturbed, even though it is not far west of the M1.

Among the picturesque 17th-century cottages of reddish stone in Moreton Pinkney (once a lace-making centre) is a modern house, **BAREWELL FIELDS**, in Prestidge Row. From its sliding glass doors is a fine view over the valley of the River Cherwell as it makes its long journey to Oxford. Out of the sloping garden comes produce for Margaret Lainchbury's table – asparagus, for instance, which might be followed by turkey from her son's nearby farm, and strawberries.

Bedrooms in pale colours are immaculate, the chocolate-brown bathroom is excellent. £15–£16. [Tel: 0295 760754; postcode: NN11 6NJ]

MANOR FARMHOUSE   S

Crackington Haven, Cornwall, EX23 0JW   Tel: 0840 230304
South-west of Bude. Nearest main road: A39 from Bude to Camelford.

5 Bedrooms. £33–£36 including dinner. Prices go up in June. All have own bath/shower/toilet. Views of garden, country. No smoking. Washing machine on request.
Dinner. 4 courses and coffee, at 7pm. Non-residents not admitted. Wine can be ordered. No smoking.
3 Sitting-rooms. With open fire, central heating, TV. **Bar.** No smoking.
Large garden

Muriel Knight so much enjoys cooking and looking after guests that she gave up her job as a teacher in order to concentrate on this, in her outstandingly beautiful home near the sea (the garden of which provides fruit and vegetables).

It is a historic manor house (named in Domesday Book), much of the present building three centuries old, and furnished with taste. Past a stone-flagged hall is a beamed breakfast-room. In the winter sitting-room is a stone pillar and wrought-iron screen concealing a log stove; leading from it is a help-yourself bar. Past the television room is a summer sitting-room with mullioned windows and lovely views of garden, farmland and hills. In the dining-room lyre-backed chairs with yellow seats surround the mahogany table which Muriel lays with silver, cut glass and starched napkins. Equal care has gone into bedrooms that have such things as 17th-century antiques, Berlin-work window-seats, lattice windows, elegant bathrooms. (One has a Sitz bath which some elderly people appreciate.) I particularly liked the rose room.

In the grounds are a sloping lawn with herb border and, beside an old water-wheel, a games room with full-size billiards and table tennis.

Muriel's pleasure in cooking shows itself in the dinners she provides. Here is just one example: choux-pastry swans with a filling of avocado and cream; coronation chicken (that is, in an apricot and curry sauce) accompanied by jacket potatoes stuffed with cheese and basil, *and* cauliflower and date salad *and* rice, prawns and eggs in prawn sauce; a lemon and orange pavlova. It hardly needs saying that Manor Farmhouse is a good choice for gourmets.

In such an idyllic spot, there is little temptation to go elsewhere. However, the resort of Bude is very near and the border of Devon. Bude is more sedate than many west country resorts, in a setting of grassy downs and golden sandy beaches on which the Atlantic thunders in.

Readers' comments: Gracious and warm, a beautiful ambience. Delightful place. We were looked after superbly. Super place, nice hosts. Peace, quiet, good food, comfort. Best holiday in 32 years. Lovely welcome. Glorious views. Food marvellous, elegantly served. Lovely relaxing atmosphere. Full marks for comfort, good furnishing and convivial atmosphere. Wonderful value for money. Quite outstanding. Like the very best 5-star establishment.

When writing to me, if you want a reply please enclose an International Reply Coupon.

MANOR FARMHOUSE

C(5) D S X

Wormington, Worcestershire, WR12 7NL   Tel: 0386 73302
(Messages: 0386 73565)
South-east of Evesham. Nearest main road: A46 from Broadway to
Cheltenham (and M5, junction 9).

3 Bedrooms. £15–£20 (less for 4 nights or continental breakfast). Bargain breaks. All have own shower/toilet. Views of garden, country. No smoking. Washing machine on request.
Light suppers if ordered.
1 Sitting-room. With open fire, central heating, TV, tea/coffee-making facilities.
Small garden

Once this house was known as Charity Farm because 'dole' was dispensed to wayfarers. The farm was connected with Hailes Abbey (in the 13th century, its phial of Christ's blood made it a centre of pilgrimage; now there are only ruins), hence some ecclesiastical touches like the pointed arch beside the log fire – possibly it was a leper window. There are leaded casements in the comfortable sitting-room, a stone inglenook in the hall, slabs of Welsh slate on the floor, steps and turns everywhere on one's way up to beamy all-white bedrooms well furnished with mahogany pieces. There's still a cheese room dating from the time when this was a dairy-farm.

What was once a cattle-yard is now a very attractive court with lawn, fountain and stone sinks planted with flowers. To one side is an old granary of brick and timber which dates, like the house itself, from the 15th century. From his stable door Monty, a big hunter, watches visitors' comings and goings. On the farm are shooting and trout-fishing.

Pauline Russell usually serves only breakfast, recommending for other meals Goblets wine bar in Broadway – that world-famous showplace, best known of all the picturesque villages hereabouts and once called 'the painted lady of the Cotswolds' because the colour of the golden stone glows so vividly here. Flower-filled, perfectly groomed gardens do their bit too.

From here one can drive to the fruitful Vale of Evesham (loveliest in spring), high Bredon Hill ringed by pretty villages, Tewkesbury to see the abbey, historic Evesham for boat trips on the Avon, Pershore (abbey church and 18th-century houses), or little Ripple with old houses around its green and quaint carvings on the misericord seats in the church.

Through the region runs the River Avon, watering the rich fields and orchards.

The area is a source of endless pleasure to anyone who enjoys discovering little-known villages and their individual treasures. Examples are Bosbury, surrounded by hop fields and dominated by a detached church tower fortified as a refuge from the Welsh raiders of the 12th century; Bredon, full of black-and-white houses and, in its church, a treasure-house of carved tombs and monuments – it also has an immense mediaeval tithe barn; Bretforton, where the ancient and picturesque inn – just one of many fine buildings here – is owned by the National Trust (look for the 'witch marks' on the floor and the splendid collection of 17th-century pewter); Colwall, which has a huge stone said to have been hurled there by a giant in pursuit of his faithless wife (the scenic Jubilee Drive high up in the hills starts here); and the two Combertons, Great and Little (the latter is in fact the bigger one, but both are beautiful) at the foot of Bredon Hill.

MANOR HOUSE   C D M PT S

Nocton Road, Potterhanworth, Lincolnshire, LN4 2DN   Tel: 0522 791288
(Messages: 0522 692852)
South of Lincoln. Nearest main road: A15 from Lincoln to Sleaford.

4 Bedrooms. £18–£20 (less for 3 nights). Prices go up from Easter. Some have own bath/shower/toilet. Tea/coffee facilities. TV. Views of garden, country. No smoking. Washing machine on request.
Light suppers if ordered.
2 Sitting-rooms. With open fire, central heating, TV, piano, record-player. No smoking in one.
Large garden

Built at a fine period for domestic architecture (1840), Ann and John Wades' home has impressive rooms – beginning with the big entrance hall which has panelled doors and a stone-paved floor from which a white and mahogany staircase winds up, its balusters elegantly turned. A coral damask wallpaper and big gilt mirror are in keeping with this setting. Off the hall is a double sitting-room, high ceilinged with a marble fireplace and, on three sides, deep-set French windows that open onto lawns. Pink brocade curtains, Chinese carpets, chandeliers hanging from the pink ceiling, a great copper vat of logs: all combine to create a handsome effect. There is also an oak-panelled television room, its alcoves filled with books.

From the windows are views of the almost park-like garden where ponies and sheep wander. Beyond rose beds is an outsize summer-house, glass-walled and with a changing-room (for the swimming-pool), table tennis, darts, etc. One can walk from here to a pond, brook and weir frequented by waterfowl.

Bedrooms and bathrooms are excellent, and varied. One, for instance, is in a modern grey and scarlet colour scheme. Another – light and airy – has pale, flowery fabrics, polished board floors and exposed rafters overhead. Families like to book the combination of a small room (with bunks) adjoining the bedroom for parents. Some rooms are in a cottage annexe, converted with much use of pine to provide not only bedrooms and family suites but also a kitchen.

Readers' comments: Superb house and charming hostess. Delightful house, beautiful grounds, a memorable stay.

A few miles south, at Timberland, is the 18th-century **PENNY FARTHING INN**, a suitable choice for anyone who likes the convivial atmosphere of a village pub combined with very good food. Behind the unassuming exterior are beamy, stone-walled bars with tapestry chairs, and a TV room for residents. To avoid kitchen noise, ask for a bedroom at the back. Tony Daniel's cooking includes such dishes as casseroled pheasant,

guinea-fowl with a port sauce and carpetbag steaks. £19 (b & b).
Readers' comments: Superb cooking, enormous breakfasts, truly welcoming. [Tel: 0526 378359; postcode: LN4 3SA]

MANOR HOUSE FARM C(8)

Prestwood, Staffordshire, ST14 5DD   Tel: 0889 590415 and 0335 43669
North of Uttoxeter. Nearest main road: A5032 from Cheadle to Ashbourne.

2 Bedrooms. £16–£20 (less for 6 nights or continental breakfast). Tea/coffee facilities. TV. Views of garden, country. No smoking. Washing machine on request.
Light suppers if ordered.
1 Sitting-room. With open fire, central heating, TV, piano. No smoking.
Large garden

Once his family farmed here, but now Christopher Ball has turned to dealing in antiques; a fact reflected in the handsome furnishings of the 17th-century house. It was built of grey sandstone from nearby Hollington quarry.

High-backed settles flank the log fire in the sitting-room, which has stone-mullioned bay windows in its thick walls – with fine hill views. On the oak-panelled walls of the dining-room hang oil paintings. One bedroom (with beams and exposed stone walls) has a four-poster – cream fabrics trimmed with pink ribbon – and a flowery washbasin. One of the two bathrooms has an outsize sunken bath.

The terraced garden is particularly attractive: weeping ash, pinnacled summer-house (it was once the cupola on a hospital roof), steps ascending between clipped yews, a tennis court and croquet. You can barbecue your own meat if you wish.

Conductor Howard Snell and his musical family live at 16th-century **HOLLINGTON HOUSE** in Hollington – another moorland village. The pretty sitting-room, book-lined, has patchwork cushions made – like the bedspreads – by Angela herself (a former Hallé violinist), lacy Victorian valentines and a modern turquoise rug on the polished floorboards. On the smallholding you can watch Dolly being milked – or have a go yourself. Outside the village is the quarry from which came both pink and white stone

for nearby Croxton Abbey, now a ruin, and for the modern cathedrals of Coventry and Liverpool. Light suppers only. £15 (b & b). [Tel: 088 926221; postcode: ST10 4HH]

> Some proprietors stipulate a minimum stay of two nights at weekends or peak seasons; or they will accept one-nighters only at short notice (that is, only if no lengthier booking has yet been made).

MAPLEHURST MILL

C(12) M

Mill Lane, Frittenden, Kent, TN17 2DT Tel: 058080 203

North-west of Tenterden. Nearest main road: A229 from Maidstone towards
Hastings.

5 Bedrooms. £18.50–£26 (less for 6
nights). All have own bath/shower/toilet.
Tea/coffee facilities. TV. Views of garden,
country, river. No smoking.
Dinner. £16 for 4 courses (with choices)
and coffee, at times to suit guests. Non-
residents not admitted. Vegetarian or special
diets if ordered. Wine can be ordered. No
smoking. **Light suppers** sometimes.
1 Sitting-room. With wood stove, central
heating, piano. No smoking.
Large garden

'It was like the Marie Celeste,' said Kenneth Parker, describing this 18th-century
mill when they took it over. It had hardly been touched since the day it ceased to
grind, and the tools of the miller's trade lay where he had left them: the governor
for the millstones, the key to open the sluices, the sack-hoist, the flour chest
beneath the chute, smutter and scourer, floury hoppers . . . On the grinding floor,
the Parkers are now creating with the help of these finds a little museum of
milling, and are researching the history of the mill, which dates back to 1309.
(One grisly item: they discovered that in the religious persecutions of 1557, the
miller and his wife were burnt at the stake.)

Their conversion of the mill has been faultless. It now has every up-to-date
comfort, yet the ambience of the past has been vividly preserved. Through
the entrance hall, which has baskets of dried flowers, one comes to my favourite
bedroom (being on the ground floor, it would suit anyone who finds stairs
difficult). There is a window right by the waterwheel and the mill-race flows
under its floor.

Upstairs are exposed wall beams, low doorways, white or pine-boarded walls,
a tree-trunk that forms part of the structure, iron pillars or mechanisms and brick
or cast-iron fireplaces. Each bedroom is different – one with lacy duvet covers and
festoon blinds, for instance; another with a pine four-poster draped with a pink
and blue honeysuckle fabric; a third with flowery Habitat linens. Bathrooms are
excellent. From some windows are views of yellow waterlilies and dabchicks on
the stream, or of cows and hayfields. You may even glimpse foxes or a heron. In
the grounds are a small vineyard, a heated swimming-pool, and a nature trail with
over 70 species of birds.

The mill would be worth going out of one's way to visit not only for all this
but because Heather's meals are so imaginative. Here is an example: Sussex
smokies (haddock) in a cheese and wine sauce followed by chicken breasts with a
sauce made from avocados, sherry and cream (the accompanying vegetables are
organically grown) and then a home-made chocolate, coffee and almond ice
cream. Afterwards, one can relax either on the waterside terrace or in the huge
sitting-room where Heather has a rare grand piano, perfectly semicircular. It is a
gracious room in which the sofas are covered with cottage-garden fabrics and
aquamarine curtains hang at the casements on opposite walls. Beauty, character,
good food and peace: what more could one want? Maplehurst Mill is also well
placed to visit such famous sights as Sissinghurst and Leeds Castle.

MARINA HOTEL

C D P T

The Esplanade, Fowey, Cornwall, PL23 1HY   Tel: 0726 833315
East of St Austell. Nearest main road: A390 from Lostwithiel to St Austell.

rear view

11 Bedrooms. Normally £27–£38 (less for 2 nights) **but for readers of this book only** there are 2 rooms at a dinner-inclusive price of £70 for 2 days. Prices go up in June. Bargain breaks. All have own bath/shower/toilet. Tea/coffee facilities. TV. Sea views, balcony (some).
Dinner. A la carte or £16 for 5 courses (with choices) and coffee, at 7–8.30pm. Vegetarian or special diets if ordered. Wine can be ordered. No smoking. **Light suppers.**
3 Sitting-rooms. With central heating. **Bar.**
Small garden
Closed from November to February.

Built in 1830 as a seaside retreat for the Bishop of Truro, this fine house has been furnished with the elegance it deserves. The handsome mouldings, arches and panelling of the hall and octagonal landing are now decorated in brown and cream; and each bedroom is different – a pale colour scheme in one; sprigged covers and pine in another (its rounded window overlooking the sea); four with covered verandahs of lacy ironwork facing the tiny walled garden and waterfront beyond it. The dining-room has Indian Tree china on peach tablecloths, with spectacular views from the big picture-windows; the bar, rosy armchairs and a thick pale carpet. Eight-foot marble pillars were uncovered in one bedroom.

David Johns gives equal attention to the standard of the food. Dinner is priced according to your choice of main dish, from a selection that includes (for instance) boned chicken in a sauce of mushrooms and cider, beef Wellington, rack of lamb and local fish in a variety or ways.

Fowey (pronounced Foy) is on that mild stretch of the coast known as the Cornish Riviera. It is an old and picturesque harbour of steep, narrow byways (parking is difficult; a minibus takes visitors to a carpark each morning), its waters busy with yachts and fishing boats. Some people arrive by car ferry. It is easy to find secluded coves and beaches nearby, or scenic walks along clifftops. The little town is full of antique, book and craft shops; historic buildings; restaurants and good food shops. Easily reached from here are Lanhydrock House and gardens, Restormel Castle, Charlestown and Wheal Martin China Clay Museum. Cornwall has a spring gardens festival – ask the Marina for a leaflet about the 55 gardens that participate. One very near here, famous for camellias in an 18th-century setting, is perched on the clifftop at Trewithen; another, with superb sea views, is Trelissick; and Polruan is a spectacular Headland Garden.

Go to Falmouth to visit Pendennis Castle, built by Henry VIII to guard the estuary, and for the maritime museum. There are rare breeds to be seen in the country park at Kea and, near the cathedral city of Truro (which also has Cornwall's county museum), is a cider farm with activities to view.

Readers' comments: Excellent; super room. Extremely helpful. Have never experienced such professional yet personal attention.

206

MARSHGATE COTTAGE HOTEL   C(5) M PT
Marsh Lane, Hungerford, Berkshire, RG17 0QX   Tel: 0488 682307
West of Newbury. Nearest main road: A4 from Marlborough to Newbury
(and M4, junction 14).

9 Bedrooms. £19–£24.25 (less for 7
nights). Most have own shower/toilet.
Tea/coffee facilities. TV. Views of garden,
country, canal. Some no-smoking rooms.
Dinner (if ordered in advance). £16 for 3
courses and coffee, at 7.30–9pm (not
Sundays). Non-residents not admitted.
Vegetarian diets. Wine can be ordered.
Light suppers if ordered.
1 Sitting-room. With open fire, central
heating. Bar.
Large garden

The marshes which give this cottage its name stretch down to the 18th-century
Kennet & Avon Canal, a haven for birds and wildflowers. Marshgate (used as a
pest-house during the plague of 1640) is even older than the canal, its thatched
roof descending almost to ground level; but it is an extension which provides
guest-rooms, in keeping with its original character. Most rooms overlook the
marshes, which are a sheet of yellow in buttercup-time. Wild orchids grow there,
frogs croak in spring and kingfishers can be spotted hunting.

Mike Walker, once a journalist, did most of the conversion himself, re-using
old handmade bricks and wrought-iron locks; laying floors of beautiful chestnut
boards. His Danish wife Elsebeth, a biochemist, has furnished the rooms with
Scandinavian taste, hunting for finds such as mirrors or stained glass in the area's
many antique shops. The breakfast-room is in white and pine with brick walls;
dried flowers are strung along the beams. From a quarry-tiled hall an open-tread
staircase goes up to some bedrooms. Most, however, are on the ground floor,
furnished with a pleasing simplicity – modern pine and various shades of pastel
predominate. A patio with garden benches allows guests to enjoy the view of canal
life including passing narrow-boats.

In the grounds are goats and ducks, also a 'dipping hole': that is, the point
where an underground stream pops up – watercress grows in it.

Dinner (for parties of six or more) may comprise such dishes as mussels in
garlic sauce, Danish roast pork with sugar potatoes and red cabbage, followed by
sorbet or cheese and biscuits.

In addition to many good eating-places, nearby Hungerford abounds with
shops selling antiques and there is scenic downland in every direction. Newbury's
Watermill Theatre is one of many interesting spots (the wheel is still to be seen).
Walkers make for the high Ridgeway Path which is of prehistoric origin. This is
also a good cycling area: bicycles can be hired at the hotel. Barge trips available,
drawn by horses.

The two most popular local sights are Littlecote, a Tudor mansion with
Roman remains and a Roundhead display; and the oldest working beam-engines
in the world, at Crofton.

Readers' comments: Agreeably cosy. Delightful river setting. Friendly atmosphere.
One of the most delightful places.

MEDBOURNE GRANGE
Nevill Holt, Leicestershire, LE16 8EF   Tel: 0858 83249
North-east of Market Harborough. Nearest main road: A427 from Market
Harborough to Corby.

3 **Bedrooms.** £15–£16 (less for 7 nights).
Tea/coffee facilities. Views of garden,
country. Washing machine on request.
Light suppers if ordered.
1 **Sitting-room.** With central heating, TV.
No smoking.
Large garden

At Nevill Holt's great 17th-century Hall (now a school) Emerald Cunard held her
salons, attended by the leading political and literary lions of the Edwardian era.
Medbourne Grange was a principal farm on its large estate, a dignified stone
house standing at the heart of 400 acres of dairy pastures and arable fields.

Sally Beaty has furnished it attractively: the capacious, cut-velvet armchairs
are of the same soft blue as the sitting-room carpet; one rosy bedroom (with far
view) has a carved walnut suite, another (overlooking the dairy-yard) is paisley-
patterned – this, though a single bedroom, has a sofa-bed too. Although there is a
dining-room, most guests enjoy eating in her big, tiled kitchen with its pretty
wildflower wallpaper.

Outside are stone troughs of flowers and, sheltered by old walls, a heated
swimming-pool; while beyond lies the valley of the River Welland which flows all
the way from Naseby (in Northamptonshire) to the Wash (in Lincolnshire).

Medbourne village has picturesque buildings and a particularly pretty stream
frequented by kingfishers and herons. In East Carlton Park are not only woods
and ponds but a heritage centre that features the history of iron-making. Market
Harborough has a great many 18th-century houses and a school (1614) on wooden
pillars. Foxton's flight of ten locks is famous, and all around are villages and
churches of honey-coloured stone – as well as such historic buildings as
Elizabethan Rushton Lodge (triangular), Lamport Hall, Rockingham Castle,
Kirby Hall, Stanford Hall and many others. Reservoirs attract wildfowl – and
wildfowl-watchers.

Readers' comments: An excellent stay, fully recommended.

Sitting-room at Wheathill Farm (see page 361)

MELLINGTON HOUSE

C PT S

Broad Street, Weobley, Herefordshire, HR4 8SA   Tel: 0544 318537

North-west of Hereford. Nearest main road: A4112.

3 Bedrooms. £15-£18. Prices go up from Easter. Bargain breaks. Some have own bath/shower/toilet. Tea/coffee facilities. TV. No smoking. Washing machine on request.
Dinner. From £10 for 3 courses (with choices) and coffee, at 7.30pm (not weekends). Non-residents not admitted. Vegetarian or special diets if ordered. Wine can be brought in. **Light suppers** if ordered.
1 Sitting-room. With open fire, central heating, TV, piano, record-player.
Large garden

Once, mediaeval houses were considered old-fashioned and so householders often put new façades on them. That is why Mellington House has a front in Queen Anne style, but its real age is revealed at the back where the original half-timbering is still exposed – typical of most buildings in Weobley, which is a particularly fine mediaeval village set in the lovely Herefordshire countryside. Although the house is in the centre of the village, it is quiet because its walls are thick and the big sash windows double-glazed (not that Weobley gets heavy traffic). It was once the home of the notorious Baroness de Stempel.

Ann Saunders has furnished the house very pleasantly (for instance, brass beds and wildflower duvets), the sitting-room is large and comfortable, and there is a downstairs bedroom which Ann (a physiotherapist) provides for people who have mobility problems. The dining-room opens onto a large, old, walled garden where, on sunny mornings, she serves breakfast.

Ann prepares such meals as: melon, roast beef with garden vegetables, home-made cheesecake, and cheeses. These can be provided for guests in the self-catering 'hayloft' too. (Baby-sitting available; walking or bridge weekends can be arranged.)

From Weobley, there are plenty of sightseeing options. The picturesque black-and-white village of Eardisland is close. There are a dozen bookshops (most belonging to Richard Booth) in Hay-on-Wye, now nicknamed 'Book City', Brecon, Offa's Dyke and numerous stately homes provide other destinations for a day out; and, as this is an area of orchards and nursery gardens, many people return home laden with pot-plants and pick-your-own soft fruits. The Malvern Hills and the Black Mountains are close, and several market towns are nearby. Add to these the Brecon Beacons, Radnor Forest, the 'Golden Valley', Welsh and Shropshire market towns, a motor museum, a lovely drive along Wenlock Edge, Ironbridge, the Wye Valley and innumerable garden centres.

Travel northward for Worcestershire, which has a tremendous amount to see. Fine scenery, historic buildings (including churches), hill walks, waterside dairy-farms, a magnificent cathedral in Worcester itself, hopfields and orchards, woods, and sights which include Elgar's birthplace (Broadheath).

Readers' comments: Could not praise more. Made most welcome. Extremely comfortable. Beautiful surroundings. I will return. Delicious dinners. Could not have been made more welcome. Spacious accommodation. Warm and friendly. Everything done to make us comfortable.

MIDDLETON LODGE
Middleton Priors, Shropshire, WV16 6UR   Tel: 074634 228 or 675
West of Bridgnorth. Nearest main road: A458 from Bridgnorth to Shrewsbury.

3 Bedrooms. £17.50–£20 (less for 2 nights or continental breakfast). All have own bath/shower/toilet. Tea/coffee facilities. TV. Views of garden, country. No smoking. Washing machine on request.
Light suppers if ordered.
2 Sitting-rooms. With open fire, central heating, TV. No smoking.
Large garden
Closed in December.

There was not even electricity when Mary Rowlands grew up here, in a 17th-century house built by the Howards (of Castle Howard, Yorkshire) as a hunting-lodge. There are modern comforts now, but old features remain unchanged.

Mary has turned the slate-floored scullery into a handsome dining-room with a hefty oak table that was once in a monastery, surrounded by William-and-Mary chairs. There is pewter on the sideboard, and the unusual brick fireplace still has an old bread-oven alongside. The kitchen, its ceiling studded with bacon-hooks, is now a sitting-room with stone fireplace and an array of willow-pattern plates. At the top of the house she is restoring a chapel.

There are two staircases leading up to bedrooms which are well supplied with armchairs. A frilled four-poster is in one, twin brass beds in another. One huge bathroom has a tiled bath on a dais, another a fine Victorian bath and an array of ferns. Some visitors appreciate having their own suite and entrance.

Outside, a great cedar and other specimen trees give the big, walled garden a stately look. Each time we arrived, a particularly small rabbit sat on guard in the middle of the drive, not at all willing to let us pass; and, given the life span of less intrepid rabbits, may still be on duty when you call.

Readers' comments: Beautifully maintained. Delightful hostess. Tasteful furnishings, and very quiet. Kindness itself.

At Aston Eyre is a little Norman church with some exceptional stone carving. Next to it is **CHURCH HOUSE** which was originally a wheelwright's cottage with a workshop. Now Margaret Cosh's home, it has some quarry-tiled floors, low beams and a brick inglenook in the sitting-room. Up a narrow staircase is a neat, cottage-style bedroom; another is on the ground floor and has French doors opening onto a terrace, garden with summer-house and Margaret's small-holding. The breakfast-room, too,

has French doors with a view of the beautiful Shropshire countryside. Light suppers or three-course dinners (by arrangement). £14–£16. [Tel: 074631 248; postcode: WV16 6XD]

THE MILL   **C D**

Mungrisdale, Cumbria, CA11 0XR   Tel: 07687 79659
West of Penrith. Nearest main road: A66 from Keswick to Penrith
(and M6, junction 40).

nights or continental breakfast). Prices go up from Easter. Most have own bath/shower/toilet. Tea/coffee facilities. TV. Views of garden, country, river. Washing machine on request.
Dinner. 5 courses (with choices) and coffee, at 7pm. Vegetarian or special diets if ordered. Wine can be ordered. No smoking.
Light suppers if ordered.
2 Sitting-rooms. With open fire, central heating, TV. Snooker. Table tennis.
Large garden
9 Bedrooms. £36–£41 **including dinner, to readers of this book only** (less for 5   **Closed from November to mid-February.**

It is only a generation since the watermill in this Lake District valley stopped working. By the old stone building which used to house the saw which the mill powered is the sawyer's cottage, now a private hotel. It is a peaceful spot, with little more than the sound of the River Glenderamackin rushing down its rocky bed.

The Mill (which is next to, but not connected with, the Mill Inn) is a simple white house with moss on the slate roof. A small conservatory, faces a stone terrace and a lawn with seats by the water's edge. Eleanor and Richard Quinlan have found sources of ingredients not usually associated with the Lake District, which explains the presence on the menu of such things as stuffed vine leaves, as well as excellent home-made soups accompanied by fresh soda bread (the last a fixture by popular demand). The main course might be quail with orange, brandy and thyme; or roast beef with mustard puddings and claret gravy.

The main sitting-room is pretty (the stone surround to the log fire bears the date 1651), and there is a small TV room with well-filled bookshelves. In the dining-room each small oak table has burgundy napkins, willow-pattern china, candles and a nosegay. Bedrooms are trim and simple, with restful colours, and each has a bowl of fruit. Early arrivals are greeted with tea and home-made fruit log. All over the house are original paintings. (Baby-sitting available.)

Readers' comments: Beautiful, quiet, excellent food. Service attentive and friendly. Food is superb. Outstanding. Interesting dinner with Mozart background.

MOSEDALE HOUSE is a neat conversion of a Victorian farmhouse and attached barn in the unspoiled fellside hamlet of Mosedale. In the big sitting-room, heavy beams contrast with new woodwork, stained green. There are groups of chairs and settles round a wood stove and, for the view, round the old barn doors. One bedroom is available with a sitting-room and kitchenette; another is fully accessible by wheelchair. For dinner (available to self-catering guests too), Lesley and Colin Smith offer, for example, carrot

soup, pork in cream or stuffed courgettes, and orange boodle, using some ingredients from the smallholding (on which they keep livestock too). No smoking. £19–£23. [Tel: 07687 79371; postcode: CA11 0XQ]

211

MILL HOUSE   C PT S X
Millgate, Bracondale, Norwich, Norfolk, NR1 2EQ   Tel: 0603 621151
Nearest main road: A146 from Norwich to Lowestoft.

2 **Bedrooms.** £18.50–£20 (less for continental breakfast). Prices go up in April. Both have own bath/shower/toilet. Tea/coffee facilities on request. Views of garden, country, river. No smoking. Washing machine on request.
Light suppers if ordered.
1 **Sitting-room.** With open fire, central heating, TV, piano, record-player. No smoking.
Large garden

It is a surprise to find this quiet backwater so near the city centre. Facing the placid River Yare, its waters a haven for coots and kingfishers, with other birds among the ivy-clad chestnuts and wild daffodils, stands a handsome 18th-century house built of flint and brick. It was originally the home of a prosperous miller (the mill – destroyed in a fire – used to grind mustard for Colman's). Behind the walled garden run the trains from Norwich to London, but all is silent at night. You can borrow Gillian Evans' rowboat and take a picnic out onto the marshes; or the strenuous might even get as far as Norwich Cathedral.

Inside the house is a higgledy-piggledy mixture of good antiques and old leather armchairs, interesting pictures (many by Gillian's husband) and pot-plants, log fire in the sitting-room, stone flags on the hall floor. There are handsome architectural details – classical archways and the plaster cornices, for example – and an elegant staircase to bedrooms that include a good family suite. (Light suppers only.) Bicycles on loan; croquet; and baby-sitting can be arranged.

A few miles southward is 17th-century **GREENACRES FARM** at Wood Green, Long Stratton, right on the edge of a 30-acre common with ponds and ancient woods. Bedrooms are spacious and comfortable, with own shower or bath; and there is a self-contained wing sometimes available on a b & b basis. Children are welcome, and in the huge games room you can peer into the floodlit depths of a 60-foot well as old as the house itself. Joanna Douglas's dinners are homely two-course meals, such as meatballs in tomato sauce and cheesecake. Those

using her self-catering wing can also dine with her. (Bicycles on loan; tennis court; baby-sitting available.) £17–£18. [Tel: 0508 30261; postcode: NR15 2RR]

Prices are per person in a double room at the beginning of the year.

212

MILNE HOUSE

C(5) **PT S X**

Millers Dale, Derbyshire, SK17 8SN   Tel: 0298 871832
(Messages: 0298 871636)
East of Buxton. Nearest main road: A6 from Bakewell to Buxton.

6 Bedrooms. £14–£18 (less for 3 nights). One has own bath/toilet. Tea/coffee facilities. TV (in some). Views of garden, country. No smoking.
Dinner. £12 for 3 courses and coffee, at 7.30pm. Vegetarian or special diets if ordered. Wine can be ordered. No smoking.
Light suppers if ordered.
1 Sitting-room. With open fire, central heating, TV. Bar.
Small garden

Soon after the watermill here ceased to function, Nick and Fran Davidson moved in, converting it into a home for themselves and for their woodcraft tools firm. Just across the little road from the mill-shop and gallery is this pale stone house, clematis rambling up its walls, where the mill-owner once lived – now providing separate accommodation for visitors. (The Davidsons are not resident at Milne House, but Fran has the support of a team of cheerful people who care for her guests.) Occasionally wood-turning courses are run.

The visitors' rooms are white-walled and simply but pleasantly furnished. A family room is conveniently situated on the ground floor, and outside is a small paved terrace on which to sit and enjoy the view of wooded hills opposite and the sound of water.

Jane Broadbent comes in to cook most nights; she is an experienced and inspired cook offering such meals as her own duck pâté, salmon en croûte, crêpes and a wide choice of English and continental cheeses.

Guests are welcome to go through the mill (its former wheelroom now displays woodware and woodworking supplies) to the very pretty garden beside the river, great crags rising up on the opposite bank.

Mid-Derbyshire is famous for its dales (river valleys) among wooded peaks: those of the rivers Dove, Noe and Derwent in particular. Wildlife, historic buildings, archaeological remains and old customs survive the years largely unchanged. This is a limestone area, dotted with pure springs around which small spas were built (Matlock and Buxton, for instance – the latter with some crescents like Bath) and caves (Matlock and Castleton). Places to visit include Ashbourne (markets, and a very fine 13th-century church with striking monuments); old Bakewell, of Bakewell pudding fame; Birchover village, surrounded by unusual rock formations; Crich – a collection of vintage trams (you can ride in a horse-drawn one); the gorge known as 'little Switzerland', through which the Dove flows – Izaak Walton fished here; and a cable-car will take you to the Heights of Abraham.

Haddon Hall is near Rowsley, a moorland walking centre. Historic stone towns include Wirksworth (of *Adam Bede* fame) and hilly Youlgreave.

Readers' comments: Warm welcome. Good value. Food very good and plentiful. Very friendly. Quite exceptional. Relaxed and friendly.

MILTON FARM

East Knoyle, Wiltshire, SP3 6BG   Tel: 0747830 247

North of Shaftesbury (Dorset). Nearest main road: A350 from Shaftesbury to Warminster.

2 Bedrooms. £19–£19.50 (less for 3 nights). Price goes up in July and August. Both have own bath/shower/. Tea/coffee facilities. TV. Views of garden, country.
Dinner. £13 for 3 courses (with choices) and coffee, at 7pm. Vegetarian or special diets if ordered. Wine can be ordered or brought in. **Light suppers** sometimes.
1 Sitting/dining-room. With open fire, central heating.
Large garden
Closed in December.

This is a truly picturebook farmhouse – a stone-flagged floor in the entrance hall, glimpse of a kitchen with pine table and a gun-case beside the gleaming Aga. In the sitting-room, which has a boarded ceiling, logs hiss gently on the stone hearth. There are old oak furniture, deep chairs, and flowers everywhere.

The Hydes removed a lot of later accretions to reveal the original beams in this mainly Queen Anne house, and then added comfortable furniture and elegant fabrics. Janice Hyde serves candlelit dinners – she is a superb cook – which consist of interesting dishes using local produce. One example: onion quiche, followed by a huge trout from the River Nadder (stuffed with almonds, mushrooms, lemon and I-know-not-what) and then the lightest of mousses. Clotted cream, milk and butter are from the farm's cows; pheasant, hare and rabbits are local. (Heated swimming-pool; hand-painted Portuguese pottery for sale.)

Readers' comments: Janice Hyde is a delight; countryside and house are beautiful. Delicious cooking. Very welcoming; delicious dinner; very comfortable. Excellent service. Splendid bedroom, most enjoyable dinners.

In a leafy valley at The Green, part of East Knoyle, is sheltered **SWAINS-COMBE**: a lovely thatched stone house with an equally lovely garden. Antiques and elegant fabrics furnish the beamed rooms, and two staircases lead to separate suites of bedrooms: in one, two bedrooms with William Morris fabrics, bathroom and sitting-area with velvet wing chairs; in the other, three bedrooms and two bathrooms – the four-poster reproduces a mediaeval design. Joy Orman is a skilled cook, serving such candlelit dinners as aubergine in cream cheese sauce, chicken breasts marinated in sherry and herbs then stuffed with hazelnuts and apricots, crème brûlée and cheeseboard. £19 (b & b).

Readers' comments: Charming and informal hosts. Extremely comfortable, excellent cooking; I have stayed four times. Delectable dinners. Superb. Most helpful, warm and welcoming. Very attractive, comfortable and cosy. Lovely garden. Well looked after. Immaculate. [Tel: 0747 830224; postcode: SP3 6BN]

Llanfair-Waterdine, Shropshire, LD17 1TT   Tel: 0547 528348
North-west of Knighton (Powys, Wales). Nearest main road: A488 from Knighton to Shrewsbury.

2 Bedrooms. £15.50–£17 (less for 3 nights). Prices go up in April. One has own toilet. Tea/coffee facilities. TV. Views of garden, country, river. Washing machine on request.
Light suppers if ordered. Vegetarian or special diets. Wine can be brought in.
1 Sitting-room. With open fire, central heating, TV, piano.
Small garden
Closed in December and January.

Here, where the border between Wales and Shropshire runs, two sisters grew up in the 1940s: Brenda and Jocelyn. Later they wrote a nostalgic history of their parish; and tiny though the village is (only nine houses, inn, church and post office), it has a 'past' which runs to 52 pages.

The girls' great-grandfather built many of the farmhouses in the area and worked on the huge Knucklas viaduct nearby, the stones of which came from a demolished castle where Queen Guinevere is said to have lived. Now a scenic railway takes tourists over its 13 arches. In the church are two unique features: farm names on each pew (recognition that each had paid its tithe to the church), and a barrel-organ which plays hymns. Outside is 'the gypsy's grave' with an inscription in Romany.

There are legends of the devil, memories of dancing in the village barn to the music of gypsy fiddlers and of the tailor sitting cross-legged on his bench as he stitched, wartime evacuees arriving (and prisoners-of-war too), and of 60,000 sheep annually thronging the lanes on their way to be auctioned at Knighton.

Monaughty Poeth itself has an 800-year-old history, for it once belonged to the Cistercians of Abbey Cwmhir: Monaughty means 'monastery grange' and Poeth 'burnt' – the house burned down and was rebuilt in the 19th century. This is where Jocelyn, now married to farmer Jim Williams, lives and welcomes visitors.

As to the accommodation at Monaughty, this is in very traditional farmhouse style, with comfort the keynote, and in every room Jocelyn's pretty flower arrangements. She serves only snack suppers (excellent salads and fruit pies), so some visitors go to the picturesque old Red Lion for steaks, duck, etc.

Sitting in the garden afterwards, one looks across to the Williams' sheep hills through which Offa's Dyke runs, and the only sound is the baaing of sheep.

Readers' comments: Treated like royalty! Enjoyed every comfort. Warmest of welcomes. Large, pretty bedroom and lovely view. Wonderful concern for her guests. Attractive accommodation. Extremely friendly. Idyllic location. Charming and unassuming people.

MOOR HALL   C

Victoria Road, Newney Green, Essex, CM1 3SE   Tel: 0245 420814

West of Chelmsford. Nearest main road: A414 from Chelmsford to Harlow.

2 **Bedrooms.** £16–£18. Tea/coffee facilities. Views of garden, country. No smoking. Washing machine on request.
Light suppers if ordered.
1 **Sitting-room.** With open fire, central heating, TV.
Large garden

Built in 1320 as a monastery, and in the style of an early mediaeval hall house (that is, one vast high chamber with smoke from the chimneyless fire wafting through a mere hole in the roof), Moor Hall has seen many transformations before becoming the very comfortable home it is today. But still there are such features as quatrefoil carvings, iron-studded doors, and a moat with ducks to remind one of its ancient origins. For centuries it has been in the ownership of Oxford University because a daughter of the estate married into the family which founded Wadham College in 1610; and she brought her husband Moor Hall as part of her dowry. The Gemmills have been tenant-farmers here for over a century. Such a historic, peaceful spot – yet only 35 minutes from the City of London (and 20 from Stansted Airport). Quite handy, too, for the port of Harwich.

Susan Gemmill has combined attractive modern colours with old features – deep coral, for instance, on walls with exposed timbers in the dining-room where a refectory table complements the brick inglenook and chamfered beams overhead. Here breakfasts and snack suppers are served. In the sitting-room, which has (like some other rooms) fluted panelling and lattice-paned windows that overlook the moat, are comfortable sofas, racing prints and a cabinet of silver; while upstairs are spacious family rooms – one in pale yellow, one in apricot with William Morris fabrics prettily draped.

Readers' comments: Charming house, tastefully and comfortably furnished. Made to feel like welcome friends. Full of atmosphere.

Dining-room at Orchard Farm, Mordiford (see page 263)

MORNINGTON HOUSE

C D S

Speltham Hill, Hambledon, Hampshire, PO7 6RU Tel: 0705 632704
North of Portsmouth. Nearest main road: A3 from Portsmouth to Petersfield.

2 Bedrooms. £14 (less for 4 nights). Tea/coffee facilities. Views of garden, country. Washing machine on request.
Light suppers if ordered.
1 Sitting-room. With open fire, central heating, TV.
Large garden

The form in which we know cricket dates from the 18th century – when Hambledon produced the first cricket club of all (still going strong) and laid down today's complicated rules (in 1760, the year when Mornington House was built). There is a cricket memorial here, and much cricketing memorabilia in the Bat and Ball Inn, where good food is served.

Charles Lutyens, for many years chairman of the club, is a great-nephew of Sir Edwin Lutyens and may show his Delhi plans to interested visitors as they relax in the bay-windowed sitting-room or the adjoining conservatory with grapevine overhead. There are splendid views over brimming herbaceous flowerbeds, beech hedges, rooftops and church, and over Speltham Down – which the villagers collectively bought for the National Trust to save it from development. The Wayfarers' Walk passes by here on its long trail from the coast to Inkpen Beacon. In the garden is a swimming-pool (unheated).

Everywhere are interesting antiques – an inlaid escritoire from Holland, Edwardian chairs painted with garlands, a clock with windjammer pitching and tossing in time with its ticking and tocking. Open fires crackle in the sitting-room and in the hall. In the dining-room (overlooking a paved courtyard), 'spitting images' of Disraeli and Gladstone preside over the breakfast table, and an unusual hide-covered rocking horse is a magnet to little children.

One bedroom, with lace spread and bamboo bedheads, leads to a strawberry-patterned bathroom with another bedroom, in blue and white, adjoining it.

Readers' comments: Delightful. Lovely welcome and attention. Look forward to returning. Delightful house, charming hosts. Excellent supper. So comfortable. Shall return.

On the other side of the village is **CAMS**: its 17th-century pine-panelled dining-room is impressive, with marble fireplace and shuttered glass doors opening onto the garden beyond the haha of which sheep graze (beside a tennis court). Spindle-backed rush chairs surround a great circular table of polished yew, where Valerie Fawcett may serve such meals as pâté, chicken breasts in lemon and coriander, and apple pie. In the sitting-room, chinoiserie curtains and pink walls make a pleasing background to antique furni-

ture. Up the impressive staircase are pretty bedrooms: the oldest, in pink and white, has beamy walls and leaded windows. £15–£17. [Tel: 0705 632865; postcode: PO7 4SP]

217

MULBERRY HALL   C S
Burstall, Suffolk, IP8 3DP   Tel: 0473 652348
West of Ipswich. Nearest main road: A1071 from Ipswich towards Sudbury.

3 Bedrooms. £16.50. Views of garden, country. No smoking. Washing machine on request.
Dinner. £13 for 3 courses (with choices) and coffee, at 7.45pm (except in August). Non-residents not admitted. Vegetarian or special diets if ordered. Wine can be brought in. **Light suppers** if ordered.
1 Sitting-room. With open fire, central heating, TV, piano, record-player.
Large garden

Cardinal Wolsey owned this house in 1523. Son of an Ipswich butcher, he had had a meteoric rise under Henry VIII (a cardinal and Lord Chancellor of England while still in his thirties) and he used his consequent wealth to commission fine properties and works of art. But in 1529, having failed Henry in the matter of divorcing Catherine of Aragon, he was stripped of nearly all his honours.

It is Henry VIII's colourful coat-of-arms which embellishes the inglenook fireplace in the big sitting-room – pink, beamed and with a grand piano. From this a winding stair leads up to well-equipped bedrooms. There is a small dining-room (green curtains and wallpaper in a sprigged Laura Ashley pattern, wheelback chairs round an oak table) where Penny Debenham serves such meals – to be ordered in advance – as trout mousse with a watercress purée; pork au poivre accompanied by dauphinoise potatoes, broccoli, courgettes and salad; fruit tartlets with elderflower cream; and cheeses. Breakfasts, too, are good, with such pleasant options as local apple-juice, chilled melon, home-baked bread and smoked haddock in addition to the usual bacon and eggs.

Outside is an exceptional garden – or series of gardens, enclosed within walls of yew or beech. Beyond a brick-paved terrace is a lawn with long lavender border, and a pergola leads past a rose garden to the tennis court.

Nearby Ipswich, a port even in Saxon times, has a plethora of mediaeval churches with fine monuments. The traffic in the town is heavy, so exploring is best done on foot. Wolsey made it a twin to Oxford, such was its reputation for learning – but only the gateway of his uncompleted college remains, near the quays where old inns and a classical Custom House survive. The town museum includes replicas of two local Saxon treasures now in the British Museum, the Sutton Hoo and Mildenhall finds; Christchurch Mansion (in a park) is a Tudor house with a collection of furniture and toys, as well as paintings by Constable and Gainsborough. Stroll down the Buttermarket to find the Ancient House, its façade covered in elaborate 17th-century plasterwork representing the (then) four continents: it is now a bookshop.

The surrounding scenery is of open farmland, dotted with particularly pretty villages.

Readers' comments: Beautiful house, outstanding food and service; will visit again. A lot of loving care. Bedrooms light and airy, extremely comfortable; excellent food, breakfast a highlight. Warm welcome, lovely house, superb breakfast. Very relaxed.

MUNK'S FARMHOUSE
Headcorn Road, Smarden, Kent, TN27 8PN   Tel: 023377 0265
West of Ashford. Nearest main road: A274 from Maidstone to Tenterden
(and M20, junction 8).

3 Bedrooms. £18–£19 (less for 7 nights). All have own bath/shower/toilet. TV. Views of garden, country. No smoking.
Dinner (weekends only). £14 for 3 courses and coffee, at 7.15pm. Non-residents not admitted. Vegetarian or special diets if ordered. Wine can be brought in. **Light suppers** if ordered.
1 Sitting-room. With open fire, central heating.
Large garden

You had better behave yourself if you stay here, for in the garden is a prison-cell. The old wood lock-up (double-walled and with tiny barred window), now a 'listed building', was moved here in 1850 from the village for, once the railway had been built, there was no longer a stream of brawling railway navvies to fill it.

The house itself has an even longer history. Weatherboarded in typically Kentish style, it was built nearly three centuries ago. Inside are beams, inglenook fireplaces, iron-latched doors, the original built-in cupboard and a very wide oak staircase: clearly the yeoman-farmer who originally lived here was a man of substance. Even the quarry tiles he laid were so large and thick that they are still as good as new. These are in the dining-room (formerly the kitchen) where guests now eat at a big refectory table. Josephine Scott serves such dinners (if these are ordered in advance) as pâté or melon, poached salmon or roast lamb with fresh vegetables, and home-made desserts or fresh fruit.

There is a sitting-room with log fire and William Morris sofa, and pretty twin-bedded rooms with sloping ceilings and country views. Outside is a heated swimming-pool. At nearby Pluckley, *The Darling Buds of May* was filmed.

Munk's Farmhouse is situated between Leeds and Sissinghurst castles and within reach of Canterbury, Rye and the Channel Tunnel.

Readers' comments: Really attractive and comfortable place, pretty garden, amiable hostess, excellent dinners.

The 15th-century **BELL INN** at Smarden has a façade of chequered brickwork overhung with scalloped tiles. Inside are Ian Turner's bars (stocked with eight 'real ales'), two with inglenooks and all paved or brick-floored. Here one can eat very well, seated on oak settles under beams strung with hop-bines. Outdoors an iron spiral staircase, wreathed in honeysuckle, leads up to the bedrooms: board ceilings, white brick walls, immaculately furnished. Visitors are provided with the wherewithal to

make their own continental breakfast. £15–£16. [Tel: 023377 0283; postcode: TN27 8PW]

NALDERHILL HOUSE X
Nalderhill Road, Wickham Heath, Berkshire, RG16 8EU Tel: 0635 41783
or 37231
West of Newbury. Nearest main road: A4 from Newbury to Hungerford
(and M4, junctions 13/14).

5 **Bedrooms.** £17.50–£20 (less for 3 nights
or continental breakfast). Some have own
bath/shower/toilet. Tea/coffee facilities. TV.
Views of garden, country. Washing machine
on request.
Light suppers if ordered.
1 **Sitting-room.** With open fire, central
heating, TV. No smoking.
Large garden

In 1876, the heir to a vast estate – all the land you can see from Nalderhill, and a
great deal more – was only four years old, so trustees were appointed, and their
chairman built this fine house for himself high up above the Kennet Valley. The
estate was cleverly landscaped to give an almost park-like view from the house:
copses were planted to conceal buildings, hahas dug to replace fences or hedges.
In the distance Coombe Hill rises 900 feet to the point where a beacon flares on
memorable occasions – for instance, the Queen's silver jubilee. The house itself is
surrounded by impeccable lawns, a flagstone terrace and rosebeds (the figure
beside these is not a scarecrow but a scare-deer!).

One enters through a hall with pale beige carpet and sofas of cut velvet. There
is a very big dining-room with a French window opening onto the terrace –
the wily pheasants know when breakfast is served and tap on the glass for
titbits (appreciated, too, by the squirrels). Everywhere the architectural details
are handsome: the solid oak of the doors, staircase and woodblock floors
came from trees felled when the house was built (the estate had its own sawmill
and brick kiln).

There are plentiful bathrooms, and all bedrooms have big windows
making the most of the fine views. In one is a 17th-century four-poster
with Indian-style hangings and cover, while another has 'thirties furniture in
palest walnut.

Across a cobblestone courtyard is a modernized cottage, its cream or pastel
rooms overlooking a Victorian rose garden. The sitting-room here has glass doors
opening into a Victorian conservatory filled with such flowers as jasmine and
plumbago. There is a kitchen (with microwave oven) in which visitors can cook
their own evening meals. A Jacuzzi and steam room are available.

Apart from Newbury's well-known association with horse-racing, other local
attractions include three golf courses, fishing on the River Kennet (which Patrick
Mackey can arrange for guests), and fine productions staged at the picturesque
Watermill Theatre nearby.

For explanation of code letters (C, D, M, PT, S, X) see page xlvi.

220

NEW CAPERNWRAY FARMHOUSE C(10) **D X**
Capernwray, Lancashire, LA6 1AD   Tel: 052473 4284
North of Lancaster. Nearest main road: A6 from Lancaster to Kendal (and M6, junction 35).

3 Bedrooms. £19 (**to readers of this book only**) –£27 (or more after Easter). Bargain breaks. All have own bath/shower/toilet. Tea/coffee facilities. TV. Views of country, garden. No smoking.
Dinner. £17.50 for 4 courses, fruit and coffee, at 7.30pm. Non-residents not admitted. Vegetarian or special diets if ordered. Wine can be brought in. No smoking. **Light suppers** if ordered.
1 Sitting-room. With open fire, central heating, books.
Large garden

Easy to reach from the motorway yet so rural, this is a place of absolute peace. The oak beams and stone walls that are features of most rooms date from the 17th century, when the house was built as a farm. Now, surrounded by lawns, it is the home of Peter and Sally Townend. They moved north, to this house, when Peter got a deputy headship locally and they say frankly that it was only when the cost of central heating soared that they began, a little doubtfully, to take paying guests – and then found they really enjoyed the experience. Sally encourages people to treat the house as if it were their own home. Dinner, after a complimentary sherry, is served by candlelight and could consist of smoked salmon, whole poussin with a sauce of wine and blackcurrants, individual chocolate tortes with cream sauce, followed by cheeses and fresh fruit.

Meals are eaten in what was once the dairy, now furnished with Ercol elm chairs and table. In the sitting-room, velvet armchairs and sofa contrast with the rugged stone of fireplace and walls. Bedrooms have doors of dark wood with brass knobs, attractive colours and Edwardian-style pine furniture. There are cane armchairs.

Capernwray not only lies in attractive countryside but is midway between the Lake District and the Yorkshire Dales, neither much more than a half-hour in a car. Scenic walks, pretty villages, market towns and inns abound.

Readers' comments: Every bit as comfortable as you describe it, if not more so! Food and friendliness first class. Four very happy nights. A real gem, superb food. Particularly enjoyable. Marvellous food, beautiful house, warm welcome.

Economical bed-and-breakfast is to be had at **THIE-NE-SHEE**, Moor Close Lane, Over Kellet. Both the neat bedrooms in this bungalow, built in 1952 as a farmhouse, are on the ground floor, and they have fine views across a luxuriant garden. Beyond Morecambe Bay, one can see on the horizon Black Combe – Wordsworth's 'completest, unobstructed prospect'. Owners are Margaret and Malcolm Cobb (he, being a railway enthusiast, was attracted

to this area by Steam Town at Carnforth, as well as by the pleasant countryside). No smoking. £10.50–£12.50. [Tel: 0524 735882; postcode: LA6 1DF]

NEW MOOR HOUSE

Edlingham, Northumberland, NE66 2BT   Tel: 066574 638
South-west of Alnwick. On A697 from Morpeth to Wooler.

5 Bedrooms. £15.50 (less for 7 nights). Price goes up from April. One has own bath/shower/toilet. All have tea/coffee facilities. Views of country. No smoking.
Dinner. £9.50 for 3 courses (with choices) and coffee, at 7pm (not Wednesdays). Non-residents not admitted. Vegetarian or special diets if ordered. Wine can be brought in. No smoking.
1 Sitting-room. With open fire, central heating, TV. No smoking.
Closed from November to February.

Once a coaching inn, at a crossroads in dramatic scenery of moorland and forests, New Moor House is set against a backdrop of the Cheviot Hills.

When Hilary and Peter Harcourt-Brown took the house over, they refurbished it to its present comfortable standard, with antiques in keeping with the age of the house. One steps into a dining-room furnished with pews salvaged from a disused church. The beamed sitting-room, with cretonne chairs and open fire, is upstairs.

Hilary prepares the home-cooked meals in generous portions. A typical meal might be home-made soup, a roast with fresh vegetables, then apple pie with cream. The house has its own soft, filtered, spring water which makes a very good cup of tea.

Peter and Hilary, who breed prize-winning collies and Afghan hounds, are keen on accommodating visitors with dogs, if inoculated.

Readers' comments: Most comfortable, delicious food. Warm welcome, comfortably furnished. Well ordered; they take pains with guests' whims. Substantial servings.

On the coast is **WESTLEA** (29 Riverside Road, Alnmouth), a very comfortable modern guest-house facing the Aln estuary and immaculately kept by Janice Edwards. One attractive bedroom opens onto the sunny front garden. All rooms, if small, are well equipped. The upstairs sitting-room has a balcony from which to enjoy the river view. Nearby are sandy beaches.

Breakfast choices are imaginative; and for dinner, there may be such dishes as Cheviot lamb with Northumbrian baked suet-puddings. £18–£20.
Readers' comments: Excellent value. A most enjoyable week. Kind and helpful. Hearty meals, beautifully cooked.

Immense trouble taken to make guests feel comfortable and at home. All sorts of little kindnesses. Food was of the best. Very impressed with warmth of welcome and unrivalled concern for their guests. [Tel: 0665 830730; postcode: NE66 2SD]

NEWBARN

CDSX

Wards Lane, Wadhurst, East Sussex, TN5 6HP Tel: 0892 782042
South-east of Tunbridge Wells (Kent). Nearest main road: A267 from
Tunbridge Wells to Heathfield.

3 Bedrooms. £18–£19 (less for 4 nights).
Prices go up in April. Tea/coffee facilities.
Views of garden, country, lake. No smoking.
Washing machine on request.
Light suppers if ordered.
2 Sitting-rooms. With open fire, central
heating, TV, record-player. No smoking.

Large garden

Sitting on the brick terrace with the blue lake view below and hills beyond, I
could have imagined I was in the Lake District – but this was Sussex, and London
only an hour away. There was a solitary angler in a boat, rabbits and wagtails on
the lawn – perfect peace!

In the 18th century this was a farmhouse, lattice-paned and tile-hung in traditional Sussex style. Indoors, knotty pine floorboards gleam with polish, there are
low beams, and the wood-latched doors were specially made by a local joiner for
Christopher and Pauline Willis, who took great care, when renovating the house,
to ensure that every detail was in harmony. Bedrooms are light and flowery,
predominantly yellow and green, or pink and blue. The sitting-room, which has
an inglenook, is decorated in apricot and cream. There is a games room in one of
the barns, and Shetland ponies roam the fields.

Usually only breakfast is served (with Pauline's preserves to follow –
marmalade made with treacle, gooseberry jam with elderflowers, for instance)
because the area is well supplied with good restaurants. Visitors are welcome,
however, to use the Aga cooker when it is convenient. (Baby-sitting available.)

The landscaped garden descends right to the edge of the lake, which is in fact
man-made: Bewl Water reservoir. Around its perimeter and many inlets is a 15-
mile footpath: there are boat cruises, a visitor centre, watersports, a wooden ark
for children and picnic spots. Sometimes there is Morris dancing or a crafts show.
Birds from the nature reserve can be spotted. Bicycles for hire, horse-riding and
fishing.

Bewl Water is on the Kent/Sussex border and there is so much of interest in this
historic area that one could happily spend a week or two without going far afield.
At Finchcocks, a Queen Anne house, is a collection of early pianos and other
instruments which visitors can hear played. Scotney is a decorative, turreted castle
with particularly lovely waterside gardens. Bayham Abbey's ruins are beautifully
sited by a river. Sissinghurst has Vita Sackville-West's gardens around its castle.

Tunbridge Wells is the nearest major town, with true spa elegance, tempting
shops in the Pantiles and elsewhere, curious 'twittens' (footpaths) twisting behind
the backs of elegant houses; and, on its large common, strange rock formations.

Readers' comments: Views and peace superb. A pleasure to stay in. Warm,
comfortable and excellent decoration. Friendly and helpful. Outstanding. A lovely
spot and very pleasant people. We will definitely return. Absolutely beautiful. The
best b & b ever. Beautiful location, tasteful decoration.

NEWLANDS MOHAIR FARM   C D S X
York Road, Barmby Moor, Humberside, YO4 5HU   Tel: 0759 380308
East of York. On A1079 from York to Market Weighton.

3 Bedrooms. £12.50–£14. Prices go up from Easter. One has own bath/shower/toilet. Tea/coffee facilities. TV. Views of garden, country. Washing machine on request.
Light suppers if ordered.
Large garden

This would be a good choice for anyone who wants to see the city of York but prefers to stay in the country (especially if they are approaching via the Humber Bridge). And they will stay on an intrinsically interesting farm as a bonus. For this is the only farm in the country where the main enterprise is angora goats, whose long silky hair provides mohair ('angora' yarn is made from rabbit fur). Originally from Turkey (the word angora is a corruption of Ankara), they are widely kept in other countries and, when Lesley Scott formed her flock about 10 years ago, she assembled breeding stock from as far away as New Zealand and Canada, travelling back with them. Visitors to the farm can get to know these friendly and intelligent animals, which now number about two hundred. They can also buy, at surprisingly low prices, garments made from their hair. This Lesley has processed in Bradford and then knitted locally to her own designs. Yarn and kits are on sale too, as are tops and fleeces for hand spinners.

In the farmhouse, which is decorated with some imagination, most rooms are rather small, and there is no sitting-room. However, the family room is spacious, with armchairs and a writing table. Ask to hear the story of Lesley's great-grandfather's will, which hangs on the breakfast-room wall.

The farm, which is well away from the road, is on the site of a Roman settlement with a pottery. A more recent installation is an outdoor spa bath, in operation during the summer.

Those who do not want to travel the 10 miles into York to dine have a fair choice in Pocklington, the nearest large village, where there is even a German restaurant.

William Wilberforce went to school in Pocklington (another village in the vicinity is called Wilberfoss) and, at Stamford Bridge not far away, King Harold defeated the Norwegians in 1066: he was less fortunate later in that year. Also in Pocklington is one of the strange museums which seem to be springing up all over the place: Penny Arcadia, which is devoted to amusement machines, from what-the-butler-saw to jukeboxes. It claims to offer 1½ hours of unique entertainment. The gardens of Burnby Hall are notable for their collection of waterlilies.

Mohair Farm would be a good base for visiting not only York but also Beverley, which is like a smaller version of the more famous city: see other pages.

Facts (prices, etc.) at the top of entries are supplied by the proprietors themselves. While every effort is made to ensure that these are correct at the time of going to press, they may alter thereafter: please check when you book.

NORTH COURT   C D PT

Shorwell, Isle of Wight, PO30 3JG   Tel: 0983 740415
(Messages: 0983 524731)
South-west of Newport. Nearest main road: A3055 from Totland to Ventnor.

3 Bedrooms. £15–£17.50 (less for 3 nights or continental breakfast). All have own bath/toilet. Tea/coffee facilities. TV. Views of garden, country. Washing machine on request.
Light suppers if ordered.
1 Sitting-room. With open fire, central heating, TV. No smoking.
Large garden

Swinburne and his girl cousin used to play the organ that stands in the hall of this great 17th-century manor house – a big stone-flagged room with pale blue walls, logs piled high around the stove.

The house is now the home of John and Christine Harrison, portraits of whose ancestors hang on the walls of the large dining-room with mahogany tables and marble fireplace. The great staircase was reputedly designed by Grinling Gibbons, and nearly every room has handsome detailing from that period – arched or scallop-framed doorways, egg-and-dart mouldings, shuttered windows in thick stone walls. At the top of the house is a games room, very suitable for family use. The prettiest bedroom is perhaps the blue-and-white one with bay window overlooking the tennis lawn. All bedrooms are large, with armchairs.

Impressive though the house is, the really outstanding feature is the large and undulating garden with many plants of botanical interest. You can wander through woodlands or down terraces to a stream with water-plants, try to tell the time from a sundial in the knot garden, look down into the ancient bath-house, wander through arches of wisteria or lilac, play croquet . . . As only snacks are served, dinner for most people always involves a stroll through this lovely garden (opened to the public occasionally) to reach the nearby Crown Inn.

The island's coastline, its inland scenery and pretty villages appealed to the Victorians' love of the picturesque, and it was they who established it as an ideal holiday destination. Some feel that this has now ruined parts of the coast but, in a village such as this, one is well away from the summer crowds and yet so central that every part is within easy reach. Small though the island is, the scenery is extraordinarily varied – and at its best in spring or autumn, when visitors are few. You could stay a month and every day find a different 'sight' to visit, as varied as Carisbrooke Castle or Osborne House on the one hand and the ferny chines (ravines) or wildlife reserves, a working smithy or a museum of clocks on the other. Some of the least famous places are the most attractive – unspoilt villages such as Calbourne, Mottistone, Yaverland and Kingston, for instance. One of the nicest, old-fashioned resorts on the south coast is Ventnor and to the east of it lies picturesque little Bonchurch, complete with duck-pond; while on the St Lawrence side there stretches a 6-mile walk or drive among myrtles and ilex – the Undercliff, created when towering cliffs broke and slid down to the sea, a disastrous spectacle until nature moved in abundantly with self-seeded plants and trees. At the end of the Undercliff is a headland, St Catherine's Point, with lighthouse and far sea views.

NORTH FARMHOUSE

C D

Station Road, Docking, Norfolk, PE31 8LS   Tel: 0485 518493
North-east of King's Lynn. Nearest main road: A149 from King's Lynn to
Wells-next-the-Sea.

4 Bedrooms. £16. Price goes up from
Easter. All have own bath/shower/toilet.
Tea/coffee facilities. TV. Views of garden,
country. No smoking. Washing machine on
request.
Light suppers if ordered.
1 Sitting-room. With open fire, central
heating, TV, piano.
Large garden
Closed in December and January.

The flint walls of this house in one of Norfolk's attractive conservation villages are
nearly two feet thick at the older, 17th-century end, through which one enters.
This part is now used as a little gallery to exhibit the paintings of Roger Roberts
(and other local artists).

Roger has stripped the pine doors and refurbished the little iron fireplaces
which are a feature of many rooms. Pale yellows and blues with much white
paintwork give a fresh and airy look throughout. There is an excellent family
suite, with Laura Ashley fabrics, consisting of two bedrooms and a shower-room;
and other very large rooms that have good bathrooms. In the sitting-room
antiques mingle with more homely furniture.

A number of visitors come to Docking in winter because the coast near here is
unique in the world for the number of migrant birds that arrive from the north.
Out on the marshes of The Wash, muffled figures brave wind and rain to see the
wading birds flock in, or they go to the many bird reserves of the area (Scolt
Head, Titchwell, Holm, Snettisham and others). Sandringham is near, and even
when the royal home is not open to the public it is worth going there to see the
buildings of the stud (its founder was the racing champion Persimmon, of whom
there is a statue); the immense gates of wrought iron decorated with grapes and
ivy; and the high encircling walls beautifully crafted from four-inch slivers of the
local, reddish stone (carr), laid with perfect regularity for mile after mile. This is
ideal country for walking or cycling (no steep hills!) and for seaside holidays. The
beach at Brancaster is one of the best, sandy and unspoilt; or go to Hunstanton if
you want a lively little resort. Holkham Hall and Houghton are two of the nearest
stately homes. At Wolferton a lovely woodland ride brings you to mementoes of
royal trains in the station once used by kings.

King's Lynn, a great port in the Middle Ages, grew up alongside the
River Ouse. One can walk among Norman and half-timbered buildings,
monastic remains, old inns and cobbled courts. The ancient parish church is
full of treasures from carvings to huge brasses; and there are two huge
market places.

Readers' comments: A wonderful stay, and very warm welcome. A very high
standard, with character and artistic flair. Very substantial breakfasts. Extremely
informative hosts. Friendly and relaxing. Excellent in all respects.

NORTHLEIGH HOUSE

C D M

Fiveways Road, Hatton, Warwickshire, CV35 7HZ   Tel: 0926 484203
North-west of Warwick. Nearest main road: A4177 from Warwick to Solihull
(also M40, junction 15; and M42, junction 5).

6 Bedrooms. £20–£26. All have own bath/shower/toilet. Tea/coffee facilities. Refrigerators and remote-control TV. Views of garden, country. No smoking. Washing machine on request.
Dinner. £14.50 for 3 courses (with choices) and coffee, at times to suit guests. Non-residents not admitted. Vegetarian or special diets if ordered. Wine can be brought in. No smoking. **Light suppers** if ordered.
1 Sitting-room. With central heating, wood stove, TV. No smoking.
Small garden
Closed from mid-December to end of January.

A former dress designer, Sylvia Fenwick – a vivacious personality – has turned her creative talents to decorating every bedroom with elegance – each is different, each memorable, and many verge on the luxurious (for instance, some double rooms have two washbasins). They are all very well equipped and heated.

The L-shaped blue suite (with kitchenette in cupboard) has a sofa, bamboo tables and a carved bed in a silk-curtained alcove. There's a huge poppy room, with white furniture, in which the pale green leafy wallpaper is matched by the carpet. Another room, Victorian and frilly in style, has a cocoa-and-white colour scheme; while yet another is in Chinese style. On two sides of the big sitting-room are garden views; the room has comfortable furniture, pleasant colours and an ornate little wood-burner.

Sylvia serves supper trays, or dinners (by arrangement) at which you might get something like avocado salad, pork chops in a sauce of mustard, sugar and almonds – served with five vegetables; and a rich strawberry trifle ('I go mad with the cream!'). But she also provides guests with a map showing a dozen local inns that do good food. Because she keeps rare breeds of sheep and poultry, her own produce sometimes features in these meals.

Rural quiet surrounds the house – and yet it is only a few miles from Birmingham's National Exhibition Centre and international airport; the National Agricultural Centre; and the bustling towns of Warwick and Coventry.

Readers of Edith Holden's *Country Diary of an Edwardian Lady* will be familiar with a number of place-names around here such as Knowle, a historic village on a hill, with half-timbered houses; and Packwood House (NT) which has a lovely garden containing conical yews representing Christ and the disciples (and fine furniture inside) – Edith did many sketches here. Mediaeval Baddesley Clinton is moated.

Readers' comments: Very superior, one of the best I have found, bedrooms spacious and breakfasts excellent. First class! Immaculate. We loved this place so much we spent an extra night there. Sylvia Fenwick is a very warm and hospitable lady. Her scrambled eggs are heavenly!

NORWOOD FARMHOUSE   C(12)
Hiscott, Devon, EX31 3JS   Tel: 0271 858260
South of Barnstaple. Nearest main road: A377 from Barnstaple to Exeter.

3 Bedrooms. £19–£22. Prices go up in April. All have own shower/toilet. Tea/coffee facilities. TV. Views of garden, country. No smoking. Washing machine on request.
Dinner. £13 for 4 courses (with choices) and coffee, at 7pm. Wine can be brought in. No smoking. **Light suppers.**
2 Sitting-rooms. With open fire, central heating, TV, video. No smoking.
Large garden
Closed from December to February.

At the heart of a hundred acres of pastureland is a 17th-century farmhouse with beams, inglenook and log stove on a slate hearth, panelled doors of pine, and furnishings chosen well for this setting. There are sofas of buttoned brocade in the sitting-room, a brass bed prettily draped, Laura Ashley and other good fabrics, dried-flower arrangements and on the walls Linda Richard's own accomplished paintings of local scenes. Her husband was born in this house, where three generations of Richards have farmed.

For dinner, Linda serves such meals as avocado pear, pork and apples cooked in Devon cider, fruit pie with clotted cream, and cheeses – after which (in what was once the dairy) guests relax in front of television (with video), with a book by the fire, in a Victorian conservatory, in chairs on the south-facing terrace, or strolling in Norwood's own woodlands. Those using the farm's self-catering accommodation are also welcome to dine in the house.

Norwood is only a few miles from ancient Barnstaple which, in addition to the centuries-old attractions of its Pannier Market on Tuesdays and Fridays, has plenty of modern shops, an antiques bazaar, and a very big swimming-pool in its leisure centre. Many 18th-century buildings and a colonnaded walk survive in the centre; there is a museum of local history in a 14th-century chapel; and the bridge of 16 arches dates from the 13th century. Recent tourist attractions include Jungleland (exotic plants), a farm park at Landkey, a sheepskin tannery with workshop tours at Pilton Causeway, and the Cobbaton collection of vehicles and other relics from the Second World War.

Good beaches lie beyond Barnstaple, at Woolacombe, Saunton and Croyde which overlook Barnstaple Bay and have National Trust landscape behind them. In this direction, too, are the wildflowers of Braunton Burrows, a nature reserve with sand dunes; and one of Devon's few very fine churches, at Braunton (which also has an excellent gallery of crafts and paintings, with wholefood restaurant).

Readers' comments: Comfortably furnished; attractive dinner – generous and healthy food. Warm welcome. Made to feel at home. A well-adorned house. By far the best.

Book well ahead: many of these houses have few rooms. Do not expect dinner if you have not booked it or if you arrive late.

NUMBER ONE   C D PT X

1 Woodlands, Beverley, Humberside, HU17 8BT   Tel: 0482 862752
Nearest main road: A1079 from York to Beverley (and M62, junction 38).

3 Bedrooms. £16–£17 (less for 7 nights). Tea/coffee facilities. Views of garden. No smoking. Washing machine on request.
Dinner. £12 for 4 courses (with choices) and coffee, at about 7pm. Non-residents not admitted. Vegetarian or special diets if ordered. Wine can be brought in. No smoking. **Light suppers** if ordered.
1 Sitting-room. With open fire, central heating, TV. No smoking.
Small garden

Like York but on a smaller scale, Beverley consists of a minster rising from a warren of small streets within what was once a moated town. Traffic is restricted in the centre, which means that streets such as Woodlands are relatively quiet. Number One is in a dignified late-Victorian terrace.

The Kings, both teachers, have furnished the house with some brio, using wallpapers and bright colours to good effect. There is an abundance of house-plants, books and pictures, the last ranging from original works, through reproductions, to old school photographs. And some quirky touches are decorative: a pair of antlers hung with assorted hats, for example. There is a grandfather clock on the landing, which leads to well-windowed bedrooms. The dining-room doubles as Neil King's study: guests particularly appreciate finding the fire already burning here at breakfast time.

Sarah King provides for dinner a choice of three or four first courses which might include a dressed avocado; a meat or fish main course (barbecued spare ribs or salmon in wine sauce, for example); and a choice of out-of-the-ordinary puddings, including locally made ices; and cheese. Over coffee, which comes with chocolates, the Kings like to talk to their guests in front of the sitting-room fire. There is croquet, and cycles can be hired; baby-sitting also available.

Beverley is best known for the minster, but it would be an enjoyable town even without it. St Mary's church is almost as fine an example of Gothic architecture: a carving in it (one of many notable grotesques here and in the minster) is said to have put the idea of the White Rabbit into Lewis Carroll's head. St Mary's is minutes from Number One, by a street with an antiquarian bookshop, a good craft gallery, and a restored arcade with dealers in such things as pot-pourri and oriental artefacts. In the opposite direction is the Westwood, a historic park-like open space with the town's racecourse. (Racing enthusiasts often use Beverley as a base for all Yorkshire's many meetings.)

For a different kind of history, the Museum of Army Transport is popular: the oldest exhibit here is the waggon used by Lord Roberts in the Boer War.

Should you tire of 'this place made for walking in', as John Betjeman called Beverley, where a Georgian frontage often conceals a much older building, there is plenty to visit within driving distance: York and Hull (see other pages) and the North Sea coast, notable mansions, and more recently created attractions such as farm museums and model railways.

OAK TREE INN   C D M PT S X
Tantobie, County Durham, DH9 9RF   Tel: 0207 235445
West of Stanley. Nearest main road: A692 from Gateshead to Consett.

8 Bedrooms. £15–£23 (less for 3 nights). 5% **off to readers of this book.** Bargain breaks. All have own bath/shower/toilet. Tea/coffee facilities. TV. Some have views of garden.
Dinner. From £8.50 for 3 courses (with choices), at 8–8.30pm. Vegetarian or special diets if ordered. Wine can be ordered. No smoking area in breakfast-room. **Light suppers** if ordered.
Bar. With open fire, central heating, TV, piano, pool table, etc.
Small garden

The inn was once a small manor house, the property of the local Member of Parliament. The rooms, some of which have four-poster or half-tester beds, still have original Victorian fireplaces, and the overall decor is Victorian in feel. Some rooms are in a converted coach house; others, less elaborate (and cheaper), in a cottage.

It is a surprising place to find in – it has to be said – an unattractive village: a combination of guest-house, gourmet restaurant and village pub, kept by a former college lecturer in fashion who describes herself as a lifelong devoted glutton!

In the dining-room, also Victorian in character, guests can have a table d'hôte meal, or they can choose from a very long à la carte menu, mostly French bourgeois in inspiration. The wine list is also long. On occasion, there are special continental evenings (Austrian, French, German, Alsace-Lorraine). And once a month there is live music – light classical, continental café-style, for example, or soloists. If this is not to your taste, there are games to play in the bar downstairs: Sylvia Hurst says the locals love to hear of 'foreign parts'. (Sunday lunch and baby-sitting are available.)

The Oak Tree would be a good haven for those whose business takes them to the north-east, but the area has much to offer the tourist too, with the city of Durham on one side and unspoiled hilly country on the other.

In particular, there is the North of England Open-Air Museum at Beamish, only a few miles away. Awarded the accolade of European Museum of the Year some time ago, Beamish has as its object the preservation of the heritage of the north-east – urban, rural, and industrial – 'in the round' and, as far as possible, 'live'. The following are some of the things which have been assembled on the 200-acre site.

There is a recreated market town of the 1820s – houses (one with dentist's surgery), shops with authentic stocks, pub with beer on sale and dray horses in the stables, fairground with working rides, and so on. A typical country station with signal box serves the railway which crosses the site, and there is a working replica of George Stephenson's *Locomotion* – or you can travel by tram or horse-drawn carriage. The farm is complete with local breeds of livestock and old implements. Pitmen's cottages (one used for demonstrations of baking) are by the recreated coalmine buildings and the drift mine, into which one can go. And there is much more: a day here would hardly be enough to make the most of the place.

OLD BAKEHOUSE   **S**
33-35 High Street, Little Walsingham, Norfolk, NR22 6BZ
Tel: 0328 820454
North of Fakenham. Nearest main road: A148 from Cromer to King's Lynn.

3 Bedrooms. £17.50–£20 (less for 7 nights). One has own shower/toilet. Tea/coffee facilities. Views of garden, country.
Dinner. A la carte (Tuesdays to Saturdays); or £12.50 for 3 courses (with choices) and coffee, at 7pm if pre-booked (Tuesdays to Fridays). Vegetarian or special diets if ordered. Wine can be ordered. **Bar.**

Over a restaurant renowned for good food are excellent bedrooms.

From 1550 until recent times, part of this house was a bakery and the old ovens are still to be seen. Above an ancient cellar bar is a large, lofty dining-room – in the 18th century it was a corn exchange. There is a great brick fireplace at one end, and huge iron-hinged door. When Chris and Helen Padley took over, they painted the walls pale pink and furnished the room with pine and rush furniture. Here they serve such delectable table d'hôte meals as fresh peaches baked with cheese and herbs (for a starter), banana-stuffed chicken with a mild curry-and-almond sauce, and ice-cream coffee-cake; with a wider à la carte choice too.

Readers' comments: Gourmet food; friendly and efficient. Loving attention to detail; food superb. Food wonderful (front room noisy).

Great Walsingham boasts a fine Elizabethan house in big grounds, **BERRY HALL**, West Gate, named after the merchant who built it in 1532. Once Rupert Brooke's family lived here. Now it is the home of Doris Wilson and Joan Sheaf. Many rooms, all very big, have fine panelling; in the hall are a flagstone floor and impressive oak ceiling; Portuguese Delft tiles decorate the dining-room. There is a great balustraded staircase and unusual antiques. Swans glide in the moat; and a peacock parades amongst the rosebeds. For dinner Doris cooks such dishes as watercress soup, lamb noisettes in sherry sauce

and meringues with strawberries. £15.50 (b & b).
Readers' comments: Most attractive, comfortable and spacious. Food cooked to perfection. Charming and characterful. [Tel: 0328 820267; postcode: NR22 6DZ]

Prices are per person in a double room at the beginning of the year.

OLD BAKERY C(6)
2 Mitchelgate, Kirkby Lonsdale, Cumbria, LA6 2BE Tel: 05242 71422
South-east of Kendal. Nearest main road: A65 from M6 (junction 36) to
Skipton.

2 **Bedrooms.** £15–£16. Prices go up in
April. Tea/coffee facilities. No smoking.
Washing machine on request.
1 **Sitting-room.** With open fire, central
heating, TV, video, record-player. No
smoking.
Small garden
Closed from November to January.

Little more than 40 years ago, the Old Bakery was indeed a bakery, and there is a
printed carrier-bag framed on one wall to prove it. When Robert and Elisabeth
Etherington were restoring the house, they found a lot of bread tins and pie
moulds in an attic (also, less explicably, a quantity of lead shot – and tailor's
pins). Entered through what was the shop, the living-room was once the front
rooms of two cottages. With small-paned windows and low beams, it is cosy
though not cramped. Guests share a long, antique-style table for breakfast and, in
the evenings, can sit by a big open fire at the other end of the room.

At the back of the house is an enclosed garden, walled and paved, with an iron
lamp-post and a stone-walled raised border which the Etheringtons have created
themselves. Bedrooms are neat and cottagey.

Breakfast can be continental or English, with Cumberland sausage and black
pudding on offer – like the bread and croissants, made in the town. Dinner is not
provided because Kirkby Lonsdale has so many restaurants.

The town also has many antique shops (and 3-day auctions), some near
curiously named streets such as Salt Pie Lane and Jingling Lane or off the
pleasant market square with its monument and cross. The church is Norman and
some of the many inns are two or three hundred years old. Signs point to
Ruskin's View (over the River Lune, which gave Lancashire its name), which he
considered the finest in England. During the first weekend in September, there is
an annual Victorian fair when the whole town dresses in period costume. The
Laurel and Hardy Museum is near.

Readers' comments: Exceptional hospitality, warmth and interesting conversation. I
can't imagine anyone regretting a stopover here.

In a backwater close to the M6,
MILTON HOUSE BARN, Crook-
lands, has been ingeniously converted
to give lots of nooks and crannies.
Guests use a characterful sitting-room
at the top of the building, and they
have their breakfast by a double-height
window where the barn doors used to
be. Rooms (except for the single) have
private or en suite bath. Pauline Jones
serves such dinners as home-made
soup, beef cooked in ale with puff
pastry crust, and sticky toffee pudding.

No smoking. £17 (b & b with light
supper). [Tel: 05395 67628; postcode:
LA7 7NL]

OLD BAKERY

C(12) D S X

Milton Abbas, Dorset, DT11 0BW   Tel: 0258 880327
South-west of Blandford Forum. Nearest main road: A354 from Blandford to Dorchester.

6 Bedrooms. £17–£22.50 (less for 3 nights or continental breakfast). Some have own bath/shower/toilet. Tea/coffee facilities. Views of garden, country. No smoking.
2 Sitting-rooms. With open fire, central heating, TV, piano.
Extensive grounds

Milton Abbas looks almost too good to be true, as if it had been created specially for a picture on a chocolate-box. Indeed, it is a special creation; for in the 18th century it was laid out as a 'model village' when the Earl of Dorchester razed a nearby mediaeval settlement to build himself a mansion (Milton Abbey) and resited its inhabitants here. The broad village street, grass-verged, slopes steeply down, lined all the way with trim white-and-thatch cottages.

One of these is the Old Bakery: the huge ovens are still there, in a vast sitting-room where guests now relax. Margaret Penny has a decorative touch, so all the bedrooms (and even the toilet) are attractive. There are small but pretty single rooms – pink and lacy. She has found interesting wallpapers – poppies for one room; in another, navy-and-white – to complement twirly cane bedheads, board doors, neat pine cupboards within which basin and shower are concealed in one room, and the antiques that feature in every room. (A suite with its own sitting-room also has its own entrance.) Behind the house are woods, pasture and stables for visitors who bring horses – this is a great area for riding and walking – and adjoining the house is a saddlery and leathercraft workshop. There are an inn and a tea-room nearby for evening meals.

Some of Milton Abbey (now a school) can be visited, notably the huge chapel and its striking monuments: part of a 15th-century church of cathedral-like proportions which the Earl retained when he demolished most of the original monastery to make his great house. The Abbey is celebrated for its music weeks.

Across the pretty Piddle Valley is Cerne Abbas and, in Duck Street, **SOUND O'WATER**, a former inn which Jean and Doug Simmonds have modernized to provide a comfortable guest-house. Some rooms are in an annexe opening onto a pretty garden that wanders down to the winding River Cerne. Light suppers provided, but all Cerne's inns do good food. Cerne is a lovely village and with the famous giant on its hillside. £15–£20.

Readers' comments: Very comfortable and friendly. [Tel: 0300 341435; postcode: DT2 7LA]

OLD EGREMONT HOUSE

31 Egremont Street, Ely, Cambridgeshire, CB6 1AE   Tel: 0353 663118

Nearest main road: A10 from Cambridge to King's Lynn.

2 **Bedrooms.** £18.50–£19 (less for 2 nights and weekends). Prices go up from April. One has own bath/toilet. Tea/coffee facilities. TV. Views of garden. No smoking. **Large garden**

rear view

The 300-year-old house, once a yeoman's farm, has been filled by Sheila Friend-Smith with attractive furnishings, the garden is lovely and there is a cathedral view.

One bed/sitting-room has a cream carpet and beribboned duvet, sprigged wallpaper and stripped pine furniture. There are armchairs from which to enjoy a view of the winding flower garden and its herbaceous bed; from the other bed-room one sees the neat vegetable garden where Victorian hedges of box flank the symmetrical paths, and the tennis lawn. The house is full of interesting things to look at: Jeremy's collection of clocks (one is silent, being gravity-operated), pretty Portuguese tiles in bathrooms (and some depicting old military costumes), embroideries from Jordan and stone-rubbings from Thailand. Breakfast is served at a big mahogany table surrounded by Chippendale-style chairs, with antique china, numerous books and prints around. For dinner, Sheila recommends the Old Fire Engine, a few minutes' walk away, but one must book ahead.

Either Ely or Norwich could be the starting-point of a cathedrals' tour up the east side of England. More-or-less linked by what was once called the Great North Road (from London to Scotland), now known as the A1, are the exceptionally fine cathedrals of Peterborough (in Cambridgeshire), Lincoln, York and Durham. As to Ely itself, the city still has an 18th-century air. There is a particularly attractive riverside walk linking its quays, and a nature trail with not only birds to be seen but also a fine view of the cathedral. Ely is one of Europe's most glorious cathedrals, a multiplicity of pinnacles and spires outside, lofty vista within.

The original **SPINNEY ABBEY** founded in 1220, near Wicken, was closed down by Henry VIII, became a private house (where Cromwell's son lived after the Stuarts were restored to the throne) and was later pulled down. Its stones were used to build a new house in 1775. This is now the home of Valerie Fuller (and of her inherited collection of Victorian stuffed birds), who has roomy and comfortable bed-rooms, a sunken bath in one bathroom and, from the farm lands, views into ancient Wicken Fen, a National Trust nature reserve. (B & b only.) £17.

Readers' comments: Excellent hostess, capable and friendly. Very comfort-able. [Tel: 0353 720971; postcode: CB7 5XQ]

234

OLD FARMHOUSE   C D

Raskelf, North Yorkshire, YO6 3LF   Tel: 0347 821971
North of York. Nearest main road: A19 from York to Thirsk.

10 Bedrooms. £19.50. Price goes up at Easter (less for 4 nights during summer). Bargain breaks. All have own bath/shower/toilet.
Dinner. £15.50 for 4 courses (with choices) and coffee, at 7–7.45pm. Vegetarian or special diets if ordered. Wine can be ordered. No smoking. **Light suppers** if ordered.
2 Sitting-rooms. With open fire, central heating, TV.
Small garden
Closed in January.

Bill and Jenny Frost's 18th-century guest-house has immaculate accommodation and decorative touches like a bouquet of silk flowers in the brick hearth whenever a log fire is not burning; and a particularly luxurious bathroom adjoining one bedroom. Dining chairs were made by Thompson, the famous 'mouse man'.

But it is the outstanding dinners which bring most visitors here. At every course there are several choices, from which one might select (for example) rabbit terrine, chicken breast en croûte, old English trifle; and finally the most interesting selection of a dozen English cheeses I have come across for some time, ranging from yarg (mild and low-fat, wrapped in edible nettle-leaves) to potted Stilton (buttery and port-laden); blue Wensleydale to snow-white Ribblesdale. Bread and preserves at the 7-item breakfast are home-made, as are the 5 kinds of cheese-biscuit.

Readers' comments: Wholehearted recommendation. High standard. Excellent and varied food, very amiable and faultless service. Spotless and comfortable accommodation. Quite outstanding. Our favourite: so friendly, and food is first class. Excellent value in every way. Imaginative cooking, friendly host.

In a barn adjoining tiny **POND COTTAGE** (Brandsby Road, Stillington) is a treasure-trove of domestic bygones. For the Thurstans are antique dealers, specializing in 'kitchenalia' and pine furniture. The 18th-century house itself is furnished with antiques, and its shelves and nooks are filled with curios. There are collections of coronation mugs and Staffordshire dogs in the low-beamed sitting-room, where high-backed wing chairs are grouped around an inglenook fireplace. This is a house of twists and turns, unexpected steps and low windows. Its pleasant bedrooms overlook a terrace, a croquet lawn and a natural pond.

Dianne serves only breakfast

because (the citizens of nearby York being great diners-out) the area is very well supplied with eating-places. £13.50–£14.50.

Readers' comments: A brilliant discovery. Fantastic treatment. Accommodation and catering excellent. Wonderful. Outstanding. Delightful and caring hostess. Nothing too much trouble. [Tel: 0347 810796; postcode: YO6 1NY]

235

OLD FORGE   **C D M PT X**

Burgage Lane, Southwell, Nottinghamshire, NG25 0ER   Tel: 0636 812809

North-east of Nottingham. Nearest main road: A612 from Nottingham to Southwell.

5 Bedrooms. £19–£22 (less for 2 nights or continental breakfast). Prices go up in April. Bargain breaks at weekends. All have own bath/shower/toilet. Tea/coffee facilities. TV. Views of garden, country. No smoking. Washing machine on request.
Light suppers if ordered.
1 Sitting-room. With open fire, central heating, TV, record-player. No smoking.
Small garden

Flower baskets hang on the pale pink house where once a blacksmith lived and worked; yet it was only about twenty years ago that there ceased to be a forge here. The forge itself, at the back, is now two bedrooms, clematis growing over its roof; and the great stone rim round which iron for wheels was hammered now lies idle by the lily-pool in the little garden. This is overlooked by a small quarry-tiled conservatory from which there is a view of historic Southwell Minster nearby.

Hilary Marston has filled the 200-year-old rooms with treasures such as a very old 'log cabin' quilt from Boston (now used as a wall-hanging), Staffordshire figures, a tapestry chair stitched by a great-aunt, and a brass bed with lace spread.

Each bedroom has its own character. One has a trellis-effect bedhead built in and tulip-bud wallpaper; another is pink and flowery; a third – with a good view of the Minster floodlit at night – has pale cottage-garden flowers.

Because there are 10 eating-places within 5 minutes' walk, full evening meals are not provided.

At the heart of the peaceful old town, surrounded by fields of red earth reminiscent of Devon's soil, is the Minster, founded in Saxon times, with remarkably fine stone carvings (in its Chapter House) of leaves from all the native trees of England. Most visitors also want to see Newstead Abbey, founded in 1170 (it later became Byron's home), Belvoir Castle on its lofty crag, Lincoln's cobbled lanes and dominating cathedral high up, the National Water Sports Centre (at Holme Pierrepont) and the Robin Hood Centre in Sherwood Forest.

Nottinghamshire is, like certain other counties, stupidly ignored by most tourists – which means it is less crowded for those who do appreciate its many attractions (not least, a multitude of things appealing to children: farm parks, shows about Robin Hood, 'adventure' parks, exhibitions about cave men's lives – at Cresswell Crags, the National Mining Museum, canal trips and so forth). The River Trent winds northward, flowing through Nottingham and past Newark – a town dominated by ruins of the castle where King John died in 1216, and centred on a big market square with 14th-century inns. There are five antique fairs a year. Near it is Hawton's church, worth a detour for its fine tower and 14th-century Easter sepulchre. Eastwood is where D. H. Lawrence grew up, in a mining cottage now open to the public.

Readers' comments: Made to feel very welcome, nothing too much trouble. Well-decorated, comfortably furnished, each room very individual. Warm welcome. Well-appointed rooms. Outstanding breakfast. First class. Excellent rooms. Superb breakfast, altogether a pleasant experience.

OLD GRANARY

C PT

The Quay, Wareham, Dorset, BH20 4LP Tel: 0929 552010
Nearest main road: A351 from Poole to Swanage.

4 Bedrooms. £19–£23. **20% discount in winter to readers of this book (2 days, excluding Fri and Sat).** Some have own bath/toilet. Tea/coffee facilities. TV. Views of country, river. No smoking.
Dinner. A la carte or £13.95 for 4 courses (with choices) and coffee, at 6.15–9pm. Vegetarian dishes. Wine can be ordered.
Light suppers if ordered.
1 Sitting-room. With open fire, central heating. **Bar.**

Standing right on the quay by the River Frome, this 18th-century brick building was once a warehouse for grain that went by barge to Poole, and it still has much of its old character.

Derek and Rose-Marie Sturton run a restaurant on two floors, with good food served on flowery china, in two dining-rooms furnished with cane chairs and attractive colours.

A typical dinner might comprise, for instance, haddock Mornay, duckling and raspberry mousse. (Sunday lunch also available.) There is a riverside terrace with seats, for cream teas and drinks (the terrace is lit up at night), and a bar with open fire. Upstairs are two floors with pretty, beamed bedrooms, their windows giving a view of the river, swans and the Purbeck Hills beyond. The local landscapes on their walls are for sale.

Wareham is a most interesting old town, a great mixture of history and of architectural styles. It is encircled by high earth banks built by the Saxons to fortify their village against Viking raids. The roads within this were laid out, Roman-style, on a grid. St Martin's church is Saxon and contains, rather oddly, a monument to Lawrence of Arabia (whose home at Clouds Hill is open).

All around this area are marvellous places to visit – the following is merely a selection. Poole Harbour, the second largest and loveliest natural harbour in the world, the Blue Pool, Corfe Castle, Lulworth Cove, the Purbeck Hills; Arne – heathland nature reserve; Swanage, old-fashioned resort with sandy bay and architectural curiosities salvaged from London; Durlston Head – cliffs, birds, country park, lighthouse; Studland's beaches with Shell Bay beyond; Wool and Bere Regis (with Thomas Hardy associations); Bindon Abbey; the army Tank Museum at Bovington; Bournemouth; Compton Acres gardens.

As a change from driving you could take a boat trip from Poole (described elsewhere) or go on Swanage's little railway. And this is, of course, superb walking country with scenery made lovely by hills and valleys, wandering streams and villages of thatch and stone cottages to be discovered among the lanes.

Readers' comments: Superb in every respect; a real find; haven't words to describe food, room and attention to detail; absolutely professional but very personal; welcoming and friendly, spotlessly clean, excellent food. Lovely situation, a personal touch. Food superb. Pretty bedrooms, high quality food. Unique place, very comfortable. Wonderful! Exceptionally friendly and welcoming. Very pretty dining-rooms. Full of character. Excellent in every way.

OLD HALL

C(5) **D PT**

Poolside, Madeley, Staffordshire, CW3 9DX   Tel: 0782 750209
(Messages: 0782 621728)
West of Newcastle-under-Lyme. On A525 from Newcastle-under-Lyme to
Whitchurch (and near M6, junction 15).

6 **Bedrooms.** £18–£25 (less for 3 nights).
Prices go up in April. Some have own
bath/shower/toilet. Tea/coffee facilities. TV.
Views of garden, country. No smoking.
Washing machine on request.
Dinner (by arrangement). £10 for 3
courses (with choices) and coffee, at 7pm.
Vegetarian or special diets if ordered. Wine
can be brought in. No smoking. **Light
suppers** if ordered.
2 **Sitting-rooms.** With open fire, central
heating, TV, piano. No smoking in one.
Large garden

Cheshire is famous for its black-and-white houses, and this – though just over the
county boundary – is a good example, with its beams and gables. Beams and fine
woodwork abound inside as well, and the house is full of old oak furniture.

In one sitting-room there is an inglenook fireplace with glittering brassware
around it; in another, a grand piano by the wood stove, and sometimes music-
stands as well, for Mary Hugh is a professional musician. She teaches the violin,
but the viola is her principal instrument, and visitors may sometimes enjoy
chamber music or even join in impromptu. Through oak-boarded doors is the
dining-room, with an old Welsh dresser and small-paned mullioned windows.
Here guests (and sometimes small private parties) are served with, for example,
watercress soup, cheese soufflé, beef sirloin in mushroom and pepper sauce,
chocolate roulade and cheeses – cooked by Ann O'Leary, a professional caterer.
Guests in the Hall's self-catering accommodation may dine in too.

Up the wooden staircase, past a coloured-glass panel for 'stolen light' to
another room, are the bedrooms (most of which are spacious) with low beams,
antiques and handsome brass door-fittings. The tiled bathroom with its huge bath
is almost unchanged since the 1920s, when it was one of the first illustrated in
Ideal Home.

Off the breakfast-room is a high-Victorian conservatory, made of cast iron at a
local foundry. The two-acre garden outside, with pond and pergola, is annually
opened to the public. In it are croquet and tennis lawns.

At the front of the house (adjacent to the village pond) are handsome yews
and cedars. The Hughs have neatly converted the stable block: there is a double-
height space with a grand piano on a dais. When not used for recitals or private
functions, this serves as a sitting-room for the bedrooms in the block, which are
reached by a staircase whose balustrade is in the form of staves of music. A family
occupying these rooms would also have the use of a private kitchen.

As well as historical appeal (Chester, Shrewsbury and Little Moreton Hall are
not far), the area has much for anyone interested in our industrial past: the
Gladstone pottery museum with its original bottle kilns and the Chatterley
Whitfield mining museum, for instance.

Readers' comments: Very good and unusual. Wonderful house. Serene atmosphere.
First-class food.

238

OLD INN   **C D S**
Burford Road, Black Bourton, Oxfordshire, OX18 2PF   Tel: 0993 841828
West of Oxford. Nearest main road: A40 from Oxford to Burford.

2 Bedrooms. £14.50. Price may go up in April. Tea/coffee facilities. TV. Views of garden, country. Washing machine on request.
Dinner. £10.50 for 4 courses (with choices) and coffee, at 7.30pm. Non-residents not admitted. Vegetarian or special diets if ordered. Wine can be brought in. **Light suppers** if ordered.
1 Sitting-room. With open fire, central heating, TV.
Small garden

No longer an inn, this 17th-century house is now the elegant home of Pat and John Baxter. It has thick stone walls, low beams in the sitting/dining-room and outside are views of the village and old houses, with the mediaeval church close by.

The bedrooms are very attractive: one is all-white (a crisp and light effect); another is a beamy room with antiques. Even the bathroom has been furnished with style – soft green carpet and William Morris wallpaper. The breakfast-room has pine chairs, scarlet cloths and a garden view. Only one family (or group of friends) is taken at a time.

Mrs Baxter provides the best of typically English food, asking her guests beforehand what they would like. Melon with port might be followed by a joint or a steak-and-kidney pie, and then perhaps brandy-chocolate cake – all served on pretty Blue Baltic china. Afterwards, when guests relax on the flowery blue-and-white sofas and armchairs in front of the log stove, the Baxters may join them for coffee. (Sunday lunch by special arrangement.) And only a minute or two away is the very pretty village of Clanfield (a tiny stream runs alongside the road) where, as an alternative, the Tavern serves meals of gourmet standard.

Black Bourton is well placed to explore the Cotswolds, Oxford, the Berkshire Downs, Woodstock and Stratford-upon-Avon. Favourite outings include Burford, Bibury, the Roman villa at North Leigh, Minster Lovell, Fairford's church, the endangered species farm at Guiting Power, Filkins woollen mill, the Cotswold Wildlife Park – and the gardens at Buscot House and at the house of *The Countryman* magazine. Antique shops abound.

Oxfordshire's long history (it was well populated even in prehistoric times) has left the fine landscape dotted with architectural and other relics of the past. Its mediaeval churches are outstanding because they were built when wool brought wealth. King Alfred was born at Wantage, Churchill at Blenheim (he is buried at nearby Bladon). Much of the area's history is explained in the Vale and Downland Centre in Wantage, and Oxford has an audio-visual show on the subject. The county museum is at Woodstock.

Readers' comments: Comfort and service superb. Excellent food served with zest and style. Extremely comfortable and pleasant; delicious dinner. Extremely good value, very hospitable. Delightful, charming – just like staying with friends. Warm, welcoming, a very high standard. Friendly and hospitable. Very pleased.

239

OLD MILL D
Little Petherick, Cornwall, PL27 7QT   Tel: 0841 540388
South of Padstow. On A389 from Padstow to Bodmin.

6 Bedrooms. £18–£24.65 **to readers of this book** (less for 7 nights or continental breakfast.) Prices go up in April. Some have own bath/shower/toilet. Tea/coffee facilities. Views of garden, country, river. Washing machine on request.
Dinner. £11 for 3–4 courses and coffee, at 7pm. Vegetarian or special diets if ordered. Wine can be ordered. No smoking.
3 Sitting-rooms. With central heating, TV. Bar.
Small garden
Closed from November to February.

This picturesque 16th-century watermill (with a working water-wheel) is beside a stream that winds its way into the Camel estuary – an area of outstanding natural beauty, along a coastline celebrated for its many beautiful beaches (a number are protected by the National Trust).

Michael and Pat Walker have furnished the Mill very attractively. The beamy sitting-room has white stone walls, one with a mural of ploughing. William Morris fabric and Berber carpet contrast with the green slate of the floor. All around are unusual 'finds': an ancient typewriter and sewing-machines, clocks, and old tools such as planes and picks. The paved terrace by the stream is enclosed by sun-trapping walls. Bedrooms are homely (very nice bathrooms); quiet ones at the back.

For dinner, at tables covered with homespun cloths, you may be offered such choices as prawn cocktail, pork chop, blackcurrant cheesecake and cheeses.

Little Petherick is a pretty village with (just across the road from the Mill) a beautiful church, close to Padstow which is still agreeably antiquated. Narrow, crooked lanes lead down to Padstow's harbour, a pretty group of houses encircles the quay, and there are several outstanding buildings including the Court House where Sir Walter Raleigh dealt out judgments when he was Warden of Cornwall. The world-famous Hobby Horse street dance takes place on 1 May here. There are idyllic, golden beaches around here (go to Treyarnon to see surfing). Near St Columb Major (impressive church) is an Iron Age fort called Castle an Dinas; St Mawgan is a pretty village in a woodland valley; by contrast, St Wenn is a wild and windy moorland spot; by the lighthouse on Trevose Head you can see the whole coast from St Ives to Lundy Island. At Wadebridge, there is a new exhibition centre, housed in a converted railway station, dedicated to the life and work of Sir John Betjeman. He is buried at St Enodoc, just across the estuary.

On the whole, north Cornwall is far less touristy than the south, its greatest attractions being scenery (not only coastal but inland too) with fewer commercial entertainments, sights, etc.

Readers' comments: Beautifully furnished. Could not be more pleasant and helpful. Lovely setting. Very hospitable. We found the service and quality of meals excellent. Excellent in every way. Greatly enjoyed our stay. Very comfortable house in picturesque setting. Very hospitable and helpful. Meals beautifully served: very good choices.

240

Waggon Road, Lower Dolphinholme, Lancashire, LA2 9AX
Tel: 0524 791855
South of Lancaster. Nearest main road: M6 (junction 33).

3 Bedrooms. £16.50–£22 (less for 3 nights in low season only or 7 nights at all seasons). Prices go up at Easter. One has own bath/shower. Tea/coffee facilities. Views of garden, country, river. No smoking. Washing machine on request.
Dinner. £10.50 for 3 courses (with choices) and coffee, at 7–9 pm. Vegetarian or special diets if ordered. Wine can be ordered. No smoking. **Light suppers** if ordered.
1 Sitting-room. With open fire, central heating, TV, record-player. No smoking.
Large garden

At the bottom of a steep little valley runs the River Wyre, and by the river stands the Old Mill House, over which – for all its three storeys – the mill itself once towered. A corn mill in the 17th century, it was used for weaving in the next century, being the world's first worsted mill, and wool was brought from as far away as Norfolk to supply it. In 1810, so that a 24-hour day could be worked, the owner installed gas lighting, from the first private gasworks outside London.

Nothing of all this industrial activity remains above ground level now, for the mill was demolished shortly after it closed, over a century ago. But interesting remains abound: the 15-foot-deep water-filled sump of the old gasometer, with a huge counterweight in the undergrowth beside it, the remains of the millpond and its race, overgrown steps and foundations. The owners, Carol and Alan Williamson, are gradually extending the already big formal gardens to take in these intriguing relics.

Not only those with an interest in industrial archaeology will enjoy exploring the wooded slopes of the grounds, which cover nearly four acres. They are a haven for wildlife (with official protection) and the river frontage provides fly fishing as well as pleasant views. Birdwatchers have counted 55 species here, and there are more to be seen on Leighton Moss.

Overlooking the trim lawn, with walnut tree and herbaceous borders where the tall mill building once stood, are spacious bedrooms (one with four-poster) and, on the ground floor, an oval sitting-room with pale green wallpaper and carpet, and maroon leather chesterfields and armchairs. For those who eat in, Carol provides, for example, mushrooms in garlic, Lune salmon and apple torte. Most of the food is home-made.

It is hard to believe that the quiet hamlet of Lower Dolphinholme is only minutes from the motorway. It is close to the enjoyable city of Lancaster and the Forest of Bowland, about both of which there is more under other entries.

Only slightly further away are the Yorkshire Dales and, in the opposite direction, Morecambe Bay and the southern Lake District, which is much less overrun than the better known central area. But rural Lancashire deserves to be seen first, especially by those who think this is just a county of derelict cotton mills!

Readers' comments: Made to feel very welcome. Excellent dinner. Most charming.

Stoney Lane, Thorpe, Derbyshire, DE6 2AW   Tel: 033529 410
North-west of Ashbourne. Nearest main road: A515 from Ashbourne to
Buxton.

3 Bedrooms. £15–£18 (less for 3 nights).
Two have own shower/toilet. Views of
garden, country.
Dinner (if ordered in advance). From 9 for
3 courses and coffee, at 7pm. Non-residents
not admitted. Vegetarian or special diets if
ordered. Wine can be brought in.
1 Sitting-room. With open fire, central
heating, TV.
Small garden
Closed from December to February.

Dovedale is one of the loveliest parts of the Peak District; and in this area there
are particularly fine views of it where the Manifold Valley runs down into the dale
(at the foot of Thorpe Cloud – one of several 1000-foot hills here).

On the edge of Thorpe village is a very prettily sited stone house in traditional
style, which stands where once an orchard of damson trees grew. This is the
comfortable home of Barbara Challinor and her husband; keen gardeners, as is
obvious from the herbaceous beds, stone terraces, rock garden and stream with
waterfalls in their sloping, landscaped grounds. Barbara has a useful arrangement
with a farm which is a few minutes' walk away: she provides bed-and-breakfast
while dinner is served at the farmhouse – straightforward soups, roasts and fruit
pies, with home-baked bread. Bicycles (either touring or mountain models) can
be hired.

This part of the National Park is known as 'the White Peak' because the
underlying rock is limestone (further north, in 'the Dark Peak', the geology
changes). There is a network of paths around here by which to explore Milldale,
Wolfscote Dale and Beresford Dale – leading to other valleys further afield. The
celebrated Tissington Trail starts 2½ miles away.

But scenery is not the only attraction of the area. There are the stately homes
of Chatsworth and Haddon Hall to visit, the old towns of Matlock and Bakewell,
and busy Ashbourne with a splendid church and antique salerooms.

It takes a long stay to do justice to the Peak District, a particularly scenic
National Park, but if you are pressed for time it would be possible to see some of
the finest parts by driving the following route. After walking in the beautiful park
of Ilam Hall (NT), continue to the head of Dovedale – a scenic route known as
Little Switzerland, with weird crags and pillars of rock, stone packhorse bridges
and a dramatic gorge – all familiar to Izaak Walton (who described them in his
Compleat Angler). Among the stone-walled fields and woodlands of Beresford
Dale is the pretty village of Hartington, its busy past as market and lead-mining
town now long gone. Arbor Law is a place of mystery – a circle of white stones
erected on a windswept site 4000 years ago and with burial mounds nearby.
Beyond it lies possibly the most perfect mediaeval stately home in this country
(parts built by a son of William the Conqueror): turreted Haddon Hall, with
terraced gardens descending to a sparkling river. Across high heather moors (with
another stone circle) lies Matlock which is in fact two towns, one a Victorian spa
– there is a mining museum worth visiting here. This is where the River Derwent
has cut a dramatic gorge through the limestone hills.

OLD PARSONAGE FARMHOUSE   D

Hanley Castle, Worcestershire, WR8 0BU   Tel: 0684 310124

South-east of Malvern. Nearest main road: A38 from Worcester to Tewkesbury (also M5, junctions 7/8; and M50, junction 1).

rear view

3 Bedrooms. £20–£22.50 (less for 7 nights). Prices may go up in April. 5% less

to readers of this book staying 3 mid-week nights. All have own bath/toilet. Tea/coffee and TV on request. Views of garden, country. No smoking. Washing machine on request.

Dinner. £14.75 for 4 courses (with choices of dessert) and coffee, from 7pm. Non-residents not admitted. Vegetarian or special diets if ordered. Wine can be ordered. No smoking. **Light suppers.**

2 Sitting-rooms. With open fire, central heating, TV, record-player. Bar.

Large garden

Closed in January.

It is not just the surrounding views of the Malvern Hills or the handsome 18th-century house of mellow brick which makes this worth seeking out: Ann Addison has a flair for both cookery and interior decoration, while Tony is a wine expert. He runs wine-tastings in the one-time cider mill adjoining the house.

You enter the house via a vaulted entrance hall (with Edwardian fireplace), then through double doors into the sandalwood sitting-room with its small library and television. On the right is the elegant, pale sea-green drawing-room with its arched Georgian windows and marble Adam fireplace. To the left is the sunflower-yellow dining-room which has the original brick hearth and bread oven.

Damask cloths and Rorstrand china from Sweden create an appropriate setting for the kind of meals Ann serves, such as mushrooms and herbs in puff pastry, chicken breasts with prawns in cream and brandy, bramble mousse, cheeses.

Upstairs are elegant bedrooms (for instance, one has fruit-and-flower fabrics complemented by peach walls, another has a vast bathroom with oval chocolate bath).

All around is superb countryside. Drive southward and you come to Upton-upon-Severn where a 14th-century bell-tower still stands near the bridge: once it was part of a church, was given a 'pepperpot' cupola in 1770, and is now a heritage centre – the church itself was dismantled in the 'thirties. The town's historic byways and riverbank inns are well worth exploring.

Westward lie the Malvern Hills, with stupendous views from the Herefordshire Beacon (over 1100 feet high) and the remains of one of the greatest Iron Age forts in Britain. Near here is the village of Eastnor which has two castles, the moated one (15th-century) is real and ruined; the other (1812) is a romantic mansion, turreted in Norman style, which was designed by Smirke – architect of the British Museum – and has armour, tapestries, etc. inside. Worcester has its cathedral, Charles II's headquarters in the Civil War (the Commandery) and good shops.

Readers' comments: Very impressed. Warm and friendly welcome, helpful and charming. Extremely comfortable. High standard of imaginative food. Superb standards and unrivalled personal service. Lovely, large bedroom. Very friendly. Most welcoming and comfortable.

OLD PARSONAGE HOUSE

C(12) **D S**

Higham, Suffolk, IP28 6NH   Tel: 0284 810308

West of Bury St Edmunds. Nearest main road: A45 from Bury St Edmunds towards Newmarket.

2 Bedrooms. £20 (less for 5 nights or continental breakfast). Both have own bath/toilet. Tea/coffee facilities. Views of garden, country. No smoking. Washing machine on request.

Dinner. £15 for 3 to 4 courses (with choices) and coffee, at 8pm (not Wednesdays in winter). Non-residents not admitted. Vegetarian or special diets if ordered. Wine can be ordered. **Light suppers** if ordered.

1 Sitting-room. With open fire, central heating, TV.

Large garden

In 1850, the local landowners brought in Gilbert Scott (architect of the Albert Memorial and St Pancras Station) to improve their estate with an unusual round-towered church of flint and brick and, alongside it, a rectory in similar style – now the home of Susan Ram and her husband Tom (who is bursar of Caius College, Cambridge, a half-hour away). As you might expect, Scott designed a very handsome building. Over an impressive, Gothic-style front door with elaborate iron hinges is a little oriel window, and roses clamber up brick-banded walls of flint – a building material much used in this area. All around is a fine landscape: fields of rich, dark soil; great beech trees in Thetford Forest Park; swans gliding on the pretty River Lark. In the village there is a working forge.

Susan's accomplishments include needlework (cushions in the sitting-room were made by her, and she upholstered many of the chairs) and pony-trap driving. She teaches pony-driving to disabled people, and sometimes takes visitors for rides in her trap. She has furnished her home beautifully, decorating the long, bay-windowed sitting-room with coral curtains and wallpaper. From the dining-hall, Gilbert Scott's elegant staircase curves up to bedrooms that have trefoil windows overlooking the croquet lawn and grass tennis court. Beyond these are fields with Susan's little Soay sheep, a rare breed now, and her hens – who contribute to the meals she cooks for visitors. A typical dinner might start with smoked salmon or a mousse before tarragon chicken or stuffed pork fillet, a rich pudding such as pears in caramel, and cheese or a savoury.

This is not a 'touristy' area, and yet there are enough things to see or do for at least a 10-day holiday (and it is only 1½ hours from London). In Thetford Forest, archaeologists have recreated a 5th-century village of wood-and-thatch houses excavated on a hillock: a 13th-century sand dune blew over it and thus preserved the ancient remains where Saxons once lived and worshipped their god Woden. (Ancient crafts are demonstrated here.) There are guided walks to discover wildlife, pick fungi or just enjoy the forest colours. Bury St Edmunds has its lovely abbey ruins and other mediaeval buildings, a clock museum and an elegant little 18th-century theatre. The colleges of Cambridge, Ely's cathedral and racehorses being exercised on the breezy gallops outside Newmarket all attract visitors. Even non-horsey people have been fascinated by the National Horseracing Museum and the guided tours of the National Stud at Newmarket. For a really purposeful holiday at Higham, you can take three-day courses in such subjects as china-mending or growing and cooking herbs; or go to craft courses at the Saxon village.

244

OLD RECTORY   C PT

Byford, Herefordshire, HR4 7LD   Tel: 098122 218
West of Hereford. Nearest main road: A438 from Hereford to Brecon.

3 Bedrooms. £18 (less for 3 nights). Bargain breaks. All have own bath/shower/toilet. Tea/coffee facilities. TV. Views of garden, country. No smoking. Washing machine on request.
Dinner. £8.50 for 2 courses and coffee, at 7pm. Vegetarian or special diets. Wine can be brought in. No smoking. **Light suppers** if ordered.
1 Sitting-room. With central heating. No smoking.
Large garden
Closed from December to February.

An enormous cedar of Lebanon dominates the garden outside the Rectory, a handsome brick house which, though built in 1830, is Georgian in style – having big, well-proportioned rooms and great sash windows which make the most of the very fine views of hills and church. Audrey Mayson and her husband have put a great deal of loving care not only into the restoration of the big house but also the landscaping of the formerly neglected garden. The house is run in an informal, caring way. (Baby-sitting can be arranged.)

The sitting/dining-room has pale green walls, deep pine-shuttered windows, pine-panelled doors, and their collection of unusual Escher pictures.

For dinner Audrey serves such dishes as grapefruit and orange, chicken breast in mushroom sauce and hazelnut meringue.

Byford is on the way to Wales, but there are many reasons to pause here for more than a stopover. Nearby are Hereford and its cathedral; Hay-on-Wye for the Lost Street Museum, rows of old shops crammed with Victoriana; the lovely River Wye with footpaths alongside (salmon fishing and tuition available).

Readers' comments: Very friendly, relaxed and roomy. Good food.

Because Monica Barker previously lived in India, **APPLETREE COTTAGE** (at nearby Mansell Lacy), built of half-timbering and brick in the reign of Henry VI, is full of exotic touches such as Kashmiri crewel bedspreads and curtains. These nevertheless assort well with pretty fabrics, antique oak furniture, and chairs covered in traditional tapestry or velvet. Previously two cottages, then a cider-house, the building still has many of its original features, such as low beams and small, deep-set windows; and when Monica had to put in a new, twisting staircase, she had it woodpegged in the traditional way. (En

suite facilities available.) By arrangement, she will cook such meals as cucumber and yogurt soup, steak pie and meringues – using wholefood ingredients. The cottage stands at the foot of a hill popular with walkers and birdwatchers alike. £13–£17. [Tel: 098122 688; postcode: HR4 7HH]

Northleigh, Devon, EX13 6BS   Tel: 040487 300
West of Axminster. Nearest main road: A35 from Axminster to Honiton.

2 Bedrooms. £17–£19.50 (less for 5 nights). Both have own bath/shower/toilet. Tea/coffee facilities. TV. Views of garden, country. Washing machine on request. **Light suppers** if ordered.
1 Sitting-room. With open fire, central heating, TV.
Large garden

It is in a conservatory – furnished with pine, and heated when necessary – that Rosemary Cohan normally serves breakfasts, so that visitors can enjoy the view to the south, across lovely Farway Valley – part of east Devon's extensive area of outstanding natural beauty, much of which is owned by the National Trust (beyond it lies a particularly fine stretch of coast). The rectory, which was built in 1825 – an excellent period for domestic architecture – has nicely arched doorways and marble fireplaces. The original rector was clearly a man of substance for the house is surrounded by stables, coach house and a big walled garden for vegetables.

Rosemary has furnished the handsome sitting-room in white and yellow; while the green-and-white dining-room has a hand-printed William Morris wallpaper and a large bay window with arched panes. As Honiton has plenty of restaurants, only light-supper trays are served here, by arrangement, for those who want to eat in. Bedrooms, too, are very pleasant: a soft green one overlooks the stables; in a rose room, are stencilled ribbon garlands. Rosemary, antique-dealer and designer, has filled the house with unusual and elegant furniture complemented by very good fabric designs, decorative bedlinen and dried flower arrangements. When I visited, she was planning to install a Jacuzzi in a mimosa-filled conservatory.

Because farming is done by old-fashioned methods round here (no 'agribusiness'), wildflowers have not been sprayed out of existence and wildlife flourishes – buzzards and even rarer birds, for instance; rare moths, badgers and deer. The narrow lanes are – typical of Devon – high-banked. Down by the sea are small, unspoiled resorts and fishing villages, such as Sidmouth, Branscombe, Seaton and Beer. In one direction is the historic city of Exeter and in the other the villages of Dorset.

Parts of the country here rise quite high, and among the hills is the old lacemaking town of Honiton (the beautiful lace is still made, but mostly in surrounding villages: the craft was introduced by Flemish refugees in the 17th century). The town is a good hunting-ground for antiques, and is endowed with handsome 18th-century houses and coaching inns. Coleridge was born in, and Thackeray spent some of his childhood at Ottery St Mary. As children they were probably taken to its great 14th-century church built in imitation of Exeter cathedral – it is worth a visit to see the fan-vaulting, Tudor clock, oldest weathervane in Britain and stocks in the churchyard. Outside nearby Cadhay Manor are statues of the Tudor monarchs.

OLD RECTORY   C(14) **D**
Patrick Brompton, North Yorkshire, DL8 1JN   Tel: 0677 50343
South of Richmond. Nearest main road: A684 from Bedale to Leyburn.

3 Bedrooms. £19 (less for 7 nights). All have own bath/shower/toilet. Tea/coffee facilities. TV. Views of garden, country. No smoking. Washing machine on request.
Dinner. £12 for 4 courses and coffee, at 7.30pm (not Mondays and Thursdays). Non-residents not admitted. Vegetarian or special diets if ordered. Wine can be brought in. No smoking.
1 Sitting-room. With open fire, central heating. No smoking.
Small garden
Closed in December and January.

David and Felicity Thomas have furnished their home in keeping with its period (it was built early in the 18th century), complementing comfortable chintz sofas with a soft green colour scheme, the mahogany furniture of the dining-room with peach walls (the table is laid with Minton china and good silver). Bedrooms (on two floors, reached by a twisting staircase) are spacious and immaculate, some overlooking a walled garden with lawns beyond. There are alcoves, bay windows and low doorways.

Felicity enjoys cooking. A typical dinner might comprise stuffed eggs, pork dijonnaise with wine sauce, and blackberry mousse, followed by cheeses.

The village is surrounded by small market towns (there's at least one market on the go every weekday), great mediaeval abbeys such as Jervaulx, two cathedral cities and two spa towns, waterfalls, famous crags and viewpoints, and the Dales – both Wensleydale and more rugged Swaledale are close by. Wensleydale is the broadest and most fertile. Heather-clad hills enclose fields marked by dry-stone walls, with stone cottages and prosperous 18th-century houses. Bolton, Richmond and Middleham have castles, the last associated with Richard III: there is a local society devoted to rehabilitating his reputation. The North York Moors and even the Lake District are accessible for a day's outing. Constable Burton Hall has a fine garden, Thorpe Perrow an arboretum. Antique sales and shops attract many visitors; and there is plenty of farm produce to buy or pick. In winter, there are activity weekends at the Old Rectory – painting, crafts, history, etc.

Bolton Castle well deserved the big restoration programme that has been going on and Bedale Hall is worth a visit for its small but very interesting museum of social history – there are folk museums, too, at Hawes and Reeth and, at Aysgarth Falls, the county's collection of 50 coaches and other horse-drawn vehicles. Working watermills can be seen at Little Crakehall and Bainbridge (at the former you can buy stoneground flour; at the latter is a dolls' house centre).

Many of Yorkshire's great abbeys are world-famous. Less well known is Coverham Abbey in a beautiful riverside setting at Leyburn, and with lovely gardens. In it are effigies of early mediaeval knights.

Readers' comments: Delicious meal, pretty rooms. The best yet! Beautifully furnished, genuine welcome, super dinner, wonderful hosts. Outstanding. Very pleasant rooms. Delightful owners. Wonderful hospitality, excellent food, most relaxing. A marvellous week. Most comfortable, so welcoming. At the very top of the tree of b & bs. A cordon bleu treat. Very comfortable, meals most enjoyable.

OLD RECTORY   C D M

Vicarage Lane, Sherbourne, Warwickshire, CV35 8AB   Tel: 0926 624562
South-west of Warwick. On A46 from Coventry to Stratford-upon-Avon
(and near M40, junction 15).

14 Bedrooms. £19–£22.50 (less for 3
nights or continental breakfast). Prices go
up in June. Bargain breaks. All have own
bath/shower/toilet. Tea/coffee facilities. TV.
Views of garden, country.
Light suppers.
1 Sitting-room. With open fire, central
heating. Bar.
Small garden

In the 'thirties a Canon of Warwick lived here, but the 18th-century house has
played many other roles too: inn, farm and now a guest-house – still with low-
beamed rooms, flagstone floors, pine fireplace and bay windows. What was once
a dairy is now a family suite at the back where, adjoining a carpark made pretty by
hanging-baskets of flowers, there are several bedrooms. The ground-floor rooms,
opening onto a lawn, would particularly suit any disabled person or visitors travelling with a dog. There are more rooms in a pair of converted cottages.

The furniture chosen by Sheila and Martin Greenwood for the old rooms is in
keeping with the historic building: old oak dressers and chests, dining-chairs of
country Chippendale, fireside armchairs covered in traditional cretonnes. Most
bedrooms have old brass beds, with flowery fabrics of pink or blue and white. As
the house, though secluded, is within the hum of traffic passing along the A46
(concealed beyond a row of lime trees and an old pump), some rooms are double-
glazed. In the sitting-room, an old pine cupboard has been converted into an
'honesty-bar' from which to help yourself to drinks and write down what you take.

The village is between those two tourist honeypots, Warwick and Stratford-
upon-Avon, and is itself picturesque with cottages and church beside a lake. In
addition, visitors make for the attractive country town of Kenilworth and its
castle, the royal spa of Leamington (pump room and lovely Jephson Gardens),
Charlecote Park (elegant interior, deer park and orangery where tea is served),
Coughton Court, Packwood House and its unusual topiary gardens, Baddesley
Clinton and Upton House. The Cotswolds are near; and within a day's drive you
can easily visit Worcester, Oxford, Cheltenham or Coventry cathedral. Plenty of
walks, fishing and golf courses too.

The very centre of England is in Warwickshire, at Meriden, around which was
once the great Forest of Arden – setting for Shakespeare's romantic *As You Like It*
(his mother's maiden name was Arden). The Woodmen of Arden, active today,
are the oldest group of archers in the country. Although only patches of the
ancient woodland survive, this is still a very scenic area, watered by many rivers
and dotted with ancient villages.

Warwick's enormous castle was described by Sir Walter Scott as 'the fairest
monument of ancient and chivalrous splendour', and the town's church is of
equal grandeur (with a number of very splendid monuments beneath the great
tower which Wren added).

Readers' comments: Everything first-rate, the Greenwoods friendly and helpful.
House and garden charming. Very welcoming hosts.

OLD RECTORY   C S

Thurloxton, Somerset, TA2 8RH   Tel: 0823 412686
South-east of Bridgwater. Nearest main road: A38 from Taunton to Bristol
(and M5, junctions 24/25).

4 Bedrooms. £13–£15 (less for 6 nights). One has own shower. Tea/coffee facilities. Views of garden, country. No smoking. Washing machine on request.
Dinner. £8 for 3 courses (with choice of puddings) and coffee, at 6.30pm (not Wednesdays). Non-residents not admitted. Vegetarian or special diets if ordered. Wine can be brought in. **Light suppers** if ordered.
1 Sitting-room. With open fire, central heating, TV.
Large garden
Closed from November to March.

At the end of the Quantocks is Thurloxton, the old Victorian rectory of which is an enticing sight in summer when flowerbeds, hanging-baskets on the white walls, and a conservatory of bougainvillaea and other subtropical flowers make a colourful scene beyond the smooth lawn. Ann Comer has put pretty sofas and chairs in the spacious blue sitting-room. The L-shaped family bedroom is excellent; and outside is a putting green, with views across the fen-like Somerset Levels towards Glastonbury. A typical dinner: home-made chicken soup followed by roast beef, then fruit pie or lemon soufflé. (Baby-sitting available.)

Thurloxton is centrally placed to visit all parts of Somerset – the Quantock Hills in one direction, the Mendips in the other, the reedy Somerset Levels, the coast, and the county town of Taunton – its secret places best discovered on foot. Beyond the early mediaeval castle (housing a particularly good museum and with a Norman garden close by) are lovely lawns beside the River Tone. A waterside path leads to French Weir – or you can take a boat trip. Vivary Park, named for the monastic fishponds (*vivaria*) which used to be there, stretches a mile out into the countryside – parts of it with flowerbeds and fountain, the rest a natural area. Near great St Mary's church (angels in its roof, an outstanding Perpendicular tower) is a network of craft studios and speciality shops. All around are interesting places to visit – picturesque villages (Bishop's Lydeard, Crowcombe, Combe Florey, Wiveliscombe), Blagdon Hill for views, the Palladian mansion of Hatch Court, steam railway to Minehead, Hornsbury watermill, the gardens at Hestercombe House, Tudor Poundisford Park and, wherever you go, exceptional scenery: in summer, wisteria against old stone walls, fields of buttercups, willow-fringed streams and thatched cottages, ponds of swans and ducks, pinnacled and crocketed church towers soaring high (often built of orangey Ham stone), buttercrosses in market squares, imposingly pillared town halls, wayside inns and sunlight flickering through trees meeting over narrow lanes.

Readers' comments: Lovely position, beautiful garden.

When writing to me, if you want a reply please enclose an International Reply Coupon.

OLD RECTORY
Wetherden, Suffolk, IP14 3LS   Tel: 0359 240144
North-west of Stowmarket. Nearest main road: A45 from Stowmarket to Bury St Edmunds.

3 Bedrooms. £17.50–£25 (less for 2 nights). Two have own bath/shower/toilet. Tea/coffee facilities. Views of garden, country. No smoking. Washing machine on request.
Light suppers only for elderly visitors.
1 Sitting-room. With open fire, central heating, TV. Piano.
Large garden
Closed from December to February.

Readers who used the first edition of this book may have stayed with Mrs Bowden when she lived near Hadleigh. Now she has an equally elegant house here, into the decoration of which she has put the same tremendous amount of care.

The house, which dates from the 18th century, stands in extensive grounds (where sheep, horses and donkeys wander in summer). There is also a croquet lawn. One steps into a hall with stone floor, a piano in one alcove and pot-plants.

Up the deep pink and white staircase are elegant bedrooms – I particularly liked one decorated in apricot with an antique brass bed and comfortable armchairs. Fine paintings, interesting fabrics and graceful curtains are features of this imaginatively renovated house. In the drawing-room is a wallpaper patterned with classical medallions; the raspberry dining-room has an Adam fireplace of pink marble and a most unusual table – immensely long, it was made in Renaissance Italy from a single piece of walnut. Pamela, a member of the Embroiderers' Guild, has made many of the furnishings herself: cushions, curtains, bed-hanging and sheets with broderie anglaise, for example.

Usually, bed-and-breakfast only. For other meals, Pamela Bowden recommends local inns: such as the King's Arms at Haughley.

Central Suffolk, once forested, is now an area of wide open fields with prairie-size farms. Villages cluster around greens, big mediaeval houses like that at Parham are often moated – less for defence than to drain the site and provide a water-supply for the inhabitants (rainfall being low in this part of England). The area has had a turbulent history, hence the presence of so many castles (the one at Framlingham is outstanding, and so are the monuments in the church).

The many attractive villages include Debenham, threaded by a pretty stream and with rush-weaving to be seen; Eye, for the fine roodscreen in its church and the Minstrels' Gallery at the White Lion; Hoxne, scene of St Edmund's martyrdom at the bridge. Earl Soham, unusually leafy, has a great variety of architectural styles from every period; Saxtead Green, a working windmill; Heveningham, stately mansion in a park laid out by Capability Brown. Yoxford is called the 'garden of Suffolk' because of the abundance of spring flowers at every cottage.

From Wetherden, so centrally situated, it is easy to motor to the coast and Ipswich (beyond it the seaside resort of Felixstowe), and even to Cambridge, Norwich and Colchester in adjacent counties. In Stowmarket, a small market town, is Abbot's Hall which has a museum of rural life.

Readers' comments: The ambience was delightful, the house beautifully furnished, the breakfast excellent. Outstanding, beautifully maintained. Welcoming atmosphere. Excellent. Friendly.

OLD RECTORY HOTEL   C D M X

North Walsham Road, Crostwick, Norfolk, NR12 7BG   Tel: 0603 738513
North-east of Norwich. Nearest main road: A140 from Norwich to Cromer.

13 Bedrooms. £20. Price goes up in April. All have own bath/shower/toilet. Tea/coffee facilities. TV. Views of garden. No smoking (in some). Washing machine on request.
Dinner. £7.50 for 3 courses and coffee, at 7pm (not Sundays). Vegetarian or special diets if ordered. Wine can be ordered. No smoking (in one part). **Light suppers** if ordered.
1 Sitting-room. With central heating, TV. **Bar.**
Large garden

When Dianne and Colin Solomon first took over this sedate 1820 rectory, they ran it as a guest-house, but they later extended it with a wing of bedrooms at the back. The dining-room became a restaurant, now very popular with local people. To one side, in what was once a coach house, is a games room with snooker, bar-billiards, table tennis and darts. At the back is a heated swimming-pool, and a garden with swings for children.

The new wing has been done to the highest standards, with sophisticated heating, lighting and fire-precaution systems. The rooms (all on the ground floor and some interconnecting for families) are stylishly furnished with pink colour schemes, and very well equipped (for instance, each has a refrigerator). There is a laundering and shoe-cleaning room for visitors' use.

In the main house is a Wedgwood-blue sitting-room with Victorian armchairs upholstered in shadow velvet, pot-plants and sliding glass doors opening onto a paved terrace and the swimming-pool.

The menu for dinner majors on such universally popular choices as prawn cocktail, roast beef and profiteroles. Some produce is from the garden. (Sunday lunch is also available.)

Crostwick is very near Norwich, one of England's most attractive mediaeval cities – dominated by cathedral and castle, but home also to the ultra-modern Sainsbury Art Centre. The town's history goes back to Saxon times but it was Flemish weavers who made it rich – hence the multitude of splendid churches and lanes of fine half-timbered houses (don't miss winding and cobbled Elm Hill, now full of antique shops, and Tombland Alley). Fragments of the town's great, flint encircling walls remain. There are four notable museums, one in the castle (archaeology and natural history; paintings), others in Strangers Hall (historic rooms recreated), Bridewell (rural crafts) and St Peter's (church art). The huge Market Place is a lively sight when the colourful stalls are trading. Old inns and churches abound, and winding through it all is the busy River Wensum – boat trips available as well as riverside walks.

Within easy reach are the Broads, the sandy heritage coastline, stately homes, craft workshops, windmills, 17th-century Blickling and Felbrigg Halls, the gardens of Swannington Manor and of the Pleasaunce, a lace museum and one of gems, the big wildlife park of Great Witchingham, and the traditional seaside resort of Cromer.

Readers' comments: No faults, clean and welcoming.

251

St James' Street, Castle Hedingham, Essex, CO9 3EW   Tel: 0787 61370
South-west of Sudbury (Suffolk). Nearest main road: A604 from Halstead to
Haverhill.

3 **Bedrooms.** £18.50 (**to readers of this book only**)–£24.50 for a suite (less for 3 mid-week nights). All have own bath/shower/toilet. Tea/coffee facilities. Views of garden. No smoking. Washing machine on request.
Dinner. £14 for 3 courses and coffee, at 7.30–8.30pm. Vegetarian diets if ordered. Wine can be ordered. No smoking. **Light suppers** if ordered.
2 **Sitting-rooms.** With open fire, central heating, TV. No smoking.
Small garden

Garden-lovers in particular should go out of their way to stay here, for the Crawshaws have created – within a remarkably few years of taking over what was then a rough field – an elegant and lovely garden, featured in several books. Its lawns are surrounded by shapely and brimming beds of shrubs and flowers, all grown from seed. Steps lead up to a lily-pool with koi carp, and at the end is hidden a neat vegetable garden which supplies the kitchen. And there's a population of little toads – hundreds of them – which come out at night.

Through the street door of the terracotta-and-white house, built in the 18th century, one steps straight into a quarry-tiled hall/dining-room. Between its ceiling beams is a trap-door, known as a coffin-door – necessitated by the narrow, former staircase – and an inglenook is filled with flowers. There are Chippendale chairs around the dining-table, and silver candlesticks on it. Here, Penny may serve such dinners (if ordered in advance) as haddock soufflé in spinach leaves, rack of lamb and a choice of puddings – chocolate pots, lemon pie, etc. Her breakfasts include such options as home-made trout fishcakes.

The sitting-room (brick-walled and with a copper-hooded fire) opens onto a paved terrace made colourful and appealing by a dozen huge plant-pots.

The principal bedroom is attractively decorated, with gaily quilted bedhead and spread, while the other has roses on walls and bed. The view from this room is of the public tennis court across the street which leads into the centre of the village (picturesque, and with interesting shops), over which the castle itself looms high. A cottage in the garden provides extra bedrooms and has its own sitting-room – these rooms are especially attractive and quiet.

This is a very scenic part of Essex, near the Suffolk border, with a great deal to enjoy, crisscrossed by footpaths and bridleways. Audley End and a large number of other stately homes are in the neighbourhood, as well as many very pretty half-timbered villages and towns: Saffron Walden and Thaxted in particular (the latter has music festivals). Mole Hall Wildlife Park is another attraction. Colchester and Dedham Vale deserve at least one whole day. Cambridge is little more than half an hour away (it, and Suffolk villages such as Lavenham and Long Melford, are described under other entries).

Readers' comments: Charming house and garden, excellent cooking.

OLD VICARAGE   S

Affpuddle, Dorset, DT2 7HH   Tel: 0305 848315

East of Dorchester. Nearest main road: A35 from Dorchester to Poole.

3 Bedrooms. £17.50–£20. All have own bath/toilet. TV. Views of garden, country. Tea/coffee facilities and washing machine on request.
Light suppers if ordered, in winter.
Large garden

Before Anthea and Michael Hipwell moved here, it was an ambassador's country home: a handsome Georgian house with fine doorways, windows and fireplaces – surrounded by smooth lawns (with croquet) and rosebeds within tall hedges of clipped yew, the old church alongside.

Anthea has a flair for interior decoration. Even the corridors are elegant, with portraits and flower-prints on walls of apple-blossom pink which contrast with the cherry carpet. In my bedroom, the curtains were of ivory moiré, the bedspread patterned with rosebuds.

Breakfast is served in the prettiest dining-room in this book. Taking as the starting-point her collection of aquamarine glass (housed in two alcoves) and a series of modern lithographs in vivid turquoise, Anthea decorated the walls to match, and chose a dramatic turquoise curtain fabric reproduced from a Regency design in Brighton's Royal Pavilion. Against this all-blue colour scheme, the pale furniture shows to advantage. As no evening meal is provided, many visitors go to the Brace of Pheasants at Plush or the Greyhound at Winterbourne Kingston.

The Old Vicarage is well placed for a stopover on the long journey (by A35) to the west country; when arriving or departing on the Weymouth-Cherbourg ferry; or while learning to fish for trout at the nearby Wessex Fly-Fishing School.

The Hipwells lend walkers Ordnance Survey maps, and will advise them on sightseeing possibilities, including less obvious ones – such as the huge bric-a-brac market held at Wimborne every weekend, or little-known beaches (one favourite is at Ringstead, surrounded by National Trust land). In addition, there are such favourites as Hardy's cottage and T. E. Lawrence's; Kingston Lacy house (near which is Walford Mill crafts centre); Maiden Castle and Corfe Castle; Studland beach and the Purbeck Hills; and several garden centres – one specializing in old roses. And, at the end of the day, you are welcome to relax in the Hipwells' garden.

There are a great many fine gardens in the county. Among lesser-known ones is Mapperton (near Beaminster), a Tudor manor house, which has pools, an orangery and fine views. In the same direction is more famous Parnham, also Tudor: as well as its large gardens, it has the workshop of Britain's most celebrated furniture designer, John Makepeace. And at Broadwindsor crafts centre you can see other craftsmen at work in a converted barn.

Readers' comments: Very pleasant. Excellent service. Delightful hosts. Our favourite b & b. Delightful decor. Tea on the porch especially nice. Delightful house, charming hostess.

OLD VICARAGE C(12) **D S**

Northington Lane, Awre, Gloucestershire, GL14 1EL Tel: 0594 510282

South-west of Gloucester. Nearest main road: A48 from Gloucester to Chepstow (and M4, junction 22).

4 Bedrooms. £17.50–£19.50 (less for continental breakfast). Some have own shower/toilet. Tea/coffee facilities. Views of garden. No smoking. Washing machine on request.
Dinner. £14.50 for 4 courses (with choices) and coffee, at 8pm (weekends only). Non-residents not admitted. Vegetarian or special diets if ordered. Wine can be brought in. No smoking. **Light suppers** if ordered.
1 Sitting-room. With open fire, central heating. No smoking.
Large garden

To complement the handsome 1820s features of the house – for instance, black marble fireplace, big sash windows and, somewhat later, a particularly splendid Victorian bathtub – May and Nick Bull have added Victorian furniture, a brass bed in one room, bevelled mirrors, button-backed armchairs and a day-bed of russet velvet. The Bulls' own glasshouses supply virtually all their vegetables (including aubergines, pumpkins and tomatoes), and all are organically grown. There is usually plenty of fresh fruit (old-fashioned varieties in particular), even at breakfast. Lamb and pork are home-reared, venison is from the forest.

They also make their own cider: you may see the old stone press in action if you stay in late September. Nick even has his own one-man coal-mine among the bluebells and foxgloves of the Forest of Dean: he owns a 'gale' of coal with a shaft dug in Victorian times by an earlier 'free-miner'.

From various choices that you are likely to be offered, dinner might comprise a courgette soufflé, wild Severn salmon with fresh dill, then pear and grapes on shortbread served with medlar cream, and double Gloucester cheese made locally.

When overseas visitors stay at **BROUGHTONS**, in Flaxley Road near Newnham, the Swinleys usually fly their national flag! The house, built by an ancestor 200 years ago, stands so high up on the eastern edge of the Forest of Dean that there are views of the Severn winding its way far below and even of Gloucester cathedral's high tower. At the front is a circular lawn with lily-pond, overlooked by a cherub at the decoratively gabled porch; at the back are a great ancient wisteria, and a hard tennis court beyond an area of woodland. Sometimes breakfast is served on the terrace. All rooms are handsomely furnished and both bedroom suites are

for sitting in too (beds are prettily canopied). Snack suppers only. Minimum stay, two nights. £18 a night.

Readers' comments: Warm and friendly atmosphere, every comfort, beautiful house, amazing views. [Tel: 0452 760328; postcode: GL14 1JY]

OLD VICARAGE

Higham, Suffolk, CO7 6JY   Tel: 020637 248

North of Colchester (Essex). Nearest main road: A12 from Colchester to Ipswich.

3 Bedrooms. £19–£25 (less for 3 nights). Some have own bath/shower/toilet. Tea/coffee facilities. TV. Views of garden, country, river. Washing machine on request. **Light suppers** sometimes. Wine can be brought in. No smoking.

2 Sitting-rooms. With open fire, central heating, TV. No smoking.

Large garden

One of the most elegant houses in this book, the Old Vicarage stands near a tranquil village and is surrounded by superb views, with the old church close by. Everything about it is exceptional, from the Tudor building itself (its walls colour-washed a warm apricot), and the lovely furnishings, to the pretty south-facing garden – which has unheated swimming-pool, tennis and river boats (it's surprising that few families with children have discovered it, particularly since the coast is near; Felixstowe and Frinton have sandy beaches).

Colonel and Mrs Parker have lived here for many years, and their taste is evident in every room. Lovely colours, pretty wallpapers and chintzes, antiques, flowers and log fires all combine to create a background of great style. In the breakfast-room, eight bamboo chairs surround a huge circular table (of mock-marble), and the walls have a trellis wallpaper the colour of watermelon. Bedrooms are equally pretty: one green-and-white with rush flooring; another has mimosa on walls and ceiling (its tiny windows are lattice-paned); the family room is in lime and tangerine. There are lace bedspreads, Indian watercolours, baskets of begonias – individual touches everywhere.

Bed-and-breakfast only; most visitors dine at the Angel, Stoke-by-Nayland.

Lynne, from the village, comes in to help and (herself a lively source of information) is evidently as greatly impressed as the visitors themselves with all that the Parkers do to help people enjoy their stay – information on sightseeing and eating-places, where to watch local wildlife, and so on. (Baby-sitting available, too.)

Higham is very well placed for a great variety of activities and outings. One could easily spend a fortnight doing something totally different each day. There are Roman Colchester (lovely gardens on the ramparts), Constable's Flatford Mill and Dedham, the seaside, racing at Newmarket, sailing, the mediaeval villages and great churches of central Suffolk, tide-mill at Woodbridge, market and Gainsborough's house at Sudbury, and lovely villages. Beth Chatto's garden, Ickworth and East Bergholt Lodge attract garden-lovers.

Readers' comments: Lovely house, very calm, beautifully appointed, charming staff. A firm favourite; superb and beautiful; hospitality outstanding. Perfect! Delightful weekend; privileged to be there. Excellent in every way. Most beautiful house. Very friendly. Thoroughly enjoyed it, superb. Very helpful. Food of highest standard, attention to detail outstanding. Splendid home and hospitality.

OLD VICARAGE

C(12) PT

66 Church Square, Rye, East Sussex, TN31 7HF   Tel: 0797 222119

Nearest main road: A259 from Folkestone to Hastings.

6 Bedrooms. £18.50–£26 for a suite (less for 7 nights). Some prices go up in April, but **5% less to readers of this book staying 3 nights from April to October, excluding bank holidays.** Bargain breaks. Most have own shower/toilet. Tea/coffee facilities. TV. Views of country. No smoking. Washing machine on request. **Light suppers** if ordered. Vegetarian or special diets. Wine can be brought in. **1 Sitting-room.** With central heating. **Small garden**

This pink-and-white, largely 18th-century house is virtually in the churchyard, a peaceful spot since it is traffic-free and the only sound is the melodious chime of the ancient church clock (its pendulum hangs right down into the nave of the church). One steps straight into a very pretty sitting-room, yellow sofas complemented by Laura Ashley fabrics and prints. Curved windows, antiques and pot-plants complete the scene. Beyond is the breakfast-room.

The bedrooms are prettily decorated, mostly with pine furniture and flowery fabrics. Two have elegant four-posters. Those at the front have views of the church and its surrounding trees; others, of Rye's mediaeval roofscape. Henry James wrote *The Spoils of Poynton* while living here in 1896 with his fat dog, servants and a canary, before moving to nearby Lamb House. He said in a letter '. . . the pears grow yellow in the sun and the peace of the Lord – or at least of the parson – seems to abide here' (no pears now, but the rest is still true).

As only breakfast is served (and cream teas in the garden on sunny weekends), for dinner Julia Lampon recommends – out of Rye's many restaurants – the Landgate bistro, Flushing Inn or Old Forge. Julia will also do snack suppers (if ordered); and all guests are invited to a complimentary sherry with the Lampons in the evening.

There is a weekly sheep market and a general market. The Rye Heritage Centre features a sound-and-light show and an authentic town model. Romney Marsh (famous for its autumn sunsets and its spring lambs) attracts painters and birdwatchers. Rye itself was the setting for E. F. Benson's *Mapp and Lucia* stories. Benson lived in Georgian Lamb House after Henry James (it is now a National Trust property).

The town deserves a lingering visit to explore its cobbled byways, antique and craft shops and historic fortifications, for there are few places where a mediaeval town plan and original houses have survived so little altered. In addition there are in the area 20 castles, historic houses such as Kipling's Batemans, Ellen Terry's Smallhythe and (with fine gardens) Great Dixter, Sissinghurst and Scotney. Battle Abbey and Camber's miles of sandy beaches are other attractions.

Readers' comments: Charming house, pretty rooms, friendly welcome. Outstanding. Charm and helpfulness of the owners gave us a perfect weekend. Very beautifully furnished and comfortable rooms. Friendly hosts. Fantastic – best breakfast I've ever had.

OLD VICARAGE HOTEL
C D PT

Parc-an-Creet, St Ives, Cornwall, TR26 2ET   Tel: 0736 796124
Nearest main road: A30 from Redruth to Penzance.

8 Bedrooms. £17–£22 (less for 3 nights). Prices go up from Easter. Some have own bath/shower/toilet. Tea/coffee facilities. TV. Views of garden.
2 Sitting-rooms. With central heating, TV, record-player. **Bar.** Snooker, piano, etc.
Large garden
Closed from November to March.

Built of silvery granite in the 1850s, the house (on the outskirts of steep little St Ives) is entered via a small conservatory and a great iron-hinged door of ecclesiastical shape, which opens into a hall with red-and-black tiled floor. Mr and Mrs Sykes have done their best to preserve this period ambience, furnishing the bar with crimson-and-gold flock wallpaper and all kinds of Victoriana. There's a piano here, which occasionally inspires visitors to join in singing some of the old songs of that period. In addition, there are a sitting-room and a blue-and-white dining-room. Big windows and handsome fireplaces feature throughout; and the Sykeses have put in excellent carpets, along with good, solid furniture – a 'thirties walnut suite in one bedroom, and velvet-upholstered bedheads. There is a refurbished Victorian loo, preserved in all its glory of blue lilies and rushes.

Jack Sykes, formerly an engineer, did all the modernization himself, even the plumbing.

There are chairs and sun umbrellas in the garden; putting and badminton, too.

Readers' comments: Beautifully restored; excellent in all aspects. Pleasant, and good value. Excellent in every way. Attention to detail outstanding. Cannot praise highly enough.

At nearby Zennor is **BOSWEDNACK MANOR**, overlooking a magnificent headland. It is run in slightly Bohemian style by Graham and Elizabeth Gynn, former wardens of Skokholm Island nature reserve. Inside are Turkish hangings, bamboo furniture, stuffed birds, dragons painted on the dining-room's blue ceiling (conservatory beyond). Outside are a studio, a games room, open-air chess and a meditation room for visitors' use. Organic garden vegetables and local

fish contribute to meals. The Gynns offer birdwatching and archaeology holidays, wildlife films, and guided walks. No smoking. £13.50–£18. [Tel: 0736 794183; postcode: TR26 3DD]

OLD WHARF FARM C D PT S X
Yardley Gobion, Northamptonshire, NN12 7UE   Tel: 0908 542454
(Messages: 0908 542844)
South of Northampton. Nearest main road: A508 from Milton Keynes to
Northampton (and M1, junction 15).

3 Bedrooms. £17–£20 (less for 2 nights).
Prices go up in April. Views of garden,
country, canal. No smoking. Washing
machine on request.
Light suppers if ordered in advance. Wine
can be brought in.
1 Sitting-room. With open fire, central
heating, record-player.
Large garden

In this idyllic canalside setting, many visitors watch traditional narrow-boats
being painted and restored in the dry dock which John Bowen has created in the
orchard. The 18th-century house has had many lives – as farm, then inn, then
wharfmaster's house and back to a smallholding before he took over. The Duke of
Grafton helped to pioneer the canal system in this area and he used French
prisoners-of-war to build the stables for horses to tow the boats along.

One enters through a tiled and beamed hall with an Orkney chair (made like
the old straw beehives), interesting pictures and rugs. There's a deep green par-
lour for meals, with mahogany furniture, and a red-tiled sitting-room where old
armchairs covered in William Morris fabrics are gathered round a log stove in the
big inglenook. Marine or canal paintings are everywhere. Board stairs lead to the
bedrooms: one has a grapevine peering through the window, while in a particularly
pretty family room sugar-pink duvets match the walls. Lying casually about are
such oddly assorted family treasures as John's own childhood teddybears and
Bonzo, and the plush top-hat of showman C. B. Cochrane: John's father was a
ballad singer in some of his variety entertainments. A bust of John's father is
topped by the flying helmet he wore in the First World War.

Outside there's a view of watermeadows, and a miscellany of animals ranging
freely about, which children in particular enjoy: dogs, cats, ferrets, chickens,
ducks, geese, pigs, calves and some Aberdeen Angus beef-cattle are usually in
residence. A rowing skiff can be borrowed, for fishing, exploring or picnicking.
Old farm machines, the original restored Victorian weighbridge (for carts deliver-
ing coal, etc. to the barges), croquet, and a rope-ladder up into a spreading willow
play-tree all contribute to the scene. (Baby-sitting available.)

Light suppers can be arranged if ordered, but most visitors go for meals to one
of the local inns (there are other choices of dining-places nearby). Tea and coffee
are free – help yourself in the kitchen.

The southern part of Northamptonshire has agreeable countryside, easily
reached from the M1, with attractive stone villages among the folds of the hills. A
special feature of the scene is water – rivers, canals, lakes and reservoirs abound
(and on many of these watersports and boating are possible). Sulgrave Manor is
where George Washington's ancestors lived.

Readers' comments: Excellent in every way. Fascinating house: even more interesting than I anticipated. Exceeded expectations. Relaxed family friendliness. Perfect
balance of attention and independence. Lovely furnishings. Wonderful breakfasts.

OLIVER'S

Church Street, Scawby, Humberside, DN20 9AM   Tel: 0652 650446
South-east of Scunthorpe. Nearest main road: A15 from Lincoln to Brigg
(and M180, junction 4).

4 **Bedrooms.** £16–£17.50 (less for 7
nights). Some have own bath/shower/toilet.
Tea/coffee facilities. TV. Views of country.
No smoking. Washing machine on request.
Dinner. £10 for 4 courses (with choices)
and coffee, at 7pm. Non-residents not
admitted. Vegetarian or special diets if
ordered. Wine can be brought in. No
smoking. **Light suppers** if ordered.
1 **Sitting-room.** With central heating. No
smoking.
Large garden

This 17th-century house in the village centre was once the post office, and what
was the shop area is now a big sitting- and dining-room, divided by cast-iron and
wooden columns, traditionally furnished. Here Hazel Oliver serves such meals as
spiced hot grapefruit, chicken in white wine, and raspberry-and-apple crumble.
Derek Oliver, who practised as a surveyor until recently, is an able watercolourist,
and his framed works (including some of the Olivers' home town of Stratford-
upon-Avon) are on sale.

Bedrooms are sizeable; one is in pink with pine fittings and velvet bedhead,
another is in cream with flowery fabrics. The best, with its own bathroom, is on
the ground floor. There is a large and pleasant garden.

The nearest town is Brigg, whose fair, at which gypsy horse-dealers used to
gather, has been commemorated in music by Delius. Cleethorpes is a traditional
seaside resort, with sandy beaches and one of the few remaining piers. Near it is
Grimsby, with a reconstruction of an Iron Age village and the new National
Fishing Heritage Centre. Westward of Scawby is the 'Isle' of Axholme, where John
Wesley's Epworth birthplace is open to the public. Bog oak is often ploughed up in
fields round here. Look out for the area's many windmills, some almost vanished
or incorporated into other buildings, a few in working order. Down a long, straight
road – surely Roman – is historic Lincoln with its grand cathedral.

To go over the enormous, modern suspension bridge that soars across the
Humber is an experience in itself; and on the other side are not only Beverley and
York (both described elsewhere) but that much under-valued city, Hull. Once a
great port – particularly in the heyday of whaling – it has perhaps the finest maritime museum outside London, a fascinating area of old wharves and warehouses
where once the docks were busy with more than today's pleasure-craft, a church
of considerable splendour (almost the biggest in England), a notable collection in
the Ferens art gallery, the 17th-century house where Wilberforce was born (with a
museum about slavery and its abolition), and much, much more. One of my
favourite cities.

Equally undervalued are the Wolds which – on this side of the Humber – run
down into Lincolnshire and Tennyson country ('calm and deep peace on this
high Wold' he wrote of his birthplace). The rich pastures of these gentle hills are
threaded by lanes where now you rarely encounter another car; but they bear
traces of extensive prehistoric habitation, of Viking settlement and of mediaeval
prosperity. Here is Gainsborough (its tidal bore described in George Eliot's *Mill
on the Floss*), with the Old Hall where Richard III once stayed.

OLIVER'S FARMHOUSE

Toppesfield, Essex, CO9 4LS Tel: 0787 237642
North of Braintree. Nearest main road: A604 from Colchester towards
Cambridge.

3 Bedrooms. £17–£19 (less for 3 nights or continental breakfast if ordered in advance). One has own bath/shower/toilet. Tea/coffee facilities. TV. Views of garden, country. No smoking. Washing machine on request.
Light suppers if ordered.
1 Sitting-room. With open fire, piano. No smoking.
Large garden

To the attraction of a very historic house (16th-century) is added that of a particularly interesting garden (created from what was a wilderness only a few years ago), for Sue Blackie is a qualified landscape gardener. And her architect husband James (whose work includes the award-winning Quay Theatre at Sudbury, a few miles away) makes wine from the small vineyard adjoining the garden: a link with the past, for Domesday Book records a vineyard here.

The Oliver who gave his name to the original farmhouse was, in 1340, a mercenary commander during the Hundred Years War with France. Later occupants were the Symonds family (from whom descended the founder of Topsfield in Massachusetts) and it was they who 'modernized' the house by putting in fireplaces and chimneys, an innovation in the 1580s.

The huge sitting-room with chamfered ceiling-beams has an equally huge brick fireplace – during summer this is filled with a display of some fifty peacock-feathers (contributed by Hector, who can often be seen peering curiously through the leaded window-panes at visitors). White linen sofas and a white flokati rug contrast with apricot walls on which hang some of the modern paintings which James collects. His paintings also fill the terracotta walls of the landing, where latched, board doors open into bedrooms furnished with antiques, old china, nosegays of such garden flowers as sweet peas or jasmine, and pleasant colour schemes. Sue brings breakfast up to the bedrooms, and if you are in luck this may include delicious jam she makes from wild bullaces – similar to greengages.

On the other side of Thaxted (a few miles from Stanstead Airport and the M11), Ugley Green is anything but! The name of this pretty spot, with thatched and pargeted cottages around the green, means 'Ug's clearing' in what was once forest. Here, in Snakes Lane, is **THATCHED COTTAGE**. The Tudor thatched house is surrounded by a large and lovely garden – a series of lawns enclosed by hedges, here an old apple tree and there a tub of colourful flowers. Past a tiled hall is a beamed dining-room with exposed rafters, and a small blue sitting-room with plenty of books. One

lattice-paned bedroom is on the ground floor. Joan Hilton serves breakfast in her pleasant kitchen; only light suppers (by arrangement). Many visitors eat at Elsenham's Crown Inn. £15. [Tel: 0279 812341; postcode: CM22 6HW]

THE ORCHARD   C(11) **PT**

High Street, Bathford, Avon, BA1 7TG   Tel: 0225 858765

North-east of Bath. Nearest main road: A4 from Bath to Chippenham.

4 Bedrooms. £19–£24. Prices go up at Easter. All have own bath/shower/toilet. TV. Views of garden, country. No smoking.
Light suppers if ordered.
1 Sitting-room. With open fire, central heating.
Large garden
Closed from December to February.

All the pleasures of Bath are within about ten minutes by car (or bus), yet this little village perched on a hillside seems deep in the country. There are stunning views over the River Avon to the far countryside and all around is peace.

John and Olga London's home is a luxurious Georgian house standing in its own grounds. In the garden are specimen trees, such as a copper beech and a Judas tree; there are terraced lawns (with croquet), and walls of creamy Bath stone – characteristic of many gardens in this conservation village. The bedrooms, with private bathrooms, are amongst the most elegant in this book; and the other rooms are equally handsome with attractive colour schemes and antique furniture. Even the landing is memorable: nicely framed etchings on russet walls, sparkling white paintwork. One bedroom (with very large bed and orthopaedic mattress), decorated in cream tones and furnished with pine and rush, has a huge bay window and armchairs from which to enjoy the view. There is an even bigger bed in a pinky-brown room, the velvety wallpaper complemented by a cream carpet. In a third room are peach fabrics, an antique settle and another big, south-facing window. 'The Folly' is a pretty ground-floor wing with separate entrance and its own patio.

Breakfasts include freshly squeezed orange juice, home-made muesli, free-range eggs and locally baked wholemeal bread. For dinner, the nearby Crown Inn is excellent.

Readers' comments: House and appointments are a delight. Complete peace, beautiful surroundings, everything done perfectly. Went out of their way to make us feel welcome. Rooms fabulous. Delightfully furnished. Outstanding. A privilege to stay there. Excellent, could not be bettered, have stayed 3 times.

A two-bedroom suite occupies the ground floor in beautifully converted **BRIDGE COTTAGE**, Ashley Road, Bathford. There is a little dining-room for light suppers; a particularly pretty bathroom, with flowery fitments; and a spacious, fitted bedroom in Laura Ashley style with windows at each end. Upstairs is a double bedroom (with bathroom and a sunny sitting-room) overlooking the tubs of begonias and petunias which fill the courtyard

garden: Ros Bright is a very keen gardener. £18–£20. [Tel: 0225 852399; postcode: BA1 7TT]

ORCHARD COTTAGE   C(5) D
Back Lane, Upper Oddington, Gloucestershire, GL56 0XL
Tel: 0451 830785
East of Stow-on-the-Wold. Nearest main road: A436 from Stow-on-the-Wold
towards Chipping Norton.

rear view

2 Bedrooms. £17–£18 (less for 3 nights). Prices go up in April. Bargain breaks. Both have own bath/shower/toilet. Tea/coffee facilities. Views of garden, country. No smoking.
Dinner. £13.50 for 3 courses and coffee, at 7–8pm. Vegetarian or special diets if ordered. Wine can be brought in. No smoking. **Light suppers** if ordered.
1 Sitting-room. With open fire, central heating, TV, record-player. No smoking.
Small garden
Closed from December to February.

A few ancient apple trees are all that remain of the great orchard which gave this 18th-century cottage its name. Originally two tiny dwellings, the house has been repeatedly modernized over the last two hundred years, most recently by its present owner Jane Beynon. She has used soft colours in the rooms – for instance, creams and pinks in a bedroom with lace bedspread; rush-seated and spindle-backed chairs in the small dining-hall; and Doulton's 'Babylon' china on the table. The garden is her pride and joy.

A typical dinner might comprise local trout pâté; chicken in a creamy piquant sauce; local fruits or tangy lemon Dutch flummery. As an alternative to a cooked breakfast, she can provide cold meats and cheeses in continental style.

The Cotswolds are not too well provided with bus services, so Jane is one of a team of volunteers who drives a community minibus around eight villages and the town of Chipping Norton once a week. She gladly takes visitors along, or will provide routes for their own car tours. Oddington itself has a very special 11th-century church; late June is a good time to stay, when a number of private gardens in the village are opened to the public.

Walking or motoring in the Cotswolds is a pleasure in itself, but there are many other things to do too – the Roman villa at Chedworth, Sudeley Castle, the Cotswold Wildlife Park, horse-racing, shopping for antiques or country clothes, visiting gardens such as those at Hidcote, Kiftsgate or Batsford (it has a Japanese-style arboretum) or the many stately homes and even statelier churches for which this county is famous.

Stow-on-the-Wold merits unhurried exploration: it's a little town of antique and craft shops, restaurants and byways – one of many picturesque villages. And there are plenty of places at which to buy farm produce.

Readers' comments: Hospitable, outgoing and kind. Every comfort. Cooking, comfort, hospitality all first-class. Outstanding meal and cheerful warmth. Accommodation and facilities excellent. Superb cooking. Very pleased.

For explanation of code letters (C, D, M, PT, S, X) see page xlvi.

262

ORCHARD FARM

C(10) **D PT**

Mordiford, Herefordshire, HR1 4EJ Tel: 0432 870253

South-east of Hereford. Nearest main road: A438 from Hereford to Ledbury.

3 Bedrooms. £15.50–£16.50 (less for 7 nights). Bargain breaks. Tea/coffee facilities. Views of garden, country, river. No smoking. Washing machine on request.
Dinner. £10.50 for 3 courses and coffee, at 7pm. Non-residents not admitted. Vegetarian or special diets if ordered. Wine can be ordered. No smoking. **Light suppers** if ordered.
2 Sitting-rooms. With open fire, central heating, TV. No smoking. Bar.
Large garden

Country antiques, corn dollies and Victorian china decorate Marjorie Barrell's rooms in this 17th-century house of reddish stone walls, inglenooks, flagged floors and beams. An old Norwegian stove (decorated with reindeer) warms the sitting-room. Pink and pine bedrooms with wicker armchairs have high ceilings and nice bathrooms; the dining-room has rush chairs and a cornice with blue china dishes. Beyond woods at the back, the Black Mountains rise high. You may spot deer, foxes and even badgers; kestrels and buzzards; cowslips and violets – for the house is in an area of special scientific interest within the Wye Valley, itself an area of outstanding natural beauty. Some visitors like to fish in the river running through the Barrells' land.

Mrs Barrell is a cordon bleu cook. With dinner – which might comprise shrimp salad, duckling cooked in honey and ginger and frangipane tart, for example – she offers you Herefordshire wine, cider or perry. Bread and jams are home-made; most produce is local.

Readers' comments: Food excellent, beds comfortable. Extremely pleasant and welcoming.

In the middle of Fownhope village, Susan and Austyn Clifford bought a 17th-century cottage (once a black-smith's), now called **OAKLANDS**, to use as both home and workshop: he makes by hand wood-pegged, country-style cabinets and other furniture, using solid oak and hand-some, traditional designs. In the house are examples of his work – notably the impressive dining suite – as well as some unusual Belgian armchairs with cut velvet facing the fireplace in the little sitting-room. Susan has used festoon blinds at most windows and

cottage-style furnishings in the bed-rooms. Her evening meals include grills and casseroles. (Baby-sitting available.) £14–£16. [Tel: 0432 860691; postcode: HR1 4NJ]

ORCHARD HOUSE   C PT
High Street, Rothbury, Northumberland, NE65 7TL   Tel: 0669 20684
South-west of Alnwick. Nearest main road: A697 from Morpeth to Wooler.

6 Bedrooms. £19.50–£22 (less for 7 nights). Most have own shower/toilet. Tea/coffee facilities. TV. Views of garden, country. Washing machine on request.
Dinner. £12 for 4 courses and coffee, at 7pm. Non-residents not admitted. Vegetarian or special diets if ordered. Wine can be ordered. No smoking.
1 Sitting-room. With central heating. Bar.
Small garden
Closed from December to February.

Rothbury, a pleasant little market town with some interesting shops, stands in the very centre of Northumberland, and so many of the pleasures of that large and underestimated county are within an easy drive: the Roman wall to the south, Holy Island to the north, and in between countryside which can change from open moorland to woods and arable fields within a few miles, with picturesque villages and historic monuments for punctuation. Castles and pele towers (fortified farmhouses) remind one of border raiders.

Orchard House is Georgian. It stands well aside from Rothbury's bustling main street. Jeff and Sheila Jefferson took it over several years ago when Jeff left the RAF after years as an engineer (some of them spent in Malaysia) and have turned it into a comfortable and unpretentious place to stay. Like many people who provide good accommodation in relatively unknown spots, they have found that guests who stayed a night or two while passing through have returned for a longer holiday.

Sheila's four-course menus are out of the ordinary and varied, the only fixture being roast beef every Sunday. Otherwise you might get (for instance) French onion soup, pork scallopine, strawberry meringue and cheese (local produce is used whenever possible). There is a cabinet well stocked with miniatures of drinks for you to help yourself and enter in a book.

The sight closest to Rothbury is Cragside, the mansion which Norman Shaw (best known, perhaps, for his government buildings in London) designed for Lord Armstrong, the armaments king. It is one of the most complete late-Victorian houses there are. Among the oddities are a Turkish bath and a hydraulic lift, but its main distinction is that it was the first house in the world to be lit by electricity. The grounds are elaborately landscaped.

Brinkburn Priory, Alnwick Castle, Wallington Hall and gardens are all near. Strange stone beasts' heads glare from the lawn in front of the last.

Readers' comments: Very impressed. A delightful couple, friendly and helpful. Outstanding food; rooms sparkling clean and spacious. Excellent food – first-rate value. Comfortable, spotless; we thoroughly endorse all you say. Excellent in every way. Exceptionally helpful, excellent food, very good value. Very good food, everything of the highest standard. Marvellous food and accommodation.

OVERCOMBE HOTEL   C D M PT S X

Plymouth Road, Horrabridge, Devon, PL20 7RN   Tel: 0822 853501
South-east of Tavistock. On A386 from Plymouth to Tavistock.

11 Bedrooms. £20–£25 (less for 3 nights). Prices go up in June. Bargain breaks. Some have own bath/shower/toilet. Tea/coffee facilities. TV. Views of garden, country. **Dinner.** A la carte or £11 for 4 courses (with choices) and coffee, at 7.30pm. Vegetarian or special diets if ordered. Wine can be ordered. **Light suppers** if ordered. **2 Sitting-rooms.** With open fire, central heating, TV. **Bar.**
Small garden
Closed in January.

Conveniently placed for one to explore Dartmoor and the coast, the Overcombe Hotel (now run by Brenda and Maurice Durnell) consists of two houses joined in one to make a very comfortable small hotel. You can relax in either of the sitting-rooms, according to what you want – a bar in one, TV in another, log fires, pleasant views. From the bay window of the dining-room, one looks across to the moors. Bedrooms are pretty (some on the ground floor) and one has a four-poster.

There is always a selection of dishes on the menu with such choices as pear and parsnip soup, salmon in filo pastry, traditional puddings and cheeses.

Visitors come here for a variety of reasons (the least of which is that it's a good staging-post if you are on that long slog to furthest Cornwall). The Dartmoor National Park attracts people touring by car, anglers, riders, golfers and – above all – walkers (for them, Maurice organizes special two- to seven-day bargain breaks, with experienced guides accompanying visitors on walks of eight miles or more, and illustrated after-dinner talks about the moors). Plymouth is near; and among visitors' favourite outings are Cotehele, Buckland Abbey and Saltram House (all National Trust), Morwellham Quay and the Shire Horse Centre.

Further east lie the delectable South Hams: flowery valleys, sands, mildest of climates. To the west is the Cornish coast: dramatic cliffs, sandy coves and some harbours so picturesque (Polperro, Looe, etc.) that popularity threatens to ruin them. But go inland, and you will still find undisturbed villages and market towns.

Plymouth was heavily bombed, which means that its shopping centre is very modern. But the old quarter, the Barbican, which Drake and the Pilgrim Fathers knew so well, survived, and it is to this that visitors throng. Here are the old warehouses and the harbours full of small boats, the narrow alleys with beguiling little shops and restaurants, the mediaeval houses now turned into museums, the fish market and 17th-century citadel. Plymouth has an outstanding aquarium, Drake's Island out in the Sound (to be visited by boat), the naval dockyard and the famous clifftop – the Hoe – with its unique seascape, memorials and flowers.

Other local sights: the 15th-century cottage where Drake's wife grew up (at Saltash); and the gardens at Bickham House (Roborough).

Readers' comments: A wonderful stay. Made us very welcome and could not have been more delightful hosts. Excellent food, fresh vegetables daily. Comfortable and warm. We will go again. A relaxed, easy atmosphere; we could recommend this hotel to any of our friends. Quite perfect in every way. Wonderfully imaginative cooking.

PARADISE HOUSE   C(5) M PT
88 Holloway, Bath, Avon, BA2 4PX   Tel: 0225 317723
Nearest main road: A367 from Bath to Radstock (and M4, junction 18).

10 Bedrooms. £20–£33 (less for 4 nights, or 3 nights mid-week). Most have own bath/shower/toilet. Tea/coffee facilities. TV. Views of garden, country, city.
1 Sitting-room. With open fire, central heating.
Large garden

It stands half way up a steep, curving road which was once indeed a 'hollow way': a lane worn low between high banks by centuries of weary feet or hooves entering Bath from the south: the last lap of the Romans' Fosse Way. It is now a quiet cul-de-sac in the lee of Beechen Cliff, with panoramic views over the city, the centre of which is only 7 minutes' walk away – downhill. (As to uphill – take a taxi! Or else a bus to the Bear Flat stop.) Look the opposite way and all is leafy woods.

The house itself was built about 1720, with all the elegance which that implies: a classical pediment above the front door and well-proportioned sash windows with rounded tops in a façade of honey-coloured Bath stone.

David and Janet Cutting took it over several years ago and have restored it impeccably throughout, stripping off polystyrene to reveal pretty plasterwork ceilings, for instance, and gaudy tiles to expose a lovely marble fireplace in which logs now blaze. They stripped dingy paint off the panelled pine doors and put on handles of brass or china. They have furnished to a very high standard indeed, with both antique and modern furniture, elegant fabrics, and well-chosen colours, predominantly soft greens and browns. The sitting-room is especially pretty, with Liberty fabrics and wallpaper, pictures in maple frames and a collection of Coalport cottages. There is also a Jacuzzi. The bedrooms, given as much care as the rest, vary in size and amenities; the new garden room has wheelchair access.

At the back, beyond a verandah with ivy-leaf ironwork, is quite a large walled garden (a sun-trap in the afternoon), with lawns, fish-pool, a rose-covered pergola and marvellous views of the city and hills all around. This secluded setting extends behind the mediaeval Magdalen Chapel next door, which was once a hostel for lepers banned from the city. In 1982 David and Janet acquired the adjoining Georgian house, which they then completely restored, furnished and decorated to the same elegant standards as the main house. (Lock-up garages for a small fee; croquet and boules available.)

As to Bath itself – which attracts more visitors than any other place in England except London – the attractions are so varied that they can hardly be compressed into one paragraph. Just wandering among the Georgian perfection of its streets and squares, which spread from the historic centre right up the sides of the surrounding hills, and in its award-winning gardens, is a pleasure in itself, and it would take many days to explore them all (the best method is to take a bus to each hilltop in turn and walk back downhill).

Readers' comments: Top-class! Truly excellent. Ideal, with excellent facilities. Superbly equipped, very attractive. Outstanding hotel. Extremely comfortable. Beautiful home; made us very welcome. Lovely house and garden.

PARK FARM
C(12) **X**

Spring Road, Barnacle, Warwickshire, CV7 9LG   Tel: 0203 612628
North of Coventry (West Midlands). Nearest main roads: M69 and
M6 (junction 2).

2 Bedrooms. £18 (less for 4 nights or
continental breakfast). Tea/coffee facilities.
TV. Views of garden, country. No smoking.
Washing machine on request.
Dinner. £11 for 3 courses (with choices)
and coffee, at 7pm. Non-residents not
admitted. Vegetarian or special diets if
ordered. Wine can be brought in. No
smoking. **Light suppers** by arrangement.
1 Sitting-room. With open fire, central
heating.
Large garden

The Roundheads burnt down the original house: several great Civil War battles
took place in this region. This one was built about 1670. Outside it stand fine
yews and within are such handsome features as the balustered staircase. All
around is the 200-acre farm.

The house is immaculate, furnished with antiques and decorated in restful
colours. In the green and cream sitting-room are flowery cretonnes and a small
fireplace of pink marble. The big dining-room has windows at each end, and here
Linda Grindal serves such meals as home-made pâté, chicken and broccoli
casserole with dauphinoise potatoes, and blackcurrant shortcake. She began
taking visitors almost by chance: some Australian farmers visiting the Royal Show
at Stoneleigh in 1979 were desperate for accommodation, so she put them up.
Having enjoyed this experience, she decided to do it regularly.

Upstairs are pleasant bedrooms – fine walnut beds in the pink one, a prettily
draped one in the green room; and a very good bathroom.

The house is well placed for visiting the cathedral at Coventry and a war spectacle there, the 'Blitz Experience' (in the Transport Museum); Warwick Castle
and Stratford-upon-Avon are only 25–35 minutes away; and there are plenty of
fine houses to visit – such as Charlecote and other National Trust properties, and
Arbury House in Nuneaton (George Eliot territory). Ryton Organic Garden
Centre attracts some visitors.

At **MANOR FARM** in Willey, the
nicest bedroom (with good shower)
has Laura Ashley fabrics and pine fitments; and all have rural views of Ray
Sharpe's grazing sheep – with lambs
leaping in springtime. A peaceful contrast to the motorways and to the city
hustle of Birmingham and Rugby, neither far away. Visitors have mixed
interests: they come for motor-racing
or the scuba-diving centre, cycling or a
miniature 'Glyndebourne' in the area.

Helen Sharpe will provide light
suppers only by arrangement, but she

has negotiated a discount for guests
dining at the Olde Watling Inn nearby.
(No smoking.) £16–£21. [Tel: 0455
553143; postcode: CV23 0SH]

PARKFIELD HOUSE

C S

Hogben's Hill, Selling, Kent, ME13 9QU Tel: 0227 752898
South of Faversham. Nearest main road: A251 from Faversham to Ashford
(and M2, junctions 6/7).

5 **Bedrooms.** £15–£16.50 (less for 2
nights). Prices go up in March. TV. Views
of garden, country. No smoking.
Light snacks.
1 **Sitting-room.** With open fire, central
heating, TV. No smoking.
Large garden

There were Hogbens on this hill in 1086 (they are named in the Domesday Book)
. . . and there still are!

It is Mr and Mrs Hogben who own Parkfield, a largely modern house with a
pretty garden, as well as the small joinery works alongside – John Hogben's principal activity. It is worth staying at Parkfield House simply to listen to him talk
about Kentish ways and history (especially his stories of past Hogbens, who were
blacksmiths, farmers, wheelwrights and smugglers). Next door there used to be
an inn called Ye Olde Century in memory of a John Hogben who lived there until
he died when he was 101.

The house, built in 1820, had become run down until about 40 years ago
when Mr Hogben renovated and extended it. Now it is immaculate and very
comfortable. In the sitting-room are big, velvet armchairs in which to relax by a
log fire.

And if you want something special for breakfast (fish, fresh fruit, ham, cheese)
Mrs Hogben will get it.

Selling is in a very beautiful and tranquil part of Kent, well situated for
touring, walking and sightseeing. It is, of course, the cathedral which brings most
visitors to nearby Canterbury: one of Britain's finest and most colourful, with
many historical associations, the site of Becket's martyrdom (commemorated in
some of the best stained glass in the world), the splendid tomb of the Black
Prince, and much more.

The ancient walled city still has many surviving mediaeval and Tudor
buildings, the beautiful River Stour, old churches and inns, Roman remains,
a very good theatre, and lovely shops in its small lanes. It is in the middle of
some of Kent's finest countryside, with a coast of great variety quite near
(cliffs, sands or shingle; resorts, fishing harbours or historic ports) and ten
golf courses. Howlett's Zoo and mediaeval Faversham are very popular, and
the whole area is full of fine gardens and garden centres. Both Leeds and
Dover castles are within easy motoring distance. One could spend a fortnight
here without discovering all there is to see in one of England's most beautiful
and most historic counties, rich in towns with antique shops and fields of pick-
your-own fruit.

In blossom-time there are car 'trails' marked out among the orchards.

Readers' comments: Excellent in all respects, exceptional hospitality. Excellent
service, well cared for. Warm welcome. Spotless. Attractive bedroom.

PEACOCK FARMHOUSE

C D M PT X

Redmile, Leicestershire, NG13 0GQ   Tel: 0949 42475
West of Grantham (Lincolnshire). Nearest main road: A52 from Nottingham to Grantham.

10 Bedrooms. £17.50–£21 (less for 7 nights). Some have own shower/toilet. Tea/coffee facilities. Views of garden.
Dinner. A la carte or £12.50 for 3 courses (with choices) and coffee, at 7.15pm. Vegetarian or special diets. Wine can be ordered. No smoking. **Light suppers.**
1 Sitting-room. With central heating, TV, piano. **Bar.**
Large garden

This guest-house with restaurant (built as a farm in the 18th century and later a canal bargees' inn) is ideal for a break when doing a long north-south journey on the nearby A1, particularly with children – or as a base from which to explore the many little-known attractions of Nottinghamshire and adjacent counties.

It is in the outstandingly beautiful Vale of Belvoir, with the Duke of Rutland's Belvoir Castle (full of art treasures) rearing its battlemented walls high above a nearby hilltop: an unforgettable sight. The topiary yew peacock on the front lawn, started in 1812, was inspired by the peacock in the crest of the Duke.

The Needs have created a happy family atmosphere here. Four upstairs rooms have views of Belvoir Castle, while others on the ground floor (with en suite bathrooms) include a self-contained pine cabin and a coach house outside the main building. Children can safely play in the garden which has a large lawn, hammock, swings, small covered swimming-pool, playroom, pool-room, bicycles, barbecue, and farm pets. Indoors are snooker and table tennis.

Food is above average, with home-made bread and soups, herbs from the garden and much local produce. Starters may include trout and cream cheese terrine or herb and beansprout omelette; main courses, beef and venison carbonnade or salmon with sorrel sauce; puddings, fresh fruit pavlova and 'tipsy' bread-and-butter pudding.

There are many popular sights in this region: Belvoir Castle, Belton House, Stapleford Park, Rutland Water and Wollaton Hall in its park; also Holme Pierrepont Hall, Doddington Hall, and Newstead Abbey (Byron's home). Eastwood has D. H. Lawrence's birthplace. Lincoln (cathedral), Southwell (minster), Sherwood Forest (Robin Hood display) and Nottingham are also near – the last a much underrated city. I recommend the arts museum in the castle and others at its foot (the lace museum is fascinating), river trips and walks through the Georgian quarter. The historic market towns of Stamford (in particular) and Newark are of great interest. One can shop for local Stilton, crafts and Nottingham lace to take home – Melton Mowbray is famous for pies and other pork delicacies.

Readers' comments: Good food, delightful hosts. Helpful, very nice people. Comfortable.

PEAR TREE COTTAGE

C(2) D PT

Church Road, Wilmcote, Warwickshire, CV37 9UX   Tel: 0789 205889
(Messages: 0789 204289)
North-west of Stratford-upon-Avon. Nearest main road: A3400 from
Stratford to Birmingham (and M40, junction 15).

7 Bedrooms. £19–£20 (less for 7 nights).
All have own bath/shower/toilet. Tea/coffee
facilities. TV. Views of garden, country.
Washing machine on request.
2 Sitting-rooms. With central heating,
TV.
Large garden

Mary Arden, Shakespeare's mother, grew up in the big half-timbered house which
overlooks this cottage of much the same date. It now holds a museum of rural
life.

Pear Tree Cottage, too, is half-timbered. From its flowery garden one steps
into a hall with stone-flagged floor, oak settle, other antiques and bunches of
dried flowers. The floor is of blue lias, once quarried at Wilmcote, and to be seen
also in Stratford's famous Clopton Bridge and the steps of St Paul's cathedral in
London.

In the beamed dining-room, country Hepplewhite chairs and colourful
Staffordshire pottery figures show well against rugged stone walls. There's a little
television room and a pretty reading-room opening onto the gardens. Bedrooms
(reached by steps and turns all the way) have very pleasant colour schemes. Some
are in a new extension.

Outside are two gardens, a stream, a pool with pink waterlilies, stone paths
and seats under old apple trees. Although Margaret Mander does not serve
evening meals, there are kitchens in which guests can prepare their own snack
suppers, and two local inns serving good food in the village.

Readers' comments: Ideal in all respects. Have always received most kind and courteous attention and a wonderful breakfast. Thoroughly enjoyed every stay.

In Stratford-upon-Avon itself is
HARDWICK HOUSE, 1 Avenue
Road – a quiet residential part of the
town. Built in 1887, it is a guest-house
of high standard run by the Coulson
family. Bedrooms vary, but most are
spacious – particularly those on the
ground floor. In an airy dining-room,
substantial snacks are served. There
is only a small sitting-reception
room but, perhaps more important
in Stratford, there is a carpark.
Furnishings are conventional and comfortable, everything is spick-and-span,
and Jill is a hospitable hostess.

The house is only a few minutes'
walk from Shakespeare's Birthplace,
the coach terminus, and the start of
round-Stratford guided tours by open-
top bus. £19–£23. [Tel: 0789 204307;
postcode: CV37 6UY]

PEAT GATE HEAD   C(5) M S
Low Row, North Yorkshire, DL11 6PP   Tel: 0748 86388
West of Richmond. Nearest main road: A6108 from Richmond to Leyburn.

5 Bedrooms. £32.50–£34.50 **including dinner.** Prices go up in April. Some have own shower/toilet. Tea/coffee facilities. Views of garden, country, river. No smoking. Washing machine on request.
Dinner. 4 courses and coffee, at 7pm. Vegetarian or special diets if ordered. Wine can be ordered. No smoking.
2 Sitting-rooms. With open fire, central heating, TV, piano. Bar. No smoking in one.
Large garden

It sometimes seems that anywhere north of Leeds now calls itself Herriot country, what with almost countless books, films and television series. Though the author actually practises to the east of the county, much filming of his books was done in the Yorkshire Dales, and Peat Gate Head is just along the moor road (with water-splash) where the opening of every television episode was recorded.

Alan Earl had long loved Peat Gate Head, a 300-year-old Swaledale farm-house built of the local limestone, and when his job as a history lecturer ended with the closure of the training college where he worked, he decided to buy it and to turn his enthusiasm for cooking to good use by opening it as a guest-house. From several choices at each course one might select, for instance, smoked mack-erel pâté, chicken breasts in orange-and-tarragon sauce, and queen of puddings. It is Alan's cooking and warm personality which bring visitors back repeatedly.

The beamed house is simply furnished. There is a vast stone chimneypiece in the dining-room, and in the sitting-room a wood-burning stove pleasantly scents the air. Two bedrooms are on the ground floor (one with own shower and toilet).

Outside, a summer-house on the lawn looks across a sweep of Swaledale, a textbook illustration of a valley, from the river running along the flat bottom, through stone-walled fields, to open moorland.

Readers' comments: Made us so welcome and entertained us non-stop; delicious meals; peaceful atmosphere. Great charm, most acceptable dinner, massive breakfast. Very good value, most entertaining too. Three unforgettable days . . . the quality of everything. A fine man, a character! Took a great deal of trouble.

Two miles above Marske near the foot of the valley, **TELFIT FARM** is at the end of a long farm road, mostly metalled. It is a totally unpretentious hill farm which walkers, painters and lovers of solitude will particularly appreciate. Young Mary Allison serves such food as fish pâté, a roast, and a gâteau or fruit salad with 'a good dollop of cream'. £11.50–£12.50 (b & b).
Readers' comments: The welcome given

set the standard for the rest of the holiday; the food was first class. [Tel: 0748 823769; postcode: DL11 7NG]

PENNINE LODGE

D M PT S

St John's Chapel, County Durham, DL13 1QX   Tel: 0388 537247
North-west of Bishop Auckland. On A689 from Bishop Auckland to Alston.

5 Bedrooms. £18–£19 (less for 3 nights). Bargain breaks. All have own bath/shower/toilet. Tea/coffee facilities. TV. Views of garden, country, river. No smoking.
Dinner. £9 for 3 courses and coffee, at 7pm. Non-residents not admitted. Vegetarian or special diets if ordered. Wine can be ordered. No smoking.
1 Sitting-room. With central heating. TV. No smoking.
Large garden
Closed from October to March.

Pennine Lodge was built in the 16th century, and it has the long and narrow shape typical of a Weardale farmhouse. Just below the windows of the corridor which connects the bedrooms is the upper River Wear, rushing over a small waterfall backed by trees, a beautiful spot. The rooms themselves are full of interest, with lots of timber and stone, antiques and bric-a-brac.

Guests dine in a long, low-ceilinged room next to the garden, with a stone inglenook at one end. There are three courses: a starter (or else cheese), with a main course which is quite likely to be a casserole of pheasant or other game from the Raby estates, and a choice of puddings or cheese from the trolley. All is home-made by Yvonne Raine, including jams and bread; afternoon tea is available. She has also researched, and sometimes cooks, local mediaeval recipes.

Raby Castle is one of the best of its kind, and High Force is England's highest waterfall. Killhope Wheel is a huge waterwheel with lead-mining displays. The Durham Dales Centre at Stanhope (craft shops, tea-room) is worth a visit.

Readers' comments: It's so good I've been back repeatedly. Lovely position, comfortable without being pretentious. Delightful old house, competent and delightful hostess, food excellent. Beautiful setting. Very friendly. Superb scenery. Excellent bedrooms and bathrooms.

A few miles eastward is **BRECKON HILL** at Westgate-in-Weardale, an old farmhouse which has been neatly renovated by Lyn and John Say. At the end of a rather steep drive, it is very peaceful. There are impressive views of the dale from the gardens and from most of the bedrooms (one on ground floor and all with bath or shower), as well as from the new conservatory. Many rooms contain examples of Lyn's skilled embroidery. She provides such meals as mushroom soup, pork in white wine (with fresh vegetables, mostly home-grown) and lemon surprise pudding. (No smoking.) £20 (b & b).

Readers' comments: Rooms delightful; magnificent views of Weardale. Facilities first class. Quiet and peaceful. Views magnificent and hospitality second to none. Food excellent. Superbly positioned. Will return. [Tel: 0388 517228; postcode: DL13 1PD]

272

PETER BARN   C(5) S
Cross Lane, Waddington, Lancashire, BB7 3JH   Tel: 0200 28585
(Messages: 0200 22381)
North-west of Clitheroe. Nearest main road: A59 from Preston to Clitheroe.

3 Bedrooms. £17.50–£18.50 (less for 3 nights). Bargain breaks. Some have own shower/toilet. Tea/coffee facilities. TV. Views of garden, country. No smoking. Washing machine on request.
Light suppers if ordered.
1 Sitting-room. With open fire, central heating, TV, balcony.
Large garden

Cross Lane – locally known as Rabbit Lane for obvious reasons – is a single-track road that runs through a tunnel of trees near the village of Waddington, which was the locale of an experiment in community television a few years ago. Peter Barn was indeed a barn until the Smiths turned it into a family home; now they use the upper floor exclusively for guests. The large, airy sitting-room is reached by an open-tread staircase and has a roof made of old church rafters. By a stone fireplace are leather-covered settees and armchairs, near the head of the staircase is the breakfast-table, and off the other end of this well-proportioned space are the bedrooms and bathroom. (The arrangement is such that a large family would have the use of a virtually self-contained flat.) Much of the furniture consists of antiques, and there is some interesting bric-a-brac around. Among the verdant houseplants are two monsteras which live up to their name: one touches the 20-foot apex of the room.

Jean Smith has the greenest of fingers, for the one-acre garden is a remarkable achievement, having been a field when the house was converted 15 years ago. Now it is beautifully landscaped and lovingly tended, with decorative conifers, a pond and a Japanese-inspired area.

There is no shortage of places for an evening meal, not least in Clitheroe, the lively market town a couple of miles away.

The Smiths also organize special weekend breaks to coincide with interesting local activities and 'hibernation' weekends from January to March.

Westward, near the picturesque village of Chipping, is **HOUGH CLOUGH FARMHOUSE**, run by cookery enthusiast Doreen Ingram. (Light suppers and Sunday lunch available.) From this Victorian farmhouse, new bow windows look across fields and meadows to the distant hills. All bedrooms have their own bath or shower-room. (Visitors can go and see calves, a donkey and other livestock at the friendly neighbouring farm.) £16.50.
Readers' comments: The nicest b & b we have stayed in. Beautiful, comfortable

accommodation. Hospitality like visiting old friends. Outstanding cooking. [Tel: 0995 61272; postcode: PR3 2NT]

273

PETHILLS BANK COTTAGE

C D

Bottomhouse, Staffordshire, ST13 7PF   Tel: 0538 304277
(Messages: 0538 304555)
South-east of Leek. Nearest main road: A523 from Leek towards Ashbourne.

3 Bedrooms. £19–£20.50 (less for 2 nights or continental breakfast). All have own bath/shower/toilet. Tea/coffee facilities. TV. Views of garden, country.
Dinner. £15 for 4 courses (with choices) and coffee, at 7.30pm. Non-residents not admitted. Wine can be brought in. **Light suppers** if ordered.
1 Sitting-room. With open fire, central heating. No smoking.
Small garden
Closed in January and February.

This 18th-century farmhouse, much modernized, stands in landscaped gardens on the crest of a hill, at the edge of the Peak District. The thick and rugged stone walls are exposed to view in a snug sitting-room which was once a cowshed - now soft lighting falls on pinky-beige chesterfields of buttoned velvet, and from the big window there is a view of the Martins' rock garden. In the dining-room are carved Dutch chairs upholstered in green velvet and a log stove on a tiled hearth.

One particularly pretty bedroom, on the ground floor, has its own verandah overlooking the hills, silky draperies and a private sitting-room with pink-and-blue sofa. Up an open-tread stair are more bedrooms, one in a former hayloft. Each has its own style: for instance, bamboo sofa in a room of peach and green; louvred cupboards, onyx 'Vanitory' and briar-rose patterns in the other.

Yvonne's dinners (available on only some evenings) include such dishes as pasta, trout en croûte, chocolate cheesecake, cheese with fruit.

Readers' comments: Made most welcome, well looked after. Warm and cheerful hostess. Excellent cook. Nothing was too much trouble. Very attractive lounge, extremely attentive service. Warm and friendly, very helpful. Excellent in every way and very good value. Breakfast here surpasses all others.

Once an inn, the 17th-century **WHITE HOUSE** at Grindon stands 1000 feet high, above the Peak District's lovely Manifold Valley. Its rooms are filled with decorative cushions, quilts, lamp-shades and so forth, made by Philomena Bunce, who puts not only flowers but fruit in each bedroom. There is a pretty garden, full of roses and cottage flowers.

Philomena's unusual breakfast options include Staffordshire oatcakes (topped with a savoury mixture), oak-smoked kippers sent from Craster, and home-baked bread. Her crafts and produce are on sale. (Light suppers only. For dinners, the Cavalier Inn is near.) £19–£20.

Readers' comments: Furnishings outstanding; highest standard of comfort, warm welcome. Our stay one of the pleasantest ever. Absolutely superb – perfection! A wonderful find. A gem! Everything is perfect. [Tel: 0538 304250; postcode: ST13 7TP]

PHEASANT INN   C D M

Stannersburn, Northumberland, NE48 1DD   Tel: 0434 240382

North-west of Hexham. Nearest main road: A68 from Corbridge to Jedburgh (Scotland).

8 Bedrooms. £20–£25 (less for 7 nights). Prices go up in May. Bargain breaks. All have own shower/toilet. Tea/coffee facilities. TV. Views of garden, country. No smoking. Washing machine on request.

Dinner. £14 for 4 courses (with choices) and coffee, at 7–9pm. Vegetarian or special diets if ordered. Wine can be ordered. No smoking. **Light suppers.**

2 Lounge bars. With open fires, central heating.

Close to Kielder Water, this is everything one wants a country inn to be – nearly four centuries old, stone-walled and low-beamed and in particularly lovely countryside. The Kershaws are determined to keep it unspoilt. The bedrooms, however, are modern, in a former hemel (farm implements store) and barn; many of them are on the ground floor. They are arranged round a square of grass where the farmyard must have been, to one side of the inn building.

The main bar (where very good snacks are served) is big and beamy, with a stone fireplace and some agricultural bygones, such as hay-knives and peat-spades; and a stuffed pheasant appropriately sits on the sill of one of the small windows. A smaller bar houses a pool table.

The dining-room is light and airy, with raspberry-coloured walls and pine furniture. Food is freshly prepared – one interesting starter is avocado with grapefruit and Stilton; trout comes with a sauce of yogurt and herbs; venison appears often. (Sunday lunch available too.)

Stannersburn is in the southern part of the Border Forest Park – 200 square miles of hills and moors that stretch from Hadrian's Wall to Scotland. Within this area is Kielder Forest with Kielder Water in the middle. The immense forest of various conifers was first planted in the 1920s, there are scenic drives through it, and the lake is a great man-made reservoir – the biggest in Europe. Visitors can take a 10-mile cruise, calling at places of interest around the 27½-mile coastline. The energetic can go in for watersports.

Eastward lies Otterburn, scene of an epic conflict in 1388, when Percy ('Hotspur') led the English against the Scottish Earl of Douglas – as related in the 'Ballad of Chevy Chase'. Among the attractions of this area is Otterburn Mill, no longer working but with bargains in knitwear and tweeds. Other local villages include Elsdon (once the Norman capital of Redesdale), its historic houses – one of them a fortified parsonage – surrounding a huge village green.

Although the area is a National Park – England's least known? – it is largely unexploited, though there are one or two such things as 'open' farms to visit. The contemplative may be rewarded by the sight of roe deer or red squirrels.

Readers' comments: It's super. A very good welcome. Delicious breakfast. Such a wonderful start to our holiday. Delightful country inn. Mr Kershaw and his family could not have been more friendly and courteous, our room was delightful and spotlessly clean, and the food was truly delicious – we look forward to a return.

PICKFORD HOUSE
Bath Road, Beckington, Somerset, BA3 6SJ   Tel: 0373 830329
South of Bath (Avon). Nearest main road: A36 from Bath to Warminster.

4 Bedrooms. £14–£15 (less for 4 nights). Bargain breaks. Some have own bath/shower/toilet. Tea/coffee facilities. TV. Views of garden, country. No smoking. Washing machine on request.
Dinner. £10 for 3 courses and coffee, from 7pm. Non-residents not admitted. Vegetarian or special diets if ordered. Wine can be ordered. **Light suppers** if ordered.
2 Sitting-rooms. With open fire, central heating, TV, piano, record-player. Bar.
Garden

Sometimes parties of friends take the whole of this hilltop house for a gourmet weekend together – for Angela Pritchard is a cordon bleu cookery writer.

On such weekends, the guests are invited to enjoy a Somerset cream tea to be followed later by a candlelit dinner of 6 courses with appropriate wines. On the next day, they explore the area's attractions (on their own or with the Pritchards at the helm), which include Bath, Wells and innumerable stately homes, before another gourmet meal. There is the heated swimming-pool or picturesque Beckington in which to pass the time before a Sunday lunch.

Even on everyday occasions Pickford House food is exceptional. Angela offers the choice of a 4-course dinner or what she calls a 'pot-luck' one of 3 courses. An example of the former: mushroom roulade, lamb en croûte, mulberry mousse (made from garden fruit) and cheeses. And of the latter: fish au gratin, carbonnade of beef, bananas baked with Kirsch.

As to the house itself, this is one of a pair that were built from honey-coloured Bath stone for spinster sisters in 1804. The furnishings are comfortable with two modern bedrooms in the old school house (one with kitchen adjoining). In addition to the main sitting-room, there is a family room which has TV and toys.

Readers' comments: Very friendly; particularly good value. Absolutely superb; food was excellent, hospitality outstanding. Delightful people, meals delicious. Excellent: accommodation and dinner beyond praise. Welcome relaxed, warm and personal. Great care to make us comfortable.

In Charlton, a few miles to the west, is **MELON COTTAGE VINEYARD** from the 200 vines of which come about a thousand bottles of dry white wine each year (go in October to see the harvest, and in spring for the bottling). It is known that the Romans, too, had vineyards in the area. The Pountneys' cottage has 39-inch stone walls, parts dating from mediaeval times. There are small stone-mullioned windows; one large bedroom is under the exposed rafters of the roof. (The

Somerset Wagon in Chilcompton serves good meals.) £12–£14.
Readers' comments: Very comfortable. Excellent hospitality. [Tel: 0761 435090; postcode: BA3 5TN]

PILLMEAD HOUSE   **C D M PT S**
North Lane, Buriton, Hampshire, GU31 5RS   Tel: 0730 266795
South of Petersfield. Nearest main road: A3 from Petersfield to Portsmouth.

2 Bedrooms. £18.50. Both have own bath/shower/toilet. Tea/coffee facilities. TV. Views of garden, country. No smoking. Washing machine on request.
Dinner. £12 for 3 courses (with choices) and coffee, at 7pm (not Sundays). Non-residents not admitted. Vegetarian or special diets if ordered. Wine can be brought in. No smoking. **Light suppers** if ordered.
1 Sitting-room. With open fire, central heating. No smoking.
Large garden

The lozenge-paned windows and brick-and-flint walls are typical of many houses in this area, but the Tudor chimneys – very elaborate, and 8 feet high – came from a mansion.

The house overlooks a valley, its lawn and rock garden descending steeply among terraced beds of roses and lavender. Visitors can enjoy a view of the Queen Elizabeth country park and Butser Hill while drinking their after-dinner coffee in the garden.

The dining-room's bow windows, too, make the most of the view. This is a pretty room, with pink wildflower curtains and Victorian mahogany furniture.

Upstairs, white walls contrast with moss-green carpets. One bedroom, cottage-style, has peach fabrics and patchwork cushions; in another primrose predominates, with a patchwork bedspread and cushions. (Baby-sitting available.)

Sarah Moss serves such meals as goose-egg soufflé, guinea-fowl and compote of figs and raspberries – using much produce from her large kitchen garden.

In Buriton, a picturesque downland village, are a Norman church and two ponds. All around are pleasant walks; and, a few miles away, the historic towns of Portsmouth, Chichester and Winchester.

Readers' comments: Excellent: our second visit.

There really are toads at **TOAD'S ALLEY** in South Lane on the other side of Buriton, home of interior designer Patricia Bushall. They can sometimes be seen heading to the stream which lies between the garden and the crest along which walkers follow the South Downs Way. The secluded house comprises three tiny farmworkers' cottages built in the 15th century, with brick-floored hall and low-sloping ceilings upstairs. Both bedrooms have splendid views of sheep grazing on the hillside. A sitting-room for guests is attractively furnished, like the other rooms, with pale colours.

Meals are taken at a handsome, oval table of oak. A typical dinner menu might include stuffed tomatoes, lemon and lime pork, and pancakes. £15–£18 (b & b). [Tel: 0730 263880; postcode: GU31 5RU]

PIPPS FORD

Needham Market, Suffolk, IP6 8LJ   Tel: 044979 208
North of Ipswich. Nearest main road: A45 from Ipswich to Bury St Edmunds.

6 Bedrooms. £17.50–£29.50 (less for 7 nights). Prices go up in April. All have own bath/shower/toilet. Tea/coffee facilities. Views of garden, country, river. No smoking. Washing machine on request.
Dinner. £19 for 4 courses (with some choices) and coffee, at 7.15pm (not Sundays). Vegetarian or special diets if ordered. Wine can be ordered. **Light suppers** if ordered, in winter.
3 Sitting-rooms. With open fire, central heating, TV, video, piano, record-player.
Large garden
Closed from mid-December to mid-January.

On a stretch of the River Gipping that has been designated an area of outstanding natural beauty stands a large Tudor farmhouse. Raewyn Hackett-Jones has made patchwork quilts or cushion-covers for every room and searched out attractive fabrics (Laura Ashley, French ones and so on) for curtains or upholstery. She puts flowers in each bedroom. Many of the beds are collectors' pieces: a four-poster, a French provincial one and several ornamental brass beds. Oriental rugs cover floors of wood or stone. Even the bathrooms attached to each bedroom are attractive. One is spectacular, with a huge oval bath. Some bedrooms are in converted stables, with sitting-room.

This is a house of inglenook fireplaces, sloping floors, low beams and historic associations, for it once belonged to Tudor chronicler Richard Hakluyt. There are three sitting-rooms and in one visitors can enjoy the family's huge collection of records. Meals may be served in a flowery conservatory, grapes overhead.

Breakfasts are exceptional. From an enormous choice, you could select exotic juices; home-made sausages or black pudding; home-made yogurt, croissants or cinnamon toast; waffles, crumpets, muffins; kidneys, mackerel, fishcakes.

Popular dinner dishes include avocado and smoked salmon baked with cheese; breast of duck with port; a roulade of salmon, turbot and spinach; fillet of beef; home-made ice creams; traditional puddings and tropical fruits.

Beyond the garden (with croquet, tennis and swimming-pool), there is coarse fishing in the river, where cricket-bat willows grow, and a Roman site. Interesting places to visit by car are Constable country, Aldeburgh and Ipswich.

Readers' comments: Most impressed; made very welcome; food absolutely super; most hospitable place; relaxed and informal, thoroughly happy and comfortable; delightful house, beautifully furnished; food and service outstanding; one of the best holidays ever; friendly good humour. A fitting climax to our wonderful trip with your book. Charming and talented hostess, food beautifully garnished.

Some proprietors stipulate a minimum stay of two nights at weekends or peak seasons; or they will accept one-nighters only at short notice (that is, only if no lengthier booking has yet been made).

POLETREES FARM
Ludgershall Road, Brill, Buckinghamshire, HP18 9TZ   Tel: 0844 238276
West of Aylesbury. Nearest main road: A41 from Aylesbury to Bicester
(and M40, junction 8).

2 Bedrooms. £16 (less for continental breakfast). Tea facilities. TV. Views of garden, country.
Dinner. £12 for 4 courses and coffee, at 6.30pm. Non-residents not admitted. Special diets if ordered. Wine can be brought in. **Light suppers** if ordered.
1 Sitting-room. With open fire, central heating, TV.
Large garden

There is clematis round the porch, baskets brimming with begonias and lobelias hang on the walls, and all around are roses, apple trees and views of fields: a scene of total peace. Inside, stone walls, oak beams and an inglenook with a rare 15th-century window beside it – tiny oak mullions and wood-pegged shutters – have survived the centuries. The water for the house still comes from a spring.

Anita Cooper has furnished her ancient home well. In the dining-room, a thick blue carpet is complemented by chair and curtain fabric of flowery blue-and-cream and bedrooms are pleasantly decorated too, with handsome walnut furniture. She caned the bedheads herself. In the sitting-room there is a collection of keys – all from the old Brill railway, closed in 1926, and a collection of earthenware boots.

Dinner may comprise such dishes as home-made soup, roast pork, chocolate mousse, and cheese with fruit.

The nearby village of Ludgershall is where Wycliffe started his great work of translating the Bible into English.

Readers' comments: Fantastic weekend! Very friendly; felt totally at home. Comfortable, and lovely breakfasts. Would recommend Poletrees time and time again.

Just over the county border in Oxfordshire, at Arncott Road, Horton-cum-Studley, is **STUDLEY FARM-HOUSE**. It is the home of Jean Hicks, a gifted flautist who sometimes organizes chamber-music sessions for guests wanting either to participate or to listen. The Victorian façade gives no hint of what lies within: oak beams, flagstone floors and inglenooks that date back to the 16th century. Throughout the house there are pale colour schemes and good carpets. Bedrooms have en suite facilities. B & b only, but there is a kitchen for

making snack suppers. No smoking. £19– £23.
Readers' comments: Comfortable, spacious, peaceful. Friendly hospitality. Thoroughly enjoyed three stays. Absolutely delightful and welcoming. Spacious, lovely room. [Tel: 0865 351286; postcode: OX9 1BP]

PONDEN HALL

CDS

Stanbury, West Yorkshire, BD22 0HR   Tel: 0535 644154

South-west of Keighley. Nearest main road: A6033 from Hebden Bridge to Keighley.

3 Bedrooms. £15–£16. Some have own toilet. Tea/coffee facilities. Views of garden, country. Washing machine on request.
Dinner. £8 for 3 courses and coffee, at 7pm. Vegetarian or special diets if ordered. Wine can be brought in.
1 Sitting-room. With open fire, central heating, piano, record-player.
Large garden

Emily Brontë knew Ponden Hall well: she often walked the three miles from Haworth and is supposed to have based Thrushcross Grange on the house. One of the objects of her visits was to use the library, which then contained books on the law of tenancy and inheritance which no doubt helped her to plot *Wuthering Heights*.

Now the library is a guest bedroom and, though the books are gone, one wall is still covered by the oak cupboards which held them (with a large portrait of Gladstone gazing at them). All the bedrooms are of interest, with mullioned and transomed windows, stone fireplaces, and beamed ceilings. A very large room, often used by parties of walkers or occasionally for courses, has a 'ceiling' consisting of woollen fabric draped from purlin to purlin. The fabric was made at the Hall, where there was a hand-weaving enterprise until a few years ago. This explains the attractive striped bedspreads, rugs and wall hangings which are used throughout the house.

Ponden Hall was occupied by the same family from at least the beginning of the 17th century until a hundred years ago (a booklet traces its history), and the house has remained almost unchanged since an extension was built in 1801. The 'great chamber', in the Elizabethan part, is now the guests' sitting- and dining-room. At one end are a big fireplace, now with an iron stove where logs burn, and comfortable settees. At the other is a dining-table which can seat as many as 18 people: it was a cloth-cutter's table. Here Brenda Taylor and her helpers serve robust and well-cooked meals, always starting with a home-made soup with good bread: then, for instance, chicken roasted with tarragon and lemon, with a big variety of well-prepared vegetables, many of them fresh from the garden, followed by plum crumble with cream or Greek yogurt.

Outside are trees and farmland, and the Pennine Way. There is a shelter for long-distance walkers by a ruined farm building, and many of them camp here or stop in the house, appreciating the welcoming and informal atmosphere. Below is a small reservoir, with some opportunities for watersports.

Haworth, which makes the most of its Brontë connections, is an obvious draw here, as is the Worth Valley Steam Railway, but there is scope for plenty of rewarding day trips: to Bradford (see elsewhere in this book for some of its attractions); and Ilkley, an old spa town which has retained much of its original character.

POOL HOUSE HOTEL   C
Hanley Road, Upton-upon-Severn, Worcestershire, WR8 0PA
Tel: 0684 592151
South-west of Great Malvern. Nearest main road: A4104 from Pershore
towards Ledbury (also M5, junction 8; and M50, junction 1).

rear view

9 Bedrooms. £17.50–£28 (less for 2
nights). Prices go up in April. Some have
own bath/shower/toilet. TV. Views of
garden, country, river. No smoking.
Clothes-washing on request.
Light suppers if ordered.
2 Sitting-rooms. With open fire, central
heating, TV. Bar.
Large garden
Closed in December.

I have included this hotel for its superb river-bank setting, with gardens that
make the most of this. Herbaceous borders wander among lawns with fruit
trees, sloping down to the waterside. The 18th-century house is simply furnished.
I thought bedroom 2 attractive: it has a rose-and-cream colour scheme and
a good view of the river. Jill Webb's flower arrangements are a feature of
the house.

Beyond the peach dining-room is a hexagonal TV room with big armchairs
and a door leading to the garden; and then a sitting-room with log fire. In the
grounds, croquet and fishing are available.

From the house one enjoys views of the Malvern Hills. Not far off is the River
Avon, the Cotswolds, 'Shakespeare country' and the lovely Wye Valley. Other
sightseeing possibilities include Tewkesbury Abbey, Cheltenham spa, Worcester
cathedral (and the Royal Worcester factory), Hereford and Gloucester (two more
cathedrals). Upton itself is a delightful old market town, as is Ledbury. The
Malverns have a spring garden show, Hidcote is near, and Pershore Agricultural
College grounds are well worth visiting. Racing, fishing, cricket and birdwatching
at the waterfowl sanctuary are other pursuits which bring visitors here.

In Upton-upon-Severn itself (a small town that needs to be explored on foot
and by boat), there are plaques dotted about on sites of historic events – the most
photographed one describes how Cromwell was acclaimed in 1651 'with
abundance of joy and shouting' after his victory at the Battle of Upton. The
town's history, which goes back to Saxon times, is displayed in its heritage
centre (in the old cupola-topped church tower). You can go as far as Tewkesbury
on the pleasure-cruiser, or simply stay in Upton to make the most of its
little shops, bistros and byways. The 'Three Counties' agricultural show takes
place nearby.

Readers' comments: Most helpful. Food and accommodation excellent. Very
enjoyable week's stay. The loveliest garden; friendly people. Beautiful setting.
An absolute gem! Best so far. Delightful house, beautiful location. Looked after
us very well. Definitely to be repeated.

Prices are per person in a double room at the beginning of the year.

PORTWELL HOUSE
C D M PT

Market Place, Faringdon, Oxfordshire, SN7 7HU   Tel: 0367 240197
South of Witney. Nearest main road: A420 from Oxford to Swindon.

7 Bedrooms. £16 (less for 3 nights). Bargain breaks. All have own bath/toilet. Tea/coffee facilities. TV. Washing machine on request.
Dinner. £8–£9 for 3 courses (with choices) and coffee, at 7–8pm (not Sundays). Non-residents not admitted. Vegetarian or special diets if ordered. Wine can be ordered. **Light suppers** if ordered.

The curiously wedge-shaped house, well over 300 years old, is run by David and Margo Manning as a small and friendly guest-house, fresh and neat. Up two winding staircases are bedrooms (each with bathroom) which have colourful curtains and duvets, comfortable chairs from which to watch television and, in some cases, views of the weekly market below. There is a ground-floor bedroom too, and a sitting-area with pot-plants, aquarium, armchairs and books. A typical dinner might be prawn cocktail, steak and apple pie.

Faringdon is a pretty town – a place of mossy roofs, old inn signs, swinging lamps and clocks on brackets, with a colonnaded Buttermarket. Brickwork, stone and colourful stucco give the streets variety, and there is an ancient church half-hidden behind great yews (one of many in this area). A good centre for public transport and for many sports, it is at the heart of an area full of interest with plenty to explore. In the spring, the grounds of nearby Faringdon House produce a wonderful display of flowers. This was the home of Lord Berners (the model for Lord Merlin in *The Pursuit of Love*), who also built the Folly Tower nearby.

In the surrounding Vale of the White Horse there are plenty of good canalside walks (with revitalizing little inns along the way); Uffington church, which has memories of Tom Brown (of *Tom Brown's Schooldays*); and the prehistoric white horse itself, cut out of the turf on the chalk downs.

Readers' comments: Kindness, attention and hospitality. Pleasant and comfortable; the best bargain for a long time. Excellent standards, friendliness, very happy atmosphere. Outstanding. Excellent in every way. Cannot praise too highly, warm welcome. Attractive, roomy bedrooms. Excellent atmosphere. Very nice.

Della Barnard's foals are one of the attractions at **BOWLING GREEN FARM** on Stanford Road, just outside Faringdon, and the pedigree Charolais cattle another. The house itself, built in 1717, has fine views across the vale. Breakfasts (and snack suppers) are served in the spacious bedrooms: one is on the ground floor, with sliding glass doors opening onto the garden – no bowling green now! There is a

sitting-room. £19–£20. [Tel: 0367 240229; postcode: SN7 8EZ]

PRESTON FARM C(4) S

Harberton, Devon, TQ9 7SW   Tel: 0803 862235

South of Totnes. Nearest main road: A381 from Totnes to Kingsbridge.

3 Bedrooms. £16–£17. Prices go up from Easter. Some have own bath/shower/toilet. Tea/coffee facilities. TV. Views of garden, country. Washing machine on request.
Dinner. £10 for 4 courses and coffee, at 6.45pm. Non-residents not admitted. Vegetarian or special diets if ordered. Wine can be brought in. No smoking.
1 Sitting-room. With open fire, central heating, TV, record-player, video.
Small garden

It's unusual to find a working farm with its house right in a village (a very quiet one), but there used to be several such clustered together in Harberton. The Steers' house, built in 1680, has been in the same family for generations. All the rooms are comfortable, and bedrooms have pretty co-ordinated fabrics. There is good home cooking at dinner, with dishes as varied as pancakes stuffed with salmon au gratin, chicken Marengo, roasts, pies, baked Alaska, treacle pudding. The ingredients are mostly home-grown or local. Breakfast comes on 'help-your-self' platters – conventional bacon and eggs or more unusual things like hog's pudding or smoked haddock.

Harberton is a picturesque cluster of old cottages with colourful gardens, set in a valley. Its 13th-century church has a magnificent painted screen and stained glass windows. The local inn is of equal antiquity. Preston Farm was once a manor house, which is why rooms are spacious.

Readers' comments: Absolutely marvellous. Excellent accommodation, super meals, everything delightful. First-class in every way. Happy atmosphere. A delight to be there – visited twice. Wonderful value. Quite the best place we have ever stayed. A perfect week. Excellent meals, beautifully served.

At the other end of Harberton village is **FORD FARMHOUSE**. Within its white walls are a low-beamed dining-room (furnished with country Chippendale chairs and a dresser with pretty plates), an upstairs sitting-room, and delightful little bedrooms, some with flowery views of the small, wandering garden and stream. Breakfast options include particularly tasty sausages, kidneys or liver, tea-cakes or croissants. Sheila Edwards will also provide light suppers if ordered. Guests also enjoy eating at the Church House Inn. £15.50–£17.

Readers' comments: Excellent. Superb breakfast. Delightful house and garden. Idyllic location. Truly welcoming. [Tel: 0803 863539; postcode: TQ9 7SJ]

283

PRIORY COTTAGE   C(5) S
Low Corner, Butley, Suffolk, IP12 3QD   Tel: 0394 450382
East of Woodbridge. Nearest main road: A12 from Ipswich to Lowestoft.

5 Bedrooms. £12.50–£20. Some have own bath/shower/toilet. Tea/coffee facilities. Views of garden, country, river. No smoking. Washing machine on request.
Dinner (by agreement). £12.50 for 3 courses and coffee, at 7pm. Non-residents not admitted. Vegetarian or special diets if ordered. Wine can be brought in. No smoking.
1 Sitting-room. With open fire, central heating, TV, video, record-player. No smoking.
Large garden

On arrival, visitors are greeted by a Muscovy duck who has made the well-head his own throne; all around is a prettily landscaped garden.

The entrance hall has an unusual floor of polished 'pamment' tiles, sofas and arrangements of dried flowers. There are velvet chairs in the pale green L-shaped sitting-room, and a log stove. In the dining-room (pine table, dresser and Windsor chairs) Rosemary Newnham serves dinner – if ordered in advance – which may comprise sherry, soup or mousse, a casserole or pie, fruit fool or meringues. Alternatively, there are several inns and restaurants in the area: at one inn, Suffolk folk songs can be heard on Sundays.

Upstairs, rooms with clear bright colours, flowery wallpaper friezes, pine doors and beds, and louvred built-ins are neat and cheerful: some have views of Butley Creek and the bird reserve on Havergate Island. I particularly liked the blue-and-white one which has a prettily draped bed and linen trimmed with broderie anglaise. (Baby-sitting and Sunday lunch are available.)

The cottage is in an area designated as being of outstanding natural beauty, and completely unspoilt. It is virtually on the Suffolk Coast Path (50 miles of footpath and bridleway) which wanders through forests where deer roam and along a shore much frequented by migrant wildfowl and by small yachts. Beyond the elaborately carved gatehouse of Butley Priory lies Orford – celebrated for its oysterage and for its huge polygonal castle (early Norman). Further up the coast is the old-fashioned resort of Aldeburgh (made famous by Britten's opera, 'Peter Grimes'), with an internationally famous music festival centred on the Maltings at nearby Snape and with events in numerous churches too. Inland lies Framlingham and another outstanding castle. South of the sailing centre of Woodbridge is the only big resort, Felixstowe: sedate and orderly, with well-tended flowerbeds along the seafront.

The sunny, breezy coast here has been much eroded (entire towns have vanished into the sea after floods or storms) and so the principal road lies some way inland (through heaths and across estuaries), with only lanes penetrating to the shore, which means the area is undisturbed by traffic or crowds. There are any number of outings: horse-drawn wagon rides, walks with a naturalist, a cruise in a motor launch, a cordon bleu picnic with champagne and much else.

Readers' comments: Beautiful location. Exceptionally well furnished. Friendly, hospitable and attentive. Food was superb. Wonderful, convivial evenings. Could not have had better accommodation, food and friendliness.

PRIORY FARMHOUSE

C D S

Hodsock Priory Estate, Blyth, Nottinghamshire, S81 0TY
Tel: 0909 591768 or 474299
North of Worksop. Nearest main road: A1 from Newark towards Doncaster.

4 Bedrooms. £14.50–£16 (less for 7 nights). Some have own bath/shower/toilet. Tea/coffee facilities. Views of garden, country. No smoking. Washing machine on request.
Dinner. £6.50 for 3 courses and coffee, at 6–8pm. Non-residents not admitted. Vegetarian or special diets if ordered. Wine can be brought in. No smoking.
1 Sitting-room. With open fire, TV. No smoking.
Small garden

No priory ever existed here; but during the Gothic Revival, when the ancient mansion of Hodsock was extended (1823–33), it was fashionable to give houses ecclesiastical names. The architect, Ambrose Poynter, was both a pioneer of the Gothic Revival style and a founder of the Royal Institute of British Architects.

In its 1000-acre grounds there are secluded walks and fine views of the mansion and its 15th-century gatehouse. At Hodsock Priory's gardens (sometimes open to the public) Lady Buchanan runs gardening courses.

The farmhouse is adjacent to the mansion, of which there is an imposing view as you approach along the narrow drive that stretches across the landscaped park.

Pat Buckley and Sylvia Mellars, the friends who together run the guest-house, live a stone's throw from the front door; both grew up on the estate and are knowledgeable guides to what to see in the neighbourhood. Rooms are light and pleasant, predominantly cream and brown; not elegantly furnished but comfortable and immaculate. Meals, too, are homely: for instance, soup, chicken and fruit crumble – with much emphasis on fresh local vegetables and fruit.

Nottinghamshire is not yet a famous tourist area, but it is full of unusual attractions: with working windmills, the Robin Hood Centre in Sherwood Forest and Tim Clarke's Modern Farm Centre at Farnsfield, it is ideal for children; while adults might prefer to wander down the longest tree-lined drive in Europe (Clumber Park) or among the outdoor sculptures in the gardens at Rufford Park. In Worksop is 'Mr Straw's House' (NT), a 1920s time-capsule.

Readers' comments: Extremely pleasant and friendly, nothing is too much trouble.

In the nearby village of Firbeck is **YEWS FARMHOUSE**, mainly 18th-century, which faces a big croquet lawn bounded by a haha, beyond which graze Jacob sheep against a backdrop of woodland and stream. It is exquisitely furnished: in one of the twin-bedded rooms, old carved oak bedheads stand against a Wedgwood blue wall. Catherine Stewart-Smith serves such dinners as home-made soup; lamb noisettes with at least three fresh vegetables; chocolate mousse

rear view

with cognac or whisky ginger syllabub, and cheeses. £20–£25 (b & b). [Tel: 0909 731458; postcode: S81 8JW]

PROSPECT HILL HOTEL   C
Kirkoswald, Cumbria, CA10 1ER   Tel: 0768 898500
North of Penrith. Nearest main road: A6 from Penrith to Carlisle
(and M6, junction 41).

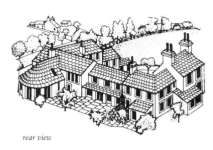

rear view

11 Bedrooms. £19–£28.50 (less for 3 nights or continental breakfast; and mid-week). Prices may go up from May. Bargain breaks. Some have own bath/shower/toilet. Tea/coffee facilities. Views of garden, country. Washing machine on request.
Dinner. A la carte or £13 for 3 courses (with choices), at 7–9pm. Vegetarian dishes available. Wine can be ordered. **Light suppers.**
2 Sitting-rooms. With open fire, central heating, TV. **Bar.**
Large garden

A group of 18th-century farm buildings close to a village that feels remote (though the M6 is only 9 miles away) has been turned into a hotel with great individuality by Isa and John Henderson (he was formerly a television designer).

They reconstructed an old gin case, a half-round room within which ponies walked round and round powering wheels to grind grain.

A collection of old farm implements is displayed on the sandstone walls in the bar (once a byre, with low-beamed ceiling and flagged floor).

Every bedroom is individually decorated, and traditional materials have been used. Many rooms still have walls of rugged stone, and a number have brass bedsteads with patchwork quilts. Homespun curtains, thick carpets and country colours like peat or moss are all in keeping with the character of the place. The former coach house has been turned into an annexe where one room is ideal for a family. There is a glassed-in porch with cane furniture and a terrace.

The menu features such popular dishes as sautéed mushrooms with Parmesan cheese, pan-fried lamb steak in a mead and rosemary sauce, hot Cumberland rum-nicky or chocolate whisky gâteau. There is a vegetarian menu and an extensive wine-list. Breakfast may include green figs and smoked haddock, as well as the more usual options.

John has produced his own leaflets of walks, from evening strolls to half-day hikes, with notes about where deer can be seen, a spectacular waterfall in a gorge, riverside paths, a forest nature reserve, caves and castle ruins. The neighbourhood is full of ancient villages, the prehistoric stones of 'Long Meg' and a pottery still using a Victorian steam-engine. Kirkoswald is a good choice for a winter break.

Maps, bicycles and Wellington boots can be hired.

Readers' comments: Comfortable and well organized; good cuisine; excellent amenities, nothing was too much trouble; very good in all respects; well decorated rooms; good and thoughtful service; value for money. Attractively converted and with good food. Thoroughly enjoyed our stay, food excellent. Full marks for service, cuisine and superb farmhouse conversion and lovely surroundings.

When writing to me, if you want a reply please enclose an International Reply Coupon.

QUARRY HOUSE S
Church Road, Newcastle-on-Clun, Shropshire, SY7 8QJ   Tel: 0588 640774
North-west of Knighton (Powys). Nearest main road: A488 from Clun to Knighton.

3 Bedrooms. £16–£19 (less for 4 nights). Prices go up at Easter. One has own bath/shower/toilet. Tea/coffee facilities. Views of garden, country. No smoking. Washing machine on request.
Dinner (minimum of 4 people, staying 3 nights). £12.50 for 4 courses and coffee, at 7.30pm. Non-residents not admitted. Wine can be brought in. No smoking. **Light suppers** if ordered.
Small garden

The small, old quarry that gives this very modern house its name lies behind it. The Woodwards cleared the quarry of debris and landscaped it to make an attractive backdrop to their architect-designed home, a feature of which is two ground-to-roof walls of glass opening onto the garden. Light floods into rooms that were created from what was once a stone barn, its great rafters skilfully re-used upstairs. The unusual floor slates are not local but came from East Africa. A staircase (with balusters perforated in varied leaf shapes) rises to a gallery that provides a sitting-area for visitors, alongside pretty blue-and-white bedrooms and attractive bathrooms. In the open-plan dining/sitting-room, divided by a hearth with big log stove, Vanessa serves such meals as home-made pâté, a roast or casserole and then one of the puddings which are her speciality.

Sheltering on the side of a valley outside the unspoilt little town of Clun is **WOODSIDE OLD FARMHOUSE**. There are fine views and much wildlife: birds, frogs, even bats at twilight. Trout inhabit a pool of pink waterlilies fringed with kingcups. The house is at the foot of a sloping lawn with willow tree, its old stone walls made colourful by baskets of busy Lizzies. Thick walls help to create a cosy sitting-room, and in the dining-room beams still carry old bacon-hooks. Cottage-style bedrooms are light and bright. (Baby-sitting available.) For dinner Margaret Wall may offer you cucumber soup, steak-and-kidney pie and a compote made from the garden's summer fruit, or

perhaps chocolate fudge pudding at other seasons. £13–£15 (b & b).
Readers' comments: Accommodation and cuisine superb. Lovely house in beautiful surroundings. [Tel: 0588 640695; postcode: SY7 0JB]

Book well ahead: many of these houses have few rooms. Do not expect dinner if you have not booked it or if you arrive late.

RACEHORSE COTTAGE

C(8) D PT

Nepcote, Findon, West Sussex, BN14 0SN   Tel: 0903 873783
North of Worthing. Nearest main road: A24 from Worthing to Dorking.

2 Bedrooms. £14. Tea/coffee facilities. Views of garden, country. Washing machine on request.
Dinner (if ordered). £11 for 3 courses and coffee, at 7.30pm. Non-residents not admitted. Vegetarian or special diets if ordered. Wine can be ordered.
1 Sitting-room. With open fire, central heating, TV, record-player.
Small garden

The flint-walled hamlet of Nepcote is almost part of 18th-century Findon village, celebrated for its three racing stables (and very ancient church). This explains the name of the cottage, for which the previous owner chose a roadside position where he could watch the strings of horses and their jockeys go by on their way to the surrounding South Downs for daily exercise. He built in traditional Sussex style: its upper storey weatherboarded, the doors panelled.

It is a pleasant, unpretentious home with an L-shaped sitting/dining-room with open fire, trim bedrooms that have velvet bedheads and views of the Downs. There is a small garden and glasshouse from which come the fresh vegetables and fruit that Jean Lloyd serves her guests. She is a keen cook and prepares such meals (if ordered in advance) as ramekins of eggs with Stilton and cream or melon with kiwi fruit; gammon with Cumberland sauce; and loganberry flan. Bread, muesli and jams are home-made. The Lloyds dine with their guests.

The area round here is not only scenic but full of gardens, stately homes, Roman remains and castles to visit. Walkers enjoy wending their way from Nepcote right up to Cissbury Ring, a prehistoric hill fort. South coast resorts within easy reach include sedate Worthing (a considerable number of retirement homes are here) and Brighton (celebrated for its oriental Pavilion and sophisticated pleasures). Arundel (castle, Catholic cathedral and wildfowl reserve) is also nearby.

Readers' comments: Everything necessary for comfort. Evening meal delicious.

Close to Worthing is the old village of Sompting, with a Rhenish-style Saxon church and, in Upper Brighton Road, **UPTON FARMHOUSE**, behind the handsome 18th-century façade of which are parts built in the 15th century. The bedrooms – which have soft colours, deep, velvety carpets and views over farmland – are all exceptionally spacious, immaculate and well equipped. Breakfast is served on lace tablecloths, with locally smoked kippers offered as an option. The massive sitting/dining-room is very comfortably furnished – its walls lined with

prints of old sailing ships. Penny Hall is a particularly caring hostess. Light suppers if ordered. £17.50 (b & b).
Readers' comments: Warm welcome, excellent food. [Tel: 0903 233706; postcode: BN14 9JU]

288

RECTORY FARM
Northmoor, Oxfordshire, OX8 1SX   Tel: 0865 300207
(Messages: 0865 300689)
South-west of Oxford. Nearest main road: A415 from Witney to Abingdon.

2 Bedrooms. £18.50–£19.50 (less for 3 nights). Both have own shower/toilet. Tea/coffee facilities. Views of garden, country. No smoking. Washing machine on request.
Light suppers only if ordered.
1 Sitting-room. With wood stove, central heating, TV, piano. No smoking.
Large garden
Closed in January.

Until a generation ago, this ancient stone farmhouse (the ogee arches of its fireplaces have been dated to the 15th century) was owned by St John's College, Oxford: college priests used to stay here when preaching at the adjacent church – which explains why one bedroom has such a finely decorated ceiling.

The deep-set windows are stone-mullioned, with views of fields, snowdrops (when I visited in February) and a great slate-roofed, timber dovecote that was built in the 18th century – like the house itself and the granary perched on its staddlestones, a listed building. The Floreys' 400 acres are used for sheep, cattle and crops – one of which is dried flowers (you can buy bunches to take home, or baskets already filled with Mary Anne's beautiful arrangements of them).

Having a growing family to look after, she provides light suppers only (by arrangement) but there are many restaurants near: I ate well at the Bear and Ragged Staff. Meals are served in a dining/sitting-room with chamfered beams overhead, red Turkey rugs on the floor, tapestry armchairs, and a sideboard laden with Victorian silver-plate.

The bedrooms are particularly spacious, light and attractively decorated, their shower rooms immaculate (outsize bath-towels much appreciated!); and their windows have farm or garden views. On the farm are Thames-side walks (fishing too). A series of lakes which were once gravel pits attract wildfowl.

17th-century **LEENA COTTAGE**, in picturesque old Stanton Harcourt, was extended in recent times by Chris Rathbone and a shapely swimming-pool put into the pretty garden. Guests sleep in antique brass beds in rooms with sprigged wallpapers and windows at each end. Some rooms have rugged stone walls, and in a stone inglenook with bread-oven, logs blaze on chilly mornings. Chris's young daughter won an award for her booklet on walks in

this lovely area. £14. [Tel: 0865 882177; postcode: OX8 1RP]

RED HOUSE

C(8) PT

Sidmouth Road, Lyme Regis, Dorset, DT7 3ES   Tel: 0297 442055

Nearest main road: A3052 from Lyme Regis to Exeter.

3 Bedrooms. £19–£24 (less for 4 nights). Prices go up at Easter. All have own bath/toilet. Tea/coffee facilities. TV. Views of garden, sea.
Light suppers if ordered.
Garden
Closed from December to February.

Delightful old Lyme has many claims to fame – Jane Austen; fossils (including dinosaur bones) found along its beaches; the landing of the rebel Monmouth in 1685 to start his abortive rebellion; and more recently *The French Lieutenant's Woman*, the author of which, John Fowles, lives locally.

When Geoffrey Griffin retired, he and his wife Elizabeth, a journalist, decided to move here and (inspired by reading previous editions of this book) run a bed-and-breakfast house. It wasn't any olde worlde cottage that they fell in love with but this dignified 'twenties house that had been built for Aldis (inventor of the famous signal-lamps which bear his name) on a superb site with a 40-mile sea view south-east as far as Portland Bill. It is a house with handsome features – iron-studded oak doors, leaded casements and window-seats, for example. On sunny mornings (occasionally even in late autumn), you can take breakfast on the wide verandah and enjoy sea breezes while you eat – at your feet, sloping lawns with colourful rhododendrons, camellias, fuchsias and wisteria. On chilly mornings, breakfast is served in an attractive room with a fire.

The bedrooms are excellent. Mine was 20 feet long, very comfortably furnished in period with the house, with a thick carpet. By contrast, there is an even larger family room in scarlet-and-white. Each bedroom is equipped with armchairs, TV, a refrigerator, flowers and books – the aim being to provide individual bedsitters for guests, as there is no communal sitting-room, only a large landing which has seats and a supply of leaflets, maps and local menus.

This is a perfect base from which to explore the locality. Sandy beaches with their shrimp-pools are ideal for children. There are excellent walks (in Marshwood Vale or along the coast) including nature trails; drives along lanes of primroses, bluebells and subtropical wildflowers in the downs; Hardy villages; National Trust houses. You can watch or take part in sea-sports and cider-making.

'They went to the sands, to watch the flowing of the tide, which a fine south-easterly breeze was bringing in with all the grandeur which so flat a shore admitted. They praised the morning; gloried in the sea; sympathized in the delight of the fresh-feeling breeze . . . "I am quite convinced that the sea air always does good".' Thus spoke Henrietta to her friend Anne, in Jane Austen's *Persuasion*; and at Lyme today the same sands, sea and air are still working their magic.

Readers' comments: Just perfect, equal to the best hotels, excellent value. Kindness itself, so caring. The best ever. Good value. Splendid views and pleasant gardens. Comfort and charm. Could not have been kinder, a marvellous place. We really enjoyed our stay. Beautiful accommodation and gracious hosts.

290

REGENCY HOUSE   C D PT X

Neatishead, Norfolk, NR12 8AD   Tel: 0692 630233

North-east of Norwich. Nearest main road: A1151 from Norwich to Stalham.

3 Bedrooms. £17.50–£20 (less for 2 nights). Prices go up in July. Bargain breaks. Two have own bath/toilet. Tea/coffee facilities. TV. Views of garden, country. **Light suppers** if ordered.
1 Sitting-room. With cassette-player.
Small garden

Former Manchester bank-manager Alan Wrigley was so touched by the friendliness of Neatishead people towards a newcomer that, after a few years here, he began planting wayside trees as a 'thank you': the total has already passed 4000. He and his wife Sue, formerly a *Daily Express* reporter, run this 18th-century guest-house to an immaculate standard.

The breakfasts are outstanding: standard issue is 2 sausages, 4 rashers of bacon, 6 mushrooms, 2 whole tomatoes, 2 slices of bread and as many eggs as you request! But if you prefer it, Sue will produce a vegetarian breakfast instead. This is served in an oak-panelled room with willow-pattern crockery on tables that were specially made by a local craftsman. Bedrooms have Laura Ashley fabrics (two have king-size beds). The sitting-room has red leather armchairs and a beamed ceiling.

Pretty little Neatishead – in the heart of the Norfolk Broads – fortunately does not attract the crowds which sometimes ruin Horning and Wroxham. There is a staithe (mooring) here for fifteen boats – and the Wrigleys have a 14-foot dinghy which visitors can use for fishing. For dinner, there is a choice of eating-places within yards of the guest-house.

Readers' comments: Welcoming, friendly, good breakfast. Large rooms, lovely furnishings. Amazing breakfasts, generous hospitality. The best b & b we've stayed in. Very neat, well-appointed rooms. Excellent in every way.

Off the Norwich Road to North Walsham is the huge, 18th-century **TOLL BARN**, now immaculately converted and handsomely furnished. Beyond two courtyard gardens with fountains are six spacious, ground-floor bedrooms. All have en suite facilities and pretty colour schemes; and are very well equipped. Annette Tofts provides good suppers which guests have in their rooms. Breakfast is served in the large, brick-and-beamed dining-room in the main house. £18–£20.

Readers' comments: Delightful home, superb conversion. Spacious, comfort-able. Ideal hosts, professional but warm and relaxed – and a half-melon for breakfast! Could have stayed forever! Food outstanding. [Tel: 0692 403063; postcode: NR28 0JB]

RICHMOND LODGE $\qquad$ C(6) D
Mursley, Buckinghamshire, MK17 0LE Tel: 0296 720275
South-west of Milton Keynes. Nearest main road: A421 from Bletchley to
Buckingham.

3 Bedrooms. £17.50–£20 (less for 3 nights). Some have own bath/shower/toilet. Tea/coffee facilities. TV. Views of garden, country. No smoking. Washing machine on request.
Dinner. £12.50 for 3 courses and coffee, at 7pm. Non-residents not admitted. Wine can be brought in. No smoking. **Light suppers** if ordered.
1 Sitting-room. With open fire, central heating, TV. No smoking.
Large garden

Just before the First World War, this house was built as a hunting lodge for a wealthy London butcher who frequented the area when buying beef-cattle and decided to make his weekend retreat in this high, windswept spot. The whole atmosphere is still one of sedate, solid comfort; and even the garden retains its original Edwardian formality (croquet and lawn tennis are available). From an immaculate lawn, with a stately blue cedar, there are views right down the Vale of Aylesbury with a glimpse of Waddesdon Manor, High Wycombe and Dunstable Downs. Yet London is only 35 minutes by train (from Leighton Buzzard).

Chris Abbey used to be a hotel manager and so her standards are very professional. Spotless rooms have well-chosen fabrics: for its view of the lily-pool, I thought the jade and strawberry bedroom the most attractive. Chris sometimes serves breakfast on a sunny patio where there are fuchsias and clematis. For dinner (if this is ordered in advance) she might cook you salmon mousse, pork chops with a celery and pineapple sauce, and (she loves doing puddings) summer pudding.

Buckinghamshire is a county of contrasts – leafy in the south, rising up into the Chiltern Hills where great beech trees flourish on the chalky soil, and then turning into a great fertile plain northwards (the Vale of Aylesbury). Here the landscape is threaded with little rivers. This is not an area for many spectacular views – that from Richmond Lodge is exceptional – but rather for the pleasures of making small, private discoveries of its beauties which include a wealth of ancient and interesting churches, for instance, and quite a lot of stately homes. These include several National Trust mansions, and 18th-century Stowe, now a school but open to the public – its landscaped gardens with classical buildings and six lakes are world-famous. You will find such varied diversions as Claydon House (Florence Nightingale memorabilia), Shuttleworth aircraft museum, and the National Rose Society's gardens. Near Milton Keynes are beautiful Fenny Lodge (18th-century waterside house now full of modern crafts) and Stacey Hill Museum of rural bygones. The Rothschilds' Waddesdon Manor and Stoke Bruerne's canal museum are also popular sights.

On the other side of the A5 is Bedfordshire – Woburn Abbey and safari park are here, Stockwood's gardens and craft workshops, Whipsnade Zoo, and the historic grounds of Wrest Park with 18th-century gardens that include a painted pavilion.

RIVER PARK FARM   C S

Lodsworth, Petworth, West Sussex, GU28 9DS   Tel: 07985 362

East of Midhurst. Nearest main road: A272 from Petworth to Midhurst.

4 Bedrooms. £16 (less for 3 nights). Tea/coffee facilities. Views of garden, country. No smoking.
Dinner. £7 for 2 courses (with choices) and coffee, at 7pm (not Wednesdays and Fridays). Non-residents not admitted. Wine can be brought in. No smoking.
1 Sitting-room. With central heating, TV.
Large garden
Closed from December to February.

The farm (of 340 acres of corn, bullocks, sheep and poultry) is in a secluded position among woods where, if you are up early enough, you may encounter deer. There is a 4½-acre lake with plentiful carp and ducks, and in front a pretty garden. The house itself, built in 1600, is old and beamy with comfortable bedrooms along twisting passageways. In the dining-room Pat Moss has a strikingly colourful collection of green leaf plates and wooden ducks. Outside are golden roses and wisteria clambering around the door. Altogether it is a tranquil spot, full of nooks and crannies – amazing, visitors think, because it is so close to London.

Pat does not do full-scale dinners (available elsewhere locally) but has a list of homely dishes like shepherd's pie or macaroni cheese, and for puddings like banana split she uses rich Jersey cream from the farm's own cows. Bread is home-baked and eggs free-range. There are flowers in every room. Pat also makes and sells marmalade, dried flowers and decorative herbal hangings. Coarse fishing available.

People come for the local walks and birdwatching (Pat has pinned up bird-identification charts and gives visitors field notes on the crops and wildlife in each season, with map, and her own daily nature notes); or to visit the many outstanding sights in this neighbourhood; or the polo or point-to-points at Cowdray; or to see the local game of stoolball played at Midhurst. There are many small country towns around here, streams running down into the River Rother, woodlands and picturesque villages with greens and duck-ponds, old inns and ancient churches, Arundel Castle, wildfowl reserves, Goodwood House and Roman remains. Turner knew and loved this area, staying at Petworth House where many of his paintings can be seen. It's a good area for antique shops, too. Garden-lovers head for West Dean and Denmans; and there is the open-air Weald and Downland Museum.

An attractive drive would be via Petworth, still with many 18th-century byways and, of course, one of the country's grandest mansions through the huge deerpark of which one can motor, to see some of the finest mosaics outside Italy in the big Roman villa tucked away among pretty lanes at Bignor. Near here is another hidden village, Bury, with thatched cottages beside the winding River Arun. On the way from here to Chichester is Boxgrove Priory, the tremendous and ancient church of which still survives.

Readers' comments: Warm hospitality, generous home cooking. Enjoyed ourselves so much that we have twice visited for a week. Marvellous setting and house, kind hosts, good food. Outstanding. Very relaxed atmosphere. Comfortable, quiet. Warm, relaxed, friendly atmosphere and lovely farm.

ROCK HOUSE X

Alport, Derbyshire, DE45 1LG   Tel: 0629 636736
South of Bakewell. Nearest main road: A6 from Bakewell to Matlock.

3 Bedrooms. £19. Price goes up after mid-April. All have own bath/shower/toilet. Tea/coffee facilities. Views of garden, country. No smoking. Washing machine on request.
Light suppers if ordered.
1 Sitting-room. With gas fire, central heating, TV. No smoking.
Small garden

The rock for which this house is named is a great crag of tufa (a type of volcanic stone, perforated like Gruyère cheese, which was formed 300 million years ago) rearing up alongside it.

Only a few yards from the 18th-century house two rivers join, splashing over weirs constructed long ago to contain trout downstream – you can watch these drifting in water so transparent that the locals call it 'gin-clear' (its purity is due to the limestone bed over which it runs). Lathkill Dale is a National Nature Reserve. Tony and Jan Statham are first-rate sources of information about the history of this most beautiful of valleys. They will lend maps, tell you the best riverside walks, and where to find river pools (created for washing sheep).

The front door opens straight into the stone-flagged sitting-room, its walls now painted mushroom, with buttoned velvet armchairs, where you will be served tea on arrival. Glass doors lead through to the breakfast-room.

By pre-arrangement, Jan may serve supper platters, beautifully presented (but most visitors go to the nearby Druid Inn or other pubs). Breakfast possibilities include muffins, poached fruit, Staffordshire oatcakes, home-made jams and some vegetarian dishes. All bedrooms are well furnished.

Alport is well placed for touring either the wild and dramatic 'Dark Peak' (the stone there is millstone grit) or the more benign 'White Peak' (limestone), a fertile and verdant region. It is close to Chatsworth House and park with garden centre.

Readers' comments: Very comfortable and a warm welcome. Breakfast excellent, rooms large and comfortable. Beautiful house, much pampering, what breakfasts! One of our favourites, lovely house; thoughtful and friendly people. A charming house with lovely walks all round, and delicious breakfasts. Sorry to leave, hope to return. Very friendly, couldn't do enough for us. One of the best.

As one of England's golf champions (1972), Mary Everard used to travel the world but eventually chose the remote hamlet of Rowland (just north of Bakewell) in which to settle down. Here, at 18th-century **HOLLY COTTAGE**, she welcomes guests to her elegant sitting-room, a raspberry-and-white dining-room furnished with old maple chairs from America, and pretty bedrooms with white board doors.

B & b only. £16–£17. [Tel: 0629 640624; postcode: DE45 1NR]

ROGAN'S C D PT

Satron, Gunnerside, North Yorkshire, DL11 6JW   Tel: 0748 86414
West of Richmond. Nearest main road: A684 from Leyburn to Sedbergh.

3 Bedrooms. £18–£19.50 (less for 7 nights). Bargain breaks. All have own bath/shower/toilet. Tea/coffee facilities. TV. Views of garden, country. No smoking. **Light suppers** if ordered.
1 Sitting-room. With open fire, central heating, cassette-player. No smoking.
Large garden
Closed in December.

When Maureen and Bill Trafford renovated Stable Cottage, they decided to call it after Rogan's Seat, the highest point in the hills that line Swaledale – though nobody seems to know who Rogan was. Visitors to this early 19th-century house have their own entrance to their sitting-room, where white-painted walls, bamboo furniture, and a colour scheme based on pink and green, together with vigorous house-plants, give a conservatory-like atmosphere. There is a large garden, from which footpaths lead directly into the countryside without the need to cross a road.

The bedrooms, also with white-painted textured walls, are fitted out in mahogany or pine; outlooks are leafy.

The house lies by the road which snakes through the series of villages and hamlets along Swaledale in the Yorkshire Dales National Park. The next village, Muker, is the largest and almost the last settlement before the watershed of the Pennines, where the River Swale rises. Here there is a shop for woollens hand-knitted by a team of farmers' wives and daughters, mostly from the wool of Swaledale sheep, the breed to which the valley has given its name. From near here, the Buttertubs Pass leads past Hardraw Force, one of the highest waterfalls in England, where brass band contests are held in a natural amphitheatre. This is a way into Wensleydale, perhaps for a particularly good pub meal at the King's Arms in Askrigg. Simpler pub meals are closer at hand: the Traffords will direct – or even drive – you to the best places.

The attractions of Swaledale, or within easy reach of it, include Richmond (with its Georgian theatre), castles, relics of past lead-mining, strange rock formations, craft workshops of many kinds, and – near the house – a bridge reputedly haunted by a headless dog.

Just along the road, **OXNOP HALL** is a working farm, where the 17th-century part of the main farmhouse has small-paned, stone-mullioned windows and oak beams. Here, a family or party could have their own sitting-room, with open fire. Some of the other accommodation is in a connecting, modernized barn. Annie Porter serves, for example, egg mayonnaise, a joint or chops, and home-made trifle.

£19 (b & b). [Tel: 0748 86253; messages: 0748 86504 or 886233; postcode: DL11 6JJ]

ROOKERY FARMHOUSE

CMS

Castle Carlton, Lincolnshire, LN11 8JF   Tel: 0507 450357
South-east of Louth. Nearest main road: A157 from Louth towards
Mablethorpe.

3 Bedrooms. £14.50. All have own bath/shower/toilet. Tea/coffee if required. Views of garden, country. No smoking. Washing machine on request.
Dinner. £8.50 for 4 courses and coffee, at 7–8pm. Non-residents not admitted. Vegetarian or special diets if ordered. Wine can be brought in. **Light suppers** if ordered.
2 Sitting-rooms. With open fire, central heating, record-player.
Large garden

Sweet peas and roses climb up the mellow brick front of the house, built in 1776, on which a sundial tells the hours. Bees and butterflies hover over catmint, hanging-baskets fill the verandah with colour, and at the back a garden wanders from one level to another: herbaceous beds, a tree peony, tai haku cherry and, in spring, drifts of daffodils and irises. Often there are spectacular sunsets to enjoy when relaxing here after dinner.

Inside the house, there are antiques; pot-plants on tiled window-sills; and a piano in the high-ceilinged dining-room which was once a barn – its original brick walls are still exposed; board-and-latch doors; low beams. In a book-lined 'snug' are comfortable velvet chairs and everywhere are pictures and fresh flowers. One (single) bedroom and a shower are on the ground floor.

Annemarie Gosse (Danish-born) makes the most of the excellent vegetables and fruit which Lincolnshire's rich fenland soil produces – growing a great deal organically herself. She bakes her own bread and croissants; honey, trout and sausages are all local. A typical dinner might start with crab, followed by pigeon or rabbit pie and then home-made ice cream with fruit sauce, and cheeses. Alternatively, you can have a simple supper (such as fish pie and treacle tart). The Gosses often dine with their guests and Peter (formerly a history teacher) is a mine of information on the local history of the area (which has special Australian and American connections) and on its wildlife too. (Baby-sitting available.)

The flat Lincolnshire coast has its own character: bracing breezes have swept the sands up into high dunes at certain points, the tides go out so far that the sea is sometimes almost out of sight, and it is still shallow when you do get to it. The North Sea constantly sweeps Yorkshire soil down here, creating (at Gibraltar Point) salt marshes frequented by seals, migrant birds and birdwatchers – a very different spectacle (with fine views over The Wash) from that offered by the over-jolly resorts, from Cleethorpes to Skegness. Inland are all the attractions of the Wolds.

If you drive north along the coast, you will come to a nature reserve with natterjack toads, Donna Nook (a good hunting-ground for seashells), Cleethorpes – from the promenade of which one can watch the procession of ships heading for the Humber, and the huge fishing port of Grimsby. It is worth pressing on to see the 600-year-old sculptures of ruined Thornton Abbey.

Readers' comments: Enjoyable experience. Warm welcome. Excellent dinner. Vast, delicious breakfast. Gastronomic delight. Good taste and good quality.

RUDSTONE WALK FARM

South Cave, Humberside, HU15 2AH   Tel: 0430 422230

CDMSX

West of Hull. Nearest main road: A1034 from Market Weighton towards Hull
(and M62, junction 38).

bath/shower/toilet. Tea/coffee facilities. TV.
Views of garden, country, river. Balcony
(some). No smoking (in some). Washing
machine on request.
Dinner. £9.50–£15 for 1–3 courses and
coffee, at 7–7.30pm. Non-residents not
admitted. Vegetarian or special diets if
ordered. Wine can be ordered. No smoking.
Light suppers if ordered.
2 Sitting-rooms. With open fire, central
heating, TV, video, piano, record-player.
No smoking (in one). **Bar.**
Large garden

14 Bedrooms. £20–£25 **to readers
of this book only.** All have own

Always painted white to serve as a landmark for sailors on the Humber estuary,
this farmhouse stands on the highest point of a plain bounded by the river to the
south and the sea to the east. It goes without saying that the views are wide: as far
as 50 miles on a clear day, when York can be seen across the lawn. The farm,
built on a site occupied since Roman times, is mentioned in Domesday Book (the
name comes from that of a vanished Saxon hamlet), and its oldest buildings date
back at least 400 years.

The main sitting-room is in the 18th-century part: a large space recently
created from two rooms, it has a big inglenook fireplace built of stone and
ornamented with copper kettles. There are chintz-covered settees and a grand
piano, and the windows have been enlarged to take advantage of the view. A
smaller, stone-walled room has been modernized and fitted with a bar and French
windows opening onto the garden which has croquet and lawn tennis.

The dining-room was once the hired hands' quarters. Here, under a boarded
ceiling from which corn dollies hang, guests dine round one enormous table on,
for instance, soup, roast pork, oranges in Grand Marnier, and cheese. There are
lots of family antiques around.

The bedrooms are attractive. In one, decorated in Wedgwood blue, there is a
damask-covered sofa; another room, in pink and green, has a lace bedspread from
Africa. Along a covered flagged path are rooms suitable for families or guests
requiring ground-floor accommodation. These are available either on a self-catering or b & b basis. Each 'cottage', in a row converted from a farm building to an
architect's design, has the use of a sitting-room and a small kitchen. French windows in most of these rooms open onto a terrace overlooking the fields of the
farm, entirely arable now except for two pet shire horses. The farm is run by
Pauline Greenwood's two sons while she looks after not only visitors but also
participants in the small conferences for which there are facilities. (Sunday lunch
is also available; baby-sitting can be arranged.)

Beverley and York (see other pages of this book) and half a dozen mansions
are easily reached by car, and there are plenty of footpaths for walking in the
Wolds. The nearest city is Hull – still a busy port after many centuries, though
the original docks, by the historic Old Town, have been filled in to create open
space or have been converted into a marina. You can visit the Jacobean birthplace
of William Wilberforce, with relics of the slave trade he helped to abolish.

RUTLAND COTTAGES   C S X
5 Cedar Street, Braunston-in-Rutland, Leicestershire, LE15 8QS
Tel: 0572 722049
South-west of Oakham. Nearest main road: A6003 from Oakham to Kettering.

5 Bedrooms. £15–£18 (less for 3 nights). Some have own bath/shower/toilet. Tea/coffee facilities. TV. Views of garden, country. No smoking.
Light suppers if ordered. Vegetarian or special diets. No smoking.
2 Sitting-rooms. With open fire, central heating, TV, piano. No smoking.
Small garden

A 17th-century bakehouse is the home of John and Connie Beadman (she taught music); and in addition they own nearby cottages let on a bed-and-breakfast basis. All guests take breakfast together in the beamed dining-room of the house (on Sundays, cooked breakfasts are available only between 7.30 and 8.30am). Visitors can eat at two inns in this pretty conservation village of golden stone, or Connie will provide sandwich suppers.

Guests have the use of the Beadmans' huge and beautifully furnished sitting-room (it has a see-through stone fireplace in the middle, and a 'curfew window' through which the village watchman could check that the baker's fires had been properly extinguished for the night). Its windows open onto a heather garden.

John and his sons are keen bell-ringers, willing to take visitors on guided tours up into the bell-towers of local churches. This is a good area for walks or cycling (maps on loan) and other country pursuits, and for sightseeing too: the historic schools at Uppingham and Oundle, the mediaeval town of Stamford, castles at Rockingham and Belvoir as well as the stately homes of Burghley and Belton – at the former, horse trials take place each September. The former county of Rutland still has its own rural museum. Connie often helps visitors trace their family history locally.

Man-made reservoirs when naturalized can be as beautiful as any lake. Rutland Water, one of the greatest reservoirs in northern Europe, is particularly fine. There are paths around its wandering perimeter, pleasure boats on it, a nature reserve and trail, and areas devoted to watersports. The road around the south side is the more scenic one. At Normanton, a classical church on a cause-way seems almost to float on the water (it is now used as a water museum); the village of Upper Hambleton is picturesquely sited too. The excellent Bay Tree Garden Centre has pre-Christmas events and a good restaurant.

Other places of interest in the area include 16th-century Lyddington Bede House – a Tudor almshouse, and Tolethorpe Hall where the founder of the Congregational church was born (Shakespeare's plays are performed in an open-air theatre here). There is a collection of steam locomotives in the iron-mine sidings at Cottesmore; and a recently opened plant centre at Bamsdale.

Readers' comments: Most friendly. Cottage excellent. B & b at its best. Nothing is too much trouble. The accommodation is first class. Very pleasant welcome, excellent. Good breakfast. Warm welcome.

ST CHRISTOPHER'S

High Street, Boscastle, Cornwall, PL35 0BD   Tel: 0840 250412

South of Bude. Nearest main road: A39 from Bude to Wadebridge.

C(12) D PT S

9 Bedrooms. £16–£19 (less for 3 nights). Prices go up during summer. Bargain breaks. Some have own shower/toilet. Tea/coffee facilities. Views of country, sea.
Dinner. £9 for 3 courses (with some choices) and coffee, at 7pm. Non-residents not admitted. Vegetarian or special diets if ordered. Wine can be ordered. **Light suppers** if ordered.
1 Sitting-room. With log burner, central heating, TV.
Small garden
Closed from November to February.

This 18th-century guest-house in an unspoilt harbour village (a conservation area) belongs to Brenda and Brian Thompson who used to run a local restaurant.

One enters it through a slate-floored hall with roughcast walls. There is a large sitting-room, well furnished with damask wallpaper and a big velvet sofa. It is heated by a log burner and adjoined by a cottage-style dining-room. Bedrooms have well-chosen colour schemes: no. 2, for instance, which is L-shaped, is decorated in celadon and white, with cane chairs.

A typical dinner might comprise a mushroom-and-wine savoury, then tenderloin of pork in a cream sauce, syllabub and cheeses. There is an extensive wine list.

This is a splendid area for scenery, birdwatching and wildflowers, and secluded beaches as at Trebarwith Strand and Bossiney Cove.

All along this coast are picturesque fishing villages such as Boscastle, Tintagel and Port Isaac, but the scenery inland deserves to be explored too. An interesting day's drive might start at Tintagel (with a visit to the romantically sited seashore castle and Celtic monastery ruins up 300 steps; King Arthur's Hall – his story told in stained glass; and the Old Post Office, in a 14th-century house).

Readers' comments: Very good. Pleasant welcome and good food. Excellent hospitality, very relaxing. Very good value. Excellent food with plenty of variety. Very comfortable. Excellent fare. A friendly and attractive b & b in a lovely area. Excellent hosts. Warm welcome. Varied meals. A lovely old house.

1683 is carved on one wall of **OLD BOROUGH HOUSE,** Bossiney, made of slate that came from England's largest quarry (at Delabole, near Camelford), a spectacular sight.

Once the house was the residence of the mayors of Bossiney (later, of J. B. Priestley). It has small windows set in thick walls, low beams, steps up and down, twisting corridors, a log stove in the sitting-room which has crimson velvet armchairs, and a bar in the roomy entrance hall. From the garden there is a sea view.

Christina Rayner serves such meals as tomato soup with cream, carbonnade of beef, crème brûlée and cheeses. £14.50–£18.50 (b & b). [Tel: 0840 770475; postcode: PL34 0AY]

ST ELISABETH'S COTTAGE

D S

Woodman Lane, Clent, West Midlands, DY9 9PX   Tel: 0562 883883
South-east of Stourbridge. Nearest main road: A456 from Kidderminster to
Birmingham (and M5, junctions 3/4).

2 Bedrooms. £18–£19 (less for 3 nights).
Both have own bath/toilet. Tea/coffee
facilities. TV. Views of garden, country. No
smoking. Washing machine on request.
Dinner (by arrangement). £12 for 3
courses (with choices) and coffee, at
variable times. Non-residents not admitted.
Wine can be brought in. No smoking. **Light
suppers** if ordered.
3 Sitting-rooms. With open fire, central
heating, TV, piano, record-player. No
smoking.
Large garden

The 18th-century cottage – once laundry to the big mansion nearby – has been
much extended over the years and is now quite a large house, surrounded by a
particularly beautiful garden. There is a willow-fringed pool which attracts
herons, rosebeds, a big sloping lawn, summer-house and swimming-pool.

Sheila Blankstone has furnished her home elegantly with, for instance,
deep-pile carpets of pale moss-green in a bedroom that has a bathroom with
pheasant-patterned wallpaper; pink chintz and a fine inlaid walnut table and
cabinet in another. Huge picture-windows make the most of garden views. In
addition to the large sitting-room there is a sun-room and a small 'snug'. Some
visitors will appreciate having their own entrance to their bedroom (with child's
room adjacent), and the choice of continental breakfast (in their room) or a
cooked breakfast in the dining-room. Everywhere are Sheila's lovely flower
arrangements. She will sometimes do dinners, such as melon, roast lamb, cheese
and fruit – or visitors may use her kitchen. Vegetables are grown in the garden.

The village is in the Clent Hills (a lovely area even though the busy M5 and
Birmingham are so near). Stourbridge has since Tudor times been famous for
glassmaking: visits to glass works can be arranged. A few miles to the south of it is
Hagley Hall, Palladian outside and ornately decorated with plasterwork inside. In
its grounds are mock ruins and temples.

On the other side, head for Kinver – not just for its historic houses and
church, but to walk to the dramatic summit of Kinver Edge, looming overhead: a
200-acre beauty-spot belonging to the National Trust, from which there are far
views of the Cotswolds, the Malvern Hills and other heights. People used to live
in the sandstone caves up here.

This is the edge of the Black Country – one great iron-furnace during the
Industrial Revolution of the 19th century. Now, proud of its past, local people are
conserving historic industrial buildings and creating museums which have turned
Dudley, in particular, into a tourist centre. Its Black Country museum recreates
life and work in Victorian times. You can go to the Geochron for a primaeval
forest experience, or view underground caverns from a canal boat. Dudley also
has a Norman castle, priory and particularly good zoo.

For explanation of code letters (C, D, M, PT, S, X) see page xlvi.

ST JAMES'S HOUSE
The Green, Thirsk, North Yorkshire, YO7 1AQ   Tel: 0845 524120 or 522676

C M PT

Nearest main road: A19 from Middlesbrough to York.

4 Bedrooms. £16–£19 (less for 7 nights or continental breakfast). Some have own shower/toilet. Tea/coffee facilities. TV. No smoking.
1 Sitting-room. With central heating. No smoking.
Small garden
Closed from November to February.

Barry Ogleby being an antique dealer, it is not surprising that every part of his 18th-century house is well endowed with period pieces. You may sleep in a room with a bedstead of prettily turned spindles or in a genuine Victorian four-poster; and in corridors as well as rooms there are such interesting pieces as inlaid blanket-boxes or unusual chairs. On the ground floor is a particularly convenient family room, looking onto flowerbeds, winding paths and lily-pool.

Only two minutes' walk from the quiet green, a conservation area, is Thirsk's busy market place and many restaurants – only breakfast is served by Liz Ogleby. This is where the world's most famous vet, writing under the name of James Herriot, has his surgery. There are local guides who will accompany you on car tours, pointing out sites associated with Herriot, his books or the films; one shows videos en route.

In the immediate vicinity are the stupendous view from Sutton Bank, Castle Howard (famous even before television's 'Brideshead Revisited'), thriving Ampleforth Abbey and its school, the pretty villages of Coxwold and Kilburn – the latter associated with 'the mouse-man' and his furniture, the former with Shandy Hall (home of Laurence Sterne). A few miles away is Northallerton, a town of fine houses, with characterful villages all around. Fountains Abbey, Newburgh Priory, the white horse of the Hambleton Hills, Byland Abbey, Helmsley (old market town), the arboretum at Bedale and Harlow Car gardens are other attractions.

There are landscaped gardens at Duncombe Park, Helmsley – a town dominated by great castle ruins on a huge earthwork. Seventeenth-century Nunnington Hall not only has fine rooms but a display of miniature rooms too. Sion Hill Hall, at Kirby Wiske, is not historic – except in style – but is notable for its displays of period furniture. What was once the home of Thomas Lord – of cricketing fame – is now Thirsk's museum of local history and of cricket. In an area of spectacular abbeys, do not overlook some of the smaller gems such as Mount Grace Priory (with 23 monastic cells) or Saxon St Gregory's Minster at Nawton.

Readers' comments: A warm welcome. Comfortable, quiet room; good breakfast. Friendly hostess, very good house, beautifully furnished. Breakfasts are something special. One of the best b & bs we have encountered. Superb hospitality. Very warm welcome. Beautiful bedroom. Wonderful breakfasts in generous quantities. Every detail perfect. We were made comfortable and welcome.

301

ST MARY'S HOUSE

C D M PT X

Church Street, Kintbury, Berkshire, RG15 0TR   Tel: 0488 58551
West of Newbury. Nearest main road: A4 from Marlborough to Newbury
(and M4, junctions 13/14).

3 Bedrooms. £16.50–£21 (less for 4 nights). Prices go up from Easter. All have own bath/shower/toilet. TV. Views of garden, country. Clothes-washing on request.
Light suppers if ordered.
2 Sitting-rooms. With wood stove, central heating, TV. Bar.
Small garden

Old-fashioned roses and a grapevine up the walls add to the picturesque look of the Barrs' unusual house. Its pointed windows are lozenge-paned, and little dormers punctuate the roof: it used to be a school from 1856 until 1963.

All bedrooms are on the ground floor, one of them (with particularly handsome bathroom, chaise longue and flowery chintzes) opening onto a paved terrace with lavender hedge. The sitting-room is furnished with antiques, and the dining-room with a great, 17th-century refectory table surrounded by leather chairs. Alcoves of books, pointed arches, three outsize sofas around a lacquer table in front of the handsome fireplace, and great copper vats of logs all add to an interior of outstanding distinction.

The lovely Kennet & Avon Canal is only a hundred yards away, for Kintbury lies midway between Hungerford and Newbury – towns described elsewhere in this book (along with the rest of Berkshire). Only a few miles south are the Hampshire Downs; and, westward, Wiltshire's Vale of Pewsey, both of which are also scenic areas which take days to explore. Northward is a region rich in prehistoric remains – hill forts, barrows, ancient tracks and so forth. The valley itself is quite different: woodland, commons and meadows as the backdrop to villages of flint, brick and thatch with narrow lanes and some richly decorated churches. Birdwatchers and walkers love the whole area (as do anglers). Favourite outings include Avebury (prehistoric ring), Marlborough, Newbury (racecourse), Bowood House, Littlecote and Highclere Castle.

Picturesque Hungerford is famous for its scores of antique shops (many open even on Sundays). And, of course, most visitors go to Windsor not only for its famous castle and Eton College but also for the 'Royalty and Empire' show.

Readers' comments: Lovely atmosphere, lovely place.

Sitting-room at Welam House (see page 95)

SAMPSONS FARM   C D PT S X
Preston, Devon, TQ12 3PP   Tel: 0626 54913
North of Newton Abbot. Nearest main road: A380 from Newton Abbot
towards Exeter (and M5, junction 31).

5 Bedrooms. £15–£20 (less for 2 nights or
mid-week). Some have own shower/toilet.
Tea/coffee facilities. TV. Views of garden,
country. Washing machine on request.
Dinner. £13.50 for 3 courses (with
choices) and coffee, or à la carte, from 7pm.
Vegetarian or special diets if ordered. Wine
can be ordered. **Light suppers** if ordered.
1 Sitting-room. With open fire, central
heating. **Bar.**
Large garden

To this traditional Devon house, all whitewash and thatch, came a Cornish farm-
ing family who gave it a new way of life – as a renowned restaurant. For one of
Hazel Bell's two sons, Nigel and Colin, who assist in the running of Sampsons
Farm trained as a chef at Torquay's celebrated Imperial Hotel, and it is he
(Colin) who cooks the gourmet-class lunches and dinners.

After scallops with garlic, I enjoyed the house speciality – a half-duckling
in orange sauce with vegetables cooked to perfection, and then a lemon ice
cream with biscuity topping. (There is a good wine-list too.) This was served in a
low, cosy dining-room, with candle-lamps and flowers brightening the plum
tablecloths and a warm glow coming from the stone hearth. Beyond the small
bar is a snug, timbered sitting-room with log fire in an inglenook thronged
with copper pans, and in the garden is a barbecue with a paddock of ducks
and geese beyond.

The way to the bedrooms is all steps and twists (one of the rooms has a four-
poster), for the house has grown in a higgledy-piggledy way since its beginnings in
the 14th or 15th century: no one is quite sure of its age. The immensely thick,
white walls are of cob – that is, built up from the clay which was added lump by
lump, slowly drying in the sun. It started as a long-house: family at one end and
cattle at the other, with a cross-passage between – the passage, with screen walls
of hefty oak planks, still survives.

Altogether an exceptional place (characterful ambience, a most hospitable
hostess, and excellent food) which would be well worth a long detour – but that's
not needed as it is so close to the main route through Devon into Cornwall. This
means that visitors staying here can quickly reach not only such historic towns as
Exeter, Totnes, Dartmouth and Tavistock but also Dartmoor and some of south
Devon's best beaches too (Torquay is only 20 minutes away and Dawlish even
nearer). There are good walks, swimming-pools, river fishing and golf close by as
well as clay-pigeon shooting. Hazel says the scenery around Hennock reservoirs is
comparable with Canada's wildernesses.

SAXELBYE MANOR HOUSE   C D
Church Lane, Saxelbye, Leicestershire, LE14 3PA   Tel: 0664 812269
North-west of Melton Mowbray. Nearest main road: A6006 from Melton Mowbray towards Derby.

3 Bedrooms. £16–£21.50 (less for 5 nights). One has own shower/toilet. Tea/coffee facilities. TV. Views of garden, country. Washing machine on request.
Dinner. £9.50 for 4 courses and coffee, at 7pm. Non-residents not admitted. Vegetarian or special diets if ordered. Wine can be ordered or brought in. **Light suppers** if ordered.
1 Sitting-room. With open fire, central heating, TV, piano.
Large garden
Closed from December to February.

In this little hamlet is an especially attractive farmhouse, tucked within a garden where willows and fuchsias flourish. Parts of it are 800 years old. Margaret Morris has furnished it with a fascinating collection of Victoriana (even in the cloak-room): little velvet chairs and chaises longues, old prints and pot-plants in abundance. Narrow passages lead to a grand staircase constructed four centuries ago in the old stone stairwell. There's even a big Victorian bath in the huge bathroom. She provides traditional 4-course dinners: for instance, prawn cocktail, the farm's own lamb with four vegetables, sherry trifle, then Stilton and other local cheeses.

On the farm are cows, sheep and beef-cattle. It provides not only free-range eggs for breakfast but very good, tested milk.

Melton Mowbray is a pleasant market town (from which you can go home laden with its famous pork pies and other products of the pig), and is well placed for visiting other historic Leicestershire towns such as Loughborough and Oakham (as well as Grantham and Stamford in Lincolnshire, and Nottingham for its castle and other historic buildings). Belvoir Castle and Rutland Water are well worth a visit. The tiny county of Rutland still keeps its identity even though it was incorporated into Leicestershire decades ago. Go to Bottesford (for its church monuments), Burghley (for views) and Wing (a mediaeval maze).

Readers' comments: Have stayed repeatedly. Another wonderful Gundrey house! Meals and lovely bedroom were first class. Nothing was too much trouble. Lovely room, wonderful meal. Good cook, charming hostess. Friendly welcome.

The conservation village of Holwell has a particularly ancient church (1200) alongside which is 18th-century **CHURCH COTTAGE**, full of steps and turns inside. Here Brenda Bailey gives visitors not only a beamed bedroom with brass bed and a spacious bathroom but their own small sitting-room too, and their own front door. Breakfasts and light snacks are served in her dining-room, which overlooks the sloping, landscaped garden. £15.

[Tel: 066476 255; postcode: LE14 4SZ]

SAYWELL FARMHOUSE

Bedmonton, Kent, ME9 0EH   Tel: 062784 444

C(12) **D PT**

South-west of Sittingbourne. Nearest main road: A249 from Sittingbourne to Maidstone (also M20, junction 8; and M2, junction 5).

3 Bedrooms. £19–£21 (less for 4 nights). Some have own bath/shower/toilet. Tea/coffee facilities. TV. Views of garden, country. No smoking. Washing machine on request.
Dinner. From £15 for 3 courses, wine and coffee, at 6–8pm. Vegetarian or special diets if ordered. No smoking. **Light suppers** if ordered.
1 Sitting-room. With open fire, central heating, TV. No smoking.
Large garden

High up in the North Downs, mossy lanes thread their way between orchards sheltered from the wind by long lines of poplars. When autumn leaves are drifting down and traveller's joy tops the hedges with its shadowy foam, the golden apples are gathered and loaded for London's markets.

Here – far from the busy world – is found a white farmhouse, approached by a long brick path across its trim lawn, roses clinging to the flint walls of the garden. The oldest part – the kitchen – is 13th-century, its low beams hung with copper pans. The dining-room is four centuries younger: '1611' and the then owner's initials are carved on a beam.

Yvonne Carter has used pale pink for walls with exposed timbers, a good foil to the oak furniture which admirably complements this background and the big brick inglenook. Some bedrooms have floors sloping with age, and windows that enjoy views of the dovecote and the Downs beyond. Colour schemes are tranquil combinations of blue and cream or pink and white.

Yvonne is an accomplished cook who sometimes does 5-course dinners for private parties; while for her resident visitors she ordinarily prepares such meals as avocado and kiwi fruit in a sour cream dressing; chicken with lemon sauce (and fresh local vegetables); profiteroles. Wine is included in the price.

The tiny hamlet of Bedmonton, although it feels so remote, is well placed for visiting most of Kent's great sights, including Canterbury itself. Particularly near are the famous moated castle of Leeds, the county town of Maidstone (a celebrated museum of historic carriages near its ancient episcopal palace and mediaeval church), Rochester – cathedral, castle and considerable Dickens' associations, and Chatham – where the opening of the great dockyard to visitors is now proving a major attraction.

The hamlet is also close to picturesque Hollingbourne: right on the ancient Pilgrims' Way to Canterbury, this village has half-timbered inns and a church which is worth a visit to see the fine tomb of Elizabeth Culpeper (1638).

And all around are the North Downs: 'turfy mountains where live nibbling sheep' is a Shakespearean definition of the Downs.

In due course, this house may prove a handy stopover when going through the Channel Tunnel by train.

Readers' comments: Wonderful food. Hosts most kind. Very peaceful and cosy. Delightful hosts. Meals were wonderful. Courteous owners, very welcoming. Food very good. Beautiful place, everything for our comfort.

SEVEN   C(14) **PT S**
Water Street, Cambridge, CB4 1NZ   Tel: 0223 355550
Nearest main road: A45 from Cambridge to Newmarket (and M11, junction 13).

rear view

3 **Bedrooms.** £19 (less for 7 nights).
Tea/coffee facilities. Views of garden.
Light suppers if ordered.
1 Sitting-room. With central heating, TV.
Small garden

An archway (built for coaches) with red painted gates leads to a pretty courtyard
and this 16th-century listed house where once bargees lodged. For Water Street
runs along a bank of the River Cam, at one time a busy waterway for trade. Now
it is a quiet backwater except when a regatta or raft race is taking place. You can
walk the towpath right into Cambridge (it is 1½ miles to King's College); or cross
a footbridge to Stourbridge Common. (The less energetic can take a bus into
Cambridge: one of Water Street's attractions is that here, unlike the city centre, it
is easy to park one's car.)

Jane Greening has put her own artistic touches everywhere, from the blue-
and-white fingerplates on pine doors to interesting pottery and paintings on brick
walls. She usually serves only breakfasts (recommending the garden restaurant of
the riverside Pike and Eel inn for other meals). There is a small sitting-area
upstairs, an elegant dining-area in the hall and an attractive walled garden.

Cambridge itself takes days to explore, and then there is a lot to see in the
vicinity. Anglesey Abbey, for instance, which was really a priory only, founded in
1135. This century, a wealthy connoisseur filled it with art treasures and around
it created one of the really great gardens of England.

Readers' comments: Could not have been better looked after. Delightful.

On this side of Cambridge is Swaffham
Bulbeck and the **OLD RECTORY**
which was built in 1818 for the Rev.
Leonard Jenyns, a distinguished
naturalist who was offered but
declined a place on the *Beagle* expedition, recommending instead his pupil
Charles Darwin – who was a frequent
visitor to the rectory.

Jenny Few-Mackay frequents salerooms to seek out all the Victoriana
which furnishes the house in the style
of Jenyns' time: one room has a handsome brass bed from which, through
big windows, to enjoy the view of

fields. There is a garden and swimming-pool; plus billiards in a converted
barn. The best place for dinner is the
Hole in the Wall at Little Wilbraham
(or the Red Lion in Swaffham Prior).
£16–£21. [Tel: 0223 811986; postcode: CB5 0LX] .

306

SEVERN TROW   **M**
Church Road, Jackfield, Ironbridge, Shropshire, TF8 7ND Tel: 0952 883551
South of Telford. Nearest main road: A442 from Telford to Bridgnorth
(and M54, junctions 4/5).

4 Bedrooms. £17–£21 (less for 3 nights).
All have own bath/shower/toilet. Tea/coffee
facilities. Views of garden, country, river.
No smoking.
Light suppers in winter only, if ordered.
2 Sitting-rooms. With open fire, central
heating, TV, record-player. Bar. No
smoking.
Small garden
Closed in November and December.

Through the deep Ironbridge gorge, scenic birthplace (in 1709) of the Industrial
Revolution, flows the lovely River Severn on its way to the distant sea. As early as
the 17th century it was a trade route, with flat-bottomed sailing-barges called
trows bearing goods downriver to the port at Bristol. After unloading, boats had
to be hauled back up again by teams of men walking the 120-mile towpath. The
Severn Trow, standing on the river bank, provided them with beer, dormitory
lodgings and (on the top floor) a cubicled brothel. Then it became a church hall.

To original features which gave the house unique character, Jim and Pauline
Hannigan have added very attractive furnishings. There are now carpets on floors
of red and black quarry-tiles, good sofas in the sitting-room where an old pine
dresser serves as a bar, and in the dining-room an outstanding and very colourful
mosaic floor. The arched entrance, big enough to accommodate a cart, once
linked malt-store to brew-house; the latter is now another sitting-room with beer-
vat openings still set in the brick walls.

Upstairs are excellent bedrooms with light colour schemes such as yellow and
white, and interesting furnishings – a net-draped brass bed, for example.

Very substantial breakfasts are provided but usually no evening meal. However,
Jim will drive visitors to and from any of Ironbridge's two dozen eating-places. In
winter (for weekend guests) the inglenook, now re-equipped with iron trivets, spit
and cauldron, is again used for traditionally cooked dinners and mulled wine.

Readers' comments: Most comfortable, wonderful welcome. Has to be seen to be
believed. Friendly couple, superb breakfasts, extremely helpful. The best we have
visited. Breakfast fruits a work of art!

On the other side of Telford is
18th-century **CHURCH FARM,**
Wrockwardine (close to the M54),
where the Savage family has farmed for
generations. It's a historic village – and
mediaeval finds have turned up in the
very attractive garden of the farmhouse. Of all the bedrooms, no. 4 is
the prettiest. One is in a ground-floor
annexe that was once a wash-house. In
the high, beamed sitting-room, notice
the side-sliding sash windows, usually

found only in Yorkshire. Jo's dinners
include home-made soups, roasts,
casseroles and traditional puddings.
£19–£23 (b & b). [Tel: 0952 244917;
postcode: TF6 5DG]

SHEARINGS

Rockbourne, Hampshire, SP6 3NA   Tel: 07253 256

North of Ringwood. Nearest main road: A354 from Salisbury to Blandford
Forum (and M27, junction 1).

3 **Bedrooms.** £19–£23 **for readers of this
book** (less for 7 nights). Prices go up in

April. All have own bath or shower.
Tea/coffee facilities. Views of garden,
stream. No smoking. Washing machine on
request.
Dinner. £13 for 3 courses and coffee,
at 8pm (not Sundays). Non-residents
not admitted. Vegetarian or special
diets if ordered. Wine can be ordered
or brought in. **Light suppers** if
ordered.
2 **Sitting-rooms.** With open fire, central
heating, TV, piano.
Small garden
Closed in January.

The house, with thatched roof and porch, overlooks a clear stream and has its
own footbridge. It was built in the 16th century (from oak beams that are even
older), and when Colin and Rosemary Watts came here they took great care to
decorate and furnish it appropriately. One pink-carpeted sitting-room has rosy
cretonne sofas facing the inglenook fireplace; another, with chintz-covered chairs,
is for television. Most meals are eaten in the beamy kitchen/dining-room.

The garden at the back (with croquet) is particularly pretty: sloping lawn,
brick summer-house, a sun-trapping brick patio.

Mr and Mrs Watts are interesting people to meet – she, musical and artistic;
he, a retired brigadier. Rosemary is an excellent cook – of such meals as iced
cucumber soup, beef, éclairs, cheeses. (Pressed flower crafts for sale.)

The village itself is picturesque, and has a Roman villa.

Readers' comments: Excellent. Made very welcome. Truly beautiful and peaceful.
Top marks. Treated like personal guests.

Towards Fordingbridge is **WEIR
COTTAGE**, Bickton, which was once
the flour store for the nearby watermill
(now converted). Seated on the sofa in
a turquoise and white ground-floor
bedroom, one has a view of the
tranquil watermeadows. On the sunny
upper floor are more bedrooms, and a
vast room with rafters above a long
chestnut table and armchairs grouped
around the open log fire. A breakfast-
table is placed to make the most of the
mill-race view. From another sash window one can see the garden – winding
herbaceous beds and a paved terrace

with swing-seat. (Philippa Duckworth
serves such meals as cucumber
mousse, local pheasant and rhubarb
fool.) £18 (b & b). [Tel: 0425 655813;
postcode: SP6 2HA]

SHIELDHALL   C(10) **D M S**
Kirkharle, Northumberland, NE61 4AQ   Tel: 0830 40387
West of Morpeth. Nearest main road: A696 from Newcastle to Otterburn.

6 Bedrooms. £16.75–£22.75 (less for 3 nights). All have own bath/shower/toilet. Tea/coffee facilities. Views of garden, country. Washing machine on request.
Dinner. £12.75 for 4 courses and coffee, at 7pm. Vegetarian or special diets if ordered. Wine can be ordered. **Light suppers** sometimes.
2 Sitting-rooms. With open fire, central heating, TV, piano. No smoking. Bar.
Large garden

18th-century stone buildings enclose a courtyard where white fantails strut, the former barns to left and right providing very well-equipped ground-floor bedrooms for visitors – each with its own entrance. Meals are taken in a beamed dining-room in the centre, furnished with antiques and an inglenook fireplace (a typical dinner might be home-made soup, a roast or lasagne, blackcurrant tart and local cheeses – with produce from the garden and orchard); and to one side are two sitting-rooms (one with library) for visitors. From a patio with chairs one enjoys a serene view; from the well comes spring water.

Stephen Robinson-Gay is an accomplished cabinet-maker, happy to show visitors the workshop where he makes or restores furniture. Most of the work in all the rooms is his. For instance, beyond the arched doorway of the mahogany room is a colonial-style bed with very fine inlay, and in the oak room a four-poster with carved canopy, copied from a Flemish bed in Lindisfarne Castle (on Holy Island), complete with a secret cupboard to hold a shotgun – necessary bedside equipment in the troubled times of three centuries ago. There is a showroom of woodwork.

Celia is a fount of information on local history and what to see. Close by is one of the National Trust's biggest houses, Wallington Hall (with very fine grounds).

Comfortable modern, leather-covered armchairs face a log fire in the big sitting-room of Christine Rodger's Victorian house, **OLD POST OFFICE COTTAGE**, at Little Bavington. Scots-born Christine calls herself a Francophile, which accounts for such dishes as garbure paysanne and carbonnade of beef, followed by a choice of puddings. John Rodger can be relied on to produce trout and game in season. This is a quiet spot, with open views from the bedrooms, and all rooms have refreshingly plain walls and carpet. As well as the notable mansions open to the public, Bobby Shaftoe's family home is nearby. Hadrian's Wall

and the city of Newcastle are other draws. £14–£15.

Readers' comments: Stayed for a week, such being the welcome, homeliness and comfort, plus good home cooking . . . Very clean, well appointed, good food. [Tel: 0830 30331; postcode: NE19 2BB]

SHOTTLE HALL FARMHOUSE

C D M

Shottle, Derbyshire, DE5 2EB   Tel: 0773 550 276

North of Derby. Nearest main road: A517 from Ashbourne to Belper
(and M1, junction 28).

11 Bedrooms. £19.50–£25 (less for 7 nights and for senior citizens). Prices go up in April. Some have own bath/shower/toilet. Tea/coffee facilities. TV. Views of garden, country. No smoking.
Dinner. £11.50 for 4 courses and coffee, at 7.30pm (not Sundays). Vegetarian or special diets if ordered. Wine can be ordered. **Light suppers** if ordered.
2 Sitting-rooms. With central heating, TV. Bar.
Large garden
Closed in November.

The guest-house is over a century old and has all the solid Victorian quality of that period: big rooms, fine ceilings and doors, dignity in every detail. Not only the bedrooms but even the bathrooms are large and close-carpeted, with paint-work and everything else in pristine condition. As well as a sizeable sitting-room, there are two dining-rooms – one is used for breakfasts because it gets the morning sun. From both, the huge windows have views of hills and of the fertile valley stretching below the house. There are a rose garden and lawns – and not another house in sight. Two bedrooms are on the ground floor; and there is a new self-contained suite, which is suitable for disabled people.

Guests enjoy Phyllis's straightforward home cooking. As well as traditional roasts, a typical dinner menu might include: mushrooms in cream and garlic, chicken with apple and cider sauce, hazelnut meringue, English cheeses, and coffee with cream. Phyllis collects antique cheese dishes; and has other antiques for sale.

Shottle is in the middle of a rural area of fine landscapes. Close by are the Derbyshire Dales and the Peak District (described elsewhere). The Matlocks are a hilly area with pretty villages to be found. The old spa of Matlock Bath has interesting places to visit (stately gardens, wildlife park, model village, a museum of mining, and the tower, terraces and caverns of Abraham's Heights). Cromford is both attractive and historic, with Arkwright's first mill, old waterside buildings, a good bookshop, etc. There are six stately homes and innumerable good walks.

Around Derby, magnates built themselves great houses such as Wingfield Manor where Mary Queen of Scots was imprisoned, the very splendid Sudbury Hall which now houses a museum of childhood, Melbourne Hall where Lord Melbourne lived (the formal gardens are particularly fine and the Norman village church is outstanding), Kedleston Hall – a magnificent Adam house, and Calke Abbey (1701), the contents of which remained scarcely disturbed over the last century. In the Matlock direction is mediaeval Carnfield Hall. The traffic of Derby is worth braving to visit the cathedral, Wollaton Hall and museums.

Readers' comments: Lovely room, excellent dinner: a winner. Good and friendly. Wonderful! Delightfully warm and friendly couple. Superb cook. Thoroughly enjoyed our stay, charming and friendly people. Very impressed; could not have been more helpful. Very good hosts. An idyllic country house. The best! Good food. Spacious, comfortable bedroom. Friendly and helpful.

SISSINGHURST CASTLE FARM   C(5) D S X
Sissinghurst, Kent, TN17 2AB   Tel: 0580 712885
East of Tunbridge Wells. Nearest main road: A262 from High Halden towards
Tunbridge Wells.

5 Bedrooms. £19–£24 (less for 5 nights). Prices go up in April. Bargain breaks. One has own bath/shower/toilet. Tea/coffee facilities. Views of garden, country. No smoking.
Dinner (by arrangement). £13 for 4 courses and coffee, at 7pm. Vegetarian or special diets if ordered. Wine can be brought in. No smoking. **Light suppers** if ordered.
1 Sitting-room. With open fire, central heating, TV.
Large garden

'Hydrangea petiolaris will grow under trees and ramble over an old stump', wrote Vita Sackville-West to her tenant at the Castle Farm. 'I asked the Director of Kew and he specially advised this.' In the same note she said: 'I can give you a lot of columbines – ask Vass [her gardener] for them.' James Stearns (grandson of that tenant, who still farms here) treasures this note from one of England's most famous gardening ladies, creator of the adjacent gardens at Sissinghurst Castle (now NT). It was in fact James's great-uncle, an estate agent, who first introduced the Elizabethan castle to Vita.

The farmhouse, which dates from 1855, was once a mansion inhabited by a substantial family – hence the row of servants' bells which still survives, along with such period features as panelled sash windows, fretted woodwork and the galleried staircase. Here hang two fine paintings lent by Nigel Nicolson (son of Vita and Harold Nicolson) who still lives in a wing of the castle. Furniture is a homely, pleasant mixture of old pieces; and one bedroom, with windows on two sides, has a good view of the castle. Beyond the croquet lawn are leafy woodlands.

Pat Stearns is an accomplished cook. A typical meal might comprise watercress soup, chicken breasts with an orange and caper sauce, pavlova with fresh fruit, and local cheeses.

It is worth climbing to the top of the tower at the splendid brick castle to look across the Weald towards the North Downs: below are woods, lakes, oast houses, Castle Farm's fields of cereals and sheep – and, of course, the world-famous gardens, with outbuildings and remnants of a moat. The castle was virtually a ruin when Vita and her husband, Harold Nicolson, rescued it in 1930. The gardens were planned as a series of 'rooms' and so although they extend to six acres the overall effect is intimate: a major part of their charm. Vistas open up unexpectedly; in every month there is something different in flower – from cottage-garden to rare species. One of the most popular of the gardens contains nothing but old-fashioned roses. Inside the castle you can see rooms where the two pursued their profession as writers.

Near here is the picturesque market town of Cranbrook (with cathedral-like church), and beyond its steep main street the biggest working windmill in the country, built before the Battle of Waterloo.

Readers' comments: We enjoy the very homely atmosphere and friendliness.

SLOOP INN   C D

Bantham, Devon, TQ7 3AJ   Tel: 0548 560489
West of Kingsbridge. Nearest main road: A379 from Kingsbridge to Plymouth.

5 Bedrooms. £20 (**to readers of this book only**)–£25. Prices go up from May. Bargain breaks. All have own bath/toilet. Tea/coffee facilities. TV. Views of country, sea, river. Washing machine on request. **Dinner.** A la carte, at 7–10pm. Vegetarian or special diets if ordered. Wine can be ordered. **Light suppers.**
Bars
Closed in January.

It goes without saying that this 400-year-old inn by the sea has a history of smuggling.

One of its owners was in fact a notorious wrecker, luring ships (by means of false lights) onto rocks in order to plunder them. Since the law was that 'if any man escape to shore alive, the ship is no wreck' – and so plundering it would be theft, wreckers were murderous wretches too. Neil Girling can tell you many stories of the smugglers and point out places in the village where they hid their kegs of French brandy. Once, the Sloop minted its own coins (some are now in the interesting museum at Kingsbridge) with which to pay for goods and services – the coins were usable only to buy drinks at the Sloop: good business!

The inn is unspoilt: everything one hopes that a village inn will be but rarely is, low-beamed, stone-flagged and snug. Some walls are of stone, some panelled.

One of its several bars is made from old boat-timbers. Here you can take on the locals at a game of darts or table-skittles after enjoying an excellent bar meal; or stroll down to the sandy dunes to watch the sun set over the sea. Bathing, building sandcastles and exploring rock-pools delight children; and there is surfing. Many of the unpretentiously furnished bedrooms have a view of the sea or River Avon. There is a yard and well at the back with seats.

Soups are home-made and ham home-cooked; smoked salmon, crabs and steaks are all local produce; granary bread is served. Fish is, of course, particularly good and fresh. All portions are generous.

Bantham is one of Devon's most ancient villages (the remains of prehistoric dwellings were laid bare in an 18th-century storm, and there was a Roman camp here later). Once, its main livelihood was pilchard-fishing – but no longer.

The whole area is remote, peaceful and unspoilt with good walks through beautiful countryside or along the coastal footpath; and yet the cities of Plymouth and Exeter are within reach, and the great resort of Torquay. In early spring, wildflowers are everywhere and the blue waves are beginning to be dotted with boating enthusiasts. This is a rich farming area ('the fruitfullest part of Devonshire'), with villages of colourwashed cottages thickly thatched.

On the other side of the Avon is Bigbury where a strange, long-legged 'tram' takes people across the sea to Burgh Island.

Readers' comments: Food very good. A most enjoyable stay. Quiet, peaceful, idyllic scenery. Excellently furnished. Food the best I've eaten lately.

SNOWFORD HALL FARM   C
Hunningham, Warwickshire, CV33 9ES   Tel: 0926 632297
East of Leamington Spa. Nearest main road: A423 from Coventry to Banbury (and M40, junction 12).

3 Bedrooms. £16–£19. Some have own shower/toilet. Tea/coffee facilities. TV. Views of garden, country. No smoking.
Dinner (by arrangement). From £12.50 for 4 courses and coffee, from 6.30pm. Non-residents not admitted. Wine can be brought in. No smoking. **Light suppers** if ordered.
1 Sitting-room. With central heating, TV, piano. No smoking preferred.
Large garden

A very long drive through fields leads to this spacious 18th-century house at the heart of a 250-acre farm (cattle and crops) with fine views around it. One enters through an interesting hall with a big, china-laden dresser and polished wood floor. The huge sitting-room is very attractively furnished. Here and there around the house are many things made by Rudi Hancock herself, a skilled craftswoman – samplers, for example, and corn dollies; and furniture which she has restored.

Dutch-born, she was previously a cookery teacher and so you can expect a good dinner, if booked in advance. She uses many home-grown vegetables and fruit, and makes her own jam.

The most interesting of the bedrooms has a very unusual and decorative Dutch bed of solid mahogany, handsomely carved. (Baby-sitting available.)

Snowford Hall is near Leamington Spa and its environs, described elsewhere, and such sights as Kenilworth Castle, Coventry cathedral and Draycote Water country park. Packwood House has an exceptional garden, and the National Centre for Organic Gardening is near. Southam is an old market town; Stoneleigh a mediaeval village (with the great National Agricultural Centre outside it). The National Exhibition Centre is within easy reach, so are Warwick University and Rugby School. And all around are some of England's finest landscapes.

Hunningham is close to the ruler-straight Fosse Way which goes all the way from Devon to Lincolnshire, built by the Romans to link their most important forts. Though not even a 'B' road now, it still survives the centuries, so well was it engineered, on the line of a prehistoric trail which was an important trade route linking the mines of the south-west to ports that traded with Scandinavia.

Leamington gained the prefix 'Royal' when the young Queen Victoria stayed there only a year after coming to the throne. Fine 18th- and 19th-century squares and terraces give the town a discreet charm. There are some outstanding gardens in the area – including the public Jephson Gardens in Leamington and those of the Mill House by the river at the foot of Warwick Castle.

Readers' comments: Lovely rooms; gorgeous, silent countryside. Wonderful reception, beautiful house, plenty of very good food, wholly pleasurable. Very comfortable. A very warm welcome and excellent breakfast.

SOMERSET HOUSE C(9) **D PT S X**
35 Bathwick Hill, Bath, Avon, BA2 6LD   Tel: 0225 466451
Nearest main road: A36 from Bath to Warminster.

10 Bedrooms. £19.60–£30.20 (less for 3 nights). Prices go up in April. Bargain breaks. All have own bath/shower/toilet. Tea/coffee facilities. Views of garden or city. No smoking. Laundry facilities.
Dinner. £17.80 for 4 courses (with choices) and coffee, at 7pm (not Sundays). Vegetarian or special diets if ordered. Wine can be ordered. No smoking. **Light suppers** on Sundays.
2 Sitting-rooms. With open fire, central heating, TV, piano. Bar. No smoking.
Large garden

Above the Doric-columned portico of this handsome Georgian mansion is a decorative iron verandah; wisteria and roses climb up the walls of honey-coloured stone.

The entrance hall (with a Greek key border round the ceiling) leads to a sitting-room, with conservatory opening onto lawn. There are two bedrooms on the ground floor. The dining-room is below stairs (it has an open fire and pine dresser).

On the first floor is another sitting-room with a particularly pretty plasterwork ceiling and very old Venetian glass chandelier. The original panelled shutters flank the high sash windows; outside is the long verandah, with fine city views.

Bedrooms are large and pleasantly furnished, many with antique fireplaces (one has an antique loo) and attractive views. Some have Laura Ashley fabrics.

Malcolm Seymour (once a tourist board director) is a mine of information on what to see in the neighbourhood. Throughout the year he arranges weekends with special themes: Georgian Bath, Herbs for Health, Brunel. (Ask for programme.) Jean, formerly a teacher, enjoys cooking recipes appropriate to each of these occasions, assisted by other members of the family.

At breakfast, few people opt for the full cooked version because there is such an array of home-baked breads (nutty, spicy or fruity), preserves, muesli, freshly squeezed fruit juice and so forth; often haddock, kidneys, Cumberland sausage or muffins are offered. As to dinner, when nothing more exotic is afoot, Jean or Jonathan may produce something like game soup, their own 'rolypoly, gammon and spinach' recipe with home-grown vegetables, and apples in cider served with home-made ice cream. On Saturdays, special gourmet dinners (at 7.30pm) are offered; Sunday lunch is also available except in summer.

Perhaps the greatest glory is the garden. Every tree flowers at a different season, and the centrepiece is a great 300-year-old Judas tree – at its purple best in May. All around, between beds of peonies and columbines, is a 7¼-inch rail track installed by a former owner. All within a 12-minute walk of the city centre.

Readers' comments: The best establishment I've stayed at, where people count; the cooking reinvigorates the taste-buds. Superb comfort and food. Excellent accommodation; the most interesting and nicest food we have ever experienced. Particularly delighted. A favourite. The Seymours make guests welcome.

SOUTH FARM
East Meon, Hampshire, GU32 1EZ   Tel: 0730 823261
West of Petersfield. Nearest main road: A272 from Winchester to Petersfield.

3 Bedrooms. £18–£20 (less for 3 nights or continental breakfast). Prices go up from April. Bargain breaks. Some have own bath/toilet. Tea/coffee facilities. Views of garden, country, river. No smoking. Washing machine on request.
Light suppers if ordered.
1 Sitting-room. With open fire, central heating, TV.
Large garden

The approach to the farm is delightful. There are specimen trees on a lawn (ash, chestnut), an old granary and a grapevine under glass. In the 500-year-old house is a brick-floored dining-room with huge inglenook, rush ladderback chairs and a big oak table. The very large sitting-room has carved furniture and chinoiserie curtains in gold and blue. Bedrooms have been very agreeably furnished by Jane Atkinson: one with poppy fabrics, for instance; in another are exposed beams and a lace bedspread. An oak-panelled room has peony fabric. All are outstanding.

The house is full of flowers because Jane, an accomplished flower-arranger, regularly has large deliveries from Covent Garden market. You can dine at the George or Izaak Walton inns in East Meon if you want more than a light supper.

The Meon Valley amid the South Downs has churches that go back to Saxon times, flint-walled houses, and prehistoric burial mounds. To the south are woodlands, remnants of the once-great Forest of Bere, and then comes Portsmouth Harbour. Despite heavy traffic on roads into the port, this is well worth a visit – to see Nelson's *Victory*, Henry VIII's *Mary Rose* and his Southsea Castle, Victorian forts up on the hills and Norman Portchester Castle down by the waterfront. There are boat trips and ferries to the Isle of Wight; excellent museums (don't miss the Royal Marines one); Dickens' birthplace; much ceremonial on Navy Days; and waterfowl on the wilder shores of the two natural harbours here. Queen Elizabeth Forest contrasts with all this (drive to Georgian Buriton, go up Butser Hill, or visit the recreated Iron Age village).

The clear chalk streams, with occasional watermills, have made this lovely area well known for its watercress and its trout: the River Itchen is famous among anglers, and its valley is outstandingly beautiful – to drive or walk along it from Itchen Stoke is an unforgettable experience, pausing at Ovington's mediaeval inn on the way. Old and New Alresford are on opposite banks of the River Alre: in the latter, colourful Broad Street, with 18th-century houses, is well worth visiting (and in its churchyard are the graves of French prisoners from the Napoleonic wars). At the north end of Broad Street are a millstream and dam built in the 12th century; and also a lovely footpath through watercress beds and past a black-and-white thatched mill spanning the river. Other villages worth seeking out include Tichborne – famous for a *cause célèbre* in 1871 when an Australian imposter laid claim to the estate here; and for the Tichborne Dole, flour given to villagers since 1150.

SOUTHFIELDS COTTAGE   C(10) **D X**
Milbourne, Wiltshire, SN16 9JB   Tel: 0666 823168
East of Malmesbury. Nearest main road: A429 from Malmesbury to
Cirencester (and M4, junction 17).

2 **Bedrooms.** £17 (less for 5 nights).
Bargain breaks. Both have own bath/toilet.
Tea/coffee facilities. TV. Views of garden,
country. No smoking. Washing machine on
request.
Light suppers if ordered. No smoking.
Small garden

Inside the 300-year-old cottage, pink walls contrast with others of exposed
Cotswold stone, and in the fireplace an old bread-oven has survived the years.
Baskets of flowering pot-plants fill the deep window-sills of the dining-room.
Upstairs, bedrooms overlook old plum and apple trees in the garden, and the
fields beyond. John Meller made many of the bedheads himself – a pair of pine
ones with fretted hearts, for instance. Christine Meller (a cookery teacher) will
occasionally provide dinners or light snacks, but many visitors go to nearby
Malmesbury for a meal at, for instance, Le Flambé, the King's Arms or other
restaurants. (Bicycles for hire.)

   Malmesbury is a delight: it needs to be explored on foot. Perched on a rock in
a loop of the River Avon, it is almost islanded. After visiting the 12th-century
abbey, famous for its splendid Norman carved stonework, and the exceptionally
fine 15th-century market cross (providing a roof for 'poore folke to stande dry
when rayne cummith'), I wandered down to the ancient almshouses and former
woollen mill opposite which is a walkway over the clear and shallow river. From
this one gets a view through the arches of an old bridge: one of six in the town.
The sound of water and the stately progress of the swans add to the delight of this
beautiful corner. (It is worth getting the three leaflets of town and river walks
available at the Tourist Information Centre.)

   From Malmesbury one quickly reaches the hills at the western end of the
Cotswolds, Badminton and Gatcombe Park (where horse trials are held), and
Westonbirt Arboretum (17,000 specimens in the National Tree Collection,
colourful with blossom in spring and russet foliage in autumn). If you are looking
for bargains in classic couture go to historic Easton Grey House – the celebrated
Saunders boutique is here – or if you want to stroll in lovely riverside gardens,
with lunch available as well. Bath is only half an hour away; picturesque Castle
Combe and Cirencester (abbey, park, Roman museum, market, crafts centre) are
even nearer, and Avebury stone circle, too.

**Some proprietors stipulate a minimum stay of two nights at
weekends or peak seasons; or they will accept one-nighters only at
short notice (that is, only if no lengthier booking has yet been made).**

316

SPION KOP C(5) **D S X**
Spring Lane, Ufford, Suffolk, IP13 6EF   Tel: 0394 460277
North of Woodbridge. Nearest main road: A12 from Ipswich to Lowestoft.

3 **Bedrooms.** £15–£17.50 (less for 6 nights). Some have own bath/shower/toilet. Tea/coffee facilities. TV. Views of garden, country. Washing machine on request.
Dinner. £12.50 for 3 courses and coffee, at 7pm. Non-residents not admitted. Vegetarian or special diets if ordered. Wine can be brought in. **Light suppers** if ordered.
1 **Sitting-room.** With open fire, central heating, record-player.
Large garden

When Colonel Walters returned from the Boer Wars he built himself a house reminiscent of his years on the veldt, with an almost conical roof of thatch and a wide-eaved verandah. Its site must have reminded him of the hill on which 300 British died at the hands of the Boers, for he named it after this.

The Fergusons have added their own distinctive touches to what was already a very unusual house. Along the verandah (hung with brimming baskets of lobelias and begonias) are life-size marble nymphs – the Four Seasons – with more among the flowerbeds. Indoors, along with much other Victoriana which surely would have delighted the colonel, are bronzes and paintings of turn-of-the-century beauties well displayed against the pale pink walls of sitting- and dining-rooms, through the lattice windows of which (or from the glass sun-room) there are wooded valley views more typical of Devon than of Suffolk. There is a meadow brilliant with kingcups and wild orchids in spring.

Bedrooms are spacious and elegantly furnished; and Susan's meals are delicious. One example – a herby soup with croûtons was followed by pork in a sauce of mushrooms, cream and wine (with vegetables cooked to perfection); raspberry meringues; and a glass of wine included.

Readers' comments: Superb food. Like being pampered by a special friend. Delighted with the reception we received. Absolutely enchanted. Charming. First-class stay. Most welcoming, excellent cook. Accommodation better than 3-star hotels.

About 50 houses, mostly in Suffolk, but some in Hampshire, are in a scheme under which one-third of whatever you pay is given to Oxfam. The participating proprietors choose a project to support (for example, a college in Kampuchea to train young men in irrigation systems), and between them over £72,000 has been raised. The scheme was originated by Rosemary and Robin Schlee, at whose own very lovely home – with equally lovely garden – visitors are also welcomed. I looked at this and one other nearby (Overdeben, 29 Ipswich Road, Woodbridge) and was very impressed with their high standards and – at the latter – a spectacular view of the Deben estuary from one of the bedrooms. All charge similar prices to Spion Kop (other, simpler houses in the scheme charge less); and all have been inspected. On departure, every visitor is given a special receipt for the one-third that goes to Oxfam. Phone Mrs Schlee to book in at any: her number is 0394 382740 (047336 619 in late July/August).

SPRINGFIELD

16 Horn Lane, Linton, Cambridgeshire, CB1 6HT   Tel: 0223 891383

South-east of Cambridge. Nearest main road: A604 from Cambridge to Haverhill (and M11, junctions 9/10).

2 Bedrooms. £15–£17.50 (less mid-week or for 3 nights, or continental breakfast). One has own bath/toilet. Tea/coffee facilities. TV. Views of garden, country, river. No smoking. Washing machine on request.
Light suppers if ordered.
1 Sitting-room. With open fire, central heating, TV. No smoking.
Large garden

The hum of bumblebees and the ringing of church bells are sounds typical of peaceful countryside. Less expected is the distant roar of lions as dusk falls! But Springfield is quite near Linton Zoo.

The spring which gives the 19th-century house its name rises in a carp-pond at the far end of the garden – or, rather, gardens; for there is a succession of hedge-enclosed areas, each with its own character. One of these (almost islanded by a twist of the River Granta) is equipped for children, with a particularly sturdy tree-house and a small raft on the river.

The house is of gracious design, its gables decorated with fretted bargeboards and at its side a spacious conservatory where breakfast is often served (or you can eat in your bedroom, provided with table and chairs for the purpose). Judith Rossiter has filled the conservatory with white flowering plants of various species – the one exception being the fluffy yellow blossoms of mimosa. Adjoining it is a sitting-room with a near-white colour scheme and Fred Rossiter's collection of model sailing-boats and paintings of boats.

Bedrooms are on the second floor, furnished with antiques including old maps of America and other Americana (the Rossiters used to live in the States). The obvious reason for staying in this pretty conservation village is to visit nearby Cambridge, described elsewhere (there is a bus).

Readers' comments: Very comfortable, and a really splendid breakfast. Charming and very comfortable. Warm welcome. Strongly recommended.

In picturesque Hadstock, just across the Essex border, is a flowery close called Orchard Pightle ('pightle' is an old word for an enclosure) within which is Gillian Ludgate's home, **YARDLEYS**. She so much enjoys looking after guests that she gave up her job to do this full time. Above a spacious and light sitting-room are well-equipped bedrooms in pale colours, neat and airy; and at the back a conservatory brimming with flowers, where meals are sometimes served. Gillian is a keen cook, serving such meals as salmon mousse, pork fillet

with apricots, and pavlova. Breakfast may include garden fruit, local sausages, her own jam, and bacon which she gets from Cumbria. (Don't miss the Saxon church on Hadstock's green.) £16–£18. [Tel: 0223 891822; postcode: CB1 6PQ]

SPURSHOLT HOUSE   C D
Salisbury Road, Romsey, Hampshire, SO51 6DJ   Tel: 0794 512229
(Messages: 0794 522670)
North of Southampton. Nearest main road: A27 from Romsey to Salisbury.

3 Bedrooms. £15–£17.50 (less for 4 nights). Some have own bath/shower/toilet. Tea/coffee facilities. Views of garden, country, river. No smoking. Washing machine on request.
Dinner. £10 for 4 courses and coffee, at 7.30–8.30pm (not weekends). Non-residents not admitted. Wine may be brought in. **Light suppers** if ordered.
1 Sitting-room. With open fire, central heating, TV. No smoking.
Large garden

In the 1830s this was the home of Lady Cowper, one of Lord Palmerston's many mistresses (he was nicknamed Cupid!).

There are paved terraces with urns of geraniums, overlooking a lawn, impressive topiary, and a view of Romsey Abbey. Beyond flowerbeds, yew hedges enclose a succession of further pleasures – one garden leading into another, a parterre with lily-pool, followed by apple trees, and a dovecote with fantails.

Rooms have been furnished by Anthea Hughes in keeping with the character of the house. The spectacular sitting-room has stained glass originally in the Palace of Westminster. One bedroom is oak-panelled, and all contain antiques. Two have open fireplaces, elegant sofas and garden views.

Anthea sends visitors a dinner menu beforehand from which to choose such dishes as: potted shrimps, marinated lamb kebabs, lemon meringue pie and cheeses. There is also self-catering accommodation, with the option of dining in.

Readers' comments: Thoroughly enjoyed staying. Made most welcome. Lovely house with beautiful gardens. Most comfortable. Couldn't have been kinder.

On Tote Hill near Sherfield English is **LITTLE FOSTERS**, Barbara Boby's fully modernized 18th-century cottage on her mixed smallholding – very much off the beaten track. Bedrooms, neat and trim, overlook fields and a lawn with weeping birch. Using local produce (much of it organically grown), Barbara provides such meals as stuffed mushrooms or fresh asparagus; River Test trout in lemon sauce or pheasant in red wine; gooseberry crumble or pears and apple with crystallized ginger, yogurt and cream. The house is surrounded by a large garden and rolling countryside threaded with footpaths for walkers. (Babysitting can be arranged.) £15–£16.

Readers' comments: Most kind. Small but comfortable room. Absolutely wonderful food and very good value. Charming cottage, peaceful setting. Most delightful place, most interesting people. [Tel: 0794 40309; messages: 0794 40558; postcode: SO51 0JS]

STANSHOPE HALL

Stanshope, Staffordshire, DE6 2AD   Tel: 033527 278

North-west of Ashbourne (Derbyshire). Nearest main road: A515 from Ashbourne to Buxton.

3 Bedrooms. £20–£27.50 (less for 3 nights and for return visits). Prices go up in April. All have own bath/shower/toilet. Tea/coffee facilities. TV. Views of garden, country.
Dinner. £16.50 for 3 courses (with choices) and coffee, at 7.30pm. Vegetarian or special diets if ordered. Wine can be ordered. No smoking. **Light suppers.**
1 Sitting-room. With open fire, central heating, piano, record-player.
Large garden
Closed in January.

Built in 1670 by Cromwell's quartermaster, Jackson, the Hall has seen many changes. It was greatly extended in the 1780s and when, at nearby Ilam, a great mansion burnt down in the 19th century, salvaged fireplaces were re-installed here. Later a theatrical designer made it his home, embellishing it with all sorts of trompe l'oeil effects. The murals with peacocks and trees in the sitting-room are in the manner of Rex Whistler, while in the entrance hall a stairway and arches of Hopton stone contrast with painted marbling.

Recently, local artists have repainted bedrooms with decorative murals (bathrooms too), each with its own theme – Moorish, Egyptian or fishy.

Not only the ambience but also the food provided by Naomi Chambers and Nick Lourie is out of the ordinary. A typical menu: carrot and ginger soup or pancakes stuffed with leeks and cream cheese, followed by lamb in red wine and honey, then either gooseberry ice cream or Bakewell tart.

Readers' comments: A real home from home. Food excellent. Very relaxing and enjoyable break. Warm and comfortable with excellent views.

BEECHENHILL FARM, just outside Ilam, is a long low house built from limestone two centuries ago. Perched on a south-facing hillside, it overlooks grazing sheep and cows. Sue Prince has painted roses on walls and drawers; and her breakfasts have won an award (there is always plenty of fruit and, in winter, porridge). No dinners, but there are local inns. There's a pretty garden with pond, hanging-baskets of flowers, and a goat wanders in the paddock. Pleasant bedrooms, one of which is a light and

spacious family room. £16–£19. [Tel: 033527 274; postcode: DE6 2BD]

STARLINGS CASTLE   C D S X
Bronygarth, Shropshire, SY10 7NU   Tel: 0691 718464
North-west of Oswestry. Nearest main road: A5 from Oswestry to Llangollen.

8 Bedrooms. £20 (less for continental breakfast). Tea/coffee facilities. TV. Views of garden, country. No smoking. Washing machine on request.
Dinner. £20 for 3 courses (with choices) and coffee, from 7.30pm. Vegetarian or special diets if ordered. Wine can be ordered. No smoking. **Light suppers** if ordered.
2 Sitting-rooms. With open fire, central heating, record-player. **Bar.**
Large garden
Closed in February.

Yes, there *are* starlings (at spring migration time, they roost here in thousands) and this *is* a castle – albeit a mock one, built in the 18th century as a hunting-lodge by the owners of nearby Chirk Castle, which dates from 1330. The windows in its sandstone walls overlook an inner courtyard (grapevine, pond, pergola and baskets of lobelias) or have views of Offa's Dyke in one direction and the Berwyn Mountains in the other, beyond groves of rhododendrons and conifers.

It is not only the memorable house and its setting 1400 feet high which bring visitors. Antony Pitt worked as a chef in Bath, London and France before setting up here on his own, with his wife Jools; and the meals are outstanding. From about five choices at each course, you might select such dishes as salmon-and-plaice terrine, chicken breast stuffed with blue cheese and leeks, and hot chocolate soufflé. Dinner is served in a light and airy dining-room with a woodblock floor, green bamboo chairs and blue china on damask cloths. (Sunday lunch available.)

There is a choice of sitting-rooms. One (a 'snug', with a pine dresser as a bar) has leather club chairs, stove, low ceiling and terracotta walls with an art nouveau frieze and portraits of Antony's 17th-century ancestors. Another, L-shaped and with windows on two sides, is full of leafy plants and sofas in pale covers: it has doors leading into the garden. Bedrooms are up a winding turret stair. Even in snowy winters visitors come here (the Pitts bring them up from Selattyn).

Readers' comments: Memorable cooking, magnificent views, comfortable rooms. Very impressed.

Lying in bed at 17th-century **FISHER'S COTTAGE**, Llanyblodwel, you may hear the splash of salmon leaping in the River Tanat which flows through the garden. They come from Greenland to spawn here, and in late autumn you can watch them pull the rocks aside to find a safe niche for their spawn – or in March spot the two-inch fry emerging. You may also see otters, brown trout, nesting kingfishers or dragonflies: an idyllic spot, with the Berwyn Mountains as its backdrop. Audrey Holder's dinners comprise dishes like mackerel pâté, steak-and-

kidney puffs and brandy charlotte – after which blue velvet armchairs around a log stove await you; and neat, trim bedrooms upstairs. £16. [Tel: 0691 828382; postcode: SY10 8NF]

STODY HALL

Stody, Norfolk, NR24 2ED Tel: 0263 860549

North-east of Fakenham. Nearest main road: A148 from Cromer to Fakenham.

3 Bedrooms. £18–£20 (less for 7 nights). Some have own bath/toilet. Tea/coffee facilities on request. Views of garden, country, river.

Dinner. £15 for 3 courses and coffee, at approx. 7.30pm (not Sundays). Non-residents not admitted. Wine can be brought in. **Light suppers** if ordered.

1 Sitting-room. With open fire, central heating, TV, piano.

Large garden

The late Rex Harrison rejected hotels in favour of this handsome flint-walled house when filming in the area, moving in with his own butler and housekeeper for several months. It is easy to see why, as one sits on one of the comfortable sofas in a sitting-room with silky coral walls and marble fireplace, log fire crackling, watercolours of local scenes on the walls. There are mementoes of Khartoum (where a family forebear served with General Gordon); and 'Spy' cartoons on the green and white panelled walls of another sitting-room. In the garden are a hard tennis court and a croquet lawn.

The dining-room is particularly dramatic, the colour of its Turkey carpet repeated in the scarlet walls that are the background to a great Regency table and chairs. Miriam Rawlinson serves such dinners as haddock mousse, beef Stroganoff (with garden vegetables) and crème brûlée.

Upstairs are attractive bedrooms with, for example, a tufted white spread contrasting with the rosy satin of bedhead and curtains, lacy cushions (made by Miriam), a fine wardrobe of figured mahogany, and draped dressing-tables. There are big bathrooms, one with blue carpet, another papered with a pink clematis pattern. Rex Harrison slept (of course) in the four-poster room.

The 400-year-old house overlooks rolling pastures and all around are quiet lanes for walks. Nearby is Holt, a picturesque market town; and the very beautiful coastline is only five miles away.

Readers' comments: Wonderful food, ambience and hosts.

Vegetarian cookery is the speciality of Liz Logan at **TRAVELLER'S COTTAGE**, Horningtoft. By arrangement, a typical dinner might consist of mushroom pâté, stuffed pancakes with cheese sauce, and ice creams home-made from fresh fruit. Bread is home-baked and bread-making tuition is available. One steps through a small conservatory into the kitchen, where meals are eaten. In the small, trim rooms beyond are rag rugs, pots of geraniums and paintings by David Logan. A modest, friendly atmosphere. £14.

rear view

Readers' comments: Very well cared for; quiet and considerate. Wonderful meals. [Tel: 0328 700205; postcode: NR20 5DS]

STOKE FARM   C S
Broad Chalke, Wiltshire, SP5 5EF   Tel: 0722 780209
West of Salisbury. Nearest main road: A354 from Salisbury to Blandford
Forum.

2 Bedrooms. £19.50 (less for 2 nights). Both have own bath/shower/toilet. Tea/coffee facilities. TV. Views of garden, country. No smoking. Washing machine on request.
Dinner. £13 for 4 courses (with some choices) and coffee, at 7pm. Non-residents not admitted. Vegetarian or special diets if ordered. Wine can be brought in. **Light suppers** if ordered.
1 Sitting-room. With open fire, central heating, TV.
Large garden
Closed in December and January.

A gracious house at the heart of a 1000-acre farm overlooking the Ebble Valley, this is very typical of many other such farms set among the rolling downs of Wiltshire: a mixture of arable fields and of pastures for beef-cattle and dairy-cows.

One approaches the house past mossy rick-stones, old cattle-troughs now filled with flowers, and tree-stumps overgrown by periwinkles. A lovely magnolia covers the front wall. Inside, the early Victorian features have been retained – panelled doors, arches and window shutters. My bedroom had windows on two sides with pretty curtains and views across fields of cows to the hills. Late in the year, the pens immediately below are full of calves. Throughout the house, soft colours predominate, with carefully arranged flowers, baskets of trailing plants and interesting paintings well lighted (one is by Cecil Beaton, who used to live in the village). There are good carpets and attractive wallpapers everywhere, even in the bathroom. In the big sitting-room, deep armchairs are grouped around a log fire and well-stocked bookshelves. Last but far from least, Janet Pickford is an excellent cook. Meals are served in a dining-room that still has the old built-in bread oven, often with local trout and pheasant on the menu. (Baby-sitting can be arranged.)

Many guests go walking. The Pickfords have produced their own map of local footpaths, all well waymarked in this region, which lead down to watercress beds in the valley or up to the Ridgeway which was once a drove road for oxen being taken to market. Croquet and tennis are also available.

I first stayed here in order to visit nearby Salisbury and its cathedral. In addition there is plenty to see in the area – Elizabethan Breamore House, attractive villages (like Downton, Fordingbridge or Tilshead), the Celtic fort on top of Figsbury Hill, Old Sarum with the ruins of its Norman castle on another hilltop, the Roman villa at Rockbourne, Wilton's historic carpet factory and Wilton House, for example. Other leading sights: Stonehenge, the New Forest, two shire horse centres, and plenty of gardens (garden centres too).

Readers' comments: The best b & b in England! Everything about Stoke Farm would be difficult to fault. Very pleasant and helpful. Wonderful! Most comfortable; huge towels, wonderful bathroom. Great kindness. Superb house, lovely antiques. Excellent on all counts.

STOTSFOLD HALL
C(5) S

Steel, Northumberland, NE47 0HP   Tel: 0434 673270
South of Hexham. Nearest main road: A695 from Hexham to Corbridge.

4 Bedrooms. £16.50. Some have own bath/toilet. Views of garden, country.
Light suppers if ordered.
1 Sitting-room. With central heating, TV.
Bar.
Large garden

Hexhamshire – the area of south Northumberland around the town of Hexham – is little known to visitors. Much of it is well-wooded countryside of steeply rolling hills. Off a quiet road which leads to nowhere in particular is Stotsfold Hall.

Once the heart of a big estate now broken up, the present house stands at the end of a long drive in a 15-acre park. There are big lawns, flowerbeds, a rose garden, and a large greenhouse. Even though the house is at 800 feet, the lie of the land is such that everything seems to flourish. Particularly impressive are the trees which are a feature of the grounds: copper beeches, lodgepole pines, larches and cedars, to name only a few.

The house was built in 1900 and is full of the monumental joinery characteristic of the time. The scale is large, ceilings high, windows big. Furnishings are conventional and comfortable. On the walls hang framed deeds and mortgages relating to the estate, some going back as far as 1662.

The Woottons do not usually provide an evening meal, and guests go to Hexham or Slaley to eat, or more often to the nearby Fox & Hounds – generally known as the 'Click 'Em In' from the cry of the waggoners who used to change horses here. On their return, visitors can make use of the house bar.

This is a place for people who want great peace in beautiful surroundings.

Readers' comments: The greatest feature for us was the way the Woottons welcomed us. Difficult to conceive of a better place to stay.

Only 10 minutes' walk from the centre of Hexham, **WEST CLOSE HOUSE** is in a quiet, private cul-de-sac (Hextol Terrace). Designed by an architect for himself about 70 years ago, it is a redbrick villa comfortably furnished in conventional style. The fine gardens, enclosed by tall, clipped beech hedges, are not large but they are beautifully tended, with a revolving summer-house at the back. Patricia Graham-Tomlinson provides simple snacks (restaurants nearby). £15–£22.

Readers' comments: The best so far: a winner. Made to feel at home. Breakfast and accommodation excellent. [Tel: 0434 603307; postcode: NE46 2AD]

STOURCASTLE LODGE

C PT X

Gough's Close, Sturminster Newton, Dorset, DT10 1BU   Tel: 0258 472320
South-west of Shaftesbury. Nearest main road: A357 from Blandford Forum
to Wincanton.

5 Bedrooms. £19.50–£32 (less for 3
nights). All have own bath/shower/toilet. TV
(some). Views of garden. No smoking.
Dinner. £14 for 3 courses (with choices)
and coffee, at 7.30 pm. Vegetarian or
special diets if ordered. Wine can be
brought in.
1 Sitting-room. With open fire, central
heating, TV.
Garden

Gourmets seek out this secluded town house, for peace as well as good food.
Although just off the market place, Gough's Close is traffic-free and quiet: a
narrow lane opening out into a green and pleasant place, with the River Stour
beyond. The 17th-century Lodge has been agreeably furnished by Jill Hookham-
Bassett, with soft greens and pinks predominating. Everything is very spick-
and-span, the bedrooms cottagey in style, and all rooms have views of the
secluded garden where one can take tea.

Ken and Jill, who achieved a gold star for cooking when she trained at Ealing
Technical College, also run a catering service, so food here is well above average.
A typical dinner might be: kedgeree, chicken cooked in a tarragon and mushroom
sauce, and charlotte Malakoff (made with cream and almonds). An unassuming
house with a lot to offer in the way of hospitality (baby-sitting available, too).

From the Lodge, it is easily possible to explore not only Dorset but parts of
Wiltshire and Somerset as well.

Mediaeval Sherborne's superb 15th-century abbey of golden stone deserves a
lingering visit because of its remarkable fan-vaulting, colourful roof-bosses and
other outstanding carvings, as well as a glass reredos engraved by Laurence
Whistler. There are two castles: one, Norman and perched on a steep mound;
the other, built for Sir Walter Raleigh and surrounded by park and gardens – it
contains a series of very fine rooms and art treasures.

At Shaftesbury, King Canute died; and the remains of King Edward
(martyred at Corfe Castle) were brought here. This ancient town is perched high
on a hilltop overlooking the lovely Blackmoor Vale, and from its centre the
picturesque cobbled street of Gold Hill makes a steep descent. Church, museum
of curiosities and the Grosvenor Hotel are all well worth a visit – the last because
it houses (upstairs) an incredible sideboard depicting the Battle of Otterburn
carved from one massive piece of wood. All around Sturminster Newton are
other places of scenic or historic interest – Blandford Forum, Milton Abbas,
Dorchester.

North Dorset is not as much frequented by tourists as the coastal area, even
though its landscape is very fine, and there is much to see.

Readers' comments: Friendly; eager to help and please. Tastefully furnished house
and spotlessly clean. Jill's cooking was superb. Delightful. Made to feel welcome
and at home. Room charming. Enjoyed our visit so much. Delicious food.

STOWE HILL HOUSE
Lichfield, Staffordshire, WS13 6TJ Tel: 0543 253098
Nearest main road: A38 from Lichfield to Burton-upon-Trent.

3 Bedrooms. £18–£25. Some have own bath/toilet. Tea/coffee facilities. TV. Views of garden.
Dinner. £10 for 3 courses and coffee, at about 7pm. Wine can be brought in. **Light suppers** if ordered.
1 Sitting-room. With open fire, central heating, piano.
Large garden
Closed in December and January.

Dr Johnson (whose birthplace in Lichfield can be visited) was a regular visitor to this elegant house built in 1745, and he used to run races with the maid-servants in the steep landscaped grounds that overlook the town and the cathedral's spires (sometimes floodlit above the treetops). Earlier, the Cromwellians used this site to attempt a bombardment of the cathedral – and Pat Rule will tell you a most unusual ghost story involving the soldiers' fried bacon!

The setting is very fine – sweeping lawns with cedars, rhododendrons and roses – as befits such a house, and indoors Pat has furnished the handsome rooms appropriately too. The Wedgwood-blue dining-room with a pretty cornice around the ceiling has gracefully draped curtains, and Sheraton chairs at the long table. Off it is a sitting-room that leads to a conservatory. A notable galleried staircase rises to bedrooms which have, for instance, festoon blinds and a pink moiré bed-spread. In one very attractive bathroom is a trellis wallpaper. For dinner, Pat serves such meals as pâté, salmon and cheesecake.

Beneath 'the Ladies of the Vale', as the three spires of Lichfield's 13th-century cathedral are known, is a particularly lovely interior and the west front is a mass of statues. Rich stained glass and the green close add to its charm. The town's history is told in a series of tableaux at the Heritage Centre.

Northward lies Abbots Bromley, in which colourfully costumed men dance in September – bearing Saxon antlers – not only along the streets but also in the grounds of **YEATSALL FARM** in Yeatsall Lane. Windows have fine views of the lake below, by which you can walk or go birdwatching. Beautifully decorated by Joyce Lawton herself, the rooms have beams and much stripped pine; the bathrooms are very good. An outbuilding holds old farm machines, a forge with great bellows, and a decorative gypsy caravan. (Light snacks only.)

Occasionally, Richard's 4-seater Piper takes off. In the town are puppet shows. £15–£20. [Tel: 0283 840343; postcode WS15 3BY]

STOWFORD HOUSE   C S
Stowford Lane, Stowford, Devon, EX20 4BZ   Tel: 056683 415
South-west of Okehampton. Nearest main road: A30 from Okehampton to
Launceston.

6 Bedrooms. £17.50–£20 (less for 3 nights mid-week **to readers of this book only**). Most have own bath/shower/toilet. Tea/coffee facilities. TV. Views of garden, country.
Dinner. £12 (or £16 to non-residents) for 4 courses (with choices) and coffee, at 7–8pm. Vegetarian or special diets if ordered. Wine can be ordered. **Light suppers** if ordered.
1 Sitting-room. With open fire, central heating, TV. **Bar.**
Large garden
Closed in January and February.

This former country rectory is now a comfortable hotel, dignified by its 18th-century features such as the fine windows, handsome front door, a graceful archway inside and impressive staircase. The large garden is at its best in May.

The hotel has a reputation for good food. With over 20 years' experience of running first a catering service for businessmen and then a restaurant in Winchester, Jenny Irwin has accumulated a wide repertoire of recipes. Typical dishes she may serve – in a dining-room with a particularly fine Victorian fireplace – include kidneys in sherry, mocca roulade, and Cambridge tart (made with mixed peel and glacé cherries).

Bedrooms are large, light and airy. Everywhere is a profusion of pot-plants; and on some walls are delicate watercolours by her father-in-law, Sydney Irwin.

Nearby is Lydford which, a thousand years ago and more, was a place of note (its tin was exported to the Mediterranean). In Saxon times it even had its own mint; and seven coins from the time of Ethelred the Unready are displayed at the Castle Inn. The neat, square castle was built in 1195 for use as a 'stannary' prison (the tin-miners had their own 'stannary' laws and courts – *stannum* is Latin for tin), with a pretty little church beside it. Lydford is also famous for its gorge – one can walk by foaming waters with oak woods hanging overhead to the roaring 200-foot waterfall known as the White Lady. Lichens, mosses and ferns give the scene a subtropical look as the waters hurtle around smooth black boulders.

Within about 30 miles are Princetown (high and bleak, famous for Dartmoor Prison, which was built by Napoleonic prisoners, and for prehistoric stones nearby), Plymouth, the sandy resort of Bude with rocky Tintagel beyond, Exeter, lovely Salcombe, Looe and Clovelly.

From here one can explore the 400 square miles of Dartmoor's wild hills, its forest and woodlands, granite tors, archaeological sites and moorland villages. As well as the famous Dartmoor ponies roaming free, there is a great deal of wildlife. Granite quarries, stone slab bridges, waterfalls, ruins of tin mines, thatched cottages – all contribute to the variety of the scene. There are guided walks with experts to explain what one sees, or National Park leaflets to consult if you go on your own (available at nine information centres).

Southward lies Tavistock, where Francis Drake grew up, and Drake's home, Buckland Abbey (with the Drake Naval Museum), is near.

Readers' comments: Made most welcome. Delightful accommodation, wonderful meals. Excellent. Very impressed with the ambience and the owners. Really beautiful house. Exceptional food. Very quiet. Warmest welcome. Food excellent.

STRATFORD LODGE   C(8) M PT X
4 Park Lane, Castle Road, Salisbury, Wiltshire, SP1 3NP
Tel: 0722 325177

8 Bedrooms. £20–£27 (less for 2 nights). Prices go up from Easter. Bargain breaks. All have own bath/shower/toilet. Tea/coffee facilities. TV. Views of garden. Balcony (one). No smoking. Washing machine on request.
Dinner. £16 for 4 courses, or fewer *pro rata* (with choices) and coffee, at 7–8pm. Vegetarian or special diets if ordered. Wine can be ordered. No smoking. **Light suppers** if ordered.
2 Sitting-rooms. With open fire, central heating, piano, record-player.
Small garden

In a quiet byway overlooking a park stands a fine Victorian house, now a handsomely furnished guest-house. Jill Bayly has taken a lot of trouble to find good furniture in keeping with the style of the house. The sitting-room has much Victoriana and a large array of African violets; the pale green dining-room, mahogany tables laid with pretty rosy china (napkins to match) and rose curtains at the windows. Bedrooms are attractive, particularly one with a cane and carved bedhead on a bed with cover to complement the apricot walls. In another room, pale pink, brass beds have lace spreads. After dark one can go on sitting in the garden which is enclosed by flowering shrubs, because Jill brings out candle-lamps. Beyond it is the vegetable plot which provides fresh produce.

Jill has a varied repertoire of dishes for dinner (only light suppers on Sundays and Wednesdays, served in the conservatory), and she cooks to a high standard. A typical meal: home-made soup, avocado with a Roquefort and walnut dressing; duckling with a sauce of port and redcurrant jelly; and a help-yourself dessert table. Breakfasts, too, are generous, with options such as kedgeree, and marmalade which she makes herself.

Salisbury is also known as New Sarum (new in 1220!) because the first town was elsewhere, on the hill now known as Old Sarum which began as an Iron Age fort – you can still see traces of a Norman cathedral up there. When it was decided to rebuild on a better site, the new cathedral, with the tallest spire in England, was surrounded by grass and big walls to keep the town at a distance.

Readers' comments: Dinner superb, a meal to remember.

FARTHINGS, at 9 Swaynes Close, Salisbury, is very central (there's a view of the cathedral spire over rooftops) yet very quiet, and it has a garden with brimming flowerbeds. All rooms are immaculate, and pleasantly furnished. Gill Rodwell's breakfast choices include croissants and much else. Light suppers if ordered. £16–£18 (b & b).
Readers' comments: Clean, quiet and excellent value for money. Very charm-

ing lady. Gleamingly clean. [Tel: 0722 330749; postcode: SP1 3AE]

STREET FARMHOUSE   C D X

South Warnborough, Hampshire, RG25 1RS   Tel: 0256 862225
South-east of Basingstoke. Nearest main road: A287 from Odiham to
Farnham (and M3, junction 5).

3 Bedrooms. £15–£19 (**less to readers of this book staying 7 nights**). Some have own bath/shower/toilet. Tea/coffee facilities. TV. Views of garden, country. No smoking. Washing machine on request.
Dinner (if ordered). £10 for 3 courses (with choices) and coffee, at 7.30pm. Non-residents not admitted. Vegetarian or special diets if ordered. Wine can be brought in. No smoking. **Light suppers.**
1 Sitting-room. With open fire, central heating, TV, record-player.
Large garden

Two 16th-century cottages were combined into one to make this attractive house, beamed and with inglenook fireplace, in an ancient village through which a stream runs. Wendy Turner's choice of furnishings admirably complements the old house. There are prettily carved chairs in the pale green dining-room; pine doors have been stripped and brick walls exposed; buttoned chairs in rust-colour covers are gathered around a log stove in the sitting-room. Bedrooms are very pleasant – for instance, furnished with chest-of-drawers of woven cane, with very good armchairs and colour schemes. One bathroom has an oval bath in peach, and a bidet. Standards throughout are high and in the garden there is a heated swimming-pool. Dinner might include pork in cider with apricots, and raspberry pavlova. (Baby-sitting available.)

North Hampshire (quickly accessible along the M3) is an ideal base from which to explore southern England: within an hour are Winchester, Southampton and the New Forest. But anyone who lingers here will find plenty of interest, not least because this is Jane Austen country (her house is at Chawton, and scenes from the area feature in her books). Farnham still has streets much as she knew them, and a hilltop castle. Not far away is Selborne where Gilbert White wrote his natural history (1789) and one can still see countryside that he saw. Both his and Jane Austen's homes are open to the public – his has a museum about Captain Oates and Scott's Antarctic expedition and it is surrounded by National Trust woodlands. Nearby Odiham, too, retains the appearance of an 18th-century market town, with ruined castle nearby; and there are pretty villages – Greywell, Upton Grey (houses encircling a pond), Sherborne St John (with a Tudor NT mansion, the Vyne, and moated Beaurepaire), Basing (castle ruins). Silchester was once a great Roman fort.

Westward lie Litchfield, a flowery village in an area of prehistoric remains; Wherwell, a real showpiece – all timber and thatch, with fine views of the famous River Test; streamside Hurstbourne Tarrant; and Highclere – castle and hilltop grave of Lord Carnarvon (who discovered Tutankhamun's tomb in 1922). In marked contrast to all these quiet pleasures are Farnborough's air show and Aldershot's military tattoo.

Readers' comments: An outstanding experience. A place of great character; seldom have we met such friendly people. Excellent in all respects.

SUGARSWELL FARM
Shenington, Warwickshire, OX15 6HW Tel: 0295 680512
South of Stratford-upon-Avon. Nearest main road: A422 from Stratford to Banbury.

3 Bedrooms. £19–£25 (less for 7 nights). All have own bath/toilet. Tea/coffee facilities. TV. Views of country. No smoking. Laundry facilities on request.
Dinner. £16 for 3 courses and coffee, at 6.30pm. Non-residents not admitted. Wine can be brought in. No smoking.
1 Sitting-room. With open fire, central heating, TV. No smoking.
Large garden

Rosemary Nunnely is a cook of cordon bleu calibre – her greatest delight is preparing meals. Visitors who stay with her are likely to get something very different from ordinary 'farmhouse fare': on the day of my first visit, she had prepared seafood gratin followed by fillet steak (home-produced) in a sauce of port, cream and garlic, with crème brûlée to finish. Rosemary uses wine and cream in many of her dishes, rum in such specialities as Jamaican torte.

The house is modern but made from old stones taken from a demolished cottage. It has big picture-windows, and a striking staircase with 18th-century portraits. Sofas are grouped round a huge stone fireplace in the sage green sitting-room. The hall, like the dining-room, has terracotta walls. Guests sit on Chippendale chairs to dine; there is good silver on the table, and one side of the dining-room consists of a glass wall filled with Rosemary's collection of Crown Derby.

Upstairs are elegant bedrooms – one with a sofa from which to enjoy woodland views beyond the fields where cows graze, and a very large bathroom decorated in bright mulberry.

Included in the price is the gift of a touring map of the region, showing how to get to (for instance) Warwick, Stratford, the Cotswold towns, Woodstock (Blenheim Palace), Oxford, Silverstone (car races) and Sulgrave (the Washington ancestral home) or such stately homes as Upton House (horse trials in autumn) and Farnborough Hall. In Shenington itself is an outstanding garden, at Brook Cottage.

As to the curious name Sugarswell, Rosemary explained its origin: shuggers (mediaeval slang for robbers) made a settlement here, which their more respectable neighbours destroyed. Vestiges can still be seen from the air.

Readers' comments: Lovely home, superb cooking. A marvellous place. Time-capsule of the good life! Excellent: very good food and well-appointed bedrooms. Charming hostess, comfortable and delightful accommodation, delicious food. Very pleasant rooms and good views. Superb welcome, superb cooking. A lovely place to stay. An outstanding cook. Accommodation excellent. *And from the former manager of a 5-star hotel:* We have been back nine times.

Prices are per person in a double room at the beginning of the year.

SULNEY FIELDS   C D P T S
Colonel's Lane, Upper Broughton, Nottinghamshire, LE14 3BD
Tel: 0664 822204

North-west of Melton Mowbray (Leicestershire). Nearest main road: A606
from Melton Mowbray to Nottingham.

5 Bedrooms. £12.50–£15 (less for 2
nights). Some have own bath/shower/toilet.
Tea/coffee facilities. Views of garden.
Washing machine on request.
Dinner. About £7.50 for 3 courses and
coffee, by arrangement. Vegetarian or
special diets if ordered. Wine may be
brought in. **Light suppers** if ordered.
1 Sitting-room. With open fire, central
heating, TV, record-player.
Large garden

Panoramic views over the great Vale of Belvoir stretch in front of this handsome
18th-century house, entered through a pretty 'gothick' porch filled with flowering
plants. A big sitting-room has a wall of tall windows making the most of this
scene. Its silky coral walls are matched by the armchairs.

Hilary Dowson's bedrooms are equally handsome. A big blue one, with fine
mahogany furniture and good paintings, has an adjoining room for children, and
a pretty bathroom; the pink room, a bay window for enjoying those views.
Outside is a sheltered swimming-pool.

As to dinner, Hilary serves meals like prawn cocktail, coq au vin and summer
pudding.

Melton Mowbray is famous for pies (visit Ye Olde Pork Pie Shoppe) and
Stilton cheese, made in Colston Bassett village where you can buy it direct; there
are riverside parks and an ancient church. Other churches (and villages) well
worth a visit include those of Waltham-on-the-Wolds (carved monks), Denton
(gatehouses; manor with lakes) and Bottesford (monuments, and witchcraft
associations). Go to Loughborough for its carillon of 47 bells and its five-mile
Victorian railway line or, if you are a walker, enjoy the wildlife reserve near
Holwell, among plenty of other possibilities.

What remains of great Sherwood
Forest lies to the north of Nottingham,
and here (in Ricket Lane, Blidworth) is
a Victorian hunting-lodge, **HOLLY
LODGE**. It is near the estate of
ancient Newstead Abbey which
became Byron's home: it and its
grounds are open to the public.
Visitors' bedrooms at the Lodge are in
converted stables opening onto a
grassy court with chairs. A Laura
Ashley suite with mahogany-fitted
bathroom is particularly attractive.
Dinners are eaten in the house, sometimes in the big kitchen with its dresser
and copper pans: by arrangement, Ann
Shipside produces such meals as

stuffed tomatoes, salmon, apple-and-
sultana custard crumble. Afterwards,
one can sit under the grapevine and
fuchsias of the conservatory to enjoy a
view of old roses and woodland, or by
a log fire in the William Morris sitting-
room. £17–£20. [Tel: 0623 793853;
postcode: NG21 0NQ]

SUNSHINE COTTAGE   C M PT X
The Green, Shepherdswell, Kent, CT15 7LQ   Tel: 0304 831359
North-west of Dover. Nearest main road: A2 from Dover towards Canterbury
(also M2, junction 7; and M20, junction 13).

5 Bedrooms. £16–£19 (less for 5 nights or continental breakfast). Some have own shower/toilet. Tea/coffee facilities. Views of garden, country. No smoking. Washing machine on request.
Dinner. £11 for 3 courses (with choices) and coffee, at 6.30–8.30pm. Vegetarian or special diets if ordered. Wine can be ordered or brought in. No smoking. **Light suppers** if ordered.
2 Sitting-rooms. With open fire, central heating, TV, record-player. No smoking.
Small garden

Neither shepherd nor well gave this pretty village its name: the Saxons knew it as Sibert's Wold. Sunshine Cottage, built in 1635, is now the home of Barry and Lyn Popple.

One steps into a cosy sitting-room with shaggy, cocoa-coloured carpet and low beams, a velvet sofa facing a brick inglenook that has logs piled high and hop bines draped across it. In a kitchen that is open to view, Lyn cooks such meals as home-made soups, chops or chicken, fruit salad or spotted dick. These are served in a dining-room where antique pine is complemented by coir matting, dressers display antique plates, old pews and stickback chairs surround tables laid with pretty china.

There is one ground-floor bedroom (with shower), decorated with Liberty fabrics. Those upstairs vary in size and style; several have antique iron bedsteads and views of village rooftops. Barry is an artist and some of his pictures are on the walls. (Baby-sitting available.)

Readers' comments: Full of treasures. A relaxed cottage atmosphere. Made us very welcome.

At Coldred, in Church Road, is 16th-century **COLDRED COURT FARM**, home of Truda Kelly. Not only does she make all the ice cream, preserves and bread (new-baked by 7am!) but she and her mother have filled the house with crochet bed-spreads, embroidered or patchwork curtains, dried flowers and other deco-rative touches. Their scented candles, herbal lotions and local honey are on sale. Windows have leaded panes; there are inglenooks, stone-paved floors and board doors. In the cellar are TV and pool rooms; a ground-floor bedroom is in what was once a dairy.

Meat, herbs and free-range eggs come from the farm – through which the North Downs Way passes. £18.50–£20.
Readers' comments: Delightful: warm, family atmosphere, food good. [Tel: 0304 830816; postcode: CT15 5AQ]

TANHOUSE FARM

Rusper Road, Newdigate, Surrey, RH5 5BX   Tel: 0306 631334
South of Dorking. Nearest main road: A24 from Dorking to Horsham
(and M25, junction 9).

2 Bedrooms. £14.50–£17. Tea/coffee
facilities. Views of garden. No smoking.
Washing machine on request.
Light suppers if ordered.
1 Sitting-room. With open fire, central
heating, TV. No smoking.
Large garden

A dozen shoes, at least two centuries old, are displayed in the kitchen of this
16th-century, half-timbered farmhouse. They were discovered at the back of
chimneys when alterations were being done – inside several children's shoes were
ears of corn (fertility symbols). The shoes came as no great surprise because,
throughout this area, these are often found: putting them up chimneys was
believed to bring good luck. This was once the house of tanners and cobblers,
who could doubtless afford to be liberal with their shoe charms.

One can see through into the kitchen from the breakfast-room (low-beamed
and with latched doors), which opens onto a terrace overlooking a small brook
and a pond with an island frequented by 40 ducks, geese and coots. There's a
76-foot well and a lily-pool too, with fields of sheep and cows beyond.

All rooms have character. In a brick inglenook is an iron fireback dated 1644;
around it are greeny-blue velvet armchairs and low oak tables, solid and heavy,
which began life as wood-chopping or pig-slaughtering benches. A carved sideboard is loaded with old china. On the landing is revealed the cruck construction
of the house (that is, massive curving tree-timbers used in their natural shape
to support the roof). Pastel walls and fabrics (complementing pale green or pink
carpets) give the bedrooms a fresh, light look.

For dinner, Nina Fries recommends either Gammages nearby or several of the
many local inns.

There's a hidden corner in Dorking:
an oval green, high up, where horses
graze (within minutes of the High
Street). Around this conservation area
pretty villas were built in 1830, one of
which, **5 ROSE HILL**, is now the
home of Margaret Walton. She has
chosen lovely fabrics and wallpapers
while retaining such features as
graceful cast-iron fireplaces and even
rather splendid Victorian baths. The
bedroom with the best view is on the
second floor: beyond Dorking's
mellow rooftops you can see Ranmore
Common (NT) and Denbies' huge
vineyard (open to visitors for tastings).
In the handsome dining-room, she

serves candlelit dinners (such as
smoked salmon, chicken fricassée,
pavlova), Sunday lunches and snacks.
Breakfast is sometimes on the sunny
terrace overlooking a secluded garden.
Baby-sitting available. £15–£17.50.
[Tel: 0306 883127; postcode: RH4
2EG]

THORNLEY HOUSE

D PT X

Allendale, Northumberland, NE47 9NH   Tel: 0434 683255

South-west of Hexham. Nearest main road: A69 from Newcastle to Hexham.

3 Bedrooms. £17.50 (less for 4 nights). All have own bath/shower/toilet. Tea/coffee facilities. TV. Views of garden, country. Washing machine on request.
Dinner. £8.50 for 3 courses and coffee, at about 7pm. Non-residents not admitted. Vegetarian or special diets if ordered. Wine can be brought in.
2 Sitting-rooms. With central heating, TV, piano, record-player.
Large garden
Closed in November.

Allendale Town is a large village in a sheltered valley amid some of the most open scenery in England – deserted grouse moors and breezy sheep pastures which stretch for uninterrupted miles, punctuated only by isolated farmhouses and the occasional relic of the lead mining which once made this area important. On the outskirts of the village is Thornley House, a large and solid inter-war house in a big garden with woods and fields around it. Rooms are spacious and light, with views of the wooded roads into the village and of the Pennines.

Eileen Finn is a keen cook, and though guests are offered conventional fare (vichyssoise soup, breaded chicken, salad, and chocolate mousse, for example, served on Wedgwood china), she needs only a little encouragement to cook a dish from Mexico, where she lived for eight years, or from another of the many countries to which she has paid long visits. Bread, yogurt and muesli are home-made, orange juice freshly squeezed. Mementoes of her journeys abound in the house: batik pictures from Kenya, onyx figures and chess sets from Mexico, Chinese paintings (one on cork), rugs from Turkey and elsewhere (and others she has made herself). As well as being a linguist and chess-player (she enjoys playing with guests), she is an able pianist, and there is a Steinway grand in one of the two sitting-rooms. Visitors may be taken on guided walks on occasion. Otherwise, they can make their way through woodland to the village. At Christmas, there is a full-board house-party.

Allendale is Catherine Cookson's country. She lives nearby and many of her Mallen stories are set here. It is one of the loveliest parts of the north country, wild and rocky, in parts comparable with some Swiss scenery. Allen Banks, where two rivers converge, is a beauty-spot. Not far off is the Killhope Pass (nearly 2000 feet high) with a great wheel once used for crushing ore when these hills were mined for lead. A long process of restoration (by Durham County Council) is approaching completion: the result will be one of the most interesting 'working museums' in the country. In Allendale Town, on every New Year's Eve costumed 'guizers' parade with blazing tar-barrels on their heads – vestige of a half-forgotten pagan fire rite. At Allenheads a few miles away, an award-winning heritage centre houses a small display about the history of the area, shops and a café. At Hexham is a great Norman abbey, well worth visiting.

Readers' comments: Very welcome. Delightful venue. Very comfortable. Friendly. Nice house, excellent room. Superbly quiet and comfortable. Wonderful food.

THORNTON MANOR

C(5)

Ettington, Warwickshire, CV37 7PN Tel: 0789 740210
South-east of Stratford-upon-Avon. Nearest main road: A429 from Warwick
to Stow-on-the-Wold (and M40, junction 15).

3 Bedrooms. £16–£17 (less for 3 nights
or continental breakfast). All have own
bath/shower/toilet. Tea/coffee facilities in
kitchen. Views of garden, country. No
smoking. Washing machine on request.
Light suppers sometimes.
1 Sitting-room. With log stove, central
heating, TV, piano.
Large garden

A stately home in miniature, this stone manor house, E-shaped in plan, declares
its date, 1658, on a doorpost. Through an iron-studded oak door with decorative
hinges, heavy bolts and locks, one enters a great hall dominated by a large stone
fireplace with log stove. Overhead are massive chamfered beams.

Through the leaded panes of deep-set, mullioned windows in the breakfast-
room (and in a bedroom above it) there are views of the garden, woods and the
fields of this farm, which is well tucked away at the end of a long drive. Little
humps in the grass show where there was once a village in view until, in the 13th
century, the Black Death killed off all its 60 inhabitants. Ancient outbuildings
include an old pigeon-house from the days when the birds were farmed.

Gill Hutsby (who occasionally sings at the Royal Shakespeare Theatre) has
used old-fashioned furniture and rosy cretonnes in the bedrooms. There is a
kitchen for guests' use, and also a tennis court. Visitors can fish for trout in the
Hutsbys' lake or enjoy coarse fishing in the River Dean. Stratford-upon-Avon
(best visited out of season) has not only Shakespeare's birthplace but also Hall's
Croft (his daughter's home), the fine mediaeval church with his tomb, and
Harvard House (after which the American university was named).

Also at Ettington is **GROVE FARM**,
a house found at the end of a brick
path, with grapevine beside it and an
old pump. It is full of character, with
unusual furniture and trifles Meg and
Bob Morton have collected: from a
spectacular carved sideboard to an old
imp's head built into one wall, an elm
manger to a collection of knobkerries.
The chased silver pheasant-gun
belonged to Bob's grandfather and the
old dough-chest to Meg's (he was a
baker). Bedrooms, under the sloping
eaves, have own bathrooms, pretty fabrics, good carpets and old-fashioned
furniture. Meg serves only light suppers. (The bar food at the Houndshill
Inn is very good.) Meg cares for elderly

horses; they are to be seen grazing in
the fields beyond which are deer
woods and a panoramic view of the
Cotswolds as far as Bourton-on-the-
Water. £14.50–£17.50.
Readers' comments: Warm, friendly welcome. Most impressed. [Tel: 0789
740228; postcode: CV37 7NX]

TIGHE FARM   C(8)
Stone-in-Oxney, Kent, TN30 7JU   Tel: 023383 251
North of Rye (East Sussex). Nearest main road: A268 from Hawkhurst to Rye.

2 Bedrooms. £17 (less for 3 nights). Views of garden, country.
Light suppers if ordered.
1 Sitting-room. With open fire, central heating, TV, piano.
Large garden
Closed from December to February.

This 17th-century house is full of works of art and unusual antiques (collected by Jimmy Hodson's father, a sculptor before he took to sheep-farming here) and also oriental pieces (Elise's family lived in India for many years). The blue bedroom, for instance, has not only a carved mediaeval table but geisha-girl prints and Numdah rugs; in the oldest room, with mullioned windows, is a Kashmir chain-stitch rug. The Hodsons have retained one very curious feature – an iron winch above the staircase, which they think was used when hiding contraband (Romney Marsh was notorious for smuggling).

One breakfasts at a polished refectory table with rush chairs in a particularly interesting room – hop-bines are strung across the inglenook, with a copy of a statue of the Virgin Mary in Notre-Dame; there's a carved oak sideboard and brass-rubbings from the local church. In the beautiful sitting-room are unusual chests and other antiques; the old iron fireback carries the royal coat-of-arms.

The garden is equally attractive, especially a paved terrace, brimming with fuchsias and roses.

As dinner is not served (only snack suppers), Elise provides visitors with menus gathered from good local inns and restaurants – and with a file in which she has detailed routes recommended for sightseeing tours.

Being midway between Rye and Tenterden (each described elsewhere), Tighe Farm is ideally placed for exploring historic and beautiful parts of both Sussex and Kent. Guests usually visit Smallhythe (Ellen Terry's Tudor house), Sissinghurst and Great Dixter gardens, Bodiam Castle, Tenterden and its steam railway, Camber sands and the Romney Marsh churches.

Readers' comments: Very welcoming and helpful. Excellent room, peaceful. Have stayed three times: so welcome; peaceful; a stately home in miniature. Made very welcome. Mrs Hodson very helpful. Very good value for money. Wish we had stayed longer. Surpassed our expectations. Made more than welcome. Fresh and polished to a glow. Shall stay here frequently. Excellent value.

The addresses of houses are geographically correct but postal addresses sometimes differ (for correspondence, the only essential element is the postcode).

Information about the nearest town and 'A' road helps you to locate the whereabouts of any village on a map; but before setting off it is necessary to get precise instructions from your host as many houses are very much 'off the beaten track'.

TILED HOUSE FARM
C(10) S

Oxlynch Lane, Oxlynch, Gloucestershire, GL10 3DF   Tel: 0453 822363
West of Stroud. Nearest main road: A38 from Gloucester to Bristol
(and M5, junction 13).

3 Bedrooms. £14–£15 (less for 7 nights). Prices go up in April. One has own bath/shower/toilet.   Tea/coffee   facilities. Views of garden, country. No smoking.
Dinner (if ordered). £7 for 2 courses and coffee, at 6.30pm. Vegetarian or special diets if ordered. Wine can be brought in. No smoking.
1 Sitting-room. With open fire, central heating, TV, video, piano. No smoking.
Large garden
Closed in December.

Long ago, this was the first house in the area to have the innovation of tiles to replace thatch on the roof, hence its name. A paved path flanked by rick-stones leads to the front door of the 400-year-old house. The ceilings are low and stairs steep. In a big sitting-room with huge stone fireplace, the original bacon-hooks in the beams and gun-racks above the hearth still remain. The green and white colour scheme contrasts with a polished woodblock floor.

From the dining-room, which overlooks a farmyard sometimes full of much-photographed pedigree cows, stairs go up to some of the bedrooms (and a very nice bathroom), the largest of which has timber-framed walls. There is also a self-contained ground-floor suite with good bathroom; here a strange little 'gothick' window was uncovered in a thick stone wall when renovations were being done.

In nearby Quedgeley there are five restaurants; but for visitors not wanting to go out Diane Jeffery will make an inexpensive supper of, for instance, tuna mousse with salad, baked potato and garlic bread, or chicken casserole, followed by apricot gâteau with cream.

Readers' comments: First-class accommodation and superb breakfast. Delightful.

At the foot of a National Trust hill is **LOWER GREEN FARMHOUSE**, Haresfield, a house of stone walls, leaded and mullioned windows, beamed ceilings. The light and spacious family bedroom is particularly attractive, with views across the Severn to the Forest of Dean (superb sunsets). Visitors to this far west part of the Cotswolds find not only lovely scenery but countless picturesque villages, inns and stately homes.

By arrangement, Margaret Reed will provide light suppers. In the garden is a stone barbecue, pool with

yellow irises and a 40-foot well. £14–£15.
Readers' comments: Can't recommend too highly. Excellent cook and hostess. [Tel: 0452 728264; postcode: GL10 3DS]

TREGADDRA FARM   **C X**

near Cury, Cornwall, TR12 7BB   Tel: 0326 240235
South of Helston. Nearest main road: A3083 from Helston to Lizard.

5 Bedrooms. £17.50–£19.50. Most have own bath/shower/toilet. Tea/coffee facilities. Views of garden, country. Balcony (two).
Dinner. £6 for 3 courses and coffee, at 6.30pm. Non-residents not admitted. Vegetarian or special diets if ordered. Wine can be brought in. No smoking. **Light suppers** if ordered.
2 Sitting-rooms. With open fire (in one), TV.
Garden

A beautifully kept garden of winding flowerbeds and spacious swimming-pool (heated) is the setting for this immaculate house, built in the 18th century but much modernized since. Two upstairs bedrooms have balconies. All around are distant views, especially fine when the sun is setting over the sea – in the other direction, Goonhilly's satellite station on the moors is quite spectacular too.

Rooms are well furnished in conventional style, with plenty of space and comfort. When evenings are chilly, logs blaze in a granite inglenook, and there is a glass sun-room to make the most of the mild climate in this very southerly part of England. (Baby-sitting available.)

For dinners, June Lugg uses the produce of the farm (vegetables, beef) whenever she can. With the beef comes something different from the usual Yorkshire pudding: Cornish cobblers. This might be followed by blackberry and apple crumble – one for each family – with clotted cream.

The Lizard peninsula is a particularly beautiful area. There are sandy beaches and coves, fishing villages, old inns, coastal walks and all the creeks of the River Helford to explore.

In the valley hamlet of Nantithet, near Cury, Jill and Harry Mizen have modernized an 18th-century cottage called **RIVERSIDE** as a small guest-house, its garden bordered by a stream. One steps straight into the sitting-room with inglenook, beyond which is a dining-room with doors to the walled garden, pine furniture and an open-tread staircase to pretty bedrooms. These include an all-cream one, with frilled bedcovers and a rocking chair; a blue-and-pink one in Provençal style; and one with a sofa from which to enjoy the view. In addition, a modern garden annexe has a ground-floor bedroom with its own sitting/dining-room (it is equipped for either self-catering or b & b visitors).

As to meals, a typical dinner might be melon balls with prawns (in a spicy dressing), steak-and-wine pie and 'granny's' rice pudding. Crafts for sale; baby-sitting available. £15.50–£18.

Readers' comments: Very comfortable. Good home cooking. [Tel: 0326 241027; postcode: TR12 7RB]

TREGONY HOUSE
Tregony, Cornwall, TR2 5RN   Tel: 087 253 671

C(7) PT

East of Truro. Nearest main road: A3078 from St Mawes towards St Austell.

rear view

6 Bedrooms. £28.75–£31.75 **including dinner** (less for 7 nights). Prices go up from May. Some have own bath/shower/toilet. Tea/coffee facilities. TV. Views of garden, country. Washing machine on request.
Dinner. 4 courses (with some choices) and coffee, at 7pm. Special diets if ordered. Wine can be ordered.
1 Sitting-room. With open fire, central heating, TV, record-player. Bar.
Garden
Closed from November to February.

Behind a cream façade is a house partly dating from the 17th century; later, additions were made – so the dining-room, for instance, is low-beamed and thick-walled while the hall and sitting-room have 18th-century elegance, particularly since the addition of a pomegranate wallpaper in the hall, rounded alcoves crammed with books, and interesting antiques. All the bedrooms have their own individual character and comfortable style. They are furnished with antiques and pretty flower arrangements. Two double rooms with bathroom in between make a self-contained suite – suitable for families.

In the dining-room (furnished with oriental rugs, oak tables and Windsor chairs) Barry and Judy Sullivan serve such imaginative meals as spinach roulade, apricot and walnut stuffed lamb, and Calvados apple mousse (plus local cheeses). Herbs, raspberries, etc. come from the cottage-garden, where you can have tea.

From Tregony you can quickly reach the warm south coast of Cornwall, with all its coves, beaches, harbours and scenic drives.

Readers' comments: Food marvellous: imaginative and beautifully cooked. Warm and friendly. Interesting food; comfortable, friendly. Outstanding: excellent, imaginative meals attractively presented. A very happy week; accommodation excellent, comfortable, tastefully decorated; delicious food.

Perched on Vicarage Hill above Mevagissey, and looking south towards the sea, is this handsome 18th-century house (once it was a vicarage): **MEVAGISSEY HOUSE**. A great picture-window in the sitting-room makes the most of the view. Dinner is served by candlelight and Diana Owen's meals are based on the best of traditional cookery – cinnamon grape-fruit might be followed by steak pie and a pudding such as almond and raspberry pavlova. I particularly liked the king-sized brass bed with crochet cover, and the huge size of the

rear view

carpeted bathroom. (No smoking.) £14–£19.
Readers' comments: Charming hosts; excellent value. Delicious meals, very friendly. [Tel: 0726 842427; postcode: PL26 6SZ]

TREMEARNE

Bone Valley, Heamoor, Cornwall, TR20 8UG   Tel: 0736 64576
West of Penzance. Nearest main road: A30 from Penzance to Land's End.

3 Bedrooms. £17.50–£20 (less for 7 nights). Prices go up in July. All have own bath/shower/toilet. Tea/coffee facilities. Views of garden, country. No smoking. Washing machine on request.
Dinner. £10 for 2 courses and coffee, at 7pm. Non-residents not admitted. Vegetarian or special diets if ordered. Wine can be brought in. No smoking.
1 Sitting-room. With open fire, central heating, TV, video.
Large garden
Closed from November to February.

The granite house was neglected and the walled grounds completely overgrown with brambles, a Sleeping Beauty scene, when Sally Adams and her family came here. They restored the 'Jubilee' rose garden (planted in the year of Queen Victoria's diamond jubilee), and found many old-fashioned varieties still surviving – such as the lovely Albertine rambler rose, the scent of which greets you as you arrive.

One enters through a tiled conservatory, decorated with garlands of dried flowers. This is where Sally serves such dinners as beef cooked in Guinness, and plum crumble, using garden produce.

In the Victorian-style sitting-room, there are carpets and armchairs of deep turquoise contrasting with cream walls, and an open fire. Bedrooms have artistic touches and features such as an iron bed showing up well against coral walls, a crochet bedspread in one, old toys in another.

Readers' comments: Thoroughly recommended. It was home from home and with very friendly attention when needed.

East of Penzance is the village of St Hilary where, in Trewhella Lane, is a mine-owner's house of silvery granite, ideal for gourmets in particular: 17th-century **ENNYS FARM**. Sue White is a dedicated cook, who prepares such candlelit meals as avocado mousseline with smoked salmon, chicken in green peppercorn sauce and iced nut-cake with Kirsch (even more elaborate menus in winter). Bread is home-baked. There are a barbecue, a grass tennis court, patio for breakfast and swimming-pool. Indoors one finds alcoves, deep-set sash windows, pretty plasterwork and a shapely staircase. Rooms have handsome beds (one a four-poster), piles of lacy pillows, leather and velvet armchairs and flower pictures by a local artist. Family suites

and a laundry-room have been created in the stables (baby-sitting available). £17.50–£20.
Readers' comments: Wonderful hostess. Beautifully situated. Super food. Happy, caring atmosphere. Food exquisite. Highest commendation. The perfect place to unwind. Total peace and quiet. [Tel: 0736 740262; post-code: TR20 9BZ]

TREVIADES BARTON
D PT S

High Cross, near Constantine, Cornwall, TR11 5RG   Tel: 0326 40524
South-west of Falmouth. Nearest main road: A394 from Falmouth towards Helston.

3 Bedrooms. £18–£22. Two have own bath/shower/toilet. Tea/coffee facilities. Views of garden, country, river. Washing machine on request.
Dinner. £16.50 for 4 courses, wine and coffee, at 8pm. Non-residents not admitted. Vegetarian or special diets if ordered. Wine can be brought in.
2 Sitting-rooms. With open fire, central heating, TV, piano, record-player.
Large garden

This most unusual, U-shaped, 16th-century house is approached through a narrow and picturesque courtyard (paved with slate and full of daisies).

From the Treviades family, named in Domesday Book, the land passed to the Trefusis family in 1349 and they held it until 1920. But long before that there was almost certainly the villa of a Roman commander on this site; *trevia* is Latin for crossroads. Some parts of the present building may be as old as the 13th century, and successive owners have discovered old wells, fish tanks, disused fireplaces and windows, ancient steps and alcoves.

The long sitting-room is 18th-century. It is lined with cream-and-white panelling and has an Adam fireplace at one end, flanked by alcoves of china. Elegant tapestry and patchwork cushions (Judy's skilled work) are on the armchairs and sofas, marine watercolours on the walls. From here one can step out to a succession of individual walled gardens where camellias (and roses) flourish, with a croquet lawn and kitchen garden. The camellias are at their best in February or March.

Judy Ford runs courses on needlework, stencilling and cookery. As to this last, here is an example of her dinners: pâté with green mayonnaise, salmon trout, French apple flan with elderflower sorbet, and cheeses (wine included).

Such meals are served in a granite-walled dining-room, Regency chairs surrounding the big mahogany table, Royal Chelsea china on the table, scarlet candles in the silver candelabra. There is a pretty French stove on the hearth, and in one corner is – surprise! – one of the earliest vacuum cleaners, bellows-operated.

Readers' comments: A unique experience. Charming and welcoming hosts. Exceptionally attractive gardens. Excellent dinner, comfortable room.

From **THE HOME** at Penjerrick you can see, between wooded hills, ships in Falmouth Bay or take a path to a sandy beach. Ann Tremayne's small hotel was built in 1872 as a convalescent home for the needy, unlikely to have enjoyed such comfortable furnishings, glass sun-room with cacti or the excellent, homely cooking. You can bus from the front gate to villages along the River Helford or to

Falmouth Harbour; or walk the long-distance coastal path. £18–£23. [Tel: 0326 250427; postcode: TR11 5EE]

TREWERRY MILL

St Newlyn East, Cornwall, TR8 5HS Tel: 0872 510345

South of Newquay. Nearest main road: A30 from Redruth to Bodmin.

6 Bedrooms. £15–£17. Prices go up from June. Views of garden, country. No smoking. Washing machine on request.
Dinner. £6.50 for 3 courses (with choices) and coffee, at 6.45pm. Non-residents not admitted. Vegetarian or special diets if ordered. Wine can be ordered. No smoking.
1 Sitting-room. With open fire, central heating, TV. Bar. No smoking.
Large garden
Closed from November to March.

Trerice is an Elizabethan manor house of stone, with lattice-paned windows (one has 576 panes) and elaborate plaster ceilings. The watermill was built in 1639 to provide flour for the household; now it is a guest-house, the wheel stilled but a stream still flowing by. Ponds attract wildfowl.

One passes through a stone-flagged hall to a sitting-room with big leather armchairs around a log fire and a window through which there is an inside view of the waterwheel. Bedrooms are small and neat (there is one large family room); and the dining-room is simply furnished with oak tables and chairs. Here Ethel Grateley serves, for instance, turkey soup, local plaice in cheese sauce, homegrown vegetables and fruit crumbles – all for a very modest price. Morning coffee, lunches and cream teas also available. (In one of the barns is an art gallery.)

Readers' comments: Food plain but well cooked, bedrooms very comfortable, garden a delight. A lovely, restful weekend. A great success. Delightful place. Hosts extremely competent and concerned about the welfare of their guests. Fabulous value for money. A very special stay with super hosts. Great value. A favourite!

At Mithian, near St Agnes, is **ROSE-IN-VALE HOTEL**, a handsome 18th-century mansion that was once the home of a local mine captain. The Arthurs, in the course of improvements, uncovered such ancient features as a fringle (bread oven) in an inglenook. There are two large sitting-rooms with fine details preserved and on a curving staircase is a decorative window. In the modern extension at the back is a very long dining-room with huge windows giving a view of the lawns and rosebeds. A small, sheltered swimming-pool, heated by solar panels, is overlooked by some of the bedrooms (all en suite), and there is also a four-poster suite. Rooms are handsomely decorated.

The chef's specialities include fish mousse in crab sauce, duck in Grand Marnier and iced soufflé of peaches. Other amenities include a bar, solarium and games room. £20 (b & b) **to readers of this book only.**
Readers' comments: Hospitality beyond reproach. Service, comfort and cuisine excellent. Charming owners. [Tel: 0872 552202; messages: 0872 540319; postcode: TR5 0QD]

UPPER BUCKTON

Leintwardine, Herefordshire, SY7 0JU   Tel: 05473 634
West of Ludlow (Shropshire). Nearest main road: A4113 from Knighton towards Ludlow.

3 Bedrooms. £14–£20 (less for 3 nights). Views of garden, country, river. No smoking. Washing machine on request.
Dinner. £14 for 4 courses (with choices) and coffee, at 7pm. Special diets if ordered. Wine can be brought in. No smoking. **Light suppers** if ordered (for late arrivals).
1 Sitting-room. With open fire, central heating, TV. No smoking.
Large garden

Yvonne Lloyd is an accomplished cook, serving such starters as bananas and bacon with curry sauce or stuffed mushrooms; then roasts, salmon or chicken with orange and almonds; vacherins or chocolate roulade. Such meals are presented on Doulton's 'Old Colony' china with Harrods silver. It is largely her reputation for good food which brings visitors here – that, and the peace and quiet of this 18th-century house (at the centre of a 300-acre sheep and cereal farm) in which antiques furnish the comfortable rooms.

All bedrooms are named after local sites (mine was Coxall, with a view of Coxall Knoll where there was an Iron Age fort). Yvonne has a decorative touch, with a taste for ribbon-and-posy fabrics in one room (used even on the scalloped and quilted bedhead), poppies in another, for instance. All the frilled or pleated valances are made by her.

Outside is a verandah on which to sit with pre-dinner drink or after-dinner coffee to enjoy the view towards the high ridge of the Wigmore Rolls. A lawn slopes down to a clear millstream fringed by hostas, to one side a tall and graceful birch and to the other a high, feathery ash and the mound where once a Norman fort stood. A granary has been equipped with table tennis, darts and snooker; there are also a croquet lawn and other games.

This is very good country for walking and birdwatching, or for leisurely drives, and only a little further afield are the Shropshire hills, Radnor Forest, Elan Valley and Offa's Dyke. There are many picturesque black-and-white villages (typical of this area), and castles (relics of the centuries of border warfare with Wales): Ludlow, Stokesay, Croft, Powis, Montgomery. Museums cover all manner of special interests from cider-making to industrial archaeology, farming to local history. The Severn Valley steam railway is popular with children and adults.

I particularly enjoyed an evening drive high up where the buzzards fly, the still higher hills a distant blue. The sun went down on the glorious colours of gorse and rose bay willowherb which adorned the ever-varied shapes of hills and valleys. The following day, we drove along lanes flanked by the blowsy hedges and golden fields of a hot summer's day: whenever the road rose up there were head-turning panoramas of landscape laid out like a relief map.

Readers' comments: Outstanding location, imaginative and generous cooking, most comfortable. Marvellous hosts, lovely house, food excellent. Warm, attractive rooms, delicious meal, we felt completely at home. Gracious country living. First-class hosts. Our stay was a treat. Outstanding meals. Welcoming and comfortable.

UPPER GREEN FARM   M X
Manor Road, Towersey, Oxfordshire, OX9 3QR   Tel: 0844 212496
East of Thame. Nearest main road: A4129 from Thame to Princes Risborough
(and M40, junction 6).

9 **Bedrooms.** £17.50–£25. Most have own
bath/shower/toilet. Tea/coffee facilities. TV.
Views of garden, country. No smoking.
2 **Sitting-rooms.** With central heating,
TV. No smoking.
Large garden

A building of whitewash and thatch overlooking a duck-pond at the front,
Marjorie and Euan Aitken's house is one of the prettiest in this book. They
uncovered 15th-century beams with the original carpenters' identification marks;
came across Elizabethan coins; restored the wood shutters which (window-glass
having yet to be invented) were all that kept out wintry blasts five centuries ago;
found a secret priest-hole where, in the days of religious persecution, a Catholic
priest might have to hide for days when the search was on. In one huge chimney,
there were still the iron rungs up which small boys were forced to clamber to clear
the soot. An old kitchen-range and adjoining copper boiler have been preserved,
together with the rack on which spits for roasting whole sheep were kept, and the
special hooks used for drying the farmer's smocks by the fire. In the hall is a
pump (still working). Across the lawned farmyard is Paradise Barn, dated 1790,
with six en suite bedrooms. Breakfast is served in the barn which has the original
hayrack (now filled with dried flowers), a beamed ceiling and brick floors.

Marjorie, who used to be an antique dealer, has filled every room with
fascinating trifles – shelves of old bottles (found discarded in the garden), bead-
work pincushions and watch-cases, huge marble washstands, naive Staffordshire
figures, old brass scales (which she uses) and tin toys.

The Aitkens not only tell visitors about the well-known sights nearby (which
include Claydon House, Ryecote Chapel, West Wycombe's 'hellfire' caves, the
horses' home of rest, etc.) but introduce them to other sides of local life. For
instance, you may go and see the sorting and grading of sheep fleeces, join in bell-
ringing, pick up bargains at local markets or auctions, chat to balloonists as they
glide by only a few yards above the farm. And, of course, their sheep, ducks,
chickens and geese are an entertainment in themselves. The Aitkens can also
arrange for visitors to be taken to and from Heathrow or Gatwick by taxi, with car
hire available at the farm itself.

Bed-and-breakfast only; there is excellent pub food within a short
walking distance. Guests who bring their own snacks will be provided with plates,
tea, etc.

Readers' comments: Charming home, warm hospitality: we arrived as guests
and left as friends. Much impressed by warm welcome, delightful house
and excellent breakfast. Wonderful couple – it always feels like going home!
Charming people, absolutely delightful house. Superb breakfast. Absolutely
excellent.

UPPER HOUSE FARM

C D

Hopton Castle, Shropshire, SY7 0QF Tel: 05474 319

West of Ludlow. Nearest main road: A4113 from Knighton towards Ludlow.

3 Bedrooms. £16.50–£17.50. All have own bath/shower/toilet. Tea/coffee facilities. TV. Views of garden, country. No smoking. Washing machine on request.

Dinner. £9.50 for 4 courses and coffee, at 7pm. Non-residents not admitted. Vegetarian or special diets if ordered. Wine can be ordered or brought in. No smoking.

1 Sitting-room. With open fire, central heating. No smoking.

Large garden

Closed from November to January.

A very beautiful garden surrounds this 18th-century house, and indoors everything is of an equally high standard: from the good carpets and the velvet armchairs grouped around the fireplace to the cut-glass and silver on the dining-table, the antiques and the excellent bathrooms. You can enjoy a huge and sunny bedroom, a game at the pool table, or a stroll on the farm to look at cattle or Clun forest sheep. There's trout-fishing to be had, free, in the river or the farm's pool.

But above all it is Sue Williams' cooking that brings visitors back repeatedly, a combination of French and English recipes. (Typically, after a vol-au-vent she may serve pheasant casseroled in red wine followed by blueberry tart and cream, then cheeses.)

The picturesque ruins of Hopton Castle are on the farm's grounds (it was built by the Normans; and in 1642 thirty Roundheads held it against 300 Royalists for three weeks before being brutally massacred). Set in the lovely Clun Valley, high among wooded hills, there are fine views and walks all around it.

If you approach Ludlow from the Wigmore side, you will see it all spread out before you – a panorama of Norman towers, soaring church pinnacles, crowded mediaeval and 18th-century houses, a hilly backdrop. Stones of varied colours went into the construction of the castle, now an impressive ruin, originally built as the central stronghold to control the turbulent Welsh border. The 15th-century church is equally magnificent in scale: look up to the roof for gilded angels and under the choir stalls (misericords) for mermaids. The Feathers Hotel is famous for its carved façade and balconies; 18th-century Dinham House is a centre for craftsmen.

Taking the road from Ludlow to Craven Arms, you pass through Bromfield with priory ruins in its watermeadows and, in the impressive church, an unusual ceiling of cherubs' heads and painted scrolls. Onward lies Stokesay Castle, a little gem, with fruit trees in its moat now but old features retained within (the carved gatehouse is still inhabited); and, at Aston-on-Clun, a historic poplar annually redecorated with flags in celebration of a landowner's wedding long ago: a popular background for wedding photographs today.

Readers' comments: Cannot praise highly enough. Glorious countryside. Meals an absolute delight. Most charming and a wonderful cook. Friendly, warm and welcoming. An excellent few days, utterly peaceful. Lovely old house, splendid meals. Most friendly and cheerful service. Courteous owners. Food very good. Made most welcome. Truly rural retreat. Food with flair and imagination.

UPPER VINEY FARMHOUSE   C D S X
Viney Hill, Lydney, Gloucestershire, GL15 4LT   Tel: 0594 516672
South-west of Gloucester. Nearest main road: A48 from Gloucester to
Chepstow (and M4, junction 22).

3 Bedrooms. £15–£17.50 (less for 3 nights). Bargain breaks. All have own bath/shower/toilet. Tea/coffee facilities. TV (in two). Views of country. No smoking. Washing machine on request.
Dinner. £10 for 3 courses (with choices) and coffee, at 6.30pm. Non-residents not admitted. Vegetarian or special diets if ordered. Wine can be brought in. **Light suppers** if ordered.
1 Sitting-room. With open fire, central heating, TV.
Small garden

Occasionally the Littens lay on two-day breaks of forest walks with an expert guide. These vary in length, and include meals along the way as well as talks in the evening. Often, participants are shown such things as salmon-net making, or a cider-press in a private house: not typical tourist 'sights'. The house is on the southern edge of the historic Forest of Dean, a royal hunting forest since before the Norman Conquest. An area of great beauty and wildlife interest, it also has coal mines owned privately by 'free-miners' under traditional forest laws. There are remains of Roman iron mines, strange rock formations, caves, rivers, gardens . . .

Upper Viney is a 16th-century house of stone walls and floors, exposed timbers and ancient, twisting staircase. The sitting/dining-room has an inglenook with bread-oven, and in an alcove are finds that have turned up in the garden (clay pipes, hand-forged nails), as well as a small child's boot which has been dated at 1835: an expert said the iron-studding shows the child worked in a coal mine.

There is a particularly big family room and very nice shower/bathrooms.

Mary Litten cooks straightforward meals like sardines on toast, chicken chasseur and apple charlotte (always with two choices of starter and pudding).

Parkend is in the middle of the Forest of Dean and here, facing the cricket green, is **EDALE HOUSE**, in Folly Road. Bedrooms are luxurious – decorated in soft blues and cream, with pretty fabrics and furniture of polished pine. Village cricket can be watched from the rooms, two of which are on the ground floor. The two rooms (one bunk-bedded) that constitute a family suite have – a much-appreciated touch! – two televisions. There is a lobby designed for walkers' wet shoes and coats.

In the comfortable sitting-room is Sheila Reid's growing collection of unusual honeypots (30 when I was there). The dining-room overlooks the

garden, with its numerous feathered visitors from the Nagshead RSPB reserve at the rear of the house. By arrangement, Sheila serves such meals as tomato and basil soup, beef braised with wild mushrooms, then a pudding or cheese. £16.50–£18 (b & b). [Tel: 0594 562835; postcode: GL15 4JF]

UPTON HOUSE   D

Upton Snodsbury, Worcestershire, WR7 4NR   Tel: 0905 381226
East of Worcester. Nearest main road: A422 from Stratford-upon-Avon to
Worcester (and M5, junctions 6/7).

3 Bedrooms. £19–£32.50 (less for 3 nights or mid-week sometimes). All have own bath/shower/toilet. Tea/coffee facilities. TV. Views of garden, country. No smoking.
Dinner. £12.50 for 3 courses or £22.50 for 5 courses and coffee, at 7.30 or 8pm. Non-residents not admitted. Vegetarian or special diets if ordered. Wine can be brought in. **Light suppers** if ordered.
1 Sitting-room. With open fire, central heating.
Large garden

Part 14th-century, part Tudor and part 18th-century, this building is full of individuality. It has been furnished in character, with antiques collected by Hugh and Angela Jefferson. They decided to take guests to help with the cost of educating four children, then found how much they enjoyed entertaining.

Their colour schemes are fresh and imaginative. In the dining-room, chairs covered in watermelon satin contrast with primrose walls (this room has a vast fireplace); in the sitting-room, sofas covered in pink or blue brocade are grouped round another log fire. A feature of this room is the pretty little bay window with wide sill, through which one looks across the lawn (surrounded by trees and rosebeds) to half-timbered cottages and the Norman church, the clock of which chimes every quarter-hour. Croquet can be played.

The pink bedroom, low-beamed, has roses on curtains, a moss-green carpet and violets on the Royal Albert china for early-morning tea. The peach room has an elegant Victorian bathroom. The green room is almost as attractive.

Angela is an inspired cook of exceptional skill – a typical meal might comprise seafood vol-au-vent, stuffed lamb, chocolate truffle cake and cheeses.

It is hoped to get the old cider-mill at the back restored in due course. Meantime, if you want to see cider being made in the traditional way (in October) there is another mill nearby which you can visit. Children enjoy exploring the orchard, and meeting the ducks. From Upton House one can readily visit the Bredon and Malvern Hills (Hereford and the Wye Valley beyond them); such Cotswold beauty-spots as Broadway or Chipping Campden; and, in the other direction, Stratford-upon-Avon in Warwickshire. Worcester (cathedral and china factory), Spetchley gardens and several garden centres are other options. When in Worcester (best explored on foot) seek out the Commandery for Civil War exhibits, 15th-century Greyfriars, the Guildhall and lovely riverside gardens.

Readers' comments: Excellent. Comfort and friendliness. Excellent, relaxing week-end. Food superb. Felt like a luxury hotel but with personal touches. Hosts care about their guests.

**Book well ahead: many of these houses have few rooms. Do not
expect dinner if you have not booked it or if you arrive late.**

Vauld, Herefordshire, HR1 3HA Tel: 056884 898
North of Hereford. Nearest main road: A49 from Hereford to Leominster.

6 Bedrooms. £15–£25 (less for 3 nights). Some have own bath/shower/toilet. Tea/coffee facilities. TV. Views of garden, country. Washing machine on request. **Dinner.** £15 for 3 courses and coffee, at 7.30pm (not Sundays). Non-residents not admitted. Wine can be brought in. **Light suppers** if ordered.
Sitting-rooms: see text.
Large garden

'Sleepy hollow', the locals call this area where the ancient farmhouse lies hidden, its creamy, black-timbered walls lopsided with age (it was built in 1510). One steps through the front door into a great room with stone-slabbed floor, half-timbered walls, log fire and colossal beams overhead. (Farming is no longer carried on here.)

Those who book the granary suite (which has its own stone staircase from out-side) have a private sitting-room, with deep velvet armchairs, bedroom, bathroom and a gallery with another bed; and, through windows with unusual crisscross glazing bars, a view of the lake. Other visitors may prefer the ground-floor oak room with a very impressive four-poster (this, too, has its own entrance and bathroom). Additional accommodation is also available in the converted, 17th-century timber-frame barn which is situated directly opposite the farmhouse. Here is also a guests' sitting-room with tea/coffee-making facilities, a television, and a patio.

Jean Bengry will prepare a meal using much local produce, for this is an area of fruit-farms; and she keeps her own poultry and goats. A typical menu: chicken-liver and mushroom pâté, turkey in hazelnut sauce, trifle and local cheeses.

Ancient Hereford, its turbulent military history behind it, is still a market town with a mediaeval network of streets. The cathedral is full of treasures and, having been built in stages, has examples of almost every architectural style. The Norman nave is exceptionally impressive, some bishops' tombs particularly ornate, the cloisters tranquil. Hereford is the home of Bulmers, whose cider museum is well worth a visit – though those with other drinking habits may make for Broadfield Manor to taste wine from the vineyard there.

Many visitors, with 'the Black-and-White Village Trail' in hand, motor from one picturesque village to the next, along the route discovering an amazing number of really huge mediaeval churches tucked away in the countryside. Others go from one stately garden to another: Hergest Croft, Burford, Dinmore Manor, Queen's Wood (arboretum) and innumerable others. Hay-on-Wye ('book city') is near.

Readers' comments: Excellent accommodation, fine food, friendly folk. None of us wanted to leave. Nothing was too much trouble. Made us completely at home. A superb break. What a wonderful place! The food was a treat. Enchanting. Very comfortable.

VICTORIA SPA LODGE
Bishopton Lane, Bishopton, Warwickshire, CV37 9QY   Tel: 0789 267985
North-west of Stratford-upon-Avon. Nearest main road: A3400 from
Stratford-upon-Avon to Birmingham.

7 Bedrooms. £19.50–£22.50. All have
own bath/shower/toilet. Tea/coffee facilities.
TV. Views of garden, country, canal.
Light suppers if ordered.
1 Sitting-room. With central heating, TV,
record-player. No smoking.
Small garden

'Invalids desirous of flying from the toilsome engagements of fashionable life, yet
accustomed to its enjoyments, might seek a retreat in this tranquil and soothing
spot', wrote Dr Granville in his guide to spas published in 1841. For the 17
springs here had made little Bishopton a spa – opened in 1837 by Victoria shortly
before she became queen. The baths are now part of a private house, but their
adjacent hotel once again accommodates visitors – you may sleep in the very
room where Victoria slept. Or perhaps in the one where Bruce Bairnsfather (of
'Old Bill' fame) later grew up: many of his pictures line the staircase.

The house is a *cottage ornée* with fretwork bargeboards projecting from the
eaves above lozenge-paned windows. Inside, Dreen Tozer has chosen appropriate
Victorian furniture and added, for instance, rose festoon blinds and quilts in one
room, which also has a pink buttoned sofa; and a grey-green colour scheme
in another that has a flowery ceiling (a particularly pretty bathroom adjoins
this). Some rooms have views of the old Stratford canal and passing boats.
For house-parties of eight, Dreen will cook a full dinner; on other nights, snack
suppers only.

'Nothing has been forgotten which can render such an establishment desirable
as well as comfortable', wrote the critical Dr Granville a century and a half ago.
Still true.

Bedroom at Northleigh House (see page 227)

VILLAGE FARM

High Street, Sturton-by-Stow, Lincolnshire, LN1 2AE Tel: 0427 788309
(Messages: 0522 730389)

North-west of Lincoln. Nearest main road: A1500 from Gainsborough towards
Lincoln.

3 Bedrooms. £16–£19 (less for 2 nights).
Prices may go up in April. Bargain breaks.
Some have own bath. Tea/coffee facilities.
Views of garden. No smoking.
1 Sitting-room. With open fire, central
heating, TV, record-player.
Large garden
Closed in January and February.

In the middle of this usually quiet village stands an early Victorian house,
now pleasantly furnished by Sheila Bradshaw – at the heart of a 350-acre farm
where pedigree cattle and sheep are raised. For the sitting-room she chose a pale
green carpet, pink velvet curtains held back in tasselled loops, and flowery
chintzes; among many Victorian heirlooms are things of her own making –
canvaswork or patchwork cushions, for instance. She is a keen Women's
Institute member, a handbell-ringer, loves flower-arranging and has made a
big sampler depicting the house itself. Her husband's family farmed in Sturton
for many generations back: among his enthusiasms are Shetland ponies and
growing orchids.

Bedrooms are very attractive: one, with matching wallpaper and fabrics, has a
sloping ceiling and odd windows; in the peach-and-cream one is a rocking-chair;
one of the prettiest has pink Laura Ashley sprigged linen and a Philippine cane
chair. A conservation area has been created on the farm, which includes a large
pond and 1500 new trees. Coarse fishing and rough shooting available.

Readers' comments: Very helpful, a lovely week. Sheer magic! Comfort, views and
value – all very good.

An alternative in Lincoln itself is a
quiet Edwardian house (5 minutes'
walk from the cathedral), **CARLINE
GUEST-HOUSE**, 1–3 Carline Road.
Immaculate and comfortable; unusually
well-equipped; and very moderate
prices for rooms with TV, own
bathroom, etc. Gill and John Pritchard
provide bed-and-breakfast only, with
eggs from their own hens. (No smoking.) £15– £18.50.
Readers' comments: Every conceivable
amenity. Most enjoyable. Highly

recommended. Best in UK! Top hotel
standards. Owners clearly enjoy their
job. [Tel: 0522 530422; postcode:
LN1 1HN]

For explanation of code letters (C, D, M, PT, S, X) see page xlvi.

350

VINE FARM

Waterman Quarter, Headcorn, Kent, TN27 9JJ   Tel: 0622 890203

South-east of Maidstone. Nearest main road: A274 from Maidstone towards Tenterden (and M20, junctions 8/9).

3 Bedrooms. £18–£20. Prices go up in April. Bargain breaks (fishing and golf). All

have own bath. Tea/coffee facilities. Views of garden, country. No smoking. Washing machine on request.

Dinner (if ordered). £12.50 for 4 courses and coffee, at 7pm. Non-residents not admitted. Vegetarian or special diets if ordered. Wine can be brought in. No smoking. **Light suppers** if ordered.

1 Sitting-room. With open fire, central heating, TV. No smoking.

Large garden

Closed from mid-December to mid-January.

Nothing could be more typical of Kent than this white weatherboarded farm-house, originally the home of a Tudor yeoman. It is surrounded by flowerbeds, lawns, landscaped ponds, paved courtyard, well, pots of flowers, a 16th-century barn and 50 acres of meadows where sheep graze.

One enters through what was the big brick-floored kitchen, its ceiling low and beamed. This is now the guests' sitting-room, with Victorian armchairs of buttoned velvet and book-lined walls. Next door is the dining-room which has a huge inglenook with log stove and is similarly furnished with fine antiques and pretty chintz curtains. Here Jane Harman serves dinners such as pancakes stuffed with shrimps in a cream sauce, fillet of lamb with home-grown vegetables, chocolate roulade and cheeses.

Bedrooms have antiques, Laura Ashley festoon blinds and fabrics, and bed-heads of brass curlicues or ladderback mahogany. There is one ground-floor room (with its own red and white bathroom).

The garden is particularly attractive, thanks to Jane's enthusiasm for gardening, with such features as a huge herbaceous bed and a landscaped pond partly surrounded by Bethersden marble. Coarse fishing available in the grounds.

The name Waterman Quarter, incidentally, tells a story. Once this quarter used to be subject to floods when the river overflowed. It was the waterman's job to fly a warning flag when the river was in spate.

Within easy reach are many of Kent's spectacular mansions and castles (Knole, Leeds and Hever, for example, Scotney with its lovely gardens, and Sissinghurst with gardens created by Vita Sackville-West), and historic cities (such as Canterbury and Rochester) and towns (Tenterden, Cranbrook). The country lanes are particularly beautiful in apple-blossom time (usually May) or even earlier, when the cherry trees are in flower. In September, the hops are gathered and taken to the oast houses for drying – a few allow visitors.

Vine Farm's ponds are 'sites of nature conservation interest' with many native species, including wild orchids, herons, nightingales and kingfishers; Wye College is conducting wildflower experiments in the meadows. Jane organizes tours of private gardens (meals as well as accommodation provided): brochure on request. She can direct enthusiasts to the many small specialist nurseries of Kent.

VINES
C D PT S X

High Street, Marlborough, Wiltshire, SN8 1HJ   Tel: 0672 516583
Nearest main road: A4 from Newbury to Bath (and M4, junction 15).

6 Bedrooms. £19 to readers of this book only (also bargain breaks, available even at bank holidays). All have own bath/shower/toilet. Tea/coffee facilities. TV and much else (see text).
Dining- and sitting-rooms (see text).

From a modest guest-house, David Ball and Josephine Scott completely transformed the Ivy House Hotel at Marlborough into a large and elegant hotel with a restaurant that has won numerous accolades. Not surprisingly, the inevitable price-rises that followed eventually took it out of the range of this book. But there is good news: David and Josie are now also running a guest-house opposite.

This is the Vines, an 18th-century terrace house converted and decorated to the same high standards as the hotel itself. Bedrooms are furnished in style, and equipped with every possible facility (remote-control TV, good armchairs, hair-dryers, mini-bars in refrigerators and – for the businessmen who comprise most of the mid-week guests – trouser-presses, telephones and radio-alarms). Those over-looking the High Street are double-glazed.

What is more, accommodation here is offered to readers of this book at a preferential rate, *provided that* the book is mentioned when making a reservation and shown on arrival. Further, there is a 10% discount on dinner in Ivy House Hotel. Breakfast can also be taken in the hotel, or will be brought to your room in the Vines. Other hotel amenities open to Vines visitors include a sitting-room, bar and sun-terrace. Clay-pigeon shooting can be arranged; and for walkers there is a drying-room and laundry for a nominal charge.

As to dinner, this is always a memorable occasion. You can choose from either a two-course or three-course menu which may include such dishes as smoked fish terrine encased in smoked salmon with a dill sauce; breast of duck, stuffed with sage and almonds, in an orange sauce; and warm sticky toffee pudding served with a walnut and caramel sauce. The wine-list features a good selection of New World wines, as well as some lower-price alternatives to the château-bottled French wines. There is also a wholefood and fish restaurant.

Marlborough is a handsome and historic town, with one of the widest high streets in the country. Many of the houses are mediaeval, though this is not immediately apparent until you explore the byways and alleys because so many frontages were rebuilt in the 18th century. It was a stage-coach centre, which accounts for the number of old inns and hotels. At each end of the broad street is a church in Perpendicular style. Its famous public school, Marlborough College, is well worth a visit when open to visitors. Every August the College runs adult summer schools (subjects range from wine appreciation to word processors, golf to country-house history) and participants can stay at the Vines.

Readers' comments: Delighted with the welcome and concern. Wonderful! The high point of our tour. Accommodation excellent, food exquisite.

352

WALLTREE HOUSE FARM   C M
Steane, Northamptonshire, NN13 5NS Tel: 0295 811235
North-west of Brackley. Nearest main road: A422 from Banbury to Brackley
(and M40, junctions 10/11).

6 Bedrooms. £18–£19.50 (less for 3 nights). Most have own bath/shower/toilet. Tea/coffee facilities. TV. Views of garden, country. Coin-operated laundry.
Dinner (by arrangement). From £8 for 3 courses and coffee, at 7pm. Vegetarian or special diets if ordered. Wine can be ordered. **Light suppers** if ordered.
2 Sitting-rooms. With open fire, central heating, TV.
Large garden

Quite a surprise to find, at the end of a long farm lane, a park-like setting in which this handsome Victorian farmhouse stands.

Pauline and Richard Harrison have transformed the house and its outbuildings. Bedrooms in the former granary are modern in style: Stag furniture in some, rosy fabrics, much bamboo and pine, very good bathrooms. You can be sure of ample warmth on 365 days in the year, for Richard installed a special straw-burner which means all his central heating costs him nothing but the labour of gathering straw from his fields after each harvest. There is a lovely sitting-room with adjoining conservatory.

Dinner (ordered in advance) may be anything from a farm supper to a gourmet menu.

It was at Brackley that the barons negotiated Magna Carta before its sealing at Runnymede later in 1215. Today the attractive town lies around a particularly wide, mile-long main street flanked by trees and little lanes, and adorned by a very fine 18th-century town hall, historic school, old inns and quaint almshouses. The church is worth a visit, for its windows and monuments are of particular interest.

The whole county is full of good things and quiet beauty, yet so many visitors merely pass through it on the way to more celebrated places of interest.

Meals under the vine at Little Parmoor (see page 192)

353

WALNUT COTTAGE   C(14) **M PT**
Old Romsey Road, Cadnam, Hampshire, SO4 2NP   Tel: 0703 812275
West of Southampton. Nearest main road: A31 from Romsey to Ringwood
(and M27, junction 1).

3 Bedrooms. £18.50–£19.50 (less for 2 nights or continental breakfast). Prices go up at Easter. All have own bath/shower/toilet. Tea/coffee facilities. TV. Views of garden. (During June–October, minimum 2-night bookings.)
2 Sitting-rooms. With open fire, central heating, TV.
Small garden

The road no longer leads anywhere (its days ended when a nearby motorway replaced it). The little white cottage, with brimming window-boxes and a red rambler-rose by the door, stands in a pretty garden (with an old well) which traps the sun. One bedroom, the garden room, opens onto this.

All the rooms have been attractively furnished by Charlotte and Eric Osgood, who did much of the work themselves (even the tiling of the showers, and the flowery china door-knobs on each bedroom door). There are two sitting-rooms with pale carpets, cretonne armchairs, flowers on the window-sills and interesting objects on the shelves. One has windows on all three sides. In the dining-room are Regency chairs, cupboard and mirror; a diminutive iron grate, as old as the cottage, has been preserved (though the only fireplace still in use is in the larger sitting-room). Here Charlotte serves breakfast on Royal Doulton vineleaf china, but for other meals, she recommends a thatched and whitewashed inn nearby.

The cottage is on the edge of the New Forest. Romsey and Broadlands are very near; Beaulieu, Salisbury and Winchester, too.

Readers' comments: Beautifully located . . . most helpful people. Delightful couple, charming rooms, comfortable; superb breakfasts. Very impressed by their care and attention. Faultless accommodation and welcome. Splendid. Brilliant hosts. Really enjoyed our stay. Lovely, and most comfortable.

On Castle Hill at Woodgreen (near Fordingbridge) is **COTTAGE CREST** where the Cadmans provide bed-and-breakfast. Bedrooms are some of the most beautiful and well-equipped in this book. A great brass bed with pink-and-white lacy linen is in one; it has an L-shaped room with windows on two sides from which to enjoy superb views of sunsets over the River Avon in the valley below. There is also a garden suite with private sitting-room facing this view. One can sit on a paved terrace with a little pool, or take a zigzag path down to a lower garden, or walk straight into the

New Forest. (Light suppers only.) £18–£19.
Readers' comments: Delightful, made so welcome, very comfortable. Most charming and friendly. Very warm welcome. Made most comfortable. Garden suite beautifully furnished, and with fresh flowers. [Tel: 0725 512009; postcode: SP6 2AX]

354

Compass, Dartmouth, Devon, TQ6 0JN   Tel: 0803 833979
Nearest main road: A379 from Dartmouth to Kingsbridge.

3 Bedrooms. £17 (less for 7 nights). Price goes up in May. Views of garden, country, sea. No smoking.
Dinner (by arrangement). £13 for 4 courses and coffee, at 7.30pm. Non-residents not admitted. Vegetarian or special diets if ordered. Wine can be ordered or brought in. No smoking.
1 Sitting-room. With wood stove, central heating, TV, record-player. No smoking.
Large garden

So beautiful is the coastal scenery beyond Dartmouth (owned by the National Trust) that today no-one is allowed to build on it: Wavenden is the only house there to enjoy the superb view of the River Dart's wide estuary, jagged headlands and, across the water, 15th-century Kingswear Castle.

When Ken (an award-winning journalist) and Lily Gardner moved here, it was a rather ugly 'twenties bungalow which they rebuilt so sensitively that even environmentalists have congratulated them on enhancing the previous scene. And the garden too has been improved by them, with grassy terraces, primrose banks and well-landscaped flowering shrubs. Guests have easy access to the shore where they can bathe or fish.

There is a large two-level dining- and sitting-room, with huge glass doors through which to enjoy the views, and also a big fireplace of polished black slate (with wood burner). Through these doors one steps onto a paved sundeck with reclining chairs from which to watch every kind of craft go by.

From every bedroom, furnished in Laura Ashley style, are glimpses of the sea and garden, colourful even in early spring because the climate here is so mild.

This is a good choice for walkers because the Devon Coastal Path and a network of National Trust footpaths lie just beyond the gate. In a hedge are traces of the first cross-Channel telegraph cable (about 1870).

In hilly Dartmouth itself is a picturesque Butterwalk with houses supported by granite pillars; 17th- and 18th-century buildings; and on a hill high above, the imposing Royal Naval College.

Readers' comments: Delicious and bountiful fare. The location, the welcome, the comfort, the food, the decor – everything was superb value. Lovely views, and atmosphere generated by the Gardners. Excellent food. Friendly and relaxed. Very well looked after. One of the most beautiful locations. Mouthwatering food. Excellent hosts.

WELLPRITTON FARM

C S

Holne, Ashburton, Devon, TQ13 7RX   Tel: 03643 273
West of Newton Abbot. Nearest main road: A38 from Exeter to Plymouth.

4 Bedrooms. £16–£17 (less for 7 nights). Only weekly bookings in high season. Some have own bath/shower/toilet. Tea/coffee facilities. Views of garden, country. Washing machine on request.
Dinner. £8 for 4 courses and coffee, usually at 7pm. Vegetarian or special diets if ordered. Wine can be brought in.
1 Sitting-room. With central heating, TV. Games room (snooker, table tennis).
Small garden

Tucked away in a fold of the gentle hills south of Dartmoor is this small farm where sheep and hens are kept; donkeys, goats and rabbits too.

Sue Townsend has furnished the bedrooms prettily (some are small), and she supplies them with fruit-squash and biscuits as well as tea. There is a family unit of two rooms and a shower, and a ground-floor suite. A comfortable sitting-room is available to guests.

After a starter such as melon or pâté, dinner will probably include a roast, poultry or steak pie, perhaps followed by fruit pie or flan, always accompanied by Devonshire cream, then cheese and coffee. Sue tries to cater for every guest individually. There is no charge for washing and ironing facilities, mealtimes are flexible, the welcome warm, and many extra services provided (loan of maps, hair-dryer, free tea on arrival). From the farm, which has a small swimming-pool, there are views of the moors.

One of the local beauty-spots is 60-foot Becky Falls in oak woodlands threaded by nature trails. At Bovey Tracey are exhibited local crafts of high quality in a granite watermill. There is a vineyard and a rare breeds farm, and the National Trust has 200 acres of riverside park.

Other local NT properties include mediaeval Bradley Manor with its own chapel, and the 16th-century Church House at Widecombe. Ugbrooke House by Adam contains a collection of armour and uniforms, Trago Mills the largest model railway in the county. Yarner Wood is a national nature reserve with a trail through heathland and woods.

Chudleigh has something for everyone: Victorian rock gardens with an 80-foot cliff and a cave, and, in a mill with working waterwheel, 17 craft workshops.

Readers' comments: We were pampered, the situation is an absolute dream. Loud praises of all aspects, especially the food. The very best: nothing is too much trouble. One of our favourites; Sue is one of the best cooks; food beautifully presented. Very enjoyable; warm welcome, good food, comfortable. Sensational cook. Caring hostess. Beautiful setting. Superb food.

When writing to me, if you want a reply please enclose an International Reply Coupon.

WENTWORTH HOUSE   C(5) D M PT
106 Bloomfield Road, Bath, Avon, BA2 2AP   Tel: 0225 339193

20 Bedrooms. £18–£23 (**but to readers of this book only, 5% less for 2 nights, 10% less for 3 nights**). Prices go up in April. Some have own bath/shower/toilet. Tea/coffee facilities. TV. Views of garden, city.
Dinner. £12.50 for 3 courses (with choices) and coffee, at 7pm (not Sundays). Non-residents not admitted. Vegetarian or special diets if ordered. Wine can be ordered. No smoking. **Light suppers** if ordered.
1 Sitting-room. With central heating. **Bar. Small garden**

The big, four-storey house was built for a coal merchant a century ago – those were the days when smoke from millions of hearths brought wealth to a few. It is a fine building of creamy stone, now furnished and equipped to very good standards. The dining-room has a glass extension overlooking the swimming-pool and a lawn with children's swings. Some of the nicest rooms are below this: they not only open onto the garden but in some cases are suites, each consisting of a small sun-room with armchairs and glass walls beyond the bedroom. At the other extreme, top-floor rooms have the finest views over the city far below.

The hotel has three other attractions for visitors. There is an ample carpark (a rarity in Bath). A six-minute bus halts just outside, saving you the steep walk up from the city after a day's sightseeing. And close by is a rural walk.

Avril Kitching cooks the meals herself – straightforward menus such as melon, haddock in cheese sauce and fresh fruit salad (there is always a fish and a meat dish to choose from). With breakfast cereals come bowls of various seeds.

Apart from Bath itself (which deserves at least a week-long stay), the tiny county of Avon is full of interest.

Readers' comments: A delightful stay. Owners kind and helpful. Charming, relaxing and home-like. Service excellent. The best to date. Exceptional breakfast choices. Lots of character and very comfortable.

Just off a steep main road out of Bath is **OLDFIELDS** (102 Wells Road), a late Victorian house (or, rather, two) of honey-coloured stone. The big sitting-room, with marble fireplace, is decorated in soft browns and mossy greens and has lace curtains at the high windows with their fine views of the city. The owners, Anthony and Nicole O'Flaherty, are great fun; breakfasts are generous (with herbal teas, if you like) and there is much emphasis on wholefoods and local produce. Care is taken over every detail. £20–£24.

Readers' comments: Wonderful! Exceptionally nice people. Spacious comfort. [Tel: 0225 317984; postcode: BA2 3AL]

WESTERN HOUSE
High Street, Cavendish, Suffolk, CO10 8AR   Tel: 0787 280550
North-west of Sudbury. On A1092 between Long Melford and Clare.

3 **Bedrooms.** £13.50–£14.50 (less for 6 nights). Tea/coffee facilities. Views of garden. Only one has basin.
Large garden

Twice made redundant, Peter Marshall decided he had had enough of industry and – his children now being grown up – would instead make a living from his best asset: his attractive 400-year-old house in the historic village of Cavendish.

He and his wife Jean (who teaches singing) are vegetarians, so at one end they started a wholefood shop, full of the smells of dried fruit and fresh herbs, and refurnished several bedrooms to take bed-and-breakfast guests. Options include all kinds of good things (such as their own muesli, eggs, mushrooms, tomatoes and home-made bread) but no bacon. They will recommend good restaurants of all kinds in the village, at Long Melford or in Sudbury.

Each beamed bedroom, reached via zigzag corridors, is very pretty, and spacious – well equipped with chairs, table etc. One at the front (double-glazed, because it looks onto the main road through the village) has a fresh white-and-green colour scheme extending even to the sheets.

One of the nicest features is the large and informal garden where paved paths wander between old-fashioned flowers, elderly fruit trees, and plant troughs.

Cavendish is one of a string of mediaeval villages described elsewhere. Clare is close, so is Sudbury town and Long Melford – very long indeed, lined with dignified houses and antique shops. Its church and its great mansions (Melford Hall and Kentwell Hall) are well worth seeing. The greatest jewel is Lavenham: lanes of half-timbered and lopsided weavers' cottages still intact, great Guildhall housing a museum of wool history, resplendent church.

Readers' comments: Excellent, with very good breakfasts. Much enjoyed it; and the shop is excellent. Extremely comfortable; warm welcome. Absolutely excellent, high standard. Charming and interesting people.

In a quiet byway of Lavenham itself, at **48 WATER STREET**, bedrooms overlook some of the picturesque and very colourful mediaeval cottages. Downstairs, opening onto a small paved garden, is the sitting/dining-room where – if you do not want to patronize the local restaurants – Margaret Morley serves such dinners as stuffed mushrooms, chicken casserole and syllabub. £14 (b & b). [Tel: 0787 248422; postcode: CO10 9RN]

WESTERN HOUSE

Winchelsea Road, Rye, East Sussex, TN31 7EL Tel: 0797 223419

On A259 from Hastings to Folkestone.

C(10) **PT X**

3 Bedrooms. £15–£18 (less for 7 nights). Prices go up at Easter. All have own bath/shower/toilet. Tea/coffee facilities. TV. Views of garden, country.
Dinner. From £10 for 3 courses (with choices) and coffee, at 6.30–7.30pm. Non-residents not admitted. Vegetarian or special diets if ordered. Wine can be brought in. No smoking. **Light suppers** if ordered.
Large garden

The mediaeval port of Rye was perched high on a thumb of land (almost an island) projecting into the sea. But centuries ago the sea receded, leaving behind dry land which became ideal pasturage for sheep. It is here, at the foot of Rye town, that tile-hung Western House was built in the 18th century, commanding far views – you can even see Hastings in clear weather – from its paved terrace (with working pump) where tea may be taken, or from the huge lawn surrounded by brilliant flowerbeds set against mellow stone walls. On summer evenings, the terrace is lit by an old Victorian street-lamp.

Artist Ron Dellar is the present owner of Western House, and his paintings fill the dining-room walls. Up the staircase, and in the bedrooms, are all manner of finds he has amassed over the years: African masks, a parrot in a glass dome, an 1820 box of paints ('Constable was alive then', he comments), Rupert Bear books, antique toys. Melanie, his wife, sells Victorian lace, linen, baby-gowns and books which are laid out in the big entrance hall. Ron's own prints of Rye are on sale too.

This is a house of character, as befits its long history. A boat-builder lived here and, later on, Members of Parliament. Among its visitors (in 1913) was the impressionist artist Pissarro; and Ron has incorporated him in a mural featuring Rye church which he painted for one of the bedrooms. All these rooms are attractively decorated, with interesting wallpapers and fresh flowers, and some have good views of the marshes across which you can walk to Winchelsea. There's a moated Martello tower out there, giant marsh-frogs croak throatily, you may see herons or marsh harriers flying overhead. (Although the house is on the road to Winchelsea I slept undisturbed.) Painting tuition and antique-hunting breaks are available.

As to dinner, a typical meal may include home-made soup, baked gammon in cassis sauce, ice cream or hot chocolate fudge pudding. Otherwise, visitors can try one of Rye's many good inns and restaurants.

The Cinque Ports (seven, in spite of the name) stretch along the south-east coast, and in the centuries before the Navy existed their seamen would serve the king in time of war. In return, they were given trading privileges which made them rich – hence the number of fine old houses and churches still to be found in most of them, from Sandwich in Kent to Hastings in Sussex (and Rye is the jewel of them all). Their history is told in Hastings museum.

Readers' comments: We were particularly delighted. View magnificent. Fabulous: great people, great room, great food.

WHASHTON SPRINGS FARM C(5)
Whashton, North Yorkshire, DL11 7JS Tel: 0748 822884
North-west of Richmond. Nearest main road: A66 from Scotch Corner to Brough.

8 Bedrooms. £19 (less for 7 nights). Prices go up in April. Bargain breaks for parties in winter. All have own bath/shower/toilet. Tea/coffee facilities. TV. Views of garden, country, stream.
Dinner. £12 for 3 courses (with choices) and coffee, at 7pm (not Sundays). Non-residents not admitted. Vegetarian or special diets if ordered. Wine can be ordered.
1 Sitting-room. With open fire, central heating. Bar.
Small garden
Closed in January.

Far more handsome than the average farmhouse, 18th-century Whashton Springs has great bow windows and other detailing typical of this fine period in English architecture. Around it is a large, mixed farm run by two generations of Turnbulls. It is high among wooded hills, with superb views of the Dales and of a stream with mediaeval bridge below.

Every bedroom is different. One, for instance, has flowery fabrics, broderie anglaise on the bedlinen, pretty Victorian antiques and a bow window; another, a four-poster with William Morris drapery and buttoned velvet chairs. Others in a converted stable-block are more modern in style (velvet bedheads, flowery duvets and pine furniture); most of these overlook a courtyard where tubs and stone troughs brim with pansies and petunias; one has a garden view.

Fairlie Turnbull provides such dinners as: cheese soufflé, home-bred roast lamb and brandysnaps (or, a typical Yorkshire ending to a meal, Wensleydale cheese served with fruitcake).

The many gardens of this region are at their best in spring, and the famous 'sights' (York, Durham, Richmond and the Dales) less crowded. One can even drive across to the Lake District from here. It's an area not only of spectacular scenery but of dramatic or romantic ruins (great abbeys and castles). Walkers seek out waterfalls and caves, fells and crags, for which the Yorkshire Dales are famous. The little cobbled villages and old inns seem hardly to change at all with the years.

Whashton's nearness to the A1 means many people use it as a one-night stopover on their London–Edinburgh journey, but it deserves better than this because there are so many good reasons to linger. Swaledale alone takes days to explore, and so does Teesdale (both described elsewhere). It is a region of contrasts. Lonely moors rise to 2000 feet (this is where to listen for curlews and plovers, and to wonder at lives passed in such few isolated farms as there are), while every dale differs – Wensleydale is wide and either pastoral or wooded; Swaledale winds between steep hills; some others are like deep clefts – Arkengarthdale, Coverdale, Bishopdale, for instance. Heather moors, houses of 18th-century dignity, the distinctive curly-horned sheep: all contribute to the individuality of this area.

Readers' comments: Very comfortable. Made very welcome. High praise. Lovely surroundings and easy access to many places. Very comfortable.

WHEATHILL FARM   C(5) S
Church Lane, Shearsby, Leicestershire, LE17 6PG   Tel: 0533 478 663
North-west of Market Harborough. Nearest main road: A50 from Leicester to Northampton (also M6, junction 1; and M1, junction 20).

4 Bedrooms. £16–£16.50 (less for 3 nights or continental breakfast). Prices go up in June. One has own shower. Tea/coffee facilities. Views of garden, country. No smoking. Washing machine on request.
Light suppers if ordered.
1 Sitting-room. With open fire, central heating, TV, record-player. No smoking.
Large garden

In 1823, the owners of this cottage (part Saxon, part mediaeval) put a new façade on the front: brick, with trim white paintwork. But behind this the old beamed rooms remained unchanged, with huge inglenook housing a log stove, and a twisting stair.

Sue Timms has a decorative touch, and uses pretty fabrics or beribboned net in cottage-style bedrooms, one downstairs (and even in one of the bathrooms too). The house is full of unusual heirlooms, including a 100-year-old pot-plant which originally belonged to a lighthouse-keeper (her great-uncle) on the wild Farne Islands off the Northumberland coast. Outside is an attractive garden with lily-pool and lake (you can feed the carp), croquet and boules; and fields of Wheathill's cows. (Baby-sitting can be arranged.)

Shearsby is, like many others around here, a particularly pretty village, not far from Georgian Market Harborough (its lively markets date from 1200) and at the centre of rich grazing country – a tranquil region threaded by waterways with, at Foxton, ten locks stacked in a tier to raise boats up a 75-foot incline.

Further north is the scenic Charnwood Forest area – a mixture of heath, crags, ridges and remnants of oak forest with fine views from its hilltops. Within a short distance are Anstey's mediaeval packhorse bridge, the pretty little spa town of Ashby de la Zouch, a particularly interesting church at Breedon-on-the-Hill, and Loughborough which has a carillon of 47 bells in a high tower in the park. Other sights include Birdland, Twycross Zoo and Stanford Hall.

Bruntingthorpe's **MANOR HOUSE FARM**, in Peatling Parva Road, is a tall stone building of the 18th century, its sash windows overlooking a carp-pool fringed with yellow irises in summer and frequented by ducks. Bedrooms, on the second floor, are beautiful and downstairs is an unusual fireplace with carved cherubs busy shearing sheep. Janet Brightwell serves snack suppers only. £16 (b & b). [Tel: 0533 478347; postcode: LE17 5QL]

WHICHAM OLD RECTORY   C S
Silecroft, Cumbria, LA18 5LS   Tel: 0229 772954
West of Ulverston. Nearest main road: A595 from Broughton-in-Furness to
Whitehaven.

3 Bedrooms. £15 (less for 2 nights). Price goes up from April. Tea/coffee facilities. TV. Views of garden, country, sea.
Dinner. £9 for 3 courses (with some choices) and coffee, at a time to suit guests. Non-residents not admitted. Vegetarian or special diets if ordered. Wine can be brought in. **Light suppers** if ordered.
1 Sitting-room. With open fire, central heating, TV, piano.
Large garden
Closed in December.

So many people head for the heart of the Lake District that the outlying areas of the National Park remain uncrowded and uncommercialized. The south-west corner in particular, around Millom, is often overlooked, even though it is within an easy drive of famous beauty-spots and has its own particular attractions – uncrowded beaches, for example, and a mild maritime climate. The last accounts for the peaches and other fruit that flourish in the garden of the Old Rectory – some appearing on the dinner-table, or going into the wine which guests usually sample.

The house is typical of those Victorian rectories built for Trollope-size clerical families with domestic staff in proportion. David Kitchener, an ex-RAF supply officer and an accomplished woodworker, has put a lot of work into the spacious house, some of it to display intriguing family possessions – Victorian dish-covers, an ancient cast-iron pressure cooker and other interesting bric-a-brac: a big model of a dhow he bought when in the Middle East, a fairground flare, woodwork from a Warwickshire church, a collection of kukris and other weapons.

He and Judy Kitchener also find time to grow most of the vegetables which she uses in her enthusiastic cooking. There is always a home-made soup, with alternative first courses, then perhaps coq au vin (which may be half a chicken per head) with at least three vegetables, to which guests help themselves, and a sweet such as raspberry mousse, to which the garden is likely to have contributed too. The freshly baked bread is David's speciality.

All the bedrooms overlook the lawn, next to which is a small semicircular conservatory which David has built onto the end of the stable, so that guests can enjoy the garden even when a sea breeze is blowing. The energetic can take a footpath to the top of Black Combe (2000 feet) for views of Scotland and Wales. The less energetic can explore the beach at Silecroft, with its sands and rock-pools. Up the coast are mansions and gardens, a narrow-gauge railway and old seaports. Eastward are pleasant market towns.

For – almost literally – a cross section of Lake District scenery, one could drive up the Duddon Valley (or Dunnerdale), which was a favourite of Wordsworth's. From Duddon Sands at sea level, the road follows the river upstream through increasingly rugged scenery. At the top, Hardknott Pass takes one westward to the coast, Wrynose Pass into the central Lake District.

Readers' comments: Lovely people. Felt really welcome and at home. Good food.

WHITE BARN

Crede Lane, Bosham, West Sussex, PO18 8NX   Tel: 0243 573113
West of Chichester. Nearest main road: A259 from Chichester to Portsmouth.

rear view

3 Bedrooms. £19–£25 (less for 4 nights or 3 mid-week). Prices go up in April. Bargain breaks. All have own bath/shower/toilet. Tea/coffee facilities. Views of garden.
Dinner. £15 or £17 for 4 courses (with choices) and coffee, at 7.15pm. Non-residents not admitted. Vegetarian or special diets if ordered. Wine can be brought in. No dinners in August. **Light suppers** if ordered.
1 Sitting-room. With open fire, central heating, TV.
Small garden

As interesting architecturally as any house in this book, White Barn is no barn but a very modern house indeed (single storey), designed by architect Frank Guy, and standing in the seclusion of a former orchard.

The dining-room is impressive: its principal features are a roof of exposed boards, and a vast glass wall on one side (opening onto a red-tiled terrace).

This room is open to the big kitchen with its scarlet Aga cooker, pans hanging from brass hooks, and solid beech work-counter with old brass grocery-scales.

Then there is an oddly-shaped sitting-room, built all around the circular brick hearth on which a modern log stove stands. Its huge sofas face a narrow window 12 feet high. Tony Trotman's coat-of-arms hangs on a central column (he can trace his family back to 1086). Throughout there are white walls and glossy cream doors.

Few visitors prefer a separate table for meals but join all the others at a huge pine refectory table, laid with flowery Portmeirion pottery, where Susan Trotman serves such appetite-whetting meals as stuffed mushrooms or Italian cheese croûtes with a piquant red-pepper sauce, before, perhaps, chicken breasts sautéed in cream and white wine (and an abundance of fresh vegetables), followed by a pavlova topped with home-made lemon curd and Jersey cream.

Bedrooms open onto the garden, or overlook it. One is an imaginatively planned family suite: the room with children's bunk beds is like a cabin.

Not far away is the Saxon harbour of Bosham (its church is depicted in the Bayeux tapestry), thronged with little boats. Chichester, described elsewhere, lies in one direction and the historic naval waterfront of Portsmouth in the other – where you can visit HMS *Victory*, the *Mary Rose*, the dockyard museum, old bastions and byways, Southsea Castle, and the ring of Victorian forts high up.

Readers' comments: Very comfortable, food superb. Excellent value, memorable – not to be missed! Wonderful. Warm and welcoming. A memorable stay; outstanding. Food is out of this world. Top class! Comfortable, restful, very good food in ample quantity. Charming, cheerful, considerate. Meals superb. Will certainly return. The very best of hosts. First-class food, warm welcome. Beautifully looked after in every way. Delicious meals. Warm welcome. A most happy visit.

WHITE HOUSE   S X

Hanwood, Shropshire, SY5 8LP   Tel: 0743 860414
South-west of Shrewsbury. Nearest main road: A488 from Shrewsbury to
Bishop's Castle.

6 Bedrooms. £20–£25. Bargain breaks. Some have own bath/shower/toilet. All have tea/coffee facilities. TV (in one). Views of garden, country, river. Washing machine on request.
Dinner. £12 or £15 for 2 or 3 courses (with choices) and coffee, at 7.30pm. Vegetarian or special diets if ordered. Wine can be ordered. No smoking.
2 Sitting-rooms. With open fire, central heating, TV, record-player. **Bar.**
Large garden

The great black-and-white building dates back to the 16th century. The sitting-room is stone-floored and brick-walled, the flue from its log stove rising up to high rafters overhead. There is a big dining-room and bar, with modern-style bedrooms above – pink-and-white, with flowery fabrics: all immaculate, and redecorated every three years. Some have views of a garden brimming with flowers, beyond which the Rea brook babbles (home to several kingfishers).

Mike and Gill Mitchell have built up a considerable reputation for their restaurant; and each night there is a choice of about five dishes at every course – including such things as stuffed tomatoes, pork brochettes à la grecque and crab-apple jelly pancakes served with cream. Many vegetables come from the garden.

The southern hills of the county attract walkers as well as visitors to historic Shrewsbury, to the many castles and abbeys of the area, and to the lakes and sleepy villages on both sides of the Welsh border.

Shrewsbury, almost islanded by a loop of the Severn, is best explored on foot. Steep byways are lined with mediaeval houses, there is a 12th-century castle, several markets take place each week, interesting houses can be visited – now museums of local history, china, etc. – and there are statues of its two most famous sons, Clive of India and Charles Darwin.

In the other direction, the Hanwood road leads to the high lookout point of Earls Hill, an Iron Age site that is now a nature reserve where you may spot kestrels and jackdaws nesting among the rocks. This is near Minsterley, notable for the skulls and cherubs around the door and windows of its church. Some of Shropshire's famous hills are here, the Stiperstones – an unusual crest of sharp crags (another nature reserve). The dramatic formations of the quartzite are due to the shattering action of the last Ice Age and the strange shapes have inspired such names as 'the devil's chair' (with legends of witches to match). Mary Webb's novel, *Gone to Earth*, is set in this area.

By contrast, the Long Mynd is flat-topped, nevertheless rising to 1700 feet of moorland above which gliders soar. From this vantage point you can see how little Shropshire has changed over the centuries: the fields below seem tiny, their ancient hedges still in place (no prairie-scale 'agribusiness' here).

WHITES' FARMHOUSE   D S
Town End Road, Radnage, Buckinghamshire, HP14 4DY
Tel: 0494 482333
North-west of High Wycombe. Nearest main road: A40 from High Wycombe
to Oxford (and M40, junction 5).

1 Bedroom. £19 (less for 3 nights). With
own bath/toilet. Tea/coffee facilities. Views
of garden, country. No smoking. Washing
machine on request.
Light suppers if ordered.
1 Sitting-room. With open fire, central
heating, TV.
Large garden

Lindsay Wilcox is chairman of the Contemporary Applied Arts gallery, so it is
hardly surprising that his home, all mellow brick and rambling roses outside, is
filled with the best in modern, craftsman-made furniture (designed by
Makepeace, La-Trobe, Bateman and others), ceramics and textiles – to all of
which the 17th-century house has proved an admirable background. Even the two
baby-chairs are craftsman-made, to the same design as Prince William's; and the
weather-vane on the roof is a modern sun-sculpture in steel.

Guests have a bedroom with views over the Radnage valley to beech woods
and a Saxon church, a private sitting-room and their own entrance.

Claudia can provide light suppers (such as pasta or chicken), after which
guests are welcome to enjoy a stroll in the garden with its collection of rare flowering shrubs and trees, or just sit with a drink and watch the tame white doves fly
across the unspoilt valley. The more energetic walk the many well-signed paths,
or even the long-distance Ridgeway footpath.

Here, and eastward to the Hughenden Valley, is such fine scenery that much
of it is owned by the National Trust, including the great house which was
Disraeli's home. At West Wycombe there is much to see and most is very unusual, including an underground cave system open to the public, and the 18th-centu-
ry church with so immense a golden ball on top of its tower that parties were held
in it by Sir Francis Dashwood – leader of the 'Hell Fire Club' which held orgies
in the caves and in the ruins of Medmenham Abbey. His magnificent Palladian
mansion is surrounded by parkland which Capability Brown laid out.

Then there are Penn, where William Penn lived, and Jordans, associated with
the Pilgrim Fathers; Milton's cottage at Chalfont St Giles; and High Wycombe's
chair museum (from the Chiltern beech woods originated the Windsor chair, and
the town is still a centre of furniture-making).

In this Chilterns area of outstanding natural beauty, are gentle drives through
beech woods and along country lanes to the old Roman road at Ellesborough –
the Upper Icknield Way. There are fine views of Chequers, the country home of
Britain's Prime Ministers, and the 17th-century home of parliamentarian John
Hampden.

**Book well ahead: many of these houses have few rooms. Do not
expect dinner if you have not booked it or if you arrive late.**

WHITESTONE FARM

C D PT S

Downdale Road, Staintondale, North Yorkshire, YO13 0EZ

Tel: 0723 870612

North of Scarborough. Nearest main road: A171 from Scarborough to Whitby.

rear view

3 Bedrooms. £12.50–£13 (less for 3 nights or continental breakfast). Prices go up from Easter. Bargain breaks. Tea/coffee facilities. TV. Views of garden, country, sea. No smoking.
Dinner. £7 for 4 courses and coffee, at 6.30pm. Non-residents not admitted. Vegetarian or special diets if ordered. Wine can be brought in. No smoking. **Light suppers** if ordered.
2 Sitting-rooms. With open fire, central heating, TV, record-player.
Small garden

Its position is a big attraction of this stone-built farmhouse (south of Robin Hood's Bay, famous for its three-mile sweep and the constant erosion which has caused many cottages to tumble into the sea). It is near National Trust coastal scenery, all with spectacular views.

There is a glass-walled sun-lounge so that you can see meadows with cows and lambs in one direction and the sea in the other – from the comfort of the large curved sofa or an armchair. A steep staircase leads up to neat, rather small bedrooms which enjoy similar views.

Adjoining the farmland are woods and Heyburn Wyke nature reserve – roe deer occasionally wander in from the reserve. There are footpaths down to the rocky shore and along a disused rail track; the long-distance Cleveland Way passes by on its journey to the North Yorkshire Moors.

Pat Angus prepares for her guests such meals as: fruit juice; tomato stuffed with walnuts, raisins, cheese and chives in mayonnaise – served with a salad and home-baked wholemeal roll; turkey breast in breadcrumbs with cranberry sauce and four vegetables; sherry trifle. Exceptional value.

Staintondale's attractions include not only the coast but also the North York Moors. Scarborough is a huge mixture of resort, fishing harbour and historic town, with superb scenery around (both cliffs and sandy bays). Some of it is now garish; but the harbour and fishmarket are as they always were, and dramatically positioned on a headland are the remains of a Norman castle overlooking Scarborough's superb bay. Staintondale's shire horse centre is popular.

Anne Brontë died and is buried at Scarborough. She wrote about 'the deep, clear azure of the sky and ocean, the bright morning sunshine on the semicircular barrier of craggy cliffs surmounted by green swelling hills, and on the smooth, wide sands, and the low rocks out at sea – looking, with their clothing of weeds and moss, like little grass-grown islands – and above all, on the brilliant, sparkling waves. And then the unspeakable purity and freshness of the air!'

Readers' comments: A lovely atmosphere, food excellent in content, presentation and quantity. A caring couple. Wonderful value for money. Very good.

Prices are per person in a double room at the beginning of the year.

WHITEWEBBS

C(7) D PT X

Grange Road (off Lower Road), **Chalfont St Peter, Buckinghamshire, SL9 9AQ** Tel: 0753 884105

South-east of High Wycombe. Nearest main road: A413 from Amersham to Denham (also M40, junction 1; and M25, junction 16).

2 Bedrooms. £17.50 (less for 4 nights). Both have own bath/shower/toilet. Tea/coffee facilities. TV. Views of garden. No smoking. Washing machine on request. **Dinner** (by arrangement). £10 for 2 courses and coffee, at 7pm. Non-residents not admitted. Vegetarian or special diets if ordered. Wine can be brought in. No smoking. **Light suppers** if ordered. **Small garden**

This house, secluded by tall oaks and pines, was built in 1928 on ground belonging to the nearby Grange, once the home of William Penn's father-in-law (who sailed with him on the *Mayflower*). Now it is the home of artist Maureen Marsh who specializes in portraits of houses and country views: visitors are welcome to enter her studio and to see the little printing-press on which she and her husband produce Christmas cards and so forth.

Often tea (with home-produced raspberry jam and cakes) is served in the garden, pretty with flower baskets and rose bushes – or visitors can use the kitchen to make their own at any hour. Maureen enjoys cooking and gives her guests such meals as a courgette and cheese gratin with a salad, followed by pecan pie into which go sherry-soaked raisins. These are served in a cream and pine dining-room with lattice-paned windows.

Upstairs are trim, cottagey bedrooms and everywhere her delightful water-colours.

This is a tranquil spot for a break from London or to recover from a flight to Heathrow. For walkers, the South Bucks Way passes close by; for sightseeing there are Milton's cottage, the Chilterns open-air museum of historic buildings, beautiful drives in the Chiltern Hills (famous for their autumn colours), the Bekonscot miniature village – 1½ acres recreating life in the 'twenties complete with a 20-locomotive railway, the Quaker centre of Jordans, and the historic streets of – for instance – Beaconsfield and Marlow. Some of the Thames' loveliest reaches are in the vicinity, as are the Italianate mansion and grounds of Cliveden and Tudor Chenies Manor, Stanley Spencer's paintings in pretty Cookham, the 'hell-fire' caves at Medmenham, the historic chair museum of High Wycombe, Gray's monument at Stoke Poges and Disraeli's house (Hughenden Manor).

Readers' comments: Warm hospitality. Large, airy and comfortable rooms. Have stayed several times. One feels like a family guest. Delicious breakfasts. Extremely pretty.

WHITTLES FARM
C(12)

Beercrocombe, Somerset, TA3 6AH   Tel: 0823 480301
South-east of Taunton. Nearest main road: A358 from Taunton to Ilminster.

3 Bedrooms. £18.50–£20 (less for 7 nights). All have own bath/toilet. Tea/coffee facilities. TV. Views of garden, country. No smoking. Washing machine on request.
Dinner. £15 for 4 courses and coffee, at 6.30pm (on 4 evenings a week). Non-residents not admitted. Vegetarian or special diets if ordered. Wine can be ordered. **Light suppers** if ordered.
1 Sitting-room. With open fire, central heating. Bar.
Large garden
Closed from December to mid-January.

It is not just the excellence of the accommodation but also Claire Mitchem's delightful personality which go to make an exceptional farmhouse holiday here – at the end of a lane leading nowhere. Part of the house dates back to the 16th century (hence the beams and inglenook of the sitting-room).

There is not only a dining- but also a separate breakfast-room; and every bedroom is attractively decorated – one with deep pink moiré wallpaper complementing the velvet bedheads and curtains of the same colour; another with festoon blinds, a sofa with embroidered cushions and a very pretty bathroom, for example. Colourful bouquets are an eye-catching feature throughout the house.

Food is fresh and attractively presented. A typical menu: vegetable quiche as a starter; boeuf bourguinonne (with beef from a local award-winning butcher) accompanied by four vegetables and a salad; 'queen of puddings' with clotted cream; cheese and fruit.

There are excellent woodland walks around here, and drives along lanes which vary at every turn. You may see a thatcher at work, pause for a drink at a cider farm, or peer over old stone walls to admire brimming cottage-gardens. The Quantocks are near.

Within easy reach are Hatch Court, Montacute House and Dunster Castle; the coast both north and south; and the county town of Taunton itself, only a few miles away (close to the M5): the Vivary and Hestercombe gardens here are well worth a visit, and also the castle (with exceptionally good museum) close to the River Tone.

Almost within Taunton is the hamlet of Bishop's Hull where, in Silk Mills Road, is much modernized **ROUGH-MOOR COTTAGE**, Joan Pape's immaculate guest-house with well-equipped rooms: excellent bathrooms, in particular; and a very good family room with sofa. An especial attraction is the log-cabin swimming-pool in the well-tended garden, which also has a good tennis court (coaching available) and a summer-house with table tennis. Four-course dinners. Nearby is Avery's large nursery garden and a stream

where a watermill is being restored. £19–£22.50.
Readers' comments: Delighted with the hospitality, have stayed repeatedly. Pleasantly furnished. [Tel: 0823 331931; postcode: TA1 5AA]

WHYKE HOUSE
13 Whyke Lane, Chichester, West Sussex, PO19 2JR Tel: 0243 788767
Nearest main road: A27 from Worthing to Portsmouth.

C M PT S X

rear view

3 Bedrooms. £18 (less for 6 nights). Tea/coffee facilities. TV. Views of garden. No smoking. Private parking.
1 Sitting-room. With central heating, TV. No smoking.
Small garden

In a peaceful suburban cul-de-sac, very close to the historic centre of Chichester (and overlooking a grassy Roman site at the back, where children now play) is an unusual bed-and-breakfast house, ideal for families.

Here Tony and Lydia Hollis provide continental breakfasts (and service rooms), give advice on sightseeing, then depart to their own home next door. There is a fully equipped kitchen which guests are then welcome to use to prepare other meals, if they do not wish to go to Chichester's many restaurants and cafés. Guests can also use the sitting-room and back garden (with croquet), glimpsed in the drawing. It is almost like being in a home of your own, with complete freedom.

(For those in the self-catering flat, breakfast can be cooked.)

The furnishings throughout have great individuality. Family antiques mingle with Russian folk art, local paintings (you may meet the artist) with soft-furnishings made by Lydia – who also has a flair for painting furniture decoratively. Adjoining the white kitchen is a dining-room with green bamboo wallpaper; the baby's highchair is a century-old heirloom, so is the grandmother clock. For some older guests, the ground-floor bedroom and shower are particularly convenient.

Readers' comments: The Hollises are so kind and helpful. Very comfortable; unpretentious and suited to young families. What good value. Comfortable, quiet, convenient; most welcoming. Pleasant weekend; a real treat to stay.

East of Chichester, the accommodation at **ST HUGH'S**, Boxgrove, is in a separate annexe in the garden. It comprises a spacious, well-furnished bedsitting-room which opens onto a private patio. There is an excellent shower room; and cooking facilities are hidden away in pine fitments. For breakfast, guests enter the main house and its dining-room (lined with ancestral portraits of Cornish farmers). B & b only: for other meals, Edwina Tremaine recommends restaurants in nearby Chichester. Boxgrove itself deserves a visit because the Norman nave of its parish church is quite outstanding. £16.

rear view

Readers' comments: Wholly recommended, beautifully furnished. Absolutely ideal. Very comfortable. Made very welcome. Helpful hosts. [Tel: 0243 773173; postcode: PO18 0DY]

WIGBOROUGH FARM

C

Lower Stratton, Somerset, TA13 5LP   Tel: 0460 40490
West of Yeovil. Nearest main road: A303 from Ilminster to Wincanton.

3 Bedrooms. £17. Some have own bath/toilet. Tea/coffee facilities. TV. Views of garden, country. No smoking. Washing machine on request.
Dinner. £12 for 3 courses (with choices) and coffee, at 8.30pm. Non-residents not admitted. Vegetarian or special diets if ordered. Wine can be brought in. No smoking. **Light suppers** if ordered.
1 Sitting-room. With open fire, central heating, TV, piano, record-player.
Large garden
Closed from December to February.

But for a fire in 1585, this mansion would doubtless have been one of England's oldest. Only one wing was rebuilt: even so, it remains among the most impressive of the houses in this book.

Outside are pinnacled gables, Tudor roses carved in the spandrels above the arched doorway, handsome dripstones above the narrow-paned mullioned windows – all in tawny Ham limestone which lichen has enriched over the centuries: the same local stone from which the National Trust's great Montacute House was built about the same time as this house.

Inside are ogee arches, stone floors and iron-studded doors; there are still spit-racks above one of the huge fireplaces. The ground-floor rooms are high-ceilinged: one has a minstrels' gallery overlooking the great refectory table and its leather chairs (this gallery is now a bedroom). The sitting-room has a quite exceptional plaster ceiling with bas-reliefs of foxes, stags, pheasants and even a unicorn (made by Italian plasterers in Elizabeth I's reign); and over its fireplace is the great coat-of-arms of a local family.

Guests' bedrooms (varying in size and style) are on the second floor: the most outstanding has oak walls, its panels decoratively carved with arches and pilasters, and a four-poster bed.

From many windows are views of lawns with specimen trees, tubs of busy Lizzies, old stables and the walled vegetable garden.

Where meals are concerned, Joan Vaux and one of her daughters prepare such dishes as mushroom soup, beef cooked in wine and fruit mousse.

Yeovil (a glove-making centre) has nine springs flowing into a very lovely lake: the walk to it, along a wooded riverside path, is well worth seeking out. All around the town are historic villages, such as Milborne Port with its old guildhall, Tintinhull which still has punishment stocks, Hinton St George with fine stone houses among its tangle of lanes, picturesque Compton Pauncefoot named after a Norman landowner of big belly ('paunch-fat') and South Cadbury, whose high and massive earthworks were reputedly King Arthur's stronghold, Camelot. Langport is a hilly market town with a chapel on top of a mediaeval arch.

Some proprietors stipulate a minimum stay of two nights at weekends or peak seasons; or they will accept one-nighters only at short notice (that is, only if no lengthier booking has yet been made).

Pasture Road North, Barton-upon-Humber, Humberside, DN18 5RB
Tel: 0652 34416
South-west of Hull. Nearest main road: A1077 from Scunthorpe to Grimsby.

3 Bedrooms. £12 (less for 3 nights). TV (in one). Views of garden, country. No smoking. Washing machine on request.
Dinner. £6 for 3 courses and coffee, at 7pm. Non-residents not admitted. Vegetarian or special diets if ordered. Wine can be brought in. No smoking. **Light suppers** if ordered.
1 Sitting-room. With central heating, TV, record-player. No smoking.
Large garden

It was the ducks on the pond that made the Howsons fall for this house a few years ago, and visitors can still watch them through the big window of the living-room. In front of the architect-designed bungalow, built in 1984, stands the weeping willow tree after which it is named, and all around it are beautifully land-scaped gardens which, with a meadow, extend to four acres (all the bedrooms overlook them). The gardens are now Bill Howson's main concern, and he pro-duces the fruit and vegetables which Joan uses for such meals as casserole of lamb, raspberry creams and cheese. Vegetarians can also be catered for (Joan being one herself), and what is not produced by the Howsons is obtained from organic sources. (Sunday lunch is also available.)

Joan is a semi-professional artist, and glazed plates decorated with wildlife subjects, which are her speciality, hang throughout the house (these and her drawings are for sale). Her studio, in a separate building beyond the pond, can be hired by visitors who want to paint.

The house, which is surrounded by trees and stands only a few feet above sea level, is a place for walkers and nature-lovers – the first because it is close to many local and long-distance footpaths (the Viking Way to Rutland and the Wolds Way from the Humber to Filey among them). The garden borders a 'site of special scientific interest', and the nearby claypits are a haven for such rare wetland fauna as the bittern. The area is looked after by enthusiastic locals, and there is an inter-pretation centre in an old boathouse. This is by the viewing area provided for people who come to admire the truly impressive Humber bridge.

Though not a well-known tourist destination, South Humberside has its appeal, with peaceful brick villages, some great houses, and the towers of old windmills, one of which has been turned into a pub restaurant in Barton. For cathedral enthusiasts, the village is conveniently situated midway between Lincoln and York, and Beverley is close.

Mallards at Willow Tree Lodge

WINDMILL HOUSE

Winterbourne Monkton, Wiltshire, SN4 9NN   Tel: 06723 446
South of Swindon. Nearest main road: A4361 from Swindon to Devizes
(and M4, junction 16).

C PT S X

3 Bedrooms. £15–£16 (less for 7 nights). Prices go up from Easter. Views of garden, country. Washing machine on request.
Dinner. £10 for 3 courses (with choices) and coffee, at 6.15pm (not Friday to Sunday). Non-residents not admitted. Vegetarian or special diets if ordered. Wine can be brought in. No smoking. **Light suppers** if ordered.
1 Sitting-room. With open fire.
Small garden

All but the base of the windmill vanished long ago and this, the miller's house, has been greatly modernized – although in some rooms the old walls made of chalk blocks are visible, one bearing the date 1711. All around are fields, with far views of prehistoric heights. Avebury is only a mile away.

A narrow spiral stair leads up to bedrooms that are simply furnished but comfortable, and the dining/sitting-room (with log stove) is unpretentious. Outside is an unheated swimming-pool. But what most impresses the walkers, game-shooting parties, and others who come here is the food. Penny Randerson comes from a family of chefs, which may be why meals are of an order to compare with some many-starred hotels. Although one-night visitors are offered a set menu (with choices at each course), those staying longer can order ahead from her considerable repertoire of such dishes as pigeons en cocotte, seafood gratin, cheese fondue (unusually prepared with cherry brandy), filet Chateaubriand, pork chops ardennaise, etc. Bread is home-baked and vegetables from the garden.

Readers' comments: Most kind. Good evening meals. Good value.

The prehistoric stone circles which surround picturesque Avebury village are even older than Stonehenge, their purpose unknown and their construction method a mystery too, as each weighs up to 40 tons. Almost opposite the Norman church is the **OLD VICARAGE**, parts of which date back to the 17th century. Jane Fry has a flair for interior decoration, so each room has beautiful colour schemes – even the blue-and-salmon kitchen, with tiled alcove for the blue Aga, 'dragged' kitchen units and festoon blinds. The front door opens into the canary dining-room with Chippendale chairs, window-seat in a bay, and Indian curtains embroidered with birds of paradise. The terracotta sitting-room

looks onto the walled garden with its begonia tubs and roses. All three double bedrooms are equally attractive. A typical dinner: smoked salmon, chicken breasts in an orange sauce with almonds and raisins, fruit and cheese. £17–£19 (b & b).
Reader's comment: Everything splendid.
[Tel: 06723 362: postcode: SN8 1RF]

WINDRUSH HOUSE   C(12)
Hazleton, Gloucestershire, GL54 4EB   Tel: 0451 860364
South-east of Cheltenham. Nearest main road: A40 from Cheltenham to
Oxford.

4 Bedrooms. £17.25–£19. Some have own shower/toilet. Tea/coffee facilities. Views of garden, country. Washing machine on request.
Dinner (by arrangement). £15 for 4 courses and coffee, at 7.30pm. Wine can be ordered or brought in. **Light suppers** if ordered.
2 Sitting-rooms. With open fire, central heating, TV, video, piano, record-player.
Large garden
Closed in January.

The greatest attraction of this small guest-house built of Cotswold stone is
Sydney Harrison's outstanding cooking. Not only is everything impeccably
prepared – vegetables delicately sliced and lightly cooked, bread home-baked,
breakfast orange juice freshly squeezed – but she has a repertoire of imaginative
dishes that puts many an expensive restaurant in the shade. With your breakfast
porridge you will be offered whisky. And all the food is served on Royal
Worcester porcelain. On nights when dinner is not served, she recommends the
Fosse Bridge or Frog Mill.

Sydney's friendly welcome is manifest the moment you arrive, and a free glass
of sherry awaits you in your room.

As to the house itself, this is furnished with much attention to comfort, and in
tranquil colours. All the rooms are immaculate, the furnishings traditional.

The house stands in a quiet spot some 800 feet up in the Cotswold
Hills, where the air is bracing and the views are of far fields and grazing sheep.
It is on the outskirts of a rambling village of old stone farmhouses with a
small church.

Hazleton – under two hours from London – is close to beautiful Northleach,
which has a mediaeval church of great splendour and an excellent museum of
country life; Cirencester, a lovely market town with the outstanding Corinium
museum, crafts, another church as grand as a cathedral and a great park; Burford
and Cheltenham, with all the elegance of a spa, particularly at the Montpellier
end of the great Promenade (another good museum and fine church). The beauty
of the Cotswold Hills needs no describing, nor its showpiece villages like
Bourton-on-the-Water, Bibury and Stow-on-the-Wold. There is a Roman villa at
Chedworth, butterfly and bird gardens, folk and farm museums, wildlife and rare
breeds parks, stately homes and gardens, castles (such as Sudeley), abbeys and
walks. Riding can be arranged.

Readers' comments: Food absolutely outstanding, even for a spoiled Swiss!
Absolute calm. First-rate; inventive menu; highly recommended. Excellent food
and genial hosts. Food outstanding; what a find! Superb cooking. The best meal
we'd had – highly recommended. Excellent in every way, especially food and
wine. The best cook we've found in England. Excellent food; very comfortable;
welcoming. Our third visit. Excellent cook and hostess; very comfortable. We
booked for three days and stayed one week.

WINDYRIDGE

Wraik Hill, Whitstable, Kent, CT5 3BY   Tel: 0227 263506

North of Canterbury. Nearest main road: A299 from Faversham towards Ramsgate (and M2, junction 7).

8 **Bedrooms.** £17.50–£19.50 (less for 3 nights). Prices go up in June. Bargain breaks. Some have own shower/toilet. Tea/coffee facilities. TV. Views of garden, country, sea.
Dinner. £9.50 for 3 courses and coffee, at 6.30pm. Vegetarian or special diets if ordered. Wine can be ordered. **Bar snacks.**
3 **Sitting-rooms.** With wood burner, central heating, TV, record-player, piano. No smoking in one. **Bar.**
Large garden

The architectural eccentricities of this house are due to the fact that a demolition contractor once lived here, and in the course of expanding what was originally a small cottage he built in all kinds of curios – even gargoyles from a chapel, and rare Norman panes of purple glass. Some iron-framed windows came from a prison. Two-foot-thick walls have a mixture of granite slabs, bricks and low stone archways combined in an odd assortment.

Cheryl and Clive Barker now run Windyridge as a guest-house. At one end of the very big sitting/dining-room, sofas and cretonne wing chairs face a great stone fireplace with log stove (there are more sitting-rooms and a cosy bar elsewhere) while beyond the tables at the other end a steep, open-tread staircase rises to the bedrooms – and there is a telescope from which to enjoy the panoramic sea views. Even without its aid, one can often see from this high vantage-point the distant shores of Essex and, at night, the twinkling lights of its liveliest resort, Southend-on-Sea. All the bedrooms are fresh and trim; there is a particularly good family room with curtained annexe for children.

Cheryl serves such dinners as mushroom soup, fresh salmon, rhubarb crumble and cheeses. Rolls are home-baked, vegetables come from the garden.

Beyond a sun-room with cushioned bamboo chairs is a rambling garden. Along the coast (15 minutes' walk away), sandy beaches are separated by the Swale from the Isle of Sheppey – this waterway is a haven for wildfowl.

Of all counties, Kent – fertile and wealthy – has played a greater part in English history than any other because its coast is only 20 miles from Europe (to which it was once joined) and because of its proximity to London.

Once, Whitstable enjoyed an important role in all this and was busy with travellers who came by coach from Canterbury to embark there for a sea journey to London (which says much about the sad state of road transport to the capital at that time). Then in 1830 the world's first passenger train took over this route: you can see its locomotive (Robert Stephenson's *Invicta*) in Canterbury.

But it was only in this century that Whitstable really prospered as a seaside resort. It still has rows of black-and-white weatherboarded fishermen's cottages to give it character, and such seafood restaurants as the Oyster House (where you can eat well). Eastward lie Herne Bay, an old-fashioned Victorian resort, and Reculver's twin towers – Norman, but within the remains of a great Roman fort.

Readers' comments: Very friendly owners, excellent food. Very kind hostess.

374

WINNACOTT FARM
North Petherwin, Cornwall, PL15 8LS   Tel: 056685 785366
North of Launceston. Nearest main road: A30 from Okehampton to Bodmin.

3 Bedrooms. £12–£19. Prices go up from July. Two with own bath/toilet. Tea/coffee facilities. TV. Views of country. No smoking. Washing machine on request.
Dinner. £9 for 4 courses and coffee, at time by arrangement. Vegetarian or special diets by arrangement. Wine can be brought in. **Light suppers** if ordered.
1 Sitting-room. With open fire, central heating, TV.
Large garden
Closed from October to January.

The remote 17th-century house has the pleasant, homely accommodation typical of most working farms.

In the oak-furnished dining-room with Royal Worcester china, Greta Bird serves such meals as courgette soup with rolls (both home-made), roast lamb with five home-grown vegetables, a spicy fruit and almond crumble (the custard is made with eggs from her ducks), unusual cheeses and fruit. At breakfast there are a dozen honeys to choose from.

Bedrooms are prettily decorated, well equipped and very moderately priced. Outside are a small arboretum above a pond with ducks; an aviary of finches; and rare breeds of chickens.

Readers' comments: Well decorated, lovely meals, friendly atmosphere. Charming, quiet. Real personal hospitality, excellent meal imaginatively prepared. Cosy and delightful. Dinner stupendous; breakfast a feast.

South of Launceston, near Treburley, is **FLEARDON FARM** and in its barns a gallery with the work of Roger Garland, creator of those brilliant and intricate covers to Tolkien's books. His mother welcomes bed-and-breakfast guests to the 250-year-old house which has a surprising interior: a big open-plan kitchen/dining area with mahogany staircase to the floor above. The large sitting-room with windows on three sides has a log stove, sofas and a profusion of pot-plants. Bedrooms (and excellent bathrooms) overlook the cobbled courtyard or a waterfall and stream. There is a deco- rative folly and a lake frequented by Canada geese. £15–£17.
Readers' comments: All in superb order. Unobtrusive help and friendliness. [Tel: 0579 370364; messages: 0579 370760; postcode: PL15 9NW]

When writing to me, if you want a reply please enclose an International Reply Coupon.

WOLD FARM

CDMPTSX

Old, Northamptonshire, NN6 9RJ   Tel: 0604 781258
(Messages: 0604 781122)
North of Northampton. Nearest main road: A508 from Northampton to
Market Harborough (and M1, junction 15).

6 Bedrooms. £18–£21 (less for 3 nights).
All have own bath/shower. Tea/coffee
facilities. Views of garden. Washing
machine on request.
Dinner. £11 for 4 courses, wine and coffee,
at 7pm. Vegetarian or special diets if
ordered. Wine can be brought in. **Light
suppers** if ordered.
2 Sitting-rooms. With open fire, central
heating, TV, record-player. Billiards.
Garden

This 18th-century house has particularly attractive and spacious rooms, and two
delightful gardens with rose pergola, golden pheasants and swing-seat. A garden-
cottage has been converted to provide more bedrooms (en suite), one of which is
on the ground floor. Throughout the house are attractive fabrics and wallpapers;
one room, for example, with 'Country Manor' pattern on walls, bed and curtains.
In the sitting-room are alcoves of Hummel figures, in the dining-room a carved
17th-century sideboard, and in the breakfast-room a dresser with the exhortation:
'Nourish thyself with lively vivacity'. Window-seats, antiques and white-panelled
doors add further character to the rooms. Throughout, standards are of the
highest. The house is at the heart of a beef and arable farm.

For dinner, Anne Engler serves – in an oak-beamed dining-room with
inglenook fireplace – such meals as home-made soup followed by a roast and then
perhaps fruit salad or Bakewell tart, and cheeses – with a sherry, wine or beer
included. (Occasional barbecues; and Sunday lunch also available.) Anne, once a
'Tiller girl', is a most warm and welcoming hostess.

A feature of the rolling agricultural landscape round here is the network of
18th- and 19th-century canals, and the reservoirs (now naturalized) that were
built to top up the water in these. At Stoke Bruerne a waterways museum tells the
whole story of the canals. The many stately homes of this prosperous county
include Althorp (childhood home of the Princess of Wales) and Boughton House
(modelled on Versailles). There are Saxon churches at Brixworth and Earls
Barton. The county is famous for its high-spired churches and for its many
historical associations: it has two 'Eleanor crosses' erected in the 13th century
by Edward I wherever his wife's coffin rested on its journey to burial in
Westminster Abbey; Fotheringhay is where Mary Queen of Scots was executed;
Cromwell defeated Charles I's army at Naseby in 1645 (good bar food at the
Fitzgerald Arms, and a museum of the battle). In the Nene Valley is a scenic
steam railway.

Looking at all the things there are to see and do – interesting to children and
adults alike – it seemed to me that staying here would be a very good all-weather
alternative to a traditional seaside holiday for the family.

Readers' comments: Cooking outstanding. Very thoughtful attention. Harmony and
friendliness. Exactingly high standard. Kind and generous. It excels. Outstanding
success. Warmest of welcomes. Attractive garden. Pretty and very comfortable
room. Food a delight; table-settings superb. Friendly, attentive and patient.

THE WOOD

De Courcy Road, Moult Hill, Salcombe, Devon, TQ8 8LQ
Tel: 0548 842778
South of Kingsbridge. Nearest main road: A381 from Salcombe to Totnes.

rear view

6 Bedrooms. £20–£32 (less for 7 nights). Prices go up from May. Most have own bath/shower/toilet. Tea/coffee facilities. TV. Views of garden, country, sea. Balcony (some). Washing machine on request.
Dinner. £15 for 4 courses (with some choices) and coffee, at 7.30pm. Vegetarian or special diets if ordered. Wine can be ordered. **Light suppers** if ordered.
1 Sitting-room. With open fire, central heating, piano, CD-player.
Terraced garden
Closed in December and January.

One of the most spectacular sites in this book is occupied by a turn-of-the-century house which seems almost to hang in the air, so steep is the wooded cliff below it. One looks straight down onto the pale golden beach of South Sands (a small cove) and the blue waters of Salcombe estuary with the English Channel beyond. Rocky headlands stretch into the distance. To make the most of this exceptional view, some bedrooms have balconies and the elegant, split-level sitting-room has huge windows that open onto a paved terrace (sometimes meals are served on a verandah). One can walk through the garden to a steep woodland footpath which goes down to the sands – but what a climb up again! – and from there take the ferry to Salcombe.

Bedrooms, on two floors, have different styles. No. 1 is all pink and white. No. 2 has a sensational bay window framing a view of the estuary; it has a canopied bed, balcony, a power shower and a whirlpool bath. No. 3, a single, is very pretty: Victorian-style cream and pink fabrics, pine-panelled doors. No. 4, with jade, peach and cream fabrics, has a balcony; as does no. 5, with four-poster and out-size bathroom. No. 6 is level with a small patio.

In the dining-room (handsomely furnished with pink velvet chairs, white-gold Minton china and linen napkins), Pat Vaissière serves candlelit dinners that use much local produce – such as cheese-filled eggs, lamb with apricot-and-almond stuffing, chocolate rum trifle, and cheeses. Rolls are home-baked.

Salcombe is Devon's southernmost resort, and arguably its most beautiful one. Even orange and lemon trees grow here which, together with palms remind one of parts of the Mediterranean. The estuary is very popular for sailing, garden-lovers come to see Sharpitor (NT), walkers make for the viewpoints of Bolbery Down and Bolt Head. All along the coast from here to Plymouth are picturesque waterfront villages, such as Bantham and Newton Ferrers, described elsewhere. In the opposite direction are Kingsbridge (old market town), Slapton Sands (nature reserve, with lagoons), picturesque Dartmouth (of outstanding historical interest – two castles, quaint quays, the Royal Naval College).

Readers' comments: Outstanding standards. They go out of their way to provide that little bit extra at every turn. Made to feel so much at home. Worth coming for the food alone! Lovely site; delighted. Superb comfort, food and hospitality.

Bramdean, Hampshire, SO24 0LL   Tel: 0962 771793
East of Winchester. On A272 from Winchester to Petersfield.

3 Bedrooms. £20–£22 (less for 3 nights or continental breakfast). Bargain breaks. All have own bath/toilet. Tea/coffee facilities. Views of garden, country. No smoking. Washing machine on request.
Dinner. £12 for 3 courses and coffee, at 8pm. Non-residents not admitted. Wine can be ordered or brought in. No smoking.
Light suppers if ordered.
1 Sitting-room. With open fire, central heating, TV. No smoking.
Large garden
Closed from November to February.

In July 1554, Philip II of Spain arrived (in the pouring rain) at Winchester for his marriage to Mary Tudor. She had spent the previous night at this house; and must have been more tense than most brides, for there had been a Commons' petition against the Spanish marriage, and a plot to depose her before it could take place.

Woodcote Manor is one of the most outstanding houses in this book. At its heart is a 14th-century building to which additions were made in Tudor and Jacobean times, with alterations in the 18th century, and a further – very handsome – extension made in 1911. Caroline McLaughlan and her family live in one part of the house, and it is her husband's paintings which hang on many of the walls.

A very long sitting-room has tall sash windows and window-seats deep-set in its pale blue walls; a marble fireplace; and Florentine cabinet with birds and flowers inlaid. At the back is a large dining-room dominated by a panel of Dutch oak carved with a scene of the Israelites escaping from Egypt.

A handsome staircase leads up to bedrooms including the one used by Mary Tudor before her wedding. Oak-panelled, it has a splendid fireplace that was specially installed for her visit. There is a very attractive attic suite with leaded casements which would be ideal for a family. Caroline has chosen attractive contrasts of colours and textures – white flokati rugs on polished oak floors; aquamarine walls with redcurrant curtains.

As to dinner, this is mostly based on the farm's own produce. A typical menu: spinach soup or pâté, roast pheasant, blackcurrant mousse and meringues, cheeses. You can work off the calories in a swimming-pool or playing tennis.

Readers' comments: Intelligent people. Beautiful house. Will return.

At hives beyond the badminton court, a swarm of two dozen veiled bee-keepers were holding a 'meet' when I arrived at **MORESTEAD GROVE**, Morestead, an early Victorian rectory with handsome rooms. Katharine Sellon serves such dinners (if ordered in advance) as smoked haddock mousse, chicken in a wine and mushroom sauce and candied oranges, using her own vegetables and eggs. No

smoking. £17. [Tel: 0962 777238; postcode: SO21 1LZ]

WOODLANDS   C PT S

Parkham Road, Brixham, Devon, TQ5 9BU   Tel: 0803 852040
South of Torquay. Nearest main road: A3022 from Brixham to Torquay.

5 Bedrooms. £18–£19.80 (less for 3 nights). All have own shower/toilet. Tea/coffee facilities. TV. Views of sea (some). No smoking. Washing machine on request.
Light suppers if ordered.
1 Sitting-room. With central heating, record-player. No smoking.
Small garden
Closed from November to February.

The morning sun streams across Lyme Bay and in through the bay window of the breakfast-room, where rainbow-bordered china is elegantly laid on navy table-cloths – just one of many attractive touches in this Victorian guest-house owned by artist Robert Doling and his wife Norma. The house is perched high (Brixham is no place for the faint-hearted or feeble-footed!) and looks down to a harbour of bobbing boats, surrounded by steep lanes of colourful houses. The sea view beyond stretches across to Dorset: Weymouth can be seen from the small top bedroom.

On Sundays, a carillon from Brixham church rings out over the rooftops (it was a Victorian vicar here who composed the hymn 'Abide with Me') but other-wise Parkham Road is very quiet.

This is an immaculate house for Robert is a perfectionist. On every wall are either his own paintings or well-chosen prints (some visitors like to see his studio in the garden – he occasionally gives tuition). And the house has – a real boon in Brixham – its own carpark a few yards uphill.

Around the picturesque and lively harbour there are still fishermen's cottages and inns crowded together in the narrow lanes. It was here that William of Orange landed in 1688 to replace James II as King of England. There is a coastal footpath which goes to the scenic cliffs at Berry Head in one direction and, in the other, an interesting route to Paignton. Also in the vicinity are sandy beaches, and, going inland, the wild expanse of Dartmoor, the beautiful River Dart, pretty countryside and stately homes. You can take the car ferry to reach historic Dartmouth to the south, or drive north to the seaside resorts of Paignton and Torquay, only a few minutes away.

Brixham is at the south end of Tor Bay, its coastline famous for golden sands and subtropical plants, its sea for (usually) an azure blue: an almost Mediterranean scene. Its mild climate has made it Devon's most popular holiday area, for better or worse, with plenty to see and do. The lush countryside, red-earthed, has been farmed from prehistoric times and every century since has contributed historic or beautiful buildings to enrich the scene: Berry Pomeroy, for instance, has a Norman castle, while little Dawlish is noted for its pretty Regency terraces (for its gardens, red cliffs and sand dunes too); most villages have mediaeval thatched cottages; in several places there are caves in which Stone Age men lived; and Paignton still has its Victorian pier.

Readers' comments: Personal attention and care. Rooms designed with creative taste.

WOODLANDS   C D M PT X

Trewollock, near Gorran Haven, Cornwall, PL26 6NS   Tel: 0726 843821
South of St Austell. Nearest main road: A390 from St Austell to Truro.

6 **Bedrooms.** £15.50–£16.50. Tea/coffee
facilities. Views of garden, country, sea. No
smoking. Washing machine on request.
Dinner. £12.50 for 3 courses (with choices)
and coffee, at 6.30pm (not Sundays). Non-
residents not admitted. Vegetarian or
special diets if ordered. Wine can be
brought in. No smoking. **Light suppers** if
ordered.
2 **Sitting-rooms.** With open fire, central
heating, TV. No smoking.
Large garden

This homely 1930s house occupies a lovely site with sea views and a 10-minute
path leading down to the sands and rocks (from which people fish). In the garden
is a pair of wild ponds – the top one has fish and waterlilies, and by the secluded
bottom one are seats from which to enjoy the sight of the sea below. There's a
verandah to sit on, too; a barbecue for visitors' use; and the long-distance coastal
footpath running just beyond the hedge.

All the rooms are very spick-and-span, some with sea views – no. 5 has the
best; and one spacious bedroom is on the ground floor. (Baby-sitting available.)

Lynn Shelton makes all her own scones, cakes and jams (cream teas are
served) and cooks such meals as celery chowder, roast beef with organic local
vegetables and apple strudel – served in a sun-trapping dining-room. Though not
very old the house has a little bit of history: after the disastrous *Torrey Canyon* oil
spill, the affected seabirds were brought here to be cared for and revived by the
then owner, Mrs Cookson.

Readers' comments: Impressed with the decor of the bedrooms and the wonderful
views.

A little way inland is Gorran village
and a spacious Edwardian guest-
house, **HIGH CLERE**. It is perched
high enough up for a good view of
the sea when one is breakfasting or
having dinner (such as corn-on-the-
cob, chicken Marengo and home-made
lemon cheesecake). In fact, from a top-
floor bedroom you may see as far as
the Eddystone lighthouse. Chloe and
Alan Birkett have decorated most of
their immaculate and spacious rooms
in a fresh leaf-green and white colour
scheme, doors have shining brass handles, and there are ample bath/shower
rooms. Outside are well-tended
flowerbeds and a smooth lawn. £15–
£16.

Readers' comments: Furnished very
pleasantly, a lovely welcome, superb
breakfast. Delightfully run by a
charming couple. Outstanding value;
excellent and plentiful breakfasts.
Beautifully situated. A veritable gem.
Surpassing friendliness, courtesy and
attention to detail. [Tel: 0726 843136;
postcode: PL26 6HP]

WOODMANS GREEN FARM   C D S
Linch, West Sussex, GU30 7NF   Tel: 042876 250
North of Midhurst. Nearest main road: A3 from Guildford to Petersfield.

3 Bedrooms. £17.50–£18.50. Prices go up in May. Tea/coffee facilities. Views of garden, country. No smoking. Washing machine on request.
Dinner. £10.50 for 3 courses (with choices) and coffee, at 7.30pm. Non-residents not admitted. Vegetarian or special diets if ordered. Wine can be brought in. No smoking. **Light suppers** if ordered.
2 Sitting-rooms. With open fire, central heating, TV, record-player. Piano.
Large garden
Closed in January.

This Tudor house has interesting features of the period, which include a particularly grand staircase, stone-mullioned windows in the gable, low doorways (on which Mary Spreckley drapes swags of dried flowers) and, in the farmyard, an unusual roofed and brick-walled midden. (There is a heated swimming-pool.)

Bedrooms are spacious and peaceful; under the beamed roof is a large and attractive family room. Adjoining the sitting-room is a bright garden-room.

By arrangement, Mary – who is a very good cook – will prepare either a full dinner (such as vegetable soup, chicory-stuffed chicken with blue-cheese sauce, and apple flan with cream) or a light supper (such as pasta with broccoli, mushrooms and ham).

This very attractive area around Haslemere, Petersfield and Petworth is a good base from which to visit Chichester, Fishbourne Roman palace, Petworth House, and the open-air Weald and Downland Museum of ancient buildings. There are good walks and country inns (mountain bicycles, wellies and maps on loan). Polo is played at Midhurst – a town with many antique shops and restaurants.

Readers' comments: Friendly atmosphere, cooking imaginative and attractively served; very pleasant indeed. Delicious breakfast. Delightful hosts.

A very large woodland garden screens **CUMBERS HOUSE** at Rogate from the road, and beyond are fine downland views. Most bedrooms are spacious, with large casement windows, and pleasantly furnished. There is a particularly elegant dining-room and in the green-and-grey sitting-room there are pretty trifles around; guests are welcome to play on the mellow, well-tuned Schiedmeyer. Mid-week, Prue Aslett serves excellent meals (if ordered in advance); bread is home-baked, eggs are home-produced. No smoking. £17.50–£18 (b & b).
Readers' comments: Full of praise –

rear view

maximum stars! Delightful hospitality. Couldn't have felt more at home. Warm and welcoming. Marvellous furniture. Delicious supper. [Tel: 0730 821401; postcode: GU31 5EJ]

WYCK HILL LODGE   C(10)
Wyck Hill, Stow-on-the-Wold, Gloucestershire, GL54 1HT
Tel: 0451 830141
On A424 from Stow to Burford.

3 Bedrooms. £19–£21 (less for 3 nights and at mid-week). Prices may go up in May.

All have own bath/shower/toilet. Tea/coffee facilities. TV. Views of garden, country. No smoking. Washing machine on request.
Dinner. £10.50–£13 for 4 courses (with choices) and coffee, at 7.30pm. Non-residents not admitted. Vegetarian or special diets if ordered. Wine can be brought in. No smoking. **Light suppers** if ordered.
1 Sitting-room. With open fire, central heating.
Garden

This picturesque house was built around 1800 as the lodge to a nearby mansion. Now it is surrounded by very lovely gardens, from which come the abundant flowers in every room. There are far views across Bourton Vale and good walks straight from the door.

In the L-shaped sitting-room are big leather armchairs and, in winter, a crackling fire. The dining-room is particularly attractive: it has three antique tables and, like some other rooms, windows set in pointed arches with stained-glass panes at the top. There is a view of the terraced garden (with pond) and far hills.

Two of the bedrooms (one opening onto the garden) are on the ground floor, and there is another upstairs – this is a big, two-level room with a cane sofa.

For dinner, Jackie Alderton serves such meals as parsnip-and-apple soup, lamb with a stuffing of mint and cucumber, and apple-and-Calvados crumble. Or you may be offered a barbecue in the garden. At breakfast there are plenty of choices – haddock, for instance, and ham.

Readers' comments: Delicious food, very comfortable. Good, careful attention. Very gracious hosts. Best we have stayed in. Beautiful home, charming people. Excellent in every way.

Nearby Bourton-on-the-Water is too picturesque for its own good (it is thronged in summer) but **THE RIDGE** guest-house, at Whiteshoots, is well away from all that. A gabled Edwardian house, it is surrounded by lawns and fine trees, with hill views. Dining-tables are in a new conservatory overlooking a sunken garden; Pamela Minchin provides light suppers, if ordered. Among the several comfortable bedrooms is one on the ground floor. £14.50–£19.

Readers' comments: Superb. Delightfully furnished, hospitable hostess. Have stayed three times. [Tel: 0451 820660; postcode: GL54 2LE]

For explanation of code letters (C, D, M, PT, S, X) see page xlvi.

YEW TREES

Silver Street, Misterton, Somerset, TA18 8NB   Tel: 0460 77192
South of Crewkerne. Nearest main road: A356 from Crewkerne to Dorchester.

3 Bedrooms. £15 (less for 2 nights or continental breakfast). Price goes up from April. All have tea/coffee facilities. Views of garden. No smoking. Washing machine on request.
Dinner. £11 for 4 courses and coffee, at 6.30–7.15pm. Non-residents not admitted. Vegetarian dishes if ordered. Wine can be brought in. No smoking. **Light suppers** if ordered.
2 Sitting-rooms. With central heating, TV. No smoking.
Small garden

Two 17th-century cottages – beamed and stone-walled – have been turned into one house, providing an unusually large sitting/dining-room, furnished with antiques. Bedrooms have pale colours and pine furniture, with low windows tucked under the eaves of the house.

Ann and Geoffrey Clifton sometimes teach English here to individual overseas visitors whom many English guests enjoy meeting at dinner, or afterwards – often sitting in the garden where flagstoned steps curve down towards the lily-pool.

Ann likes cooking for her visitors such meals as the one I enjoyed: courgette soup, delicious silver chickens (I won't spoil the surprise by describing what these are!) and Somerset applecake.

Misterton is a quiet and friendly village with lovely countryside around, and is an excellent centre for visits to famous old buildings such as Sherborne Abbey, Montacute House, Forde Abbey and Parnham House, a beautiful Renaissance manor house where John Makepeace has a world-famous school for craftsmanship in wood. Or you can explore a host of picturesque hamstone villages with their thatched cottages and fine mediaeval churches. Visit, too, some of the beautiful gardens – East Lambrook Manor (designed by Margery Fish), Tintinhull House, Hadspen House (once the home of Penelope Hobhouse), and the tropical gardens and famous swannery at Abbotsbury. At Hornsbury Mill you can have cream teas in a 300-year-old mill with large waterwheel.

There are lovely walks in the surrounding countryside, or along the spectacular Dorset coast a short drive away (maps can be borrowed), while towns such as Crewkerne, Lyme Regis and Honiton provide happy hunting-grounds for collectors of antiques or crafts.

Readers' comments: Most delightful house of great character, beautifully furnished, food and hospitality exceptional. Most friendly welcome, good and ample food. Have booked again. Very comfortable, food excellent, service first-class. What a find – enjoyed every minute. Super hosts.

Facts (prices, etc.) at the top of entries are supplied by the proprietors themselves. While every effort is made to ensure that these are correct at the time of going to press, they may alter thereafter: please check when you book.

YOAH COTTAGE

West Knighton, Dorset, DT2 8PE Tel: 0305 852087

South-east of Dorchester. Nearest main road: A352 from Dorchester to Wareham.

C(8) D S

2 Bedrooms. £14.50–£16.50 (less for 7 nights). Prices go up in June. Tea/coffee facilities. Views of garden, country. No smoking. Washing machine on request.
Dinner. £10.50 for 3 courses and coffee, at 7.30pm. Vegetarian or special diets if ordered. Wine can be brought in. No smoking. **Light suppers** if ordered.
1 Sitting-room. With open fire, TV. No smoking.
Large garden

In every room of this picturesque cottage, all whitewash and thatch, are terracotta sheep, pigs, Noah's Arks or Gardens of Eden – which both Furse and Rosemary Swann make in their studio at the back. (There is a garden-house with a display of them for sale.) 'Becoming redundant was one of the best things that happened to me', says Furse, who changed career in mid-life (he previously taught English).

The great beam over one of the inglenook fireplaces carries the date 1622. Rooms are low and white-walled, the staircases narrow and steep, floors stone-flagged, windows small and deep-set. Until 50 years ago, the cottage was divided: a carter living in one end, a shepherd at the other.

The Swanns have filled the house with an immensely varied collection of treasures, from a 19th-century glass painting of a bull to modern abstracts, pictures of Borzoi dogs by Weschke and prints by Munch to a portrait of 'Mrs Darling' (in *Peter Pan*) by a great-uncle. There is a collection of green Bristol glass and another of Breton plates, a splendid samovar of Polish brass, odd-shaped pebbles from the nearby beach at Ringstead, oriental rugs and Victorian raised-cotton bedspreads, metal animals by an award-winning sculptor whose work they spotted in India . . . in every room there is a visual feast. Bedrooms are equally attractive (the pretty bathrooms are on the ground floor).

The large garden is a romantic spot, with flagged paths wandering among cottage flowers, hedges separating one secret spot from another.

Rosemary produces not only imaginative dishes of her own (for instance, pork tenderloin with mushrooms in a green pepper and cream sauce) but also specialities from Sweden, where she lived for many years. Furse prepares breakfasts, which can include such unusual options as scrambled eggs on anchovy toast or kedgeree; and he makes all the jams. When not busy with visitors, Rosemary accepts other dinner bookings.

Next door is the friendly 18th-century New Inn. Thomas Hardy is said to have owned the cottage opposite and, when writing his last major novel, *Jude the Obscure*, he also undertook the restoration of West Knighton's church. In this western part of Dorset, a lovely area, you will find Hardy's birthplace, 'Egdon Heath', an exciting coastline, the market town of Dorchester, Iron Age hill forts, and a great many literary associations.

Readers' comments: Most beautiful and characterful. Warm and welcoming, most interesting people. Comfortable and extremely well fed. A most enjoyable week, super experience. Delightful atmosphere.

ALPHABETICAL DIRECTORY OF
HOUSES AND HOTELS IN
WALES

Prices are per person sharing a double room, at the beginning of the year. You may be quoted more later or for single occupancy.

Prices and other facts quoted at the head of each entry are as supplied by the proprietors.

Sitting-room at Upper Trewalkin Farm (see page 412)

ABERYSCIR OLD RECTORY   C D
Aberyscir, Powys, LD3 9NP   Tel: 0874 623457
West of Brecon. Nearest main road: A40 from Brecon to Sennybridge.

3 Bedrooms. £17.50 (less for 7 nights). All have own bath/shower/toilet. Tea/coffee facilities. TV. Views of garden, country, river. Washing machine on request.
Dinner. £8.50 for 4 courses (with some choices) and coffee, at 7pm. Vegetarian or special diets if ordered. Wine can be brought in.
1 Sitting-room. With central heating, record-player. Piano.
Large garden

Well tucked away in the hills, this Victorian stone house, standing in large grounds, has been furnished by Elizabeth Gould to high standards of comfort and solid quality. A horse, ram and squirrel greeted our arrival, and there is poultry too. I particularly liked the pink bedroom which has windows on two sides and very lovely views of the Brecon Beacons. Dinners include generous quantities of such dishes as smoked haddock ramekins, beef Stroganoff and Elizabeth's Malibu dessert – coconut liqueur combined with tropical fruits and whipped cream. Afterwards, there are velvet chairs and a chaise longue in the attractive, green sitting-room from which to enjoy the views or watch Elizabeth use her New Zealand spinning wheel. (Baby-sitting available.)

The Brecon Beacons are the highest mountains in South Wales, with several peaks over 2000 feet. Ice Age glaciers scored deep valleys in the red sandstone; to the south, the underlying rock is limestone or millstone grit, producing different scenery and a multitude of cave systems, gorges and waterfalls.

The Eppynt Hills to the north are softer (at their feet runs the lovely River Wye) but even here you can enjoy panoramic views all the way to Carmarthen.

Scenery is the main but not the only attraction of the area. There are plenty of castles to visit: for instance, Y Gaer (very close to the Old Rectory) was the Romans' largest inland fort, and mediaeval castles are at Builth Bronllys and Crickhowell among other places. Brecon has a Norman cathedral, and in many villages are churches with fine rood screens. Zulu War relics can be seen in the museum of the South Wales Borderers regiment which fought at Rorke's Drift; and everywhere are craft workshops (excellent tweeds and flannels).

However, it is outdoor activities which bring most people here. There is superb walking country, even if you do not want to tackle the mountain paths. Forest trails are well waymarked; and there are guided walks, too. Vast areas around Builth are relatively unexplored (the Tourist Information Centre there has a leaflet of walks). For the intrepid, caving, climbing, hang-gliding and watersports await.

Good day trips by car along scenic routes include the Usk reservoir (visiting the Black Mountain bird park on the way), and also the Llyn Brianne reservoirs (perhaps picnicking in the Gwenffrwyd bird reserve, or following a riverside nature trail to the cave of outlaw Twm Catti, before arriving at the dam viewpoint).

The Elan Valley has a chain of lakes and five dams extending over nine miles; a short detour brings you to yet another stupendous dam at the Claerwen reservoirs.

Readers' comments: Outstanding value, lovely scenery, food and people. Wonderful accommodation and food. Exceptionally generous portions. Excellent. Most restful. Absolutely spotless, food delicious and attractively presented, warm welcome.

BRON HEULOG   C D PT X
Waterfall Road, Llanrhaeadr-ym-Mochnant, Clwyd, SY10 0JX
Tel: 0691 780521
North of Welshpool (Powys). Nearest main road: A483 from Welshpool to
Oswestry.

3 Bedrooms. £13–£15 (less for 3 nights).
Tea/coffee facilities. TV. Views of garden,
country. Washing machine on request.
Dinner. £8 for 3 courses and coffee, at
6–8pm. Non-residents not admitted.
Vegetarian or special diets if ordered. Wine
can be brought in. **Light suppers** if
ordered.
1 Sitting-room. With open fire, central
heating, TV, piano, record-player.
Large garden

There is an especially lovely drive through hills, moors and woods from Bala to
the Tanat Valley. Here, on the way to the country's highest waterfall, is this handsome stone house of 1861 which, as its name (*bron*) suggests, is on a hillside.

Lorraine Pashen has filled it with her collection of antiques, oil-paintings and
Blüthner grand piano: the curving staircase is almost an art gallery. One bedroom,
with prettily draped bedhead, looks onto the unusual tortuosa willow (as depicted
on willow-pattern plates). Lorraine's dinners include dishes like avocado mousse,
sweet/sour pork, and home-made rum-and-raisin ice cream, served on
Wedgwood's Florentine china in a blue and gold dining-room with crystal
chandeliers and 17th-century portraits. (Baby-sitting can be arranged.)

Llanrhaeadr, surrounded by the Berwyn Mountains, is very near the English
border, Offa's Dyke and the Shropshire towns of Shrewsbury and Oswestry. In
the opposite direction lie lakes Vyrnwy and Bala (described elsewhere) and
Llangollen (on the way to it, call at Llanarmon's curious church with two
pulpits), home every July to the world-famous *eisteddfod*. Salmon leap beneath its
14th-century bridge over the Dee (one of the 'seven wonders of Wales'), castles
crown the peaks surrounding the vale. In the richly carved church of St Collen's
are buried the 18th-century 'ladies of Llangollen' whose black-and-white house,
Plas Newydd, was a tourist attraction even in their day. From here one can take a
canal boat or steam train.

Readers' comments: Rooms, food, hostess a delight. Best meals I had. Will return.

Further along the beautiful and little-
known Tanat Valley is Pen-y-Bont-
Fawr. Enid Henderson and her niece
live at 17th-century **GLYNDWR**.
Behind is a pretty riverside garden.
Beams, low doorways and open fires
give the house character. There is good
home cooking, and bedrooms have
their own bathrooms. £14–£18 (the
latter, an adjoining cottage).
Readers' comments: Superb meals, cosy
and warm. Everything possible was

done to make us feel at home. [Tel:
069174 430; postcode: SY10 0NT]

WALES

BRONANT
Bontnewydd, Gwynedd, LL54 7YF   Tel: 0286 830451
South of Caernarfon. Nearest main road: A487 from Porthmadog to
Caernarfon.

C D S X

3 Bedrooms. £15–£17 (less for 2 nights or
continental breakfast). Tea/coffee facilities.
Views of garden, country, sea. No smoking.
Washing machine on request.
Light suppers if ordered.
1 Sitting-room. With open fire, central
heating, TV. Organ in dining-room.
Large garden

On the north side of the Lleyn peninsula (looking over the Menai Strait to
Anglesey) is Bronant, a handsome Victorian house, kept in immaculate order by
Megan Williams and her nieces who run a tea-room here. Their traditional Welsh
teas are really authentic: the gingerbread, *bara brith* (speckled bread) and Welsh
cakes regularly take first prizes at county shows.

Most rooms are spacious, with Welsh tapestry bedspreads in rich colours and
views of sheep, pine trees and mountains. Some windows have stained glass
depicting apples and pears, appropriate to a house where good, natural food
excels. The light suppers are quite substantial. (Baby-sitting available.)

The peninsula is one of the most Welsh parts of Wales, with the native
language still very much alive. It has wild and dramatic scenery inland, sandy
beaches along its shores – many secluded. Past Trefor (near where a 1700-foot
mountain looms above the sea, with deserted quarries in its sides) are the secret
valley of Nant Gwrtheyrn, a shadowy place of old legends, and the Lleyn's highest
peak – Yr Eifl. Porth Nefyn is a particularly long and lovely bay with a safe, sandy
beach and clifftop walks; and still further west you can find the 'whistling sands'
of Porth Oer (at times, the grains of sand squeak when you walk on them). Right
at the end of the Lleyn is Mynydd Mawr, a National Trust headland with coastal
views comparable to those of Cornwall's Land's End. Over two miles of choppy
waters lies Bardsey Island (known to pilgrims as the isle of 20,000 saints).

Along the south coast, in a wilderness of subtropical flowers, are the little
manor house (part mediaeval) of Plas-yn-Rhiw; another great bay – Porth Neigwl,
otherwise known as Hell's Mouth because of the treacherous rocks on which so
many ships foundered; and Abersoch, a busy little harbour, near which is the
showpiece village of Llangian. Seek out the old part of Pwllheli to find a Georgian
arcade and canopied Victorian shops in sharp contrast to the popular modern
attractions of this resort. Penarth Fawr is a rare survival, a stone hall house –
basically one great room in which family and servants all dwelt together in the
15th century. A mossy stone path leads to the clear waters of St Cybi's well,
behind Llangybi village; and at Brynkir you can see traditional Welsh cloth being
woven in the watermill.

The Lleyn's most famous village is, of course, Portmeirion, an Italianate
waterside fantasy designed by Sir Clough Williams-Ellis in 1925. Every architectural style, and every colour of the rainbow, seems to be represented here: Sir
Clough himself described it as a 'gay, light opera sort of a place'.

Readers' comments: Tasty, well-cooked meals. Spacious, comfortable bedroom.
A great place with spectacular views. Very good value. Marvellous cakes.

BRONIWAN

DSX

Rhydlewis, Llandysul, Dyfed, SA44 5PF   Tel: 0239 851261

East of Cardigan. Nearest main road: A487 from Cardigan to Aberystwyth.

3 Bedrooms. £16 (less for 5 nights). Some have own bath/shower/toilet. Views of garden, country. No smoking. Washing machine on request.

Dinner. £8 for 3 courses and coffee, at 7–7.30pm. Non-residents not admitted. Vegetarian or special diets if ordered. Wine can be brought in. No smoking. **Light suppers** if ordered.

1 Sitting-room. With open fire, central heating, TV, piano. No smoking.

Large garden

On a rocky hillside (*bron*) stands an ivy-clad, grey stone house, sheltered by beech trees and looking across to the Frenni Fawr Hills where Pwyll, prince of Dyfed, fell in love with a lady in gold brocade riding a pale horse and made her his bride: 'The countenance of every maiden he had seen was unlovely compared with her countenance.'

It was built in 1867, with much use of pitch-pine (this is a distinctive wood, imported from America in Victorian times) for doors and the panelling of its big bay windows. Outside, a decorative white iron fence encloses the front garden.

Carole and Allen Jacobs combine organic farming with teaching English. They have Aberdeen Angus beef-cattle, sheep, hens and a vegetable garden – all of which supply their table and in the care of which visitors are welcome to join if they wish (there is a donkey too). The rooms are very attractive with, for instance, striped wallpaper, Welsh tapestry bedspreads, watercolours, books and old Staffordshire pottery figures. On chilly evenings they light a log stove which stands in the stone fireplace. Below the terrace is a barn equipped with table tennis, paints, books and games.

A typical dinner: watercress soufflé, New Quay mackerel in oatmeal (with garden vegetables and a salad of cucumber and yogurt), pears in white wine. On some winter weekends, 'man-in-the-kitchen' courses are organized.

Broniwan is well placed for a holiday full of varied interest. In one direction is the long sandy coastline around great Cardigan Bay, dotted with such pleasant little fishing villages as Aberaeron and Llangrannog and with seals to be seen; while inland are hill walks among gorse and heather where butterflies and buzzards fly. There are old market towns along the banks of the River Teifi, waterfalls (and fishermen in coracles) at Cenarth and a mill at Cwm Cou. The ruins of Cilgerran Castle are perched high on a rocky spur above the river gorge: Turner was one of many artists to paint the great circular towers and gatehouse which still stand, along with crumbling but massive outer walls built by the Normans – Owaîn Glyndwr devastated it when he led his great revolt in 1405.

Cardiganshire is the place to go if you like wide open spaces. The windswept moors, where skylarks soar, rise up towards 2000-foot peaks and along the way are views to far horizons. It is a great area for birdwatchers who may spot kestrels, red grouse and even the rare kites. This is one of the least populated parts of Britain, except in the leafy valleys or at resorts along the coastline of cliffs, coves and golden beaches. There is no industry to mar the scene but plenty of craft workshops.

BRYNARTH
Lledrod, Dyfed, SY23 4HX   Tel: 09743 367
South-east of Aberystwyth. Nearest main road: A485 from Tregaron to
Aberystwyth.

CDS

7 Bedrooms. £16–£18 (less for 7 nights or
continental breakfast). Prices go up from
Easter. All have own bath/shower/toilet.
Tea/coffee facilities. Views of garden,
country.
Dinner. £8 for 3 courses and coffee, at
7–7.30pm. Vegetarian or special diets if
ordered. Wine can be ordered. **Light
suppers.**
1 Sitting-room. With open fire, central
heating, record-player. **Bar.**
Large garden

A very pretty group of white stone buildings, three centuries old, encloses a big
courtyard with lily-pool, flowering shrubs and benches of stone and timber –
inviting one to linger.

Inside the guest-house is a sitting/dining-area where the slate-tiled floor and
stone walls are complemented by old pews and a chunky pine table. There is a
small bar adjoining this; and an inglenook with a large, open log stove.

Brenda Ball serves such meals as ratatouille, lamb fricassée (with egg and
lemon sauce), and plum or apple pies, often using organically home-grown
produce.

Attractive bedrooms have king-size double, or twin, beds with panelled bedheads and wardrobes, flowers painted on their doors, and stone walls. There is
also a games room with snooker, darts and table tennis. Water comes direct from
a pure spring. Painting courses are run throughout the year.

The seafront at Aberystwyth still has a sedate, Victorian air along the
promenade. But it is much more than a resort – near the pier is the main building
of its university and on a headland, its ruined castle. Fishing boats come and go.
The university has an outstanding arts centre (with gallery, theatre and cinema)
high above the town and with views across the bay. The town also houses the
distinguished National Library of Wales, a museum of rural and maritime history
in what was once an ornate music-hall, and the biggest *camera obscura* in the
world (over 400 feet up a hill and reached by a near-vertical railway) which gives
you a view of over two dozen distant mountain peaks. Or you can take a steam
train which goes from the town up to its mountainous destination, Devil's Bridge:
a 12-mile valley ride. Waterfalls plummet 300 feet down a wooded ravine, and
three bridges span a dizzying gorge. By car, you can get as high as 1200 feet.

Readers' comments: We give them the highest marks. Could not have been happier
with food and accommodation. A delightful setting.

**Book well ahead: many of these houses have few rooms. Do not
expect dinner if you have not booked it or if you arrive late.**

BUCK FARMHOUSE   C
Hanmer, Clwyd, SY14 7LX   Tel: 094874 339
South-east of Wrexham. On A525 from Wrexham to Whitchurch.

4 Bedrooms. £17 (less for 3 nights). Price goes up from April. Views of garden, country. No smoking. Washing machine on request. (Bathrooms are downstairs.)
Dinner. £10.50 for 4 courses and coffee, at 7.30pm. Vegetarian or special diets if ordered. Wine can be brought in. No smoking. **Light suppers** if ordered.
2 Sitting-rooms. With wood stove, central heating. TV. No smoking.
Small garden, and woodland.

In this 16th-century house a surprise awaits. For both Frances Williams-Lee and Cedric Sumner were much travelled before they decided to settle here among the pastoral scenes of Clwyd – and this is reflected in the wide range of dishes you may be offered, with much emphasis on organic produce freshly and simply cooked.

Frances, though of Chinese ancestry, comes from Trinidad – a meeting-place for a variety of cuisines – and worked under an accomplished French chef in Normandy. Cedric lived in Canada, another country where a mingling of cultures has influenced cookery. The result is a series of very varied and imaginative menus. Just one example: celery and almond soup; a pie of sweetcorn, leeks and red peppers (the range of vegetarian and vegan dishes is particularly wide) or perhaps pork with onions, tomatoes and garlic; and Nova Scotia bread-custard. Breakfast options include home-made muesli or granola, fruit compotes, omelettes and much else.

Such meals are eaten in a low-beamed dining-room and prepared in a kitchen lined with jars of spices and other ingredients, through which visitors walk to reach the pretty little garden of herbs, rock plants, shrubs and lawn (unless they prefer to sit after dinner in the snug sitting-room, well stocked with books).

Steep stairs lead to neat bedrooms furnished in cottage style: necessarily double-glazed as the house is, despite its rural surroundings, on a main road.

Readers' comments: Have returned 3 times. Fascinating house, interesting meals.

Beyond Malpas (Cheshire) lies the pretty village of Tilston, surrounded by the Peckferton and Bickerton hills. **TILSTON LODGE** is now home to Kathie Ritchie and her collection of rare breeds. The original Victorian features include a handsomely tiled hall with pretty marble fireplace and galleried mahogany staircase. Kathy has made patchwork bedspreads; stencilled woodbines on walls; draped a four-poster with lace; and collected an array of Victorian jugs. In the raspberry-walled dining-room – with William-and-Mary style chairs, good linen and silver – she serves imagina-

tive meals using home-grown produce, free-range eggs, local lamb, Cheshire and other local cheeses. £17.50–£21 (b & b).
Readers' comments: Excellent in every way. Fine bedroom and bathroom. Very good, quiet setting. [Tel: 0829 250223; postcode: SY14 7DR]

CAERNEWYDD FARM

C M PT

Pembrey Road, Kidwelly, Dyfed, SA17 4TF   Tel: 0554 890137

North-west of Llanelli. On A484 from Llanelli to Carmarthen.

rear view

6 Bedrooms. £15 (less for 3 nights or mid-week). All have own shower/toilet. Tea/coffee facilities. TV. No smoking. Washing machine on request.
Dinner. £7 for 2 courses and coffee, at 6pm. Non-residents not admitted. Vegetarian or special diets if ordered. Wine can be brought in. No smoking. **Light suppers** if ordered.
2 Sitting-rooms. With open fire, central heating, TV. No smoking.
Large garden

Despite its position on the road, all is peace once you are inside the house for rooms are at the back. The huge sitting-room is where the stables used to be: its sliding glass doors open onto a sheltered, heated swimming-pool and it is furnished with handsome and ample modern sofas. There is much polished pine, bedspreads are of Paisley-patterned fabric (all are ground-floor rooms), and everything is neat as a new pin. (Baby-sitting can be arranged.)

Dinners prepared by Margaret Beynon often consist of a roast joint followed by a gâteau or meringues, and then cheeses.

This would be a good choice for families wanting to enjoy the miles of clean, golden beaches along this coast, for walkers (who can follow footpaths on the sheep-farm's own land) or for birdwatchers who want to visit the nearby wildfowl reserve.

All the area around Carmarthen Bay has a serene beauty (unlike the rugged coast further west). You can still see salmon fishermen in coracles – small, bowl-shaped boats, just as were used in pre-Roman times.

There are legends of Merlin; and innumerable ruined castles as well as the site of a huge Iron Age fort, 1½ miles across (Carn Goch). Splendid though Kidwelly's own moated castle is, it is not the most impressive – that is Carreg-Cennen, near Llandeilo, perched above a 300-foot precipice. Built in the 14th century, it has a long underground passage to a spring.

Nearby Pembrey is famous for its miles of sandy dunes by the sea, a particularly ancient church with barrel-roof of timber, and the landing place of Amelia Earhart on her record-making Atlantic flight in 1928. In the opposite direction is Laugharne, where Dylan Thomas's boathouse home can be visited. It is a delightful little harbour, with fine estuary views and a castle. Yet another coastal village with castle is at Llanstephan, to which you can cross by boat. In a cave along here fossilized mammoths were found; and at the resort of Amroth a prehistoric forest reappears as petrified stumps whenever tides are very low; the long Pembrokeshire coastal path starts here.

Readers' comments: Excellent. Ample food. Made very welcome. Very good value.

COACH HOUSE COTTAGE

D PT S

Glendower Square, Goodwick, Dyfed, SA64 0DH   Tel: 0348 873660
North-west of Fishguard. Nearest main road: A40 from Goodwick to
Haverfordwest.

1 Bedroom. £12. Price goes up in March.
Tea/coffee facilities. Views of country, sea.
No smoking. Washing machine on request.
Dinner. £8.50 for 2 or 3 courses (with
choices) and coffee, at 7pm. Non-residents
not admitted. Vegetarian or special diets if
ordered. Wine can be brought in. No
smoking. **Light suppers** if ordered.
1 Sitting-room. With open fire, central
heating, TV, video, piano, record-player.
No smoking.
Small garden

The harbour of Fishguard with its ferries to Ireland is actually at Goodwick, a
little further along the bay. In this village, tucked away behind the inns and shops
of its small square, Max and Elizabeth Maxwell-Jones found a quaint little
stone cottage, part of which had once been a coach house. Both are artistic (he a
calligrapher and sign-writer, she a catering lecturer with a talent for making
intricate bobbin lace) and this shows in the way they have converted the house, in
its colour schemes and the multitude of pictures, books and interesting objects
which fill every surface. It's a house of pretty colours and patterns, fresh and neat.

One reaches it up 20 steps beside a rushing mountain brook and enters
through a stable-type door, straight into the dining-kitchen where one is immediately given a friendly, conversational welcome. From the little bedroom are hill
views and a glimpse of the sea.

Elizabeth is an accomplished cook who served, on the night when I stayed,
cauliflower soup, excellent chicken Marengo and summer pudding – all made
with organic ingredients. She teaches lace-making and Max runs occasional drawing and calligraphy courses in his studio at the cottage. Many of the shop and inn
signs around the area are his work.

Readers' comments: Extraordinarily kind and considerate.

In the main street of Fishguard (but
with quiet rooms overlooking the sea at
the back) is **MANOR HOUSE
HOTEL**, built in the 18th century,
where the staff are accustomed to
welcoming travellers by ferry who
land in the middle of the night (by
pre-arrangement). Most rooms are
spacious, with a good deal of 'thirties
furniture, crochet or patchwork spreads
and interesting objects around. In a
room on the ground floor antiques are
for sale. Austrian-born Beatrix Davies
has given the small hotel a reputation
for its food. There is always a wide à la
carte choice that includes such dishes
as mussel pâté; chicken cooked in a
purée of plums, garlic and parsley; a
syllabub of blackcurrants and sherry.
From the garden (where you can take
breakfast) there are fine views across
the sea to Dinas Head. £16–£22. [Tel:
0348 873260; postcode: SA65 9HG]

CWMTWRCH

Nantgaredig, Dyfed, SA32 7NY   Tel: 0267290 238   C D M X

North-east of Carmarthen. Nearest main road: A40 from Carmarthen to
Llandeilo (and M4, junction 49).

6 Bedrooms. £20–£24 (less for 7 nights).
Prices may go up at Easter. All have own
bath/shower/toilet. Tea/coffee facilities. TV
(some). Views of garden, country. Washing
machine on request.
Dinner. £15.50 for 4 courses (with choices
including vegetarian) and coffee, from
7.30pm. Special diets if ordered. Wine can
be ordered. **Light suppers** if ordered.
2 Sitting-rooms. With open fire, TV,
record-player. Restricted smoking. **Bar.**
Large garden

The name of this farmhouse-turned-hotel means 'valley of the wild boar'.
Nothing so wild now disturbs the peace of this civilized spot where Jenny
Willmott and her husband have transformed a group of old farm buildings with
great sensitivity. The restaurant, run by the Willmotts' three daughters, has stone
walls painted white, slate floor and boarded roof above. At one side, the kitchen is
open to view; on the other is a conservatory overlooking the courtyard, pots of
flowers, and sheep-fields beyond. The food is exceptional, with such dishes as
individual quiches as a starter, followed by fresh salmon or boned Barbary duck,
and a flan of grapes with sponge and almond topping among the varied choices.
Bread is baked daily. All rooms have interesting and lovely objects, paintings and
pottery (for sale). Bedrooms (full of character) are in the house or (at ground
level) in former stables. There is a 9-hole golf course and an indoor heated
swimming-pool.

Readers' comments: Excellent. Charming owners. Superb cooking. Marvellous.
Most comfortable, made to feel at home. Food excellent. Really good.
Helpfulness and friendliness had to be seen to be believed. First class.

Also in this area is Llanpumsaint and
FFERM-Y-FELIN or 'mill farm', the
18th-century home of Anne and David
Ryder-Owen: a place of particular
interest to birdwatchers. David, a keen

ornithologist, can tell you where to spot
pied flycatchers, buzzards and even the
rare red kite. Beyond the dining-room
is a sitting-room so large that it has a
fireplace at each end; pink, buttoned
velvet sofas and a walnut piano contrast
with rugged stone walls. Anne serves
such meals as corn-on-the-cob, wild
trout with home-grown vegetables, and
apple crumble; breakfast options
include laverbread and cockles.

This would be a good place for a
family holiday (baby-sitting available):

the children's bedroom (with toys) has
a picture-window overlooking the lake
and its waterfowl, and there is a pet
donkey as well as other livestock. Self-
catering accommodation too, with
meals provided in the main house if
wanted. Non-smokers preferred. £16–
£18.50.
Readers' comments: Wonderfully looked
after. Food excellent and plentiful.
Kind, considerate, welcoming. [Tel:
0267 253498; postcode: SA33 6DA]

DEWIS CYFARFOD

DEWIS CYFARFOD   **C(8) D M X**
Llandderfel, Gwynedd, LL23 7DR   Tel: 06783 243 (Messages: 0244 313522)
North-east of Bala. Nearest main road: A494 from Corwen to Bala.

5 Bedrooms. £18–£24 (less for 7 nights). Prices go up from June. All have own bath/shower/toilet. Tea/coffee facilities. TV. Views of garden, country, river. Washing machine on request.
Dinner. £11–£14 for 2 courses (with choices) and coffee, at 7.30pm (not Tuesdays and Wednesdays). Vegetarian or special diets if ordered. Wine can be ordered. **Light suppers.**
1 Sitting-room. With open fire, central heating.
Large garden

On the way to beautiful Lake Bala is one of the most attractive houses I found in Wales, Dewis Cyfarfod – 'the chosen meeting-place'. Drovers used to meet at this spot where road and river converge, a convenient place to water their livestock. Now the pair of 17th-century cottages is the elegant home of Peter and Barbara Reynolds, furnished with antiques and pretty chintzes, good paintings and well-chosen colour schemes. The spacious sitting-room has groups of comfortable armchairs, a log fire, and panoramic valley views through its picture-windows. In one bedroom, William Morris's 'strawberry thief' fabric complements a white wallpaper with cherries, and other rooms are equally pretty – one with a walnut bed and wildflower fabric, another (in a ground-floor cottage close by) with an oyster and charcoal colour scheme. One bathroom is particularly sumptuous (two basins, royal blue and gold fittings).

Meals here can comprise such feasts as celery and lemon soup, beef braised with oranges and wine (accompanied by savoyard potatoes), fromage frais with strawberries and then farmhouse cheeses.

Readers' comments: Decor lovely, meals delicious. Informal and relaxed.

Along the same road is a 13th-century watermill, **MELIN MELOCH**. The galleried house has pretty bedrooms. Through an arch by the fireplace is a great table flanked by pews, where Beryl Fullard serves (by arrangement) such meals as melon with raspberry coulis, lamb, brandy-cake and cream. A trout pool in the garden provides fish for the table. The miller's cottage has a ground-floor bedroom and spacious family suite; other rooms are in a granary. Everywhere are lovely arrangements of dried flowers and 'finds' such as a milkchurn and mangle colourfully repainted by Richard in between landscaping the large water-gardens and restoring a Victorian

turbine. (Self-catering, too, plus dinner.) £15–£18.50.
Readers' comments: Spectacular. Food and location excellent. Lovely house. Perfection. Spoilt me with excellent cooking. The house is a beauty. Absolutely wonderful time. Never-to-be-forgotten, unique house. [Tel: 0678 520101; postcode: LL23 7DP]

WALES

DYSSERTH HALL
C(10) **S**

by Powis Castle, Powys, SY21 8RQ   Tel: 0938 552153
South of Welshpool. Nearest main road: A483 from Welshpool to Newtown.

rear view

4 Bedrooms. £16–£18 (less for 3 nights). Prices go up in June. Bargain breaks. Some have own shower/toilet. Tea/coffee facilities. Views of garden, country, river. No smoking. Washing machine on request.
Dinner. £14 for 3 courses (with choices) and coffee, at 7.30–8pm. Non-residents not admitted. Vegetarian or special diets if ordered. Wine can be ordered or brought in. No smoking. **Light suppers** if ordered.
1 Sitting-room. With open fire, central heating, TV, piano, record-player.
Large garden with tennis court.
Closed from December to February (except for shooting parties).

A crag of red rock and a moat provided strong defences for 13th-century Powis Castle, from which the princes of Powis ruled much of Wales. The management of their descendants' estates was in the hands of Paul Marriott until he retired. His 18th-century manor house is close to the castle (now NT).

Paul and Maureen's elegant home is furnished with fine antiques, well-chosen wallpapers and fabrics – delicate clematis paper in one bedroom, blue brocade on the walls of the dining-room, for instance. There are good paintings everywhere. From a paved terrace with rosebeds one can enjoy the view across the Severn Valley to Long Mountain.

Dinner (by arrangement) may be a candlelit meal of avocado and prawns, Welsh lamb or pheasant, meringues or, possibly, local cheeses.

On the other side of Welshpool, at Trelydan, is mediaeval **BURNT HOUSE**. Above a big, open-plan sitting/dining-room with ample sofas are attractive bedrooms. One has a pink wall with exposed timbers and pretty walnut beds; its bathroom is outstanding – textured tiles around the built-in bath. A soft green and cream room, with 'Country Diary' fabrics, has a view of the Berwyn Mountains. Tricia Wykes used to cook cakes professionally and so, after perhaps home-made pâté and pork fillet in a sauce of cream and sherry, one may be offered a gâteau or a tempting meringue confection. £15–£16 (b & b).

Readers' comments: Lovely views, welcoming hostess, excellent cook. Delightful, cooking admirable. Lovely old house. Hospitality and cuisine excellent. Truly marvellous. Enjoyed every minute. Excellent value for money. Have never been so spoilt. [Tel: 0938 552827; postcode: SY21 9HU]

EYARTH STATION C D M X
Llanfair-Dyffryn-Clwyd, Clwyd, LL15 2EE   Tel: 0824 703643
South of Ruthin. Nearest main road: A525 from Ruthin to Wrexham.

6 Bedrooms. £19–£20 (less for 3 nights or continental breakfast). Prices go up in April. All have own bath/shower/toilet. Tea/coffee facilities. Views of garden, country.
Supper. £11 for 2 courses (with choices) and coffee, at 6–7.30pm. Wine can be ordered.
2 Sitting-rooms. With open fire, central heating, TV.
Large grounds

I, like many people, had underestimated the county of Clwyd. No national park here, but superlative scenery nevertheless in the range of the Clwydian Hills running south. Ruthin is an attractive little town with half-timbered houses and a craft centre (at its castle, really good mediaeval banquets are held).

Just south of here, a disused railway station is now an unusual – and unusually excellent – guest-house. It has been imaginatively converted and furnished by Jen Spencer. Outside, all is white paint and flowers. Ground-floor bedrooms have such touches as festoon blinds and canopied bedheads in pretty floral fabrics; some (more simply furnished) are in what were the porters' rooms. Excellent bathrooms (even a bidet). What was once the waiting-room is now a very large sitting-room (one of two) with a balcony just above the fields: big sofas, modern marble fireplace with log stove and thick carpet make this particularly comfortable. The conservatory/dining-room – once the station platform – overlooks (as do two bedrooms) a small, well-heated swimming-pool which gets the afternoon sun. Jen offers suppers of such dishes as chicken and leek pie followed by chocolate fudge cake.

Northward, Denbigh's high castle overlooks the Vale of Clwyd all the way from Ruthin to the sea. At Dyserth, waterfalls drop a spectacular 60 feet, there is a ruined castle, and a stately home (Bodelwyddan Castle) with fine gardens – it was nominated National Heritage Museum of the year in 1989. It is an outstation of London's National Portrait Gallery.

At Rhuddlan is an even more impressive castle, the parliament house of Edward I and the viewpoint of Bon Hill. Holywell had a shrine to which even kings came as pilgrims; many visitors still come to the beautiful friary at Pantasaph (and to the cave museum of military vehicles with tableaux of war scenes).

Mold is worth visiting for the animal frieze in its ancient church, and its theatre; and Nannerch for the watermill craft centre. Above Cilcain rises a great peak with Jubilee Tower on top, a landmark for miles around, and a country park. Llanarmon-yn-Ial has an unusual church, with effigies.

As to the landscape on the way to all these towns and villages, Gerard Manley Hopkins wrote: 'There can hardly be in the world anything to beat the Vale of Clwyd.' One route which shows the area at its best is via the Horseshoe Pass.

Readers' comments: Excellent accommodation, and welcoming. Delightful lounge and grounds. Meals superb. One of the best places. Exceptional food, wonderful hosts.

FAIRFIELD COTTAGE C(4) D PT S

Knelston, Gower Peninsula, West Glamorgan, SA3 1AR   Tel: 0792 391013
West of Swansea. Nearest main road: A4118 from Swansea to Port Eynon
(and M4, junction 47).

3 **Bedrooms.** £16. TV. Views of garden, country. No smoking.
Dinner. £8.50 for 3 courses and coffee, at 7pm. Non-residents not admitted. Wine can be brought in. No smoking. **Light suppers** if ordered.
1 **Sitting-room.** With open fire, central heating, TV. No smoking.
Small garden

The Gower peninsula (especially its cliffs, bays and sandy beaches) is so scenic that at peak periods the traffic occasionally makes movement difficult. But at other times there are few more attractive places.

Knelston is roughly equidistant from north, west and south coasts – a tranquil hamlet within what was the very first region to be officially designated an 'area of outstanding natural beauty'. I came to it across Cefn Bryn ('the brown ridge'), a stretch of moorland where ponies roam free and yellow waterlilies brighten the pools. It is an area dotted with castle ruins, prehistoric burial chambers and other traces of a far distant history.

Caryl Ashton's 18th-century home is a little white cottage made colourful by window-boxes, tubs and hanging-baskets of flowers. One steps straight into the sitting/dining-room from which a staircase rises between the joists to small but pretty, cottagey bedrooms in which she has used sprigged or tulip-patterned fabrics to complement simple bamboo furniture and white walls. There is a very good bathroom.

One can take a complimentary aperitif by the inglenook fire or in the garden (it has a summer-house) before enjoying such a meal as gratin of haddock, roast beef accompanied by creamed parsnips with almonds and baked potatoes in cheese sauce, and home-made lemon meringue pie. Fruit and vegetables come from local farms, and yogurt is home-made. Caryl is a dedicated cook.

Readers' comments: Kind and well-organized. Very well kept and comfortable. Treated with particular care and love.

Just across the lane is a modern house called **STONEY FORGE** because it was built from the stones of a derelict forge. Everything in it is spick-and-span and Margaret Davies is a good cook of such meals as mushroom soup, roast turkey and pineapple upside-down pudding. (Baby-sitting can be arranged.) £15–£16. [Tel: 0792 390920; postcode: SA3 1AR]

FFALDAU

Llandegley, Powys, LD1 5UD   Tel: 0597851 421

East of Llandrindod Wells. Nearest main road: A44 from Kington to Rhayader.

4 Bedrooms. £18–£22.50 (less for 3 nights or mid-week). All have own bath/shower/toilet. Tea/coffee facilities. TV (some). Views of garden, country. Washing machine on request.
Dinner. £10.50–£18 for 2 or 4 courses (with choices) and coffee, at 7–9pm (not Sundays and Mondays). Vegetarian or special diets if ordered. Wine can be ordered. **Light suppers** if ordered.
2 Sitting-rooms. With log fires, central heating, TV. **Bar.**
Large garden

Set back from the road is one of the prettiest mediaeval houses in this book: roses climb up stone walls, rustic seats overlook colourful beds of heather. Beyond the lawns are grazing sheep and distant hills.

Ffaldau ('sheepfold') began life around 1500 as a long-house: people lived at one end, livestock at the other. When the Knotts took over, the ceilings leaked, floors had rotted, and all around was a litter of railway wagons and hen-houses. Not only have they transformed the house and garden but – with no previous experience – they run a restaurant which has an ever-widening reputation for fine food (even bar meals are exceptional).

Old features have been retained and restored, from a wig-cupboard built into one thick wall to a characterful old iron grate with Prince of Wales feathers in its decoration. Upstairs one can see the cruck construction of the house: the great tree-trunks used to support the roof. Mullioned windows are set into the stone walls, slabs of slate floor the hall, a log stove stands on an old inglenook hearth.

All this is complemented by the taste of Sylvia and her daughter Sara who made the swags of dried flowers and chose waitresses' floral dresses to match the pink linen and walls of the dining-room, where candles with nosegays deck each table. On the landing is a sitting-area well stocked with books.

As to the food, there is a simple 'country' menu, as well as a more expensive 'gourmet' menu from which to choose such imaginative dishes as a tartlet of smoked tuna in sour cream and horseradish, veal fillet with a sauce of green peppercorns, Grand Marnier and orange, and brandy-snap cup filled with ginger-and-raisin ice cream and hot brandy. There is a wide list of wines.

Nearby Llandrindod Wells has the faded charm of a one-time spa (indeed, you can still 'take the waters' there) and stands in an area of great beauty, little troubled by traffic or tourists. One can drive almost without sight of another car among hills like dusty velvet, with mountain sheep occasionally silhouetted on the skyline.

Readers' comments: Excellent cooking, most welcoming and obliging, most tastefully furnished. Thoroughly enjoyed good hospitality. Good cooking; caring and informal. Extremely hospitable. Best steak and breakfast that we can remember. Exceptional food, wonderful hosts. Perfectly situated. Wonderful atmosphere. One of the happiest and most comfortable stays anywhere. Food beautiful. Family most welcoming and helpful. Very comfortable. Food excellent and imaginative.

399

FLICKERING LAMP D

Elan Valley, Powys, LD6 5HS Tel: 0597 810827 (Messages: 0793 611687)
North-west of Llandrindod Wells. Nearest main road: A470 from Rhayader
to Llangurig.

3 Bedrooms. £14.50–£16.50. Bargain
breaks. Two have own shower/toilet. Views
of garden, country, reservoir. No smoking.
Washing machine on request.
Dinner. £13 for 3 courses (with choices)
and coffee, at 8pm. Non-residents not
admitted. Vegetarian or special diets if
ordered. Wine can be ordered or brought in.
No smoking. **Light suppers** if ordered.
1 Sitting-room. With open fire, central
heating. No smoking.
Large garden

Every so often I make a really exciting find – and this is one.

So spectacularly beautiful is the Elan Valley that I wonder why it is not world-famous in the way that, for instance, the Lake District is. Long may it stay so: there is not a trace of commercialization and traffic.

The miles of wooded valley hold a chain of enormous man-made lakes, each more lovely than the last, and each with its dramatic dam towering high – best seen in October or November, for instance, when there has been enough rain to send the overflowing waters from the reservoirs cascading down the surface of the dams and when the surrounding trees are ablaze with autumn colours.

The whole area belongs to the Water Board, who allow no buildings other than their own. They have a village of silvery granite cottages for workers, on the pretty banks of the downstream Elan (there is a good interpretation centre here). Up in the mountains is this biggish house built for the estate managers in the early 1900s. It is now the home of Laurence and Maggie Dowden. So remote is this spot that they rely not only on filtered spring water but on their own generator for electricity – with somewhat fitful results, hence the name they gave their house.

Maggie has chosen very attractive and original colour schemes for the rooms – silvery-greens and soft blues, tomato-red duvets, tartan in one lavatory, stripped pine walls. There are several paintings of red kites by local naturalist Dee Doody. This is a splendid area for spotting birds of prey such as peregrines and merlins.

Maggie enjoys cooking, and produces such meals as nut pâté, lamb steaks with tomato and coriander, and chocolate/chestnut slice.

Towards Rhayader is 18th-century
ARGOED FAWR, Llanwrthwl, once
owned by James Watt of steam-engine
fame. Overlooking the River Wye, it is
now the home of Maureen Maltby;
and although old features have been
retained – such as a ham-rack, slab
floors and slate hearths – every room is
comfortable and immaculate; the bathroom is excellent. Breakfast choices
often include kidneys, black pudding
and Ayr haddock. Supper is a help-
yourself buffet of such things as chick-

en, salmon, quiches and pâtés. Spring
water. Exceptional garden. £12–£16.
Readers' comments: Delightful. Nicest
ever visited. Breakfast fit for a king!
[Tel: 059789 451; messages: 059789
367; postcode: LD1 6PD]

GLANRANNELL PARK HOTEL

Crugybar, Dyfed, SA19 8SA   Tel: 0558 685230

South-east of Lampeter. Nearest main road: A482 from Lampeter to Llanwrda.

C D

12 Bedrooms. £15–£31 (less for 2 nights). Bargain breaks. Some have own bath/toilet. Tea/coffee facilities. Views of garden, country, river. Washing machine on request. **Dinner.** £15 for 3 courses (with choices) and coffee, at 7pm. Vegetarian or special diets if ordered. Wine can be ordered. No smoking. **Light suppers** if ordered.
2 Sitting-rooms. With open fire, central heating, TV, piano. **Bar.**
Large garden
Closed from November to March.

About 1830, a great 14th-century mansion was torn down and its stones used to build this elegant house, extended in recent times to provide more bedrooms.

The Davies' hotel is spacious – there is not only the big sitting-room through which one passes on entering, but also a large cocktail bar and a snug retreat with red leather armchairs and a library of books, for residents only.

The least expensive bedrooms – in converted stables – are simply furnished but have the advantage for some visitors of being on the ground floor and with space to park immediately outside. Those in the house vary in size and outlook. From three (one small) you get a lovely view of lawns and the hotel's private lake; in another, birdwatchers can do their viewing in armchair comfort, for the old apple tree outside is a tenement of pied flycatchers' nests. As Glanrannell stands in 23 acres of grounds, much of what you see is available for visitors to roam in, and there are plenty of footpaths in the rest of the lovely Cothi Valley too. The hotel's name comes from the Annell trout stream which runs along its boundary.

Dinner always includes much local produce (such as rack of Welsh lamb served on a coarse tomato sauce) or lemon sole from the coast.

Reader's comment: A delightful holiday.

From Pumpsaint, a long and devious track leads up into the forested hills, past the Roman gold mine, to remote **ERW HEN** ('old acre'). This valley is an 'area of special scientific interest' for its wildlife (especially birds of prey) and Roman remains abound. The 400-year-old house has been furnished by David and Brenda Vockings with individuality: plum-coloured tiles and wallpaper, a carved Burmese table, prints of hawks, salvaged black and red quarry-tiles. Dinners comprise such things as peppered mackerel, chicken

chasseur (with four vegetables), mandarin flan and cheeses. David will take visitors in his four-wheel drive to remote mountain spots or advise on walks. £13–£17. [Tel: 05585 495; postcode: SA19 8YP]

401

LLWYNDÛ FARMHOUSE HOTEL   C D PT S X
Llanaber, Barmouth, Gwynedd, LL42 1RR Tel: 0341280 144
West of Dolgellau. Nearest main road: A496 from Barmouth to Harlech.

7 Bedrooms. £19–£22 (less for 3 nights). Bargain breaks. All have own bath/shower/toilet. Tea/coffee facilities. TV (in most). Views of garden, country, sea. No smoking. Washing machine on request.
Dinner. £12.50 for 3 courses (with choices) and coffee, at 7–7.30pm. Non-residents not admitted. Vegetarian or special diets if ordered. Wine can be ordered. **Light suppers** if ordered.
1 Sitting-room. With open fire, central heating, TV, record-player.
Large garden

In the year that the youthful Shakespeare wrote *The Taming of the Shrew*, an even younger man made his way from remote Llwyndû to London, to study law in the Inner Temple. It was 1597, and this house had already seen generations of his family grow up. Peter Thompson, whose home it now is, researched the history of the house and its inhabitants for a university dissertation: he even has some of their very early wills.

This, therefore, was a house of considerable consequence in the neighbourhood, and handsomely built. The walls are immensely thick, and the living-room huge; one ceiling-beam is over two feet thick, and great blocks of granite form the fireplace. New discoveries continue to come to light – for instance, a 16th-century oak-mullioned window which had long been blocked up.

The bedrooms have, in most cases, views (and sounds) of the sea waves – and excellent bathrooms (one with oval bath and bidet, for example). One room has a dressing-room, another its own stone stair to the garden; some are in a converted granary. Everywhere are attractive furnishings, and great pieces of driftwood from the beaches stand here and there like sculpture.

Peter and Paula are very keen cooks, preparing such meals as parsnip-and-apple soup, lamb in a mushroom and cinnamon sauce, rhubarb-and-banana pie.

Readers' comments: House has tremendous character. Lovely food, great value. Delightful situation, friendly welcome. Food superb. Excellent hostess and cook. Stunning views.

On the water's edge of Mawddach estuary is **HERONGATE**, at Arthog, the simple and inexpensive but pleasant home of Pat Mallatratt whose late husband's paintings line the walls of the small sitting-room. Herons, oyster-catchers and tame sheep seeking titbits can be seen from the bay windows. The house is in a small, isolated crescent built by a Victorian entrepreneur as part of a grander plan that never materialized, in an excellent area for walks. (Light suppers

only.) £12–£13. [Tel: 0341 250 349; messages: 0341 250 207; postcode: LL39 1BJ]

OLD VICARAGE　　　　　　　　　　　　**C M P T S X**
Moylegrove, Dyfed, SA43 3BN　Tel: 023986 231 (Messages: 023986 646)
West of Cardigan. Nearest main road: A487 from Cardigan to Fishguard.

5 Bedrooms. £15.50–£18 (less for 7 nights). Prices go up in April. Bargain breaks. Some have own bath/shower/toilet. Tea/coffee facilities. TV. Views of garden, country, sea. No smoking. Washing machine on request.
Dinner. £12.50 for 4 courses (with choices) and coffee, at 7pm. Non-residents not admitted. Vegetarian or special diets if ordered. Wine can be ordered. **Light suppers** if ordered.
2 Sitting-rooms. With open fire, central heating, TV, piano, record-player. No smoking in one.
Large garden

An air of quality and comfort pervades every room in this substantial Edwardian house, set on a sweeping lawn with glimpses of Cardigan Bay not far away. The unusual slate and turf wall of the garden is traditional to the area. High up in the countryside, the house has superb views for it is in the middle of the Pembrokeshire Coast National Park.

Peach, brown and green predominate in the restful colour schemes of the rooms, many of which have bay windows. Crystal glasses and fluted white china on blue cloths help to create a particularly attractive effect in the dining-room. Here Peggy Govey serves imaginative meals such as smoked salmon quenelles, chicken breasts cooked with apricots and brandy, praline mousse, and cheeses.

The large bedrooms have flowery duvets and good bathrooms, and there is a recently built 'patio suite' with sliding glass doors opening onto the lawn.

Within a mile, the long Pembrokeshire coastal path passes on its way, following the dramatic cliffs, beaches and steep valleys that make this coast so outstanding. Further afield the Preseli Mountains rise high. It was from here that the Ice Age swept immense blueish stones over 200 miles, from which Stonehenge was built; and the deep river valleys in this area are full of prehistoric remains.

Offshore, seals and seabirds have their colonies among sunlit isles buffeted by Atlantic winds and waves. There are picturesque villages such as riverside Cilgerran (Turner's painting of castle ruins above its ravine is one of the Tate Gallery's jewels) and Nevern, its mediaeval bridge, Norman church and Celtic cross providing landmarks for pilgrims going to St David's birthplace (where there is now a cathedral, Britain's smallest, built by the Normans).

Fishguard is a picturesque little port on a great bay sheltered by cliffs: in the Napoleonic wars the French landed here, the last ever invasion of British soil. For a museum interpreting the history and ecology of the whole county, head for the castle in Haverfordwest, a market town, beyond which are more little seaside resorts with sandy beaches to discover.

> Some proprietors stipulate a minimum stay of two nights at weekends or peak seasons; or they will accept one-nighters only at short notice (that is, only if no lengthier booking has yet been made).

403

PARK HALL   D S
Cwmtydu, Dyfed, SA44 6LG   Tel: 0545 560306
North-east of Cardigan. Nearest main road: A487 from Cardigan to
Aberystwyth.

5 Bedrooms. £18–£23 (less for 7 nights).
Bargain breaks. All have own bath/
shower/toilet. Tea/coffee facilities. TV.
Views of garden, country, sea. Washing
machine on request.
Dinner. £14.50 for 4 courses (with choices)
and coffee, or à la carte, at 8pm. Vegetarian
or special diets if ordered. Wine can be
ordered. **Light suppers.**
2 Sitting-rooms. With open fire, central
heating, TV, piano, record-player. Bar.
Large garden

In a wooded valley protected by the National Trust is this turn-of-the-century
mansion which is decorated with flair, using much Victoriana – the table linen
and silver, the brass beds (one four-poster), the leather chesterfields and even the
bath with brass claw feet are in period. Antique lace has been used quite a lot,
and Laura Ashley Victorian-style fabrics as well as patchwork, Welsh tapestry
bedspreads, and a wallpaper of sweet peas in a bathroom. From pine-panelled bay
windows, there are views of Cardigan Bay between the hills and of the picturesque valley running down to it. Chris Macdonnell's dinners are of a high
order. A popular starter is prawn and avocado salad; main courses can include
salmon poached in vermouth; with such puddings as profiteroles – and then
cheeses. Dinner, teas and lunches are served in a large conservatory which overlooks the sea.

   Cardigan's ancient bridge straddles the Teifi, a salmon river. There are a
castle, abbey ruins at St Dogmael's, and a park of native wildlife. Upriver (at
Cilgerran) you may see coracle fishing – a coracle regatta is held each August –
and there is a romantic castle ruin; at Henllan, beautifully sited, or Llanbydder
are little woollen mills open to visitors; and at the valley's 'capital', Lampeter, one
can visit St David's College or attend the horse fairs in May.

Readers' comments: Impossible to find criticism. Very friendly, superb accommo-
dation. Excellent value. Very good hosts, food excellent. Splendid house.
Outstanding hospitality. Nothing too much trouble. Food and rooms excellent.
Felt we had made genuine friends. Most relaxing. Good food. Very enjoyable.

Also at Cardigan Bay is a picturesque
cove – Llangranog – popular in high
summer. But set aside from the throng
here is quiet **HENDRE FARM**,
unpretentious but very comfortable
and with good home cooking by
Bethan Williams, using the farm's own
fruit, vegetables and other produce: a
good choice for a traditional farmhouse holiday. £16–£18. [Tel: 0239
654342; postcode: SA44 6AP]

404

PLAS TREFARTHEN   C
Brynsiencyn, Isle of Anglesey, Gwynedd, LL61 6SZ   Tel: 0248 430379
South-west of Menai Bridge. Nearest main road: A4080 from Rhosneigr to
Menai Bridge.

8 Bedrooms. £16.50–£20. Some have own bath/toilet. Tea/coffee facilities. TV. Views of garden, mountains, sea.
Dinner. £10 for 3 courses and coffee, at 6.30pm. Non-residents not admitted. Vegetarian diets if ordered. Wine can be brought in. No smoking.
1 Sitting-room. With open fire, central heating, piano, record-player.
Large garden

It had seemed an ordinary day. True, the house is a handsome 18th-century mansion at the heart of a 200-acre farm, and its waterfront site is outstanding (there are superb views across the Menai Strait to Snowdon). But suddenly the experience became exceptional for me . . . in fact, unique. Standing by her piano in the dining-room, Marian Roberts began to sing impromptu (to my husband's accompaniment). Her voice soared effortlessly, true and clear, to the highest notes. I have rarely heard such a lovely and unaffected sound from any singer.

Marian, after repeatedly winning the highest accolades at the international *eisteddfod* each year and spending much time on concert tours in America, Australia and elsewhere, is now a 'bed-and-breakfast lady', welcoming visitors to Plas Trefarthen.

In the sitting-room, a big picture-window makes the most of the view across the water to Caernarfon Castle. The green brocade walls and a big Welsh dresser display souvenirs of Marian's travels; musical mementoes are gathered in the dining-room. Bedrooms are roomy – the pink one has an outsize bathroom and windows on two sides; the pine-fitted one has the best views of Snowdon. There are also attic rooms with large skylights.

Marian serves such dinners as home-made soup, Welsh lamb and apple tart.

The house stands in an area of outstanding natural beauty. Unlike the rest of Wales, Anglesey's 300 square miles are rocky but not mountainous: they have other charms.

The island, connected by bridges to the mainland, is still a centre of Celtic culture. There is a great deal to see: a huge nature reserve of dunes at Newborough (wildfowl and wading birds); Holy Island reached by a causeway from which there are views to the Isle of Man and Ireland, glimpses of seals or seabirds on South Stack, and vast caves on North Stack; Cemaes Bay for good bathing and clifftop walks; Amlwch, a resort surrounded by fine coastal scenery; the picturesque fishing village of Moelfre; Penmon with mediaeval remains and trips to Puffin Island; and weekly markets at Llangefni. One of Anglesey's claims to fame is the village with the longest name in Britain: Llanfairpwllgwyngyllgogerychwyrndrobwillantysiliogogogoch.

Prices are per person in a double room at the beginning of the year.

TALBONTDRAIN
C PT(limited) S

Uwychygarreg, Powys, SY20 8RR Tel: 0654 702192
South of Machynlleth. Nearest main road: A489 from Machynlleth towards Newtown.

6 Bedrooms. £15–£20 (less for 7 nights). Some have own bath/shower/toilet. Views of garden, country. No smoking. Washing machine on request.
Dinner. £10 for 2 courses and coffee, at 7.30pm. Non-residents not admitted. Vegetarian or special diets if ordered. Wine can be brought in. No smoking. **Light suppers** if ordered.
1 Sitting-room. With open fire, central heating, piano. No smoking.
Large garden
Closed in January.

Hilary Matthews abandoned a London career as a social worker to restore this remote, slate-floored house, high in the hills, furnishing it very simply – for people who travel light – but with attractive colours and textures. Inexpensive guided walking holidays are an extra attraction here (no car is needed: Hilary will book a taxi at Machynlleth station to drive you up her long, twisting lane); and she provides particularly well for children (baby-sitting available). She serves such two-course meals as bacon-and-leek flan with vegetables, followed by nectarines in a creamy sauce. Occasionally she does fungus identifying (and cooking) weekends or others on map-reading, singing, story-telling, etc. Her breakfasts feature Welsh specialities: I recommend 'Glamorgan sausage', a type of cheese croquette. Some guests enjoy her excellent pianola as an after-dinner treat. Talbontdrain (its name means 'thorn tree at the end of the bridge') is in a varied area of woodland, waterfalls, moors and sheep pastures; utterly peaceful. Around the house are goats, bees, big tubs of petunias, wagtails and chickens; inside are warmth and comfort.

The market town of Machynlleth, at the head of the Dyfi estuary, did not grow up in the higgledy-piggledy way of many mediaeval towns but was laid out systematically in the 13th century, with its main streets forming a 'T'.

Readers' comments: Friendly; good food and company; extremely comfortable. Beautifully situated.

Southward, at Llangurig, is the **OLD VICARAGE**, a late Victorian building now run with great efficiency as a guest-house, a model of its kind. Everything is immaculate and comfortable. Anna Rollings has an à la carte menu on which local lamb chops are one of the most popular items, with her fish pie and steak-and-kidney pies close runners-up. Cream teas on the sunny lawn include several cakes which are Welsh specialities. As two 'A' roads cross at Llangurig, it is a good base from which to explore Wales in all

directions. Brian Rollings helps visitors trace their family history. £18–£20. [Tel: 05515 280; postcode: SY18 6RN]

THORNTREES
Cwm Lane, Govilon, Gwent, NP7 9RY   Tel: 0873 831686
West of Abergavenny. Nearest main road: A465 from Abergavenny to Merthyr Tydfil.

3 Bedrooms. £14.50–£17.50 (less for 5 nights). Some have own bath/shower; all have own toilet. Tea/coffee facilities. TV. Views of garden, country. No smoking. Washing machine on request.
Dinner. £7.50–£10 for 2–3 courses and coffee, at 7pm. Non-residents not admitted. Vegetarian dishes if ordered. Wine can be brought in. No smoking. **Light suppers** sometimes.
1 Sitting-room. With open fire, central heating, record-player. No smoking.
Small garden
Closed from December to February.

Panoramic views of the Brecon Beacons National Park surround this house in the beautiful Llanwenarth Valley, where visitors can choose between a room in the 18th-century cottage or simpler accommodation in a pine cabin (self-catering if preferred). The cottage has two bedrooms, one of which is beamed. The cabin has a small double-bedded room, a sitting-room, shower and cooking facilities.

Carys Westfield serves such traditional country dinners as celery soup, Thorntrees' own beef or lamb with red cabbage and apple, or perhaps pork cooked in cider with prunes, her own organically grown vegetables, raspberry trifle or raisin-and-brandy pudding. Welsh dishes are often included in her repertoire, and Sunday lunch is available too. She is a fount of information on local history – the ancient iron-smelters of these hills, the burial-place of Olympics champion Foxhunter, etc.; she spins, makes and sells patchwork, and also sheepskins which she has cured in the traditional way that goes back thousands of years; she occasionally arranges barbecues; and will tell you of scenic walks and drives. The Westfields keep Jacob and other sheep, and hens for free-range eggs. One of their rams was star of the Elan Valley's 'ram spectacular' one year. Water is from a pure spring.

In the unspoilt countryside around Govilon you may spot peregrine falcons, owls and wild trout. Sheep-fields alternate with woods, and over all looms the distant Sugarloaf mountain: there are hilly walks right from the door, or follow the more leisurely path alongside the lovely Brecon canal.

A writer of 1800, Alexander Cordell, described the valley as it was two centuries ago – and, miraculously, still is now, with the stream which 'like white blood spewing from a wound in the mountain, ran through the valley of Llanwenarth in a torrent to the mothering river. On its way, in a paradise as yet untainted by the hand of man, it forms deep pools where trout and dace and little minnows lie.

'Herons stand here in statuesque silence, contemplating the earth; coloured birds hunt the shouting water: it is a poetic frenzy of unspoiled Nature.'

Nearby are several attractive market towns: Abergavenny, Brecon and Monmouth. Most visitors also go to the Big Pit mine, the Rhondda Heritage Park, and St Fagin's museum with its collection of rebuilt Welsh homes.

Readers' comments: Looked after magnificently. A great success. Excellent meals.

THREE WELLS FARM HOTEL C(8) **M PT S**
Howey, Powys, LD1 5PB   Tel: 0597 822484
South of Llandrindod Wells. Nearest main road: A483 from Llandrindod
Wells to Builth Wells.

15 Bedrooms. £17–£20 (less for 7 nights).
All have own bath/shower/toilet. Tea/coffee
facilities. TV. Views of garden, country,
lake. No smoking.
Dinner. £9–£10 for 4 courses (with
choices) and coffee, at 7pm. Vegetarian or
special diets if ordered. Wine can be
ordered. No smoking. **Light suppers** if
ordered.
2 Sitting-rooms. With central heating.
TV, piano, record-player. No smoking. **Bar.**
Small garden
Closed in December and January.

There are indeed three wells here, capped; and between them they pump 400,000 gallons a day into the Water Board's supply, from an enormous underground lake. There's also a lake on the surface with carp, tench, elusive trout and ducks: a sight that can be enjoyed through the restaurant's windows, from the ample armchairs of the big sitting-room or from the glass sun-room.

For less agile visitors it is an advantage that the stairs are fitted with a chair-lift, and there are some ground-floor bedrooms too. The rooms vary in size and facilities. One has a pink-draped four-poster made of pine, and a lake view. Several have their own sitting-rooms; and one family suite consists of two inter-connecting bedrooms plus a bathroom. Unusually, several good single rooms have been provided, so visitors on their own are unlikely to be the only singles around.

Margaret Bufton chose emerald linen for tables at one end of her restaurant and sugar-pink at the other, where there is also a bar with a silver rose-bowl displayed – her award as 'best small hotel in Wales', 1990. You may be offered such a meal as broccoli-and-cheese soup, ham with parsley sauce, a choice of puddings (typically, apricot pie, pear belle Hélène and pineapple mousse) and cheeses.

On the farm are sheep, pedigree black cattle, horses and poultry – not to mention the wildlife that flourishes here undisturbed. Fishing is also available.

Ancient wells, as in this area, often carry ancient beliefs – that their water cures eye ailments, for example. Not only did the Romans (whose fort at Castellcollen you can visit) believe this of the waters of Llandrindod Wells, but in 1983 a bottle was sent to Margaret Thatcher when she had eye trouble. The town used to be a flourishing health spa (hence its elegant architecture); its heyday is now annually recreated during a summer week when shopkeepers and others don Victorian dress and the town turns festive. Builth Wells, too, owes some of its finer buildings to its period as a spa: on the way there, pause at Disserth to see a perfect 18th-century church with box pews (each bearing its occupant's name), three-decker pulpit and wall paintings all intact.

Readers' comments: Good atmosphere, hospitality, excellent food, nice people. Dinners very well done and the owners work hard to provide the best of lodgings.

TREGYNON

C M X

Gwaun Valley, Pontfaen, Dyfed, SA65 9TU   Tel: 0239 820531
South-east of Fishguard. Nearest main road: B4313 from Fishguard to
Narbeth.

8 Bedrooms. £20–£29.75 (less for 6 nights). Prices go up in April. Bargain breaks. All have own bath/shower/toilet. Tea/coffee facilities. TV. Views of country. Smoking discouraged.
Dinner. £14 for 3 courses (with choices including vegetarian) and coffee, at 7.30–8.30pm. Wine can be ordered. No smoking. **Light suppers** if ordered.
2 Sitting-rooms. With open fire, central heating, piano. **Bar.** Smoking discouraged.
Large grounds

In the heart of the Pembrokeshire Coast National Park is something quite exceptional. Of all the places I have stayed in Wales, this remote, 16th-century country farmhouse hotel, restored by Peter Heard, has some of the most spectacular scenery around it, including an Ice Age ravine with waterfall, ancient oak woods, countryside where badgers and polecats or buzzards and red kites are sometimes spotted, wild moorland and a prehistoric fort. From nearby peaks of the Preseli Mountains, one can sometimes see Ireland and Snowdon. Not far away are some of the sunniest sandy beaches in the country, renowned for their pure air.

Jane Heard's meals are exceptional, with emphasis on wholefood, and the wine-list is also outstanding. Speciality breads, sausages, traditionally smoked ham, cheeses and Tregynon's own spring water and trout ponds contribute to the experience of eating here. You can relax afterwards by a log fire in the beamed sitting-room which has a massive stone inglenook and button-backed chesterfields of raspberry and grass-green velvet, with a snug stone-walled bar adjoining it. Some bedrooms are in the house, others in converted stone outbuildings – spacious, pretty and well equipped.

The National Park extends round almost the entire coast from Cardigan Bay to Carmarthen Bay (there is a coastal path all the way) and inland to mountains.

Readers' comments: Excellent host. Varied and original menus of excellent quality (best ice cream we have tasted). Nothing too much trouble. Very comfortable.

For anyone tracing their family history, I recommend a stay at inexpensive **MOUNT PLEASANT FARM** at Penffordd because Pauline Bowen is an expert on the subject, while Peter collects vintage cars and bygones. A warm, hospitable couple, their small, beamed farmhouse of rugged stone is immaculate and comfortable. Good home cooking, and then relaxation in big armchairs of pink velvet. Fine views of the Preseli Mountains –

superb when heather is in bloom. (No smoking). £14.
Readers' comments: Exceptional value. [Tel: 0437 563447; postcode: SA66 7HY]

TY CROESO HOTEL
C(5) D PT

The Dardy, Crickhowell, Powys, NP8 1PU   Tel: 0873 810573

North-west of Abergavenny (Gwent). Nearest main road: A40 from
Abergavenny to Brecon.

8 Bedrooms. £18.50–£25.50 (**less to
readers of this book** and for 7 nights).
Prices go up from June. Bargain breaks. All
have own bath/shower/toilet. Tea/coffee
facilities. TV. Views of garden, country,
river. Washing machine on request.
Dinner. £12.95 for 3 courses (with choices)
and coffee, from 7–9pm. Vegetarian or
special diets if ordered. Wine can be
ordered.
1 Sitting-room. With open fire, central
heating, record-player. **Bar.**
Large garden

The name means 'house of welcome', a far cry from its early Victorian origins as a
workhouse infirmary. It was used as such up to the Second World War. Now it is
run very professionally by Peter and Kate Jones as a small hotel of character, in a
rural setting.

Bedrooms vary in size. Those at the front have lovely valley views, for the
hotel is perched on a hillside above the River Usk. Kate has used pinks and greens
a lot, in rooms that have much pine furniture, and sometimes draped effects. Bath
and shower rooms are very good, and single rooms as attractive as doubles. One
huge and particularly elegant bedroom has a big curved sofa.

The restaurant has a similar colour scheme, stencilled decorations on some
walls (one is of rugged stone) and pretty arrangements of dried flowers. Here are
served such meals as avocado and grapefruit with coriander dressing, chicken
breast in a plum and brandy sauce and a syllabub of honey and ginger (there are
several choices at each course) A 'Taste of Wales' dinner is available: you may be
offered such things as a salad of goat's cheese and samphire; loin of pork with
Caerphilly cheese, cider and apple; honey and lemon yogurt; and Welsh cheeses.
(Sunday lunch is also available.)

The little town of Crickhowell, right in the Brecon Beacons National Park, has
many quiet attractions: old coaching inns, castle ruins, cobbled lanes, an ancient
bridge and church, and some fine architecture from the 18th century. The whole
of the town centre is a conservation area.

Northward is an interesting drive to ancient Llanvihangel (sited where a river
cleaves it way through the Black Mountains), pausing at the historic Skirrid Inn
which, dating from 1110, is where Owain Glyndwr gathered his troops. Flagstone
floors and ancient beams are still as he knew them; upstairs was a courtroom and
from the great oak staircase at least 200 sheep-stealers were hanged. Near it is
Tre-Wyn, an imposing 17th-century mansion with very splendid woodwork inside
and outstanding mountain views from grounds that include terraces, arboretum
and walled gardens. At hilly Grosmart, the skyline is pierced by the 13th-century
church spire and by romantic castle ruins – it was here that Prince Hal (later
Henry V) defeated Owain Glyndwr. The sinuous river below borders England.

Another scenic drive leads to an even more impressive 12th-century castle,
with moat, where Rudolph Hess was held: the White Castle, Llanvetherine.

Reader's comment: A wise choice!

TY GWYN

Betws-y-Coed, Gwynedd, LL24 0SG
On A5 from Betws-y-Coed to Llangollen.

C D M PT S X

Tel: 0690 710383 or 710787

13 Bedrooms. £17.50–£40. Bargain breaks. Some have own bath/shower/toilet. Tea/coffee facilities. TV. Views of garden, country, river. Balcony (one).
Dinner. A la carte or £17.95 for 3 courses (with choices) and coffee, at 7–9.30pm. Vegetarian or special diets if ordered. Wine can be ordered. **Light suppers.**
1 Sitting-room. With central heating, TV, tape-recorder. **Bar** with open fire.
Small garden

A former coaching inn, Ty Gwyn ('white house'), although on a road, has quiet bedrooms at the back. Sheila Ratcliffe has a flair for interior decoration, and every bedroom – small or large – is beautiful, many with en suite bathrooms (prices vary accordingly). The most impressive is an attic suite with four-poster and sitting-room; the most convenient for anyone with mobility problems, a pretty ground-floor room. A mountain rises up sheer at the back, where one tiny room has stone walls contrasting with a cane bedhead. Even in the ancient, beamed bar (fire glowing in the old black range, copper pots, carved oak settle) Sheila's colourful patchwork cushions are everywhere. There is also a very comfortable sitting-room and another where she sells antiques and old prints.

Cooking is done by chef Martin, the Ratcliffes' son, whose specialities include exotic dishes like pigeon with oyster mushrooms in Madeira or Thai-style king prawns (the table d'hôte menu is simpler). These meals are served in a picturesque dining-room: antique furniture, crochet, crystal and silver on the tables. Even the bar snacks include such options as parrotfish in lemon sauce.

Four wooded valleys meet at this village, with a high plateau looming above it. Walkers use it as a centre to explore in every direction, the serious ones making for Snowdon but most for the riverside paths, Gwydyr Forest or any of several lakes.

Readers' comments: Lovely setting, wonderful room. Good food.

Also in Betws is a small, partly 14th-century watermill: **ROYAL OAK FARMHOUSE**. Although so central, the mill is hidden in a little valley with a deep salmon pool close by. The lattice-paned windows, great stone fireplace, carved oak settle and small but very pretty bedrooms (one en suite) give this guest-house great character. Elsie Houghton serves only breakfast, but there are good eating-places in Betws. £13–£15. [Tel: 0690 710427]

Equally attractive (and with en suite bathrooms) is **ROYAL OAK**

FARM COTTAGE, run by Elsie's daughter-in-law Kathleen. £15–£16. [Tel: 0690 710760; messages for Farmhouse and Cottage: 0690 710632; postcode for both: LL24 0AH]

411

UPPER TREWALKIN FARM
C PT S

Pengenffordd, Powys, LD3 0HA   Tel: 0874 711349

East of Brecon. Nearest main road: A479 from Talgarth towards Crickhowell.

3 Bedrooms. £18 (less for 7 nights). Two have own bath/shower/toilet. All have tea/coffee facilities. Views of garden, country. No smoking. Washing machine on request.

Dinner. £10.50 for 3 courses (with choices) and coffee, at 7pm (not Thursdays). Non-residents not admitted. Wine can be brought in. No smoking. **Light suppers** if ordered.

1 Sitting-room. With log burner, central heating, TV. No smoking.

Small garden

Closed from December to March.

The reputation of hospitable Meudwen Stephens has spread far and wide: she is often invited to do overseas tours promoting Wales and its food. So one thing of which you can be sure is a good dinner – such as courgette and tomato soup, lamb chops cooked in white wine and mushrooms (accompanied by garden vegetables), and a lemon-and-orange mousse. (Free home-made cakes and tea on arrival.)

But there is more to Upper Trewalkin than this. In the 16th century it was a long-house (animals at one end, family at the other), built on a site previously owned by a Norman knight. It was updated in the 18th century, although, behind the sash windows then let into the thick limestone walls, many original features were retained.

From many rooms there are superb views of the Black Mountains. Some walls are of exposed stone, some attractively papered. At every turn are paintings of poultry by local artist Alex Williams, and others of country crafts by Zoe Short. Patchwork cushions decorate all beds.

The farm is in the Brecon Beacons National Park, an area of great interest to birdwatchers and walkers alike. Llangorse Lake is near and here, at the quieter end, grebes nest. Most visitors enjoy the immense variety of this area, in which can be found Tretower Court, little steam trains, craft workshops, waterfalls and the Big Pit museum of mining. On the farm itself you will see sheep and cattle.

Just outside Llangorse is Victorian **TREWALTER HOUSE**, the stone-built home of Jean Abbott (some readers of earlier editions enjoyed staying at her former home, Peterstone Court) who has renovated and decorated it to very high standards: everywhere is immaculate. You can wake to a panoramic view of the Brecon Beacons from some rooms, and of the Black Mountains (across the neighbouring farmyard) from others. Jean's ornamental 'bits and pieces' decorate every room. For dinner (by candlelight) she

serves such straightforward meals as melon, roast lamb, raspberry charlotte russe and Welsh cheeses. £19 (b & b). [Tel: 087484 442; postcode: LD3 0PS]

WENALLT FARM

Gilwern, Gwent, NP7 0HP Tel: 0873 830694

West of Abergavenny. Nearest main road: A465 from Abergavenny to Merthyr Tydfil.

8 Bedrooms. £14.50–£17.50 (less for 7 nights). Bargain breaks. Some have own bath/shower/toilet. Tea/coffee facilities. Views of garden, country. Washing machine on request.
Dinner. £9.50 for 4 courses (with choices) and coffee, at 7.30pm. Non-residents not admitted. Vegetarian or special diets if ordered. Wine can be ordered or brought in.
2 Sitting-rooms. With open fire, central heating, TV, record-player. **Bar.**
Large garden

The name, 'wooded mill', was given to this remote stone house when it was first built as a long-house: though most of it dates from about 1600, some parts are a good deal older. Oak beams and mullioned windows are still the same as when Oliver Cromwell reputedly stayed here on his march to Monmouth. What is now a bar once housed cattle, and the bedroom above, hay to feed them; the sitting-room was a dairy. And from many windows in this hilltop house you can see for miles. Farmer Brian Harris made many improvements when he came here and in the new dining-room installed a stone fireplace from Tredegar House (ancestral home of buccaneer Henry Morgan who became governor of Jamaica). He converted a stone cow-byre to make more bedrooms.

There are scores of cups won at horse shows (Brian is now a judge at these), and other touches that give the house individuality – from a stuffed pheasant on a hearth to the beribboned fabrics in one of the bedrooms.

Meals are well above average and after stuffed courgette flowers followed by turkey in a walnut sauce, I enjoyed the lightest apple strudel I have ever tasted. The table was laid with distinctive Black Mountain pottery.

Although it is the scenery that brings most people here, there is much else to enjoy, for this is a historic area. Henry V was born in the castle at Monmouth, a town with other royal connections. Nelson stayed in Monmouth – hence the naval temple on Kymin Hill, commanding far views. There are two Norman churches in the vicinity (the one at Over Monnow has a wonderful doorway and, near it, a mediaeval bridge with fortified gate). Then there is Raglan, with few old houses left by its church but with spectacular castle remains nearby: each of its two 15th-century courts has its own gatehouse and they are linked by a bridge to a massive, polygonal tower with a moat round it.

There are fine drives and walks in the Wye and Llantony valleys as well as along the Usk; and up into the Brecon Beacons and Black Mountains – the former can be explored on a steam railway too. Llangorse Lake is used for sailing. A very popular outing now is the Big Pit (coal mine) at Blaenavon.

Readers' comments: Friendly and helpful. Food excellent. Our spacious room was furnished with lovely antiques. Enjoyed so much that I extended my stay. Food and service excellent. Welcoming and friendly.

WEST USK LIGHTHOUSE   C PT
Lighthouse Road, St Brides Wentlooge, Gwent, NP1 9SF
Tel: 0633 810126 or 815860
South of Newport. Nearest main road: A48 from Newport to Cardiff
(and M4, junction 28).

4 Bedrooms. £18–£21 (less for 4 nights).
Some have own shower/toilet. Tea/coffee
facilities. TV. Views of garden, country, sea,
river. No smoking.
Dinner. £10 for 3 courses (with choices)
and coffee, at 7pm. Non-residents not
admitted. Vegetarian or special diets if
ordered. Wine can be brought in. No
smoking. **Light suppers** if ordered.
1 Sitting-room. With open fire, central
heating, TV, video. No smoking.
Large garden

Perhaps the strangest house in this book, the ex-lighthouse – found at the end of a
very long, stony track – is an unusual example of its kind, built to a unique
design: not tall as most lighthouses are, and considerably bigger in circumference.
In 1821, it was on an island where the Severn and Usk run into the sea, with
views far out into the Bristol Channel. Since then, land has been reclaimed and
although on one side the loudest sound is of the sea when the tide (second fastest
in the world) comes racing in to the foot of the building, on the other only the
occasional mooing cow can be heard. The walls are over two feet thick, with
rooms on both floors wedge-shaped. From the slate-paved hall a spiral stair rises
to the bedrooms, above which is a flat roof with seats from which to watch ships
go by and the spectacular sunsets – or, facing the other way, sunrises. Occasional
barbecues are held up here. Old features have been retained, such as the indoor
well for collecting rainwater, but everything else is comfortable and immaculate
from the sparkling white walls outside to the thick carpets within.

Bedrooms have been pleasantly but simply furnished with, for example, rattan
bedheads and pretty fabrics, and in the sitting-room are unusual rococo armchairs
from Italy. Modern sculptures stand here and there, and on many walls are framed
record-sleeves: Frank Sheahan used to work for a major record company before
turning his hand to restoring the derelict lighthouse, four years of hard slog.

The house is run in an informal, sometimes slightly scatty way, and often
with an assortment of other enterprises on the go – from relaxation classes to
aromatherapy sessions. An unusual and very popular facility is the flotation tank:
an hour lying in warm and buoyant brine, lights dimmed or off, all sound
silenced, is calculated to ease away every kind of stress.

You can sit by a log fire or watch satellite television, go birdwatching or
wander along the reedy dykes, looking for the plants that botanists find of particular interest. Rabbits scamper beneath the willows, butterflies flit among the blackberry bushes and the burdocks – and all within ten minutes of busy Newport.

Meals are chosen from a short list of conventional choices, from pizza to steaks.

Quite close to the lighthouse are palatial Tredegar House (lake and craft shops
in its grounds) and romantic little Castell Coch ('the red castle'). Also well worth
visiting are the Roman city of Caerleon, and the castles of Cardiff, Caerphilly and
Penhow. Both the Usk Valley and the Brecon Beacons are scenic.

Readers' comments: Charmingly and artistically furnished and very unusual; peaceful. An inspired conversion.

WYE BARN PT(limited) S
The Quay, Tintern, Gwent, NP6 6SZ Tel: 0291 689456
North of Chepstow. Nearest main road: A466 from Chepstow to Monmouth.

3 Bedrooms. £17–£19 (less for 7 nights). One has own shower/toilet. Tea/coffee facilities. TV. Views of country, river. No smoking. Washing machine on request.
Dinner. £8.50 for 4 courses and coffee, at 7pm. Non-residents not admitted. Vegetarian or special diets if ordered. Wine can be brought in. No smoking.
1 Sitting-room. With open fire, central heating, TV. No smoking.
Small garden
Closed in January and February.

Perched right on the river bank, the house is occasionally islanded when the Wye's spring tides rise 20 feet. (Which is why the house itself is built up, with steps to the door.) Four centuries ago, the monks of Tintern Abbey built it as a bark house – oak bark, needed for tanning hides, used to be stored here.

From an exceptionally pretty garden, one steps through French doors into a pleasant sitting-room of soft blues and greys which complement the fireplace of grey stone quarried in the Forest of Dean.

Because Judith Russill used to work for Britain's most celebrated furniture designer, John Makepeace (she was responsible for his students' welfare), she has a number of very lovely and unusual pieces of furniture made by his students – to which she has added other finds of her own, such as Welsh cottage chairs with acorn or spindle backs, and an art nouveau one inlaid with mother-of-pearl.

Bedrooms are just as attractive – for instance, one has lotus-patterned spreads that match the pinkish carpet and Chinese silk pictures; in another, blue and pink, is her collection of teddy bears. From their windows are views of the River Wye.

Judith specializes in traditional Welsh cookery and you may be offered, for example, Anglesey eggs (they are cooked with leeks and cream en cocotte), Wye salmon with a herb sauce, and – the Welsh answer to cheesecake – a sour-cream and sultana tart. These may be followed by various Welsh cheeses.

Out in the garden (with a sun-trapping, glazed summer-house) you get a good view of Tintern Abbey's particularly beautiful ruins. The whole of the Wye Valley is famous for its beauty, with the nearby Usk Valley giving it some serious competition too.

Sedbury, not marked on all maps, is tucked between Chepstow and the Severn estuary – quite close to the Severn Bridge. In rural Sedbury Lane stands an old farm, **UPPER SEDBURY HOUSE**, with cottagey bedrooms; and also an attic flat, usually let for self-catering but Christine Potts is happy to do meals for those guests too. (A typical dinner, using garden produce: egg mayonnaise, roast lamb, fruit crumble.) There is a swimming-pool, unheated; badminton, croquet,

etc.; and the Offa's Dyke footpath runs by the house. £14.50–£17.50. [Tel: 0291 627173; postcode: NP6 7HN]

415

WYNN HALL
Penycae, Clwyd, LL14 1TW Tel: 0978 822106

C(12) **PT S**

South-west of Wrexham. Nearest main road: A483 from Wrexham to Chirk.

3 Bedrooms. £16–£18 (less for 4 nights or continental breakfast). Tea/coffee facilities. TV. Views of garden, country. No smoking. Washing machine on request.
Dinner. From £8.50 for 3 courses and coffee, at 7–8pm (not in early July). Non-residents not admitted. Vegetarian or special diets if ordered. Wine can be brought in. No smoking. **Light suppers** if ordered.
2 Sitting-rooms. With open fire and other heating, TV, video, record-player. No smoking.
Large garden

Construction of this historic house was completed – by a Roundhead officer – in the year that Charles I was beheaded (the date, 1649, is on the façade). The gables have decorative timbering, the front door great wrought-iron hinges.

The Wynns were nonconformists who, during the years of persecution, held secret religious meetings at the Hall: the head of the family was imprisoned for his faith. Some of them sailed with the Quakers to America.

The Hall remained in the same family's hands until Elian and Ian Forster came here in 1970 – by which time the ancient house was almost falling apart. Gradually they restored it, adding oak furniture to rooms that have exposed wall-timbers, stone inglenooks and low ceilings. Up the oak stair with its original finials are beamed bedrooms, one with a locally made patchwork duvet, some with pretty curtains that match the paper on walls and ceilings. The bathroom is excellent.

From the dining-room one can step straight into the garden with its winding lawn, badminton and croquet. Some guests enjoy the company of the dogs, others Ian's classic cars. As to dinner, typical of what Elian serves is leek soup, Welsh lamb and pavlova (Sunday lunches available). Small antiques on sale.

Readers' comments: All rooms delightful – large, beautifully decorated and furnished. Owners very friendly and go to great lengths. It really is something special.

Just beyond Llangollen, perched high in the hamlet of Rhewl, is **DEE FARMHOUSE** – so named because the River Dee lies just below its garden. Once this was a slate-miners' inn (hence the slate floor downstairs). From the garden come artichokes, spinach, herbs, etc. for the soups which form part of Mary Harman's snack suppers (served in a huge dining-kitchen), as well as roses and lavender for her rooms. In the small and pretty sitting-room are antiques; cases of butterflies are in a sitting/bed-

room suite upstairs which used to be a hayloft. £15–£17.
Readers' comments: Peaceful. Fine old furniture, extremely comfortable. Concerned for one's comfort. Lovely view. [Tel: 0978 861598; postcode: LL20 7YT]

Fodor's Travel Guides

Available at bookstores everywhere, or call 1-800-533-6478, 24 hours a day.

U.S. Guides

Alaska

Arizona

Boston

California

Cape Cod, Martha's Vineyard, Nantucket

The Carolinas & the Georgia Coast

Chicago

Colorado

Florida

Hawaii

Las Vegas, Reno, Tahoe

Los Angeles

Maine, Vermont, New Hampshire

Maui

Miami & the Keys

New England

New Orleans

New York City

Pacific North Coast

Philadelphia & the Pennsylvania Dutch Country

The Rockies

San Diego

San Francisco

Santa Fe, Taos, Albuquerque

Seattle & Vancouver

The South

The U.S. & British Virgin Islands

The Upper Great Lakes Region

USA

Vacations in New York State

Vacations on the Jersey Shore

Virginia & Maryland

Waikiki

Walt Disney World and the Orlando Area

Washington, D.C.

Foreign Guides

Acapulco, Ixtapa, Zihuatanejo

Australia & New Zealand

Austria

The Bahamas

Baja & Mexico's Pacific Coast Resorts

Barbados

Berlin

Bermuda

Brazil

Brittany & Normandy

Budapest

Canada

Cancun, Cozumel, Yucatan Peninsula

Caribbean

China

Costa Rica, Belize, Guatemala

The Czech Republic & Slovakia

Eastern Europe

Egypt

Euro Disney

Europe

Europe's Great Cities

Florence & Tuscany

France

Germany

Great Britain

Greece

The Himalayan Countries

Hong Kong

India

Ireland

Israel

Italy

Japan

Kenya & Tanzania

Korea

London

Madrid & Barcelona

Mexico

Montreal & Quebec City

Morocco

Moscow & St. Petersburg

The Netherlands, Belgium & Luxembourg

New Zealand

Norway

Nova Scotia, Prince Edward Island & New Brunswick

Paris

Portugal

Provence & the Riviera

Rome

Russia & the Baltic Countries

Scandinavia

Scotland

Singapore

South America

Southeast Asia

Spain

Sweden

Switzerland

Thailand

Tokyo

Toronto

Turkey

Vienna & the Danube Valley

Yugoslavia

Fodor's Travel Guides

Available at bookstores everywhere, or call 1–800–533–6478, 24 hours a day.

Special Series

Fodor's Affordables

Caribbean

Europe

Florida

France

Germany

Great Britain

London

Italy

Paris

Fodor's Bed & Breakfast and Country Inns Guides

Canada's Great Country Inns

California

Cottages, B&Bs and Country Inns of England and Wales

Mid-Atlantic Region

New England

The Pacific Northwest

The South

The Southwest

The Upper Great Lakes Region

The West Coast

The Berkeley Guides

California

Central America

Eastern Europe

France

Germany

Great Britain & Ireland

Mexico

Pacific Northwest & Alaska

San Francisco

Fodor's Exploring Guides

Australia

Britain

California

The Caribbean

Florida

France

Germany

Ireland

Italy

London

New York City

Paris

Rome

Singapore & Malaysia

Spain

Thailand

Fodor's Flashmaps

New York

Washington, D.C.

Fodor's Pocket Guides

Bahamas

Barbados

Jamaica

London

New York City

Paris

Puerto Rico

San Francisco

Washington, D.C.

Fodor's Sports

Cycling

Hiking

Running

Sailing

The Insider's Guide to the Best Canadian Skiing

Skiing in the USA & Canada

Fodor's Three-In-Ones (guidebook, language cassette, and phrase book)

France

Germany

Italy

Mexico

Spain

Fodor's Special-Interest Guides

Accessible USA

Cruises and Ports of Call

Euro Disney

Halliday's New England Food Explorer

Healthy Escapes

London Companion

Shadow Traffic's New York Shortcuts and Traffic Tips

Sunday in New York

Walt Disney World and the Orlando Area

Walt Disney World for Adults

Fodor's Touring Guides

Touring Europe

Touring USA: Eastern Edition

Fodor's Vacation Planners

Great American Vacations

National Parks of the East

National Parks of the West

The Wall Street Journal Guides to Business Travel

Europe

International Cities

Pacific Rim

USA & Canada